THE SECOND
VATICAN
ECUMENICAL COUNCIL

THE SECOND VATICAN ECUMENICAL COUNCIL

A Counterpoint
for the History of the Council

By
Agostino Marchetto

Translated from the Italian by

Kenneth D. Whitehead

Library of Congress Cataloging-in-Publication Data

Marchetto, Agostino, 1940-
  [Concilio ecumenico Vaticano II. English]
  The Second Vatican Ecumenical Council : a counterpoint for the history
of the council / by Agostino Marchetto ; translated from the Italian by
Kenneth D. Whitehead.
    p. cm.
  Includes bibliographical references.
  ISBN 978-1-58966-196-7 (pbk.)
  1. Vatican Council (2nd : 1962-1965)--History. 2. Catholic Church--
Doctrines--History--20th century. I. Title.
  BX8301962 .M35413 2010
  262'.52--dc22

      2009050750

Distribution:
UNIVERSITY OF SCRANTON PRESS
Chicago Distribution Center
11030 S. Langley
Chicago, IL 60628

TABLE OF CONTENTS

IV. Other Histories of the Council and of the Popes of the Council

V. Particular Themes and Questions

vii

TRANSLATOR'S INTRODUCTION

POPE BENEDICT XVI, in a Christmas address to the Roman Curia in 2005, called attention to the many problems the faithful have had in understanding and implementing the teachings of the Second Vatican Council. A central factor in this was what the Holy Father called "a hermeneutics of rupture or discontinuity" that informed both the mass media reporting on the Council as well as views of many theologians. The "event" or "spirit" of the Council was praised more than the actual documents the Council Fathers and Popes promulgated. By way of contrast, Pope Benedict called for "a hermeneutics of reform or renewal within the two millennia tradition of the Catholic Church" – a hermeneutics of continuity so evident in the Conciliar proceedings, documents, and the teachings of all the popes from Blessed John XXIII through Paul VI and John Paul II to Pope Benedict himself.

In the pages that follow Archbishop Agostino Marchetto provides much of the evidence for these contrasting ways of interpreting Vatican II. Indeed, as a good friend of Pope Benedict, Cardinal Ruini, commented on introducing Archbishop Marchetto's book, it is a "counterpoint", or indeed a polar opposite, to the interpretations of Vatican II that until now have tended to monopolize Catholic historiography in many circles. A hermeneutics of discontinuity is to a great extent advanced by the five-volume "History of Vatican Council II" directed by Giuseppe Alberigo and published in six languages between 1995 and 2001 in conjunction with the Bologna Institute. The English edition is published by Orbis Books with editorial assistance by Fr. Joseph Komonchak. Cardinal Ruini concluded by remarking that the careful scholarship of Archbishop Marchetto, as well as of other theologians following Pope Benedict's hermeneutics of renewal within tradition, will eventually replace the histories of discontinuity produced by Alberigo and others. "The interpretation of the council as a rupture and a new beginning is coming to an end. This interpretation is very feeble today, and has no real foothold within the body of the Church. It is time for historiography to produce a new reconstruction of Vatican II which will also be, finally, a true story." Archbishop Marchetto does not take popular short cuts in his treatment of the histories of the Council. These are scholarly reviews that provide the evidence so that the reader can judge for himself the accuracy and import of the histories being reviewed.

Pope Benedict XVI, in his first message to the cardinals the day after his election to the papacy, spoke of his "determination to continue to put the Second Vatican Council into practice." He noted that "this very year [2005] marks the 40th anniversary of the conclusion of the Council (8 December 1965). As the years have passed, the Conciliar Documents have lost none of their timeliness" (Initial Message of Pope Benedict XVI to the Cardinals, April 20, 2005).

Speaking to the College of Cardinals immediately following *his* election in 1978, Pope John Paul II similarly pointed out "the increasing importance of the Second Vatican Ecumenical Council, and we accept the define duty of assiduously bringing it into effect" (To the Cardinals and to the World, October 17, 1978).

Even the "September pope," John Paul I, who reigned for only one month in 1978, inaugurated what would prove to be his very brief pontificate by announcing to the College of Cardinals at *his* accession to the papal chair that he wished "to continue without interruption the legacy left us by the Second Vatican Council" (To the Cardinals and to the World, August 27, 1978).

Thus, all three of the popes elected since Vatican Council II (1962-1965) declared at the outset of their respective pontificates, and as their first order of business, their firm intention and determination to implement the Second Vatican Council. In the eyes of these popes there was evidently not much that could take precedence over Vatican II. All three of them, of course, were present *at* Vatican II, they had each played important roles there, and hence they were all well aware of the Council's epochal importance. And it is certainly clear in retrospect that these post-conciliar popes have in fact treated the acts and decisions of this twentieth-century ecumenical council of the Catholic Church as the source of the Catholic "marching orders" for our times. The Council issued the documents and directives which essentially govern the Church today and will continue to do so for the foreseeable future.

Yet in spite of the Council's obvious and very great importance in the on-going life of the Church, no really sound and serious history of the Council has appeared in English since the "instant histories," compiled mostly of contemporary journalistic reporting on the Council, came out during or shortly after the Council itself, a generation ago. I refer to such books as the pseudonymous Xavier Rynne's *Vatican Council II*, consisting of the four successive volumes of the author's reporting on the Council originally published in the *New Yorker* magazine; and the massive *Drama of Vatican II* by Henri Fesquet, consisting of translations of that author's almost daily reporting on the Council that appeared in the Parisian newspaper *Le Monde*. Then there was the excellent and perceptive but very brief early history of the Council published in 1967 by the very well-informed Father Ralph M. Wiltgen, S.V.D., *The Rhine Flows into the Tiber: The Unknown Council*. This book remains today one of the best histories of the Council.

Other books on the history of the Council were published as well, especially while interest in the Council was running high. Yet, again, however, these works have belonged mostly to the same journalistic-type *genre*; they are not really "history" in the true sense. Yet these kinds of books are what those interested in the Council in the English-speaking world have for the most part had to depend on for their knowledge of what the Council was all about and what happened at the Council.

Following the appearance of these earlier books, many years have elapsed during which scarcely any sound and serious history of or pertaining to the Council has been written or published in book form in English. Books in which the Council is mentioned or treated have generally been primarily on some other subject rather than on the Council itself. The sixteen documents issued by the Council, of course, have long since been translated and are available in English in more than one edition, along with an extraordinarily long list of "post-conciliar documents" (themselves testifying, again, to the enormous importance of the Council). A number of memoirs and reminiscences by participants at the Council have also been published, some of them of great interest, in fact.

Much of what has been written and said *about* the Council, however, such as it is, has too often been "agenda driven," and has also almost been written from a distinctly "liberal" or "progressive" point of view by advocates seeking to validate in some cases what they think the Council *should* have been rather than what the Council actually was. More often than not, this kind of advocacy (as contrasted with true history) has been concerned with "the spirit of Vatican II" rather than with the actual Council and the true facts that pertain to it. Some of the books of this type go even farther and claim that the Council was an "event" which effected a distinct "break" with the Catholic tradition and created an entirely "new" kind of Catholicism. This is not true, of course, as any serious and careful study of the documents of Vatican II will show. However, this kind of interpretation of the Council nevertheless remains all too common in the published works available on Vatican II, including especially recent ones.

By comparison with the very real importance the Council manifestly has for the Catholic Church, as the popes themselves have testified, the paucity of solid scholarly material about it, indeed the lack of any serious general history of the Council written in English since the Council ended more than forty years ago, is really quite startling.

The same thing is not as true in Europe, however, where a fair number of histories and collections of historical studies and articles on Vatican II written in several major European languages have come out in recent years. Indeed, a veritable "cottage industry" of conciliar studies seems to have sprung up in Europe in recent years, and the continuing interest in the Council indicated by these studies has only intensified as successive volumes of the official *Acta et Documenta* of the Council (beginning in 1960), and the *Acta Synodalia* (beginning in 1970), have continued to appear, published by the Vatican Polyglot Press. These official sources are now virtually complete, in fact, and thus the materials necessary for a serious history of the Council now are available.

Although the continuing interest in the Council evinced by the studies that have been coming out in the major European languages is commendable, there nevertheless remains at least one very serious drawback in all this scholarly activity, and that is that many, if not most, of the recent conciliar studies have been written from a one-sided "liberal" or "progressive" point of view not dissimilar from the emphasis on "the spirit of the Council" that has long been prevalent in the English-speaking world. Just as the Council itself was dominated in its on-going operations by bishops and theologians from Western European countries north of the Alps—the "Rhine-flows-into-the-Tiber" phenomenon—so the writing of the *history* of the Council has been, and still largely is, dominated by those possessing a decidedly one-sided and usually "liberal" point of view that in a number of ways tries to contrast the Council with the authentic tradition of the Church.

This "progressive" point of view was already prominent at the Council, of course, although the burden of a number of the current writers on the subject is that this point of view, unhappily in their view, did not end up adequately reflected in the Council's actual decisions, that is, in the documents issued by Council. During and after the Council there were the appearances—often sensationally reported on at the time—that Vatican II had been engaged in "changing everything," and, in fact, largely did change everything, at least in the minds of some. Church tradition and what had gone before had supposedly gone by the board, to be replaced by an entirely new vision of the Church.

None of this was entirely true, to be sure (although there were sometimes elements of truth in this general point of view). But the finished, approved sixteen documents of Vatican Council II, promulgated by the pope, are remarkably solid and well-balanced documents. They generally respond to the real hopes Pope John XXIII had when he convoked the Council, but at the same time they are certainly in full conformity with the authentic Catholic tradition as well. Nevertheless, historians and writers with a point of view similar to those at the Council who *wanted* it to be a wholly new thing are still prominently to be found today in the ranks of those who are now writing the history of the Council. The result is too many one-sided and even skewed histories of the Council and studies about the Council.

To counter this unfortunately marked tendency in so much of the current scholarly work on Vatican II, the Libreria Editrice Vaticana published in 2005 a remarkable collection of reviews and essays examining in careful detail the greater part of the current European historiography and other scholarly output that has been appearing over approximately the past two decades. Entitled *Il Concilio Ecumenico Vaticano II. Contrappunto per la sua storia* [The Second Vatican Ecumenical Council: A Counterpoint to the History of the Council], the author of this book is a prelate currently assigned to a curial office, Archbishop Agostino Marchetto.

Archbishop Marchetto was born in Vicenza, Italy, in 1940. He is currently the Secretary of the Pontifical Council for the Pastoral Care of Migrants and Itinerant People in Rome. For more than thirty years he served in the Vatican's diplomatic service, including some twenty years in Africa; but during this time he continued to maintain his historical and scholarly interests, going back to the dissertation he had produced on the subject of the "Episcopate and Papal Primacy in the Pseudo-Isidorian Decretals" (Rome, 1971). He has degrees or diplomas in canon law, theology, and pastoral theology. He is the author, previously, of *Chiesa e Papato nella storia e nel diritto. 25 anni di studi critici* [Church and Papacy in History and Law: 25 Years of Critical Studies]. Among Archbishop Marchetto's major interest is the hermeneutic or proper interpretation of what the Council was, what it did, and what the meaning of it is.

Given the nature of his diplomatic work and his various postings and changes of residence, however, his scholarly work often had to take the form of reviews and articles that have appeared in various scholarly periodical publications. The present volume consists mainly, though not entirely, of review and articles written by him between 1992 and 2003 on the subject of the Second Vatican Council.

As the reader will discover in the following pages, Archbishop Marchetto's knowledge of the background and sources on the Council is immense. It is also detailed and accurate. At the same time, his judgments about the nature and the tendencies of much of the current historical writing concerning the Council are both acute and critical. He has mastered the review and article form almost as a special "literary *genre*," and in the absence (up to now) of a good contemporary general history of the Council written in English from an unbiased point of view, this collection can now serve as an unparalleled source of knowledge about what really happened at the Council, what the Council really decided, and how all of this should properly be judged today.

Archbishop Marchetto's focus is mainly on continental European works. He reviews or discusses more than thirty works in Italian, nine in French, and one each in German, Spanish, and Latin. The original title of only one of the works reviewed in this book is in English in the original, and this book is actually a collection of articles in multiple languages. The English-speaking reader may be surprised at how much has been written and published about the Council in these other European languages; the English-speaking reader will also discover here that, just as the often invoked "spirit of Vatican II" has sometimes crowded out or obscured what the Second Vatican Council actually decided and did, so a similar revisionist "spirit" has apparently inspired some or even much of today's historical writing about the Council. In reviewing not a few instances of this, as well as in explaining the proper sources of the Council's history in general, Archbishop Marchetto succeeds in seeing the Council steadily and seeing it whole. His main interest is conciliar hermeneutics and he proves eminently qualified to say what the Council really *was* all about! He knows how to give credit where credit is due, of course, but he also knows a great deal about *whether* credit is due. This volume can thus be considered a major contribution to a correct interpretation of the Second Vatican Council these forty years and more after its conclusion.

In addition to the major recent histories of the Council, Archbishop Marchetto also reviews and discusses a number of the biographies, diaries, and memoirs of some of the principal protagonists at the Council, many of which are not available in English (although a few are). In his conclusion, he also includes several essays on hermeneutics laying out his very informed viewpoint of what the Council was all about and how its history ought to be written. In the absence of an actual history of the Council written on the basis of the sound principles he sets forth, this collection of the author's periodical reviews and articles is indispensable for the proper understanding of this most important event in the recent history of the Catholic Church.

Among the major concerns he deals with here is the unfortunately widespread treatment of the Council not so much as the twenty-first in the long series of the ecumenical councils of the Catholic Church, but rather as a unique twentieth-century "event" in its own right and *sui generis* in what it was and did. What this approach entails, as the author abundantly shows in some of the studies he covers, is that *if* the Council was indeed merely or primarily such an "event," then it is entirely open-ended; its meaning and significance are not defined or limited by the Council's actual decisions or the documents it produced; they can be interpreted or re-interpreted to mean what some people would like them to mean—in the same way that "the spirit of Vatican II" has so often been substituted for the actual Council. (In this connection, we should recall that what Pope Benedict XVI spoke about at his accession was the importance and timeliness of the Vatican II *documents!*)

The idea of Vatican II as primarily an "event," though, is an idea that has been steadily promoted by one school of thought that Archbishop Marchetto is obliged to engage virtually throughout his narrative. The school of thought in question is the "School of Bologna," exemplified by the work of its leading spirit, the late Professor Giuseppe Alberigo of the University of Bologna. Alberigo has been a nearly ubiquitous figure in contemporary Vatican II studies, and he also collaborated on and even orchestrated Vatican II studies internationally. Among other things he was the general editor of a massive, five-volume *History of Vatican Council II* co-authored by many scholars from a number of different countries. This *History* is critically reviewed over several chapters by Archbishop Marchetto, and is referred to in some of his other studies. It has unhappily dominated the current historiography of the Council nearly everywhere up to now. It has even been translated into English and published by the usually left-leaning Orbis Books. But this tendentious history does *not* really qualify as the sound and serious history of Vatican II that ought to be available in English, as Archbishop Marchetto abundantly shows.

In the absence of a sounder, more objective history of the Council, the kind of trenchant critique of the five volumes of the Alberigo-edited *History*, and of some of the other studies so markedly influenced by it, that Archbishop Marchetto has successfully produced in this book, is essential for a proper understanding of the Second Vatican Council.

Other concerns of the archbishop are equally important and are quite extensively also treated in this book, for example: excessive reliance by many authors on unofficial diaries, memoirs, and the like in preference to the now available official *Acta* of the Council; journalistic and even sensationalist treatment of the conflicts and "clashes" that supposedly took place at the Council; invidious accounts of Council participants thought to be too "conservative"; sometimes rather fanciful, adulatory accounts of those such as Pope John XXIII and Cardinal Giacomo Lercaro of Bologna who were thought to embody the hopes of what the "liberals" still today think the Council should have been; celebrations of such "liberal" theologians as Karl Rahner, S. J., and M. D. Chenu, O.P.; interpretations based on analogies with secular political movements and parties which simply do not apply in the case of the Church; adoption of the secular political categories of "liberal" and "conservative" to describe elements within the Council; and, finally, the exaltation of Pope John XXIII, usually at the expense of Pope Paul VI, the latter widely but wrongly held to have stifled the plans and hopes of the former. A thorough and honest analysis of all these and other Vatican II themes awaits the serious reader in this authoritative book by Archbishop Agostino Marchetto.

The titles and publication data of the works reviewed or mentioned in this book are generally given in full in the original language, with a translation then provided in nearly all cases. This allows the English-speaking reader to refer directly to any of the original works that he might wish to consult. Some words and phrases in the text have occasionally been added by the translator for clarity and understanding (shown in brackets where necessary).

The publication of this work in English is a major event in the better and more accurate understanding of the Second Vatican Council.

PREFACE

FOLLOWING THE PUBLICATION by the Libreria Editrice Vaticana of the Volume *Church and Papacy in History and Law*, with its Part IV dedicated to Church councils, in which numerous essays focused on Vatican Council II, there arose in me the desire to separate these latter essays out from that rather hefty volume and then to add to them a number of successive contributions of mine in the same area of research, twenty-eight in all, in order to make up a new publication.

The intent has been to arrive, finally, at a history of Vatican II which gets beyond the serious situation created from the time of the Council on by a vision of the Council which I define as "ideological"— hence the reference to what I style a "counterpoint" to the history of the Council in my title. It is an ideological vision which has been monopolistically imposed on most publications that have come out about the Council.

Hence what I offer here is a volume somewhat more slender than the preceding one. Yet it is a more unitary volume. It is entirely dedicated to that great Vatican Synod which has had such importance for the renewal of the Church in the century now past, and which shows every sign of continuing to have relevance at the beginning of this new millennium.

I have tried this time to respect the chronological order of the publications covered in my contributions to on-going conciliar research, but the arrangement is also "logical", that is, it begins within the framework of all the Church's councils, including Vatican II (Chapters 1-3), treats the two councils held at the Vatican itself together (Chapter 4), and then moves the focus of its attention to Vatican II alone (Chapter 5-9). Following this there is a fundamental and detailed critical analysis of the five volumes on the history of the Council produced by Professor Giuseppe Alberigo and his "School of Bologna," extended as it is rather considerably beyond the city of Bologna itself (Chapters 10-14). There follows an appendix entitled "Faces at the End of the Council" (Chapter 15); then there is a glance at the Church of Vatican II (in two parts which comprise Chapter 16); and then a look at a relatively widely distributed periodical (Chapter 17); and, finally, there is a perspective from Moscow (Chapter 18).

At this point in the volume the two popes of the Council are considered, that is, Blessed John XXIII and Paul VI (Chapters 19-22). Following those chapters are examinations of various publications of general conciliar interest (Chapter 23-27).

Attention is then directed to *Lumen Gentium* (Chapters 28-29) and to an explanatory note, on *veritas salutaris*, "saving truth" (Chapter 30). This is followed by a reviews of the themes of primacy and collegiality in three recent works (Chapters 31-33), as well as by analysis of the link between the contemporary development of ecclesial movements and the Council itself (Chapters 34-35).

In connection with all this, another fundamental question cannot be forgotten, and that is the question of the private sources of the Council (Chapters 36-45). These chapters cover works about or diaries of Giuseppe Siri, Marie-Dominique Chenu, Neophytos Edelby, Augustin Bea, Joseph Ratzinger, André Charue, Gérard Philips, Albert Prignon, Umberto Betti, and Yves Congar. These private sources are also covered in a small volume by Massimo Faggioli and Giovanni Turbanti (Chapter 46). The official sources (to which the private sources have to give way) are covered in the "Synodal Acts" edited by Vincenzo Carbone and in his book on the preparations for the Third Millennium (Chapters 47-48).

We also report here on the intervention of Leo Scheffczyk, later made a cardinal, in "Towards a Correct Interpretation of Vatican Council II" (Chapter 49). This is followed by a contribution of our own in the same vein with the title: "Tradition and Renewal together: Vatican Council II" (Chapter 50).

Two summary articles on hermeneutical tendencies in the years 1990 to today bearing upon the Great Synod conclude the volume (Chapter 51-52). The first of these takes things up to June, 2000, and the second covers the time after that up to October 2002.

As before, we have grouped these chapters into seven (7) parts or sections. The titles of each of these sections have the advantage of enabling the reader to scan the subjects desired, depending upon the reader's particular interests. These seven section titles include: 1) "The Context of the Councils"; 2) "Preparations for the Council"; 3) "A History of the Second Vatican Council"; 4) "Other Histories of the Council and of the Popes of the Council"; 5) "Particular Themes and Questions"; 6) "Official and Private Conciliar Sources"; and 7) "For a Correct Interpretation of the Council." The lists and index included are the customary ones.

And so now I wish you good reading, even if *"per partes"*!

ABBREVIATIONS

AAS	=	*Acta Apostolicae Sedis*
AD	=	*Acta et Documenta Concilio Oecumenico Apparando* (ed. V. Carbone), *Typis (Polyglottis) Vaticanis,* 1960ff.
A.H.C.	=	*Annuarium Historiae Conciliorum*
A.H.P.	=	*Archivum Historiae Pontificiae*
Apol	=	*Apollinaris*
art.	=	article
AS	=	*Acta Synodalia Sacrosancti Concilii Oecumenici Vaticani II* (ed. V. Carbone), *Typis (Polyglottis) Vaticanis,* 1970 ff.
cf.	=	confer
CICO	=	Code of Canon Law of the Eastern Catholic Churches
CIC	=	Code of Canon Law
Civ. Catt.	=	*La Civiltà Cattolica*
Doc. Cath.	=	*La Documentation Catholique*
ed., eds.	=	editor[s], edition[s]
e.g.	=	for example
esp.	=	especially
ff	=	following
GS	=	*Gaudium et Spes*
Ibid.	=	same
LG	=	*Lumen Gentium*
loc. cit.	=	place cited

L'Oss. Rom. = *L'Osservatore Romano*

n.   = note; number

N.E.P.   = *Nota Explicativa Praevia*

N.R.T.   = *Nouvelle Revue Théologique*

op. cit. = work cited

p., pp.   =   page, pages

para.   = paragraph

P. L.   = *Patrologia Latina* (ed. J. P. Migne)

Rev. des sc. Rel. = *Revue des sciences religienses*

Riv. della Dioc. di Vicenza = *Rivista della Diocesi di Vicenza*

RSChIt. (or R.S.C.I) = *Rivista di Storia della Chiesa in Italia*

tit.   = title

vol.   = volume

I

THE CONTEXT
OF THE COUNCILS

1

A History
of the Ecumenical Councils

Alberigo Giuseppe, ed., with Various Authors, *Storia dei Concili ecumenici* [A History of the Ecumenical Councils], Brescia 1990, 479 pages.

"The celebration of the great conciliar assemblies constitutes a scarlet thread that extends through the whole of Christian history." Thus Giuseppe Alberigo, in the preface to this book.

The book thus addresses a theme of particular interest in the life of the Church, and it is therefore very welcome. However, once again, the characteristic "line" of the well-known professor at the University of Bologna becomes immediately visible, beginning with his brief introduction prepared in his capacity as "conductor of the orchestra" for the entire volume.

Speaking of the great councils of antiquity, convoked, as he says, "on the initiative of imperial authority, and carried on under its auspices," he offers the following characterization: "Three elements emerge: a primary concentration on the formulation of a 'profession of faith'...to which are then added disciplinary statutes governing the internal life of the community. In the second place, participation in the work of the council appears to be open to both theologians and laymen, although the work of the bishops does appear to be essential, even if it is not exclusive. Little by little, the involvement of the five apostolic patriarchates (the Pentarchy), becomes a *conditio sine qua non*. Finally, the participation of representatives of the monastic communities becomes a factor of particular importance" (pp. 5ff). The reader must take note here of the muting of the role of the Bishop of Rome, and also of how the *conditio sine qua non* mentioned came about "little by little."

In contrast to this description—which seems to be the ideal one for this author—the general councils of the Middle Ages, he says, "present a substantially diverse physiognomy, not only by being limited to the Latin Church—except for the unproductive cases of Lyons and Florence—but also in other significant respects. Above all what made its appearance, in an always more consistent way, was an abstract acceptance of *fides*, of faith, always understood as doctrine, and *veritas*, truth, always conceptually formulated and defined"—but then what else was it that the Christological councils of antiquity were also trying to define if not the doctrine of the faith and truth?

Then there was the fact that "canon law acquired...an ecclesial centrality that was unknown in the first millennium" (p. 6). But even the author himself has had to admit that this was a reality that has changed over time.

Again, "participation in these 'papal' councils"—thus does the author posit a new category of general councils—"was dictated by the pope. Moreover, the cardinals also took on a conspicuous role, even though they were not normally bishops. Nevertheless the most incisive role belonged to the orders of mendicant friars, owing to their unanticipated but wide-ranging successes" (*Ibid.*). Again here we must ask if these judgments are really well-founded.

After having characterized in his usual fashion both the Councils of Trent and of Vatican I and II—and having drawn from his characterizations a number of conclusions concerning the composition and "physiognomy" of general and ecumenical councils, Professor Alberigo then briefly treats the "crucial aspect" of their ecumenicity. In doing so, however, he somehow never gets around to mentioning the Bishop of Rome, except in connection with what he calls "the Roman Catholic tradition," which "especially in the late Middle Ages placed the emphasis on referring questions to the pope, to whom came to be credited the overall direction of general councils (their convocation, the fixing of their rules, and their agendas, transfers, and closings). Thus, according to some—though their viewpoint is actually contradicted by Vatican II—conciliar authority itself would supposedly depend upon papal authority, and hence it would fall to the pope to give binding efficacy to the decisions of a council" (p. 9).

The equivocal character of the affirmations that are made here is evident. It is necessary for the reader continually to make the proper distinctions for himself. This is shown by the author's own successive attestations concerning the fact that "it was difficult for many medieval councils to distinguish the decisions of the councils from those of the pope who presided" (p. 10). But we must ask ourselves in this regard if there were any final conciliar decisions if the Bishop of Rome did not accept them.

The author concludes: "The historical evolution of these councils seems to be characterized by a progressive reduction of their 'ecumenicity'—from universal to occidental, and then from occidental to Roman. There was also a reduction of their horizons. The hegemony of the lived faith of the community seems little by little to have been taken over by the functionality of the ecclesial institution" (*Ibid.*). The use of the verb "seems" here does not remove the heaviness and unfoundedness of this viewpoint. Nevertheless, the volume does accept "for reference purposes the list of councils maintained in the Roman Catholic tradition" (p. 10)—but only for reference purposes, it seems.

The *first part* of the work, which goes "from Nicaea (325) to Chalcedon (451)" (pp. 11-118) consists of five chapters entrusted to Lorenzo Perrone, professor of the history of Christianity at the University of Pisa. The subtitle reads as follows: "The First Four Ecumenical Councils: Their Institutions, Doctrines, and the Processes of Their Reception."

The beginning, "from Nicaea," is premised on "the primacy of the first four ecumenical councils" that formulated the fundamental dogmas of Christianity and established the "essential foundations for the ecclesiastical order of the Pentarchy (the regime of the five great patriarchates, with their hierarchies)." All this was then sanctioned by Chalcedon. Here again is to be noted the "silencer" that is imposed concerning the Bishop of Rome, since it was supposedly always "the council that provided the only opportunity to give expression to the unity of the Church" (p. 15), while in the third century "no representative instance of the 'universal' had yet emerged" (*Ibid.*). "On the other hand, the synodal component was not absent even where ecclesiastical instances of regional or greater scope were emerging, such as in the situation of the 'mother Churches' of Rome in Italy or of Alexandria in Egypt." Here is seen "the dialectic between the primatial claims of the major sees, especially that of the Bishop of Rome, and the powers of a council, not only local, but even universal, although this dialectic remained in a latent state as far as the ancient ecumenical councils were concerned" (*Ibid.*).

The same minimalistic tendency regarding the role of the pope can also be found in the author's treatment of the Council of Arles. This regional synod supposedly "manifested its autonomy with regard to both the emperor and the pope, and, precisely in view of its geographical location [*sic*], it exhibited...a treatment of special reverence with regard to the pope—to whom it gave [*sic*] the task of publicizing its decisions, thus guaranteeing in particular the reception of its canons" (p. 17). Then, going back to the earlier Synod of Antioch, the author thinks that "the decisions of the latter, although significant, are not more binding than the Roman decree of 313 for the Council of Arles" (p. 22).

The same spirit informs the author's treatment of the Council of Nicaea. Thus, with regard to Bishop Hosius (Ossius) of Cordova, whose presence at the side of Constantine, while it may have contributed to allowing the voice of the Occident to be heard, "in no way can be considered a formal representation of Rome" (p. 24). Or again: "It is thought that the council presidency was exercised by Hosius of Cordova, not as a Roman legate, but simply as a trustee of the emperor" (p. 26).

The unfolding of the presentation of the history of the Council is often conjectural in form; it proceeds from the convocation of the

Council to its development, with indications of the circumstances surrounding it; it speaks of the content of the Nicene Creed (rather resembling the Jerusalem-Antioch Creed); and it analyzes the *Homoousious* in a way which is thought to refute Arianism.

Some space is devoted to explaining the disciplinary texts of Nicaea (the dating of Easter in alignment with the use in vigor in Rome, the solution to the Meletian Schism, the regulating of public penances, and important norms relative to the structure of ecclesial governance). Also tendentious in this context are the author's treatment of considerations bearing upon entrance into the episcopal college (p. 38) and the role of the Roman See: "Political-geographic reasons as well as the claim of apostolic origin perhaps constituted the premises for the new 'patriarchal' structure. The same canon recognizes as obvious a prerogative of the Roman See analogous [to that of Alexandria], although spelling out the context of this prerogative with precision is avoided. As for the geographical extension of such a primacy, it is presumed that the canon makes reference to the position of the Roman Church in Italy—more precisely in central and southern Italy, as well as in Sicily and Sardinia—before the time that the Roman Church occupied the leading position in the Occident as a whole, where Rome would eventually come to constitute the only patriarchate" (p. 39).

Also with regard to the discipline of sacerdotal celibacy and the validity (or illicitness?) of ordinations, we would have preferred to see more precision and definiteness applied to these cases, along the lines of the well-established solutions proposed by other authors.

There follows a chapter entitled: "From Nicaea to Constantinople I: The Reception of the First Ecumenical Council." This account is in conformity with the special interest in the question of the reception of councils regularly manifested in this work.

"Between Silence and Reaction"—thus does Professor Perrone describe the comeback of the Arian followers of Eusebius of Nicomedia up to the death of Constantine, and then during the reign of Constantius II. In Rome, meanwhile, Pope Julius I invalidated the depositions from their sees of both Athanasius and Marcellus of Ancyra. The story is taken up to the advent of the emperor Theodosius I. We must, however, take note here of a discordant expression that occurs. It may just be a question of language, but it is not only that. It is the way the author speaks of "communion with the Occident" when he is actually referring to the ecclesial communion with Rome that was brought about by Meletius.

This use of improper formulas, both earlier and subsequent to this particular instance, points either to badly assimilated theological terminology on the part of the author, or to a systematic intention to make as few references as possible to the Bishop of Rome, and to communion with him. But this ecclesial communion was always what was decisive, and not only in the Occident. There is also a marked tendency here to refer to "churches" even when what is meant is the universal Church (and her common patrimony: see, e.g., p. 57).

There follows the treatment of the Council of Constantinople in 381. Considered are its convocation, its initial phase, the negotiations for union with the Macedonians, as well as canons 2 and 3 (concerning the "primacy of honor" of Constantinople in the East), including the anti-Alexandrian and anti-Roman developments that emerged. Then, finally, there is the treatment of the Niceno-Constantinopolitan Creed which emerged from the Council of Constantinople.

The chapter following is dedicated to "The Christological Question and the Rupture of the Oecumene from Ephesus (431) to Chalcedon (451)." It deals with the Nestorian crisis and the reactions of both Rome (the condemnation of Nestorius by a Roman synod held at the beginning of August in 430) and of Alexandria. Again in this case, the author makes a point of adding, significantly, an observation that the recourse to Rome exercised by St. Cyril of Alexandria involved "in substance tactical reasons rather than any admission of the doctrinal primacy of the pope" (p. 77).

With regard to Ephesus, Professor Perrone describes the two opposing assemblies which convened—the first one concerned with "the condemnation of Nestorius and the break with the Orientals," and the second one presided over by John of Antioch, and concerned with "the deposition of Cyril of Alexandria and Bishop Memnon of Ephesus." Both sessions were held in the absence of the papal legates, who had not yet arrived in Ephesus. When they did arrive, they gave their formal approval to the deposition of Nestorius. Only when the council was over did negotiations for reconciliation begin with a letter from St. Cyril to the bishop of Antioch.

But then the Eutychian crisis began, issuing in the false "robber council" (*latrocinio*) of 449, as well as in the appeal to the Roman See by Flavian, the patriarch of Constantinople; this was followed by the appeals of Eusebius of Dorylaeum and Theodoret of Cyrus. Here the author comments that "such recourse to Rome must not be seen as constituting an explicit recognition of the pope's primacy of jurisdiction" (p. 91). Was this at least "implicit"? Equally limiting in scope is the author's later affirmation having reference to a letter from Pope St. Leo I to the emperor and calling for the convocation of a council in the West. "This request...revealed how the pope...neither wanted nor could disregard the opportunity of using a council to settle a dogmatic question. This was vitally important"—we would note, rather, that it was not possible at that time to convoke an ecumenical council without the intervention of the emperor. "The sum total of the pronouncements of Pope St. Leo I, before and after the council of 451, demonstrates that the rapport between the pope and the council proved to be rather in the nature of a dialectical correlation, and was thus not merely a relationship involving the superiority of the pope and the subordination of the council. Although the bishop of Rome... authoritatively intervened...expounding his own decision concerning the faith and claiming the supremacy of the apostolic see in a way entirely different from the way of all his predecessors"—here we must again register our dissent—"in the last phase of the pontificate, reflecting the experience of Chalcedon, the idea of the significance of a council that was independent of any adhesion to Rome became more and more pronounced" (*Ibid.*).

We arrive at the Council of Chalcedon, the council most heavily attended in antiquity. It saw the rehabilitation of Flavian, carried out in accordance with a Roman decision, and in the end it saw the formulation of a dogmatic text, not to speak of the approval of important disciplinary canons relating to the structure of the Church; among these stood out the solution to the question of the rights of the See of Jerusalem, as well as the famous "canon 28" regarding the privileges to be granted to Constantinople, which Rome declined to "receive." In this regard, the judgment of the author, according to which "Chalcedon reversed in some measure the doctrine [of Ephesus] that insisted on the humanity of God" (p. 99), seems rather strange, while much more apt is his observation that the council's dogmatic formulation "successfully mediated between the various Christological models in both the Alexandrian and Antiochan traditions, and, for the first time, included in a really decisive way in a conciliar dogmatic formulation the contribution of the Occident brought about by the intervention of Pope Leo" (*Ibid.*).

Professor Perrone adds: "It was a tragedy of the Church of antiquity that the harmonizing tendency of Chalcedon was not properly understood in large areas of Eastern Christianity" (*Ibid.*). An ample bibliographical note concludes this first part of the volume—although it lacks any reference to important articles of V. Monachino; see, for example, the article "*Communio e Primato nella controversia ariana* ["Communion and Primacy in the Arian Controversy"], in A.H.P. 7 (1969), pp. 43-48. However, the mere inclusion of this bibliographical note does not succeed in filling the gap created by the lack in the contribution of this author of an adequate critical apparatus.

The *next part* of the book covers the councils "From the Second Council of Constantinople (553) to the Second Council of Nicaea (786-787)" (pp. 119-154), and it is contributed by Panayotis A. Yannopoulos.

Briefly stated, the fifth ecumenical council treated the questions of Monophysitism and Origenism. As regards the first of these questions, "the decree of 544-545 and the policy which it inaugurated constituted the line that the council basically followed. It was thought necessary to condemn the 'Three Chapters' in order to bring about a reconciliation with the Monophysites. After the *constitutum* I [of Pope Vigilius], the council condemned, in its eighth session, various Western ideas as well as the 'Three Chapters.' Imperial policy thus triumphed and Rome suffered a hard blow...It is certain that the council did condemn Origen (p. 132). This council of 553 finally re-established the order and unity of the Church, but it failed in its other objective, namely, a reconciliation with the Monophysites, who did not accept its decisions."

Introducing the sixth ecumenical council (the third in Constantinople in 680-681), the author notes that "after the death of Justinian, relative calm characterized the ecclesiastical scene. Monophysitism found a refuge in both Syria and Egypt. Theodosius of Alexandria, and, especially, Jacob Baradai, organized the Monophysite Churches on a solid basis. The Monophysite Church of Syria, down to the present day, bears the name 'Jacobite' from this same Jacob Baradai, while the Monophysite Church of Egypt is known as the Coptic Church...This serene climate was worsened by the emperor Phocas (602-610)...[but his successor] Heraclius appealed to the wisdom and political sense of the patriarch of Constantinople, Sergius...[in order to] find a formula capable of reuniting all Christians and restoring the unity of the Greco-Roman world" (p. 135).

Unfortunately, however, the Pact of Union that was drawn up in nine chapters, allowed the acceptance of monoenergism in its seventh chapter. At this point, Yannopoulos follows the path of these various contrasts all the way up to Constantinople III, which proclaimed the orthodox faith admitting two wills in Christ, of which "the human will was submissive to the divine will" (p. 139).

This council had an unexpected and unforeseen prolongation in the form of a fourth council held in Constantinople, the so-called Quinisext Council (692), which adopted decisions of a purely practical nature, but when "the canons and the acts of this body were sent to Rome to be signed by Pope Sergius I, he proved unwilling to subscribe to them" and "his successors did the same" (p. 143).

The seventh ecumenical council, the Second Council of Nicaea (786-787), rejected "the iconoclastic decisions of the Council of Hieria and affirmed the representation of the sacred and the veneration of icons"—which had been banned owing to "abuse by the Orthodox, the influence of heretics, the example of the Arabs and the Jews, certain oriental traditions, and the theology of some of the fathers of the Church" (p. 146). "Both Rome and the Eastern Patriarchs viewed this council favorably and accepted its final decisions, but no happy sequel stemmed from this" (p. 150).

This rather concise contribution to the volume leaves a number of things to be desired, especially regarding the references made to Rome. To illustrate what we mean, we need to cite several examples: "Rome never wanted to recognize the loss of its political primacy and the raising of Constantinople to be the capital of the empire, with all of the consequences which followed from that as regards the hierarchy of the Churches. Under pressure from the imperial power, Rome was constrained to accept the new position of Constantinople, but without accepting the canons of the councils which granted to Constantinople a position equal to its own" (pp. 123-124). "Rome profited from the period of the occupation of Italy by the Goths to develop a spirit of independence for itself" (p. 124). "Alexandria came to be eliminated in the race for the primacy: and the battle became one strictly between Rome and Constantinople" (*Ibid.*). "Pope Theodore, a Greek from the East [take care!] maintained the idea that the pope is the supreme head of the Church and hence has the right to intervene in the internal affairs of other Churches" (p. 137). "Martin I...convoked in 649 a synod in Rome without asking permission from the emperor as was normally done" (p. 137). "Even though some contemporary historians have cast doubt on whether Pope Honorius was actually condemned [during the Third Council of Constantinople], this condemnation effectively was voted in the thirteenth session...without any reaction from the Western representatives" (p. 139). Finally, we note that the two "supposed" representatives of the pope, as well as those of Antioch, are described here as being "suspect."

The *third part* of the book was given back into the hands of Professor Lorenzo Perrone under the title: "Constantinople IV (869-870). Roman Primacy, Pentarchy, and Ecclesial Communion on the Eve of the Separation between East and West" (pp. 155-181). Everyone must recognize the problem of the ecumenicity of this council, and it must also be asked whether the inclusion in this volume of this account signifies an affirmative answer to that question. Of course the title given here does not affirm this.

For this author, the pontificates of Leo IV, Benedict III, Nicholas I, Adrian II, and John VIII all "together represent on Rome's part the claim of a universal primacy of jurisdiction with a firmness never seen before." This is the case, but does the author simply wish to see the expression of this "claim" deferred as far into the future as possible? However, Professor Perrone does admit that Pope Leo IV, in the matter of the deposition of Gregory Asbesta, criticized the fact that Rome was neither questioned nor otherwise involved in the matter, and this occurred before the pseudo-Isidorian Decretals were known in Rome (see p. 161).

The advent of Photius as the patriarch of Constantinople signaled the beginning of a crisis in the relations between Rome and Constantinople, following the condemnation of his predecessor Ignatius. But Rome reserved to itself judgment in the matter, "limiting the charge of [its] legates to the role of inspectors who should have controlled the way the facts unfolded, meanwhile reiterating the privileges of the Apostolic See with respect to the Church of Constantinople" (p.162).

Although the author indicates the fact that "Constantinople reacted rather critically to the Roman pretension of being able to judge the internal problems of the Byzantine Church" (p. 164), he is obliged to recognize, with regard to the question of "the rights of the Roman Church...to intervene in questions concerning the Church of Constantinople, including in disciplinary cases," that this is not an attitude that is "new in its essential motivations, but goes back to and is based on principles already formulated by Leo the Great and Gelasius." The most relevant consequence of this is shown in the relationship of a pope to an ecumenical council, "the superiority of the former over the latter being expressly affirmed" (p. 164). But there is also nothing new about this. "Without the authority of the Apostolic see—as Nicholas I made a point of affirming on numerous occasions—councils have no value; for papal approval is necessary for their validation" (p. 164). But this also—we hasten to add—is not new.

It is pleasing for us to take note of the fact that Photius, "in breaking with the pope, would be automatically excluded from the Church" (p. 165). But this was already the case in the primitive Church, and it was precisely the granting or withholding of Communion, *in nuce*, that represented the exercise of the papal primacy. This was not properly noted by Professor Perrone, as we mentioned in the first part of this book.

Ignatius was reinstalled as patriarch on November 23, 867, and the condemnation of Photius was carried out during the Fourth General Council of Constantinople. The author observes apropos of this: "If Rome was preoccupied with reiterating its role of supreme judge and arbiter, which had been so strenuously contested by Photius, the Byzantine emperor appeared to be disposed to accept it, on condition that the autonomy and dignity of the Church of Constantinople not be diminished thereby. It was in that perspective that Constantinople IV affirmed the Roman primacy alongside of a marked recognition of the Pentarchy" (p. 166). With regard to the role of Rome, Perrone points out that the Roman legates finally succeeded in getting the sanctions specified by Rome applied, "although only as an autonomous pronouncement of the Council." But what significance can the word "autonomous" possibly have here when it is stated that the sanctions were specified by Rome? "The canons approved by Constantinople IV mostly reflect a problematic narrowly linked to the problem of Photius, but these canons are not without more general language touching upon the themes of the Roman primacy, the pentarchy, and the relations of the Church with the civil authority."

There follows the question of "the revision of the judgment against Photius at the Council of Santa Sophia (879-880)," which concludes on a note that points to future conflicts. The difficulties between Rome and Constantinople dragged on until the end of the century. "Only in 899 did John IX finally succeed in putting an end to the controversy by means of a conciliatory formula which did not directly displease either the Photians or the Ignatians; nor did it abdicate the rights of the Roman Church; at the same time, though, it indirectly reconfirmed the illegitimacy of the first patriarchate of Photius as well as reconfirming the judgment of Adrian II" (p. 176). Finally, the author provides an explanation of "the separate fates of the two 'councils of union'" (p. 176) in both the East and the West, and he also supplies a good bibliographic note.

The *fourth part*, entitled "The Seven Medieval 'Papal' Councils," was assigned to Alberto Melloni (pp. 183-218). Allow us to state at the outset that we are not pleased by the use of the adjective "papal" here, even when it is placed between quotation marks. The author justifies it by saying "it explains how the Latin synodal tradition arrived back where it ended up"; from the papal point of view, such councils were seen as "a point of force for the pope in his effort to free his power from the bonds imposed upon him by the symbiosis with the authority of the empire, as well as from local traditions and rights stemming from collegiality with the cardinals, all of which limited his power." But practically every word of this explanation requires an even more precise explanation. The "transformation" into "ecumenical" (or general) councils of the seven councils in question was, he says, due "to the work of certain post-Tridentine canonists and theologians" (but the Council of Constance had expressly claimed "to represent the universal Church" well before that).

Melloni notes: "The entrance of the Rus into the Christian world, the break between the pope and the patriarch of Constantinople, the victory of an ecclesiology based on the *Ecclesia Romana*, the success of the reforms carried out with such vigor by Gregory VII and various small groups of 'Gregorians'—all these things were factors which contributed to turn an on-going historical process into one of epochal scope, and one which, in the course of some two centuries, had made the successor of Peter the true ruler and supreme legislator of the Western Church" (p. 187). Here must be clarified the very concept of *Christianitas*, for the Roman pontiff was already the true ruler and supreme legislator of the whole Church. Historical questions are not resolved—we repeat—by deferring at the time to some elements that were in fact already present *in nuce* in the Church of the early centuries.

The undertaking of the author to try to differentiate synods from ecumenical councils is rather labored (see esp. p. 196), as is his research into the *Dictatus Papae* of Gregory VII. Does he not know that the latter simply crystallized in a fundamental way what had long been the Occidental understanding with regard to the privileges of the Roman Church, and which was also not without its ecumenical foundations as well? Drawing out the consequences of principles which had been in place for centuries was somehow something "unexpected and revolutionary"? (p. 188).

The first so-called "papal" council, the First General Council of the Lateran of 1123 sanctioned the end of the schism of Gregory VIII, but exhibited some resistance about ratifying the Concordat of Worms. "However, the half-century of hostility and non-availability of the pope with regard to consideration of revisions persuaded the council in the end" (p. 189). "It also provided for the regulation of various outstanding questions destined to undergo strong development" (*Ibid.*). These were later explained. 22 canons were promulgated by Lateran I.

Then, in April of 1139, Innocent II convoked in Rome a *plenaria synodus*, which is today counted as Lateran Council II. Among other things it annulled "the conflicts which had arisen in the East between the patriarchs" (p. 192).

At this point the author inserts a number of considerations concerning "the 'turn' at the middle of the 12th century"—which, according to him, was linked to Gratian. Is he not aware that this *Magister* was merely a compiler of past decisions? Various affirmations of his with regard to the "turn" in question leave us perplexed. Can it be said that there "existed a tendency, at bottom anchored in practices attested to thanks to the 'Gregorians' [without making any distinctions!] which pointed towards refusal of the administration of the sacraments by unworthy clerics"? (p. 194). And with respect to the Council of Rheims (1148), in which there was delivered to Gilbertus Porretanus a list of "corrections" to be inserted in his works, what can be said about the assertion that there was "usurped (by the consistory or reunion of the pope with his *fratres cardinales*), in the name of the

Ecclesia Romana, of a conciliar prerogative (up until then normal and necessary for judgments on a bishop)" (*Ibid.*)?

"Such institutional crumbling"—according to Melloni— "indicated a qualitative jump which showed how the Latin Church in the middle of the century was witnessing the birth of canon law as a science" (*Ibid.*). But was this in fact *ius novum*? The acts recorded as belonging to the government of Alexander III," the author concludes, "represent so many steps toward this new conception of papal power and of Christianity itself." And yet, here again, perhaps, it is necessary to make distinctions.

The accords of Anagni (1176), and the agreements between the pope and the emperor reached at Venice in July of 1177, provided for a general council that could ratify and pacify. It finally took place in Rome itself. This was the Third General Council of the Lateran (1179), which was followed in 1215 by the Fourth, and was due to Pope Innocent III; this latter council approved 70 chapters which later on were inserted into the *Compilationes*.

These important topics are briefly explained. Let us note in this connection, however, an incongruence with respect to canon 9, which prohibited more than one bishop for one see. It was supposedly this regulation that was to be "the instrument by which Latin bishops would be imposed on the Greek Church in accordance with an idea of reunion already worked out in terms of uniformity and of a necessary 'return'" (p. 203). Instead, it is precisely in this canon 9, as reported by Melloni himself, for that matter, that we read: "We strictly command the bishops...to name men capable of celebrating the divine offices and administering the sacraments in the various rites and languages." Thus, at least the accusation of uniformity certainly does not apply in this case.

The First General Council of Lyons (1245) was convoked by Innocent IV in order to heal the five wounds afflicting the Church, the image of Christ. These were "the corruption of the faith and of customs, the failure to recover the Holy Land (Jerusalem had passed back into Muslim hands in 1244), the Eastern Schism, the peril from the Tartars, and the conflict with the contumacious Frederick II" (p.

205). "The *negotium* with the emperor gave rise to a quick trial... Frederick was stripped of all his royal and imperial rights, including that of the *fidelitas* towards him on the part of his subjects" (p. 206).

Some thirty years passed before Gregory X developed the idea of holding a fully ecumenical council at Rome that would include both the Greeks and the Armenians, and would aim at the reconquest of the Holy Land for the benefit of the Christian oecumene; it would also seek ways to convert the Tartars to Christianity, and would try to effect a reform of the Church. This was the Second General Council of Lyons (1274).

A rather bitter account by Melloni records how ephemeral the effort was that was made to overcome the schism; he says it was based more on a desire "to overcome weaknesses impeding the Crusade; meanwhile there was bargaining going on over questions of convergence of interests between Roman ambition and Constantinopolitan weakness" (p. 209). It was therefore not possible "to take into consideration the theological depth of the unresolved questions, the first among them being the ecclesiological divergences among the Churches" (p. 210).

In this connection, for example, two positions adopted by the council are criticized, the first of them deriving from an analogy. As for the second one, he says that Lyons II established the fact that "all the causes relating to episcopal elections or arising out of those elections are to be listed among the *major causes* (*causae maiores*), and hence the treatment of them, in whatever kind of recourse, must be given to the Apostolic See" (*Ibid.*). But this judgment was related to considerations already several centuries old—considerations to the effect that any judgments related to bishops were, in fact, always *causae maiores*.

Weighing upon the next council, the General Council of Vienne (1311-1312), "in a very significant way, according to many, was the legacy of Boniface VIII...[including] the judicial inquiry carried out against the military order of the Knights Templar and the accusations against them, as well as questions relating to the Holy Land and plans for a Crusade—all these things became bargaining factors between Clement V and Philip the Fair; they were related to the inquiry into what would have been an improbable posthumous condemnation of the Caetani pope, Boniface VIII; or else they counted at least as an accumulation of as many advantages as possible in return for dropping plans for such a condemnation" (p. 211 ff.).

In his "conclusions," enumerated just ahead of a rather good bibliography (pp. 216-218), the author repeats: What "henceforth defines a council in medieval Christianity is the papacy, which replaced an ecumenicity considered impractical and in fact not even desired. The genetic function of the council with respect to canon law became profoundly changed when, in a macroscopic measure from Lateran III on, conciliar decisions of a universal juridical nature came to be taken in the application of previous papal decretals. Only in the niches of the law or of political theory was there preserved an awareness of the difference between pope and council, thanks to which it might have been possible to heal the schism in the Occident" (p. 214). With regard to the relationship between conciliar canons and decretals, it should be noted that even before the influence was mutual. And as for the difference between a pope and a council, it was a problem *sui generis*, since there never is a council without the Bishop of Rome, legitimately elected and never deviating in the faith.

The *fifth part* of the volume is the work of J. Wohlmuth, professor of the history of the Church at the University of Bonn. His contribution covers the Councils of Constance (1414-1418) and Basel (1431-1449) (pp. 219-281).

For the first time among the various contributions to this book, we find the author's purpose as well as his plan of work clearly laid out: "My personal effort here," he says, "will be satisfied with a rather reduced chronicle of events, while concentrating on the sequence of the various sessions and their texts…I will therefore deal first with the development of the two councils separately, and then I will sum up the theological developments along the same fundamental ecclesiological lines that tie the two councils so closely together. The chronicle of the various sessions represents the practical background in which the conciliar texts are situated" (p. 221). This approach turns out to be quite interesting, and, while working it out in practice, the author remains on the same high level as in his original premises. It is worthwhile

also noting his view that "the chronicler of two such vast councils...
must limit himself to what is indispensable, all the more so because,
while there is a huge mass of partial research, the history of these two
councils has not yet been written up to the present day" (*Ibid.*).

Constance, "the greatest and most important assembly of the late
medieval period" (K.A. Fink), was convoked in order to overcome the
grave crisis of a duplicate series of popes, in Rome and in Avignon.
We will not follow the author in all of his meanderings, but will only
mention some of the more interesting items he covers, to which we
will then add some personal interpretations. The famous fifth session,
he says, brought things to a head, thanks to "a deepened theological
understanding...of very great importance" (p. 226). "Even after the
flight of the pope, in fact, precisely on account of his absence, the
united council needed to have the competence, and dispose of the
necessary forces, in order to recreate the unity of the Church. This
claim of competence for the council was motivated by Christological
considerations: a council legitimately assembled in the Holy Spirit
(as was the claim contained in the introductory document) draws
its *potestas* directly from Christ. The consequence of this claim is
evident: even a pope owes his obedience to this *potestas*, and precisely
in matters pertaining to faith, unity, and reform. Another consequence
was added in the fifth session: any believer obstinately opposed to a
conciliar decision, even the pope, must be punished. However, if the
council was to achieve its primary objective, that is, the reunification
of the Church, putting an end to the schism, it had to find the necessary
means and methods to proceed towards this goal. The decree of the
fifth session therefore arose out of the particular historical situation in
which this council (*Haec sancta synodus Constantiensis*) must find a
solution to the problem for which it could then assume responsibility
before the entire Church and for which it considered that it was
truly representative, that it possessed the proper 'representation'
(*repraesentatio*)" (p. 226).

Wohlmuth continues as follows: "However, a distinction was made
between the historical conditioning which produced the text and the
theological motive for it. The fact that behind the council's decision
stood the highly contingent emergency situation of the papal schism

must be considered a condition and not the motivation of the text: since the situation was so precarious; and since the Church could not long live subject to three obediences, a theologically based solution was sought, and this was found in the notion of the immediate relationship between Christ and his assembled council. This relationship called for absolute obedience." (p. 226 ff.). It would normally occur to us to ask whether this condition was a *conditio sine qua non*, but from the context we conclude that the author does not think that was the case. The conclusion that Constance (and also Basel) had "other aims than that of abolishing the papacy" seem to us to be of little weight. Rather, the intention of the council was to elect a pope. There is thus opened here a door that was...already open! In effect, it was a different papacy that was envisaged here, "one with limits imposed on the part of the Council" (p. 228).

Another culminating point is touched upon later, which would have directed the judgment of Benedict XIII (Session XXXVII) towards a more "traditional" solution, namely to declare Pedro de Luna a heretic. He could then no longer have served as pope, according to the received canonical judgment. The grounds for his heresy would have been failure to believe in the article of faith concerning "*una* (sic) *sanctam catholicam ecclesiam*" (p. 233). The author comments here that "with this accusation of heresy, the text no doubt arrives at the authentic kernel of the council's approach: without establishing heresy on his part, the council could see no valid way to proceed against Pedro de Luna, as had already been the case with regard to [the anti-pope] John XXIII" (p. 233). We too believe that a deepening of the investigation of this aspect of the case could indeed illuminate our understanding, from a truly Catholic point of view, of the meaning of the Council of Constance. (One should also look at the question of the *plena fides* of the pope on p. 237 of the book.)

However, the decree *Frequens* of the XXXIX session arose out of a new situation of crisis within the council. Comparable as it was to what had occurred earlier in Session V, the decree was considered non-binding since it had never been observed in practice.

In any case, taking into account the history of the reception of the council, the judgment concerning both of these texts has fluctuated.

According to Wohlmuth, "the most important dogmatic element of session XXXIX can be seen in the fact that the papal office, precisely insofar as it constitutes the major charge confided to the Church by Christ, was linked to the *plena fides* of the Church. On the one hand, this faith involved a link to the diachronical history of the faith. On the other hand, there was a binding relationship, in each era, to the universal council. It was possible, therefore, to think of a constitutional link or tie of the highest papal power to the *plena fides* to which the council was also subject" (p. 237). But how must this *plena fides* be understood in case of a conflict? And how should we understand the term "binding" relationship"?

The General Council of Basel (1431-1449), which today is being rescued from virtual oblivion in order to be now considered a "historical phenomenon of universal reach" (Helmrath), undoubtedly witnessed, on an ecclesiastical plane, a "decisive battle between papalism and conciliarism" (H. Jedin).

The aims of the study are here again indicated in an exemplary fashion by Wohlmuth. Included are the aims of bringing out the most important themes for ecclesiology and for the history of dogmas, as well as describing the constitutional conflict (which was also important in its ecclesiological aspects). These themes included the projects for reform, the ecumenical efforts of the council in its negotiations with the Bohemians, and the efforts to restore union with the Greeks" (p. 241). In orienting himself, the author makes use of the documents of all of the 45 sessions held in Basel as well as of the 5 held in Lausanne (these last being mostly irrelevant); he notes that "turning to this entire *corpus* of texts may seem obvious to the historian, but up to the present day it represents a problem of the first order for a certain type of theological approach committed to a systematic orientation. For it is well known that with the convocation of the council in Ferrara-Florence, papal recognition was withdrawn from the Council of Basel in such a way that the Catholic reception of this council (where it exists) becomes interrupted with the session XXV of May 7, 1437" (*Ibid.*).

After having briefly explained the unfolding of synodal events from the inauguration of the council on July 23, 1431, up to the XIX session and then to the XXV session in order to arrive at a conclusion in the end, Wohlmuth then expounds "some important ecclesiastical guidelines which left their mark on the two councils" (p. 242).

We shall pass over the facts (noting only with "theological" regret two affirmations reported in order by the author that are both "theological" and "political" and are found on page 254, note 74). The author places in evidence the *tres veritates* of the council in which "conciliarism arrives at its dogmatic summit"—but it is a summit, we hasten to add, that is non-Catholic. And we then come to a "panoramic presentation of the ecclesiological acquisitions of the two councils."

The author appraises the work of the councils aimed at the reform of the Church, considering this rather poor and "incomplete" at Constance, but he states that "the results of the reforms passed at Basel have come to be recognized with less hesitation" (p. 260). He cites Meuthen, who considered Basel to be a "stage in the elaboration of a Catholic ecclesiology that was both systematically constructed and consistent." Wohlmuth explains: "It was in the context of this council...that were born the first great treatises on the Church; and they came from both the papal and conciliar sides" (p. 263).

At any rate, the fundamental question posed by the author to himself is whether one can indeed speak of an ecclesiology evolving from Constance to Basel on the basis of the conciliar texts (synodal rulings and daily interpretations made by the *Haec sancta,* as received by Basel). There was evolution.

In the end, we were pleased by Wohlmuth's way of proceeding, especially from the theological point of view proper to him. His is a major sensibility for a Catholic vision of the relations between pope and council. In any case, he affirms that "both councils were deeply rooted in Catholic constitutional principles, to which belonged not only the tradition of the *papa qui potest dici ecclesia,* but from the time of Zabarella on, also l'*universalis ecclesia id est concilium*" (p. 268). But it is necessary to make explicit that the very term "council" also *includes* the pope. Besides, this very same author himself notes, successively, that when at Constance a "council" is spoken of, "presumably it is intended that the question be left open as to whether a council with or without the pope is meant" (p. 269). Basel, however, in its interpretation of the *Haec sancta*, effectively meant only a council without the pope.

In this regard, and without getting into the replies of various scholars to the question posed by this author above, we would like to note the conclusion reached by Wohlmuth and indicate its application today. Departing from the conviction that "conciliarism should not be linked, either in its proposals for reform, or with regard to its theoretical foundations as related to pope and council," the author notes how "the equilibrium between the monarchical and corporative principles is extremely precarious." However, to state the case in words that recall less plainly the logic of domination, and with respect to the responsibility of one for the whole—and the inclusion also of the responsibility of all for the sake of this same whole—Wohlmuth observes that "the solution does not lie in eliminating one of the two principles in question" (p. 276). We certainly agree with such a conclusion.

The author continues: "The struggle to find an equilibrium between these two principles has not ceased to shake the Church up to the present day. The historic failure of conciliar ecclesiology should not induce anyone today to renounce the constitutional element that is inherent in universal councils" (*Ibid.*). In order to be able to agree with this, however, we would have desired to see greater precision from the author on what is meant by "conciliar ecclesiology" (or "conciliarism"?). We also need to know if for Wohlmuth there could be "universal councils" without the pope. This is not a case—take note!—of any "monarchical principle"; but it is rather the personal exercise of the Petrine responsibility in and for the Church. This is the way the question must, frankly and radically, be posed.

The *sixth part* of the work was assigned to Umberto Proch, under the title: "Union at the Second General Council of Lyons and at the General Council of Ferrara-Florence-Rome" (pp. 283-319).

For the first of these two synods, traditionally considered "ecumenical" by Catholics but not by the non-Catholic Eastern

Churches, the first priorities were "relief for the Holy Land and finding the necessary funds to organize a crusade" (p. 287). The second priorities were "union with the Greeks and 'peace'" (that is, peaceful relations between the Christian East and the Western powers and among the Churches). "These two elements, *unio et pax*, had to be kept distinct in order to avoid confusion with regard to Lyons II" (p. 288). A third priority area concerned intra-ecclesial reform. The author describes the preparations for union (*reductio*) with the Greeks as well as the political interests involved; he offers a judgment which, from the theological aspect, is more positive than that offered, for example, by Melloni (see p. 209ff). Proch concludes that "it was not simply a case of playing a game consisting of political compromises" (p. 291; but see also p. 292). For the Latins, "union" had to include "acceptance of the faith as prescribed by Rome" (p. 291). This came about in Februrary, 1274, at Constantinople, and this acceptance was officially confirmed in the name of the emperor a few months later at Lyons by a Palaeologus delegation that arrived there on June 24.

After presenting the work of the council according to the *ordinatio*, Proch analyzes the outcome of the efforts to achieve union and the causes of the lack of success of these efforts.

There is a great acuteness of vision here: "Precisely...in the unsuccessful ecclesiological explanations can be discerned probably the most profound cause of the failure of the unionist colloquies of the thirteenth century. In spite of sporadic efforts here and there, no one ever succeeded in arriving at any in-depth confrontation with at least two different—though not necessarily discordant—theological attitudes: namely, the scholasticism of the Latins and the Greek approach focused more on patristics, and also less inclined to accept a philosophical methodology in theological inquiry. The Greek approach was also more tied to the tradition of formulas of faith" (p. 296). The author's bibliography, as always, concludes his treatment.

After presenting the historiography of the Florentine council, and after having expounded the context in the Fifteenth century as well as the preliminaries of the council, the author presents both facts and practices. "During the conciliar sessions, five principal factors of division were identified and discussed: the Creed, the procession of the Holy Spirit, Purgatory, *epiclesis*, and papal primacy. The Greeks gradually began to see the light regarding the idea that the Fathers of the Church had always maintained, within a Trinitarian context, similar views on these issues. This was a surprise" (p. 307). Proch takes particular care to describe the evolution and the perfecting of the methods of the work as well as the discussions that took place at the council.

The decree of union, *Laetentur Caeli*, consisted of two parts: an ample and rather pompous introduction and another more sober text of a doctrinal character, "consisting of texts practically juxtaposed of the various formulas which had been proposed, discussed, emended, and then approved."

The author presents all these things in order and then concludes: "A few weeks later [the Greeks] left Italy, without great enthusiasm and in uncertain spirits, without having procured much economic and military aid, and with the difficult task ahead of them of having to explain back home the developments of some fifteen months and more. Considering the uncertainty of the Emperor John VIII himself in proclaiming the union; the battle that had already opened up between those who supported the decree and the intransigents [who opposed it]; the failure of the crusade and of the promised military aid (the defeat at Varna in November, 1444); the disappearance over a fairly brief time of the men who had crafted the union; and, especially, the failure to develop a more substantial theological and ecclesiological plan—all these reasons make understandable the failure of a union that was valid though in need of greater development" (p. 311). *In nuce*, the author's reply to the question: "Was the Council of Florence a 'failed success'"? He follows his presentation of the union of the Churches and precedes his final analysis of the affinity and diversity of Lyons II and Florence.

The *seventh part* of the book, "The Fifth General Council of the Lateran and the General Council of Trent" (pp. 321-368), is the work of Mark Venard. With balance and clarity he synthesizes the research devoted to these two councils.

Lateran V opened in Rome on May 3, 1512. It was convoked by Pope Julius II, in part in order to deal with the anti-papal *conciliabulum* convened in Pisa from October, 1511, on. The council was assembled through the initiative of the king of France, who was supported by the emperor. Their motive was to promote Church reform, in favor of which two Venetian nobles, Giustiniani and Querini, had written a *libellus ad Leonem X*, drafted in 1513, which Hubert Jedin considered "the most ample and radical of all the programs of reform proposed in the conciliar era" (p. 325).

The work of Lateran V is then presented in its doctrinal aspect, including its terms for the reform of the curia, the clergy, and the Christian people. The events that were soon to follow, the entrance upon the scene of Martin Luther, made "laughable the reform measures which the Council had in mind, even if they had been carried out" (p. 328). Hence "the most lasting achievement of this miscarried council was to put an end to conciliarist theories and to recognize the superiority of a pope over a council" (*Ibid.*).

"From Lateran V to Trent" includes an analysis of appeals to a council, as well as of the convoking of one, in order to confront the evils from which the Church was suffering. These evils included "a poor selection of bishops, the ordination of too many priests who were ill-prepared as far as their formation was concerned, the accumulation of benefices and the abuses of the curia conniving in this, decadence within the religious orders, a decline in preaching, and a slide into impiety in the schools" (p. 334). This was the situation of Christianity in various nations.

In "The Council of Trent," the author describes the operation of the synod in question, along with the personalities and vicissitudes involved, up to the XXV session (December 4, 1563), during which "the closure of the council was celebrated with solemn acclamations" (p. 344). The unity of the Council of Trent was manifest in the fact that in the course of the closing meeting all the canons and decrees voted under Paul III, Julius III, and Pius IV were read again and approved in bloc. The work of the council was thus brought together into an indivisible whole" (*Ibid.*). "The council fathers delivered all of their work to the Roman pontiff for his approval and confirmation." Pope Pius IV, perhaps under the influence of his nephew, Charles Borromeo, with the Bull *Benedictus Deus*, dated January, 1564, but only published in the following June, confirmed the council's work and appointed a commission of cardinals to follow up with its implementation. Venard then explains the doctrinal and disciplinary results of the council following its approved texts. "Bishops at the head of their dioceses, and priests at the head of their parishes: these were the twin pillars of the restored Church of the Council of Trent" (p. 352). Following the Council of Trent, the entire ecclesiastical institution was henceforth oriented towards "the prospects of the salvation of souls" (*Ibid.*). To sum up, "the Council of Trent was a product of the Catholic Reform at least as much as it was its guide; and many of the council's realizations, which have so marked modern Catholicism, have not so much stemmed from the application of the conciliar decrees as they have been creative innovations" (p. 353).

In chapters entitled "The Completion of the Work of the Council," "The Reception of the Council," The Implementation of the Council," and "The Post-Tridentine Church" (this last covering the Roman Church, the "clerical" Church, and popular Catholicism), the author succeeds in giving us an essential perspective, and he worthily concludes his graceful and objective treatment with both praise and just criticism of Jean Delumeau. "The Catholic Reform," he writes, "did not indicate a passage from paganism to Christianity. Medieval historians have justly reacted against this vision of things. Rather, it indicated the introduction of a new reaching out, carried forward with both method and efficiency, of a new model of Christianity, namely, modern Catholicism" (p. 367). "Once it was realized that the break [with the Protestants] was definitive, the Council of Trent, at this, the beginning of modern times, gave to those who remained faithful to Rome something all Western Christians had long aspired to, namely, a catechism and authentic pastors" (*Ibid.*).

The *eighth* and *ninth* (and last) *parts* of the book are treated by Giuseppe Alberigo himself (pp. 369-396 and 397-448, respectively.

These parts are entitled "Vatican Council I (1864-1870)" and "Vatican Council II (1962-1965)."

For the first of these modern councils, the premises and preparations covered lead into the first phase of the work and the debate on *Dei Ecclesia* and the constitution *Dei Filius*; and they then go on to the *Schema De Romano Pontifice* and the constitution *Pastor Aeternus*. There follows then the "suspension of the council and the reception of its decisions."

We shall limit ourselves here to making a few critical points, especially as regards the precision of the language employed. This is the case with respect to the "definition" of titular bishops: namely, "those lacking a proper diocese of their own" (p. 373). But there is more: an affirmation of the author that "the personal relationship between the apostle (Peter) and the bishops of Rome...leave obscure the situation of the Roman Church, which played a decisive role in the theological tradition of the primacy" (p. 389). Again, the word "unexpectedness" seems out of place for describing "the interpretation maintained by the German episcopate, which discovered in Pius IX a zealous and unconditional supporter" (p. 392). In fact, however, it is not a question, as the author contends, of "a moderate interpretation of *Pastor Aeternus* that would marginalize the 'integrist' position of the type exhibited by Manning" (p. 392).

Another objection of ours enters more profoundly into the merits of the case. This pertains to the following judgment, which we do not share: "It was the first time that a general council had a plan of work prepared in anticipation of its meeting without the participation of the Council Fathers themselves" (p. 375). "Even more alarming," the author thinks, "was the norm in accordance with which an absolute majority was sufficient to approve a decision definitively" (p. 381). In this regard, it is worth noting that Wohlmuth affirmed the contrary (see p. 253). But, again, Alberigo: "Only the affirmation of the third chapter, concerning the obligation to accept the teaching of the ordinary magisterium, aroused some perplexity" (p. 383). "Once again, the crucial point was found in the relationship between the pope and the Church: how did it come about that the pope had the capacity to proclaim a doctrine infallibly, entailing the agreement thereby of the whole Church, and, in particular, that of the body of bishops? In actual fact, was the pope over the Church or was he *in* the Church, although with a responsibility *sui generis*?" (p. 387). "The solemn vote took place on July 18, when a significant part of the minority [but how significant, in relation to the whole assembly?] decided not to take part in order to attenuate the scandal of a conciliar definition not approved unanimously but only by a majority" (p. 388). Did this *ex sese* "not affect the very traditional criterion according to which any ecclesiastical decision—including the venerable definitions of the first ecumenical councils—could not fail to be received into the life and faith of the universal Church, even in spite of its irrelevance?" (p. 390) "The tensions that developed in the course of the council, as well as the final laceration by which the minority [?] abandoned the assembly before the vote on the constitution *Pastor Aeternus*, made one fear that there might be troublesome questions concerning the unity of Catholicism" (p. 391). "Thus was created the impression that the liberty of the council was very precarious. The assembly as such underwent a very labored existence on account of the tendencies whereby the directions taken by the council were charted outside itself by various pressure groups" (p. 393). "The impact of the council and its decisions...on the Catholic faithful was modest" (*Ibid.*). The conclusion reached by the author prepares the way and sets the tone for the way Vatican II will be treated, since "such a council, even while preparing the way for an expansion beyond Eurocentrism, did not know how to transcend the defensive attitudes and the siege mentality that afflicted Catholicism" (p. 394).

After having described the main features of what would be the second meeting of an ecumenical council in the Vatican—the "unexpected announcement" of it, its "pre-preparation period (1959-1960)," and its full-fledged "preparatory phase (1960-1962)"—Alberigo then launches into the treatment of the great synod itself, properly speaking, beginning with its solemn opening. He then divides up his study in accordance with the four conciliar periods (I-IV) when the Council Fathers were in session, and then he goes into the "inter-sessions" in between, when the conciliar commissions continued to function.

The author shows great familiarity with the subject matter he treats. However, two recent articles have enriched our knowledge of two of the more delicate areas he covers; these are the role of Cardinal Tardini (pp. 401-402) and that of the Roman Curia (pp. 401, n. 6, 403 and 408, n. 12). There was also "the pole of resistance to the authority [of the Moderators]...constituted by the General Secretariat and, in particular, by Archbishop Pericle Felici himself, who feared a reduction in his ability to function, particularly if the groups of moderators had succeeded in institutionalizing their own secretariat, a task confided to Father G. Dossetti" (p. 418, n. 17). The two recent articles we refer to are: *"Il Cardinale Tardini e il Concilio Vaticano II"* ["Cardinal Tardini and the Second Vatican Council"], by Vincenzo Carbone, in R.S.C.I., XLV (1991), n.1, pp. 42-88; and the earlier article of Michele Maccarrone, *"Paolo VI e Il Concilio: Testimonianze"* ["Paul VI and the Council: Testimonials"], in R.S.C.I., XLIII (1989), pp. 101-122.

In any case, in this essay, there re-appears Alberigo's well-known line, his one-track sensibility, and his pre-conceived judgments—we have taken note of these in other places. What is in play here is an "ecclesiology of communion" as he understands it (see esp. pp. 425 and 426), namely, an ecclesiology that is closed to the "hierarchical communion" taught by the Church (pp. 441 and 434), and one which, even when it is expressed in new language, is nevertheless grounded on a secure historical basis. Besides, the *Nota Explicativa Praevia* employs precisely this expression, "hierarchical communion," in its ecclesiology. But then for Alberigo, this *Nota* was "neither introduced into the discussion nor signed by the pope; it thus remains extraneous to the true and proper conciliar decisions; it is a working document of the theological commission" (pp. 434 and 433). Such a view confirms his incomprehension of the laborious and far-seeing work of mediation carried out by Pope Paul VI between the majority and the minority at the Council; it was a work aimed at reducing the distance between the two sides (p. 436); it was done out of the fear of a loss of "doctrinal clarity" and "historical incisiveness" (*Ibid.*, and esp. p. 438). But it seems to us that what is most important for this author is above all his own view of the papal-episcopal relationship, in order, he says, "to get beyond the isolation of the papal office" (p. 414). More than isolation, however—we know this from seeing it re-appear over and over again—there is the "problem of the exclusively personal dimension of the papal office" (p. 420; see also pp. 429 and 433). But this, however, forms part of the integral belief of the Council.

Other points in the essay form corollaries to these difficulties of his particular vision, towards which we can only be highly critical. They include: his marked and studied silence with regard to the universal Church ("the importance of the local Church as the authentic realization of the Church must be recognized"—p. 441 and esp. p. 430 and 436); the unsuitability, at the very least, of the language he employs relative to the origin of episcopal *auctoritas* (pp. 427 and 437; see also p. 400, n. 3); his extreme sensitivity about citing the language of the ordinary magisterium in the conciliar texts relating to "procreation" (p. 440)— language used "to underline the continuity and irreformability of the magisterium, even though documents of varying authority are cited which are certainly on an inferior plane by comparison with conciliar decisions" (*Ibid.*); his negative judgment concerning *Optatam Totius* ("a decree...among the least adequate to the deal with the exigencies of the Church, not only because it did not explore more thoroughly the difficulties of clerical celibacy, but also, especially, because it failed to provide the Council with a lucid perception of the grave crisis of identity which for decades had been undermining priestly formation and, indeed, the very condition of being a priest" (p. 442); the supposed diminishing hierarchy of theological value in the chapters of *Lumen Gentium* ("In the third chapter, the ecclesiological hierarchy was treated...in such a way that its diverse theological importance was respected in the very succession of topics covered" (p. 419); his gibe against the "Roman Church" which, in the case of *Dei Verbum* [where his presentation is also very imprecise: see pp. 409 and 415], "rediscovered a correct realization" of its subordination to the Word of God (p. 444); his anxiety to demonstrate that Pope John did not intervene in fixing "the agenda of the Council" (pp. 402 and 407) and to show that he exhibited great "sensitivity" for the *Ordo agendorum* (p. 412) as well as for the way it was handled (pp. 405 and 416).

Another serious deficiency in our opinion is the inexact presentation of the relationship between Church and Kingdom, which, as is well known, is pregnant with consequences. The Kingdom is not only considered to be "distinct from the Church" (p. 435), there are differences "between the Kingdom of God and the Church as well as between the Church of Christ and ecclesial traditions" (p. 437). The Church would perhaps *not* be, then, for the Council, "the seed and the beginning of [the] Kingdom" which, in fact, *Lumen Gentium* says that it is? (LG # 5).

Finally, with regard to the question of a "just war" (pp. 415 and 432), it is not proper to speak about "theology" here, just as it is not exact to speak of the "condemnation" of those Catholics "who collaborated with the Communists, excluding them from participation in the sacraments" (p. 400, n. 4).

The volume is enriched by the inclusion of an index of abbreviations as well as analytical and general indices. A brief indication is also included of the professional specialties and works and studies of the various contributing authors. A subject index arranged according to the various topics covered would have been a helpful service to the reader.

As for *errata corrige*, we may note such errors as those on p. 13, para 1, where "*sinodi*" is rendered "*snodi*"; p. 231, para 3, where "*Il regolamento*" should be "*di regolamento*"; p. 233, para 3, where "*una sancta*" should be "*unam sanctam*"; p. 301, para 1, where "*s mento*" should be "*strumento*"; and p. 418, para 2, where "*e gi*" should be "*e-gli.*"

In conclusion, going back to what was said at the beginning with regard to the first essay by Professor Perrone, the bibliography included by each author at the end of his particular contribution does not succeed in removing our discomfort concerning the rather generalized lack of an adequate critical apparatus—notes and references—, that is to say, referring to the varied thought of those who, prior to themselves, ventured to make in-depth historical studies on the topics at hand. We can grant somewhat of an exception here in the cases of A. Melloni, J. Wohlmuth, and Professor Alberigo himself, who do employ rather restricted criteria concerning Vatican II itself. May we be pardoned for repeating it, but in our day, the typical judgment made in cases of omissions of this kind is: "The work is unscientific." What has been included, in a few cases, in the text referring to general sources is simply not sufficient, and, on the other hand, no reason is given explaining the absence of any such critical apparatus in this work.

2

A History of the Councils

R. Aubert, G. Fedalto, D. Quaglioni, *Storia dei Concili* [A History of the Councils], Edizioni S. Paolo, Cinisello Balsamo, 1995, 476 pages.

This volume is introduced by Elio Guerriero with a gibe which we believe from all indications must have been inspired by Professor Alberigo: "The unique and truly consistent characteristic" of all ecumenical councils is the "great attention that has been accorded them by Christians although their actual participation in them has always been both external and marginal" (p. 5). In this same vein, the questions of the pontifical convoking and "ratification" (we would say "confirmation") of councils "at most" (p. 6), appear to us to have been treated in a rather "casual" fashion. There are also problems concerning the relationship between pope and council, and concerning the ecumenical councils themselves and their place in history. There are things here that we would have liked to see treated in a different perspective, one more respectful of the specific nature of the Church—and not merely in terms of the difference between an "absolute monarchy" and a "constitutional monarchy." Even the author adds in this connection: "It is probably not possible to push the image of a parliament too far, and it is better to think in more specifically theological terms" (p. 7). Also, the criterion chosen here for recognition of a council as ecumenical, namely, ecclesial *consensus*, must be modified to include the role of the Bishop of Rome. In any case, the present history ends up agreeing with the Catholic Church's traditional list of which councils are to be considered ecumenical councils.

The *first part* of this volume is entrusted to Giorgio Fedalto, and consists of "The Councils of Antiquity," including the first eight councils (pp. 11-97). The result is a clear and fine synthesis apt to furnish fundamental elements for discussion and judgment, with a good presentation of the various perspectives. See, for example, the subject of *libertas ecclesiae* (pp. 68-69 and 98). There is also a marked equilibrium in the various evaluations offered. One thinks of the one pertaining to Pope Vigilius (see pp. 65 and 68 and n. 15 on p. 67), as well as the one pertaining to Pope Honorius (p. 76). Proper attention is given to outlining the development of the Roman primacy, especially within the context of the institution of the patriarchates, which took place during the period being examined here (see pp. 33, 39, 49, 56, 72, 74, 75, 84, 89-90, and 94).

In the *second part*, Diego Quaglioni takes up the subject of "The Councils of the Medieval Period and the Modern Age." He moves forward the question of the *libertas ecclesiae*, and he supplies a happy, telegraphic-style synthesis of the era between Constantinople IV and Lateran I; this period extends from the end of the ninth century up to the beginning of the twelfth century, and is described as "an epoch of tormented gestation towards the birth of a new world" (p. 103).

The First General Council of the Lateran initiates the new series of "papal general councils." This is an expression which is not satisfactory in our view. Concerning Lateran I, even though he cites the negative judgment of Giuseppe Alberigo, according to which the council's decisions are only of "circumscribed and fragmentary interest," the author notes that the canons issuing from this council have had "no small or secondary role in the life of the Church and of the history of canon law" (citation from C. Leonardi); they provided the basis for "the process of rational adaptation which soon found its completion in the *Concordia Discordantium Canonum* of Gratian" (p. 107). In any case, for Hubert Jedin, Lateran I was already "to a high degree a point of meeting and a forum for Christendom."

As for Lateran II, we may be permitted two observations and a judgment: there is a failure to cite the vigorous confutation by Fois in the *Archivum Historiae Pontificiae* of Alberigo's work on "The Cardinalate and Collegiality" (see p. 108, n. 2). Alberigo is a reliable authority in Quaglioni's eyes, although we have made clear our reservations concerning his methods. But there is another equivocal interpretation by the same Alberigo of Canon 28 which "sanctioned the end of the election of bishops by the clergy and the people and recognized the exclusive competence here of the cathedral chapters" (p. 113). But a simple reading of the text is alone required in order to understand that what was at issue here was a prohibition "against the canons of an episcopal see that might exclude religious from the process of the election of bishops; with their advice and counsel, honest and suitable persons might more readily be elected" (p. 377). We must also distance ourselves from the positive judgment rendered on a work of Landi ("Between Collegiality and Curialism") cited by Quaglioni (p. 114, n. 18); we find this work very biased and artificial.

Concerning Lateran III, we consider yet another citation from Alberigo to be out of focus; according to him, with regard to the Cathars, "it was no longer the Church defending the purity of her own doctrinal teaching, but rather it was society as such seeing itself menaced and reacting by striking out at persons and no longer merely at ideas" (p. 120). But has it not always been like that in the case of persecutions? To realize this, we need think only of the deposing and exiling of bishops by the Eastern emperors or even by the Merovingians or the Carolingians.

Particular attention is rightly given to the Fourth General Council of the Lateran. It certainly constitutes, along with the Council of Trent, "the great arch on which developed"—as the late, lamented Monsignor Maccarone so splendidly expressed it—"the life of the Church from the end of the Middle Ages to the beginning of the modern era." "To the bishops is given back the entire *negotia ecclesiastica*, as well as the responsibility for the *cura animarum*," while "the jurisdictional authority of the Roman pontiff is reaffirmed" (p. 122). The 70 Lateran constitutions enacted placed the seal on the politico-religious movement that constituted the program of Pope Innocent III.

The First General Council of Lyons provided the occasion to recall the "papal monarchy" and the same idea of *plenitudo potestatis*, of sovereignty. We would have liked to see a less *ex abrupto* beginning, as well as some clarifications, especially concerning the aforesaid ancient formula. Versatile as it might be, here in another context and with its second term removed (*in partem sollicitudinis vocatus*), it takes on a new meaning of sovereignty, resembling theocracy (see also p. 142). Frederick II emerged from this council defeated and condemned. "His despotism signified the collapse of the power of the House of Swabia...Europe changed its face, contributing to the rise of the Kingdom of France as the hegemonic power, once a creature of the papacy, but now destined to exercise a rather burdensome power over the papacy" (p. 135).

Everything contributed to placing before the bishop of Rome tasks that were gigantic in scope. But Rome was to provide a *salubre remedium* to them. Pope Gregory X summed up these tasks in three points: reunion with the Greek Church, the crusade, and ecclesiastical reform. These he proposed to the Council of Lyons ("which undeniably had the character of an ecumenical assembly") (p. 137).

After the General Council of Vienne—which, again, had "three points under discussion: the trial of the Knights Templars, recovery of the Holy Land, and ecclesiastical reform" (p. 143)—we arrive at the General Council of Constance, *Haec sancta synodus*, which presented "a new idea of a council from the ecclesiological point of view: here we read that the general synod congregated at Constance was an image of the Church militant and received its powers *immediately* from Christ himself; and therefore everyone, even one invested with the pontifical powers, owed obedience both in questions of faith and in those aimed at the extirpation of schism and at reforming the Church *in capite et in membris*" (p. 150). This was—if only within the framework of a contingent emergency, as Hubert Jedin has prudently observed— "the foundation of every successive affirmation of the superiority of a council over the pope in matters of faith and ecclesiastical reform" (p. 151). In any case, with Pope Martin V, the schism came to an end and the council concluded its work—on April 22, 1418. Of the 18 points aimed at ecclesiastical reform, the council had succeeded, a month earlier, in regulating only six. We should take note, finally, that

"Martin V did not promulgate in any way the decisions of the Council of Constance, as a result of which, in scrupulous obedience to what the council had enacted, another council was convened at Pavia in 1423," and a later one at Basel.

There appeared a tendency here "on the doctrinal plane to present the decrees of the Vth and XXXIXth sessions of Constance as dogmatic definitions" (p. 158). The contacts with the Greeks "constituted the object and cause of the turn at this council in the spring of 1437" (p. 159). In contrast with the choice of Ferrara, agreed upon between Eugene IV and the Greeks for a council of union, at Basel there was a schism. The minority, headed by Nicholas of Cusa and in agreement with the pope, accepted Florence or any other site, and abandoned Basel. Quaglioni concludes: "The conflict was resolved in favor of the pope and signaled the re-emergence of the papal *plenitudo potestatis*" (p. 159).

At Ferrara and at Florence, Eugene IV achieved the major successes of his pontificate, while "the papal primacy, which had been questioned in the discussions at both Constance and Basel, found its full re-affirmation and was placed on an even solider base, by its formal and solemn acceptance by the Christian oecumene" (p. 161).

After lingering briefly on the subject of Lateran V—"emblematic of the least happy epoch of the papacy" (p. 163)—Quaglioni presents his synthetic study of the Council of Trent, in which space is not lacking for the opinions of Paolo Sarpi, "a perhaps tendentious commentator," he adds. We can certainly drop the "perhaps" here. Very briefly, the author covers the troubled course of this council, its various phases, and its decrees. Regarding the decree on episcopal jurisdiction, there was a tendency to consider the bishop's residing in his diocese to be a matter of divine right; this viewpoint was not adopted by the council, and, in any case, it did not imply a redimensioning of papal primacy, but was rather an "enlargement" of the episcopal *ius divinum*. Still we would have liked to see at least a mention of the studies of Father W. Bertrams; this would have been helpful for the study of Vatican II as well.

But Quaglioni still cites Alberigo: "All of this normative complex emanating from the Council of Trent was dominated by one supreme criterion, namely: to fulfill the task of the care of souls. Except for this, there came about an almost total silence on the subject of the reform of the papacy and of the Roman Curia; this silence was in fact a tacit condition for the willingness of the papacy to participate in any effective policy of reform" (p. 175). However, we ask ourselves if the major cause of all the evils was not precisely the fact of the neglect of the care of souls. To have "rediscovered" this at Trent as the primary concern was already a reform of very considerable magnitude. And it came about "without getting into any discussion of papal primacy or of the temporal power of the Holy See" (p. 176).

In the *third part*, Roger Aubert presents "The Councils with Worldwide Dimensions," beginning with Vatican Council I (pp. 179-273).

This is basically a good article on the general subject chosen by the author though he does focus on various points of emphasis. He begins with "the preparations and the first polemics" (p. 183); here we would not speak of "foreign consultants" to indicate those who were not Italians, but would simply describe them as "non-Italians." The author goes on to describe "the opening and the divisions of the Fathers," whom he describes as "preponderantly Latin." Here again, we would speak, rather, of neo-Latin languages, but in any case we note in Aubert a strong preference for thinking in terms of nationality; note, for example, the way he uses "Italian authorities" (p. 188), which absolutely does not apply. More precision would have been welcome with regard to what he calls "the centralized decisions of the Roman Curia"—we would speak rather of the Holy See. The same thing is true where he speaks of the influence of political ideologies on the Fathers; for example, he writes that "now all those who believed that on the political plane the future belonged to liberal institutions thought that the Church had everything to lose by presenting itself as the champion of autocratic authoritarianism" (p. 189). Then, worthy of note, there are his treatments of "the minority," "the organized opposition," and "the elections"—"from then on in various quarters there began to be doubts about the real liberty of the council" (p. 191), though he does also add that "the council possessed more freedom than some had feared would be the case."

There follow the author's treatments of "the first conciliar debates," where the tractability of "the Roman managers" is emphasized (p. 192), and of "the maneuvers surrounding the question of the infallibility of the pope," beginning with the petition of more than 450 Fathers which was received by Pius IX. The author goes on to cover the minority's organized opposition, the "true tower of strength" of which was Lord John Acton (pp. 194-195). Then there was the counter-petition, which attracted 136 signatures, in which the pope was called upon to reject the definition. The opposition did not hesitate to try to involve public opinion and even some governments. Meanwhile, on the pope's part, there was an increased willingness to intervene more directly in the question in the conviction that he was responding "to the desire of the greater part of the assembly...to defend the liberty of the Church in the face of inadmissible interference from the secular world" (p. 198).

Thus was born the brief separate constitution, *Pastor Aeternus*, which the author covers in four dense pages. Following the "provisory vote," which revealed 88 *non placet* votes, and the failure of one last attempt at compromise, around sixty bishops decided to leave Rome before the final vote. As a result, the solemn approval of the constitution attained the quasi-unanimity of those present, "in spite of the fact that at the last minute an awkward new formula was added, *"ex sese non autem ex consensu Ecclesiae"* ["of themselves, not from the consent of the Church"] (p. 202). "Two days earlier, the assembly had unanimously rejected two French works which had cast doubt upon the real liberty of the council" (*Ibid.*). With regard to the work by Hasler which is cited, he is judged to be "tendentious" (p. 200, n. 29). Later, in the bibliographical note, he is described as "lacking in critical and historical sense" (p. 206), and such is indeed the case.

The final point of emphasis is dedicated to "the conclusion of the council and the final agitations." In the end, defections were rare, except in the case of the Germans, especially with regard to the schism of the "old Catholics" (p. 203). "The greater part of those who had refused to be present for the vote of July 18 very quickly manifested their own adhesion to the new dogma" (*Ibid.*). The entire question saw its completion after the council in the significant approval which Pius IX gave to the declaration of the German bishops in response to an incorrect explanation of the papal primacy given by Bismarck.

The final and longest chapter deals with Vatican Council II. Let us state immediately that we found this text to be better than the one on the same subject by the same author which appeared in the *History of the Church* by Fliche-Martin (Editions San Paolo). It is less "journalistic," more concise and measured, and in the end more objective. Nevertheless, we should note the presence of some *clichés*—which are not always easy to overcome, even for well-trained authors.

Did John XXIII wish to convoke a council of union such as those at Lyons or Florence? Did he want such a council while the Roman Curia wanted something else, which the latter then succeeded in imposing on the Church? These questions are not clearly posed and answered by the author, certainly not with regard to "the preparations" for the council, where he writes that Tardini "did not discourage" the pope concerning the convocation of the Council. In fact, Tardini showed himself to be very favorable to the Council, indeed almost enthusiastic, and he even said that he liked things that were "great and beautiful." But the author makes no general case that any such situation obtained. He writes that "the announcement of the Council was received with reticence by the cardinals" (p. 207). He provides no specification, however, nor does he attribute to the Roman Curia any precise information concerning any so-called council of union. We know that this was not what it was all about. The uncertainty *in capite* during the initial phase is a reality that can result in the case of advice and counsel coming from the Churches; and it can be unfavorable. In this and other respects the discussions concerning the nature and aims of the Council continued to multiply, and this was true inside as well as outside of the Roman Curia. In the end, we find that from the beginning of Aubert's researches on the Council there are three fundamental "apples of discord" in his supposedly "fresh" conciliar historiography. They are: the relationship of Tardini (or Felici and Cicognani) with John XXIII, obscuring the role of Paul VI; the "mind" or "sentiments" of the cardinals; and the role of the Roman Curia (was it monolithic?).

These questions recur in the text in accordance with the tendency noted above. For example, the responses of the bishops were supposedly synthesized "in a rather tendentious manner" (see p. 208, n. 1). "The desire inside the Roman Curia to limit severely the *aggiornamento,* or updating, announced by John XXIII was evident" (p. 209). "There were two tendencies within the Central Preparatory Commission, one open to the world and with faith in the future, and the other fearfully on the defensive and often apt to confuse customs and habits with the authentic traditions of the Church" (p. 212). While the opinions attributed to John XXIII on the work of the preparatory commissions sometimes seem forced, it was true that his final conclusion included an expression of "great satisfaction for the texts that were presented to him" (p. 213).

The author's second point of emphasis concerns "The Assembly and Its Functioning." This begins with the analysis of the various episcopacies present, along with judgments on their positions, roles, and the like—not always impartial, in our opinion. There is a discussion of the majority and the minority, characterizing them in a way which inflates the importance of those attitudes concerned with dealing with the "modern world." With regard to the incessant activity of the minority, "at times judged severely," the author observes: "In reality, beyond the fact that for the greater part of its members, it was a question of a true and proper problem of coherence, it is necessary objectively to recognize that the minority constrained the majority to examine with greater attention and completeness the texts being proposed; however, it is also necessary to state that in some cases, beyond having recourse to debatable methods—something that for that matter was true of the majority as well—its obstructionist maneuvers led not so much to greater clarification as it led to the adoption of compromise formulas that were ambiguous, to the detriment of the quality of the texts" (p. 220). However—we say—what was sought after was unanimity, and as for ambiguity, it needs to be demonstrated concretely.

At this point, there are "introduced" the *periti* (or experts), the observers, and the auditors at the Council, not to speak of the conciliar regulations, the upholding of which provided occasions for severe and we believe unjust judgments against Archbishop Felici (pp. 224-225). On the other hand, nothing is said about Father Dossetti and those who favored him (three out of four of the Council Moderators), although he held no official conciliar position.

In the subchapter on "The Popes and the Council," it seems useful to quote a statement about Pope Paul VI as indicating the position of the author concerning that pontiff, who had so much at heart the aim of achieving a consensus of the entire assembly as near to unanimity as possible: "This preoccupation caused him several times to reduce the scope of certain texts; however, it cannot be affirmed that he ever really allowed himself [we would drop the adverb "really" here] to join in the maneuvers of the minority; faithful to his role as arbiter, he listened attentively to the various points of view; in the end, however, he always succeeded [we would say "almost always"] in seeing that his own point of view as a prudent reformer should prevail" (p. 227).

The question of "information" at the Council is yet another subject that is given some rather benign attention. We would have preferred to see some attention also given to the problem of "disinformation"; and, in addition to noting the pressure exerted on the majority "when it tended to relax its own efforts" (p. 229), attention should also have been given to the "bombardment" to which the minority was subject.

One then arrives at "The Unfolding of the Council," its opening, and the debates of the first period. One has the impression that for many Fathers—an attitude that seems to us unworthy of them—"a course of theological re-qualification," given to them by experts present in Rome, was sufficient to qualify them finally...to be instruments of the Holy Spirit. For them also, the relationship between Church and State in the preparatory documents reflected a "medieval perspective"

(p. 235). It seemed to them sufficient that "a few small corrections personally written by the pope" on a text of Cardinal Suenens—a text that was in fact important—should have sufficed to prove that the pope had "adopted the cardinal's discourse practically as his own" (*Ibid.*). It was also assumed that, in the unfolding of the Council's work, "the distinction between those responsible for the conciliar work and the Roman Curia was henceforth clear" (p. 236). This confirmed the view of those who had distinguished the preparatory phase of the Council's work from the later phase of its realization.

The first "intersession," or period between the sessions, provides the author an opportunity to mention various interventions of illustrious personages at the Council, whose role is rightly underlined, although a bit to the detriment of the collective (we would say conciliar) role of the Central Coordinating Commission, which in fact brought together the work of the various conciliar commissions.

There follows then the treatment of the second session, about which many questions arise: Paul VI "did not yet have a definite viewpoint on the problem of collegiality" (p. 242)? Regarding the liturgy, was it really a question of "eliminating the limitations that the Congregation of Rites wanted to impose on the leaders of the liturgical movement" (p. 243)? And with regard to the intersession of 1963-1964 prior to the third session, and concerning the question of religious liberty, was it really the task of the majority to "defend a point of view on religious liberty more modern than that of the *Syllabus of Errors*" (p. 248)? On the other hand, the account provided on the question of "the historicity of the Gospels" is exact. Yet it sounds strange to state that "in order to spare Cardinal Agagianian an unpleasant disavowal concerning the document on the missions that was being rejected, a formulation was devised inviting the commission to redraft the text according to the indications expressed in the course of the debate" (p. 251).

In effect, during the Council, there were cases where not too much subtlety was exercised with respect to persons. Yet there was an excessive "personalism," and even extreme manifestations of power by Cardinals Döpfner and Suenens during the conflict on the subject of the religious orders (*Ibid.*). We did find particularly appropriate, however, some of the author's observations on the minority and the majority, and also on the formation, on the "left," of a new opposition which accused the Theological Commission of having made concessions to the minority that were excessive (see p. 252). Aubert rightly identifies this faction as being mostly composed of "certain French and Melchite bishops, supported by a French expert in the Secretariat for Promoting Christian Unity, by numerous Dutch and German experts, and by "the Bologna group" (*Ibid.*, n. 16). With regard to this last reference, it is extremely revealing to read *Il Vaticano II: Frammenti di una riflessione* ["Vatican II: Fragments of a Reflection"], by G. Dossetti, ed. Il Mulino, 1996, especially pp. 23-102.

It was in such an atmosphere that the *Nota Praevia* was born. It is necessary to add some more precise comments about the drafting of this *Nota*; these comments, of course, were fundamentally formulated by Monsignor G. Philips, as Aubert attests (though we no longer think this to be the case). With these comments, the impression was "given to many of wanting to attenuate the range or scope of the text in Chapter III of the Constitution [*Lumen Gentium*], while, in reality, the substance of this text was in no way modified" (*Ibid.*). In this connection, the citation of J. Grootaers (in n. 17) should be accompanied by a notation that this author does not accept the judgment of Philips, for whom the *Nota* had no effect on the substance of the conciliar text. It does seem to us, however, that the fundamental research contribution of Monsignor Carbone on this subject ought to have been at least mentioned here. Similarly, Aubert's judgment concerning the papal initiative in proclaiming Mary to be the Mother of the Church does not seem to have been well enough "fused" or developed—giving an "appearance of a disavowal of the Council on the part of the pope" (p. 254). The same thing is true of the author's comments relative to *Lumen Gentium*, especially his critical comment that there were "too many elements of a juridical nature that were destined to calm the fears of the defenders of the papal primacy" (p. 235). In effect, too often, according to him, there is a deep discomfort in the document "based upon the not always happy blending of two ecclesiologies, one of a juridical inspiration...and the other, in the aggregate predominating, but centered on the concept of communion resulting from renewal movements in biblical, patristic, and liturgical studies" (p. 255; but see also p. 269). We insist, however, upon the fact, quite apart from the necessity, of a complete fusion or interpenetration of the two ecclesiologies; this in fact emerges clearly from the conciliar texts, thanks to the concept of the life and reality of a communion which is and remains hierarchical. While it would take much to explain all this, it should at least be mentioned.

The final "intersession" is presented in bold strokes and leads to the fourth session as well as to the implementation of the conciliar documents, where the *animus* of the author against the Roman Curia re-appears (see pp. 260, 265, 266, and 267). A single citation will suffice here: "The systematic delay (of the Roman Congregations) in officially implementing the reforms established by the Council was such that, in various areas, many of the impatient faithful begin to put them into effect in an improvised way, resulting in the inevitable excesses of such a way of acting" (p. 267). May we be permitted to cite one simple example in reply. We believe that it is not possible to say that with regard to the liturgy there was any delay or holding back; new things were constantly appearing and being applied; in fact, it can be said that the most serious and visible abuses occurred in this very area in which the Church had acted most promptly in response to the call of the Council.

In his closing subchapter entitled "The First Reactions," the author places in evidence his judgment that "the reaction to the Council set in motion by John XXIII, and confirmed by a majority of the assembly [no mention is made of Paul VI], against the myopic immobilism and the prevalence of juridical preoccupations outweighing evangelical inspirations which had progressively characterized post-Tridentine Catholicism, was quickly greeted with enthusiasm on the part of the most dynamic of the clergy and the faithful. Following this brief period of euphoria, however, there soon came a period of disillusionment. In fact...among simple priests many became supporters of an *aggiornamento* that was consciously radical; they plunged into a series of improvised reforms, preoccupied more than anything else by being conformed to the modern world...Numerous errors were made and at times actual improprieties occurred, particularly in such areas as liturgy and catechesis"—but it needs to be asked *why* these errors were made. For the errors in question "were fatally bound to provoke reactions...Hence the crisis of the Church came to be denounced by adversaries of the Council as if the latter had been the direct cause of all the troubles" (p. 268).

Aubert concludes: "There were, therefore, among the results of Vatican, loopholes and ambiguities and even some cases of excessive prudence, but on the final balance sheet of the Council the 'passive' voices should not cause the importance of the 'active' voices to be forgotten" (p. 269). After having listed many of the latter, in a very brief but effective synthesis based upon the conciliar documents, the author adds that "there was more"—because, he said, "a council is also an historical event." In applying this concept, however, the author returns to the synodal or conciliar motto, since, in the end, "the new climate which undeniably took hold in the Catholic Church, in spite of numerous attempts at 'restoration'" (p. 270), was the fruit of the texts that were promulgated by the Council itself, and it is not possible to separate the historical event—"the fecund inspiration which animated the leaders of the Council" (*Ibid.*)—from what was quite tangibly "created" by it. It is on this basis that one can judge and evaluate concretely, in the perennial conciliar documents themselves, what is unique and unrepeatable in the Council beyond the features of the otherwise transient conciliar climate.

The fourth part of the book (pp. 275-439) consists of an anthology of texts and documents ranging from Nicaea up to Vatican I. This anthology precedes an index of names (pp. 461-471) and a general index (pp. 473-476).

3

The Church
and Her Conciliar Focal Points

Klaus Schatz, *Storia dei Concili: La Chiesa nei suoi punti focali* [A History of the Councils. The Church and Her Focal Points], EDB, Bologna, 1999, 351 pages.

There is no lack in Italy today of "conciliar publications," indicating among other things a renewed interest in the noteworthy expression of episcopal collegiality which re-emerged and took on new life following the Second Vatican Council. The most recent publication of this type is the work of Klaus Schatz, which has enjoyed some rather benevolent "attention" on the part of Italian "Catholic" publishers.

This is a slender volume, with few notes; however, sources and a bibliography are placed at the end of the volume (pp. 317-325). We also note the very serious lack of any reference to the very important 10 tomes of the *Acta et Documenta Concilio Oecumenico Vaticano II Apparando* (4 tomes) and the *Acta Synodalia Sacrosancti Concilii Oecumenici Vaticani II* (6 tomes), edited by Professor V. Carbone, with a "partisan" Italian integration supplied by R. Burigana (pp. 325-329). This work by Schatz exhibits the usual characteristics typical of this author. As a result, there is an undue attenuation of the testimonials to the primacy of the bishop of Rome, especially in the early centuries; there is also to be found vagueness, imprecision, and even impropriety in language usage (for example, in the use of such terms as "Ultramontanism," "Gallicanism," "papal absolutism," or "ecclesiastical proletariat"). The "prophylactic" use of quotation marks, employed by the author in excess, does not succeed in overcoming these deficiencies.

There is likewise lacking any distinction made between the Catholic Church *ad intra* and the Catholic Church *ad extra*. Also, there are too many divisions and subdivisions in the cataloguing of the councils, and these seem to diverge from the general, habitual, and canonical listings, namely, ecumenical and particular councils, with a division of these latter into plenary and provincial councils. Finally, the relationship of councils with the See of Peter is much too relativized.

The last three ecumenical councils, moreover, take up the lion's share of the book: 48 pages are dedicated to Trent, 45 to Vatican I, and 66 to Vatican II, where Schatz seems to be most at his ease; but this only compounds the seriousness of our criticism. The syntheses, however, are quite good, *in genere suo*, especially considering the intent of the author to seek a broader readership.

In his Introduction the author first of all poses the question of what ecumenical councils are, expounding the modern problematic concerning this question (pp. 10-11). He thus detaches himself from the traditional enumeration of the ecumenical councils recognized by the Catholic Church. In any case, and also with regard to these recognized ecumenical councils, the author expresses his fundamental reserve with regard to the idealization of the councils of the first millennium. According to him, there are three types of councils, which are "structurally diverse" (p. 13). These are, first: Imperial Councils— these councils obtained their validity and were generally recognized in the Church in the form of imperial laws; still, it remains necessary to distinguish and deepen the understanding of the role of the bishop of Rome in these councils. Then there are the Medieval Councils convened in Western Christendom, among which are to be counted the "conciliar" councils as well as the special case of the "papal" [!] Council of Florence. And, finally, there are the Great Councils of the Catholic Church of the modern era—"uniquely assemblies of the

(Catholic) Church," he thinks. In the context of these distinctions, the author maintains that "the relationship between the council and the pope…comes out as a problem still not resolved in the history of the Church" (p. 15).

The first chapter treats the beginnings of councils as institutions to which belong continual facts which it is necessary to distinguish (pp. 17-22). There follows "Nicaea, its reception and the battle over the Trinitarian dogma," and then Constantinople I. For such a presentation, note should have been taken concerning the *iter* for the selection of the bishop (p. 30); the limits of suburbicarian Italy (*Ibid.*); the question of clerical celibacy (the study of Cochini is now available); the question of deaconesses (p. 31); "the enormous danger for the Church represented by a Christian state" (*Ibid.*); "conciliar infallibility" (p. 37); and the relationship of a council's teaching to sacred Scripture (*Ibid.*).

The author then follows with a chapter, "Nicaea Alone? From Ephesus to Chalcedon." He overvalues the human component in these councils, the power struggles, and the absolution of Nestorius (pp. 46-47); at the same time, he treats the "pretensions" of Rome. He analyzes Canon 28 in particular (p. 58). His conclusion is that "from the sixth century on, it was the Pentarchy that certified ecumenical councils" (p. 60). And his Sibylline conclusion concerning the "reception" of the councils—a theme which, understandably, recurs—is the following: "To receive a council means to enter into the process of transmitting the faith, a process which by itself constitutes the essence of a council. Naturally, this process of reception can fail. On the other hand, the decisions of 'true' councils are never conditioned upon a future reception. They claim to have authority *ex sese*. Yet the validity of this claim of theirs is obviously demonstrated by the fact of the council's being received—after this occurs" (p. 65).

There then follows the chapter "Patriarchates, Autonomous National Churches, and Fragile Unity: the Councils of the Ancient Church following Chalcedon." As a measure of the battle that went on against this council, the author treats with much, indeed, excessive, underlining, both the royal influence and the autonomy of Rome.

Schatz attests, in fact, to "the energetic rejection of every attempt at correction on the part of Rome" (p. 69). He notes the constraints against recognizing Rome "in the role of defender and savior of Chalcedon" (p. 69). How much the meaning of the Roman primacy is actually affirmed in the pages that follow, however, needs to be indicated.

The author briefly explains the controversy over the Three Chapters and he also treats Constantinople II and III. His treatment is moderated this time around in the cases of both Vigilius and Honorius (pp. 74 & 76). Following on this, he continues to take "the measure of the disaggregation of the Christian world" with a not very happy mention of the Pseudo-Isidorian Decretals in the context of the "ratification" of councils on the part of the Holy See" (p. 81ff).

Another theme of study is "the controversy over images [iconoclasm] treated at Nicaea II in 787, and the Occidental reaction to it: it was here that "the Byzantine era" in the history of the papacy ended (p. 84). This time the role of Rome is rightly placed in relief, including in the context of the Pentarchy; it was a "specific role which could not be renounced" (p. 87), although any contemporary application of how things went then would be highly speculative (p. 88). Finally, the careful examination of the Constantinopolitan councils involved in the Photian Schism seems to us well done.

As for the so-called "papal councils" of the medieval period, according to a formula that has now become standard, the author first presents the "imperial-papal" councils. This formulation, however, has become irksome for us because, as he himself writes, "the emperor and the pope collaborated closely together as the supreme authority" (p. 95). Then he presents the "councils of the Gregorian Reform, both "the Lenten Synods," which are critically judged by him (p. 97), and the "general synods," which simply raise questions. At this point, we come under the sign of "papal rule over Christendom" with particular characteristics that the author sees and presents according to his own way of seeing things. Lateran IV and Lyons I are briefly described along with the illusory unity after Lyons II. Following the acme represented by this last great council, the decline of papal power begins with the General Council of Vienne.

"On the Unity and Reform of the Church: the Councils of the

XV Century" is the next title covered. Here Schatz confronts both the Great Schism and conciliarism, namely, the old question of whether or not a council is superior to a pope. This question arose in both extreme and more moderated forms (in ecclesial emergencies, in cases of grave crisis, in cases of an actual schism). We do not follow B. Tierney here as this author does (p. 119). For Tierney, conciliarism would have derived its own roots from the tradition. Schatz believes "the *Ecclesia Universalis* to which is promised truth is represented by the council" (p. 119); at the same time, he does not overlook "the conciliar connection with the socio-political conceptions" of the times, that is, corporate models, the model of the *universitas*, or the *regimen mixtum* (p. 121).

This *via concilii* began at Pisa with the deposition for heresy of two rival antagonists; it was then carried on at Constance ("a confirmation of Pisa or a new attempt"?) (p. 125ff.) *via facti*, it was carried on up until "the crisis and the dramatic culminating point when a council was finally placed on a level above the papacy" (p. 129).

The author's analysis continues with the condemnation of John Hus, *causa fidei* (p. 133), and goes on with the study of the conciliar decree *Haec Sancta*. For Schatz, this decree, "from the point of view of its content, is difficult to understand except as an exceptional measure drawn up to deal with the particular crisis situation represented by the schism" (p. 137). It certainly "was not intended to be a dogmatic definition" (*Ibid.*), with reference to "a conciliar superiority as that idea is generally understood" (p. 138); but it applied only "in analogous cases involving an extreme failure on the part of he papacy (schism, heretical pope)" (*Ibid.*).

The high points of the crisis of conciliarism are viewed in three parts, namely, in the activities centered on Pavia and Siena; at the Council of Basel (including its structure, composition, ideas, and tendencies, and its continual conflict with the pope); and, finally, at the Council of Florence, leading up to the union of the Churches. On the subject of the primacy of the bishop of Rome, there was recognized at this last synod the supreme magisterial and jurisdictional authority of the pope, as expressed in the classical terminology of the Western Church, and "as attested also in the acts of the ecumenical councils and sacred canons" (p. 146). Another paragraph, however, was dedicated to the way in which the five patriarchs also fit into the established order, "without any prejudice towards all their rights and privileges" (p. 147).

Schatz notes that "it was not stated in what relation these two affirmations stood, if and in what way they limited each other reciprocally" (*Ibid.*). Nor was it stated that for the Greeks the union should be understood in limited sense, as "attested" (as already mentioned above). For that time it was certainly a good result, both theologically and ecumenically, even if the union failed in the end.

"The Final Schism in the Occident" precedes the author's synthesis and balance sheet; according to these, "the papacy won a Pyrrhic victory against conciliarism" (p. 150). There were more losses than gains, in other words, and some of the most radical ideas survived well beyond the XVI century, especially in Germany and France; some of them also came together in the Reformation or found a refuge in Erasmian circles (cf. p. 151). In France, some of them issued in "Gallicanism." However that may be, it is still worth recording that in 1460 Pius II forbade upon pain of excommunication any appeal to a council.

The chapter concludes with "A Council as Alibi: Lateran V," which, however, adopted some important decisions in the matter of the reform of the Church. "Its fundamental orientation, however, was that of a 'conservative' reform: the ancient laws of the Church fully sufficed; it was simply a matter of requiring a more punctual observance of them" (p. 154). In any case, there was lacking "any serious will on the part of the pope to see that these laws were respected" (*Ibid.*).

The author presents a good synthesis of the Council of Trent in the context of "confessionalization." There are points of emphasis concerning the pressing demands for a council and for reform; the first phase of the synod; the crisis and then the interruption of the Council; the last phase; and, finally, the council's influence and historical importance.

Beyond this initial word of praise, however, we must note judgments of Schatz's that are excessive with regard to his awareness of the full historical dimensions of his subject as well as to his view of the sacraments—it is necessary to recall that our Oriental brothers also count seven of them. He also evidences some difficulties of expression with regard to the Eucharist (p. 180); but he provides a good solution to the question of the completeness [or rather, the sincerity] of confession for the remission of grave sins (*Ibid.*).

His vision of the ultimate phase of the Council of Trent is greatly enlarged by his treatments of "changes in the general situation," "the last attempt at a council of union," "the crisis of the council," "Morone saves the council" ("passing over fundamental ecclesiological questions…with solutions less binding on the question of reform"—p. 190ff.), and, finally, "the doctrinal decrees of the final session."

We note, though, that the "appellants" (to the pope) are considered to be "lacking in autonomy on the decision-making level" (p. 186). They must be seen, however, as council Fathers desirous of giving back to the superior authority things which they thought were very much in need of a vision from above. This is what happened, as a matter of fact (see pp. 195 and 198).

As for the origins of episcopal authority, having recourse to "the traditional formula of Innocent III" (p. 187) was a minor thing, since it went back very far.

Better judgment would have been desirable in treating such questions as the refusal of "French prelates" to accept the Council of Florence as ecumenical (*Ibid.*); the election of the bishop by the clergy and people (p. 189); the seminary (p. 191ff.); the significance of the "anathemas" at Trent (p. 193); and the indissolubility of marriage ("the canon…left the way open on the level of canonical and pastoral practice"—p. 197). And it should have been demonstrated that "purgatory and indulgences [were] more important than anything else" (p. 198).

The author lists Trent right after Vatican II in terms of its influence and its historical importance, particularly with regard to the structures it established and the way it transformed the face and image of the Catholic Church (p. 199). We harbor our doubts in that regard, particularly at the present historical juncture, just as we question the correctness of underlining the "social disciplinary" aspect of Trent (*Ibid.*) as well as "confessionalization" (p. 200), not to speak of the foundation for the criticism made by Lortz (*Ibid.*). Also, the influence that the Council of Trent had on the mentality of the times, even if it only came about slowly, seems to us quite excessively underlined here (p. 201). Similarly, we question the judgment that "the reform depended essentially on the papal nuncios" (*Ibid.*).

In this regard, the opinion expressed here that all these issues "emerged with the Council of Trent and thanks to it" must be rejected (*Ibid.*). Instead, it would be better to recall, because it is true and actually the case, the conclusion that "only through the papacy can a council develop a durable influence...of a kind to put its stamp on the whole Church" (p. 202).

The First Vatican Council is presented under the heading: "Council and Principles of Authority." From the outset, Schatz examines the historical factors in accordance with a lapidary formula to the effect that "no event more than the French Revolution prepared the terrain for the definitive victory of the papacy within the Church" (p. 203). Lapidary also is the affirmation that "Gallicanism was defeated not because it was theologically mistaken, but because it was no longer historically possible" (p. 205). Misleading, however, is the attribution "the end of the XV century" as the time when the doctrines of papal infallibility and papal primacy became established (p. 205)—"Philo-Romans" should take care! Did not these doctrines exist earlier? Was not the Roman *inviolabilitas* recognized earlier? However that may be, at this point we are faced with a continuing need to dissent from, and, indeed, add glosses or comments to, much of the work of this author. This, however, is not really possible here, owing to questions of space (see esp. pp. 206ff and 210ff). On the other hand, we must note as something fundamentally unacceptable, as we have already mentioned, the author's notion of "ultramontanism" (where "ultramontane Catholics" supposedly stand against "liberal Catholics"). The same thing is true of the author's so-called "papal absolutism." We deny that this "definitively represents the image and role of the Church in the modern world" (p. 215 and p. 239).

Schatz goes on to treat "questions concerning the council," namely: council and politics; public opinion; the composition and tendencies of the synod considered "according to the standard of two political parties" (p. 224 and p. 232); the beginning of the division; the discussion of the first *schemata*; "the aggravation of the collision"; the consensus concerning the *schema* on the faith; and, finally, the discussions on infallibility.

While we rather liked the author's treatment of the *consensus unanimis*, that old warhorse of the conciliar minority ("mistaken," he says—p. 233), we cannot say the same concerning his "letting fall historical reflection" (he claims that "the integrated *ratio* of the Constitution *Dei Filius* is ahistorical"—p. 236). The same thing is true of his treatment of the conflict between science and faith and of "the jurisdictional power of the pope" (p. 237). The same thing is true of how these questions were handled on the part of the minority. The author does appear to be more balanced in treating the historical "objections" to infallibility of the minority, even if, according to him, the minority "demonstrated a decisively superior historical sensitivity" (p. 240). Moreover, for us, that "terrible phrase [of Pius IX]: 'I *am* tradition'" (p. 242) is not an established fact.

In his after the council treatment, Schatz finally notes that by the end of 1870, "nearly all had accepted the dogma" (p. 245). Not very happy, however, are the conclusions he draws from the fact that Rome did not contest some of the pastoral letters that were written. The author asks: "Was this an experiment in possibly adopting a more moderate interpretation of the dogma"? Or again: "Could it be interpreted in the sense in which the minority understood it?" (p. 246) It appears to us that here the author deliberately adopts a stance of ambiguity. It was definitely the case, however, that "no bishop belonging to the minority separated himself from Rome" (*Ibid.*).

Moving on to Vatican II, Schatz treats it generally under the heading of "Council and *Aggiornamento*." He certainly presents the precursors of the Council in a surprising way. Thus, he speaks "of ecclesial directions and currents which for centuries had been relegated into the category of heresy, or at the very least were considered 'non-ecclesial'" (p. 250). He adds, though: "If this is true, it is also true that from a 'genetic-historical' point of view; there are few cases where a direct line exists between these opposition currents and Vatican Council II" (p. 250). This kind of writing is perplexing, and it continues with both ambiguity and confusion on the subject of ultramontanism (pp. 250-255). And this is even more the case with the call to claim that "we are the Church" (p. 252).

The period of the preparations for the Council is divided into subsections dealing with the following subjects: surprise concerning the calling of "an ecumenical council" (including a good "demythologizing" page—p. 258); the expectations for the Council; the *vota* (wishes) of the bishops in anticipation of the beginning of the assembly; the changing opinions of some of the Fathers (p. 261 ff.); and the closed-door preparations for the Council (with the necessary distinctions made with regard to the Secretariat for Promoting Christian Unity—p. 263). There are some good observations made however, regarding the preparatory commissions—in spite of the author's anti-curial prejudices and some of his rather sentimental comments on the pastoral nature of the Council, on *aggiornamento*, and the *Romanitas,* as well as on the position of Geiselmann about the subject of tradition (pp. 263-265). Finally, he provides the agenda for the Council and speaks of the contacts and fears prevalent on the eve of the Council.

A part of the chapter covering "composition and tendencies" makes reference to the distinction favored by the media between "progressives" ("innovators" would have been a better term) and "conservatives." It would have been just, however, to refer consistently to the "majority" and the "minority." The assertion cannot be accepted that "the minority corresponded somewhat to the tendencies of the majority at Vatican I," and vice versa (p. 273). And it is also an error to say that Cardinal Ruffini "gathered around himself the *Coetus Inernationalis Patrum* (or International Group of Fathers—p. 274 and also p. 312). It is, however, correct to say that "an essential trait of Vatican Council II is precisely the attention given to the principle of moral unanimity which was neglected at Vatican Council I...there cannot be victors and vanquished at an ecumenical council" (p. 274ff.). The author's comments about the theologians and experts at the council are greatly exaggerated (p. 277).

With respect to the treatment of "beginnings and surprises: the first conciliar period," reserve must be expressed concerning the author's treatment of the Council's "initial directions" (p. 278ff); of how he handles the subject *de fontibus revelationis*, or the sources of revelation (p. 280); and also of the comparison he makes between episcopal conferences and the "nations" assembled at the Council of Constance.

There follows his treatment of "important turns and first results: the second conciliar period" dealing with the change of pontificates and the consequences of this; the author also mentions the strategy of G. Philips who "sought to preserve conservative theology while cautiously adding deep new accents to it" (p. 288). The author does, however, show his lack of understanding in his treatment of episcopal *numera et potestates* of the bishops; and of *communio*, where he writes as if it was not hierarchical. He also shows the relationship between "the power of ordination and jurisdiction," and between "sacrament and jurisdiction" (p. 291). With regard to the distinction between the two powers, that goes back for him to the XII century, it lacks the adjective 'reflected'.

We find his disappointment concerning the Constitution on the Liturgy to be well-founded. He recognizes that "however one might evaluate the thing, post-conciliar developments, even the official Roman ordinary of the Mass, certainly went beyond what the Constitution on the Sacred Liturgy had sanctioned" (p. 295).

The subsequent section, regarding the third conciliar period, and entitled "Objectives Achieved and Disillusionments," is thoroughly dramatized by the author. This is the case, for example, when he speaks of "sliding towards the pole of primacy in ways that would be expressed in the *Nota Praevia*" (p. 297). He soon passes on, however, "to more tranquil topics—a forest of texts" (p. 299). This goes up to the "crisis of November." Although he accepts the designation of "Black Thursday" for the day the pope agreed on the *Nota Praevia*, what he attests to in his narrative are the benefits flowing from this papal decision, and so he should have abandoned the use of this gloomy and funereal qualification. It is also necessary to make clear that the signatures gathered in favor of an immediate vote on and promulgation of the Declaration on Religious Liberty were around 450 and not "around a thousand" (p. 303). It is also out of place, considering the character of the man, that the pope "was assailed by the conservatives" for having proposed modifications in the text of a Council document.

However, for this author, "that which continued to weigh was the *Nota Praevia* alone. It certainly did not change any of the affirmations of the Constitution on the Church, but simply succeeded in underlining, in a rather excessive way and with anxious pedantry, the primacy and fullness of power of the pope. This produced a lack of balance and was an instance of unilaterally emphasizing the line followed by the First Vatican Council" (pp. 304-305).

On the other hand, the conciliar balance sheet, for this author, is positive, even though, in our view, the following statement of his is quite unjust: "*Lumen Gentium* insisted...on pluralism, change, and historicity within the Church, and at the same time on the relativization of those 'exclusivistic' features of the faith that came up against the paradigms and central values of modernity—such as those things judged 'necessary for salvation,' the Church's claims to exclusivity, the immutability of her teachings, her hierarchical structure, obedience..." (p. 305).

Very much dramatized in the author's account is the period between the third and fourth sessions. During this "intersession," while the conciliar texts were being refined, public opinion supposedly constrained the Vatican to continue on the road the Council had taken (p. 306). Concerning the question of religious liberty, however, the notion of Schatz is inexact when he asserts that "the Church accepted in principle the central points that liberty had acquired in the modern era" (p. 307). The Church's traditional line of anti-liberalism was, rather, opposed to the European type of ideological liberalism which was so different, for example, from North American liberalism.

His comments apropos of the inerrancy of Scripture, however, are significant (p. 310, and earlier, p. 280), as are those on the sufficiency of the contents of Scripture (*Ibid.*). It is a fine thing to learn from this author that "tradition has now become the current of life of the Church that brings forward Scripture, attests to its truth, and explains its message" (*Ibid.*).

Another fine thing is the author's treatment of the final exchanges on the subject of *Gaudium et Spes*. On the [non]condemnation of Communism, however, Schatz should have consulted the clarifying intervention of Monsignor V. Carbone in the *Rivista di Storia della Chiesa in Italia* [Review of the History of the Church in Italy] (1990, N. 1, pp. 10-68). However that may be, we again find ourselves in disagreement with the author concerning many of the ideas expressed by him in these final pages (p. 313ff.). Equally, we would like to conclude by quoting a question he himself poses in the last paragraph of this work: "Does not a certain way of continually invoking 'the spirit of Vatican II,' which in some ways was the spirit of the 1960s, retard rather than hasten the true reception of the Council?" (p. 315).

4

The Vatican Councils

Annibale Zambarbieri, *I Concili del Vaticano* [The Vatican Councils], Edizioni San Paolo, Cinisello Balsamo, 1995, 406 pages.

St. Paul Editions, the publishers, in a rather brief lapse of time, have published a second important historical work on the Second Vatican Council, even though, this time, it bears a non-accidental, combined relationship with the history of the First Vatican Council. It represents another sign that publishers are seriously trying to "do history," rather than to publish mere chronicles—and perhaps even get beyond "ideology" and hardened established positions concerning material that remains sensitive because the great conciliar event is still so near in time (see p. 27, n. 44). We hasten to mention the value of the research of Zambarbieri; set forth in these well written pages. We are dealing here with a good synthesis along with rapid summaries and the presentation of various documents—all of it based on an in-depth bibliographical knowledge. The discourse is clear and the judgments are balanced; a "journalistic style" is avoided; see, for example, how for this author "black week" becomes merely a "difficult week" (p. 271); although he does also refer to it later (p. 302), he relies on the sure guidance of Father G. Caprile; he also makes precise, concrete references to the *Acta* of the Council; this proves to be the case when he reports on the most important interventions by the most prominent speakers in both the minority and the majority (making use of these terms, however, is not necessarily evidence of the influence of a parliamentary mentality, as the author asserts—pp. 19, 56, 215, and also pp. 262, 375, and 377).

We think we are able to affirm that what we have here is the best conciliar synthesis of Vatican II that has yet appeared. This is true from the point of view of the "historical sense" which pervades it, even if we must later manifest some reservations, especially when the author gets caught up in the vortex of the influence of "the School of Bologna." As an example of this, we note the author's great preoccupation with collegiality instead of with the primacy (see pp. 280ff., and p. 297). Both are legitimate subjects; the "disharmony" between them that is mentioned simply disappears, however, when the phrase *hierarchical communion* is employed; this phrase is capable of uniting the two poles of this binomial without doing harm to the terms of the relationship. At least this is the position that we very firmly hold.

But we need to look at the text. Following the Preliminary Note and a list of abbreviations, the volume offers an interesting introduction to the "Two Catholic councils" (pp. 9-27); it is rhythmically balanced "between history and Christian memory"; the problematic concerning their ecumenicity is included, as is their "parliamentary connection," on the one hand—along with a discussion of how such a comparison could arise—and their connection "to the Vatican," on the other hand.

The treatment of Vatican Council I (the first part of the volume) begins with "The Preparation," that is, of a "Catholic" council of the nineteenth century. Its "physiognomy" is described in "The First Phase" (pp. 62-88); this includes the beginnings of the council, the ecclesiological problems involved, and the discussions on the *schema De Doctrina Catholica*. "Papal Prerogatives" are then described (pp. 89-114). There is an in-depth analysis of the precedents for both the primacy and the infallible magisterium of the pope; there is similarly an analysis of the Constitution *Pastor Aeternus*, its proclamation as dogma, and the successive reactions to it. The author concludes—and it is a sign of his well-balanced position—that "during the debate at the council, both freedom of expression and consideration of more than one point of view were guaranteed, even if at times they seemed to be quite notably restricted. This was the case in spite of the interventions of Pius IX, which became rather pointed during the last phases of the debate; yet there continued to be carried on in depth a lively debate which was not lacking in incidents and which had a significant effect on the final results" (pp. 113ff). Finally, the fourth chapter, "A Council between Two Epochs" (pp. 115-118), is not without its own interesting considerations bearing upon the watershed event that Vatican I was.

The second part of the volume is devoted to "Vatican II" (pp. 119-351) and is better developed than the first part. The story it tells is laid out in short, easy sections, beginning with "A New Council" (pp. 121-134) where, among other things, the question of the ecumenicity of the Council is treated, along with a discussion of the "surprise" that resulted from the convocation of the Council. Yet we know that the immediate predecessors of Pope John, Pius XI and Pius XII, had both studied the possibility of convening an ecumenical council—not to speak of "the superior and transcendent intentionality" to which "the pope wished to attribute his design" (p. 130). This is well stated.

In "A New World" (pp. 135-146), the author presents us with no small profundity of vision what he calls "a diverse and contradictory civilization." He includes in his description both modern religious changes and "the new developments of modern times." Following this is "The Physiognomy of the 'New' Kind of Council according to John XXIII" (pp. 145-155). This covers both the spiritual dimension and ecumenical fraternity. (But allow us here to register a critical dissent concerning a supposed "Roncallian intention of signaling an implicit distancing not only from Vatican I, but also from the 'papal' councils of the Middle Ages" (p. 147). We are obliged to take the same view regarding all the "exegesis" he mentions of both the official and unofficial channels of the Holy See (p. 149), as well as of the ideas of "*aggiornamento*" and of the "pastoral" nature of the Council—the latter being the ideal "physiognomy" of an ecumenical assembly).

We then arrive at "The Preparations for the Council" (pp. 156-177). We would have added the word "concrete" to the word "preparations" here. The preparations are presented in an orderly manner, if at times one rather lenient in its approach, following the current "fashion" of rendering judgments that are not very well founded. (By the way, we must also note here that the idea of a "pontifical representative" is a broader term than the term "nuncio" to which the author makes reference—adding in a note "probably," which is out of place (p. 162). In this same vein, we anticipate here an observation concerning the "positioning of the papal nuncios" or the political-diplomatic precedence which they enjoy. Zambarbieri lists them after the auxiliary bishops, but in fact they are archbishops (see p. 186, n. 19). It is at this point in the text that the author presents with great exactitude the preparatory conciliar *schemata* as well as the discussions concerning them by the Central Preparatory Commission. We cannot fail to record the impression here that Zambarbieri's judgments on these topics are much more balanced and objective than those of, for example, Aubert or Alberigo.

There follows the treatment of "The First Period" (pp. 178-217), including Pope John XXIII's famous "Opening Address to the Council." This is accompanied with a good note to Monsignor G. Zannoni, "a silent and unknown protagonist," according to the happy expression of the late, lamented Monsignor Michele Maccarrone (note, p. 179). There is also the Regulation, the *Ordo Concilii Oecumenici Vaticani II Celebrandi*, "modeled in considerable measure on its counterpart Regulation from Vatican I." Such exact observation is valid for many other aspects of the Council, as the authoritative voice and testimony from the Secretariat of State could confirm, going back to the very beginnings of the preparations, when the documentation of Vatican Council I was being consulted. The analysis continues here covering the "physiognomy" of the assembly, the beginnings of the Council's work, the discussions on the *schema De Liturgia*, the divergences that developed on the theme of revelation, ecclesiological questions, and, finally, the author's "Evaluations and Prospects." For Zambarbieri, "this period was not traversed in vain" (p. 214). This judgment tells us much about his well-considered perspective, which is also reflected in his criticism of the typical classification of bishops into "progressives' and "conservatives." This classification, he says, "risks simplifying a fabric that is much more tightly woven with many convergences and divergences" (p. 217). The same thing is true, he thinks, of the *cliché* of the "two theologies" and the "two ecclesiologies" which weighed down the work of the Council in no small way, and, especially, affected the work of the theologians.

And then there is "Towards the Second Period" (pp. 218-245), with an explanation of the conciliar plan of work and of the revisions of the *schemata*, as well as of the initiatives of the new pontificate of Paul VI. There is also a reference to Jedin here, to a very exaggerated judgment of Father Dossetti for which Zambarbieri appears to show, as he does later, a particular "sympathy": "perhaps he [Dossetti] scored a bull's-eye." What the Bologna priest thought was that "this Council, unlike the two most recent general councils, did not have a bi-polar (pope-council) structure, but rather a tri-polar structure, that is, pope, curia, council" (p. 226, n. 31). "The Second Period" (pp. 227-245) as such is divided into the research on "the thought of the pope concerning the Council and on the new version of the Regulation" (with diversified judgments concerning the contribution of Father Dossetti himself, but with a propensity in his favor). In addition, there are discussions on the Church, the episcopate and ecumenism, as well as on the final approval of the Constitution on the Sacred Liturgy and the Decree on the Means of Social Communications (*De instrumentis communicationis socialis*). Finally, there appears an inquiry on the subject of the formula for conciliar approvals and promulgations and of the work of the pontificate itself—all of this being the fruit of in-depth study.

In "Between the Second and the Third Period" (pp. 246-256), the author deals with the recasting and revisions of the various *schemata* (for us, the "insinuation" on page 249, paragraph 2—see also, successively, page 278—is not a happy addition to the text; the same thing is true of the "denigration" on p. 251 with reference to *Schema XIII*). The author also deals here with procedural problems and with the tensions arising from conflicting ideas. There follows then "The Third Period" (pp. 257-289), and this treatment is divided up into a number of subjects, including: "a developed articulation of the debates" (worthy of note here is the observation on page 260 (n. 13) on the "conditioning" role of the press); "collegiality": "discussions on other subjects"; "a difficult week" (with mention of the adjective "black" used by some to describe the week in question); "the Constitution on the Church" and "the Decrees on Ecumenism and the Eastern Catholic Churches." A critical note is necessary here regarding the discussion of the Constitution on the Church, especially when the *Nota Explicativa Praevia* is referred to; the deficiency in the treatment of this subject is the most serious deficiency in the book. A sign of this deficiency is the author's failure to explain the fundamental points about it; nor is there even any mention of the distinction that was established between *munera* and *potestates*. And in the bibliography, in this same connection, he initially cites only Alberigo (p. 271, n. 53); but, in fact, note 63 on page 273 should have been incorporated into any discussion of such a delicate matter—for the sake of proper balance. In this case, the "extremist" vision of Father Dossetti is the one provided, while the judgment is lacking concerning a witness as well-qualified, for example, as Monsignor Philips, for whom there is no contradiction between the conciliar texts and the *Nota*. And, finally, with regard to several of the "neuralgic" episodes that are recounted, we would have preferred to see them characterized as "precise" or "exact"—based on the well-founded analysis of Vincenzo Carbone— not as "punctilious," as the author characterizes them.

At this point we arrive at "The Preparatory Phase for the Final Period" (pp. 290-295)—it is seen as "a troubled watch," and covered here is the work of both the bishops and *periti* in their re-elaboration of the various *schemata*. This leads up to: "The Final Period" (pp. 296-342). In this chapter, the author looks in an orderly fashion at the various divergences, debates, and votes; and then at the re-examination of *Schema XIII* and the proclamation of the approved decrees and declarations; and, finally, he looks at the very intense finale of the session itself. We would like to quote here a passage emblematic of this author's value judgments on various aspects of the Council. This passage has reference to *Gaudium et Spes*. The document is considered—though the author adds a "perhaps"— as a document which, as a whole, shows signs of "the impact of a historical movement which was perceived, precisely during the 1960s, as a rapid flood-tide, though one that was receding. The repercussions from it, along with the objective difficulty of integrating sociological, scientific, and theological language about it, resulted in a certain reserve, noticeable in various sections of the document, which prevented traditional Christian thought from being used to pronounce upon events considered radically new, and which motivated a search for ideals and images imbued with evangelical inspiration to be projected upon changing events, sometimes ephemeral ones" (p. 341). This is well said.

The conclusion of the book concerning Vatican Council II is placed "among the signs of 'modernity' and of the Word of God" (pp. 343-351). Encountered in the process is both a relative problematic and the difficulties this poses for historical research. The author speaks of "the attempts to arrive…at an organic hermeneutic at a depth adequate to the needs of the Council," and he believes that these attempts "have met with many problems that have still not been resolved" (p. 344). Nevertheless, some aspects appear to be firm and solid for him: the great scope of the celebration of the Council itself; the acquisition of a sense of co-responsibility on the part of the bishops; and, on the level of the content of the documents, the prominence assigned to the celebration of the liturgical mystery in the Christian life. Further, there was now a new ecclesiological vision that recognized the originality of local Churches; there was greater autonomy assigned to the laity; there were benefits arising from the union between all those who mutually recognized themselves as Christians, and even positive consideration for those who did not actively share the faith; hence there was a need for religious freedom for everybody as well.

Then, again, principles that were decided upon often found an immediate, tangible outlet, even if they were sometimes judged differently in various ways; examples of this included recourse to national languages, the constitution of various synodal structures, and so on. In any case, "although the 'thematization' of the conciliar documents, especially *Gaudium et Spes*, showed some signs of insecurity, and even evidenced some theological impasses, the pastors of the Church had without any doubt taken note of and heeded, and then had manifested and exercised their proper responsibility towards, the great modern revolutions in the affairs of the human race...But over all stood the tension inherent in the return to the sources of the faith itself...Similar instances were not unusual in the history of Christianity, but they tended to occur in waves, sometimes unexpectedly strong, other times more calm, but they were always bearers of new and surprising potentialities" (p. 350).

In a way that is both significant and emblematic, the author, in his final conclusions, begins "The Vatican Councils between Tradition and Renewal" (pp. 352-388) in a rather curious way. He begins it with an analysis of the relationships between the two councils that were held at the Vatican. For Zambarbieri both were "perhaps" situated "on a plane where there was mutual communication; however, it was dissymmetrical" (p. 353). But it certainly does not appear to us that this judgment can be based upon the fact that "John XXIII did not consider the new Council to be a reconvening of the earlier meeting of 1869-1870" (*Ibid.*). Nor can it be based on any of his other couplings, appeals, or exclusions. Rather, the opinion found in most serious thought today, namely, that Vatican I was definitively linked to Vatican II, is surely correct. It was linked along well defined "thematic lines," including especially the questions concerning the *Ecclesia ad intra*—"with a particular emphasis on those questions related to the hierarchy" (p. 360). With respect to research into the questions of which we speak, the author may have desired to move in another direction, for example, in the direction of analyzing the work of the development of the conciliar texts; however, this seemed to him to be "still not practicable" (p. 361). In any case, the study of the discussions that took place in the assembly (the other possible way to proceed) came out too sharp—see, however, his judgment on the social question on page 363; this should be revisited comparing it with note 91 on page 385. It remains certain, in any case, that with Vatican II there is a redefinition of ecclesial tasks with regard to the human race as a whole (p. 363): the *aula* of St. Peter's became the arena for the entire world.

And with regard to conciliar citations (*Inhaerens vestigiis...*), the frequency of the references made to Vatican I in the texts of Vatican II are more numerous than references made to the Council of Trent. However, there are still decidedly fewer of them than there are references to the magisterium of the recent pontiffs, where Pius XII dominates. In any event, in the case of a fundamental theme such as collegiality, if there is an inconclusive discrepancy, or a dispute, this furnishes an occasion to Zambarbieri to present the various currents of thought on the subject at hand. He provides several analyses in this way, using citations from *Dei Verbum* and *Gaudium et Spes* and comparing them with the approach of the earlier council; but even here the impasse remains when looking at the "vocabulary" employed in the two assemblies. "Both connections and disjunctions between the two councils are identifiable also on other planes," the author observes in a section entitled "Symmetries and Disymmetries." We cannot follow him in all his observations; they have a certain interest, but they do not go beyond a fairly exact analysis indicative of the complexity of the fundamental relationship between fidelity and renewal. This latter aspect, renewal, presented under the label of "modernity"—when this word is placed between quotation marks, watch out!—is supposed to indicate, "efficaciously, an epochal turn in a civilizational direction" (p. 379). Following a brief historical *excursus* regarding the positioning of the Catholic Church in confrontation with, precisely, modernity, the author explains the forging within the Church of "her own version of modernity" (p. 382). In fact, "Catholicism had arrived at a point where the modern world was considered an appropriate interlocutor, apart from any logic of anathema. This appeared with clear evidence in a place that was almost symbolical, namely, at Vatican II itself" (*Ibid.*). At bottom, this represented a perception of the true dimensions of the Church's own existence.

In all of this. Zambarbieri presents a picture of the historical investigator as a lover of uninterrupted continuity, but here we have to disagree since he can allow himself to be dragged along by ideologies and, for example, he can prefer the tendency to consider innovation as "revolution." I believe that we are required by a general obligation to strive towards difficult and objective research, no matter how long and toilsome, on the subject of the Church's most recent conciliar event. In this connection, it would have been good if the author had taken up in this volume the subject of the Extraordinary Synod of Bishops session in 1985 ("20 years after the Second Vatican Council"). The author cites this Extraordinary Synod in notes, but he does not enter into any interpretations of the Extraordinary Synod event as such (p. 387).

The text is followed by a good, indeed, by an exhaustive, bibliography, as we have already noted above (pp. 389-392). To this should be added the small volume of G. Martelet, *Les idées maîtresses de Vatican II* [The Major Ideas of Vatican II]. There is also an Index of Names (pp. 393-401) and a General Index (pp. 403-406).

II

THE PREPARATION
FOR THE COUNCIL

5

Particular Italian Churches
at the Council

Alberigo Giuseppe, ed., with Various Authors, *Chiese italiane a concilio* [Italian Churches at the Council], Marietti, Genova 1988, 322 pages ("Dabar," Essays in Religious History, 6).

This volume presents, as its subtitle indicates, "Pastoral Experiences in the Italian Church between Pius XII and Paul VI." Fundamentally, it consists of a number of contributions to the historical-pastoral research on the Church in Italy in the 1950s and 1960s.

Contributors include Giuseppe Alberigo himself ("The Italian Church between Pius XII and Paul VI"); A. Riccardi ("The Italian Bishops' Conference in the 1950s and 1960s"); E. Bianchi ("The Diocese of Turin and the Bishopric of Michele Pellegrino"); G. L. Potestà ("The Bishopric of G. B. Montini in Milan—1955-1963"); A. Niero ("The Patriarchate of Venice and the Patriarchs A. G. Roncalli and G. Urbani"); G. Batelli ("Between the Local Church and the Universal Church: Pastoral Choices and Governing Policies of the Archbishop of Bologna Giacomo Lercaro—1952-1968"); B. Bocchini ("The Bishopric of E. Florit in Florence: Themes and Governing Policies of the Florentine Diocese"); A. Giovagnoli ("The Diocese of Naples and the Bishopric of C. Ursi"); D. Farias ("A Quarter of a Century of the Church in Reggio—1950-1977"); and G. Dossetti ("Memories of Giacomo Lercaro").

An index of names is usefully placed at the end of work, which opens with a preface by G. Alberigo, and a suitable "salute" by Cardinal Giacomo Biffi.

Professor Alberigo rightly observes that this volume—the fruit of a study conference that took place on October 24-25, 1986, on the occasion of the tenth anniversary of the passing of Cardinal Giacomo Lercaro—is "an encouraging sign of the kind of study and reflection that has been attempted for a number of years concerning the affairs of the Church in Italy in recent decades. Books produced by contributors to this conference include, for example: *Le Chiese di Pio XII* [The Churches of Pius XII], ed. A Riccardi Laterza, Bari 1988; Various Authors, *La chiesa e i problemi del Mezzogiorno—1948-1988* [The Church and the Problems of Southern Italy—1948-1988], Nuova Minima AVE, Rome, 1988; *Pie XII et la Cité* [Pius XII and the City]: Acts of the Colloquy of the Law Faculty, Presses Universitaires, Aix-Marseilles 1987; A. Riccardi, *Il potere del papa: Da Pio XII a Paolo VI* [The Power of the Pope: From Pius XII to Paul VI], Laterza, Bari 1988; G. Verucci, *La Chiesa nella società contemporanea: dal primo dopo-guerra al Concilio Vaticano II* [The Church in Contemporary Society: From the Second World War to Vatican Council II], Laterza, Bari 1988; *Papa Giovanni* [Pope John], ed. G. Alberigo, Bari-Rome 1987; and, finally, the acts of the conference held in Lucca on the subject of Bishop E. Bartoletti, *Un vescovo italiano del concilio. Enrico Bartoletti, 1916-1976* [An Italian Bishop of the Council, Enrico Bartoletti—1916-1976], Marietti, Genoa 1988.

Alberigo adds: "These are important steps, although they are still fragmentary ones, if we are to overcome our still necessary daily empiricism, which is always exposed to the risk of becoming dissolved in myopic activism and in the temptation to self-justification. The need and the availability of a type of study and reflection critically informed about its own past points to the formation of a new consciousness for Italian Catholicism, one with an ecclesial reality properly speaking, that is, beyond an identity that is predominantly a socio-political one ("a Catholic movement"), or one essentially identified with the Roman papacy" (p. 7).

Significantly, Alberigo is here continuing on with his customary—and well-known—point of view: "It is a question of taking a committed direction, not only for the sake of the strength and fecundity of our local Churches, but also and especially for the sake of holding out against reducing the pilgrim people of God on Italian soil to an instrument for the safeguarding of the papacy, or to social or political aggregations dedicated primarily to that end."

Beyond this "proclamation," the noted professor demands that historical work exhibit "authentic cognitive validity leading to proper conclusions that go beyond apologetical or polemical pre-conceptions...without confusion or undue shifts in one's level" (p. 8).

Thus, within the framework of the particular decades being considered in this book, what "emerges above all is the weight of Vatican Council II, which constituted for the Church in Italy an epochal watershed—which was not the case with the Council of Trent." In fact, "although there are lacking any completely adequate investigations, both concerning Italian participation at the Council, and concerning the reception of the Council in our country"—but see however, *Vatican II and the Italian Church: Memory and Prophecy*, by various authors published in Assisi in 1985—;"the impetus is already clear concerning what the Council contributed to today's new consciousness of a unitary Italian Catholic identity as a Church. Although with a differentiated intensity, this consciousness has characterized the bishop of Rome as well as all the Italian bishops, the clergy as well as average Christians, and, finally—although not without some difficulty—it has characterized lay public opinion as well" (p. 9).

"An attentive revisiting, going back to these past decades, permits us to bring to light the density and fecundity of faith and testimony, in spite of the accelerated changes in Italian society and the accumulated delays dating from the first half of the 20th century. The pilgrim Churches in Italy knew how to generate a harvest of evangelical engagement worthy of the past fertile seasons of the Christian presence in our lands" (*Ibid.*).

"Another tendency which is also significant concerns the acceptance on the part of the Church of a common condition in a pluralistic society and a democratic juridical order...The proposal to look ahead, to recognize an occasion for the re-evangelization of the Church itself, will attract approvals with conviction as well as resistance of a complex kind. The backwardness of Italian Catholicism with respect to various modern movements (liturgical, biblical, patristic, ecumenical), which have so animated other ecclesial areas between the 19th and 20th centuries, seem to have offered to this Church an occasion for a less gradual renewal, but also one more directly measured by the demands of a post-modern society and assisted by the authoritative conciliar directions" (pp. 9-10). We would add here "pontifical directions." "In the 1960s and 1970s", Alberigo concludes, "numerous indications pointing in such directions became manifest."

We think that many people might agree with this provisional interpretive line. However, the analysis offered by Alberigo in his own contribution to the volume, "The Italian Church between Pius XII and Paul VI," seems rather radical and partial. It is true that certain methodological choices, frankly admitted, help us to understand (pp. 15-16), but the impression nevertheless remains—an impression which has been respectfully recorded elsewhere—that an excessive dependency on personal visions and options ends up obfuscating an objective observation of the facts, and contributes to partial and distorted judgments on persons, movements, and associations, and, in the final analysis, on the "Italian Church" itself—which one wants to consider as "fundamentally an unknown planet." However, Alberigo himself, with regard to the Johannine and conciliar eras, is wont to define as superficial the thought of those who reach "a predominantly negative judgment about these same eras" (p. 28). In support of such an affirmation, however, he reveals the fact that his own sensitivity goes down a one-way street—as appears in his analysis of the 1970s (see pp. 31-34).

The study of A. Riccardi follows that of Alberigo. It is a precise and well-documented study of the Italian bishops' conference in the 1950s and 1960s, in the period, that is, when a "physiognomy" was being sought. Le us note, however, the difficulty of expressing the very "concept" of any "Italian Church," for, to a certain degree, this Church derives its existence from the necessary acceptance of the

Roman Church; it is an integral part of the latter, which also enjoys the prerogative of the primacy (see pp. 36-37 and 55-56). And with regard to Paul VI "The Italian episcopacy comes to be considered the episcopacy of the pope, near as it is to the Holy See. The pressures and actions of the Secretariat of State brought to bear on the leadership of the Italian bishops' conference are decisive for the directions taken by the Conference."

In the next research, E. Bianchi, however, contributing a testimonial rather than an article about a local Church (Turin) and the work of its pastor (Pellegrino), writes that he "does not pretend to furnish a complete and balanced interpretation," but rather "wants to bring out features either not sufficiently made prominent or actually forgotten in the person and activities of Cardinal Pellegrino."

Following this contribution, there is that of G. L. Potestà. Even if he does not entirely succeed in carrying out his initial plan—delineating a pastoral portrait of G. B. Montini—Professor Potestà does give a valid and accurate essay. Because he wanted "to move his research beyond a strictly doctrinal circle," his plan included study not only of "the doctrinal enunciations, but also those of the governing style" of his subject, along with "the initiatives and decisions effectively assumed by him in the diocese" (p. 91).

Speaking about an important question which remains an open one, namely, whether the Montini bishopric should be divided into periods, he notes that "in the course of time the archbishop changed his focus and concentrated his attention on certain grand themes," even if he remained faithful to a vision of the Church in the contemporary world and to a perception of his own task which had been rigorously spelled out in the first documents he issued following upon his installation.

We would have liked to see in these pages a better developed presentation of the future Paul VI as a *pastor*, rather than as a doctor. We would also have liked to know more about his relationships with his clergy and his seminarians, especially with regard to the formation of these latter as future priests. (In this regard, see "Montini, Educator of the Clergy," by Cardinal Carlo M. Martini, in the *Notiziario* of the

Paul VI Institute, N. 19, pp. 60-70.) We would also have liked to see how he interacted with the people of God, including the most humble among them, in the eyes of the world. This is not the case.

However that may be, the various sections that are included in this study by Potestà succeed well enough in delineating the fundamental traits of the bishopric of G. B. Montini in Milan. These sections include: the patrimony of Christian civilization faced with modernity; the character and the limits of innovative actions; Christian proclamation of the truth and the hierarchical constitution of the Church; religious pastoral practice; Christianity as a "new form of life"; "the bishop of the workers, the archbishop of the employers"; the "opening to the left" and the autonomy of the Catholic laity; the conciliar period between a "welfare civilization" and evangelical poverty.

By the way, with regard to Potestà's opinion that the naming of Monsignor Sergio Pignedoli as auxiliary bishop of Milan was "engineered...directly by Rome" (p. 95), we hold instead to the view that this action was originated by his friend, Archbishop Montini himself. The Holy See left Pignedoli totally free to accept or not to accept. (See *Il Cardinale Sergio Pignedoli, amico indimenticabile* [Cardinal Sergio Pignedoli, Unforgettable Friend], by Various Authors, Collegio Missionario S. Cuore, Andria, 1989, p. 393).

What G. L. Potestà was not able to do for Milan and for Archbishop Montini, A. Niero has done for Venice and its Patriarchs, A. G. Roncalli and G. Urbani. His attention, in fact, is directed towards capturing the *animus*, or spirit, of these two pastors, for "this, as we might say, is... the key to their pastorships" (p. 129).

In this regard, the character of Roncalli is described: his *paternitas* "is inserted into the wider and deeper context of his *humanitas*, understood in the full creative sense of that Latin term" (*Ibid.*). This *humanitas* was exercised in his dealings with his priests, "the principal concern of each bishop" (p. 130), and was also manifest in the climate of confidence that he knew how to establish. He truly was both a *pastor* and a *pater*—"goodness and charity: what great graces!" he was wont to say. Or, again: "Don't chase after flies! Better in all things to practice goodness, forbearance, and patience." The same *humanitas* was evident in his preaching, his pastoral visits, his seminaries, and his meetings with religious women, the sick, and those in prisons—not to speak of his dealings with the worlds of culture, art, tourism, and work.

The author's research on the Urbani patriarchate continues, taking the same happy tone as initially applied to his predecessor.

In two further contributions, G. Battelli and G. Dossetti treat the archbishop of Bologna, Cardinal Giacomo Lercaro. The first of them, "Between the Local Church and the Universal Church," goes beyond the "myth," whether it is considered positively or negatively. He prefers to focus on a specific and important aspect of the bishopric of Lercaro, namely, the relationship between his pastoral orientation and his mode of governance in his archdiocese. The author attempts to push the analysis beyond consideration of specific projects in order to achieve a concrete realization of the style of pastoring and governing of Cardinal Lercaro, and thereby briefly show how his bishopric developed, "including its results" (pp. 152-153). The author accomplishes this quite happily, even though in the final part of his work there is to be found—it seems to us—some judgments that are a bit too personal.

On the other hand, the presentations of the collaborators of Cardinal Lercaro, Monsignors Baroni and Bettazzi, and then that of Father Dossetti himself, are very interesting, especially where this last collaborator speaks of "the attempted passage from the monarchical image of the bishop to the theology of the local Church." The collaboration of Dossetti provides a key to the decisions of Cardinal Lercaro, whether those that "characterized the post-conciliar opening up in Bologna" (p. 178) or the "second beginning" of the bishopric of Lercaro (p. 182).

For G. Battelli in this connection, "there are not lacking...elements that permit one to assert how at bottom the external reactions to the diocese that were unfavorable to the cardinal matured, while from inside the diocese there emerged obvious symptoms of a negative response or, more precisely, of a non-response, to the demands which the Council through Lercaro was introducing into the ordinary life of Bologna" (p. 184).

Much more personal is the "remembrance" of Father G. Dossetti with his inquiry concerning "a certain division" in the soul of Cardinal Lercaro with respect to mental and liturgical prayer (a working hypothesis), which, however, resulted in a harmonious integration towards the end of his life, *sub unica conclusione*, one might say, in liturgical piety, enriched by conciliar thought that was far from mere "voluntaristic efficiency"—excessively denounced by Dossetti, by the way, for whom others ("semi-Pelagians") are specifically pointed out.

However, the citation, in a very long note, of the contribution to the Council of the archbishop—and of the diocese—of Bologna, as this was delineated by the author at San Domenico, is quite significant. It is significant "especially in the conception of the Council itself as a celebration and as an irreversible sacramental event and hence as influencing the fundamental modality of its own operation as well as influencing ecclesiology generally, particularly the relationship between Church and Eucharist. The same thing again applies to the "originality" of the local Churches, to episcopal collegiality, and to the relationship between episcopal collegiality and the primacy of the pope" (pp. 300-304). (On the other hand, in this connection see the critical notes on Dossetti by M. Maccarrone in R.S.C.I, n.1, 1989, pp. 104-109.)

Then comes the presentation of the thought of Cardinal Lercaro on the poor and on poverty in the Church, and, more specifically, on the manner of the Church's presence in civil society, as well as on peace. There quickly follows the final point: "The distancing of the cardinal from the see of 'St. Petronius,'" as it is called. The very choice of terms here reveals the interpretive key used by the author; in our opinion, it turns out to be a very narrow view.

The remembrance of the bishopric of Cardinal Ermenegildo Florit in Florence was assigned, as indicated above, to B. Bocchini Camaiani. The limits of his research are quite frankly set forth. It was fundamentally a question of "the closing of the archives of the diocese and the non-accessibility of a great part of the existing private records." This impeded "an examination close to the actual motivations of the bishop, as well as of his analyses and judgments on the religious situation in his diocese and on his relationship with the Vatican" (p. 188).

Notwithstanding this, however, the judgments expressed—which turn out to be strongly critical—do not seem consistent with such a premise. A certain reductionism is evident in the section he includes about "accentuating a crisis": "In reality," he writes, "tensions and polemics were very much a part of the history of the Italian Church generally in those years, not just in the Church in Florence; most of these arose out of the politicization of ecclesiastical life, which has been well noted; and all of it had a very strong effect. In this perspective, it is easy to understand how the actions of Cardinal Florit could have obtained a certain consensus" (p. 211).

The examination of the Neapolitan bishopric of C. Ursi, "which presents multiple points of interest," offers reasons that make any placing of this bishopric in a simple historical framework difficult. This is certainly the case because "it is not solely a question of events rather recent in time, but rather of a parabola of events not yet concluded. For this reason, it is difficult to maintain the necessary distance from them; any attempt to draw up a complete balance sheet is impossible. More than a history of this bishopric, there has been an attempt to trace an essential chronicle of some of the events, accompanied by a few reflections and questions which could be useful for a future and more complete historical work" (p. 217). Thus A. Giovagnoli.

The close ties of Archbishop Ursi, with the pope are taken for granted, at least as regards the early years of his bishopric, and in the light of the expressed wish of Paul VI to guide the implementation of the Council in Italy (p. 219). The analysis offered here turns out to be both a valid and an in-depth one, especially with regard to the main lines of conciliar renewal pursued in Naples. The author presents the grave difficulties encountered as well as the unsatisfactory results obtained. The fact is that "beyond the complex intertwining of reciprocal incomprehensions and reciprocal delusions," there emerged, beyond the main events of the bishopric of Cardinal Ursi, "many problems, both old and new, in the diocese of Naples" (p. 244).

In short, "the efforts at reform involved complex changes in the relationship between the Church and society, in Naples as elsewhere, and these were characterized by a close interpenetration along with a certain subordination. In a city where the Church had adopted the Tridentine model only in a limited way, where no strong organized Catholic movement had ever developed, where both Fascism and the monarchy had been able to count on Catholic support, there was lacking a robust "autonomy" in the Church capable of offering support for actions for renewal on the religious and social planes. In this sense, it is possible to say conciliar renewal met with long-standing problems which had emerged in the pre-conciliar phase—for example, with the bishopric of Cardinal Mimmi, opposed on account of his Tridentine intransigence. The problem with a clergy only loosely bound to residential obligations but with close family ties and very sensitive to its economic and social status, while also being anchored in a specific tradition of spirituality, represented a situation that was more general" (p. 244).

A. Giovagnoli concludes by posing questions valid for Italy as a whole. For example, in spite of the diversity between Naples and the northern dioceses, "minor Neapolitan developments suggest a more complex...is required. From this particular history there arose...the need to lay out a balance-sheet of the efforts of Montini to guide the implementation of the Council in Italy, or at least to ask what modifications needed to be made in the demands for 'conciliar innovations; as far as the bishop is concerned, or what changes should have been introduced to the clergy in the post-conciliar era. The examination of the concrete post-conciliar situation suggests that the investigation should not be limited to the question of the reception of the Council or to the diffusion of new theological, pastoral, and organizational tendencies...If the Council introduced substantial novelties into the life of the Church, it would be important to inquire into the question of what impact this had on the essential elements which constitute the heart and bones of the body of the pre-conciliar

Church. The problems of the episcopacy and of the clergy in this sense appear to be problems of the first order, while perhaps the importance of the best-known developments involved in the so-called disputes which occurred need 're-dimensioning.' In the absence of any other points of reference that might be nearer to us, one's thoughts naturally go back to the Council of Trent for the main terms of the discussion and also to the great areas of restructuralization which resulted from it" (p. 245). Such suggestions seem to us to be particularly pertinent and worthy of a planned response.

An example particularly rich with valid considerations which apply to Southern Italy as a whole is the fine essay of D. Farias on the bishopric of Bishop Ferro, "A Quarter of a Century of the Church in Reggio." The presentation of the author's judgments concerning Bishop Ferro's episcopal service done with neither partiality nor factiousness, seems to us rather complete. There is likewise an examination of his service at the Council as well as the reverberations of this in the diocese. And there is recorded the opening up, finally, at the meeting in Paola in 1987, of the wider question of a "Communion on a regional level" that was indispensable; it was a meeting that was both "promising and disquieting" at one and the same time (p. 280).

In conclusion, this volume might appear to many as "passionate." In fact, it re-lives recent history and deals with some rather incandescent issues. The question can therefore legitimately be posed whether the necessary distance from the subject has been achieved, and whether it is even possible to attempt to produce a balance-sheet on any ecclesiastical history as recent as this. Giovagnoli himself raises this question, and he himself replies to it by saying that it is quite proper to present an essential chronicle of the major events, accompanied by questions and reflections useful for a future and more complete investigation.

We are inclined to take the same view, also because, only in the future and with the help of documents which are not yet accessible (or which have been "filtered" by thinking which may be legitimate, but which may also be too personal in the case of some documents that are available or happen to be already in the possession of some scholars) will it be possible to clarify, in a longer and hence less partial historical perspective, the real merit of Churchmen who too often, and sadly, have suffered from the impact of the modern world.

Yet they responded to the challenges they faced with important contributions to Vatican Council II. They were engaged in a difficult and thought-out implementation process in the midst of the rapidly changing vortex of the recent past. In this connection, finally, it is worth adding that the proper implementation of the Council, based on a fully documented history, is unfortunately not something that has yet been achieved.

6

Conciliar Preparation

Alberigo G. and Melloni A., eds., with Various Authors, *Verso il Concilio Vaticano II (1960-1962): Passagi e problemi della preparazione conciliare* [Towards Vatican Council II (1960-1962): Passages and Problems related to the Preparation for the Council], Marietti, Genoa 1993, 503 pages.

In the preface to this volume, right after the index, G. Alberigo and A. Melloni write as follows: "Knowledge of the preparations for Vatican Council II, up to the present time, has been both circumscribed and only approximate. The period between 1959 and 1962 seems on the one hand to have been consumed by the process of killing many preparatory *schemata* brought to birth in that same period, while, on the other hand, the non-availability of documents and sources has frustrated any possible attempts at carrying out serious historical-critical investigations. This is an attitude shared and faithfully recorded in the valuable and even monumental series of *Acta et documenta concilio oecumenico Vaticano II apparando*, which has postponed the publication of the acts of the intermediate preparatory organs and has instead limited itself to the acts of the principal organs only: the Central Preparatory Commission, on the one hand, and the Pontifical Ante-preparatory Commission in the appendices of the *Acta Synodalia*. Thus, in this area of research, considered both in its depth and its entirety, we have concentrated our attention on the work of the team at the Institute for Religious Sciences in Bologna, integrated with some added contributions from specialists. All of this

87

lies within the framework of the international project for the history of Vatican II. We began with the volume of A. Indelicato on the work of the Central Commission, and now we present this collection of essays which for the first time focus on the work and the debates of the preparatory commissions and secretariats to which were assigned the task of drafting conciliar *schemata* in view of the future Council" (p. 11). The context of this study is thus given.

The basis of the present publication is not solely official documentation but includes material from various private archives. The consistency of this material can be judged by looking at the list of sources at the end of the volume (pp. 483-492); it owes a lot to a meeting on "The Local Sources for Vatican II" held in Louvain in 1989 (This list of sources also includes some works not consulted). In order to understand both the underlying thought and the preconceptions (in an etymological sense), it is necessary to transcribe yet another passage from the preface, namely, the following: "Prescinding from the complaint in traditionalist circles about a 'failed Council,' by which out of conciliar triumphalism it was too quickly believed that what was discarded in 1962 had in fact been completely eclipsed, the preparations for Vatican II appear like an alabaster monument where what is seen on one side shines through from the other side: so much were the conflicts from the 1950s reflected in the debates of the 1960s. The same thing was true of the alterations in the relationships of the various forces at work, as well as in the overturning of the definition of what constituted a priority" (p. 12). I believe that what is expressed here is the image of a Council already seen as "revolutionary." The conflicts in the "relationships of the various forces at work" are what characterize the vision of the "School of Bologna." But there is a notable lack of historical sensitivity here, particularly as regards the presence of continuity, even in *aggiornamento*, of fidelity even in renewal. These things have always been present at councils, as indeed they are qualities of the Catholic Church herself.

Following the book's list of abbreviations, the initial contribution to the research here is that of G. Alberigo himself, with his "Crucial Aspects of the Ante-preparatory Phase (1959-1960)" (pp. 15-42).

At the heart of his analysis is his observation that the Church has "an institutional allergy for councils—something that became fixed and interiorized in Rome following the Councils of Constance and Basel" (p. 15). But was there not also another council celebrated after these two, at Trent? Still, for Alberigo, the supposed "institutional allergy" in question "suggested that the unknowns of a council should be avoided," that councils should take place in Rome, and that they should be "brief and without surprises." But was it not John XXIII himself who convoked Vatican II, and who wanted a brief council? As for the place, for this author, Rome stands fundamentally for the Curia, as he will continually show in the course of his engagement with the subject. We are faced here with a nodal point of the "Bolognese" interpretation of the Council; it is an element that we have already in the past identified as "ideological"; above all, no distinctions are made regarding the internal composition of the Curia. The essence of the Bolognese position is found in the author's conclusion: "What is seen here…is one of the dominant characteristics of Vatican II, namely, the tension between the conciliar assembly itself on the one hand, and the Roman Curia on the other hand. This phenomenon of an inherent conflict between Council and Curia…visibly leapt to the eye at Vatican II. The historical dialectic between pope and council was transformed into an inextricably complex three-way dialectic [that is, among Pope, Council, and Curia]" (p. 42). The other nodal element of the School of Bologna—and here we anticipate—is the interpretation of the role of Cardinal Domenico Tardini and his characteristic thinking (especially in relation to Pope John XXIII). The proof of how this was lies in the interpretation of how the entrusting of the preliminary phase of the conciliar preparation to the Congregation for Extraordinary Ecclesiastical Affairs was "a choice motivated technically by the greater bureaucratic ability of Extraordinary Ecclesiastical Affairs to circulate to the bishops the requests for their opinions" (p. 17, n. 5). But we can literally multiply the many objections to this contention that occur (see pp. 18, 19, 25, 27, 37, 38, 39, 40, 41, and 42).

The author treats the following subjects: "Preparation for the preparation": "a curial commission"; "a new council: Vatican II";

"Roman preparation for a 'universal' council?"; "the choice of themes for the preparation"; and "preparation without any 'soul'?"

The second study by A. Indelicato analyzes "The Formation and Composition of the Preparatory Commission" (pp. 43-66); this presentation is structured around "the beginnings of the preparatory work"; "a global image"; "presences at the places of work"; "by nationality"; "the weight of the Roman Curia": "the presence of religious and of cultural institutions"; "analysis of the individual commissions." There is provided, finally, "some keys to understanding the criteria for nominations" which are more carefully articulated than is commonly the case, it seems. The numbers given, however, are numbers. I limit my observations here to noting that the "peripheral representatives" of "the Secretariat of State" mentioned here actually represented the bishop of Rome (p. 62).

Then we come to the good chapter, a consistent one, by Maria Paiano; it is entitled: "The Renewal of the Liturgy: from the Movements to the Universal Church" (pp. 67-140). In it are indicated various problems and interventions. At the very beginning, though, there is a statement that is not so well balanced; it is the following: "On the eve of Vatican II, and it was quite widespread, there was... especially in Roman circles a conception of the liturgy understood as an external cult, managed by the priestly hierarchy through the rigid observance of rubrics, and tending to exclude the conscious and active participation of the faithful" (p. 67). Was it the case, we ask, that the liturgical movement in Italy accomplished nothing? And what can we say about a phrase such as the "Catholic reconquest" that supposedly aimed "to re-establish the control of the Church over society and over the political powers that be"? (p. 68). Using the term "restoration" in this same way is both equivocal and dangerous, even when it is placed between quotation marks (p. 75).

The research of Paiano includes the following divisions: "The liturgy prior to the Council: the main lines of reform and restoration in the 20th Century"; "the liturgical movement enters into the history of the Council"; "the project for the reform of the liturgy in the first plenary session: a doctrinal foundation with a pastoral aim"; "the movement (and movements) for the reform of the liturgy in the work of the subcommissions"; "tensions in the period between the first two sessions"; "the second plenary session: the liturgical reform from the movements into the universal Church"; "the first organic *schema* of the Constitution: active participation the aim of the reform"; "the role of Vagaggini in the development of the first chapter"; "active participation between general principles and actual translations"; "the clash over the first chapter: incarnation or paschal mystery?"; "the *schema* of November 15"; "towards the definitive *schema*: incarnation and eschatology"; "the preparatory liturgical commission"; and "conclusions."

We are pleased to record here two statements that are indicative of the value of this essay: "In the preparatory liturgical *schema*, even with the variations and mutilations dictated by the subcommission for amendments, the general results of the work of the liturgical commission were not changed. Such results were not lacking in sensitivity to diverse instances of the reform of the liturgy" (p. 134). "The mediation effected by Bugnini and Vagaggini represented a fundamental role in making acceptable new initiatives, though both traditional language and traditional theological categories were employed in the process" (p. 137).

Riccardo Burigana addresses: "The Dogmatic Project of Vatican II: The Preparatory Theological Commission (1960-1962)" (pp. 141-206). His work is consistent: following an introduction in which the ecumenical, liturgical, and biblical movements are treated, in wide ranging "approximations" (a term of the author's)—and in which ecclesiological reflections in the light of the encyclical *Mystici Corporis* and the development of moral teaching are covered—the true and proper theme of the chapter is then treated after ten pages or so. Valuable here is a rather notable rectification contained in a note which we would have liked to see introduced into the text (p. 141); that is, it would have been "more exact to speak of 'Roman theologies' rather than simply of a 'Roman theology.'" Proceeding on this basis, we could have gotten a proper start and would have avoided "improper *clichés* and mistaken preconceptions."

The author's true and proper analysis thus only begins with "'Physiognomy,' Organization, and Periodization of the Commission"; following this comes "the Preliminary Works and the Order of the S*chemata*" and "the Thematic Nuclei in the Individual Subcommissions and in the Plenary Sessions" (*de Ecclesia, de fontibus revelationis, de deposito fidei pure custodiendo, nova professio fidei, de ordine morali individuali, de ordine sociali, de castitate, virginitate, matrimonio, familia, de beata Virgine Maria*). The phrase on page 175 concerning "a formulation which confirms the unicity or singleness of the Catholic Church as the Church of Christ" is equivocal; and it is also misleading to say that Cardinal Ottaviani imposed the term *damnandi* (p. 181). Moreover, the existing Regulations in fact provided that in case of a parity of votes, the president would have the decisive word.

With regard to this last consideration, the examination of the question of the "relationships" between Vatican I and Vatican II, between Ottaviani-Tromp-Felici, between the Theological Commission and the Secretariat for Promoting Christian Unity, and so on—this examination turns out to be very interesting. The same thing is true of the author's observation—for us fundamental—of the need "to go beyond a simplistic placing in opposition of Romans and non-Romans. To the extent that there was any truth in this, with time it carried less and less weight with the break-up of the apparent unity of the Romans, and the greater and greater involvement of theologians not resident in Rome" (p. 202). The last paragraph on page 206 seems to be providing a too simplistic explanation concerning what is called "the failure of the project of a council aimed at the completion of the papal magisterium from Vatican I on, and, in particular, that of Pope Pius XII; and also for the purpose of condemning errors present in the Church and the world."

"The Laity in the Church and the World" is the title of the next contribution; it is by Giovanni Turbanti, and it is well done, precise, and consistent (pp. 207-271). It is divided into the following sections: "The preparatory commission for the apostolate of the laity": "the laity in the Church and their apostolate": "presence in society": "between charitable action and public assistance"; "forwarding the *schemata* to the Central Preparatory Commission: a balance-sheet of the work of this commission."

"The Ecumenical Proposal of the Secretariat for Promoting Christian Unity" (pp. 273-350) was committed to the pen of Mauro Velati. Here the divisions are: "The first steps of the Secretariat" (alluding to the singularity of this new Church body characterized by its freedom of operation and its openness with respect to the other preparatory commissions—p. 282); "the theological debate on the Church"; "a controverted question concerning the members of the Church" ("the ambition of the Secretariat was precisely to contribute to the development of a new theology adapted to the times"—p. 290); "papal primacy and episcopal collegiality"; "the common priesthood of the faithful": "the liturgy: unity in diversity" (the question of the use of Latin); "Scripture in the life of the Church" (offered along with the Volk report and several subsections, namely: "the rediscovery of the Bible" and *"de traditione et S. Scriptura*); "truth and charity in matrimonial pastoral practice" (the theme of mixed marriages); "prayers for unity: spiritual ecumenism"—I would not have used the word "conversion" to describe the adhesion to Catholicism of Paul Watson; see page 315. Velati's topical divisions continue and conclude as follows: "what is ecumenism?"; and "tolerance or religious freedom?"—here the question is not correctly formulated; see page 326. Finally, there are included "The Church and the people of Israel" and *"Veritatem facientes in caritate."*

We cannot agree with Velati's conclusion about the Secretariat for Promoting Christian Unity; it should have been formulated more carefully and precisely. Here it is: "In a situation strongly conditioned by the hegemonical pretentions of the Theological Commission of Cardinal Ottaviani, which reserved to itself all decisions touching upon doctrine, [the Secretariat] represented an element of great originality and at the same time one of clear opposition to what the Theological Commission wanted to impose upon the whole Council. It was evidently an unequal situation for a new organism such as the Secretariat that did not enjoy any precise institutional guarantee, and counted solely on the support of Pope John XXIII, assured through his relationship with Cardinal A. Bea. The fact itself that it was not a true and proper commission situated it in a position of weakness within the great preparatory machinery that was so strongly conditioned by the Roman Curia" (pp. 338-339). (At the end of this essay, there also appears an *excursus* on "the Preparatory Commission for the Eastern Catholic Churches)."

The author of the next contribution entitled "Towards an *Aggiornamento* of Pastoral Practice" (pp. 357-395), Maurilio Guasco, paints his subject with a very broad brush; he dedicates some thirty pages to the background of the Council before he arrives at his particular study. His treatment consists of a rather descriptive narrative, beginning with pre-conciliar pastoral practice, before arriving (only on page 373) "on the eve of the Council."

His analysis includes the topic of "bishops and the governance of dioceses"—but can the episcopate be defined as "the completion of the sacrament of orders?" (p. 374). Other topics include "the Commission for Seminaries, Studies, and Catholic Schools" as well as "clergy and faithful people"—but can we speak seriously about any "mandate" for the lay people, elevated here almost to the dignity of a sacrament? (p. 388); or about a "point of reference" which remains "the regime of Christendom"? (p. 390). Here is his conclusion: "That people of God who, in the preparatory texts, seemed to consist only of those with duties to perform and with rights limited to receiving that which others were responsible for providing, became instead in the new scheme of things almost the major protagonists in the history of the post-conciliar Church" (p. 395).

To Giuseppe Butturini was confided the treatment of "Missions and Council: the History, Texts, and Criteria of the Preparatory Commission" (pp. 397-423). After his presentation of the actual state of the research on the topic, the author, although with some asperity and exaggeration, diligently does explain "the Church's missionary character"; "missionary adaptations": "the missions in the *vota* [Latin, "desires"] transmitted by the bishops to the Ante-Preparatory Commission"; "adaptation and Catholicity"; "the necessity of the missions"; "the mission of the Church and the missions"; "the pre-conciliar commission: history, texts, and criteria"; and "the missionary commissions: changes and problems." This last topic concerns the influence of Cardinal Tardini on the preparatory work, yet nowhere is the important and clarifying study of Monsignor V. Carbone cited. Finally, Butturini treats "the *schemata* of the preparatory commission," "orientations, content, and criteria," and "conclusions."

"For the Renewal of the Religious Life" (pp. 425-444) is the title of the research conducted by Luiz Carlos Marques. In spite of two or three questionable passages ("in his own way," p. 427; on "Opus Dei," pp. 429 and 438; and "concerning matrimony and the religious state," p. 444), the analysis navigates quite conveniently from "the requests for advice and counsel" to "the commission"—consisting of the membership of the latter, which includes consultants, the chronology and the methods of its work, and, finally, the *schema* entitled *De Statibus perfectionis adquirendae*.

The reservations we harbor concerning this volume find particular reference in the final contribution of one of the editors, A. Melloni himself. His title is: "Parallelisms, Common Themes, and Conflicting Hypotheses in the Preparations for Vatican II" (pp. 445-482). Our objections begin with his initial affirmation, which by itself injects a note of destructive criticism: "No council...underwent such a vast and sterile preparation," he writes (p. 445). Was it sterile? The author himself, for that matter, responds in another vein, when he admits that "disregard [of the preparations] perhaps resulted in not taking adequately into account the influence—both from a thematic point of view and from that of the procedures that were established for the entire four years of the Council, 1962-1965—that these preparations had on both the characteristics and the weaknesses of Vatican II."

His research begins with the topic of "the preparations and the fears of the coming Council"; here he rightly places in relief the great themes of the question of the Roman Curia and that of Cardinal Tardini, as we mentioned earlier. It is particularly in his evaluation of Tardini that we disagree with Melloni. Why, we ask, does he require that the then Secretary of State had to be "neutral and unfocused"? (p. 447). Then there is his take on the subject of the Roman congregations and their relationships with the conciliar commissions, as well as on the question of the number of the latter; with two exceptions, he refers to the latter as virtual replications of the former. But this was equally a characteristic of Vatican I, which was always referred back to at need. As for his negative opinion on the grillwork of readings on the synthesis of the suggestions received from the bishops in view of the coming Council, they were contemporaneous—it is necessary to recall it—with the existing "pre-conciliar" mentality, such as it was (with no judgments offered here on the use of that particular adjective).

There follows his treatment of the "personnel" involved in the conciliar preparation phase; he speaks of the "struggle for the Council" and of "the struggle in the Curia," as if these were characteristic interferences "signaling the crucial passage from the 'ante-preparatory' phase to the 'preparatory' phase" (p. 448)—we would prefer to say "anti-preparatory" as one says "anti-pasto" [i. e., "before the meal," the "appetizer"]. His topics include: "the exceptions," "the rules," and "the objectives of and protagonists for the selections"—here too Tardini is treated, it seems to us, according to a preconceived judgment. The author's assertions seem ponderous and bear the distinct mark or flavor of research and thirst for power; he speaks about ambitions to the point where the author declares "that in a certain sense the pope remained the prisoner of all this preparatory machinery" (p. 456, n. 44). Along the same lines is the description of the role played by the pope in the selection of the personnel for the commissions; the pope's choices "did not prevail" (p. 457), we learn. And we encounter again a rock thrown into the smooth mirror surface of the conciliar water with the inclusion of the famous opinion that "perhaps beyond Capovilla [the pope's secretary], and Msgr. Angelo Dell'Acqua, there did not even exist anyone very faithful to John XXIII" (*Ibid.*). In this regard, is it exact, though, to affirm that the pope "candidly admitted, for example, that he was removed from involvement with the naming of the secretaries of the Pontifical Ante-preparatory Commission, the Central Preparatory Commission, and then of the Council itself" (*Ibid.*)?

Another section concerns "the other ante-preparatory groups:

working groups and the environment in which they worked." The kind of language he uses here to describe these groups does not seem quite proper—or at the very least it is "journalistic." He speaks of "lobbies," of the "leaders" of such "lobbies," and also of a "shadow cabinet" (p. 460). Sociology and political science certainly do play their part in valid research, but their importance should not be exaggerated, especially when there is a risk of characterizations which are unsuitable or which lower the tone of the whole study.

There follows the topic of "the weakness of an imperfect parallelism" in which the author asks why "the Tardini hypothesis" does not work. The response he gives, although it is not the only one possible—he even mentions the fact of the death of the cardinal ("also")—can be reduced to the statement that "at bottom Tardini bequeathed to his successor, if not hegemony over the Council, at least the pretense of such hegemony (whether actually or theoretically does not matter)" (p. 461). Another topic covered by the author is that of "parallelisms." On this subject he offers highly disputable conclusions in language that should have been kept under better control; he uses terms such as "schizophrenia," referring to a supposed "dream book" of the Roman congregations, speaks of "jealousy" and of the "banalization" of the intuitions of Pope John. Pursuing the further topic of "differentiation," he describes the Secretariat for Promoting Unity as a "subversive element."

Under the umbrella of "the themes of the work," Melloni then expatiates on "the sources and limits of the *quaestiones*." Here it is asserted that "there was a very doubtful degree of fidelity for the synthesis of these various points of view" (p. 465). He goes on to treat "themes and schemes" and "the management and reception of the *quaestiones*." On this last topic, he asserts that "even the pope made use of the liberty accorded to the *quaestiones*" (p. 469).

Melloni brings his contribution to a conclusion by dealing with "the methods and machinery of the work." Here he declares that "all the commissions exhibited in some measure the typical habits familiar in regular curial practice; Monsignor Bugnini is identified in passing as "an inspired conservative" and also as a "moderate reformist" (p. 472). The author covers "common procedural data" and "norms and practices of secrecy"; he describes the rule of secrecy as "functional in the interest of internal aims" (p. 474). He also treats of "the articulation of the subcommissions," and these turn out to represent a rather diverse reality. It can be asked what was intended by stating that "the secretariat served a policy position, not just an organizational one" (p. 476). Note 119 includes what we believe to be an unjust observation on "Ottaviani-Tromp and the commission they created," which is referred to as "obtusely omnipotent" (p. 477). The author passes on to what he calls "pre-disposing the canons *sub velamine schematum*"; here again his comments on the Council and the Code of Canon Law as well as on its preparation are unfair (see pp. 478-479). "Growing out of all these preparatory elements was a set of relationships difficult to reconcile with the Council; this indicated nothing else but the weaknesses of the preparations that were carried out" (pp. 479-480). But we need to take note of the fact that the Council had not yet taken place at this point. Yet the above assertion constitutes the premise and pattern of others in the same vein. We cannot agree with this approach.

In this text incongruous concerns are also often noted among the various commissions; theological idiosyncrasies are encountered, along with a widespread "objective...of surmounting" what was considered to be "the parenthesis of the Council." Then there were the cases of actual blindness concerning the *status ecclesiae* (whether this meant overvaluing their own actual power on the part of the groups directing the preparatory phases or undervaluing the problems that were agitating the Church). "Certainly the preparatory commissions, in their ensemble," the author writes, "reflected the knowledge and image of a milieu that was both unfocused and ideological; the dominant note was rigidity." For this author, "the possibilities offered by the Council, its consciousness of what was needed, were consistently undervalued." Moreover, "the isolation of the pope from any examination of the preparatory work created an unfillable gap" (p. 481). And the end result of all this became a prophecy of the present post-conciliar era (not the era of the Council itself), exhibiting indications of the problems that we would be facing today. "During the preparation period there emerged already a 'symptomatology' of an 'adult' Vatican II and even of the post-conciliar bureaucratization that would come about. Similarly, there were unresolved ambiguities in the curial-conciliar-papal relations, taboos on theological questions, and denials of the obvious discontinuities that were occurring. Only the actual convening of the conciliar assembly itself could interrupt these effects and constrain everyone to move from an image of the Council (poor and skeletal as it was) to the vital experience of the *aula* itself" (p. 482). The volume then concludes with an index of names (pp. 493-503).

7

On the Eve of the Council in Europe and in the Eastern Catholic Churches

Lamberigts M. and Soetens Cl., eds., with Various Authors, *Á la Veille du Concile Vatican II: Vota et reactions en Europe et dans le catholicisme oriental* [On the Eve of Vatican Council II: *Vota* and Reactions in Europe and Eastern Catholicism], Bibliotheek van de Faculteit der Godgeleerdheid, Leuven, 1992, 277 pages.

This volume includes texts and interventions presented on the occasion of a meeting in Houston held on January 12-15, 1991, on the subject of "Christianity and the Churches on the Eve of Vatican II." Added to these contributions are some additional ones from an earlier conference of the same type which took place in 1989; and still others prepared for yet another conference in Rome organized in 1986 by the *École Française* [French School] there. The main objective of the publication was to illustrate and explain some examples of the *vota*, [recommendations] sent in by various national hierarchies in view of the upcoming Council. These *vota*, it was thought, could provide a picture of the general situation of the Church in the years immediately preceding the Council. Also included in the volume are some reactions by non-Catholics to the calling of the Council.

Following an introduction and general index, the volume opens, by way of a more explanatory introduction, with a contribution by M. Velati entitled "Christianity and the Church on the Eve of Vatican Council II" (pp. 1-11). It is a rather superficial effort, it seems to us, if it seriously aims to characterize the ecclesial reality of the Church on various continents while claiming to show the "institutional solitude" of Pope John XXIII, not only in relation to the Roman Curia (a claim that has become almost the customary one to make) but also in relation to the entire Catholic episcopate. These are claims that have been underlined by G. Gutierrez and by others, including in the present volume. There is a sense in which the enunciation of such a thesis could be properly understood; there is even a sense in which "solitude" could indeed be considered constitutive of the personal exercise of the papal primacy; but this is not the sense in which the idea is intended to be understood here. And, indeed, there is considerable exaggeration in how the idea is presented here (see p. 6), just as there is considerable exaggeration in attempting to "accredit" the Council more as an "event" than as a "magisterial assembly," that is, as an assembly with concrete doctrinal and pastoral responsibilities.

It was surely fundamental for any effort of this nature that Professor Giuseppe Alberigo would want to lend a hand where there was the prospect of the publication of a history of the Council defined itself as "pluri-dimensional." His contribution is entitled "Hermeneutical Criteria for a History of Vatican II" (pp. 12-23). It would not be a question here, to employ the terms of the author himself, merely to have a well put-together perception of the "internal" development of the conciliar assembly; rather, this would involve "also its relationship with external factors relative to the social, political, economic, and cultural contexts on the various continents." The author then adds: "To reconstruct the phenomenology of the conciliar work, along with the spirit and the dialectic that characterized and animated the assembly in its various phases, requires a constant encounter between the development of the work of the Council and the evolution of the consciousness of the assembly itself...as well as of its components. The great doctrinal, institutional, and pastoral themes must be followed also in their 'intersecting' developments, that is, independently of the strict order of the conciliar work itself. A similar kind of attention must be given to the dialectical relationship between the internal climate of the Council and the external context in which it was operating— Roman, certainly, but also in a more general sense" (p. 12).

But when Alberigo applies all this in a concrete way we can no longer follow him. On the subject of the Council as an "event," he asserts that "it will therefore be a question of applying other and different hermeneutical criteria—even if they are in a close and complementary relationship—than the canonical qualities required for the institutional legitimacy of a council and the criteria required for the interpretation of the corpus of its decisions" (pp. 2-13). Thus, "the hermeneutic developed for the interpretation of historical sources" would here be "inadequate on account of its defects" (p. 13). Similarly, the "pastoral" character of Vatican II leads to the conclusion that only in an "analogical way" could the hermeneutic developed for the history of other councils be utilized, while the hermeneutic used for the documents of the ecclesiastical magisterium "appear to be even less adapted" [to Vatican II]. Quite obviously, we cannot agree with the author here, as unfortunately happens quite often, much to our own displeasure.

Moving on to his actual concrete hermeneutical examples, Alberigo speaks about what he calls "an integralist reading" of Vatican II which would consider the Council to be a break in the continuity of the Catholic Tradition. To this interpretation is opposed the vision of those who perceive in the Council a legitimization of a radical turn away from the preceding Catholic Tradition. It seems to us that here the extremes actually touch each other, although the author in no way perceives this. For others Vatican II was rather a case of a "minor" council, or, for those among whose number we believe the author includes himself, it was a synod of "transition"—in the strong meaning of that word. It was a Council "which moved the Church out of the Tridentine era—indeed, out of the Constantinian era—and marked the beginning of an entirely new era."

At this point, Alberigo enumerates what for him are the most important hermeneutical criteria. They include: the intentions of John XXIII; the "pastoral" nature of the Council; the *aggiornamento* [updating] as the principal aim of the Council; the practice of compromise; and the search for unanimity. We shall limit ourselves to making a few observations concerning the intentions of Pope Roncalli, which can be considered "the will of the legislator." Yet it is not often remarked that John XXIII was *not* the "legislator" in the strict sense of that word. That role belonged to Paul VI, who, we recall, was not obliged to re-convoke the Council. But in any case, what comes out here, when going back to "the intentions of John XXIII," amounts to a depreciation of the actual documents of the Council on the part of Alberigo and the exaltation of the synod as an "event" (see p. 18).

However, even in this perspective, the role of Pope Montini must not be downgraded. That John XXIII wanted a "new" council with respect to Vatican I—that is to say, he did not want just a continuation of Vatican I—in no way signifies that he intended to convoke a "new" [type of] council that, notwithstanding its particular characteristics, was different in its nature from all the other ecumenical councils which had preceded it. Similarly, the fact that the Council was to be "pastoral" did not mean that it was not also "doctrinal"—as well as very positive and even joyously suffused with truth.

We find we can agree with some of the author's enunciations on the subject of *aggiornamento*, in particular, with the idea of being open to contemporary research and to the inculturation of divine Revelation into newer cultures. However, we would have to add the significant phrase "in fidelity" (see p. 21), as he himself actually does, and beautifully, in a subsequent paragraph. Nevertheless, this author is not impeded on the following page from also producing contrary affirmations, e.g., "interpreting Vatican II in the light of preceding councils appears…anachronistic, but, especially, alien to the intentions of John XXIII as well as to the spirit of the Council itself." He does not seem to see that he himself produces contradictions more than once (see n. 20). It also seems to us that, certainly in the context of the search for conciliar unanimity, some of his observations on the "majority" and the "minority" at the Council are not exact (see p. 22).

In the next chapter on "The Bavarian Bishops prior to Vatican Council II" (pp. 24-37), K. Wittstadt describes the gallery of these diocesan pastors, examines their roots and some of their characteristics as well as their episcopal service, along with the *vota* (or at least some of them) and their roles both at the Council and on the commissions. Outlining some of the common themes contained in the responses from these bishops, this author also mistakenly makes a distinction between the conciliar texts ("which are one thing") and the spirit of the Council ("which is something else"). He speaks of "reform," and refers often to it, rather than speaking of *aggiornamento*, which is what he should have referred to.

C. Soetens, meanwhile, deals with the *vota* sent in by the Belgian bishops and religious superiors (pp. 38-52). He divides them into various categories, 22 responses in all. We ask why the elaborations worked out by the apostolic nuncio are simply incorporated with the responses submitted by the three auxiliaries? The thematic analysis which precedes the general observations offered evidences of "disappointment" with the proposals, when the aims of John XXIII are taken into account, and also when the behavior of the bishops at the Council itself is considered. This study concludes with a good comparative list, in alphabetical order, of the themes touched upon.

"The *Vota* of the Spanish Bishops following the Announcement of Vatican Council II" is a presentation (pp. 53-82) resented by E. Vilanova, "in the context of a politicized theology and a theologized politics." These are characterized as neo-Thomist, anti-modern, anti-ecumenical, "a-historical," restorationist, "ecclesiocratic," and "hierarchiocratic." We certainly would not want to deny that, more than elsewhere, the Spanish politico-religious situation could have brought about some radicalized tendencies rather generally in the pre-conciliar era. These are here described in very negative terms. This is a rather common type of exaggeration, in fact. Later on, the author speaks about "a timid opening to European theology and pastoral practice" and also about "surprise and disenchantment" in relation to Vatican II. There follows a sufficiently well-developed analysis of the responses to the consultations organized by Cardinal Tardini; from this analysis is deduced what was supposedly the Spanish bishops' conception of Vatican II; the desire of the majority of them, it is asserted, was to "define and condemn." Vilanova, "with regard to doctrinal and liturgical questions," reveals his own reductive position concerning these pastors as "teachers of truth"; he does not consider "teaching as the final instance of discernment [or judgment]" (p. 68). He accuses the Church of historical insensitivity when asking, for example, that an exposition of the foundations of moral theology be established deductively *ex lege naturali*" (p. 72). Another indication of the position of this author is his use of the term "reform" when referring to the Council—something that the episcopate itself never does. For that matter, even John XXIII defined the finality of the Council as *"aggiornamento,"* even if a certain "dynamic of reform" appeared in the *vota*. Thus, this Spanish episcopate was not entirely "retrograde," as was contended earlier. The study concludes on the high point of Catholic Action and a theology of the laity; several opinions are offered on the subject of ecumenism and on the mission and universality of the Church; and, finally, some conclusions are likewise offered. One could synthesize all of this as follows: "The majority of the Spanish episcopate paid only marginal attention to the changes taking place in society and to the adaptations to those changes being made by the Church...The response to the crisis essentially took place on the ideological plane...and there was an absence of historical categories and a predominance of moral categories instanced in judging of the reality being encountered" (p. 82).

There follows "The Recommendations and *Vota* of the Italian Bishops" (pp. 83-97), covered by M. Velati. Because they were produced on the eve of Vatican Council II, these recommendations had "a special importance in the worldwide ecclesial panorama, and not only from a quantitative point of view," but also because they were produced "in the shadow of the Holy See" (p. 83).

The author confirms the judgment of R. Morozzo della Rocca: "In the thinking of the Italian bishops, the Council needed to respond to precise and urgent demands for clarity with definitions identifying all controversial matters, whether in the doctrinal or in the disciplinary and canonical fields...This did not exclude exhibiting at times a desire for renewal; however, this occurred on a rather superficial level; it was a more 'pragmatic' version of John XXIII's *aggiornamento*; at times it amounted to nothing more than a simple revision of the Code of Canon Law or to the correction of certain dysfunctions in ordinary pastoral practice" (p. 87).

Even at first glance, the proposals advanced bring into prominence the question of the condition of the clergy; in them there is a "decisive re-affirmation of the norms of celibacy" (p. 89). "In the opinion of the bishops, the *aggiornamento* of the Church must come about through the sacerdotal role and function of the priest, but in an ecclesial context where the diocesan authority residing in the person of the bishop remains uncontested" (p. 90). And with regard to "the very close ties between the Italian episcopate and the Holy See that had been created in the course of a century," to which the author refers, we should recall that these particular ties go back many centuries; they go back at least in part to the existence of the three zones of the influence of the *potestas* of the Bishop of Rome of which Pierre Batiffol speaks, writing about the very first centuries in the life of the Church.

Velati then explains those aspects of the bishops' proposals which have reference to the magisterium of the Church and of the Council. He underlines the "evident...preponderance of negative examples calling for the condemnation of erroneous doctrines such as Marxism, existentialism, secularism, and so-called neo-modernism" (p. 92). But his conclusion seems both hasty and rash: "Evident in the kinds of positions taken is a conception of the Council involving forms in opposition to the orientation Pope John XXIII was laying out" (p. 93). Yet it was none other than Pope Roncalli who wanted the bishops to give voice freely to their true opinions on the occasion of these consultations.

In the end the author asks: "Was it renewal or preservation?" He claims that there was some openness on the part of the Italian bishops with regard to the liturgy ("a certain desire for reform was undoubtedly present"—p. 96). But there was "greater hesitancy and reserve on their part with regard to the biblical and ecumenical movements" (p. 97). However, they were generally "ignorant of the dominant themes current in international political and ecclesiastical life; at the same time only with difficulty did they grasp the changes in the culture and customs within Italian society itself...in many ways they lacked a proper vision—we could even say a 'pastoral' vision—of current problems" (*Ibid.*). Thus "the limits and incapacities of the greater number of the Italian bishops at the Council were very clearly manifested in the recommendations they submitted here." I do not find this observation very pertinent, considering that the responses of the other episcopates in the course of the same consultations differed little from the responses of the Italian bishops.

The *vota* of the Dutch bishops are synthesized next by J.Y.H.A. Jacobs (pp. 98-110). He first presents their authors, and then discusses the origins of their responses. The influence of the Executive Committee of the Catholic Conference on ecumenical questions is evident here. The author also discusses the content of the various responses. Among the observations made by way of evaluating the content, we would like to quote the following: "When the *vota* are analyzed...we discern a clear image of great expectations on the part of the Dutch bishops towards the Council at a time when little was known about the course the Council would take; these expectations were contained, but they were there" (p. 109). While it seems to us that such an observation is certainly pertinent, it could also well be considered to apply to virtually all of the responses received in Rome.

Jacobs concludes, however, as follows: "While the Dutch bishops, in their normal administration of the Church, were still acting with great circumspection, and were still leaning strongly towards conservative positions...in their pre-conciliar expectations—never made public, by the way—the majority of them, without any doubt, were opting clearly for the way of renewal" (p. 110).

The *vota* of the Swiss bishops, seven texts in all (pp. 111-118), were assigned to Ph. Chenaux. Above all, he provides evidence of their failure to produce a common, agreed-upon response, as had been suggested by the apostolic nuncio. This failure came about primarily because of the opposition between Bishop Charrière and Bishop Caminada.

The lines of force regarding the expectations of the Swiss bishops included the doctrine of the episcopate (the re-evaluation of the episcopate), the liturgical renewal, ecclesiastical discipline, and the opening to ecumenical dialogue. Yet what is striking is that "for the greater number of the Swiss bishops, there was an absence of any concern for the political or social order" (p. 117).

R. Morozzo della Rocca, in a solid study—even if it is a rather sharp and cutting one towards any "Latinizing" positions—analyzes the *vota* of the Eastern Catholic bishops in preparation for Vatican II (pp. 119-145). Responses came in from three-quarters of those who were canvassed. However, there was a notable fragmentation of opinions among them so as to reduce them, taken together, to the lowest percentage as a minority of any grouping at the Council (5 percent), even though they were weak to begin with. Notwithstanding that, "and in spite of the diversity among them, the term 'Eastern-rite' was not just a negative label attached to all the non-Western Churches" (p. 122). In any case, two orders of distinction clearly appeared in the preparatory material prepared for the Council by the Orientals, namely: in the first place, and most importantly, there was the question of the degree of fidelity to the Eastern origins of their Churches (note, for example, the differences between the Melchites and the Maronites); and secondly, there was the division of their origins into three great cultural areas which may be labeled European, Greco-Slavic, and Afro-Asian.

Moreover, the author, following the opinion of Roger Aubert and others concerning the typical judgments ("generally disappointing") rendered on the recommendations sent to Rome in preparation for the Council, declares that those sent in by the Eastern Catholic bishops "constituted an important exception to the general tone registered in this great consultation" (p. 125). In effect, "in the conciliar recommendations of the Eastern Catholic bishops and religious superiors—as contrasted with those of the Western bishops—requests for the condemnation of errors and historical movements were rare; so was any insistence on the juridical aspects, whether *ad intra* or *ad extra*, of the Church; so were any proposals for the formulation of any new dogmas." The dominant preoccupation and most particular fact about the Eastern Catholic bishops was their concern for the unity of the Church—with particular (though not exclusive) reference to the various Orthodox Churches of the East. For the most part, the "Churches" stemming from the Reformation were disregarded.

But what kind of unity was envisaged? The ideas about this were quite various, and the author sorts them out rather well in his treatment. He starts with the thinking of Cardinal Gregory Agaganian and proceeds to that of the Melchites, who claimed that a reform of the hierarchical structure of the Church was necessary, along with a "downgrading...of the absolute power of the papacy." They called for the restoration of the ranks of the patriarchs as they had existed in the course of the first millennium; in such a context, "papal diplomacy would lose its significance" (pp. 130-131). Then there were the positions of the Catholic Copts as well as those of the Pontifical Oriental Institute. There is likewise presented here some critical comments on the Melchite position which, we would say, shows some signs of the times in which they were formulated.

For us, however, it seems that the will to defend the two degrees of the *ius divinum*—that is, the supreme pontificate and the authority of the diocesan bishop—should be present for all purposes (see p. 134); and that the situation existing within the Latin patriarchate should not have been modified, for it was the fruit of a long historical development: It should not have been modified either for any ecumenical aim or in order to "demonstrate" to Eastern Christians what their situation might be if full communion were re-established. The Church's "two lungs," to employ the language that has now come into common use, should both retain their characteristics, which are the fruits of the laborious activities of centuries and, in the Occident, of the experience of the *libertas ecclesiae*; meanwhile, both the patriarchal rights and duties of the Bishop of Rome should be preserved.

The author further concentrates on the complaints of the Eastern Catholics and on their fears of being considered "second-class" Christians. It was from this that their desires for greater autonomy from Rome arose, that is, from their dependence on the Roman Curia and pontifical diplomacy. The same thing was true of their convictions concerning the necessity of "de-Latinizing" the Eastern Catholic Churches, and their criticisms of Latin Catholic missionaries and of the

Latin Catholic presence in the East. Their desire was for an effective equality of rites, allowing even for the possibility that "from time to time the rite most adaptable to the local culture and mentality might be chosen" (p. 143). There was, in addition, a desire for a revision of the norms concerning *communicatio in sacris* and mixed marriages, as well as of the rules concerning fasts and abstinence, etc.

We repeat, however, that these Eastern Fathers were by no means unanimous in the formulation of their *desiderata*, also because there was among them a variety of positions and opinions more or less inspired by Western and Latin culture. The author points out, though, a lack of interest on their part in the Muslim world—an interest manifested, however, by the Archbishop of Algiers, Léon Duval, who was not an Eastern-rite bishop.

"The Roman *Vota*" (pp. 146-168) by A. Riccardi are of particular interest and worthy of attention; this is the case even for purposes of "re-dimensioning" facile preconceptions. However, the "liberating effect" of which the author speaks, "was lacking in Roman circles," which by nature exhibited continuity. Moreover, this "liberating effect" must be reduced to rather limited dimensions, if we go by how much we are told about the "generally disappointing responses" received in the course of these pontifical consultations prior to the Council. For these responses were supposedly the cause of the effect in question. Still, this preoccupation, however circuitous, affected those "managing the immense conciliar machine" (p. 146); indeed, it was a precedent from Vatican I; but we would add that it did not last long.

As for the considerations concerning the Curia of John XXIII, we are inclined to be more cautious than Riccardi, even though he correctly recognizes the presence of groups whose line "was not at all homogeneous"; it was not a question of any monolithic reality. It does not appear to us possible to place on the same plane, for example, the treatment accorded to worker priests and that accorded to Communism. Nor can we rely unduly on an offhand remark of Pope Roncalli—if, indeed, he said it as reported—to the effect that: "I have nobody except Archbishop Dell'Acqua and Father Loris [Capovilla]."

There comes to mind, in fact, if we are seeking to characterize a man (even if he is the pope) by something he has said; another reported Johannine exclamation of the same type, namely: "I love Archbishop Dell'Acqua, while I esteem Cardinal Tardini." We can surely conclude here that collaborators do not necessarily have to be friends, or even "sons." What even a pope can require, though, is both loyalty and honest collaboration. And in the case of Cardinal Tardini, for example, who at his death was described as "the aide both strongest and closest to the pope in his governance of the Church," John XXIII got what he asked for. And he granted that.

A principal aim of this study of Riccardi "is to show how to identify some of the ways in which those in charge of things in Rome prepared themselves for the Council" (p. 148). "In Rome there were many silences and one proposition," the author writes. We would make a distinction here which should serve to lessen the scope of this assertion: among the cardinals and bishops, the bishops engaged in pastoral work in the diocese of Rome and in the suburbicarian dioceses, and those working in the Roman dicasteries, only these latter were called "to screen the *vota* of all the bishops and to shape them in accordance with the general overall orientation" (p. 149). This fact alone explains the psychology of Roman expectations, without immediately having to interpret them in terms of detachment from or indifference to the Council. The author correctly adds here that it was no "consultative obligation that was recognized, but rather an orienting function" (p. 148).

The Roman ecclesiastical universities, however, were much more involved. "Among them the Gregorian University stood out, especially as giving notable attention to biblical questions. The Lateran University actually sponsored a 'week' in preparation for Vatican II" (*Ibid.*). This latter institution, in fact, going beyond prejudices, appeared to be very well disposed, conciliar-wise, including with regard to proposals for innovations. It was not for nothing that Riccardi attests to the fact that "the preparatory work done by the Lateran faculty was among the most notable accomplishment of any Roman university" (p. 157). One indication of this was the attention given to the question of non-Catholics, for whom a new dicastery was proposed (see p. 160).

The *vota* of the other Roman theological institutions were much less focused than those of the Gregorian University and the Lateran University. Following "so many voices, so many problems," reference is made to the *Proposita et monita SS. Congregationum Curiae Romanae*. The author sees this as an "undeniable work of synthesis," and he discovers in it "an original contribution, noting that "in a certain sense these *Proposita* [constituted] the true *vota* of the Roman Curia" (p. 163). However, they are only very briefly explained, and then only in their most salient and interesting aspects. Riccardi concludes that "Reading over these *vota* does not appear to have motivated a more open attitude towards the requests made on the periphery (naturally alongside many that were condemned). For that matter, the *vota* of the Fathers contained many elements that were objectively contradictory and that could confirm the typical Roman view of things or introduce new problems and requirements for renewal...In the aggregate, reading through these *vota* submitted by the Curia brings one to a perspective which confirms the traditional line of the pontificate of Pius XII" (p. 167).

The Roman dicasteries, however, "began to sense the existence of an uneasiness in the relations between the central governance of the Church and the episcopate" (*Ibid.*). In his opinion, the Congregation for Extraordinary Affairs not only perceived this problem, but undertook to interpret it.

Moving on, the *"Ante-preparatoria Vota"* submitted by the Faculties of Theology of Louvain and Louvanium (Zaïre) are successively explained by M. Lamberigts (pp. 169-184). As regards Louvain, the text consists of two major sections, one dealing with the question of what the Church should be, while the other refers to specific *desiderata* (24 *vota* included); these submissions are not lacking in either new perspectives or interest. The same thing can be said of the *vota* from Louvanium. As a conclusion, there is an attempt to compare the contributions of the two faculties; there are elements in common and some differences. Collegiality, ecumenism, and liturgical renewal, however, were recognized as impulses necessary for the Church today. Thus, what would turn out to be the spirit and ideas of Vatican II itself were not unknown at the two "Louvains."

Then comes the chapter entitled "The Council and Contemporary Theological-Spiritual Movements between 1959 and 1962." This chapter was entrusted to E. Fouilloux, and the usual things can be said about it. With a certain "spirit of initiative," the author undertakes to present the *vota* of the various movements, but this turns out to be rather complicated given their "informality" and the difficulty of identifying objectively the "representatives." But the author manages to extricate himself from these difficulties well enough, especially with regard to questions of ecumenism, concerning which he notes "a state of unpreparedness not only among communions separated from the Catholic Church but also within her ranks" (p. 197). Fouilloux concludes his survey with a balance-sheet that is rather personal concerning the "success" of various religious movements today. His judgments concerning the ecumenical and liturgical movements are positive, while he finds even the Marian movement "far from having lowered its arms" (p. 198). The biblical movement, in his view, "remained in travail" (*Ibid.*). In the end, this author asserts that: "Almost nothing of what figures in the conciliar texts was new, properly speaking; yet the overall expression of the Catholic faith came out rather differently than was the case for the former reaction of anti-Protestantism, anti-liberalism, and anti-modernism that characterized its expression in preceding centuries" (p.199).

The chapter following continues to pay close attention to ecumenism, focusing on "The World Council of Churches and the Convocation of the Council" (pp. 200-213). The author here is, again, Ph. Chenaux, who shows himself to be both balanced and possessed of expertise. He subdivides his study into three sections concerned with "the Uncertainty of the First Months"—there was then, indeed, uncertainty (along with hope), though there was "a definite lack of clarity in the heart of the Vatican itself" concerning the nature of the conciliar event and its object (p. 203). The second section concerns "the Torments after Rhodes" [the 1959 WCC meeting], and goes up to the establishment of the Secretariat for Promoting Christian Unity. Then there is the section "Towards the Council," properly speaking, evidencing some quieting of anxieties, but also a certain "disinteresting" themselves in the event on the part of the World Council's leaders. Their principal requests for allowing a favorable response to the Council's invitation was to ask for the presence of Catholic observers at the World Council's own meeting in New Delhi, for the Church to acknowledge the need for religious liberty, and for the Church to initiate theological conversations that would go forward on parallel lines on international questions. Once they had participated at the Council as observers, and following the visit of Cardinal Bea to Geneva in February, 1965, however, a new era in ecumenical relations became a reality. Of interest in the end is the analysis here of the psychological and diplomatic bases for the eventual decision to invite observers to the Council (see p. 213). Dr. W. A. Visser't Hooft, World Council of Churches Secretary General, appears here in all his "humanity," along with the conditions he laid down regarding WCC participation the Council.

"Governments and Diplomacy Faced with the Announcement of Vatican II" (pp. 214-257) is the chapter treated by A. Melloni. The reactions recorded here consisted fundamentally of those from the French and Germans, but to a lesser extent there were also reactions from the Italians, English, Portuguese, Spanish, and Americans. The initial soundings concerned "earlier conciliar endeavors and the situation on the eve" of the Council; these helped in a better understanding of the Johannine "inspiration" to convoke a Council. This was especially true when we take into account the intervention of Cardinal Ernesto Ruffini in favor of it. The "papers" of Pope Roncalli do not provide evidence of who it was who first raised this issue, but it is easy to deduce that it was not the pontiff himself. This study goes on to consider "the status of and the main lines in the tendencies evident in the diplomatic relations of the Vatican at the end of the fifties and later" (the term "Holy See" instead of "Vatican" should have been used here). Following this, prominence is given to the question of the lack of a validating line of communication between Tardini-Montini and Pope Pius XII. The problem here was that the pope continued to consider himself to be his own Secretary of State, and hence there was presumably no need for any such line of communication.

Well, in view of the Council, the conclave of 1958 had preoccupied the chancelleries, even if, for the author, they failed by their inattention to understand the importance of the statement of January 25, 1959, announcing the Council. In this regard, the idea that the Church seemed "disoriented," as the author asserts, must be attributed to the minimal clarity *in capite* of exactly what it was that was wanted from the Council (see likewise p. 234); this is confirmed also by the reaction of the World Council of Churches. One therefore had to "seek to understand both the project and the program," resulting in this case in one interesting observation that goes against the grain of much actual historiography to the effect that "far from fearing the Council, [the Roman Curia] saw it as an opportunity to recover its proper role, which had become obscured during the years of Pope Pius XII" (pp. 229-230). We must note also the curious ecumenical observation favorable to the Curia that comes on the following page. There is also another one, a judgment on the homogeneity of views between the pope and Cardinal Tardini (p. 234). In any case, "the consensus of the press and of public opinion was generalized and was reflected in the views of diplomats" (p. 231). Thus, we encounter here an important "diplomatic source," namely, the press.

After "the failed steps of the spring," we arrive finally at the "ante-preparatory phase" proper; it is entitled "From Idea to Fact." It appears to us in this connection that the author draws conclusions here from citations both from the theological faculties and from canon law that are not pertinent (see n. 89, p. 242). The author's conclusion's would lead us to understand—even though the author states them in interrogative form—that there was much overlapping between the proposals for an ecumenical council and those for a revision of the Code of Canon Law and a citation of Cardinal Tardini's (p. 243, n. 95). The next phase, the preparatory one, properly speaking, is characterized by Melloni as "the agenda that didn't happen" (p. 246). There are "diplomatic" comments here on the make-up of the various conciliar commissions; at times these comments seem to us particularly fine (see p. 248), although they do not harmonize to the extent desired by the author. Yet he actually manages to pose the question in terms of what he styles "a superficial diplomacy or a silencer Church" (p. 249). He is also free with his own rather questionable judgments, such as the one, often repeated, of the "institutional solitude" of John XXIII, which certainly does not have any reference to the personal exercise of the supreme magisterium. And in this connection the whole note 120 deserves a suitable "exegesis."

"The Parallel Optic: The Political Context of the Concilar Preparation" discusses such things as the fears of Portugal for her colonies and also contains a diatribe against the Jewish people and the state of Israel—what factiousness resulted from the convergence of the views of the Holy Office with those of the Arab countries! (p. 254, n. 139). Anti-Franco sentiments are similarly included. All this precedes the "intermediate annotations." The question of "the difficulty for the ambassadors in trying to discover the proper interpretation for the event of the Council" thus returns. By "proper" here seems to be meant "true" interpretations, that is, interpretations in accord with the thinking of the author. A number of conclusions, finally, do not result from any research at all, we would say; rather, they arose and arise in the mind of A. Melloni (see page 257 in its entirety).

J. Famerée concludes the volume with a study entitled "Instruments and Prospects for a History of Vatican Council II: Papers from Private Sources" (pp. 258-268). Once the importance of non-official sources for historical research has been admitted, even though this opens up the questions of their credibility and objectivity, the author feels able to propose a panoramic synthesis of the whole situation, especially in Europe, beginning with the "Acts" of the *Symposium Vaticanum Secundum* held in 1989 in the "new" Louvain.

Incidentally, Famerée takes note of the new material that has come to his attention, especially since this 1989 *Symposium* just mentioned. In his presentation, he follows the chronological order of the interventions at the *Symposium*, distinguishing between the archives of bishops and those of *periti*. The countries he revisits include France, Germany, Belgium, Great Britain, Spain, Italy, the Low Countries, and Africa. But why does he speak of the "shame" of opening up these archives? Shame does not seem to us to fit the case, even if one might arrive at a greater reserve in this respect from the fact that there are rules which fix the opening of such archives only after a certain number of years. For some of these archives (e.g., in Africa) the author speaks about the "unfortunate" influence of Rome. Does this refer to the Missionary Congregations?

The volume ends with an index of the names of the persons mentioned (pp. 269-277).

8

Christianity and the Church
in Latin America
on the Eve of the Council

Beozzo José Oscar, ed., with Various Authors, *Cristianismo e iglesias de América Latina en visperas del Vaticano II* [Christianity and the Churches of Latin America on the Eve of Vatican II], Cehila-Editorial D.E.I., San José, Costa Rica, 1992, 216 pages.

It suffices to read the introduction to this volume to discover the spirit of the work, which could be defined as "vindicating." It aims to vindicate the Council for what it styles the "near contempt" for it and for its "great inspirations," and to overcome "indifference" to it and "programmed disregard" of it—these were the considerations that led to the publication of this book (p. 14 and also p. 16). It adopts an accusatory tone towards Rome, which "filtered" the episcopal recommendations it received for the realization of the aims of the great synod (p. 15). Once again, this book was published in the context of the preparation of the history of the Second Vatican Ecumenical Council orchestrated by Professor Giuseppe Alberigo of Bologna. It is another one of the fruits of the 1991 conference held in Houston on the subject of "Christianity and the Churches on the Eve of Vatican II."

The studies included here are grouped into three sections. The first of these contains the famous introductory article by Professor Alberigo—which continually reappears and which has already undergone a critical evaluation by us. This first section, by L. J. Baraúna, also presents the Brazilian sources for the history of the Council along with the creation of the Vatican II Fund. Worthy both of note and of appreciation in this connection is the discretion of Archbishop Helder Camara, who declined to make available his documents referring to the Council. His papers were "inaccessible to the public, as long as he was alive, considering that they refer to still living persons or those only recently deceased" (see p.43). And in this case, it was a question of the "most prominent piece" in the collection (p. 44).

The second section of the book is dedicated to presenting an analysis of the Latin American Church on the eve of the conciliar event. It consists of two studies, the first one by the editor, J. O. Beozzo himself, entitled "Christian Life and Society in Brazil." This is an ample though rather unfocused text, exhibiting its author's marked partiality; his conclusions should have been subjected to a better filtration process (see, for example, p. 81). The second study is by G. Meléndez, and has the title "Christian Life and Society in Central America." The analysis offered in its final pages calls for particular reserve (pp. 92-94).

The third part of the volume finally brings together in a study, the *vota* of the bishops of the southern continent submitted in response to the famous letter of Cardinal Tardini. "It presents a radiograph or image of the life of the Latin American Church and that of the Caribbean area at that particular time, (at least in its episcopal aspect); and it constitutes a precious source for understanding the pastoral preoccupations of the bishops. It also permits one to delineate a realistic picture of the ideas the bishops had of what an ecumenical council was and what some of the themes that they could and should be occupying themselves with were" (p. 15).

"Almost all the countries [in Latin America] were studied, and many authors completed their research, furnishing a panorama of local Churches—their tendencies, tensions, and preoccupations at the time of the presentation of these *vota* for the Council" (*Ibid.*). In this connection, it is worth remarking that we are dealing here with a text—and the same thing goes for the preceding second section of the book—that is a markedly "ideological" text, one that is more ideological than historical, in fact, and one with a pronounced Marxist tone as well. All of this sets up a "progressive-conservative" division in a way that is unacceptable for us.

F. Mallimaci contributes the research on Argentina; he seems to be objective and even manages to give some space to the apostolic nuncio, whose contribution possesses a value rather rare in this volume, although the same thing is repeated in the pages on Central America (see p. 186ff.). M. Salinus covers Chile and appears to be both strict and one-sided. M. Durn Estragó handles Paraguay and employs language that is simply not proper in such a book. For Peru, it is J. Klaiber, whose comments are also rather severe (p. 162ff.). I. Madera Vargas provides a good and simple exposition on Columbia and Venezuela. In his treatment of Central America, J. Delgado almost seems to be attributing to all the bishops the proposals of just one of them. J. Garcia covers Mexico, reaching clear conclusions. Finally, A. Lange deals with the Caribbean, although he writes about Cuba in a way that suggests a serious distortion of history.

The index is found in the front of the book. The *errata* include: *es* (p. 67); *Cathollicisme* (p. 98, n. 1); *cest* (p. 104); *cleryman* (p. 106); *bautissomo* (p. 108); *toda* (p. 112); *Mooni* (p. 117); *Lateinamerika Lowen* (p. 163); *EL* (p. 173); *deben diaconos* (p. 175); Raymundi (p. 204); *monenor* (p. 210); and *e Cantoz* (p. 213). These errors should be corrected to: *el, Catholicisme, c'est, clergyman, bautismo, todo, Mozzoni, Lateinamerika, Lowen, El, diáconos deben, Raimondi, monseñor,* and *Centoz.*

9

Expectations from and
Celebration of Vatican Council II

Alberigo Giuseppe, ed., with Various Authors, *Il Vaticano II fra attese e celebrazione* [Expectations from and Celebration of Vatican Council II], Il Mulino, Imola 1995, 250 pages.

This work opens with the study by Professor Alberigo on the "Hermeneutical Criteria for a History of Vatican II" that was also published in the volume *Á la Veille du Concile Vatican II* which we examined in Chapter 7. We must also make reference to the very critical position we have already taken on this essay, which we originally published in *Apollinaris* LXIX (1996), pp. 444-446, and which was reprinted as Chapter 7.

Following this study comes the research of Giuseppe Butturini on the missions entitled "Mission and Council: Missionary Requests of the Bishops in Preparation for Vatican II" (pp. 29-74). On this same subject, this same author had already contributed to the volume *Verso il Concilio Vaticano II*, which we examined in Chapter 6—on the basis, again, of another analysis of mine in *Apollinaris* LXVIII (1995), p. 852. In the text before us there is revealed a certain interest on the part of the bishops in the theme of the missions at the time of the preparations for the Council; and the text records a valid contribution made by the bishops on this same subject. This results in a contradiction, at least in this particular area, of what has been thought to be the case on nearly all sides. There was even talk of a "deceptive impression" created by reading these *vota* of the future

Council Fathers. However, the notes here leave much to be desired; it is not possible to gather from them, for example, just who might be the "associate" in a particular episcopal see. Was it the apostolic nuncio, a coadjutor bishop, or an auxiliary bishop?

G. Butturini begins by recounting the difficulties he found in the way of accomplishing his research (in general, encountered only at the beginning of it). These difficulties limited the number of the above *vota* that touched upon "the subject of the missions, even implicitly, to around 35 percent of the responses received" (p. 33). After ascertaining whether there was any mention of the missions, the author then examines the terms and contexts in which the mention was made—whether in terms of "territorial conceptions," or those that were "religious" or the ones that pertained to the "charitable assistance" carried on by the missions. "The responses of the bishops arose out of this kind of a particular background, although there were not lacking new criteria and emphases" (p. 37). Sources and models were also mentioned, whether papal encyclicals or the missionary revival of the nineteenth and twentieth centuries. Finally, there were the requests of the various episcopates themselves. The Western bishops were interested in Catholicity (the missions caught between incarnation and transcendence), and in the missions themselves, in the need for the Church, and in the question of universal salvation. The Eastern bishops, among whom the social question predominated, were interested in the relationships between religion and culture, including political, cultural, and ecclesial aspects, as well as with both Latin American and African rites.

The author's conclusion pulls together and adapts as his own the opinion of P. J. Schütte—"His view is not far from the reality," it is stated. Schütte found a "surprising concordance" between the declarations issued by the Council on the missions and the pre-conciliar recommendations for a renewal of the missionary work of the Church (p. 72). This was perhaps a sign that "the missions were one of the areas...where the Church was renewing herself" (*Ibid.*). Certainly, the author adds, "the *vota* of the bishops were taken into particular consideration during the ante-preparatory phase of activities prior to the Council": but, according to him, "it was equally true that there was quite a leap between the *schemata* elaborated upon by the Pontifical Ante-Preparatory Commission on the missions and the *vota* of the bishops; this was the case whether in the area of context or that of expression." In any case, Butturini concludes, "in the *vota* of the Fathers, there was reflected the spirit of the missionary movement" (p. 73).

Then comes Mauro Velati taking up again a theme very dear to him, namely, the origins and workings of the Secretariat for Promoting Christian Unity. His title is "An Address in Rome" (pp. 75-118). (See, again, our review in Chapter 6 of *Verso il Concilio Vaticano II*; this volume was originally reviewed by us in *Apollinaris* LXVIII (1995), p. 851ff.).

This contribution is more than anything else a very quick glance at a temporal arc covering the entire nineteenth century which saw the emergence of the ecumenical movement. It was a movement which grew out of a vision arising from premises very different from those of the Secretariat. And also here, as in the aforementioned case of the missions, there was "in the ante-preparatory consultations desired by Pope John XXIII...a consistent number of proposals...which accorded with the intuitive vision of Pope Roncalli; and which showed a profound awareness of the problems posed in relationships among diverse confessions. Precisely among these proposals, we can find some mention of the one to create a new "ecumenical office" (p. 84ff.). These mentions are examined and discussed—badly, however, in the case of those referring to the Lateran University (pp. 88-89). There was also an attempt to re-launch the Oriental Congregation, but "the repercussions of the incident on Rhodes (p. 95 ff.) proved decisive" for the success of the actions by A. Bea and L. Jaeger, with the help of J. Höfer (p. 103). This involved a substantial change in the existing curial equilibrium" (p. 105), as did the instinctive decision of John XXIII to place the new organism within the existing structural framework involved with preparations for the Council; this involved "leaving between two parentheses the question of the permanent character of the new creation" (p. 106; but see also p. 116ff.).

However, this initial exclusion of "the ambitious project of Bea" is explained by the existing *sollicitudo* for the problems of the Eastern Catholic Churches (for the cardinal's version, see page 110). Yet there was an interrogatory mention as early as April of 1960 "on the possibility and eventual modality of the participation of other Christians at the Council" (p. 113). There remained questions of "complete and correct information," and on both the statute and the structure of the Consilium—"never promulgated officially" (p. 116). Yet it is an error to say that "the incident on Rhodes" exposed and highlighted the failure of the curial apparatus; this was so because the Curia itself was not involved. Velati concludes his treatment with the following judgment: "The new organism...played a fundamental role in the transformation of Catholicism" (p. 118). For us, rather, it was a question of the *aggiornamento* of Catholicism.

The long contribution of Alberto Melloni (pp. 119-192) is entitled "Influential Spectators: Reviews and Religious Information during the Preparations for Vatican II (1959-1962)." This essay, made possible from a background of wide collaboration with the circle of Bologna, begins with assertions that subvert the *schemata* being discussed with negative judgments virtually as soon as they are mentioned at all. The "leadership" of the preparatory organs are judged to be "irrelevant" and the "degree of synergy between pope and curia" is judged to be "modest" (p. 119). It is high time to recognize that such opinions are fluid, mixed, and ill-formed.

Though we agree, we nevertheless find that the subsequent evaluation concerning the necessity for an accurate account of the role of one of the protagonists involved in the conciliar preparation— and not only one of them, we add—turned out to be more influential than had been perceived in the beginning, in the debate which took place in the arena of public opinion, that is, the press which proved to be the vehicles for what became a closely-argued historical and theological debate. Before going on to examine, as a beginning, some of the "lectures," a critical look at *La Civiltà Cattolica* (p. 120, n. 2) is worthwhile. This journal illustrates the "method" involving the very serious kind of biased partiality which Melloni himself employs in his writing of history; it also ends up involving the analysis or exegesis of things not published rather than concentrating on what was in fact said. As usual in such cases, and as is the case here, there is a depreciation of Italian realities which is promoted independently of the lines actually taken by those involved, whether by Bea, Frings, or others…or by Siri. The same thing is applied to the great man that was Cardinal Paolo Marella, who had served as a nuncio in the Far East; he is described as having been "perfectly placed in the line laid out by Siri" (p. 123, n. 9). However, the judgment on Cardinal Bea's Secretariat is surprising; it is noted how, in the first place, it was an organ dealing with the relationship of Catholics to Eastern Orthodox (p. 124).

The author goes on to the books involved, beginning with the history of H. Jedin. Who would consider it "innocuous"? Melloni asks (p. 125). We do not intend to cite all the possible examples of the books involved here, but only to point to the usual biased partiality that the author continues to show as he goes along in his exhaustive presentation of them. A sufficient indication of this is the emphasis he places on the treatment of a press conference held by Cardinal Tardini and Archbishop Felici reported on in a publication entitled *The Dangers of the Council*, which is described as "published in Rome by the Fascist publisher *Il Borghese*"—as if there were some connection between the author of this book, M. Tedeschi, and the two prelates in question (p. 131).

His analysis continues with an examination of the journals and reviews of the various movements, paying particular attention to ecumenical journals. He mentions periodicals in French, English, German (with exaggerations on page 163), Spanish, Portuguese, and "in minor languages and on the 'periphery' of the Churches."

He terminates his review with a conclusion: "The debate as conducted was selective" as far as the development of any non-directed attitude was concerned; and the ecumenical "misunderstanding" was solidified, in fact; also the "bluff involved in the creation of a Secretariat for the press did not resolve these contradictions" (p. 190).

Using a colorful expression to the same effect, Giuseppe Alberigo reaches the same conclusion, as follows: "A headless Council? In fact, this describes the evolution of the directive organs of Vatican

II" (pp. 193-238). But everyone knows that despite Alberigo's *pro forma* question mark, this was not the truth; it suffices to cite the initial decision on the voting of the members of the various conciliar commissions to show this. When Alberigo instead wishes to say that "[preparations for] Vatican II underwent complex problems of functioning and direction" (p. 192), that is quite another thing. Instead he speaks of the Council Presidency as "deficient," "lacking," and "excessive." Instead, in the initial vision of things, and in the tradition of the functions of the Secretariat of State, it should have been considered as the most suitable and proper papal source of support. It was not for nothing that John XXIII had selected Cardinal Domenico Tardini for the high "conciliar" task he assigned to him. That the actual journey going down the road proved to be difficult is quite understandable; but I would not de-legitimize the Council Presidency on account of the wise and beneficial decision of John XXIII concerning the *schema de fontibus revelationis*. The pope, *ex officio* president of the council, can always personally decide concerning any matter that is particularly delicate, without thereby harming the normal organizational structure established by him.

As for the Secretariat, and with regard to conciliar questions *extra ordinem*, it is not exact to assert that "the direction of the Council during the entire first period of work never got linked up with this organ" (p. 195). Better: its function was strongly reinforced by the guidance it did receive from the Secretary of State, the first and principal collaborator of the pope and the latter's natural spokesman (see for that matter the affirmation in this vein by Cardinal Agaganian reported by Father Dossetti at the end, on page 234). Nor was this merely because Cardinal Cicognani was "desirous of exerting a significant influence on the Council," as Alberigo claims (p. 196; but see also pp. 208 and 216). It is not necessary to know Cicognani and his "fraternal" relationship with John XXIII in order to attest to this. But in any case, the conclusion is inexact when the author says that "the assembly as such was headless." He also says this in connection with the Rescript that was "never officially published" (p. 197). In this connection, the "irritation" of Archbishop Felici needs to be shown (p. 198, n. 14). The hypothesis concerning Cardinal Bea is likewise simply out of bounds (*Ibid.*). Similarly, the author says he "reads" about those who spoke out in some of the meetings of the aforementioned Secretariat. Here he seems to have combed carefully through the diaries of Siri and Döpfner.

He then goes on to the Central Coordinating Commission, still presided over by the Secretary of State, who, willy-nilly, reconfirmed his proper role as we have described it above; he further confirmed the procedure "of three" (with Cardinals Ottaviani and Bea) that we would call informal and amicable, in order to reach an agreed-upon solution to the problem of the three preparatory *schemata* on the subject of the unity of Christians. There follow a number of inferences made by Alberigo; he speaks of clandestine talks, lively and vigorous debate within the Commission, and he also offers suppositions concerning the various points of view expressed. He finds space to describe the actions of the "workshop" that assisted Cardinal Lercaro. The latter made many suggestions; there was also the anxious (the adjective belongs to Alberigo) diligence of Father Dossetti with regard to the work that took place in between the conciliar sessions "from which the group of Bologna was formally excluded" (p. 209). "A collaboration destined to be fulfilled within the group of the Cardinal Moderators" got introduced into their deliberations early, resulting in the informal group of "three" of the Moderators [Döpfner, Lercaro, Suenens]. This was a serious matter. The conclusion concerning the conviction of Pope John XXIII "about the insufficiency of his own involvement with respect to the first period of the Council" (p. 210) is both harsh and prematurely formulated, as was the author's judgment about this at the beginning (see p. 211). Meanwhile, in his Note 37, the author begins to understand that there were at times meetings going on of which no records were made.

The coming upon the scene of Pope Paul VI is linked by Alberigo to the developed conviction of Pope John concerning the necessity of making the role of the Bishop of Rome more effective in his capacity as President of the Council *in maximo iure suo*. In fact, the new pope decided to create a "leaner organ of direction...along with adding a package of modifications in some of the regulations" (p. 212). The Moderators "worked almost exclusively during the periods of activity of the conciliar assembly or immediately on the eve of those periods. This was what specified and identified their respective roles. "There thus emerged from all those facts a distinction concerning the competences of the various organs." This conclusion seems to be correct, even if what immediately follows it is not exact. In his own way, the author defines the Central Coordinating Commission as "more directly sensitive to the requests of the Roman Curia." The Moderators, meanwhile, supposedly constituted "a more direct expression of the Council" (p. 213). It is here that the matter of Father Dossetti is inserted into the text; this reveals the mind and disposition of Alberigo himself as very much in favor of Father Dossetti. Here was someone doing something, he says, that "escaped the control of the Secretary General of the Council, Archbishop Felici" (p. 215). May we be permitted to say that viewing the affair in terms of "control" already misstates the whole question? The question itself appears in all its complexity only when Alberigo publishes it in an appendix. Father Dossetti is seen here along with all his activism and grandstanding. We are not attempting to deliver a moral discourse here, of course, but see pages 216, 226ff., 231 and 237. One example was his call for "an abridged law" for the immediate application of the Constitution on the Sacred Liturgy." (Incidentally, none of this material was forwarded to the Archive for the Second Vatican Council instituted by Pope Paul VI precisely in order to collect—it was the papal wish—all the material pertaining to the diverse conciliar commissions and organisms.)

Objectively speaking, to try to reduce the four Cardinal Moderators to "three" [Cardinal Agaganian was also a Moderator] cannot be tolerated. Nor can the idea of "independence" with regard to the General Secretariat of the Council, which, according to Alberigo, "always appeared to be in solidarity with the orientation of the preparatory phase" (p. 215). But this still remains to be demonstrated. Then to be further noted is the interpretation of Father Dossetti himself. According to Alberigo—"and the case is a singularly delicate one" (p. 217)—Pope Paul VI...supposedly approved the idea that there should be conciliar votes that were binding upon the commissions in the case of some of the most serious questions (for example, the diaconate, episcopal sacramentality, etc.). Everyone understood where they were supposed to be going...but it is certain, on the contrary, that the pope ordered to destroy the cards prepared in order to solicit opinions precisely on the famous questions of the diaconate and the episcopate. Also on the subject of the "spontaneous" withdrawal of Father Dossetti from assisting the Cardinal Moderators, there are many comments that could be made. He supposedly continued, however, on the same "route." (p. 217, n. 49). But history should remain history, quite apart from the desires of the heart. On the other hand, the solution offered by Alberigo with regard to the creation of minutes or a written record of the meetings of the Moderators can be accepted. There were in fact a number of meetings minuted or recorded by Father Dossetti himself and yet others minuted by Archbishop Felici. But the informal, "ordinary" meetings were not minuted or recorded, barring proof to the contrary.

The index of names concludes the volume (pp. 241-250). With regard to *errata*, we note: "E. Roberts, former bishop of Bombay" (p. 35, but see n. 13); "fidels" (p. 36, n. 15); "Ambrosi" (p. 39, n. 20); "Laghonut" (p. 40, n. 21); "Kampela" (*Ibid.* and p. 65); "Seckan" (p. 45, n. 38); "Reus" (*Ibid.*, n. 39); "Sheen, coadjutor" (p. 48); "Montreal" (p. 49, n. 52); "Mistici" (p. 52, n. 57); "in Germany" (p. 55); "Amazzonias" (p. 68, nn. 114 and 71); "la" (p. 83, n. 16); "ou" (p. 142, n. 94); "an" (p. 150, n. 26); "tollerance" (p. 165, n. 190); "grands" (p. 166, n. 193); "Salamanticensis" (p. 180); "Criterion" (pp. 182, 191, n. 309): "Meja" (*Ibid.*); "paroquea" (p. 183, n. 283); "invence" (p. 186, n. 289); "Oestpolitik" (p. 190, n. 306); "di Roma" (*Ibid.*); "parroissiales" (p. 192, n. 309); "Reformierte" (*Ibid.*); and "Telogia" (*Ibid.*). Finally, on page 200, a line is repeated and on page 215 an extra "with" is included. *Corrections* to the above are: T. Roberts, Titular Archbishop of Sugdea; *fideles;* Locri-Ambrosia; Laghouat; Kampala; Seckau; Reuss; Sheen, auxiliary bishop; Montréal; *Mystici*; in France; Amazonias; là; où; and; tolerance; grandes; Salmanticensis; Criterio; Mejia; paroquia; invece; Ostpolitik; a Roma; paroissales; Reformierten and Teologia.

III

A HISTORY OF THE
SECOND VATICAN
COUNCIL

10

For the History of Vatican Council II
(Announcement and Preparation)

Alberigo Giuseppe, ed., with Various Authors, *Il Cattolicesimo verso una nuova stagione. L'annuncio e la preparazione, gennaio 1959-settembre 1962* [Towards a New Season for Catholicism. The Announcement and the Preparations, January 1959-September 1962]. Volume I of the *Storia del Concilio Vaticano II* [History of Vatican Council II], directed by Giuseppe Alberigo, Il Mulino, Urbino, 1995, 549 pages.

A recent work, the first in a series of volumes celebrating the history of the Second Vatican Ecumenical Council, permits us to evaluate the historiographical debate around an event that has characterized in a pre-eminent way the Catholic Church, along with Christianity as a whole, in this twentieth century now moving towards its end.

In the "Premise" to the work, following the index, the general editor, Professor Giuseppe Alberigo, explains his role as "the conductor of the orchestra" for the entire project and draws some conclusions accordingly. He writes as follows: "Thirty years after Vatican II...it is useful to inquire what the state of knowledge is about the Council: its development and its significance" (p. 9). He adds: "Shortly after its conclusion, there was a concentration on commenting on the texts approved by the Council. This was the task of the 1970s...Thus, Vatican II came to be known a bit too abstractly, as if it were nothing but a collection of texts—to the point of being carried to the extreme. Thirty years later it appears more as an event that has made actual the hope and optimism of the Gospel; this is the case in spite of the Council's limits and gaps. To continue to dwell on a vision of the Council as the sum of hundreds of pages of documents—many of them prolix and some of them transitory—has impeded the perception of the Council's more fruitful significance as the expression of the impulse of the community of believers to accept an uneasy confrontation with the Word of God and with the mystery of the history of men" (*Ibid.*). This particular "iron" is struck while still hot in order to indicate the nodal point of a vision about which, from the outset, we must express our serious reservations. It is a vision that goes back to the old letter-spirit antithesis applied to the Council—but for us the letter and the spirit of the Council are indivisible.

For Alberigo the time has arrived—actually, though, it could just as well be considered premature—to "work out a 'historicization' of Vatican II, not in order to distance ourselves from it...but rather in order to facilitate the overcoming of the many controversies regarding its reception by the Church" (p. 10). But is all this really the case? In the paragraph that follows, significantly, the term "dialectical" is twice employed in connection with identifying hermeneutical criteria which might be adequate to judge the "event" in question. These criteria, the author tells us, are "distinct, even if they are interconnected or complementary with respect to the canonical requisites related to the institutional legitimacy of a council and to the interpretation of its decisions." However, the pendulum still continues on its oscillating course, as follows: "It is obvious that the history of the Vatican Council cannot be reconstructed solely on the basis of a rigorously critical analysis of its sources." However, and significantly, the question placed in relief, to which the answer must be given, is not only "how the decisions approved by Vatican II were arrived at, but *especially* how the work of the Council itself developed and what the significance of this development was" (*Ibid.*; emphasis added). The fundamental problematic of this work thus clearly appears from the very beginning.

Four more volumes will follow this one, each dedicated to one of the working periods of the Council. The first chapter of this volume is by Professor Alberigo himself, and bears the title: "The Announcement of the Council: From the Security of the Fortress to the Fascination of the Search" (pp. 19-70). In this chapter, the author, following the impulse of his own "Premise," and his vision of the Council as an "event," underlines the "spirit" of the Council in an almost "mystical" way. This is quite naturally the way of Alberigo, in fact, and it entails the devaluation of the conciliar texts. Attention to the "ecumenical" aspect of the Council also prevails here, as does attention to questions that conform to the well-known sensitivities of the School of Bologna (someone, quite significantly, even if writing in a purely journalistic mode, has characterized the whole publication project under review here as "the Council according to Dossetti"!). The key word in this chapter is "renewal" (see, for example, p. 58). We, however, would prefer to identify the Council more with the term *aggiornamento*, or updating. In some ways this word is *passé* and it is untranslatable into any other language; yet it points to both the originality of the Council and to its promise, not to speak of its quality and its ability, essential to any council, to bring together both *nova et vetera*, both tradition and "opening" (or incarnation)—and this is precisely what is needed.

Without entering here into the problem of the "ecumenicity" of Vatican II (see pp. 19 and 24), many questions arise in our mind while following this author along the lines he has chosen. These questions concern such things as whether "it can be concluded that the decision to call the Council was solely that of Pope John" (p. 21). But even the context in which this question is raised here is misleading (see, for example, p. 31). However, the problematical mention made here relative to the dialogue of Pope John with Cardinal Ruffini is also to be noted (*Ibid.*; and pp. 25, 30 n. 21, 31, and 32). Other questions that arise in our mind include: "overcoming the problems related to the Cold War" (p. 22); the judgment concerning the "minimal consensus" accorded to the project of the Council (p. 23); what disguises or camouflages were used by the opposition, and also the question is raised of the "sincerity" of the affirmations of Pope John XXIII (G. Martina was critical here) along with an attempt to influence his biography. Still other questions include: the convocation of councils generally (pp.

83ff); the canonical "appeal" to the Council (p. 34): post-Tridentine Christianity (p. 35); the unnuanced evaluation of the Curia (p. 40; taken up from Father Yves Congar); and the "vindication of Roman primatial claims" (p. 40).

A very small thing here is the treatment of "diplomatic sources and journalistic commentaries" (pp. 47-50). The author affirms that "almost without mediation, the Johannine initiative reached millions of women and men and convinced them of its importance" (p. 49). Following this there is a small section described as "towards a characterization of the Council, its scope and nature," as progressively sketched out by John XXIII. Such a recognition of the progressive nature of the "revelations" delivered by the pope should have led to a greater comprehension of the human element in the conciliar preparations, without any preconceived mistrust of the conditioning of the persons and offices assisting the pontiff (see, for example, the "demands" and "omissions" on page 55). However, such is not the case with this author.

Moreover, he writes, "also in the hints and allusions of John XXIII, oscillations were not lacking" (Note 89 on page 56 is simply out of bounds). However, "Pope John did not have any hesitation in characterizing the coming Council in absolutely traditional terms" (p. 58): as "a free and responsible and thereby effectively deliberating body" (Ibid.). We would add here, "along with him." It was not a Council of all Christendom, nor one of union; nor was it a "fighting" Council, or one taking contrary positions, or offering resistance to modern society. The author provides a summary of some of his points, as follows: "Pope John wanted a Council of epochal transition, a Council, that is, that would move the Church out of the post-Tridentine epoch—and, in a certain measure, out of the centuries-long post-Constantinian epoch as well—into a new phase of proclamations of and testimonials to the Gospel. Strong and permanent elements of the tradition judged to be suitable to nourish and guarantee fidelity to the Gospel during such an arduous transition were to be retained or recovered. In this perspective, the Council assumed a very special importance, but, once again, primarily as an 'event,' and not as a source for the elaboration and production of norms" (p. 58). Is all this the thinking of Pope John, we ask, or of Alberigo?

The emphasis on the vision of the Council as "a new Pentecost"—a vision dear to the heart of Pope John, in fact—leads this author to a conclusion that we can regard as excessively "charismatic." He writes in this connection: "The reference to Pentecost...brought to the fore an emphasis on the acts of the Spirit, not those of the pope or of the Church; this had been the case with the apostles and the disciples, who found themselves to be the object of the powerful and overwhelming actions of the Spirit" (p. 59). However, at the Council of Jerusalem, the decisions were attributed "to the Holy Spirit and *to us*" (Acts 15:28; emphasis added). It was a formula of synthesis, not of antithesis. Yet other affirmations of this author seem to us jarring and discordant, for example, the one on the relationship between the Council and Pope John, [said to be] determined by his "profound and immovable conviction, on the one hand, of the need of a great leap forward; and, on the other hand, it was conditioned by the deafness or at least the initial myopia of a large part of the episcopacy—even of the most open and informed part of the episcopacy. Some of the bishops may have been convinced that the Council must fill up the gap between the backwardness of the Church with regard to modern times, but they were oblivious to any wider and more ample perspectives and they disinterested themselves in any such perspectives...To this must be added the institutional allergy of the Roman Curia towards the Council, an allergy that the Curia seemed disposed to overcome only by preparing for a Council that would be an appendix to Vatican Council I, as well as the occasion for producing a solemn endorsement of an omnipotent Pacellian magisterium" (*Ibid.*). This viewpoint seems to be out of focus if not simply erroneous. The same thing seems to be true of the author's judgments concerning the appointment of Cardinal Tardini to the presidency of the Pontifical Ante-preparatory Commission and also of the presumed attitude of Pope John not to "let himself get involved in a dialectical confrontation with various ante-preparatory developments being carried out" (p. 64). The same thing is true again of the mention of a supposed parallel route of "preparations" supposedly being followed by the pope himself, clearly differentiated from the preparations being carried out by Cardinal Tardini's Commission. Were these supposed parallel preparations "tendentiously contradictory" to the official ones, as is suggested here? A hermeneutical hypothesis of Cardinal Lercaro's concerning a possible "institutional solitude" supposedly destined to characterize the entire Johannine episcopacy here becomes a fixed conviction for Alberigo (see p. 60). In a certain sense, one could affirm the same thing of the pontificate of Paul VI, and, indeed, that of any pontiff in his personal exercise of the primacy. But we believe that this is not exactly what the author wanted to say here.

The author moves on to an analysis of the "constitution of the Pontifical Ante-preparatory Commission," noting from the start that "in 1959 for almost four months (January 26-May 17), no institutional decisions relative to the Council were taken" (p. 60). On the other hand, it is stated that "the first draft of a text establishing an ante-preparatory Commission was dated February 6, 1959. It was drafted on the model of what had been prepared for Vatican Council I."

With regard to this last observation, we are finally back on the track, that is, we are focusing on the work of the collaborators of Cardinal Tardini. See notes 104 and 106 (p. 61) on making one's way with a symmetry of treatment on the subject of the areas of competence of the various Congregations of the Curia (p. 62). All this should re-equilibrate the judgments made about Cardinal Tardini. Calling the official named to be secretary to the Commission, the then "auditor" of the Roman Rota, Pericle Felici, "obscure," represents an observation that is wholly out of place; it was certainly not the case that he was unknown in Roman circles. And in this connection, we ourselves have vivid recollections and, indeed, positive judgments of the late, lamented Father G. D'Ercole, who later had a role in the launching of the journal *Concilium*.

With regard to the name of the coming Synod, "Vatican II," the author presumes that Pope John arrived at the decision [of where the Council was to be held] autonomously, always in line with his point of view that his "supreme obligation" was to "concentrate on safeguarding the liberty of the Council," while not giving up on "pointing out particular ends or goals to the conciliar assembly" (p. 67).

Then there was the fact itself of the decision to choose Rome as the locus of the Council (we would prefer to use "Vatican" here, rather than Rome). This decision "could assure the 'Romans' that they could easily influence the Council" (*Ibid.*), Alberigo writes. And it was both "a challenge and an obligation" (p. 68) to "involve" in the conciliar "renewal" also the center of the Catholic Church. But all these ideas represent really doubtful points of view. And with respect to the "policy" of Pope John, the author floats some really novel ideas here about previous pontificates. "The fight against Communism no longer dominated the papal magisterium," he writes. "Pope John did not underestimate it; he simply relativized it" (*Ibid.*; but note 119 here requires that a distinction be made, though what is said does fit the text on page 70). "John XXIII showed greater interest in the various aspects of the problem of peace...his political horizon was worldwide" (p. 69). We should note, however, that Pope John's Italian origin was always more obvious than any worldwide perspective (see note 122, which is more balanced); this was certainly obvious from his letters, both published and unpublished.

Finally, as to the role of Monsignor Lardone, described as "destined to become the pope's trusted adviser in the matter of approaches to the Soviet Union" (p. 69), we find this evaluation to be rather excessive. In addition to that, we feel we have to register some reservations concerning the use of the term "pre-history" to describe the half year following the announcement of the calling of the Council by the pope.

In the second chapter of this book, E. Fouilloux analyzes "The Ante-preparatory Phase (1959-1960): Slow Beginnings, Overcoming Inertia" (pp. 71-176). This chapter too is above all structured around the idea of "Vatican II: An Event?" It starts out with the question of whether the "21st General Council of the Catholic Church" was linked to the typical climate of the "safe" years between 1950 and

1960; this climate is described in broad strokes covering four dense pages. He asks, here, again, whether the Church "was afflicted with 'council sickness'". Should it be understood that by this was meant "the survival of a conciliar tradition"? It appears to us that his initial affirmation on page 80 that Pope John was unaware of any proposals for a council previous to his own is not exact. The same thing is true of his affirmation that the concept of an ordinary magisterium of the Church appeared only in 1863. The ecclesiastical vision underlying such an assertion is equally inexact; the pope, he writes, represents, "the apex of Catholicism; he is a kind of absolute sovereign in doctrinal matters, unimpeded by any form of countervailing power." He is wrong again about the spread of personal devotion to the pope, which is ancient in the Church (see, however, page 87). He is also wrong about the conciliar "typology" of Vatican II, where the term *aggiornamento* is degraded into a kind of "new look reformism" (pp. 87ff).

The author then analyzes "The Catholic Church at the End of the 1950s." Here he treats, among other things, the "Roman model." In a way that is quite out of focus and is susceptible to serious criticism, he covers such subjects as the papal nuncios "with their informal religious functions, who are nevertheless the true heads of episcopates largely named by themselves and lacking inner cohesion of their own" (p. 89, and see also pages 118 and 162 for other prejudiced comments about these nuncios). Other subjects that get the same kind of treatment include a history sketched out in too-large brushstrokes on the Roman Church as a prisoner within "a fortress of truth under siege" (p. 90); the contemporary idea of a Christianity that still remains to be explained and specified, but does nevertheless possess an integrative and positive underpinning; and, finally, he speaks of the pontificates from Pope Pius X on "with their not negligible attempts at reform" (pp. 94ff), though he says they were afflicted with "a certain malaise nonetheless." All this surely represents a back-dated version of the well-known "anti-Roman complex," including excessive criticisms and characterizations of Catholicism and Romanism, not to speak of highly tendentious descriptions of various "movements": Christological, biblical, patristic, liturgical, catechetical, ecumenical, etc.

The author passes on, finally, to "The Roman Consultations." There was a change of procedures. No longer was a complete questionnaire sent out. Instead, there was a simple letter of a very general nature dated June 18 and reading "Such is the will of John XXIII" (p. 107). Worthy of note here are the comments of the author, since they exhibit a certain tendency in conciliar history that we would define as "anti-curial"; they speak of "Roman divergences on the subject of the future Council manifested among the very first preparatory steps taken" (p. 110; see also pp. 144 and 168). But this merely confirms the fact of a diversification within the Curia that we have always maintained was there; the fact of this diversification should always have been kept in mind in order to avoid any undue generalizations. The criticism of Monsignor Vincenzo Carbone offered here, however, is unjustified; his opinion is described as "verging on self-satisfaction" (p. 111). The further criticism of the "conceptual schemes employed" in the analysis of the replies to the aforementioned letter of June 18 of John XXIII is similarly unjustified.

There follows the replies to this letter which neither merit "an exaggerated appreciation nor an excessive depreciation" (*Ibid.*). The first subtitles here are "On the Proper Use of the *Vota*" and "Three Types of Replies." The treatment of the former features a rather special presentation on the *Vota*, focusing upon those that are most interesting to the author. We question also his method of cataloguing these *vota*, as between "original" and "conformist," or "canonical" and "pastoral"; the sympathies of Fouilloux naturally go to the "original" ones. It is a good presentation on the whole, however, guided by a sense of wisdom after the fact. But how can anyone pretend that all these *vota* were somehow sifted through a Roman grill, defined as "scholastic-canonical" (p. 155)? Could it have perhaps been a "progressive" grill, representing a sentiment that was hardly majoritarian at the time? Did not these *vota* show signs of the pre-conciliar climate? (see pp. 144ff). Still other serious criticisms and accusations of ulterior motives are offered, along with claims of a lack of neutrality—the latter of an "order...not innocent" in the examination of the responses and in the compilation of the *Analyticus Conspectus*, which "did not faithfully echo the ante-preparatory consultations" (pp. 152ff.) How truly ugly, finally, is the author's characterization that: "Then come the divine and equal Persons: God the Father is given seven pages, the Incarnate Word rates five pages, while the Virgin Mary gets the sum total of them, namely, twelve pages in all"! (p. 155).

On the other hand, Fouilloux does conclude his treatment, by admitting "that such criteria"—the Roman cataloguing criteria—"can be questioned, but [this is not the case] with either the seriousness nor the steadiness with which these *vota* were incorporated into the operation from the very beginning of the process" (p. 156). However, there follows a further strong criticism of the document entitled "Final synthesis on the Recommendations and Suggestions of Their Excellencies the Bishops and Prelates around the World for the Future Ecumenical Council" (p. 157). This represents the final apogee of the deductive method which reduces the complex to the simple, the heterogeneous to the homogeneous, and a plurality to a majority (cf. p. 157); it arises right out of criteria focusing on number and moderation (cf. p. 158), as well as on other criteria of "a conservative tendency." But there is nothing ambiguous in the way it links together "the grand lines emerging from the consultations and even some of the nuances" (p. 160). The conclusion, however, is as follows: "In spite of everything, it is not possible to avoid the conclusion that it [the "Synthesis"] orients things along three axes or lines that are evident throughout; they are: 1) 'ecclesiocentrism'; 2) an obsession with defensiveness; and 3) a preoccupation with protecting the faithful. These priorities were to be served by the erection of a wall of words and paper: a dogmatic constitution on the Church; a *summa* of social teachings; and a "collection of the principal modern errors" (p. 160; see, however, p. 164).

The author opts instead for a selection based on content and not on the category of interlocutors or by continents—which is the division found in the *Acta et documenta*. "Geographical" considerations do appear evident in his treatment, however.

"The Roman *Vota*" are then examined—characterized as "between diffidence and indifference" (p. 146). The responses of the prelates in the Curia like those of the superiors of religious congregations, turn out to have an "ultramontane spirit"; the responses of the Roman universities and of officials in the dicasteries are not analyzed here, but later (characterized, though, as moving "from disdain to pigeon-holing"). Included, though, is "the analysis of the work on the results of the consultation by the Secretary of the Ante-preparatory Commission" (p. 123). The result of this analysis is not a happy one, however, and shows much partiality. "We decided to divide up roughly into three categories," the author explains, "the material sent to Rome from all areas of Catholicism—dioceses, universities, and non-Roman religious congregations." But what does the author mean here by "non-Roman" religious congregations? (See also pp. 146 ff.).

The three categories into which the author decided to divide all these *vota* included those in which "the papal objectives"—"crowning four centuries of intransigence"—were not taken into account; those which were engaged on the path indicated by Pope John XXIII (labeled "Towards Vatican II"); and, finally, those which it was impossible to place in either of these two categories. These last, responses impossible to place, were characterized as "Contrasts and Uncertainties"; innovative positions were sometimes taken, though these were often "diluted with a mass of timorous responses, sometimes even decidedly stupid ones, and these latter were found in fair numbers" (p. 144). The author adds, however, that "this typology should be considered provisory." Yet the whole things remains charged with consequences. He arrogates to himself the interpretation of the papal objectives, although this should have been considered an arduous and difficult task (see p. 163, where Fouilloux is forced to admit that "the praise which John XXIII lavished upon these proposals does not cease to amaze"). But all this has been subject to personal interpretations, as is well-known, even beyond the ecumenical aspect so evident with this author.

After this, we must learn all about "Roman Theology Faced with the Council" (p. 147). Although the word "theology" is recorded here in the singular, it is all the more interesting that the text provides evidence, rather, of the contrasts and differences found in the various

Roman study circles. There follow, then, "The Reactions of the Roman Congregations," which are presented, significantly, "in a way that shows very little homogeneity: they are distinct from each other in almost every way" (p. 161))—but then we have always maintained that such diversification was present.

"Towards the Preparations Properly Speaking" is the final subtitle in this chapter. This section treats the structure of the preparatory organs and the suggestions (*Quaestiones*) made for their program of operations, these latter to be placed in a "strict relationship" (p. 165) with the final synthesis: "Each preparatory commission developed its own *schemata*, based on the segment of the *Quaestiones* allotted to it, resulting in the dispersion and overlapping of subjects, which the review by the mixed subcommissions did not correct to any great extent." While the *Quaestiones* "more or less played an intellectual transition role between the ante-preparatory and the preparatory phases" (p. 166), "intermediate links between the two preliminary phases leave unsettled the basic question of the coherence of the preparations for the Council; there was operative, however, as noted in the *Conspectus*, an abbreviated version of the method applied by the Tardini commission to the ante-preparatory consultations." But "could no one any longer find even a distant echo of the questionnaire initially favored but then set aside by John XXIII"? (p. 165). The insinuation suggested here must be questioned in the context of the pope's basic motivation—he wanted to leave maximum freedom to those being canvassed for their *vota*—but this did not mean "rejection" of the aforementioned questionnaire, as Fouilloux seems to believe. However, the linkage to the model of Vatican I was valid; it was a source of inspiration for the preparations that were approved by Pope Roncalli (cf. p. 167). Similarly valid is the background of the *motu proprio* entitled *Superno Dei nutu* that is analyzed here, which the author identifies as a victory of the Curia; for him it "made complete the sweep of June 6, wherein the presidents of the preparatory commissions turned out to be the prefects of the corresponding congregations, with the exception of Cardinals Cento...and Bea" (p. 170; see, however, p. 171ff.). The decision by the pope on what had been proposed by Tardini—"a dedicated worker for the Council, but one who favored a low-profile gathering" (p. 173)—amazes the author, because the pope had shown himself so preoccupied with avoiding any confusion between the Council and the Curia. But the justification for this was supposedly "the desire to bring along and obtain the adhesion of his closest collaborators" (p. 171; cf. p. 173). This represented "a tacit compromise in which his desire for *aggiornamento* could only be the loser" (p. 172). Hence Fouilloux concludes, after briefly describing some of the conciliar figures (Bea, Tardini, Felici), that "the men chosen, their conceptual positions, as well as their methods of work, eventually led, after considerable effort, to a result that was foreseeable, namely, to a tangible Romanization of the whole conciliar project, both in what concerned the structure for the preparations and what the basic themes of these latter would be" (p. 176).

We come next to the long and consistent Chapter III of Joseph Komonchak. Its title is "The Battle for the Council during the Preparation Period" (pp. 177-379). The term "battle," we believe, conveys the "tone" of this research (it would be sufficient, in this regard, simply to consider the infelicitous adjectives so often employed by this author). At times the tone is frankly displeasing, also because the author's historical sense is often held in check because of his penchant to display "wisdom after the fact." He evidences a personal interest in both ecumenism and religious liberty. There also appear in this essay indications of internal diversification in the Roman Curia, in the theological studies being carried on in Rome, and in the papal horizons and desires described (it is not easy to classify these tendencies, on the other hand, particularly as to their value as fruits of the preparatory work: see pp. 368, 370, and 376) and, especially, of the work of some of the commissions. Arising out of all this is an erroneous idea of the author's concerning a presumed "papal delegation of authority" with regard to the question of episcopal jurisdiction (pp. 194 and 314). Yet even before Vatican Council I, there was no question in this case of any *potestas delegata*.

The author's research is divided up as follows: "The Organization of the Preparatory Work" (in general, internally, the distribution of roles, secrecy, the absence of any laity, and the need to prepare for a "pastoral" Council); "The Reform of Pastoral Practice" (including an examination of the work of the various commissions and a critique of their positions, which for this author, always entail a mention of the minimal concern or the lack of any concern for "modern problems"— themselves defined almost exclusively in terms of how the deposit of faith needed to be defended against error); "The Theological Preparatory Commission" (its members and their competencies, the subjects covered, the methods employed, the texts of the Secretariat for Promoting Christian Unity, doctrine and dialogue, the Word of God, the Church); "Revision and Amendment of the Preparatory Texts" (discussion of them in the Central Preparatory Commission, the subcommission for amendments, the degree of attention given to important *schemata*); "The Ecumenical Presence at the Council" (establishing of the principle, extending the invitations, fixing the rules—with an inexact evaluation of supposed new elements which were in fact not new—preparing the Regulations); "The Date, the Duration" ("The pope wished to see the Council open in October of 1962 and to conclude, if possible, before the end of the year"—p. 360); "The Agenda of the Council" (determining a "plan"); and "Pope John and the Preparations for the Council."

The final pages of this chapter, in particular, contain some points that we can agree with or at least be detached about. For instance, there is the fundamental question of "the relationship between Pope John and the conciliar preparatory process" (p. 373). This question has not often been dealt with before, or with such clarity. We find the question fairly and concisely stated here, even though the basic problem still remains, namely, how to link the papal desires and intuitions with the satisfaction he manifested towards the actual results that were submitted to him (see p. 374 ff.). Other instances are concerned with concrete situations, for example, the place of Latin (see p. 379); or with the pope's silences related to tensions and to his failures to engage (on ecumenical questions with the Orthodox, and on biblical questions—with regard to the latter, the author writes: "In reality Pope John seemed disturbed by recent developments in

Catholic biblical studies"—p. 378). But was he up to date in judging these results, or was it that he had confidence in what the Council would do? Our mention of being "detached" also has reference to some of the "accusations" made against Archbishop Felici (p. 368), to the presentation to the pope of the preparatory texts as a *fait accompli* (p. 370), to the evaluation (excessive) of the influence of an approach to John XXIII made by Cardinal Léger (p. 373), and to the author's final judgment according to which the bishops at Vatican II, "in order to demonstrate that they were consistently in agreement with the vision of the pope, found it necessary to repudiate a great part of the work carried out in preparation for the Council" (p. 379). But who was the interpreter of what the pope's "vision" was?

J. Oscar Beozzo handles Chapter IV. Its title is "The External Climate" (pp. 381-428). The general theme is the relation of the mass media to the Council. But the problematic of the possible influence and conditioning through the modern means of social communication on the Council Fathers is not brought out. The author examines the public information issues that are available on the preparatory work (obtaining information, setting up the press office of the Central Preparatory Commission, spontaneous initiatives). Similarly, he treats information as well as the spontaneous debates that came about (informants from religious orders, theological debates, journals and reviews, the book circuit); and also preparations for the Council by the episcopates and the ordinary life of the Church (the new "style" of John XXIII is treated rather idyllically, following the approach of Alberigo—cf. p. 405). Other topics treated include: the tensions involved in ordinary governance, the College of Cardinals, the appointments of bishops, the Roman Synod (on which his judgments are not very balanced), the World Eucharistic Congress in Munich, and the World Council of Churches meeting in New Delhi. Yet other religious, political, and ideological areas treated include: contemporary attitudes in the Muslim world and the situation of Catholics there; attitudes among the Jews, and John XXIII's relationships with them; the initiative of Jules Isaac [on behalf of the Jews]; contemporary attitudes in the Marxist archipelago; bishops and observers from the East; and, finally, the Russian Orthodox observers. With regard to the Eastern questions, though, can one really speak about "a success as considerable as it was unexpected"? (p. 427).

The volume's Chapter V, "On the Eve of the Council" (pp. 429-517), was entrusted to the pen of Klaus Wittstadt. In this essay, the first seven *schemata*, principally, are examined; they are described and judged more or less hastily, though, and, with accompanying observations that arouse in us strong reservations of the kind already aroused by some of the affirmations of the other authors in this volume. Then there are the rather refined reactions of the episcopate along with illustrations of the general attitude of expectations that obtained in various countries in the three months that preceded the opening of the Council.

There then follows an analysis entitled "John XXIII on the Immediate Eve of the Council"—but is it possible to say, apropos of this, that Vatican II *was* "The Council of John XXIII"? (p. 451). We are also obliged to register our dissent concerning other points, in particular those treated on pages 452, 456 ff., and 461. On the subject of the relationship of the Church to the Kingdom of God, a passage is cited from John XXIII that is contrary to what Pope Roncalli actually expressed! And what can be said about linking John XXIII to St. Francis of Assisi, describing both as "reformers" of the Church, one in the Middle Ages and the other in the contemporary period? (pp. 466 and 471). Other subjects treated include: organizational and spiritual preparations for the Council; the naming of *periti*; the structure of press and information services; the preparations of the conciliar *aula* in St. Peter's Vatican Basilica; and the arrival of the Council Fathers in Rome.

In the very brief Chapter VI, entitled "Preparations for What Kind of Council?" (pp. 519-526), Professor Alberigo himself concludes as follows: "The preparations for Vatican II were both extensive and prolific. They not only endured beyond the unfolding of the Council itself; they established and put in place institutional features that continued to be very relevant. The pope was established as the supreme moderator, and the Roman Curia as the principal protagonist; the episcopate as well as the theologians, especially those from Europe, were very heavily involved. Yet in the face of these developments stood the fact of the radical refusal of the great majority of the Council Fathers and their collaborators to recognize themselves in the responses that issued from the preparatory process itself" (p. 519). The author mentions successively some of the points which are problematical for him concerning the "original intention" of John XXIII in convoking the Council (his anxious desire to bring about the unity of Christians); concerning the lengthiness of the preparatory period; concerning the mystery, as we might style it, of the lack of significance in the responses received in the course of the pre-conciliar consultations ("a plethora of texts almost all of which were of very low profile, inspired by a defensive attitude mostly preoccupied with preserving the condition of the Roman Catholicism of the 1950s"—p. 520). Yet another problematical point for this author was the "timid and ill-at-ease" behavior of certain Council figures who "only twelve months later would be playing determining roles in conciliar developments" (p. 522).

Summing up the results of the years 1959-1962, Professor Alberigo, correctly, observes that "however brief the perspective might be, it requires going beyond Manichaean evaluations that would demonize as wrong the preparations for Vatican II or exalt them as representing the only "sane" moment in the course of the entire conciliar adventure" (*Ibid.*). This is correct. However, it does not remove our reservations concerning the conclusions of this same author which go back especially to the "selective filter" of the preparatory structure which, in the author's view, resulted in proposals reflecting "strange and confused forms alien to the Johannine spirit in search of *aggiornamento*" (p. 523). Similarly, we harbor reservations concerning his references to the alleged "hegemony," whether "tinged with the jealousies of the various Roman universities," or of "Roman and curial theology" (*Ibid.*); to the "influence" (judged excessive) of Cardinal Bea on Pope Roncalli (p. 524); to the "parallelism" between the conciliar Commissions and the Roman Congregations; to the "hiatus, not merely in sensitivity, but in the consciousness and the mode of perceiving the meaning of faith, and between the groups with the central ecclesiastical responsibilities and the great majority of the faithful" (p. 525); to the limits and deficiencies of the conciliar preparations he mentions which "conditioned the results of the Council to a greater extent than might have been suspected" (*Ibid.*); and, finally, to the evaluations concerning the tensions that arose in what the author calls "the historical dialectic between pope and council"—in this case, "a conspicuously explosive conflict" is mentioned, while the "dialectic" in question supposedly got transformed into "a complex and at times inextricable three-way dialectic" between pope, Roman Curia, and the conciliar assembly" (*Ibid.*), "which the pressures exerted by public opinion inevitably entered into as well." (p. 526).

And in addition to such points as these, our reservations extend to the final "sociological" vision of Alberigo. From this point of view, the conciliar preparations "appeared concentrated in the hands of a proportionately very restricted group composed exclusively of males, celibates, generally fairly advanced in age, and mostly European in culture. The composition of such a body, although not without its own dialectical tensions, nevertheless favored a very strong impermeability as far as its general social situation was concerned" (*Ibid.*).

The volume concludes with the usual indices: thematic and of names, as well as a table of contents.

11

For the History of Vatican Council II
(First Session and In-Between)

Alberigo Giuseppe, ed., with Various Authors, *La formazione della coscienza conciliare* [The Formation of the Conscience of the Council]. Volume II of the *Storia del Concilio Vaticano II* [History of Vatican Council II], directed by Giuseppe Alberigo, Peeters-Il Mulino, Bologna, 1996, 464 pages.

In his brief "Premise," Professor Alberigo makes a point of emphasizing the complete adequacy and suitability of the historiographical criteria used to reconstruct, and the literary criteria used to expound, the history of the preparation for the Council covered in the first volume of this series [reviewed by us in the previous chapter]. In the end, he writes: "We refrained from trying to benefit by attempting to unravel the actual experiences of the Council, especially in their undeniable tortuousness. So we opted for a thematic reconstruction instead, certainly a more linear one, although one less respectful of the concreteness of the event" (p. 11). This was a choice that had its advantages.

As regards sources, he goes over the situation in haste. For us this means, once again, that a historical enterprise of this scope and ambition was undertaken prematurely (see, for example, p. 104). Perhaps the authors were thinking of the Latin American saying, "*se hace camino al andar*" (that is, "we will chart our path as we go along"). But there are those who do not see the applicability of such an approach to the present case. In fact, in this volume, unpublished sources are not lacking, especially some of those that refer to the supposed "agenda" of John XXIII; and some of the latter are exhaustively mined *ad usum delphini*. Even the official sources do not, in general, seem to have been very well "digested." There are many volumes of these latter, of course. But this limitation restricts some of the collaborators to rather general citations, as well as in some of their detailed and critical observations. On the other hand, it is true that this book does begin to move beyond a mere recording of facts amounting to mere "chronicles." That much we can willingly concede to Alberigo.

Chapter I comes following the list of abbreviations and sources. It is the work of A. Riccardi, and it bears the title: "The Tumultuous Opening of the Conciliar Work" (pp. 21-86). This adjective seems to us overblown, however, and could well have been replaced by "surprising"; but it does indicate the kind of dramatization of events (words like "contradiction" and "confusion" are regularly employed) that characterizes this entire volume.

The climate in Rome is said to have been one of "uncertainty" (p. 22), even if there were those who did reveal themselves as in favor of the conciliar event that was desired by John XXIII (see p. 23). The names of Cardinals Confalonieri and Cicognani are mentioned in this connection, leaving an opening to cite other cardinals of the curia as well. This statement is important because it confirms what we have maintained from the beginning—against the prevailing winds and tides—namely, the need to recognize that the Roman Curia was not a monolithic reality. It is necessary, therefore, to diversify and make distinctions. Outside Rome, however, there prevailed a preoccupation, "indeed, a kind of pessimism, concerning the material that the bishops were going to be judging" (*Ibid.*). But in all this the author is considering rather, the opinions of theologians. In such a context, the idea of sending a message from the Council to all humanity was attributed to Father M.- D. Chenu; he was known for his interest in, and sympathy for, "the world" (as we might say). To speak truly, though, while relying on another source (Gabriel Garrone), we know that this particular project was already, in fact, underway (see p. 77ff). This is just one example of the difficulties of attribution that can present themselves to historians, especially if they are given to reading "Council diaries"—and, especially, if one thinks he has mounted a "winning horse."

Even the lapidary formula, "great expectations, huge unpreparedness, little experience" (p. 24), should be explained. Why in the world did this ecumenical Council require such a long preparation period? Was that because those involved had little experience of a Council? It is obvious that none of the participants in the Council would have had any such experience of actually participating in one.

A number of other pertinent considerations come next, however, one of them on "the place" where the great Synod was to be held; to this subject are added some further correct observations on the position of the patriarchs, and on how much was implicit in an ecumenical point of view. Another pertinent consideration covered here deals with the opening of the Council, the procession and the opening liturgy. We note in passing that the remarks of Congar are more diversified, especially in the earlier part of his reflections, than Riccardi allows us to observe (p. 31). Then there were the actual words of the pope in his opening speech, *Gaudet mater ecclesia*, described as "one of the most complete expressions of the Roncallian vision of the Council" (p. 34). "It was here that the term *'aggiornamento'* entered into the Church's official language" (p. 35). The address signaled "a strong distancing...from a 'catastrophic' reading of the current situation of the Church and of the world" (*Ibid.*). Then there was the important distinction the pope made between the "substance of the ancient doctrine of the *depositum fidei* and the way in which it is presented" (p. 37). In describing the impact of all this, the author says that "John XXIII opened the Council by indicating a path to be followed rather than laying out a program" (p. 39). Then came the three successive audiences granted by the pope which are analyzed by the author: the audience with the extraordinary missions, with the journalists, and with the non-Catholic observers.

With regard to the "extraordinary second day of Vatican II," however, there are a number of inaccuracies in this account. Should we indicate some of them? For instance, the "self-governance" of the Council is referred to (see also p. 53); but here it is necessary to record that the presidency of the Council was appointed by the pope—just as the pope approved the basic Regulations for the Council—and it was this same papally-appointed presidency that approved the proposal to postpone the session that would be electing the members of the conciliar commissions. In this connection, it is also important to note that the eventual confirmation of the list of bishops "already taking part in the work of these preparatory commissions" (p. 45) would not have meant "automatic acceptance of the *schemata* already prepared" (pp. 46, 53, and 60); nor would it have meant that "the choices made by the Roman Curia in the preparatory phase would have been confirmed" (p. 46).

It is here too that the negative role played by the "fantasy list" placed in circulation by the dicastery of Cardinal Ottaviani comes in (p. 46). Some Council Fathers interpreted this as an attempt to dictate the work of the conciliar commissions. But the proposal by Cardinal Liénart, seconded by Cardinal Frings—and also including the names of Cardinals Döpfner and König—to postpone the voting on the conciliar commission members was accepted. Riccardi expatiates on the significance of this postponement, citing an unhappy observation by Archbishop Neophytos Edelby, who considered the postponement to be the "first failure inflicted upon the General Secretary of the Council, who wanted to orchestrate the Council as with a conductor's baton" (p. 48; see also p. 53). It was, in fact, the presidency of the Council, not the Secretary General, from the outset, that had the responsibility to oversee the voting. The task of the Secretary General was to carry out the decision when it was made—which, in the end, seems to have been the work of the Secretary of State. A certain weight has to be given here to the point made concerning the enhancing of the role of intermediate bodies and areas (read: "episcopal conferences"—p. 49). But with regard to the "behind-the-scenes aspects of the proposal of Cardinal Liénart" [to postpone the voting] (p. 50), it is necessary to ascertain on what true foundation the chronicle presented by this author is based, since the critical apparatus employed by him does not show the sources for what he asserts. But these sources are necessary in order to judge how well founded his conclusions are: he writes that "there was no conspiracy here, but rather a real and widespread discomfort resulting in a very concrete initiative" (p. 51).

With regard to "the new role for the episcopal conferences," there is an exact description of this role as it unfolded at the Council (p. 52; see, however, pp. 53ff). It is necessary to recognize the organizational difficulties that were encountered and the merit with which they were faced (pp. 52 and 54ff.); only seven out of forty-three of them had approved statutes as conferences, and this in spite of the fact that they were strongly favored by both Popes Pacelli and Roncalli. In this same connection, the judgment rendered here on the various congregations surely sins through an excess of zeal (p. 55); and we would add a critical judgment of our own concerning the image presented of Archbishop Felici as a "man of the Curia." Rather, he seems to have been chosen for his important role precisely because he was independently situated on the margins of the various curial tendencies—a characteristic which pleased Pope Roncalli, who seemed to share an understanding with him regarding his own [the pope's] "agendas" for the Council. For that reason, we do not believe the pope was capable of using "irony" at the expense of Archbishop Felici, nor of speculating about his "resignation" (see p. 59, n. 101).

The author goes on to analyze the formation of the lists of the conciliar commission members elected, as mentioned above. In our view, it was the "currents" or "tendencies" within the Council that got organized for these elections, not the national episcopal conferences as such, although there was no rigid pattern followed here (see p. 64). The subsequent proposal of Cardinal Ottaviani, who ceased calling for an absolute majority for all those voted in, was at first rejected, but later wisely revived by a papal intervention. The interpretation that Riccardi puts on all this is a bit specious, since it seems to be aimed at making the reader believe that it was not the opinion of Ottaviani that finally prevailed—but also to attest to the non-applicability of certain aspects of the Regulations. But this was rather a case of narrowing the Regulations in order to make them more flexible at a time when various unforeseen difficulties presented themselves to the conciliar assembly. The Regulations did not set up some kind of a taboo, and it is important to remember this even while continuing to respect the Regulations for what they were, it is also important to remember that the General Secretary was not engaged in "obstructionism" when he applied the Regulations, as is stated here (see p. 65); nor was this the case when "Higher Authority" saw fit to modify them. That this was both obvious and legitimate followed from the fact that it was this same Higher Authority that authorized the Regulations in the first place, and in the present case it did not mean skipping over or "by-passing the Council" (see p. 65).

The author concludes that, as a result of the postponed vote and the consequences which followed from it, "a notable discontinuity...was created" (p. 60) with regard to the criteria and the prospects which had been adopted in the pre-conciliar phase. Yet he himself adds a little later that "at bottom the organizational chart of the conciliar commissions meant the preservation of some of the typical characteristics of the preparatory phase" (*Ibid.*). This was one more instance of the beneficial "dialectic" that developed between the tendencies of continuity and those of innovation; this kind of "dialectic" was implicit in the on-going development of the Council, and, I would say, of the Catholic Church herself. Yet farther on in the volume we will find Alberigo and Grootaers both undertaking to divide up and place in opposition the preparatory phase and that of the actual unfolding of the Council; they even introduce a new, "anomalous" phase, which they style a "second preparation." What is actually the case here, however, is one of the operative phases of the Council itself; the preparatory phase itself was long completed and there was no "second" preparatory phase.

In Riccardi's own presentation of the commission members named by the pope, he finds that only 27 of the 90 were Italian and that 30 percent of them had played no part in the conciliar preparation work. Then there was the announcement of the elevation of the Secretariat for Promoting Christian Unity to the rank of a commission. Thus, the author writes, "the curia-commission speculation that persisted from the preparatory phase on into the actual conciliar operational phase fell apart" (p. 65). We disagree (see also p. 85).

Following this, the author discusses at length the language question, including whether Latin was obligatory in the *aula* of St. Peter. Judging from his "agendas," the importance which John XXIII attributed to the Latin question should be clear, and hence this whole subject required that careful distinctions be made. Riccardi does not do this. He establishes a link between the question of Latin in the *aula* and the "problem of the preservation of Latin as the language of the Roman liturgy" (*Ibid.*). This is the route by which we arrive, following the pontifical interventions on this same subject mentioned earlier, at the following conclusion (which should have been softened): "The pope did not wish to govern or manage the Council directly, either through the Curia or through the conciliar commissions. His involvement in the work of the Council needed to be very discreet, and his powers used sparingly" (p. 69; see also p. 85). Or again: "The pope had no intention of functioning like a film director manipulating the conciliar apparatus." The motto of his whole life, after all, was: "Let be, allow others to act, give to others something to do" (pp. 86ff.).

After this came the "messages, programs, and plans." There is a good characterization here of the "rather different positions" of Cardinals Bea and Montini respectively, even if, as regards the latter, we do not share the too strict conclusion of the author, namely, that Montini "did not have a plan for the Council nor the means to put one into practice" (p. 75). The author nevertheless pursues the same line further: "The direction the Council should take was not very clear in the vision of Pope John." However, it is evident that the really "extraordinary" role of the Secretariat of State, presided over by the Secretary of State himself, *was* truly *extra ordinem*: "He represented directly the will of the pope, whether through his office or through the constant access he had to the pontiff" (p. 77).

Then there are what the author styles "the Roman parties"—which we would prefer to call "tendencies" or "currents." The author groups them around names such as Ottaviani-Browne (to whom should be added Ruffini and Siri, and, with lesser frequency, Pizzardo, Marella, and Aloisi Masella). Another grouping, in the middle, was that around Cicognani.-Confalonieri, characterized as more balanced and moderate; John XXIII is said to have always had "a good understanding" with Cardinal Cicognani. Moreover, even as regards the "Roman party" of Cardinal Ottaviani, it is important to recall how much diversity of both thought and strategy there was among this group—whether or not it actually constituted a "bloc" (see p. 80ff.).

Continuing his analysis of the direction and orientation of the Council, Riccardi reports the judgment of Cardinal Giovanni Urbani of Venice for whom "the presidency was unprepared" (p. 81). We do not share that opinion, for it was not a question of preparation in any case, it seems to us, for something that was entirely new, for which there was no way they could have been prepared beforehand. We find excessive also what this author says about the General Secretariat of the Council; this is confirmed by the judgment of John XXIII himself; and it was as a result of papal confidence that from the role and work of the Secretariat *extra ordinem* emerged the necessity "to provide a harmonious plan for Vatican II" (p. 83), even if in the same Secretariat two "blocs" could indeed be delineated (p. 85).

"Setting the Assembly in Motion" is the topic of Chapter II, entrusted to Gerald Fogarty (pp. 87-127). His work is divided into several subject areas, including, first, the topics of "the first contacts among the bishops and theologians" (with various subtitles); the initial inquietude among them (with reactions more or less negative); the burdens of the theologians; the observations of Karl Rahner (with his request to the Council Fathers to replace the *schema* that had been prepared on the sources of revelation); the animadversions of Edward Schillebeeckx; the contacts among the bishops (along with their "evolution") as well as among the theologians: particular judgments on various American conciliar figures; extra-conciliar meetings (including dealing with a "refusal"); the divergent views on the four dogmatic *schemata*, along with German and Franco-German initiatives. With regard to the last topic: "For the first time the central

European episcopate, a "thinking" group, found itself united" (p. 100), although, in general "the French were taking a softer line" (*Ibid.*, p. 47); but there was also an alignment with the successful Suenens-Philips tactic, which "did not pursue alternatives, but worked for a revision of the existing theological *schema* that would be acceptable to all," involving in this approach the theologian of Cardinal Montini, Carlo Colombo (p. 102 and pp. 105ff.). There were also alternative *schemata* (a German proposal and a global preface of Father Congar).

We do not intend to go deeply into this presentation with any detailed examination of these topics, especially considering the kind of narrative which this author has fashioned. In any case, we find all of it rather unduly dramatized, as we mentioned earlier. [To see what is meant] in this connection, it suffices to quote sentences such as "the collaboration between bishops and theologians succeeded in forcibly wresting control of the Council away from Ottaviani" (p. 104). This author is jaunty and unconstrained in his use of adjectives, in fact, and he employs language which would seem to exclude "conservatives and the Curia" from the Council altogether (see p. 113); at the same time, theologians *are* included as an integral part of the Council; he writes of how "the bishops and theologians...took control of the Council"—all this even though, as we have already seen, the Curia was not a monolithic body. There should have been an end put to such a generic characterization of all this.

Another division in this chapter deals with the crisis of the placing of missiles in Cuba [by the Soviet Union]. The author deals with the initiatives of Pope John XXIII with regard to this Cuban crisis. Let us state at the outset that the author's treatment of this subject issues in a happier result than his work in the previous section; this is true in part because here he does take into account quite "dispassionately" the fact of the difficulty of reconstructing the acts of the pontiff in this crisis (see nn. 83-84, p. 115; and also pp. 119ff., p. 121, n. 103, 122, 125). The mountain gives birth to a mouse here as far as bilateral relations were concerned.

The author's final section refers to "the health of the pope." According to him this "overshadowed the triumph of his [the pope's] vision within the Council itself" (p. 125). We would not say so. Besides, at this time the pope did not know the nature of his gastric problem; he himself called it "gastritis" or "gastropathy." The attestation of Zizola here (see n. 117 on p. 126) thus falls to the ground. The idea that the pope's invocation of the Virgin Mary on December 5, 1962, was "a gesture of pacification towards Ottaviani, whose *schema*"—but was it *his?*—"had just been blocked" (p. 1256) is a very superficial idea.

Chapter III is the work of Mathijs Lamberigts and has reference to "the debate on the liturgy" (pp. 129-192). Above all let us take note of the many times this author has recourse to the verb "seems" in his narrative. This, once again, indicates how necessary it is for a historical subject to mature before it can be properly treated, if it is going to be more than a mere chronicle. This is also true because the sources cannot be easily assimilated; see a clear example of this on page 168, first paragraph, with an incomplete cross reference (p. 181). Lamberigts slavishly follows, surely to excess, two paths, one blazed by H. Jenny, and the other by Archbishop Paul Hallinan (covered in the volume of T. J. Shelley). The result is a focus resembling something of an *idée fixe* on the subject of internal regulations. The author's perspective is based predominantly on the situation in the United States, and even then he draws false conclusions from his premises.

His excessive use of adjectives and of charged language is improper, and his imprecision and his inexactness in other ways such as in the names and responsibilities of various Council Fathers—unique in this volume—result in not a few *errata*. Following his chosen method the author, perhaps understandably, attempts to present the substance of various interventions in the words of those opposing them; he deals with the questions of Latin versus the vernacular, concelebration, communion under both species, adaptations, the power of bishops (and of episcopal conferences) in the reform of the liturgy, and the issues of the breviary, missal, and ritual books; and, finally, he deals with unction, or the sacrament of the sick.

Descriptions of the various votes are followed with comments which could, indeed should, have been discussed more thoroughly.

All in all, the research of Lamberigts turns out to be weak, if not quite simply deficient.

Chapter IV presents "The Initial 'Physiognomy' of the Assembly" (pp. 193-258). It is the work of Hilari Raguer. The principal question with which it is concerned is the application of political, parliamentary, sociological, and psychological criteria to the Council. It utilizes a political model *tout court*, as a matter of fact. This alone suffices to arouse our reservations, even though the study itself is well enough done *in genere suo*. We must recognize human conditioning, of course, but we must also leave room for the action of the Spirit. The research here is fundamentally based on a non-published thesis of S. Gomez de Arteche on the subject of "conciliar groups *extra aulam*," or outside the Council floor. Some good points are made; we need cite, in this connection, only the very objective observation that in the Roman Curia there were "two sectors of contrary tendencies and unequal importance" (p. 236, n. 120). The study begins, however, with a harsh, exaggerated judgment concerning the world episcopate (p. 193), which is based on the *vota* sent in by the bishops in anticipation of the Council. So the author proposes to inquire how it came about that the Council moved from such initial positions [reflected in the *vota*] to a new consciousness which permitted the assembly to set forth another vision entirely.

Having examined the composition of the Council (Council Fathers as well as non-Catholic observers and invited guests), the author turns his attention to the "role played by a number of groups to which the official Regulations of the Council attributed no role whatsoever: first of all, the episcopal conferences" (see pp. 214, 216, 218, 219 and 220). I would have a number of critical observations to make here. But the author also treats other "informal groups" in the same way, specifically the *Coetus Internationalis Patrum*, or International Group of Fathers (p. 194). On page 226 there are two erroneous statements, one concerning the Lateran University and the other one concerning Archbishop Felici alleging that he had close ties with [the conservative] Bishop Luigi Carli of Segni, Italy, because the archbishop originally came from there. Then there is the author's mention of "the Church of the poor" containing two more observations that are out of focus (p. 227). He also treats the "central European bloc" or "Universal Alliance," "the Conference of Delegates," and the curial area, or area of a certain Curia. Everything said in the study on this last point deserves critical comments and precisions, particularly the judgments rendered on Archbishop Felici. Yet other groups treated by the author are the "French", the "Latin American", the "religious superiors," "religious bishops," and "missionary bishops."

Reflected in this chapter is the background concerning the available sources of information at the council. There is another diatribe aimed at Archbishop Felici in the context of the operations of the Vatican Press Office; this needs to be compared with what is said later and more correctly and objectively on page 603, bearing in mind also the observations in the "Tucci Diary" of which the author makes use. The Press Office did not simply hand out information on the event that was the Council; it did so with "a width and breadth that no preceding council had ever employed"; yet in the opposite direction, it influenced the actions of the Council Fathers themselves" (*Ibid.*). The "people of God" is also spoken about; it was not merely a question of being a simple spectator in this case; but rather, "acting through the modern means of communication, it became a sounding board with undeniable repercussions." On the other hand, the key to the interpretation of how "the overturning of the positions between majority and minority" came about was none other than "the person of John XXIII himself, who provided the catalyst which allowed the small number of progressive bishops to act; they also knew how to stir up the enthusiasm of the people of God and world opinion in favor of his conciliar project. The universal sympathy aroused by the pope's person and by the Council provided the moral force to vanquish the predominant opposition in the Curia to any Council of 'renewal'" (pp. 194ff.). Where this author stands is thus made clear. However, it all seems to us to be too simple to be true, especially since the real key to the pontiff's thinking was *aggiornamento*, and that entailed a mediation between the old and the new.

Chapter V by Giuseppe Ruggieri deals with "The First Doctrinal Conflict" (pp. 258-293). The doctrinal conflict in question had to do with "a contested *schema*...object of an on-going debate within Catholic theology." It bore upon the question of the relationship between oral tradition—the preaching of Christ himself—and "the subsequent transmission or handing down of that preaching, whether by means, on the one hand, of what was written in the New Testament itself, or, on the other hand, of what is expounded by the ecclesiastical magisterium" (p. 259). In the exaggerations of expression that this author is given to, as in the way he simplifies things, it is worthwhile reporting on his thinking concerning the debate on this *schema* on "the sources of revelation" (*De Fontibus Revelationis*). This debate took place between November 14, 1962, and December 8 of the same year. This writer's work conveys the spirit of the debate though not the entire truth of it. For him the debate constituted "a decisive turn for the future of the Council, and thus for the Catholic Church: that is, for the 'Pacellian' Church, still substantially the enemy of modernity, and heir to the 'restored' Church of the nineteenth century. [But this turn was towards] a Church that had now become the friend of all men, even if they were the sons of modern society, and a friend also of its culture and history" (*Ibid.*). It was here—Ruggieri goes on—"that the Council came into its own, discovered its own true nature and aims, and entered into accord with the intentions of John XXIII—an accord which in some ways had been impeded by the work of the preparatory commissions, especially the Theological Commission." Concerning this last point, as is also the case with some of the other things emphasized by this author, we must dissent, even though the author qualifies his judgment by adding "in some ways" (*Ibid.*). Farther on he speaks of "curial strategy" *tout court*, especially with regard to the question of the election of the members of the commissions; we are obliged to repeat, almost to the point of exhaustion, that it is necessary to distinguish and not just fall back on "collective responsibility." This is always a delicate matter. History teaches us this. The same thing is true of the author's idea that the bishops had to "go to school" (p. 260) and of his treatment of the passage in the basic text, concerning "the inerrancy of every single affirmation, whether religious or profane," in Scripture (p. 261). The author's treatment of these questions, however, is superficial. Alternative texts had meanwhile begun to circulate, about which the author delivers himself of equally mistaken judgments, for example, in his assertion that "the *schemata* of the Doctrinal Commission were outside of the boundaries of the Church of its own time" (p. 264, n. 10).

With a title such as "The Eve of Battle," the author announces that there were going to be "bitter battles" (p. 272). He explains the nature of the discussions that were heating up concerning the proposed *schema* and the positions that were being taken concerning whether fundamentally to reject it or to revise it, perhaps after debate and a test vote—although these were questions that should have been left to the discretion of the Council presidency.

The debate on *De Fontibus* brought out what the author calls "the conciliar choice to emphasize the pastoral nature of doctrine" (p. 276; see also p. 293). The author's presentation of the substance of this material is useful and complete enough. He also includes the ecumenical dimension, making a pertinent reference to the "ecumenical method" of Father Yves Congar (p. 286). He also makes reference to what he calls a "Council of theologians" (p. 282), although for us there is no such thing. The pope himself rather soberly noted about all this "that contrasts were foreseeable at an opening such as this...May the Lord help and unite us"—an admirable observation, which should have formed the basis of all of these analyses and judgments on the Council and on the Church.

Some of the author's affirmations on page 290, however, lend themselves to some confusion—concerning the papal approbation of the preparatory *schemata*, for example. This approbation certainly did not affect the pope's *nihil obstat* concerning free discussions on the Council floor. In some cases, the pope offered his opinion concerning the "value" of certain positions, but this still left the bishops at liberty to make up their own minds on the questions at issue, bearing in mind all the factors. When it was clear that things had reached an *impasse*, though, the author correctly points to the role of Cardinal Cicognani, even while he recognizes that "it is impossible to reconstruct in the present state of our knowledge the exact manner in which certain important figures influenced the decision of John XXIII" (p. 291). This is certainly also indicative, although Ruggieri does not strictly adhere to it (see n. 91 on p. 292, where the tenor of his remarks on Cardinal Cicognani contrast with what was said about him two pages earlier). Eventually, the contested document was sent to a mixed commission, a solution that could have been called "Solomonic."

There follows the very short Chapter VI entitled "A Pause: the Means of Social Communication." It is by the already mentioned M. Lamberigts. To begin with, he briefly sums up the contents of the *schema* on the media and describes its presentation and the debate concerning it that took place in the *aula*, "where it received a positive reception for the most part" (p. 300). Following its acceptance in principle, "at least in its essential aspects" (p. 307), revisions were made by the Commission. The author notes in conclusion: "It received the same kind of marginal treatment that the press itself was getting from the Council" (p. 308). This judgment seems excessive to us, also because it presages the further judgment made subsequently that "the debate [on the media] was not given much attention, probably because of the Council's own poor relations with the press" (*Ibid.*).

Chapter VII (pp. 309-383) is also by Ruggieri and is entitled: "The Difficult Abandonment of a Controversial Ecclesiology." On the whole, it is not a bad piece of work, although it is not well "centered." The initial note *Auctoritas ante omnia et super omnia* ["authority before and over everything"] gives an idea of the approach of the piece with regard to its main ecclesiological theme; at the same time, some variants and counter-positions are also presented. The theologian G. Philips attests to the fact that, as early as October 18 [1962], he had been charged by Cardinal Suenens to "revise, complete, and improve" the whole *schema De ecclesia*. In his own person, Philips occupied a kind of *via media*, or "middle way," and thus the decisive choice of him for this task dictated that the ultimate result would be an accomplished fact; noted theologian that he was, Philips began the process of establishing the relationships that would lead to an eventual consensus concerning the *schema*.

At this point, the author describes its original text, including the various chapters it contained, meanwhile, however, delivering himself of comments not always of the happiest kind—for example, on the subject of ordinary power, which can be either proper or vicarious (p. 316). Following this, he explains the "diverse" views contributed by Philips. The latter showed himself to be very able in a tactical sense (with some exceptions) (pp. 325ff.). Treated as a "work in progress," after three successive drafts, the character of the *schema* became less juridical and more coherent, using more ecumenical language and language linked to Scripture; this was especially true with regard to the question of collegiality. All this made it more feasible for practically everyone (see p. 326). And Ruggieri exerts himself to provide a characterization of the various drafts. In each case, Philips did not offer an alternative *schema*, but rather presented "a nucleus to which everything else could be attached" (p. 332); this was the basis of his success. However, "apart from the subtle tactics of Philips there were...the observations made by Schillebeeckx and Rahner"—also on the alternative proposals—which the author strains to explain (pp. 332ff.). Father Otto Semmelroth, S.J., also collaborated here. The common objective of all of them, though, was the elimination of the preparatory *schema*. They did not entirely succeed in this intention. In this regard, the claim that the Philips project allowed the *Nota Praevia* to be brought forward is not accurate; the *Nota Praevia* became necessary in spite of the efforts of this noted theologian, even though he did make clear that the *Nota* in question was in no way in contradiction with the *schema* itself. It was, in fact, an unavoidable addition, if the overwhelming consensus in favor of the approval of the *schema* that was desired was to be achieved.

Echoing Archbishop Edelby, there came then "the Melchite moment" (p. 345), when it was necessary to elaborate a "strong strategy" with respect to the *schema* on the Eastern Catholic Churches.

On this occasion, while not calling for the *schema* to fail, but rather "distancing themselves...strongly from the other uniate Churches, the Melchite episcopate put itself forward more as the representative of the Orthodox Church within Catholicism than as an example or expression of Catholicism vis-à-vis the Orthodox" (p. 346). However, the reasoning of Archbishop Tawil (p. 347) apropos of this is not at all exact. Here too exaggerations are not lacking (see, for example, pp. 348 and 354). The Melchites were not, in fact, "sadly solitary" or isolated. Precisely because they undertook not to allow the *schema* to fail, they were very much engaged. However, it is necessary to recognize the "position of strength" of Cardinal Cicognani in defense of the text; he influenced not a few to draw back, including Cardinal Bea (p. 353). However, the *schema* should not be described as "low." This text is described more than any other in terms of the Melchite criticism of it. The conclusion of Note 64 on page 349 is in error. We might add in passing that the caption on one of the photographs included in the volume here erroneously refers to "the arrival of an observer accompanied by J. Willebrands and P. Duprey." In fact, the photograph is one of the Russian Metropolitan Nikodim Rotov.

We arrive next at "The Future of the Council" (p. 354), which begins with some rather weak observations (p. 355), and then goes on to offer on a vast scale an analysis of the various theological positions taken on the theological *schema*; the author covers the interventions of a long list of Council Fathers: Ottaviani, Gagnebet, the German and Austrian episcopates, Montini, Siri, Florit, Carli, Ruffini, Bueno y Moreal, König, Alfrink, Bea, Döpfner, Volk, Frings—the intervention of this last prelate "was perhaps the most incisive discourse of all from a critical point of view" (p. 361). The contributions of Maximos IV Saigh and the Eastern Catholic bishops were "more compact this time" (p. 361). The contribution of Cardinal Lercaro sounded his usual "unique note with regard to the entire Council, namely, the Church of the poor": it was "a pebble cast into the pond" (pp. 371f.). The author concludes concerning all this: "At this point, rather than setting forth a determined or specific doctrine concerning the Church, the Council was thinking rather of the future of the Church" (p. 366). This future "appeared uncertain" at this point, even though certain decisions taken by the Council's Secretariat for Extraordinary Affairs at the end of November suggested that some re-assuring and important choices were being made. In confirmation of a new more positive and creative direction towards "unity," there came then the discourses of Cardinal Suenens and Montini at the beginning of December (see p. 369ff.). For Ruggieri, this development indicated, as far as Montini was concerned, "an implicit commitment to the future election of a new supreme pontiff disposed to carry on with the Council by means of a program of moderation" (p. 370). His statement that "I cannot be silent concerning the fact that the *schema* is not adequate" signaled "an open distancing from curial circles in a way that no one would have dared to do earlier" (*Ibid.*). This conclusion, however, seems excessive to us.

"The Resistance of the Past" (p. 373) consists of a quite superficial treatment which precedes the presentation and discussion of the rather salutary papal decision to set up a "commission to coordinate and direct future work presided over by the Cardinal Secretary of State" (p. 372). Meanwhile, the work of the "Mixed Commission" specially appointed to deal with the *schema De Revelatione* went on, the account of it here accompanied by a number of "partisan" remarks pointing to the impossibility of arriving at any single solution regarding the relationship of Scripture and Tradition. There is a good reconstruction here of the discussion relative to this question based on the background established by McGrath and on the protocol of Laberge (published by Sauer—p. 380). The author evaluates the final discourse of John XXIII delivered to the First Session of the Council as follows: "Everything considered, it was a humble discourse intending to take leave from his Council, which he would not again address while it was in session. It was very different from his Opening Address to the Council" (p. 383).

Chapter VIII begins with the title "The Second Preparation and Its Opponents" (pp. 385-558). The Council was moving ahead. The writing of this chapter was assigned to Jan Grootaers. This author attempts to promote the idea that this session represented, for all practical purposes, a new beginning on the part of the Council; the author introduces the idea that it represented a total abandonment of the initial *schemata* (p. 386ff.). He includes a summary where he drops the "for examples" in order to downgrade the idea that *schema* XIII originated with the several *schemata* originally proposed. To validate such an approach—brought forward in order to depreciate or even cancel out the first true and unique conciliar preparatory phase—the author introduces the idea of a "second preparation"; sometimes he places this term between quotation marks, perhaps to make it more acceptable. For us, however, this is inadmissible, even when we bear in mind the tenor of the letter of Pope John XXIII, *Mirabilis ille* (dated January 6, 1963) from which emerges the evidence of a sense "of the continuity of the Council, even though the bishops, united with the pope, constitute the structure of it; this is true even when they are physically far removed." Thus, even between the conciliar sessions, we are still "in Council."! In this particular study, however, the dramatization of such ideas abounds, as can be seen from the exaggerated language regularly employed by this author and by the "colored" adjectives he also, unhappily, repeats very often. In this approach, there is both a polemical spirit and an open adoption of extreme positions. It is unpleasant to have to speak about his use of terms in this way, but he constantly uses such words as battlefield, defeat, disaster, failure, trauma, sabotage, rents and tears, indignation, traps, pitfalls, explosions (three times on one page he employs this last term—p. 437). He speaks of "revolution" twice on page 441. He also has a tendency to turn issues into personal matters, for example, he speaks of the susceptibility of the drafters of texts supposedly unwilling to "sacrifice" their "creations." But it does seem to us that "sensitivity" of this type hardly characterized the unfolding of the First Session, and quite properly not. The author, however, refers to efforts "not to humiliate those who had managed the preparatory phase" (see pp. 387, 406, 446, 462ff., 466ff., and 504); on page 462, it even seems to be a question of "nationalism," and on page 504 the author speaks of "saving face for the Cardinal Secretary of State."

But the Council Fathers were not children pouting in a corner (see p. 452), even if many individuals and many ideas were indeed in play and some were opposed to each other—but respect for persons was still maintained. Yet, even today, an anti-curial spirit persists with respect to all this, and, we would say, it persists on principle; the proper nuances, revisions, and evaluations are not even attempted. This is most unfortunate for the sake of history, not necessarily for the sake of the Curia.

Coming to the "intersession," or period between the First and Second Sessions, the author begins with a section entitled "Uncertainties and Confusion" (p. 385). He recounts how things went in the cases of the various *schemata*, and then he speaks of a case of "confusion" to which we would certainly have added a qualification such as "certain" or "relative." It had to do with the "overlapping and superseding of the various draft texts" (p. 387). For that matter Cardinal Cicognani had declared, following the first meeting of the Central Coordinating Commission, that it was "necessary to rule out the substitution of new *schemata* for the material prepared with such care during the preparatory phase, but nonetheless leaving open the possibility of introducing amendments to it" (*Ibid.*; see also pp. 401, 407ff., 428 and 549). Cardinal Confalonieri echoed these same sentiments, and even Cardinal Suenens associated himself with them. This guaranteed that at least 60 percent of the original *schema De Ecclesia* would be retained in the new revision *De Ecclesia* (see p. 388).

Another section of this chapter concerns the Central Coordinating Commission itself. It was activated, the author says, "in view of a second preparation for the Council" (pp. 391ff.). It had authority over the other conciliar commissions with respect to the revision of the various *schemata*. It was here that "norms, directives, and agendas" were examined (p. 392), and it was here too that 20 new draft texts were considered (later reduced to 17, as recommended by Cardinal Urbani; note 44 on page 408 refers to this, but it must be supplemented by note 140 on p. 373 of the chapter given to Ruggieri). The 20 new draft texts had been chosen from among the 70 original texts originally produced some of which were combined with others. The author then treats a number of topics, including: "The Charter of the Central Coordinating Commission"; "The 'Composition' of the 'Supercommission'"; and "The Assignment of Tasks." This last topic speaks of a reduction in the role of Cardinal Spellman, defined as "marginal," which was not justified by the facts; his role was supposedly reduced because he was given a "minor" text to deal with; but the text in question did not deal merely with "chastity," as Grootaers avers, but also with "virginity, marriage, and the family."

The author also treats what he calls "the ties between curial elements and the enemies of the so-called 'second preparation'"—we would add, "as the author understands the situation." This section includes a renewed attack on the dicasteries of the Roman Curia as well as on the Cardinal Secretary of State—not to speak of an attack on Cardinal Confalonieri as well. It was simply not a question of "commissions," whether conciliar or coordinating, that were somehow "tied" or, as the author says, "subservient to" (p. 465), or "under the authority of" (p. 526), or "under the tutelage of" (pp. 551ff.) the Roman dicasteries. Rather, they were bodies that corresponded to curial offices in the same area of competence. This should be made clear once and for all. As for the "enemies' [of the author's supposed 'second preparation'], their actions are examined from the procedural point of view, revealing, perhaps, certain human weaknesses and defects—even if, for example, in the case of Cardinal Alfredo Ottaviani and Father Sebastian Tromp, as the latter revealed, they were not even invited to the "famous meeting." This would surely have justified their absence; but Grootaers interprets all this as being done instead "in reprisal" or "retaliation" (see also pp. 411 and 451). The author's analysis of the whole business continues with his treatment of "the development of the internal coordinating sessions" (including their continuing development into January, March, and July of 1963). He also deals with "the working commissions of the Council."

The author goes on to enlarge in a thematic way on the material in the three principal *schemata*, namely, the *schema* on revelation, the one on ecclesiology, and the one on the Church's relationship with the world. The state of these drafts certainly indicated the transitory character of the first intersession [in between the First and Second Sessions]. The draft on the Church and the world included an extensive analysis of the Malines text, which, in 1963, was still *Schema* XVII, although it became *Schema* XIII from 1964 on.

We will not follow the author closely in all this, even though it would be interesting to do so, and would also provide the occasion for commenting on a number of things, especially with regard to the Church (see pp. 422, 425, 430—for example, this last page records the author's ironic *boutade*, or jibe, about "oral tradition"—, 432, 433— on this page is also found the author's statement about "numerous instances of Roman ignorance concerning even basic information... about the movements that had been primary sources of inspiration for the current majority at the Council"—, p. 434—which includes an "insane" claim about the supposed practice of "a policy of 'so much the worse' or 'too bad'"—, 435 and 461—where responsibility for the "failure" of the Malines text is unjustly attributed to Cardinal Cicognani and Archbishop Felici, when it was Cardinal Confalonieri who "took it upon himself" to supply a draft which many members of the mixed commission considered both "undesirable and risky").

Next is explained the progress of two other drafts, *De Oecumenismo,* and the one on the apostolate of the laity. These appear, along with a reference to "the lack of success of the 'second preparation'" (p. 483). Treated here are texts referring to the bishops and the regime of dioceses. The author speaks of the "ruthless reaction of the conciliar assembly" to them, and, by November, 1963, of "a broken system of commissions"—broken into smaller subcommissions consisting only of those members still remaining in place along with a few experts." Other texts treated include the one on the missions, with judgments on it offered that are contrary to those of such authoritative writers as Schütte and also at variance with the praise by Felici, who "pretended to be" a good judge, yet who here demonstrated "greater realism than Cicognani, Confalonieri, and Agagianian." Still other texts covered are those dealing with the Eastern Catholic Churches; what the author styles the "lack of success" concerning these latter Churches was supposedly due to the impotence of the Orientals themselves, in failing to arrive at even a minimal consensus among themselves; it was also due to the growing influence of Cardinal Bea (a "friend" of John XXIII?). But none of this represented a "defeat" or a "disaster" in the way that Grootaers likes to dramatize these things; nor was there any "obligation" for the Melchite Patriarch Maximos IV Saigh to accept the cardinalate, as the author asserts (p. 511, n. 292). And among the other failures there is his inclusion of "the adaptation and renewal of the religious life"; this came about as a result of "tensions between the leadership of the majority forces at Vatican II, on the one hand; and, on the other hand, the concerted campaign organized by a number of the bishops and religious superiors" (p. 516). Finally, the author treats the *schemata* entitled *De Beata Maria Virgine* and *De Cura Animarum*, as well as those on the sacrament of matrimony, on the ministry of priests, on the seminaries, on university studies, and on Catholic schools.

He then moves on to deal with the topic entitled "From the Council to the Conclave." Here occur various exaggerations concerning retrenchments of initial judgments which John XXIII himself, cited by Grootaers, supposedly made. Certainly, the "turn" of December, 1962—if turn it truly was (see pp. 549ff.), and concerning which the author himself realizes that maintaining Cicognani and Felici in their directive functions was actually a moderating action—became possible in the light of actual conciliar experience and as a result of a calculation of the tendencies and forces actually in play at the Council. These, of course, had been unknown earlier during the preparatory phase. Then, the hypothesis of the influence on the pope of "the pressure of time"—because he had been "informed of the fatal diagnosis"—is in contradiction with the mind of the pope, who up until virtually the end, continued to "believe" his doctors, who went on to tell him that his symptoms were not serious. Notwithstanding this, the pope always placed himself in the hands of God.

"The Last Three Months" of the pontificate are thus presented with a renewal and with even a more pronounced radicalism evident in the judgments of the author, especially as regards his judgments concerning the Roman Curia. There are also various, quite inexact, observations made concerning Italian politics in an Italy seen as "the footstool of the papacy" (p. 523). Nor is it pleasing to see the word "plebiscite" used to indicate the "extraordinary unanimity" of hearts (as Yves Congar more aptly described it) that surrounded the dying and the death of the pope.

We can register the same sentiments concerning the next subtitle: "From a Council to a Conclave." It was, the author says, "a privileged moment for the liberty of expression and for collegiality, experienced at the very center of a rigid and monarchical structure" (p. 534). This interpretation goes back to the assertions of Zizola; this author speaks further of a "Roncallian revolution," a "Suenens reformism," of "the scars of the conclave," and of "the minimal percentage of Italian bishops prepared to accept the adventure of the Council." It would appear that the "progressives" were the only ones who were prepared to accept it.

The author then turns to the subject which is labeled "From the Conclave to the Council." He speaks of "the debut of Montini," who is covered only sketchily at first. Too much is made of his supposedly "marginal role" within the Italian episcopate and during the first months of the Council. There was a certain indecision evident in the first months of his pontificate, even though "the first ten days that followed his election were spectacular" (p. 539). In any case, the insinuation is beyond the pale that there was "a commitment—more or less formal—assumed by him in the conclave in the face of the two opposing camps, where the future of the Council itself was in play" (p. 538). It was precisely to preclude such speculation that Cardinal Montini did not arrive in Rome for the opening of the conclave until the very last minute.

Besides, the new pope proceeded to carry out a detailed reorganization of Vatican II's structures; he did so "in order that what would be said, either individually or collectively, would appear to be both more ordered and more clear" (p. 540). It was a process that moved from the lesser to the greater, not from the disordered to ordered. This needs to be correctly understood. But on the subject of the Moderators, everybody has his own opinion (see p. 541); and even on this subject, the Moderators themselves (or, at least, Suenens and Lercaro) maintained at almost any price the validity of the set of Regulations enacted by the Council itself" (*Ibid.*). But this was never conceded, and for the pope there was never even any idea of such a thing. For this reason alone, I do not believe it is correct to speak about any papal promise in this regard (p. 545, n. 384). And also the behavior manifested in relation to Cardinal Agagianian, who was appointed by the pope, explains a great deal. However, the "Bolognese" text for the Regulations of the Council (cf. n. 371 on p. 541) arrived late, and the Moderators either did not know how to interpret the papal "signals" involved, or did not want to interpret them; this situation obtained up to the time of the "Dossetti crisis." Some of the other things covered here demonstrate that Grootaers really does not understand Pope Paul VI; see, for example, note 377 on page 542 on the supposed behavior of Cardinal Cicognani. The author really does not accept, or does not want to accept, that Cardinal Cicognani really was the Secretary of State, and, as such, was necessarily "the closest collaborator of the Pope." John XXIII made this absolutely clear *in mortem* of Cardinal Tardini (see p. 543, with its "out-of-place" note 379).

The "first decisions of the Moderators" were based on a "dynamic conception of their responsibilities"—always a favorable and "justifying" characterization. According to the author, the Moderators operated "independently of the Secretary General." This claim is more than a stretch, however, objectively speaking. The author regularly refers to the three Moderators who, according to him, represented the majority current at the council. But there were *four Moderators*, not three—what was the fourth one doing all this time? Again, were the Moderators "representatives" of the conciliar assembly, or were they "representatives" of the pope? Yet it is even said that the "three Moderators planned to create their own infrastructure, with an independent base and with a group of their own *periti*" (p. 547). These were all suggestions of Father Dossetti, as is fairly well known. And with regard to the conflict between the various competences of Archbishop Felici and Father Dossetti, respectively, which to some extent comes out here, the language employed by Grootaers, similarly, goes beyond anything that might be considered acceptable—just as this author's hypothesis recorded in note 391 is quite beyond anything that one might be able to accept.

The final section in this long and tortuous chapter is entitled "Results Obtained in the Midst of Tensions." This text, again, pays particular attention to the so-called "enemies of 'the second preparation,'" who were defenders of the actual preparatory phase. The final disclosure here speaks of "a decisive contribution to the coordination of the various efforts"; this proved to be "the determining influence in bringing about the success of the preparations for the Second Session"; it also gave to the Council "a certain dynamism" (pp. 554ff.). In this context, the author's judgment on the small redaction *équipes* (teams), again, seems exaggerated; he calls them "the true motor of Vatican II" (p. 555, n. 405). In conclusion, though, there is mentioned those texts that were sent out to the Council Fathers in April and May of 1963, and then two more texts, that followed in July of that year, along with a new agenda, which the author calls "relatively homogeneous" (p. 556). It included revised procedures, as well as an organization chart, indicating the new directions of the Council and showing "the participation of the representatives of the laity" (*Ibid.*).

In Chapter IX, the same Jan Grootaers continues his investigations, this time employing maritime language and that related to rivers and bodies of water. He gives the chapter the title: "Flux and Reflux between Two Seasons." We certainly prefer this kind of language to the military or "warlike" language that he has long been employing.

Citing an observation of Father Yves Congar on the relationship between *Urbis et Orbis* ("The City of Rome and the World")— Congar said it better and differently than Grootaers does—he tries to apply here his idea of flux and reflux to the movement between the "center" and the world which the Council was then experiencing outside its own boundaries. But merely "to outline or sketch the many relapses and regressions connected with the start-up of Vatican II and its first period would be...rash" (p. 560), he says. However, he attempts to concentrate his efforts on some of the more significant events that occurred. For him, these events are often those related to the ecumenical camp. He says, however, that his commentaries amount to no more than summary indications.

He begins with what he styles "The Reflux of Concentric Circles" moving out from the center. A first circle deals with the pastoral letters of bishops—Dutch, German, and the pastoral letter of the archbishop of Malines-Brussels [Suenens]. He expresses some general disenchantment with the fact that the accents and emphasis of these pastors differ, depending upon whether they are speaking primarily for Roman consumption or for that at their places of residence. Then he examines the various "nominations and promotions"; this leads him to his second circle, that is, to the commentaries and testimonials of observers at the Council, more precisely, those of H. Roux, L. Vischer, and the Orthodox Archbishop Cassien. With "the rear guard moving into the first rank," we arrive at his third circle, that of the zones of the Hispanic tradition; of an Italian Catholic revival (which he describes, erroneously, and with a lack of any real seriousness, as "out of the catacombs...a clericalist and often triumphalist Church"—p. 57). He speaks also of an Irish-influenced Church (which includes that of the United States and England, where the young clergy, he says, were "silenced"—p. 574). Raising these questions allows the author to get into a discussion of both birth control and "secularization" as well.

His developed discussion of the ecumenical question is summed up under the unfortunate title of "The Ecumenical Movement: A Promising Disorder" (this title was inspired by the "promising chaos" mentioned by the Anglican Bishop Tomkins). The fascination of many journalists with attention-grabbing pronouncements is characteristic of this author, who is evidently trying to pass on some kind of historical "joke" here. He provides a very attenuated and speculative evaluation, evidencing strong partiality for the World Council of Churches in its various expressions and "confessional families." He does the same thing for the Eastern Orthodox Church and its various "meetings."

And this author goes on to treat the subject of information at the

Council according to what he calls "the boomerang effect" (p. 591); he speaks of the preparations for a new "flux and reflux" of the Council in the subsequent session. He also attacks the Secretary General of the Council for the information policy in place. According to him, the Council Press Office existed in a state of "feudal submission." But it was precisely Archbishop Felici who created new openings aimed at loosening up on conciliar secrecy (p. 602). He also praises Father Roberto Tucci for his work as an "intermediary," and later he praises Monsignor Fausto Vallainc too (p. 603), as well as lauding the particular role of the Central Coordinating Commission. His final section bears the title, "New Policy towards the East" (p. 605). It describes an obvious intensification of the Council's contacts with Communist regimes. Grootaers explains this movement, setting down the more salient events of the period under investigation (on one point: yes, Cardinal Testa *was* a friend of John XXIII's, but the same *cannot* be said of Cardinal Bea—p. 609). The subtitle of this final section, "Sentiments and Resentments," concludes the chapter. There are brief mentions and descriptions of Cardinals Mindszenty and Wyszyński and of Archbishops Slipyi and Sterniuk.

The final chapter, "Learning by Experience: The Conciliar Experience" (pp. 613-631) is reserved by Professor Alberigo to himself. Evidently he wished to draw out and discuss the conclusions of the volume in his own voice.

The first question to which he wished to respond was posed as follows: were the conciliar preparation accepted? Following his discussion of various considerations, several of which should have been restated, it is clear that it is his conclusion that this preparation must be rejected. It is not possible to argue, as he does argue, that because the first period of the Council's work ended without the approval of any decisions concerning the *schemata* that had been prepared, there was therefore "an unequivocal rejection of these preparations and a clear testimonial to the fact that the Council had become aware of its own identity and of its own proper historical role" (p. 615). In what I believe is a reference to himself and to those who have followed him in his brand of historical interpretation, the author adds that "only slowly and gradually have we come to perceive that the conditioning that grew out of the preparatory period was resistant to change in a high degree and that the council transcended this condition only partially and much less thoroughly than some have appeared to believe." (*Ibid*.; see also p. 618). But the question remains whether in the quest for unanimity one does not have to take into account the historical period comprising the entire second millennium.

Moving from "The Search for an Identity" to "Walking on One's Own Legs" is the path the author follows. He lays a special claim to John XXIII's *Gaudet mater ecclesia*, where the pontiff announced *aggiornamento* as the way towards arriving at the primacy of pastoral practice. Yet taking a stance which is quite unjustified and out of place, he continues to refer to "curial direction." He calls the Council's discussion of the means of social communication, or media, "a loss of time" (p. 616), and he speaks of the *schema* on Revelation as having been "buried"—an observation which is surely misleading. And one can only shake one's head with regard to his preoccupation with the fact that the preparatory *schemata* were supposedly "covered" by papal authority simply because the pope had given the authorization that these texts could be submitted to the bishops. That the pope had also expressed his personal approval of and his appreciation for these same texts when transmitting them to the bishops is another question that needs to be judged separately. But we can only ask: were not the bishops assembled precisely in order to discuss these texts and the subject matter they dealt with? Was this not a Council? Is nothing known about the history of the Church's councils?

Alberigo goes back and speaks again about his impression that the Council was something of a headless operation. This is an idea that we have confuted elsewhere. Alberigo modestly mentions again the lack of any "mature doctrinal elaboration" that could serve to realize authentic "Roncallian thought" (p. 619). But with all due respect, may we be permitted to ask whether this idea of "Roncallian thought" was even all that extraordinary? It seemed to have flashed out in very concrete and reconciling terms [when the Council was announced] in January 1959; hence the later eclipse of the scope of the reunion, in spite of the participation of numerous Christians, was not without cost. But as we read on about the proposal for the sending of an *apocrisarius*, or legate, from Constantinople to Rome, we have to say that it is not correct to refer to an ancient practice in this way, using this word. The ancient official who bore this title was a representative of the bishop of Rome in Constantinople; moreover, he represented the pope at the court of the Byzantine emperor [not of the patriarch of Constantinople]; it was, in fact, the first instance of sending out Apostolic Nuncios from Rome (p. 620). Also, the notion that Cardinal Bea was a protagonist at the Council second only to Pope John XXIII himself is a notion we believe we would have to ponder much more carefully, just as we can help doubting some other assertions of this author on page 620. It is useful, though, to recognize that "even the pope's ideas evolved as a result of the actual experience of the Council." That the pope should have wished to take his proper place at the Council, "contrary to what happened in the first two months" (p. 621), when "the bishops had to learn by experience" (p. 622), represented an intention to act in the role of "mediator" in which the pope in any case will not have been very greatly helped by his confessor, Monsignor A. M. Cavagna. Moreover, Alberigo's judgment concerning Cardinal Cicognani is quite prejudiced; the latter was naturally "the pope's man"—"his closest collaborator," in fact. He certainly did have an impact at the Council, along with the other protagonists in the gallery assembled by Alberigo. In any case, it is not exact to speak of the "disintegration" of the Italian bishops (p. 622), as if—we repeat—it really were a case of this author's "second preparation" for the Council. We will not repeat here what we have already quite amply said in covering the chapter by Grootaers, but it does appear to us that this is a fundamental point. Alberigo nevertheless proceeds along the same lines, judging and linking together very diverse personalities. He speaks of preoccupations with "doctrinal clarity and with the expectations for renewal" and with "a consistent recovery of the preparatory texts" (p. 624; it was not as presented). Supposedly it was Suenens and Philips who chose the way to go. But where were the others all the while? "The conciliar spirit overflowed into Catholicism everywhere," the author writes. But if that were the case, it is not clear how he could harbor any doubts about whether "the heady and even tumultuous experience of the ten weeks of the First Session could survive the dispersion of the bishops and their return to the normality of everyday life" (pp. 624ff.).

The "Unfolding of the Conciliar Experience" covers such things as adherences to this or that leader as well as theological up-datings—[the latter considered necessary] because the bishops were supposedly still back at the level of their own "seminary studies" (see also p. 631). But was that truly the case? Is this not a great simplification? Then there was [the question of] the improvement of the bishops' conferences; this was "a true and proper ecclesiological choice," the author says. If so, why did he feel the need to add that "it was tranquilly accepted and considered to be a functional necessity"? "The Council gave to Catholicism a liberty unheard of up to then" (p. 625). There was a reshuffling of "certainties," and the emergence both of a "new orthodoxy" and a "new conversion." The author judged those to be fragile, however, on account of the test case of the debate on the "religious life" (p. 626). This does not appear to us to be emblematic of the problem, however, particularly since it cuts to the heart of "deep fidelity," and is not just a matter of ideas.

The text continues with "From John to Paul," smoothly, we would say, but the differences [between the two popes] "were considerable, also in relation to the way they conducted the Council"—take, for example, the choice of the Moderators. "Very soon a new atmosphere was perceptible, one that was determined not just by the character of the new pope, but also by the particular formation that he had received...and also by his acute preoccupation with guaranteeing the greatest possible consensus concerning the decisions that were maturing, and that the Council would soon be taking" (p. 627).

"The Church in Council" provides the occasion to the author to take advantage of a certain conciliar triumphalism in dealing with such subjects as "the effects of the Council," "the mythical authoritativeness of the Council" (p. 631), and the fact that the Council truly "coincided with the end of the Constantinian era." Then there was the question of "the future the Council was moving towards." Certainly there was no way to anticipate an "assassination" (of John F. Kennedy; see p. 629). Indeed, no one could go far in attempting to predict the future.

But the author then returns to his "new initiative," though what was really at issue was the beginning of a new period. Alberigo concludes with another question: [did the First Session amount to] "eight useless weeks"? This was because the Council had not approved any document up to this point. Yet this provides the occasion to raise the question again of the famous downgrading of conciliar documents characteristic of the School of Bologna, namely, that "they were too abstract." How does this amount to saying, "no texts were approved, hence we can skip over studying the period in question"? But among other things, was it not necessary to prepare the texts carefully after examination and discussion of them? The study of the evolution of how certain texts came to be written and issued surely also counts as conciliar history. Who could possibly doubt this? Certainly the bishops acquired a greater consciousness of their own responsibilities towards the universal Church, but just because they recognized themselves to be "protagonists," why did it have to be added that they were also "no longer 'minor' obedient representatives of a 'higher authority'" (p. 631)? But who summoned these bishops to the Council in the first place, if it was not that same "higher authority"? Who invited them to list their true *desiderata* freely, even abolishing a prepared list of questions to be asked in order to accord greater liberty to them? Was not all this in view of having free debate at the Council? How difficult it is to overcome prejudices and preconceptions! The author, for his part, continues on with his criticism of "yes-men"—but would the ideal be, rather, "no-men"? Or would that depend on the circumstances or the material placed before them? The author's accusation is that there was "a uniformity of inspiration that was ideological rather than evangelical" in the Catholicism of the pre-conciliar years. And besides why limit to the First Session alone the idea of the great Synod as the New Pentecost? This was an idea dear to the heart of John XXIII, of course. Yet Pentecost is precisely what the Council did give us: it gave us the Word of the Spirit. Or, better still, it literally spoke to us in tongues, since men of many languages, cultures, and mentalities, working together within the same framework of faith and charity, gave us the authentic work of the Holy Spirit for today.

Although we must maintain our distances from much that is said in this volume, we can nevertheless endorse the book's last two lines, namely, that "those eight weeks occupy an indispensable place in the history of Vatican II, and for that reason figure in the history of this great event of the Spirit" (*Ibid.*).

An index of names and one of themes along with a Table of Contents and a few miscellaneous notes conclude the volume.

12

For the History of Vatican Council II
(Second Session and In-Between)

Alberigo Giuseppe, ed., with Various Authors, *Il concilio adulto. Il secondo periodo e la seconda intersessione, settembre, 1963-settembre, 1964* [The Adult Council: the Second Session and the Second Intersession, September, 1963—September, 1964]. Volume III of the *Storia del Concilio Vaticano II* [History of the Second Vatican Council], directed by Professor Giuseppe Alberigo, Il Mulino, Imola, 1998, 590 pages.

Following the index, but prior to the table of abbreviations and sources, this volume opens with the typical "Premise" of Professor Giuseppe Alberigo. From this it appears once again that, through no fault of the authors, access was lacking to some documents of great importance. For example, two volumes of "the titanic publishing enterprise of V. Carbone" (p. 10) necessary to bring out the full official conciliar sources were not available; these volumes related to the functions of the directive apparatus of the Council, specifically to the General Secretariat of the Council.

Also in this volume, however—Professor Alberigo hastens to note—"we have refrained from trying to untangle the lived experience of the Council, including in all its tortuousness, in favor of a thematic reconstruction of the Council, which is certainly more linear, but also less respectful of the concreteness of the event" (p. 9). "We understand" this choice of direction. We said so earlier in covering the second volume of this vast "history" (See the previous chapter). Moreover, conscious of the possible negative consequences of ending up, not with a true history of the Council, but rather almost with a kind of encyclopedia of the Council, in which each author promotes his own themes or points of view, we understand as well that "the differences in points of view of the various collaborators have been respected; indeed, that is one of the great values of the work" (*Ibid.*). This is true, especially given the present state of research on the great Council that Vatican II was. However, a "work of many hands" should not fail to arrive at critical solutions to some of the rather important questions concerning the Council.

Let us take one single example, that of the analysis of the papal formula used to promulgate the conciliar documents. In one and the same volume, Soetens treats this question one way (pp. 344-349), while Alberigo himself mentions it on another page (p. 525). And then, on the next page (p. 526), Alberigo treats it in a way rather different from that of Soetens. This latter scholar recognizes, in effect, that through the influence of Archbishop Pericle Felici (see p. 349, n. 286), as Pope Paul VI had wished and hoped, a formula beyond the mere expression of consensus was found. This formula was "more appropriate and more in conformity with the reality of what was being celebrated"—but it was "not exactly the one that had been proposed by the experts" (p. 348). It was decided at a high level to employ the term *potestas* rather than *auctoritas* [referring to that which was possessed by the pope], and the drafters were well aware of the difference. Then, the original term, "entire consensus," was replaced by three verbs which specified the character of the pope's power received directly from Christ; this was true even though the pope also declared himself to be acting in unity with the Fathers of the Council. All this was expressed in the following precise terminology: "The decrees...have pleased the Fathers. And we, by the apostolic power committed to us by Christ, along with the venerable Fathers, *in Spiritu Sancto*, approve them; we define, establish, and order that these things thus approved synodally in this manner are hereby promulgated, *ad Dei gloriam*" (*Ibid.*). The expressions that we have left here in the Latin, ["in the Holy Spirit" and "for the glory of God"], do not appear in the Italian text. Was it Soetens who left them out, or the translator? It is a bad sign, regardless. In any case, the formula, as Soetens himself observes, tends to turn the pontifical approval into an act of the primacy of the pope. For the author, on the other hand, it was an editorial improvement in comparison to the text that was envisaged in the conciliar Regulations. In the light of this background, though, we invite the patient reader to go himself to the page of Alberigo's text indicated above (p. 345) in order to verify for himself that the director of this vast study still goes on speaking of "consensus" (better, for us, would have been "in union with," which, by itself, though, does not express the idea of the pontifical power). In any case, the wording that was actually chosen—in the end by the pope himself—was actually inspired by the expression *una cum concilio*, ["one with the Council"], that was used by the Council of Florence. This formula was thus in no way a new one, and certainly it did not in any case change the substance of things (see p. 345). Why then does Alberigo insist on being different in this case in comparison to what he calls "a long period in both medieval and modern times"? (p. 526).

But we do state here at the outset, however, in favor of this volume III, that we found it to be greatly "matured" by comparison with the previous two volumes. To confirm this, we have noted that the sources published up to now—I refer to official sources in particular—have been much better assimilated this time. On the other hand, the influence of various "ideological" blocs continues to be in evidence. Thus, we consider that the knowledge and viewpoints of the authors should, in general, have been enlisted in a much better cause—that of seeking the greatest possible objectivity.

The first contribution to the research contained in this volume is that of A. Melloni. He covers the entire Second Session of the Council along with the great ecclesiological debate that took place then. His care and attention are good and his writing is compact. Unfortunately, however, his text is marred with serious errors stemming from his faulty vision of things. It is not pleasing to us to have to identify them and to have to describe them as "preconceptions." But we are obliged to do so.

The first of them concerns the role of Father G. Dossetti. This is hardly surprising since "the School of Bologna" was actually founded by him (see pp. 24ff.). "Dossetti proposed to endow the assembly with instruments of self-government that would be both efficient and functional" (pp. 25 and 27). He wanted to "disengage the conciliar commissions from their condition of servitude to the Holy Office" (p. 27). The author adds: "Cardinal Agagianian was out of the picture" (p. 28). But who engineered this and with what right? (see p. 64). Would the cardinal have chosen a role of what the author calls "passive collaboration"? (But see p. 100, n. 335). The Council's Moderators, as is well known, "named" Father Dossetti as their secretary. Would they not have been aware that he was not actually a Council *peritus,* and "did not enjoy access to the *aula*"? The view is also not to accept that Dossetti's project for the Regulations was not brought forward in time and so the Council went forward along other lines (p. 29, n. 45; p. 30, n. 46; and p. 100). But it is quite certain, however, that authoritative historians (e. g. Carbone, Maccarrone, and Martina) have made clear that Alberigo has greatly exaggerated the role played by Father Dossetti at the Council. We would add that his "progressive extremism" involved a great deal more than just "simple anti-conservatism" (p. 104, note 350); it actually harmed the "cause" being defended by the "majority." Undaunted, however, Melloni follows Alberigo in the latter's usual friendly overvaluation [of the role of Father Dossetti]. And we should note well that none of this judgement of mine had anything to do with internal Italian politics.

In the second place, it is necessary to recognize Melloni's mistaken vision of Vatican Council I (see pp. 81 and 123). According to him, this Council was dominated by "a lobby which had the capability of getting its own viewpoint adopted"; he carries on with his usual anti-curial viewpoint; this is seen in his mention of the "doctrinal commission," which was supposedly "a faithful mirror of the Curia's organization chart," and which "reflected the typical curial ecclesiological positions" (pp. 19, 25, and 119). Those who seem to be particularly blameworthy here were Cardinal Cicognani and Archbishop Felici, who supposedly formed an "axis," dedicated to limiting the agenda of the Council, among other aims (p. 25). They are seen as agents of the Secretariat of State and the Curia generally, especially the former, Cardinal Cicognani, who "acted on the work of the assembly as the curial instrument aimed at carrying out the will of the pontiff" (pp. 22, 26). But was he not, as the Secretary of State, by his office the principal collaborator of the pope? (p. 30, n. 1; pp. 31-32). In any case, it was not the task of the Curia to reform itself; it was the pope's task.

To this supposed "axis" the author opposes the Moderators (delegates), who received "from Pope Paul VI himself the task of representing him in the *aula* and providing direction to the debates" (p. 22; then see p. 27, n. 36 esp.; pp. 28-29). The Belgian Monsignor Albert Prignon, however, judged "the Dossetti Project" with the Moderators to be "exaggerated, imprudent, and very dangerous." But in the end, were not the Moderators representatives of the pope? Cardinal Cicognani certainly thought so (p. 26). On the contrary the definition of "representative" of the assembly is rather indicative a certain way of "thinking democratically"—in a matter which is not political.

It is in this context that the author considers the actions of Pope Paul VI, whom he views too readily as a "novice" (p. 33). "The work of running a Council represented a novitiate within a novitiate"— which included, we should realize, dealing with a variety of persons, opinions, proposals, etc. But the power of decision on all this was reserved to him in the end (see, for example, pp. 22ff., 25ff., and 29ff.). The whole affair should have been instructive; in general, however, the appropriate consequences with regard to the working of the Regulations, for example, should have been drawn following "the vote of October 16," the destruction of the ballots prepared by the Moderators, and the presentation of a text "controlled" by Dossetti.

It was on this occasion that Pope Paul VI said that the position of "secretary" of the Moderators was not the place of Father Dossetti. The latter's consequent withdrawal was euphemistically characterized by his friends as a "voluntary withdrawal" (p. 99, n. 332). Yet it was the same Father Dossetti who subsequently wrote an "extremist" paper for Cardinal Lercaro in preparation for the meeting of the supercommission (p. 100, n.335). Following this, while the iron was still hot, he prepared yet another paper along the same lines (p. 100, n. 339). "Will we succeed in saving the Council"? he is said to have asked. But who was saving whom?

However, at the outset, in the text of Melloni there appears the "scandal" of the supposed intervention of [German Chancellor] Konrad Adenauer and [Italian President] Antonio Segni, which had already been reported in newspapers in search of "sensationalism." In fact, it was simply an expression of opinion in Adenauer's case, of judgments of his and of a "dream" of his, as came out in a Report sent to Paris; as for Segni, he supposedly told (through Luigi Gedda) the Italian cardinals and others that if Cardinal Montini were to emerge victorious from the conclave, it was his conviction that he would commit the Church to a policy in favor of a political "opening to the left" in Italy. All of this depended on a number of "ifs," of course, as we should note well. Moreover, it was only Segni's "conviction" anyway, even if this conviction was that of a prominent man. There was no "coercion" here; he merely "made his conviction known, if indeed he did" (p. 20).

It is in this same vein that the author continues with his suppositions and speculations concerning the conclave and a supposed "commitment"—or, rather, "an informal though explicit accord between the cardinals and the one they elected." This accord was supposedly concluded in order to obtain votes that would guarantee "the continuation of Vatican II along the lines of *aggiornamento*." Melloni echoes in yet another vein another hypothesis according to which there was also a "Spellman-Montini" meeting which supposedly "garnered conservative votes for the Milanese cardinal" (p. 21). Poor Cardinal Montini! What he had to go through to get elected pope!

This type of "research" continues with the topics "preparations for the assembly"—and here, in terms that are quite inappropriate, the author again speaks of a "second preparation for the Council" (p. 25). Further topics include: "the meetings of the bishops," "problems, comments, and 'a-Catholic' positions," and "the work" of the various commissions. Yet, even here, the terminology can be deceptive when mention is made of "new" *schemata*. It is often noted, though, that a revision is what is actually being discussed. A Moderator—certainly not a member of the "minority"—maintained that the "new" *schema De Ecclesia* contained 60 percent of the "old text (see p. 98 of *Acta Synodalia*, Vol. 6). The author then covers—but always in line with the same train of thought (see pp. 61 and 63ff.)—"the new initiatives: the return of the Council." He explains this through what he calls "voyages and arrivals" as well as through listing various "participants" (including bishops, theologians, laity, journalists, and observers). How much more precise and measured is the treatment of these same elements by M. Velati in the book *L'evento e le decisioni. Studi sulle dinamiche del Concilio Vaticano II* (The Event and the Decisions: On the Dynamics of Vatican Council II], Imola, 1997; see, especially, page 389 of this book. Velati accurately judges their contribution to the development of the conciliar texts. Melloni, in fact, mentions only two theologians, Marie-Dominique Chenu and Joseph Fenton. He also provides a summary of the allocution of Paul VI and mentions several courtesy audiences granted by the pope, notably the one granted for the journalists at the Council.

The author quite appropriately gives specific attention to the ecclesiological question, particularly in what he calls "the first steps" in the debate (pp. 58-80). He does the same for "the debate on collegiality" (pp. 80-96). And we have already offered some critical observations above in anticipation of the false conclusions that Melloni draws on the subject of the Church as sacrament. The new vision was extended "to make more acceptable the idea that this terminology (sacrament) could go beyond the Tridentine limitations that recognized only the seven sacraments, *nec plures, nec pauciora* ["neither more, nor less"], which were supposed to have marked the difference between Catholicism and Protestantism" (p. 65). Also to be taken into account here is the rather heavy language with which Cardinal Alfrink admitted to Cardinal Ruffini (p. 67, n. 191, the point of this extension beyond the seven sacraments. Does the author realize the seriousness of what he is saying here? Does he not understand that our Eastern Christian brothers have preserved and confirmed "the seven sacraments"?)

Before getting into his treatment of collegiality, Melloni proceeds with his interpretation of what he calls "substantive and procedural interferences and debates." He presents the concrete results of all the work of the commissions carried out between the sessions. The subjects covered include: missions, religious life, seminarians, clerics, and subjects of the *schema XVII*, the apostolate of the laity, the liturgy, and Christianity. Meanwhile, he writes, "the doctrinal commission was experiencing a time of dramatic indecision" (p. 77). He takes note of the actions of various "informal groups," some of them pressure groups. In this connection, he incorrectly and unjustly refers to the well-known *Coetus Internationalis Patrum* [International Group of Fathers], which he styles "the nucleus of what would prove to be the anti-conciliar splinter group at the Council" (p. 78). Here his judgment should have been more measured so as not to fall into the trap of condemning as "anti-conciliar" the group which merely had a few "extremists" in its ranks—as, indeed, was the case for the conciliar "majority" as well, *mutatis mutandis*.

Coming to his treatment of the subject of collegiality, we clearly see the great confusion of the author, who uses terms indistinctly and in a way that lacks precision. At bottom his error is the same as that of those who considered themselves harmed or injured by the famous *Nota Explicativa Praevia*. This *Nota*, crafted in order to achieve the much desired consensus among the Council Fathers, actually—and happily—clarified and made more precise the terms of the overall debate. Many Council Fathers were not so much opposed to collegiality as they were to certain personal visions of what was supposedly involved in it. The same kind of thing proved to be the case with regard to the debate concerning the revival of the diaconate (pp. 82ff., n. 256). In this connection, it would be instructive for any reader who might wish to check on what Melloni says to read the actual words contained in the interventions of Cardinals Spellman, Ruffini, and Bacci (they can be found in *Acta Synodalia*, Vol. 2, pp. 82-89). Moreover, this author should never have had recourse to the much abused category of "Roman Canonists" in discussing the debate on collegiality. Similarly he should never have tried to make look ridiculous those "adversaries" he identifies who were allegedly still back "in the Middle Ages." There was a millennium of careful thought, after all, none of it monolithic, behind what had emerged at Vatican Council I.

In any case, with the author's treatment of the "partial and directional votes" (pp. 87-96), we arrive at the heart of the matter for this particular phase of the Council. It is here that all the complications connected with the role of Father Dossetti came out, as we have discussed above. Things were also complicated by the immediate implementation of the reform of the liturgy, which was occurring at the same time. An "abridged law" was spoken about (p. 87). There was also the "journalistic counterattack" of the *Avvenire d'Italia* (p. 93), and the reaction of Father Dossetti himself, who "goaded" both Cardinal Lercaro and Cardinal Suenens on the matter (p. 95, n. 312, p. 99). The ambiguity of his own interpretation, which was echoed by others, of the words of the Holy Father—considered to be a "green light" by many (pp. 87ff. and 94)—caused Dossetti to formulate his "propositions" (or questions) in four (later five) points. The mistake became glaringly evident to all when the pope himself decided to destroy the ballots prepared for this purpose. Whatever benefit is to be derived from this inventory can be gathered, along with numerous "*distinguo*," on pages 92-93.

Indicative of the misunderstanding of the Moderators themselves is the way the whole affair was viewed by the Secretary General of the Council, who was officially charged as the appropriate conciliar "executive organ" with regard to...the press (p. 92). We refer to the first volume of the *Acta Synodalia* (AS), page 552, where Archbishop Felici, in a note to the pontiff dated December 12, 1963, writes as follows: "The Most Eminent Moderators, at the beginning of the work of the Second Session, believed that they could act independently of the Secretary General, basing their actions on the work of the Reverend Father Dossetti. Following the intervention of the Holy

Father, the relationship with the General Secretariat has improved." What follows in this text regarding this same question speaks volumes about the attitude of Melloni and of the School of Bologna (p. 92). However, to understand this question, it would be worthwhile to read the *Commentarius* of Archbishop Felici, dated October 17, 1963 (always in AS, vol. 6, p. 374, 7) and his later one dated October 21. His reservations concerned both the content of the "propositions" as well as with the manner in which they were drafted. But it is enough, although it is rather difficult, to examine the synopsis showing the evolution of the text of the propositions which is printed as an appendix in the book (see pp. 536-553). This examination makes clear that, in spite of efforts to the contrary (see p. 100, n. 337), the difference between the first draft and the final one approved by the pontiff is very great. The pope himelf made personal corrections (see p. 118). The efforts to the contrary amounted to a weakening of the text where a Dossetti-Philips convergence was proposed (p. 107, n. 362).

However, the crisis was resolved for the most part, although there was some foot-dragging, thanks to the work of a "super-commission" on which there was representation of all the directional entities of the Council, that is, the Council Presidency, the Central Coordinating Commission, the Moderators, and the General Secretariat.

Melloni allots space here to the lively and spirited Cardinal Eugène Tisserant, whose presidency he describes as "free and easy" and "energetic," as well as to his liking (p. 104), and who from time to time showed the "polemical" quality of his "thought." But this case too calls for an invitation to the reader to refer back directly to what was really said, without the mediation of this author. Two citations should suffice here. The first one presents Felici taking down the minutes, and then, in difficulty, supposedly saying that "no one here has understood anything of what we have said" (p. 120). Thus, for Melloni, he is apparently not accurately summarizing in the minutes what was actually being said at the meeting. However, this was done by Carbone and Fagiolo, whose papers Melloni claims were "inaccessible at the time" (p. 105, n. 352). However, we challenge the reader to try to understand, by going over the true minutes of the meeting, what was actually said. Turning to Tisserant, what Felici actually said was: "It is necessary to call for the vote. And then, secondly, on the procedure for approving amendments, which no one here has understood anything about. We have to know this because we have to act properly in regulating it" (see AS, vol. 1, p. 732). The second citation we wanted to mention contains a very serious accusation to the effect that "the minutes record the meeting as the Secretary of State wished to have it recorded" (p. 105). But let's be serious and not throw out accusations of falsehood without proof!

Along the same lines, and at the very last equivocal, is another citation by the author concerning a papal invitation to the Doctrinal Commission to speed up its work. The author only gives half of the pope's statement (p. 105). He leaves out the first part of what the pope said, where the latter clearly recognized the enormous amount of work, the Doctrinal Commission had to do (see AS, Vol. 2, p. 12). The entire tone of the pope's communication was different from the way it is presented by Melloni. In the end, the pope was fully appreciative of the difficulties involved.

There follows the author's treatment of "the intersection of the debates," "the Marian question," and "the meeting of the Doctrinal Commission on the 29th." In this connection, Melloni mentions again "the immense and useless preparatory machinery of the Council" (p. 116). He also goes back to treat several questions already mentioned above, including "the choices and the voting," where his comments and evaluations are at the very least tendentious (see p. 122ff.). He also treats other points concerning Dossetti, the "investiture" of the Council Fathers with the Moderators, and what he calls "tri-polarity" (which for him consists of the Council-Moderators, the Curia-Secretariat of State, and the Pope). He speaks of Pope Paul VI as "serving as a 'filter' between the *aula* and the conciliar commissions," and also of "the non-consideration of the local church." In any case, for Melloni, "from the 30th of October on, collegiality and Vatican II were synonyms, and to call one into question was to call the other into question as well." But we have to ask: what kind of collegiality is he talking about? Then, apropos of the expression, "we won," with which

Paul VI supposedly received the Moderators, following the famous vote, it is necessary to recall that it was Cardinal Lercaro himself—if we do recall correctly—who put this into its proper perspective, ascribing it to the elevation of the personality of Pope Montini, a man *super partes.*

Subsequently, the author anticipates—usefully, he says—"a lengthy work of revision" of *De Ecclesia*, which he describes as the "Philips *schema.*" He makes no mention of the around sixty percent of the original text that was still included in the final draft. There remain many other questions and clarifications concerning some of the affirmations of Melloni here—on the magisterium (pp. 125 and 128), on the *ordo episcopalis* (p. 129), and on the question of infallibility (p. 130). But our critique of this author has already gone on long enough and needs to be brought to a close.

Chapter II of the volume was assigned to J. Famerée, and treats the subject of "bishops and dioceses-November 5-15, 1963." Following what he calls the "total defeat of the minority on *De Ecclesia*" during the month of October—we would tread very softly with regard to a claim such as this—the author first discusses the *schema* entitled *De episcopis ac de dio ecesium regimine.* Here again we encounter a lack of precision in this author's use of terms, concerning collegiality, for example though he does not always get this one wrong. But he also speaks of "radical ultramontanism," the "monarchical power" of the bishops, their "individualistic ardor," and even of "the papal monarchy," as well as employing yet other exaggerated expressions (see pp. 140, 144 and 149). He further speaks of "emotional argumentation" rather than using the word "traditional." Cardinal Lercaro is presented as "without any doubt the greatest moral and religious authority in the conciliar assembly." He also freely employs military terminology in a way that is not pleasing: we read of "laying down arms" (p. 140), "gun sights" (p. 141), "launching an attack" (p. 143), "shots exchanged" (p. 146), "duel" (p. 152), the "conciliar tempest" (p. 156), to "disarm" (p. 160), a "combative minority" (p. 163), a "conflict" (p. 169), and an "exchange of fire" (P. 191). This kind of vocabulary seems excessively bellicose for a Church council of our day. And in spite of the considerable critical work on the *schema*, the text nevertheless successfully "passed" on to the next conciliar phase with the approval of 1610 of the Council Fathers who voted for it—and that was no small thing.

Famerée divides up his presentation among a number of topics such as "the apology for centralization" (there wasn't one) and the "Frings-Ottaviani duel: conflict between the majority and the minority at the summit. Instead of bearing in mind what Cardinal Frings actually said, however, the author minimizes the whole controversy (p. 147, n. 52). Other topics included are: "retirement at a fixed age" and "Ruffini against Maximos IV [Saigh]," where the author quotes the "Solomonic" comment of Cardinal Tisserant (p. 55, n. 72). Then comes "an authorized reply [by Cardinal Döpfner] to attacks by the minority," followed by "episcopal assemblies without juridical power," and "a purely pastoral foundation"—these latter two topics being closed with question marks. Finally, there is "a divided majority," the division in question coming particularly on the subject of the foundation and authority of episcopal conferences.

The author's analysis continues with the topic of "a new attack on collegiality." We would say, more properly, a new attack on a certain vision of it or a certain direction taken by the discussion of it. Yet other topics include: "dioceses neither too large nor too small," "a minor and pragmatic chapter (IV)," and "a beginning more pastoral than theological." We still have to ask this author if the "new" *schema* to be revised was truly "new," after having been approved by 1610 Council Fathers, as we have just noted (p. 174; see also p. 184, n. 160). Since there is a distinct tendency in some of today's "exegetes" of the Council to separate preparatory work from later developments and revisions, almost as if each version had been produced from scratch—and since we have also noted this same tendency in the work of Melloni—we are obliged to note here that "amendments" and "revisions" to the text and such must be carefully considered by those doing research on the Council—as we ourselves are endeavoring to do.

The author proceeds with his examination, presenting what he calls a "balance-sheet in chiaroscuro" in which we are happy to report the author's view that "the theme of the modality of selecting bishops... was not discussed as such" (p. 174). But Famerée is forgetting here that the Congregation *de Propaganda Fide* and the pope in fact select the bishops in the Western Church. This fact should lead us to think—what almost never happens—of the pope's status also as patriarch. Professor Alberigo, for his part, will regret later on the lack of any discussion of this subject (see p. 521); and he does so using inexact language applied in a context that is simply false, for example, when he refers to the false judgement of "the heterodoxy of the conciliar majority."

The author then continues, speaking about the relationship of Cardinal Lercaro's program to the conciliar activity of the Second Session. He also speaks about "the many meetings that took place on the margin of the assembly." These included meetings among the members of the Secretariat for Promoting Christian Unity as well as "the Tuesday meetings of the observers." In this last case, it would have been better if he had taken into account the more balanced and "historical" judgments of M. Velati mentioned above. The other groups covered by the author include the group known as "Jesus, the Church and the poor" and the "conciliar commissions."

Famerée devotes particular attention to the *Coetus Internationalis Patrum* which he presents as more institutionalized than it actually was; he speaks of "inscribed members" and "Curia members." We must ask who those latter Curia members were. His view contrasts with that of L. Perrin, whom he otherwise cites quite often (see p. 188, n. 176), particularly from an article by Perrin included in the work *L'evento e le decisioni* [The Event and the Decisions] (p. 172).

But as far as Perrin is concerned, "there does not exist any archive of documents or records" for the *Coetus*. The documents that exist, according to him, are "uneven and mediocre." He does indicate some "convergences that vary geometrically" (p. 185), and he also speaks of "the complexity of the world of the Curia" (*Ibid.*). The research of Famerée, though, basically follows the study by S. Gomez de Arteche. We cannot therefore agree with his characterization of the *Coetus* as "an anti-Council bloc" (p. 187, n. 171). Nor can we accept the title "the catalyzer of the minority" (thus, of the Council itself). Nor can we agree to characterize its actions as "parliamentary" (p. 188). The "abundant ramifications" of the *Coetus* that he mentions seem to us to have resulted from a variety and amalgamation of various positions, all tending in the same general direction, in fact, more than they seem to be the results of any particular investigation by the author (see, for instance, the first part of his n.183).

In this connection, we quote the following passage: "As for the content, it included a number of the typical characteristics of the minority: a radical ultramontanism opposed to anything that even appeared to be an attenuation of pontifical absolutism (the *relatio* of Carli, Ruffini, Batanian, Ottaviani, Browne, Lefebvre); tenacious opposition to the 'new' doctrine of episcopal collegiality (Ruffini, Florit, Del Pino Gomez, Ottaviani, De Castro Meyer, Lefebvre, Carli); a quibbling opposition to the directional vote of October 30 and the final decision of the Council, or, rather, of the Doctrinal Commission (Ruffini, Browne, Florit, Ottaviani, Carli)" (p. 191). A more serious problem for this author in the context of the presumed "antennae" of the *Coetus* in different strategic positions within the official organs of the Council (p. 192, n. 190) is that the *Coetus* "benefited from important sources of support and also enjoyed access to the directing organs of the Council: to the Council Presidency, thanks to Cardinals Ruffini and Siri; and to the General Secretariat and the Central Coordinating Commission through Archbishop Felici, who was originally from Segni, and was a valuable ally of Bishop Carli of Segni, and hence of the *Coetus* itself. Then there was Archbishop Dino Staffa [Secretary of the Sacred Congregation of Universities and Seminaries]." The reader will have caught the drift of the seriousness of the author's assertions here: apparently it was enough to have come from Segni in order to be classified as an "ally" of Bishop Carli…

The author concludes, however, that "only on September 29, 1964, did a cardinal—Cardinal Rufino Santos of Manila—officially offer his support to the organization…though other cardinals (Ruffini, Siri, Larraona and Browne) hosted the meetings of the group on Tuesday evenings. The attention thus given to the *Coetus*, once it was fully organized, made it possible for the group to gather as many as 450 signatures of the Fathers in support of determinate positions" (p. 192). We believe that this fact alone constitutes a sufficient reply [to the accusations lodged against the *Coetus*], and it should be kept in mind in the interests of objectivity.

The eighth and last point analyzed by Famerée has to do with the instruments of social communication, which the Council considered between November 14 and 25, 1963. The author speaks of an approval "rushed through the various conciliar stages" and also of "growing opposition that arose too late." There was an "incident" that grew out of the distribution of a critical document that opposed the *schema*; according to the author, this was "revelatory of the dissatisfaction" with the Council's documents in this case. The Cardinal President, however, dismissed such opposition to "a *schema* that was duly prepared, duly presented and debated, and duly approved" (p. 206). The author discovers here an ideological bias, and he is not alone in doing so. The bias in question was supposedly that "the content of the preparatory texts should be modified as little as possible"—but he reveals *his* "ideology" in making this charge (*Ibid.*). It is worthwhile stating in this regard that "the preservation of the preparatory *schemata* as the basis of the Council's work" was a "Belgian choice" (see, for example, Perrin at page 187). Certainly there was an established conciliar strategy aimed at working for a *consensus*, but this was hardly "ideological." Hence it would be useful for this author to read the "Observations on the Conciliar Treatment of the s*chema* entitled *De mediis communicationis socialis*" which Archbishop Felici presented to the pope on December 19, 1963 (see AS, Vol. 6, pp. 568-570).

Chapter III, "Towards the Liturgical Reform," is the work of R. Kaczynski. He follows the conciliar process that applied to this subject from its beginning stages all the way through to the approval of the finished text at the end. He examines the definitive text and goes on to look at developments following the issuance of various documents (see "Institution of the *Consilium ad exsequendam constitutionem de sacra liturgia*" [Consilium to execute the Constitution on the Sacred Liturgy]). The research here is interesting and timely, but often it is not balanced in the judgments that are derived from it. Some asperity appears, especially with regard to Archbishop Dante (see pp. 224, 228, and 230) as well as towards other "personages"—see, for example, pages 258 and 260, in which it becomes clear that the procedure of the Holy See with respect to documents "in formation" (p. 267) is not understood. The same case is taken up again against "the functionaries of the Congregation" and is repeated on page 269. To us it seems that anyone prepared to appeal to the Regulations, even if merely for the purpose of maintaining what is "just and convenient" (in the ecclesial sense), is on the right track. Such a person should not lightly be accused of holding up the work of the Council. The author, meanwhile, evidences difficulties in his comprehension of juridical and canonical language (pp. 247ff.; 251, n. 154; 252; and 276, n. 222).

Let us also take note of serious deficiencies in the author's treatment of the question of not allowing regular "Communion from the chalice" (p. 250), as well as of his radical judgments concerning the Middle Ages (p. 251) and his view of the relationships between the universal and the local Church (p. 255). He employs a most unhappy expression here when he speaks of "a magical understanding of the sacraments" (p. 237); this idea would seem to have been derived from one of "maintaining Latin at least in the formulas for the sacraments." He also exhibits a certain ambiguity in his interpretation that favors new rites within the Roman rite (p. 244). His is a very superficial interpretation of what brought about the diminution of participation in the sacraments following the reform of the liturgy (p. 254). Let us take note also that Joseph Reuss was the auxiliary bishop of Mainz, not an archbishop (p. 231). Also, Father Giulio Bevilacqua was a "great friend" of the pope, not his "collaborator" (p. 259). Moreover, conciliar texts *can* appropriately cite Roman pontiffs (p. 233). And the author's reference to the feminine presence at the Council seems rather malicious (p. 243, n. 143).

This author's judgment seems heavy indeed when he delivers himself of such dicta as this: "With the publication of the *Motu*

Proprio"—he styles it "disappointing" (p. 269)—"*Sacram Liturgiam* in *Acta Apostolicae Sedis*, the Roman way of acting aroused indignation" (p. 276). Still it is a bit much to declare that "the bishops...no longer gave their support to the Roman Curia" (p. 272).

The topic in Chapter IV, "The Ecumenical Commitment of the Catholic Church," is handled in a study that is rather good by C. Soetens. His work is divided up into a number of topics: "From Theory to Reality" discusses the fact of the issuance of an official conciliar document on Christian unity; the conciliar debate on ecumenism; the existence of two delicate problems, namely, the Jewish one and religious liberty; and the views of the non-Catholic observers. The next division of Soetens is entitled: "A Difficult Problem: the Organization of the Council." This topic covers the question of who was supposed to direct the Council; the Doctrinal Commission that was at the center of so many controversies; and the further question of whether the conciliar commissions should be reorganized and expanded. Soetens then deals with "The Final Days under a Cloud," which includes a number of issues and proceedings: the recognition of the faculties of the bishops; the closure of the Second Session; the two documents that were promulgated [liturgy and media] in the first two Sessions; the closing discourse of the pope; impressions of the Second Session as a whole; and the "extension" of the Council as a result of the visit of Pope Paul VI to the Holy Land.

While we can basically accept the research of this particular author, we nevertheless feel obliged to offer some critical remarks. They concern such things as the author's judgment on the message of Paul VI to Constantinople (p. 276) and to the Theological Commission (p. 301). The author lacks, as we said earlier, an initial approach that would change the tone of the whole presentation so that it would not elicit a *non placet* reply (p. 323, n. 172). Then there is his evaluation of the Commission for the Oriental Churches (p. 285, but with an attenuation on p. 288, n. 45). This is followed by his views on Roman theology (p. 290); on the "papal monarchy" (p. 295); on "the men of Ottaviani" (p. 301, n. 96, but with a qualification of Congar); on anti-semitism (p. 304); on religious liberty (p. 305, n. 114, adhering to an erroneous judgment of D. Gonnet, p. 308); on "modern conscience"; on "the effective direction of the Council"; and on "the curial counteroffensive." With regard to the "role" of the observers, we refer to the citation quoted above from Velati. And as for the "role" of Dossetti (pp. 321 and 322ff.), we have already expressed at the beginning our critical point of view about him. Soetens' entire introduction in these pages on the Doctrinal Commission (pp. 321 and 322ff.) conveys the viewpoint that everything was intensely and inevitably polarized. He uses words such as "hegemony," as is the case also in his discussion of the faculties of bishops (p. 340). This phraseology he uses identifies his viewpoint unmistakably (p. 341).

A bit of confusion emerges, finally, apropos of the question of the theological character of the conciliar texts. He is very desirous of going beyond classical "juridical distinctions" (p. 344). But he is also confused about "collegiality" (p. 355), as he is about the differences between recognition of the state of Israel and establishing diplomatic relations with Israel (p. 363).

The longest chapter in this volume, Chapter V, is the work of E. Vilanova (pp. 367-512) and concerns the "intersession," [that is, the period between the Second and Third Sessions], in 1963-1964. This period was characterized by a "spectacular dynamism" (p. 369). The author appears to have made a good effort to bear in mind the difference between official and personal sources. His work is precise and fundamentally valid, although there occur several defective judgments which we believe were too easily thrown out; they are excessive or unbalanced, and lacking in objectivity. We shall take note of them as we go along.

His treatment is satisfactory, however, in terms of his respect for history and his practice, in general, of making the proper distinctions regarding the Roman Curia (see p. 371), this is true also of his coverage of the interventions which many bishops thought they were obliged to make, particularly Cardinal Döpfner, with "his" famous "plan" to reduce the number of *schemata* and their content almost to the bone

(p. 377, n. 29). This author is also correct, in general, in describing the development of the various conciliar texts in relation to their origins. He speaks, for example, of *textus correctus, emendatus,* I, II, III, IV, V, and of "version" or "draft." He does mention, quite improperly, however, a "second preparation" (p. 367), and he even refers to a "third," in the manner of Grootaers (*Ibid.*, n. 1).

In any case, his treatment at the beginning is more subject to concentrated criticism (see p. 368) because he repeats a number of commonplaces, for example: "The Roman atmosphere was such during the intersession that some of the representatives of the majority were often virtually isolated" (*Ibid.*). Supposedly there were various "mixed" situations from which inferences are drawn concerning the "Cicognani-Felici axis and the adversaries of renewal in general" (p. 379). He speaks of a "triumvirate" of Tisserant, Cicognani, and Felici (p. 368). In this regard, there must be borne in mind what even John XXIII had to say, namely, that during the intersession, "we are [still] in Council," and not in a minor phase of it, either, just because the assembly is not sitting. This is a point made by Alberigo himself (p. 368, n. 2). It is therefore necessary to proceed with caution with respect to the plainly "many-headed" structure of the Council itself. (pp. 372, 374, 383 and 469). Vilanova's view is even more open to criticism, though, when we recall his own reference to the word "headless...*paradoxically* employed by Alberigo." Above all, we must recall that Pope Paul VI left vague and indefinite the role of his "representatives" ("directing organisms") so that he could protect his own role as the "head" of everybody. In any case, we do not believe it is exact to describe the Secretary General as the "intermediate organism between the pope and the assembly" (p. 373), and then to attribute to him at a certain point the removal to a distance of the Moderators (*Ibid.*). Rather, along with Dossetti, they considered themselves to be independent from the Secretary General and, indeed, they regarded him almost as their "agent to carry out their orders." The notable episode of the destruction of the prepared ballots proves this.

Further on, Vilanova's examination of the working procedures followed by the conciliar commissions seems to be rather "ideological."

This is the case with regard to his attribution to the ecclesiastical hierarchy of a "preoccupation" with the laity. According to him, the hierarchy feared "to lose its juridical and theological position," which was considered to be that of a "superior caste" (p. 410). Similarly, his judgment concerning the relationship of Catholics "with believers of other religions" is surely unbalanced (p. 413). The same goes for his views on "worker priests," not to speak of those on the "medieval *contemptus mundi.*"

And as for the "certain ambiguity" (p. 441) with which the author describes the papal initiative presenting thirteen "suggestions" for Chapter III of *De Ecclesia*, this ambiguity must certainly be qualified by Vilanova's own presentation. In passing, let us note that "the third meeting of the Central Coordinating Commission" (p. 436) was actually the thirteenth; and that "Professor Dino Staffa" (p. 444) was not a professor but an archbishop. And regarding the "boycotting' of the ecclesiological constitution (p. 446), we refer the reader to what we said above regarding the use of the Regulations; the same goes for all the references to "innovators" and "conservatives" found here. And with regard to the "pressures" from the Secretary of State" (p. 452), we refer to what the author himself said earlier, when he added "probably," suggesting doubt (p. 451).

Regarding religious liberty, clarification can be obtained by the perusal of a study by Joseph Komonchak that appeared in the volume *Vatikanum II und Modernisierung. Historiche, theologische und soziologische Perspektiven* [Vatican II and Modernizing: Historical, Theological, and Sociological Perspectives], Paderborn, 1996, page 167 (This volume is reviewed in Chapter XXIV of the present work). Komonchak distinguishes between American-style liberalism and European; this second type of liberalism is ideological and is riddled with relativism and indifferentism. Also ambiguous here is the author's accusation to the effect that the conciliar preparation represented an "overfull approach" (p. 465) as far as the conciliar *schemata* were concerned. In truth, however, the true case here was that the liberty was granted to the bishops to present their own conciliar proposals; this liberty was expressly granted by Pope John XXIII.

We observe further that Vilanova has not taken cognizance of the fact that the proposal of Father Dossetti for the Regulations arrived too late to be considered (pp. 467ff.). Note 344 is indicative of the "general absolution" imparted to Dossetti in absolute and unfounded subordination to the line of thought of Alberigo, who was his friend. Dossetti exhibits in his judgments uncritical assumptions concerning "parliamentary usages" and "imperial ones (senatorial or other)" (p. 468).

At this point, the author offers a broad analysis of Pope Paul VI's encyclical *Ecclesiam Suam* and its impact on the Council. Here again, there are some deficiencies (see pp. 475 and 478ff.) such as those on the theme of "the statutes of the episcopal conferences" (pp. 490ff.). With regard to the launching of the liturgical reform, the author again employs two weights and two measures; see, for example, the judgments he offers on Holland (p. 496), on what he calls "the positive liberalization with regard to the Latin rites" (p. 498), and on what is styled "the theodicy of domination" in Africa (p. 505).

We arrive at the "conclusion" of the book. Entitled "The New Physiognomy of the Council," it was written by Giuseppe Alberigo himself along the lines of this professor's well-known "theses." There is the one of the "new beginning," for example, indicated by "the second preparation" (p. 514). This was already adumbrated on the previous page, as follows: "The imposing material produced by the complex machinery set up to prepare for the Council was criticized, challenged, and refuted." The author should at least have added "in part" here; instead, he goes on to say: "It continued to weigh on the work of the Council, whether as a renewed *apologia* on the part of its protagonists, or in the form of a tenacious resistance to the image of the Council that in fact developed" (p. 513).

What is assumed here are the ideas of a necessarily "revolutionary" Vatican II as well as a so-called "institutional solitude" (p. 514) which "isolated John XXIII," the new Moses who had brought to the people of God new "tables" inscribed with the words "pastoral practice" and *"aggiornamento"*—which then became "the platform of the Council itself."

Professor Alberigo, however, in a subtitle, writes of "continuity in innovation" (p. 515). On the face of it, this [reference to continuity] aroused in us a hope for a more balanced reading of the Council. But in vain. He immediately turned right back onto the same old track where he had experienced such "frequent impressions" of a "headless" Council (p. 515); where he had encountered "the intransigence of Felici" (*Ibid.*; but see also p. 516); and where "Cardinal Cicognani had transformed the Central Coordinating Commission into the supreme authority for the direction of the Council" (p. 515). Would it not have been the pope who made the basic decision for such a "transformation"? Again, the curial organisms are seen by this author in a very indistinct manner; they are amalgamated together as a single, distinct whole, "a pillar of stone" (pp. 520 and 529). Here it only seems necessary to think of the characteristics of a Cardinal Confalonieri, as they clearly emerge from the acts of the Commission mentioned above (pp. 520 and 529). Also, the "original sin" which is spoken about here—attributed by Father Congar to John XXIII—refers to the statement of the same Father Congar's that the pope established conciliar commissions "corresponding to the Roman Congregations" (p. 516). This kind of speculation should be discounted by the reader, however, for exactly the same procedure was followed by the First Vatican Council.

With reference to the Second Session, it is simply a misunderstanding to refer to "the difficult novitiate of a new pope, elected in the course of an on-going Council" (p. 517). Certainly one cannot draw the conclusion from this that "this period seemed to be a part of Pope John's Council" (*Ibid.*). Meanwhile, "following the intersession of 1963-1964, both pope and the assembly were henceforth conciliar 'experts'" (*Ibid.*). Thus, "Pope Paul's Council" would only have begun in December, 1963. This claim—or stretch— is surely made to give as much space as possible to John XXIII, for whom Alberigo has so much "sympathy"—as is well known. At the same time, such sympathy is correspondingly reduced in the case of Pope Paul VI.

The director of the whole work under review here then deals with a number of crucial passages related to the period October-November, 1963. As for the *schemata De Ecclesia* and *De Liturgia*, "there was manifested a reluctance in those sectors of the Council hostile to the decisions relative to the involvement of the bishops in the management and direction of the universal Church (through episcopal collegiality)." Further, the point is raised concerning "the co-responsibility of each member of the episcopal college with regard to the universal Church as a whole" (p. 519). Here it should have been explained in what sense the various modes of collegiality were to be understood. Also, this same subject is pursued with regard to the "passive resistance" of the "powerful Doctrinal Commission" (*Ibid.*). This resistance was supposedly overcome only when "the entire assembly was called upon to express clear doctrinal directions and did indeed manifest such directions." However, this does not seem to correspond to the whole truth. In effect, considering the difficulties successively encountered on the road to the desired conciliar consensus, it is necessary to recognize that consensus was only achieved after the introduction of the *Nota Explicativa Praevia*, which supplied clarity for those who had been doubtful or were simply uncertain. If the vote, such as it was, had still been hostile, this would not have been because of the vote in itself—consider the position of Archbishop Felici, for example—but it would have been because of the content of the *schema* and of the "independent" way in which it had been brought forward. A considerable part of the "minority," after all, accepted the vote after the clarification of [the meaning of] the text and its context provided by the *Nota*.

Proceeding from this distinction concerning the internal state of the "minority," one can raise the same question with regard to the "majority," which was in no way monolithic (see pp. 521 and 531 for that matter). If there was an "attempt" to "demonize" the majority, accusing it of a "supposed heterodoxy" (pp. 520-521), then it is important to remind Alberigo that the same indications apply to the minority as well. The extremes meet each other here.

As for the liturgy, the claim of the author of "parliamentary filibustering," linked with a plan to call for repeated voting "in order to impede the movement in the direction the majority was going" (p. 520), surely represents a judgment that is excessive. The same thing is true of the author's reference to the "master law" for the Constitution on the Liturgy, given that the Council was trying to get up to "cruising speed" following its difficult launching. As we remarked above, the respect of the Regulations attests to a "regular procedure" without getting into what the various intentions of the participants may have been. Besides, it is well known that attempting to enforce restrictions on the liberty of the Council was considered forbidden territory. It was only towards the end of the work of the Council that limits were established (concerning the number of interventions permitted and requiring them in the name of a certain number of Fathers). These limits were established by the wish of Pope Paul VI himself.

On the other hand, later on, while pressing forward with his interpretation, the author "excuses...the taking over of a number of the properly conciliar decisions" by various Church entities "in order to implement without delay" the Constitution on the Liturgy. The author remarks that "the enthusiasm of the popular base frequently served to remove normal restraints" (p. 524). But such "Garibaldian" language cannot conceal the fact that liturgical norms were not being respected here.

On the subject of the *schema* entitled *De Episcopis*, the presentation offered is not lacking in indications of the author's usual point of view in favor of the institution of a collegial entity similar to the "permanent synods" of the Easter Churches. The author remarks in this connection that "the concentration in the hands of the pope and the Roman Curia of the decisions pertaining to *causae maiores* seems both excessive and intolerably onerous, if not injurious to the very identity of the single Churches" (p. 521). The author's use of the term *causae maiores* for major issues here is in any case unfortunate, even though the author adds "understood in an always greater 'omnicomprehensiveness.'" We need to go slowly also in mistakenly confusing the Pope with the Curia.

Along the same line of seeing one's own desires being projected, we find ourselves looking at the subject of "the selection of new bishops," a theme on which we have already made critical comments above concerning the position of Alberigo (see the "more historical" affirmations of Famerée). Whether the "interested community" was marginalized or not can be determined by a simple reading of the norms currently in vigor in the Latin Church.

And with regard to ecumenism, the author describes what he calls "a profound renewal of the Catholic attitude in the sense of adopting a pluralistic vision of Christianity and accepting the possibility of going beyond present divisions on the basis of 'that which unites and with the prospect of a convergence of all' in order that all might be one" (p. 522). But Alberigo greatly exaggerates the contribution of the observers here—as is confirmed by the considered judgment of Velati mentioned above.

As for the Decree on the Means of Social Communication, the author believes it remained "predominantly the prisoner of worn-out rhetoric on 'the Catholic press'" (p. 524). For him the whole document constituted a "wasted opportunity."

And with regard to the laity, Alberigo takes note of the text "in *De Ecclesia* reserved to the people of God." According to him, this would modify completely the dominant point of view in the *schema* on the laity, which he thought was "predominantly the prisoner," again, of the so-called "theology of the laity" (p. 525). He appeals to the late medieval distinction between "doctrine" and "discipline," which he believes were detached from each other "by the insistence of Pope John XXIII concerning the pastoral character of the Council" (p. 525). Thus, there is supposedly no longer any distinction between doctrine and discipline. And was this distinction "late medieval" anyway? And does the Council's use of such terms as "dogmatic constitution," "pastoral constitution," "decree," and "declaration" indicate that we have indeed "gone beyond the dichotomy doctrine-discipline" (*Ibid.*)? Furthermore, to assert that the Theological Commission represented *tout court* "the conciliar projection of the Holy Office" (p. 520) is badly in need of proof.

At the beginning of our presentation, we addressed the question of the papal *consenso* and promulgation of the conciliar texts as indicative of Alberigo's lack of understanding of the relationship between the pope and the Council. He claims that "the primacy of the bishop of

Rome" does not indicate "superiority" [over the Council]. Here he goes back to this same well-known thesis of his according to which "the development of the conciliar texts in the commissions and in the *aula* does not exhaust all the impulses and meanings of the Council, and perhaps it does not even touch upon them in their most profound sense" (p. 526; but see p. 531). Along these same lines, he goes on to mention "the great problem of the reception" [of the Vatican II documents] (p. 526), and the need to draw inspiration from "the spirit of Vatican II," that is, from "the totality of all the examples, sensitivities, and proposals that were generated as a result of the meeting together of the universal episcopate and of the common evangelical quest that was undertaken thereby" (*Ibid.*). For the author, all this testifies to a new movement going beyond what had been the case in the past. He writes, for example: "Centralized functioning based on sanctions and norms of the kind that followed the Council of Trent belonged to a type of council and to a cultural epoch that was now completely superseded" (*Ibid.* and p. 529). Three lines suffice, then, to describe the destruction of an entire past? Let us take one single example, which resolves itself into a question: Who, if not the pope, made possible for the universal Church the reform of the liturgy in the first place? Digressing only slightly, we also ask: Who, if not the bishop of Rome, and by means of issuing general norms, proved able to bring about a "reasonable" *reception* of Vatican II as well? Perhaps the new entity, the *Consilium ad exsequendam constitutionem de sacra Liturgia*? For some, this Consilium "threatened to make permanent, under another name, the Council itself, and to go on interfering structurally with the Roman Congregations" (*Ibid.*). Besides, this author has already applied, in an ever more radical fashion, the same procedure for the "liquidation" of the past to the First Vatican Council, which, for him, "was not followed by a true and proper period of reception" (pp. 529 and 532).

And on the subject of "the echo of great external events" (p. 526), it would seem to be necessary to add a number of things with respect, for example, to "the long Pacellian pontificate" and to the "philo-occidental and philo-Atlantic orientation" (p. 527). Then, again, there was the subject of the persecution of the Church in Eastern Europe.

And the author once again reveals his "political" incomprehension when he describes Pope Paul VI's pilgrimage to Jerusalem as "a primatial and monarchical act of genius" (p. 528). He characterized it thus because of the pope's choice "to entrust the preparation of the visit to a political organism, the Secretariat of State, rather than to one of the organs within the conciliar structure."

The last three pages of Alberigo's "Conclusion" seek to present a kind of balance sheet of the positive and negative aspects of the Second Session. To accomplish this, the author cites the judgments of theologians such as Laurentin, Ratzinger, Chenu, Congar, and Schillebeeckx, and he also mentions the undertaking of the launching of the journal *Concilium*. It is significant, for those who wish to understand, how "in these circumstances," it was "the general Council that imposed itself on the Roman pontificate"; the reference here is to "the decision of Paul VI for the continuation of the Council" (p. 532). There would not, in fact, according to Alberigo, have been any "alternative to the prompt and loyal decision to continue," since "even a pope with the great prestige and authority of Pope Paul VI could not but—politically speaking—accept the Council and carry it forward to its logical conclusion. Something of the same sort of thing occurred also before and during the Council of Trent..."

And here the author emphasizes the "vitality" of Vatican II, its "capacity to overcome the uneasiness...the exasperation...[and] the inertia which the great majority of the bishops at the Council exhibited"—but what a separation between Vatican II, the bishops who composed it, and Pope Paul VI this assertion indicates!

Even here it is "understood" that Alberigo contrasts the *schema* entitled *De Ecclesia* with its *Nota Explicativa Praevia* and considers it "a new crisis" (p. 533). Certainly, he continues, "at that time it could seem that the votes of October 30, 1963, had been in vain or at least inadequate" (*Ibid.*). Yet this "would not be an entirely convincing conclusion, since the maturing of the Council on the one hand, and that of the pope on the other, were in continual evolution, and no historical reconstruction can prescind from that fact" (*Ibid.*). And so? The author declares himself content, however, that questions concerning such conciliar problems were raised in other circumstances; and even though they remained without resolution, "this method" of proceeding at least brought about "a change in the strategy of the minority." The minority preferred to "increase the pressure on the pope" and "relied less and less on discussions and arguments within the assembly itself" (p. 534). Certainly this last assertion here amounts to a rather weak conclusion.

The author's final judgments, in the end, focus on Vatican II as "an occasion for renewal." At the same time, "the impression is given that the results could not be considered entirely satisfactory. It was not a case where one looked forward to the post-conciliar era...the Council itself was a stage on the road" (p. 534). The dice was cast for the post-conciliar era in which it would be asked whether the Council, or, better, the conciliar documents, might not have conceded too much.

St. Augustine was right when he wrote: *Sic amatur veritas ut quicumque aliud amant velint esse veritatem* (Conf. 10, 23, 34; P. L. 32, 794); that is, "the truth is so much loved that those who love something else besides the truth want that which they love to be the truth."

13

For the History of Vatican Council II
(Third Session and In-Between)

Alberigo Giuseppe, ed., with Various Authors, *La Chiesa come comunione. Il terzo periodo e la terza intersessione, settembre 1964-settembre 1965* [The Church as Communion: the Third Session and the Third Intersession, September 1964-September 1965]. Volume IV of the *Storia del Concilio Vaticano II* [History of the Second Vatican Council], directed by Professor Giuseppe Alberigo, Peeters/Il Mulino, Bologna, 1999, 706 pages.

As a continuation of a publication in progress, this fourth volume of the *History of the Second Vatican Council* directed by Professor Giuseppe Alberigo has recently appeared in bookstores. As has been the case for the previous volumes in the series, this large book, well made and presented, constitutes a notable encyclopedic effort on the subject of the great Vatican Synod. The director himself emphasizes its nature and importance in his usual "Premise" introducing the work: "The differences between the various points of view of the collaborators have been much discussed, but this represents one of the costs of realizing a truly common enterprise. We have carried on with the ambitious project of producing a work by several hands" (p. 10).

We note with great satisfaction in general—what was already the case for the most part with the volume preceding this one—the systematic use by the various authors of "the titanic enterprise of Monsignor Vincenzo Carbone in editing the indispensable official sources relating to the work of the general congregations and to the functioning of the directional organs of the Council and its General Secretariat" (*Ibid.*). With regard to this project, with 61 volumes completed, only one more is still lacking of the number originally projected; and, all together, these volumes containing the official sources furnish the key to open a door that up to now has been closed to an authentic conciliar hermeneutic. It may be a small key by comparison with the whole; it certainly is an indispensable one. For opening the safe door of the authentic synodical hermeneutic. But I would have to add to Professor Alberigo's remark about how indispensable these official sources are that they are also the key, if we may then continue to employ the same term, to the proper interpretation of the other conciliar documents and sources as well. I refer in particular to the many private sources for which these official sources provide the litmus paper to test the true "conciliar authenticity" of the private ones. They furnish, in brief, the criteria for the truthfulness of what is asserted; they go beyond partial interpretations based on personal impressions, gossip, and even the egocentricities, vanities, and pettiness that are revealed in some of the various "diaries" that chronicle the unfolding of what was no doubt the greatest ecclesiastical event of the twentieth century.

However, there continues to hover over the present "history" an element that we find to be unduly "ideological." It is present from the beginning, and it manifests itself in various unjustified—and certainly unscientific—animosities against persons belonging to the conciliar minority. In this respect, this volume is "one-stringed." One of the results of this way of proceeding is that the only "true" Vatican Council II comes to be the one supposedly called by John XXIII to be "innovative" and "progressive." This vision of the Council is held to have continued virtually up to September, 1964: "With the work of the autumn, 1964, as reconstructed here, Vatican II was now unfolding within the climate of the pontificate of Paul VI, and Pope Montini was showing a greater awareness of his responsibilities as the 'natural president' of the Council" (p. 9)—and this was not just the "other" Council (presumably co-inciding with his own vision). However, this great Synod was and is one and indivisible: Vatican II.

Along the same lines of a subjective and unfounded interpretation of the Council is the basic idea which underlies the type of conciliar hermeneutic of which this volume is a prime example. The idea in question is the vision of a great assembly as a novel "event" characterized by a complete break with the past and a rupturing of continuity with respect to the tradition (see p. 9, n. 1; but also see Chapter 23 of the present volume).

Finally, we need to note that, as with the previous volumes, this book claims to explain the experience of the Council by means of a thematic reconstruction of the events of the Council alone. The difficulties inherent in this kind of approach are not lacking; these difficulties could have been avoided. Leaving aside cases I could mention, I will cite only one example here, namely, the severe and partisan bias consistently exhibited toward Archbishop Pericle Felici, the General Secretary of the Council, particularly in the matter of the question of religious liberty and "the crisis of October" (pp. 192-219). No account of the papal mindset is provided here—the same mindset that would reveal itself during the famous "Black Week" of November, 1964. This expression, "Black Week," also continues to be used here, even though it is both inexact and "journalistic." By now it has come to be understood by all—even those who were viscerally opposed, at least as far as the *schema* on religious liberty is concerned—that during the week too often commonly designated as "Black Week" the Supreme Pontiff made some correct decisions which had very positive consequences for the ultimate "synodal economy." As can be verified in the *Adnotationes (manu scriptae Summi Pontificis Pauli VI* [Handwritten Notes of the Supreme Pontiff Paul VI]) for September 24, 1964, the pope noted that "the *schema De libertate religiosa* does not appear to be well prepared"; and again, on September 29, he wrote; "Regarding the *schema De libertate religiosa* (1) it is necessary to redo it: and (2) to associate with the Commission some other person competent in theology and sociology" (See the *Acta Synodalia* (AS), vol. 6, p. 418).

I could and perhaps should say more, but I will stop here with only this general introduction mentioned in order to situate the reader within the by now well-known critical point of view that I have adopted.

Chapter I, "The Ecclesiology of Communion" was entrusted to J. A. Komonchak. He establishes his bases solidly on firm ground, exhibiting the results of a good assimilation of the official conciliar sources; he also establishes from the outset the *status quaestionum* ("expectations and anxieties") and he also lays down the lines of force for the period being covered (pp. 22-26). The considerations he presents are interesting, even if for our part we cannot always share them. He employs expressions such as "behind the scenes," "us and them," and "pressures" (which "Paul VI did not always resist in the end"). He exaggerates the "role" of the *Coetus Internationalis Patrum*, or International Group of Fathers. He similarly speaks about the "left," which we would characterize rather as "extremist." He chronicles the growing differences within the majority and the inadequacy of dividing up the Council Fathers identified as "progressive" or "conservative."

In this regard, the author himself delineates a profile of the participants and describes the leadership of the Great Council (see p. 30 and also pp 49ff., 57, 61, 86, 92, and 102), though it is not completely clear if "leadership" is the proper term here—and, in any case, the author sometimes confuses it with the leadership of the pope. Questions are raised which are not entirely exact, knowing the uneasy situation created in the relations between the Moderators and the Secretary General of the Council (p. 31). This situation is presented in terms that neither reflect the truth nor are they otherwise justified (see p. 31 and then pp. 52, 55, 60, and 93). The role of Felici, which was positive for the majority with regard to Chapter III of *Lumen Gentium*, is not brought out and made explicit here (p. 96ff., 106ff., 112 and 115). The subtitle "The Laity: Men and Women" (p. 40) provides the occasion for a presentation which is rather American in its sensibility, especially (but not only) with regard to the role of women. At the same time, the author does not appear to "understand" the developments in the mindset of the Pastors. The tone continues to be negative in its judgment on the type of presence exhibited by "parish priests" at the Council (p. 48).

The third section in the Chapter deals with the new rules—five of them were added to the Regulations—and also with the question of the duration of the Third Session and with the "swiftness" of its "operations." In the fourth and fifth sections of the chapter, the author deals with the central points of his subject matter, namely, "the Constitution on the Church" and "the Episcopate and Collegiality (Chapter III)." We cannot follow him in the laying out of his analysis, which is nevertheless rather well done. For us he reveals tendencies towards simply leaving out of consideration what had preceded the completed text [of *Lumen Gentium*]; Monsignor Gérard Philips noted, however, that some sixty percent of "his" *schema* was taken from the original. Komonchak also reveals a tendency towards considering as "adversaries of collegiality" even those who merely had serious reservation about a certain type of collegiality. The final "plebiscitary" vote on the *schema* proved this. He also questions unduly the "dogmatic character" of the Constitution and defines uncorrectly as "papal delegation" the jurisdiction of the bishops.

There are also in these pages many citations from private sources which cannot but leave us perplexed, particularly those concerning the "pressures" supposedly exerted on Paul VI, especially those which led to the drawing up of the *Nota Explicativa Praevia*. The author underrates the value of "recourse" to the supreme authority in these cases, it seems to me. At bottom, this recourse is merely an exercise of the right to appeal, the right to a second judgment. This right is ancient and goes all the way back to the beginning of the papal primacy. The author also underrates the force of character of this pope and his determination to examine for himself—he described the necessity for this in his own handwriting—the conciliar documents which, after all, would bear his signature (following his "confirmation" of them as pope). He also had both the right and responsibility to allow ample time for the maturing of his particular decisions, freely and in conscience. He too had a conscience, after all!

Following "the war of the amendments" (?) and "the idea of giving some satisfaction to the minority" (?)—what miserable language!— the author takes up the theme of the interventions of Paul VI and then of the *schema* on the bishops, where a number of the echoes of the debate on the Church still reverberated.

In Chapter II, two key issues, religious liberty and relations with the Jews, are taken up by G. Miccoli. He shows himself to be particularly critical of the work of Archbishop Felici connected with these two issues. His reconstruction of events appears to us to be one-sided; this can be seen in the way he almost always keeps his distance from the testimony of Monsignor Carbone. Among other things, this author asserts that "given the continuing substantial inaccessibility of the official archives of the Council, it is not easy to evaluate the presence and influence of 'Catholic anti-Semitism' among the fathers" (p. 167). But besides the published volumes of the *Acta*, there is the opposing opinion on this issue of A. Melloni, curator of the Italian edition of the volume; for him the desired archive concerning Paul VI has in fact been opened "to scholars by the zeal of V. Carbone" (p. 15).

In any case, Miccoli follows, thanks to the official sources published by the monsignor charged with responsibility for the archive, the various interventions of the Council fathers, and indeed of Paul VI himself, although only within the limits of the knowledge of the pontiff's actions that is current at the present day. However, with regard to religious liberty, there are not lacking some rather firm instances of pontifical interventions (see, for example, the *Acta Synodalia*, Vol. 3, pp. 417, 440-443, 462ff., 501ff., 530; and see also Vol. 2). The one whom the author takes as his "guide" and "counselor" here, beyond the official guidance, however, is Father Yves Congar in his *Journal* of the Council. But this work hardly stands out on account of its "balance." The author's other guides include Hamer, Murray, Dossetti, Rouquette, Scatena, Wenger, Bergonzini, Grootaers, Oesterreicher, etc.

On the subject of religious liberty, Miccoli first of all explains "the two diametrically opposed conceptions" of it. From the very beginning in its preparatory phase, the Council was confronted with those two opposed conceptions; they served to enlarge the reflection that had to take place on this very large subject and, especially, on the issue of "the development of doctrine" which underlay it. It was truly "the great battleground at Vatican II" (p. 123). The whole subject of religious liberty thus constituted a privileged moment in the conciliar debate, which did not disavow the past. The basic problem was brought out often *cum fundamento in re*, though, and it was Bishop Émile de Smedt who properly explained the whole issue a way that we think was correct (pp. 125, 129, and 153ff.). This author, however, sides with those who see opposing positions between the earlier Magisterium on the subject and what was now being proposed for the Council.

Successively, the author reports the interventions of the Fathers, and he also takes note of the silences of those who were considered "progressives" (pp. 141 and 143) and even of Congar himself, who was "uncomfortable" (p. 152) up until the time various ambiguities and misunderstandings were finally cleared up (these pertained both to the definitions of religious liberty and to some of the motivations offered for favoring it). The most positive contribution on this subject was that of Bishop (later Cardinal) Carlo Colombo, whose intervention is rightly accorded major attention by the author (pp. 156-158). The same thing is true of the interventions of Monsignor Pietro Pavan and of Father John Courtney Murray.

At this point the author gets into the treatment of the *schema* entitled *De Judaeis et de non-Christianis*. He first briefly recalls the greatly tormented route followed by this document up to this point, but then he becomes exceedingly mixed up concerning the whole issue, particularly since he fails to make a distinction between anti-Judaism and anti-Semitism, a deficiency which has very serious and very deleterious consequences. Here, more than was the case earlier, the author shows his "prejudices" against the Secretariat of State (p. 162, n. 164; pp. 163, 166, 168ff., 182, and 201). He shows the same "prejudices" against "the local Vatican missions," arriving at erroneous interpretations and generalizations (p. 202, n. 311). This is particularly the case with regard to the question of "Deicide" (pp. 170, 172, 178ff., and 182). He ends as follows: "The hypothesis is not forced that the opposition to the text, motivated by reasons of political opportunism, concealed their true motives and offered a screen behind which lay another and more substantial opposition" (the traditional anti-Semitism with its religious roots: p. 176; but see p. 190 with even greater conviction). Also, the view of Miccoli on the subject of the *Coetus Internationalis Patrum* is not sound. One cannot just identify with this group those with "ideas substantially similar" or those who constituted "at least a part of the conciliar minority" (p. 184 and also pp. 189 and 196) just because they opposed the text. This is especially true when the "mobility" of this group is considered.

Following this, the author takes on the subject of "the crisis of October." He tries to establish some solid points about it, but he does not do it with a very firm hand. At bottom he does not understand the position of Paul VI; as the pope himself wrote, he had a great sense of his own responsibility, his own conscience, for he had to confirm the Vatican II documents with his approval. Thus, it was not just a question of the pressures on him, or of his legitimate search for a consensus; it was a question of his personal conviction; he was prepared to go against winds and tides, from whatever direction they came. We would say that his main tendency was conservative rather than innovative (but this author, again, supplies an inexact identification between "the curialists and the other members of the minority" (p. 196). This was not a case, however—as Father Congar wrote that the pope "was closely tied to a Roman optic" (p. 197). If with such a phrase this theologian wished to say that the optic in question stood for "universal" and "Catholic," then he would have been right. We doubt, and legitimately so, that this was Congar's intention. In any case, the analysis itself reveals the difficulties of "acting together" on the part of the conciliar commissions (see p. 199ff.). There were equally strong difficulties in attempting to institute practices that the General Secretary of the Council could in no way approve—or in attempting to go beyond the rules of the Council for its own supposed good (see the first very important citation on p. 215). Archbishop Felici is much criticized, unduly so, in our view, because the pope (not the Roman Curia) wished to foster a real exchange, and he entrusted to the Secretary General the task of insuring this. Given the reactions that ensued, however, the pope found himself personally obliged to conduct the conciliar ship back into port (see pp. 204-215, and, especially, pp. 216ff.). This way of proceeding proved valid for all of this material, as it would later for the *schema* that became *Gaudium et Spes*. Moreover, the *schema De libertate religiosa* cannot be described as "a victory of Cardinal Bea's," even when this statement is qualified by the adjective "substantially" (p. 217). This becomes clear when we take into account the other contributions [to this volume]; we note a number of other "disconnections" in the contributions of the different authors. The "new" text was reviewed by the "mixed" group of experts after receiving a *nihil obstat* from the Theological Commission. Following this, it was to be transmitted directly to the Central Coordinating Commission. It was thus that it was withdrawn from the competence of the General Secretariat, not because the latter body did not have competence, as the author incorrectly says in order to justify the judgments made by him earlier.

Furthermore, the judgment made by the author on *De Judaeis*, which takes him back to the *status quo ante* after "the crisis of October," is not correct, especially when we consider the context in which it was revised and eventually placed among the "non-Christian religions."

Finally, we continue to be resolutely opposed, as we noted earlier, to the use of the journalistic expression "Black Week," as if it pertained to history in a true sense. In fact, everybody now admits the benefits that resulted from the pope's decision taken at this time to postpone the discussions and the final voting on these two *schemata* into the Fourth Session.

In the next chapter (Chapter III), the topic entitled "Doctrinal Problems as Problems of Pastoral Practice" was confided to H. Sauer. This title is quite equivocal, however, and it does not completely correspond to the contents of the chapter. It is devoted to the conciliar discussions concerning the *schema* on divine revelation. The treatment is chronological, and after a brief pre-history of the problems of the document, the interventions of the Fathers are summarized along with some comments. In addition to the *Acta Synodalia*, the author cites a number of other judgments, some of them not very balanced, as, for example, from the rather extreme Father Otto Semmelroth, who called Bishop Franjo Franić "a true and genuine reactionary" (p. 236) and styled the intervention of Bishop Luigi Carli as "abject and demagogic" (p. 257, n. 128). In order to show his one-sidedness concerning one of the major themes of the *schema*, it suffices to cite the subtitle he employs: "In this *aula* we raise sacred Scripture up high, not Tradition." He says this in connection with the liturgy, something he borrowed from Bishop Hermann Volk of Mainz.

It is the same H. Sauer who continues on with the Chapter IV which follows next. It bears the title "The Council Discovered by the Laity." He again treats the interventions on this subject in chronological order, following the *Acta Synodalia*. In conclusion, he quotes a long citation from Father Karl Rahner which contrasts greatly from the *schema* itself. He also mentions the founding of the international theological review, *Concilium*, which according to him, was directly "inspired by the Council" (p. 291). The extent to which this project, up to the present time, has truly reflected the Council, can be left to informed readers. The author also mentions the proposal to canonize Pope John XXIII. In all this material covered by Sauer, there are not lacking indications of the tendencies he champions in his particular vision of the Council. The emphases he exhibits are not at all impartial in his judgments concerning such subjects as the majority and the minority, as well as other topics. On the whole, however, his work is serious, *de actis et probatis*.

Chapter V was entrusted to N. Tanner and bears the title, "The Church in Society: *Ecclesia ad Extra*." Although it covers *Schema* XIII [which became *Gaudium et Spes*] it also covers, with some thematic incongruencies, the topics of the missions, priestly life, ministry and formation, the religious life, and marriage.

Also in this case, the discussion of *Schema* XIII is rather straightforward, consisting mostly of the author's summary of the interventions of the various Fathers. His discussion is somewhat "spiced up" with the "reactions," in the background, of the observer from the World Council of Churches, Dr. Lucas Vischer, and it also includes a reaction of Father Yves Congar.

The position of Tanner in opposition to Archbishop Felici is quite evident, even though one must recognize the personal difficulties of the latter with regard to *Schema* XIII. See, for example, the question of its appendices (or *adnexa*) to the document. Even Father Congar was not in agreement on a number of points here. The narrative begins to warm up to its subject matter on page 294, though, and it is necessary to keep one's distance from [the way the author decides to go]. Then, on page 353 and following, the author latches on to the idea of the Council as an "event." In this regard, the author says, "it is important to pay attention to what the Fathers actually said, without getting into the question of whether their interventions had any effect on the final text of *Gaudium et Spes* or not" (p. 353; see also pp. 354ff). There is no one, I think, who cannot see the grave theological risk involved in such a vision of the Council [as a mere event]. I dealt with this subject in an article in *L'Osservatore Romano* for August 12, 1998 (p. 6). And in the same vein, we note that the *L'Avvenire d'Italia* was not the official organ of the Italian bishops' conference.

As for the missions, the author reports that the discussions were "inevitably dominated by the speech of Paul VI in favor of the *schema* and the reluctance of the Council Fathers to follow his recommendations" (p. 360). There were many good and pertinent observations made along the way, but the conclusion is seen as "a defeat for the pontiff" (p. 362 and p. 372). The interpretation in Note 104 to the effect that "the contrary votes were those favorable to the *schema* recommended by Paul VI" was not well considered, since the votes in favor came to 1601 and not 1914, as the author says. These kinds of mere impressions must not be taken at face value—like the very harsh judgment of Father Congar on "papal theology" (pp. 363f.).

Regarding the priestly ministry and the formation of priests, the author continues to follow his chosen method; he sums up and presents the main points of the various speeches of the Fathers, always with reference to what is contained in the *Acta Synodalia*. We are pleased to be able to report that "a good equilibrium between preservation and innovation" (p. 386) was achieved in the matter of priestly formation;

this, after all, was the kind of fundamental synthesis desired by Pope John XXIII when he convoked Vatican Council II, as it was also the desire of Pope Paul VI when he carried the Council on to its completion.

In Chapter VI, L. A. G. Tagle deals with "The Tempest of November: 'Black Week'" (pp. 417, 427, 434, 436, 446, 467, 470, 475, 477, 479ff. and 481ff.). The abundance of funereal "color" within the tempestuous framework found here provides a good indication of the interpretive direction favored by this author; he nevertheless directly mentions the mysteriousness of the whole affair on page 418. Yet it is a rather rich and even profound study in some ways, although it has no center. Also, the author likes to enclose words and expressions within quotation marks, and he is given to journalistic language as well; he reports the immediate reactions of some groups, including some within the Council, without much sense of what was to come later or without a necessary perspective on the whole thing.

Moreover, from the very outset, Tagle adopts the historical category of an "event" for the Council (see above). Thus, for the famous week that has been regularly presented as garbed in mourning, he creates "a sort of event within an event" (p. 417). He speaks of "a series of incidents which badly disturbed the assembly" (*Ibid.*), including the approval of texts seriously weakened because of concessions made to a disloyal minority which should have been "left behind" (*Ibid.*). With phraseology more appropriate to a sporting event, perhaps, we learn of such developments as the postponement of the vote on religious liberty and the presentation of the *Nota Explicativa Praevia*, which explained how Chapter III of *Lumen Gentium* was to be understood. Then, there was the introduction [by Pope Paul VI] of the nineteen amendments to the Decree on Ecumenism, and, finally, there was the declaration by the pope establishing Mary as "Mother of the Church."

The attitude of Tagle becomes clear about all this when he writes that "the Fathers together with the pope would vote definitively on texts already approved by the general congregations" (p. 419). But the Bishop of Rome did not vote "with the Fathers"; his responsibility was to "confirm" and "promulgate" texts approved by the Council, according the synodal Regulations themselves. And he could always "intervene" as well. He was in no way the "notary" of the Council as Paul VI, in a colorful expression, once actually said.

Along the same lines, the author, with this critical vision of how the great Synod was "conducted" by Pope Montini, in a section entitled "the Role of Paul VI" (pp. 434 and 474ff.), describes the pope's conduct of the Council as having caused "deep wounds" (p. 425) and as having provoked "responses" (p. 462). He subjects the pope's closest collaborators to the same critical treatment, specifically Archbishop Felici, the Secretary General of the Council (see pp. 420, 421ff., 453), and even Cardinal Tisserant [the dean of the Council Presidents] (pp. 422ff., and 432ff.).

In the acts of the assembly the author examines "the antecedents of the crisis" concerning "the four crucial incidents of 'Black Week'" (p. 426). We cannot follow him in this presentation. However, we shall indicate in what follows the pages we found most lacking in the objectivity required of any true historian and also the hypotheses to which we cannot give our adherence (pp. 427ff., 430, 432ff., 435ff., 439, and 440). "It should not surprise anyone," the author writes, "that this series of incidents and exchanges represents a series of highly ambiguous transactions in which the promulgation of the text depended upon the modifications requested by the pope" (442, 444, 446); "it would be no exaggeration to say that the *Nota Praevia* was the fruit of a 'black period' in the Constitution on the Church" (p. 449); "the minority considered that it had been able to extort the pope's agreement...Paul VI desired unanimity at the Council at whatever cost" (p. 451); "another cause of fear among the minority was the strong distinction being made between 'order' and 'jurisdiction.' This was a disjunction unknown in antiquity." We, however, would add here that the deepening of the theological meaning is found in the reflected distinction and not in what the author calls the "disjunction."

The author continues in the same vein: "The minority exploded in potentially subversive acts" (pp. 457, 459ff., 463ff., 468ff., n. 228); "the analysis of the *Nota Praevia Explicativa* by C. De Rossi showed that this document was mostly a *collage* of the principal amendments, presented by members of the minority and rejected by the commission as contradictory to the text being voted on"—so much was this not the case, however, that Monsignor Gérard Philips himself found nothing contradictory at all here, nor in the key concept of a *hierarchica communio* introduced by Father Wilhelm Bertrams, S. J. (see the *Acta Synodalia* (AS) vol. 3, p. 647); this latter concept could provide the bridge between the first and second millennium of christianity as far as the organic constitution of the Church was concerned (pp. 469, 471). [But the author instead claims]: "The *Nota* offered a restrictive interpretation of Chapter III, though not totally so" (p. 473); however, "the *Nota* did not give the only possible interpretation...it should not be absolutized" (p. 474); "Paul VI wanted the *Nota*...in order to avoid a schism similar to that of the *old Catholics* after Vatican Council I. Besides he also wanted to prevent the Roman Curia from falling into a permanent antagonism towards the bishops of the world" (pp. 475, 477). Moreover, Father Otto Semmelroth, S. J., was not "mild," as the author describes him, relying on his diary, as it relates to the citations reported; Note 276 on page 478 demonstrates this. The author goes on to speak of how "the innocuous title of *Mater Ecclesiae* ["Mother of the Church"] became the symbol for various complaints related to the emergence of a diverse form of the Church" (p. 480). Again: "The minority...banked on the temperament of Pope Paul VI...Both the strategies and the disputes that developed during 'Black Week' brought out into the open the ambiguities of the conciliar documents; but in order to take into account the many objections leveled against them, theological compromises proved to be necessary in the texts" (p. 481); "the interventions [of Paul VI] were seen as defenses of papal prerogatives, while perhaps the pope himself imagined that he could participate in the Council exactly as any other bishop might" (p. 482). This was supposedly true as regards Marian piety every bit as much as collegiality. However, the author's conclusion is positive in the end (though it is something of a *felix culpa*, or "happy fault") since for him the so-called "Black Week" proved to be one of the events which made Vatican II a source of grace.

In Chapter VII, the longest in the book, R. Burigana and G. Turbanti deal with the intersession, [or period between the Third and

Fourth Sessions]. There appear in their treatment the usual points of view typical of the School of Bologna; these points of view are clearly ideological as far as we are concerned. I refer in particular to the martial vocabulary, the excessive dramatizations, the pessimism, the animosity towards Paul VI, and so on (see, e.g., pp. 484, 510, 512ff., 515ff., 527, n. 103, 533-536, 542ff., 549, and 577). This animosity is usually expressed by comparisons with John XXIII; the two popes are seen as pursuing different paths. [These authors declare]: "For those most committed to the renewal of Catholic doctrine by the Council, the *Nota Praevia* came along to empty of its principal significance for them the great step forward that Vatican II had represented...For them the Council came to an end on November 21, 1964" (p. 487). On that date the conciliar majority was "robbed," according to them (p. 486).

I take note once again of the negative—if not entirely ill-disposed—attitude here with regard to Archbishop Felici, the Roman Curia (without any distinctions), the Secretariat of Sate, and *L'Osservatore Romano.* The same thing is true of the constant appeals made here to the "spirit of Vatican II" (covering whatever content one might wish to insert) rather than being bound "by the letter" (p. 499). There are established improper and undue ties between the Secretary of the Dutch bishops' conference and "the *Domus Mariae* Group" (p. 488)—between the satisfaction of Cardinal Giuseppe Siri and those who stress implicitly the continuity of Vatican II with Vatican I, they underline this point without sharing the Genoa cardinal's other views. We think in this connection rather of the views of such thinkers, after the Council, as Jedin, Carbone, Ratzinger, Kasper, and finally, Poulat.

And with respect to such theologians and historians as these, we take note especially here that undue stress is laid upon the role of *periti* at the Council, especially the one of Father Yves Congar, who seems to have become for them the true and just measure of the thought of the whole Church in his judgments of men and things, but it should be made clear that, by analogy, theological research occupies the position of the *acceptio rerum* in the case of the Sacred Authors—that is to say, conciliar decisions are not the work of theologians, even if the latter could have humbly woven, at least in part, the fabric of the texts adopted. But they and the decisions are episcopal or papal in the measure that they are adopted as acts of the Church's Magisterium. If then, later, we wish to know what the "material" contributions of the theologians to the approval of texts consisted of, then we must carry out a patient and objective work of comparison between what was proposed and what was decided as the end result. A comparative examination also of such sources as "diaries" is also required, particularly where the work of the conciliar commissions is concerned. Besides, precisely in the case of Father Congar, his diary records a number of passages in which it is quite evident that he was simply mistaken concerning some of the changes made and also concerning the rejection of some of his scenarios. The same thing is true of some of his affirmations: "consultations" on a text are not equivalent to "drafting" it (see Chapter 45 of this book for a detailed discussion of Father Congar and his diary; see also pp. 555, n. 160, 547, n. 208, 603, n. 272, 609, and the notes on pp. 612, 614ff., and 678).

In this chapter, we did find interesting the research on the "Mixed Commission" appointed to deal with *Schema* XIII; there is much about Congar there as well, as also later, and much as well about the emergence of the one who would eventually become pope [Karol Wojtyla].

The treatment of the *schema* on non-Christians religions with its declaration on the Jewish people is, however, way off the track, especially considering that there is lacking any distinction between anti-Judaism and anti-Semitism as the authors go round and round about the extent to which the accusation of "Deicide" should figure in the document.

There are, however, interesting discussions concerning the other conciliar commissions, those on revelation, the apostolate of the laity, the missions, and the clergy; on this last topic, the authors exhibit great leniency for those who insisted on raising the question of clerical celibacy in the Latin Church, as well as for those not favorable to the celebration of daily Mass with no faithful present and also in the case of the missions.

To be deplored here is the evidence of a preconceived negative attitude towards Cardinal Agagianian and the Congregation *de*

Propaganda Fide; in the end, this entailed a negative attitude towards Pope Montini himself as well, and this in turn leads to a false judgment on the subject of the vote on a question proposed by the pope to the Council Fathers. The Secretary General of the Council concluded in this connection: *"Ergo placuit Patribus propositio facta a commissione de missionibus. Quapropter propter hoc schema...perpolietur, perficitur et, ubi opus erit, reficitur iuxta Patrum animadversiones"* (*Acta Synodalia*, vol. III/6, p. 457). For that matter, even Father Congar found that he had to be accommodating on this issue in order to preserve in the *schema* the broadening of the vision of the missions; he had to accept along with the others that once this vision was stated, it was necessary to return to a discussion of "the history of the missions" in a strict sense. Here again, then, the method of the synthesis prevailed: there had to be mediation and compromises, putting things together rather than separating them out disjointedly and in accordance with radical thought (see p. 610ff. and p. 614, n. 300)—the latter practice, however, being the tendency in this volume under review.

The labors of the conciliar commission on the religious life are also of interest. Cardinal Ildebrando Antoniutti is reproved for his "precise ideas on what needed to be done" (p. 618). Then there was disagreement on the part of Bishop Karl Leiprecht, who was against the cardinal's "not very definite role and his frequent absence" (p. 622). Bishop Leiprecht thus assumed a "primary role." In the discussion of the commission on seminaries and Christian education, there are mentioned "strong pressures" and "significant contrasts." There follows the treatment of the *schema* on the bishops involving some particular burning issues; they are treated rather confusedly and with discrepancies between the text and the corresponding notes (p. 632); there is also mention made by Father Congar of "a terrible offensive" launched by the opposition in "a battle on the question of the bishops' conferences" (p. 633).

Finally, the task of the Central Coordinating Commission is examined. These authors tend to reduce the importance of this body, although, it was decisive (pp. 634-639); but emphasis is correctly placed on the role of Archbishop Felici with respect to *Schema* XIII, which was the result of "two requirements in part contradicting each other, namely, the need to articulate universal principles...and at the same time to deal with concrete and contingent problems...the text never fundamentally resolved this contradiction," the authors state (p. 636, n. 367).

The chapter then concludes with "Observations Near and Far," in which it is once again found necessary to speak of the division already claimed between the modes of operation of John XXIII and of Paul VI (p. 645). There is also a basically superficial and polarized account concerning "The Communist World at Vatican II."

The final chapter in the book, as has been the case for all the previous volumes in the series published to date, provides the occasion for Professor Alberigo to draw his usual conclusions. While he speaks of "great results," he sees them as overshadowed with "bitter and heavy" clouds of uncertainty. His conclusions are very personal, as is immediately evident in his initial summary of the two approved conciliar documents, namely, *Lumen Gentium* and *Unitatis Redintegratio*. The typical and familiar Alberigo is present here in his tendency to consider the synodal assembly almost as a civil parliament. He uses such phrases as "the minority at the limit of its parliamentary filibustering" (p. 649) and of "the democratic principle" (p. 661). This principle provides the basis for his judgments of the Church. He speaks of a "Christian and particularly Catholic hostility" to democracy, which he greatly reproves. There is found here also his typical distinction between "the pilgrim Church" and "the Kingdom of God" (pp. 649 and 651); but this distinction of his does not allow him to take in the true conciliar vision, which is that the Church is "the seed and the beginning" of the Kingdom (see *Lumen Gentium* 5).

There is also present here another characteristic of Alberigo's, which is his understanding of the collegiality of "the sister Churches" (the dioceses) with the primacy—and which does not tally with the account found in the Council's own texts; nor does the author show himself objective in analyzing the contribution of the "ecumenical observers" at the Council (p. 653ff.; see also p. 664).

Thus it is too that Alberigo continues not to see the link, fundamentally Catholic, between Vatican Council II and the councils which preceded it (see p. 659 on the subject of the Council of Trent); he also denies that Vatican II was "the logical continuation" of Vatican I (p. 655); this very expression, though, comes from Pope Paul VI (p. 664). That Vatican II operated in "watertight compartments," as the author claims (p. 655), is also not true; nor is the *schema* on the bishops the proof of this, as he contends (p. 659).

Moreover, the irreducible opposition that he finds between the inductive and deductive methods, to the point where only the former is supposedly valid (p. 655ff.), is quite forced and artificial, and, at bottom, is not even Catholic, especially if "the signs of the times" are somehow supposed to be considered equivalent to "revelation": supposedly, of course, "they reveal in the light of faith the unfolding of history, the riches contained in the sovereignty of the word" (p. 656).

Among the "movements" cited by Alberigo as having furnished preparations for Vatican II, there is notably lacking any mention of the "patristic" movement. To have recognized this would have aided the author in moderating somewhat his search at almost any cost for conciliar "newness," going beyond genuine Tradition and the continuity found in it (p. 656). "The search for Christ takes place among men and events," he writes, "and not in spite of them...and also along a road where everything is called to be changed except the Gospel itself." (p. 657). Along the same lines, the author finds "the messianic significance of history in the events of history itself" (p. 657). He speaks of the persistence of what he calls a "Christomonism" and of the insufficiency and even of the marginal importance only of "pneumatology in the economy of the conciliar decisions" (p. 657). He shoots an arrow at the idea of what he calls a "simplistic reading" of the documents pertaining to the Council; according to him, these documents cannot be understood without "rising to a new level of comprehension" (p. 657). Whose level? His?

One example that he provides for us is found in his analysis of the *sensus fidei* and *fidelium* and in an order of thought which produces a virtual avalanche against what he calls an "essentialist ecclesiology." He favors the "priority" of what he calls "the proclamation over every other form of doctrinal or scholarly pronouncements by the Magisterium." He also favors "an autonomous statute to govern the Church's teaching function, as compared with the sacramental and governing functions." Indeed, he sees the need for "a rethinking of the magisterial service—at times too narrow—conducted apart from the governing function and the hierarchical structure itself, which came about essentially in order to provide Church government" (all these statements are found on p. 658). Always on the subject of the Magisterium, he believes "the ordinary Magisterium of the bishops dispersed in their various dioceses—the infallibility of which is recognized" by the Council—needs to "balance...the emphasis placed on the authority of the pope by himself" (p. 659).

The author continues this line of deductions exhibiting thereby his "dialectical" tendency to oppose rather than try to mediate or reconcile the differences between the various tendencies. Even Father Congar, in the end, found it necessary to follow the latter course, for example, in the *schema* on the missions (see pp. 612-615). Alberigo, however, would prefer to see the approved texts overturned; he speaks of a new "climate quite remote from the conciliar preparatory period," and he dismisses with only a very few words the *schemata* on priests and on the religious life (p. 660). As for *Schema* XIII, however, he notes that "it is today still difficult to decide whether we are dealing with courageous and far-seeing decisions here, or with premature and imprudent decisions" (p. 661). Thus, he associates himself in this instance with the judgment pronounced by Archbishop Felici in May, 1965 (see p. 636ff.), and, in part, with the contribution of Cardinal Walter Kasper at the *Synodus Episcoporum* in 1985.

With a certain insensitivity to the question of the *libertas ecclesiae*, and continuing to make no distinction between anti-Judaism and anti-Semitism, the author pursues his negative judgments on the Secretariat of State (p. 661); he does not notice that Bishop Jan Willebrands, after his travels in the Middle East, arrives at the same conclusion of that Dicastery. But as regards the issue of the freedom of the Church, it should be recalled that Father Yves Congar himself wanted to devote a paragraph to this specific subject in the Declaration on Religious Liberty (see p. 576, n. 21).

Another subject dear to the heart of Alberigo is the degree to which "first the Catholic conflict with modernity [which modernity?] and then the persistence of 'baroque' theology" impedes the development of modern theological reflection (p. 662). Here again, though, he does not seem to realize the degree to which he appears to be in contradiction with himself, since earlier he had claimed that "the ecclesial community....does not identify itself with any condition in particular, whether historical, social, cultural, or racial" (p. 650). In this connection, we should recall what the Argentinean Bishop G. Zazpe wrote in his diary: "The Church and the Council are in the hands of the European Alliance. Nothing counts except what they say. There is no other current or group on the other side that can restrain or balance them. Even the pope cannot be considered a factor able to restrain them. Not America, not Africa, not Italy, not Spain have any weight by comparison" (see p. 662). This is a very serious statement, which should be carefully pondered.

Here, however, as we have noted before in connection with the School of Bologna, the characteristic themes appear: amid all the "tensions and uncertainties," there is the unjust historical judgment that weighs upon Pope Montini (see p. 664ff.) by comparison with Pope John XXIII; there is a continued incomprehension of the historical continuity of the Council (see p. 666); the same thing is true concerning the incomprehension of the proper role of the Roman Curia, in particular the roles of Archbishop Felici and Cardinal Cicognani (see pp. 669ff.), but also the roles of the supposed "yes-men"; and there is the keen regret expressed that the pope did not leave free without interference the development of the conciliar reforms (p. 665). The author also denounces the "weighty compromises" and deplores "expressions contradicting the principal doctrinal line being pursued" (p. 666). He regrets manifestations of the weakness of the conciliar majority towards "the recalcitrant children" (namely, the "minority," as Yves Congar reports a characterization of them made by Henri de

Lubac). On the subject of contradictions, however, it is worth recording the judgment of Gérard Philips and some others that there was, in fact, no contradiction between Chapter III of *Lumen Gentium* and the *Nota Explicativa Praevia* (see pp. 441 and 444). The same thing was true for both Father Congar and Cardinal Bea as regards the acceptance of the amendments proposed by Pope Paul VI in the text of Decree on Ecumenism.

We have made many critical comments up to this point, yet we still cannot fail to mention, in conclusion, the initial attempt of Professor Alberigo to establish what he calls "the historical validity of the Council" (p. 668). This is contained in a "letter on the subject of the Constitution *Sacrosanctum Concilium*." According to Alberigo, "the implementation and reception of the Council constitute the proof beyond any appeal" of the validity of the Council. And so now we come to today, but with due respect to the conciliar texts, and also independently from their reception and of all *clichés*, even if borrowed from a leaf of a letter by Father Giuseppe de Luca written to Cardinal Montini in 1959 (p. 670); or from a text of M. D. Chenu, O. P. (preceded in writing the "Message to Humanity" by Gabriel Garrone) with regard to the Council's first "Message to Humanity." The Council Fathers approved and issued this message on October 20, 1962.

An Index of names and of subjects, as well as a Table of Contents conclude this volume.

14

A Counterpoint for the History of Vatican Council II

Alberigo Giuseppe, ed., with Various Authors, *Concilio di transizione. Il quarto periodo e la conclusione del concilio, 1965* [A Transition Council: The Fourth Session and the Conclusion of the Council, 1965]. Volume V of the *Storia del Concilio Vaticano II* [History of the Second Vatican Council], directed by Professor Giuseppe Alberigo, Il Mulino, Bologna 2001, 791 pages.

The ponderous *History of the Second Vatican Council* concludes with this fifth volume with the same kind of "monopolistic" interpretation. The Council was a defining event of the century just passed, and will no doubt continue to project itself well into the present century. This volume is again elegantly put together, speaking typographically. Moreover, it has been able to take advantage of all 62 volumes of the published official conciliar sources. This means that, beyond the problem of the management of data stemming from sources such as personal diaries, one can verify both the authenticity and the credibility of the claims of the various authors.

Nevertheless, we are obliged to record here again at the outset the painful impressions we have long since had stemming from our reading of the four previous volumes in the series: in these pages private views supplant public views; conciliar commissions turn out to be more important than the Council as a whole (although the latter is necessarily the center of gravity of the entire operation); these same conciliar commissions turn out to be more important than the assembly of all the Council Fathers together, as expressed in their interventions and their votes. These same tendencies have persisted in this series, even though there has been some improvement in the course of the publication of the entire five volumes. And again, the authors often turn out to be both monolithic and partial in their views; they tend to favor what we have identified as an interpretive "ideology" which it does not suffice to label merely "progressive" or "innovative." For it turns out to be a far-reaching and radical "progressivism" or "innovative tendency," far removed from the authentic conciliar spirit of trying to seek a consensus among those actually making up the Council. This is the case even while respecting the initial and legitimate positions of all the participants (see Chapter 51 in the present volume for more on this subject).

We are able to use the term "conciliar event" to signify an important and decisive fact about what the Council truly was without implying that it was a revolutionary break with the Church's past, or an organized process of demolition of what had gone before. That this particular reconstruction of the Council represents something "serene and faithful" (p. 15) is not something we can credit, even if some sense of insecurity in this regard can be gathered in the following attestation: "In spite of careful oversight and a common commitment to objectivity, it is possible that some subjective views may have gotten included in this historical reconstruction" (*Ibid.*). This possibility is for us a certainty, and it is not, unfortunately, just a case of "some subjective views." However, in his usual "Premise," the director of the whole project again summarizes his by now well-known criteria. He warns that the narrative included in this volume is "less linear than in the preceding ones; it was inevitable that various and different subjects would overlap in the same chapter, simply because they occurred around the same time" (p. 11).

Let us then enter into the various pathways of the work. The first chapter, "Towards the Fourth Session" was assigned to G. Turbanti. Seeking to provide illustrative examples of the profound uneasiness found among various elements of the Council, the author brings forward some of his ideas about the Council in order to provide a context for his own commentary. The ideas in question are not new. He throws into the mix the supposed thoughts, preoccupations, and sentiments of Pope Paul VI, as well as describing some of the pontiff's actions (p. 44, 47, and 56). According to him, the pope feared "an excessive assimilation of the Church with the modern world" (p. 45). Out of this grew the pope's preoccupation with the post-conciliar period; but there gradually emerge in the text the signs of the author's difficulties in understanding the pontiff's very personal task of exercising his supreme authority in the governance of the Church and in the defense of the Catholic Tradition. One example is provided to us from the pope's encyclical *Mysterium Fidei*, for example, in which the author notes that it "had an evident judgmental character against certain doctrines indicated, and against the theologians who had championed those doctrines; the style of the encyclical reminded one of the documents issued by the Holy Office, and it is probable that the encyclical originated in that congregation" (p. 53).

On the subject of "The Central Coordinating Commission: Review of the Work of the Other Commissions," the author gives the results of the Commission's meeting of September 13, 1965; he sees a marked weakening in the results achieved, and this does not redound to the advantage of the Moderators, he thinks; the latter, according to him, "were beset by the diffidence of the Curia, which never missed an occasion to attack their authority" (p. 59). These seem to us to be hasty summary judgments, as are those expressed concerning Archbishop Felici (p. 61). However, for the other commissions, the author underlines the existence of a presumed climate change; meanwhile, the difficulties posed by the minority are also brought out. Once again, the "maestro" for this author, Turbanti, is Father Yves Congar, even though the latter expressed considerable perplexity concerning *Schema* XIII (Father Louis Lebret and Father Karl Rahner similarly expressed some perplexity on this score).

The second chapter of this volume was entrusted to G. Routhier. It is entitled: "Bringing the Work to a Close: the Difficult Experience of the Fourth Session." The discourse of Turbanti is in effect continued here all the way up to page 76. In addition, the theme of "weariness" is brought in. Certainly some weariness had set in, but it seems to me to be much exaggerated here, especially in whatever degree it is supposed to have indicated resignation or diminished interest, in particular on the part of "the cardinals who had guided the majority during the two previous sessions" (p. 76). However, according to Routhier, "the minority seems to have profited from the situation" (*Ibid.*).

But it was in this situation that "the announcement of the Synod of Bishops" supposedly "took the Fathers by surprise" (p. 79). The planning stage of the new Synod was made by what is today the Second Section of the Secretariat of State. Monsignor Albert Prignon is way out of line in his comments on this (see note 130; yet he is cited so often in this volume as to be considered one of the major sources of information). The author himself, along with Father Congar, became aware that "something had occurred to change the course of so many long centuries of the centralization and the 'self-referencing' of the Roman Curia." However, a careful reading of the pope's *motu proprio* establishing the Synod "soon revealed its limits" (p. 84). The Synod "was subordinate to the power of the pope with respect to its convocation and its agenda; it possessed only the power granted to it by the pope" (*Ibid.*). "In spite of these limitations, however, the announcement of Paul VI contributed to the calming of the atmosphere at the beginning of the Fourth Session and helped to consign the dramatic end of the previous Third Session to forgetfulness. Paul VI delivered a clear signal that he was not a prisoner of the 'old guard'" (*Ibid.*). In Note 36, however, this author resolves in his own favor a debate with Carbone, making a distinction in the process that is simply incomprehensible; the same thing recurs in Note 132.

Treating the theme of religious liberty, Routhier returns one more time to the "dramatic" (and "frustrating") end of the Third Session (p. 87). Yet he recognizes that the postponement of the vote on this *schema* was actually beneficial (p. 87). It is also worthwhile noting, as the author himself does in Note 41, that in a lecture by Father John Courtney Murray, S. J., the noted American Jesuit showed that "the teachings of the popes, from Pope Leo XIII on, gradually developed the doctrine of religious liberty" (see, however, pp. 111ff.); for "the American bishops the *schema* on religious liberty was not opposed to the traditional doctrine of the Church" (see also p. 112). We would hope that these points, which we too have many times found occasion to emphasize, could now be considered established—if only to lay to rest the journalistic expression "Black Week" (which, however, occurs here too! See pages 108 and 121). For the week in question was actually "the week of truth"!

The author then presents, under the subtitle, "Between Two Minorities: the Church in the Diverse Worlds of Catholicism," a "majority in the process of recomposition and a minority in need of recomposition"—both "actuated by the victories of the Third Session" (p. 98). "Henceforth there would be two components which, although not wishing to be confused with one another, nevertheless shared certain interests in common, namely: the cardinals of the Curia and the *Coetus Internationalis Patrum.*" Routhier cites (n. 93) L. Perrin, who on the subject of the *Coetus* has a very different point of view than Routhier himself concerning this so-called "organization." However that may be, the author speaks of a "different historical context" for the Fathers, depending on where they came from, and for whom "the majority was no longer successful in guiding a Council that had now become enlarged to the dimensions of the whole world" (p. 101). This is a rather serious claim.

In "Waiting for the Vote," Routhier asserts further that "the multiplicity of conciliar directive organs and the 'many-headedness' of the Council contributed to complicating the whole mix further. One must add that the absence of any formal procedure for the meetings of the Moderators with the pope contributed to watering down all the decisions that were made, leaving to the intermediaries the task of interpreting the decisions of 'higher authority'" (p. 106). We do not agree with this judgment at all. In language which becomes progressively more bellicose, the author presents here various opinions of Council Fathers, and then he presents "The Battle for the Vote and the Initiative of the Pope." The Vote, he reports, "seemed to be taboo" (p. 116).

Then comes "the big day," a section entitled "A Day of Destiny" [in English in the original] (p. 122). It is on the subject of religious liberty, and it develops that the uproar expected from the minority turned out to be a "paper tiger" (p. 126). The author also complains about the non-representative character of the "directive organs" of the Council (p. 126); but he praises Paul VI for wishing that "the Declaration should clearly bring out the continuity of the teaching of the Magisterium" (p. 130). Nevertheless, the "paper tiger" proved to be still rather "tenacious," while the promoters of the religious liberty *schema* evidenced some "exhaustion" (p. 132). The pope, meanwhile, "required only that the text should clearly affirm that the Church [?] is the sole true religion, that all are obliged to seek the truth, and that it had to be clearly demonstrated that this teaching was in continuity with the teachings of the pope's predecessors" (p. 133). Among other aspects of the question, more or less reported on by Routhier—often in rather unfortunate language—he reaches the point where he finally defines "the object of the religious liberty spoken about in the *schema*" (p. 141). It was anticipated that the Declaration would be promulgated on December 7, 1965. The author observes: "In spite of all his efforts, Pope Paul VI did not succeed in obtaining the consensus he had so much wanted, and this at the price of compromises which many faulted him for making" (p. 141).

The author then goes on to deal with *Schema* XIII, again, guided by Turbanti, and without coming up with any surprises, therefore, but presenting the material with proper precision with respect to his colleague on the subject of Father M. D. Chenu, O. P., "who was practically excluded from participating in the preparation of the *schema*" (p. 149). Routhier discovers the first difficulty with the *schema* in what he calls "a revision of preceding teachings" (p. 144). This is not the case, however. He also describes an unraveling here of "the coalition...that from the beginning of the Council had exercised a true and proper guiding role...[This coalition] with some geographical variations consisted mostly of a French-German alliance, or, more widely, a Central European one" (p. 145). This was the European Alliance, which, in this case, had to be re-formed, since another alliance had become manifest, "a Mediterranean bloc, with a Latin American fringe, corresponding to the conciliar minority" (p. 152). This new formation showed that "the line of the division among the Fathers…was not simply a regional or geographical phenomenon" (p. 153). There was thus a very fluid situation created concerning positions adopted, sensitivities, philosophical presuppositions, and theological opinions (pp. 155 and 158). There were "two readings of the contemporary world," or, better, of its impact on contemporary realities and history. "The most significant debate thus concerned the title, the scope, and the theological note of the *schema*" (p. 156).

The treatment of "Atheism and Communism" here introduces nothing new. The following section, "From *Casti Connubii* to Vatican II," reveals two different tendencies. Bishop Carlo Colombo, speaking in the name of 32 Italian bishops, tried to present himself as a "mediator" for a *via media*. Some of the Fathers even raised questions about the indissolubility of marriage and divorce. Archbishop Elias Zoghby can be mentioned in this connection, although Patriarch Maximos IV Saigh dissociated himself in this case. The scourge of abortion was raised. In the author's judgment, the Church can "speak securely" on these issues if she remains "outside time and history"; "confronted with the Catholicity of the Church herself," however, he thinks it is hard to maintain the same stance (p. 176).

On the subject which then follows, "Culture, and Economic, Political, and Social Life," Routhier speaks of a "radical opposition between a theology of the incarnation that accords great value to human culture, and a theology of redemption according to which culture must be redeemed, and science falls under even greater suspicion" (p. 180).

Following this comes "War and Peace" (p. 185). Here the position of Cardinal Lercaro is heavily emphasized. In his intervention he revealed "a perspective completely different from that adopted by the pope during his visit to the United Nations [in October, 1965]… His position was also more radical than that of the majority of the

Fathers as well as of Paul VI." The Bologna cardinal moved on "to echo, rigorously and faithfully, and without equivocation or thoughts of prudence, positions of Pope John XXIII aiming to go beyond the idea of 'the just war'" (p. 185). But this idea was one of the themes that dominated the debate, along with nuclear deterrence and conscientious objection. The author evidences no little displeasure when he reports that the debate on this subject "concluded in an atmosphere of general calm, no doubt because of the general weariness. It was understood that the Council had become a 'voting assembly' more than a deliberative one, and the Fathers would have easily accepted by then whatever was put before them" (p. 189). We do not believe this at all. And cannot even the results of true deliberation also be expressed by a vote? Yet, in spite of everything, "*Schema* XIII...survived the debate on the floor, even though the Germans and Spaniards would have preferred a sort of 'message from the Council' in its place" (p. 189). So once again the text went back to the conciliar commissions for a final re-working.

Prior to its final conclusion, this chapter includes another section on "The Office of Bishops and the Governing of Dioceses." Here some attention is given to the Decree which would begin to implement in practice the Dogmatic Constitution on the Church, *Lumen Gentium*. Nor are burning issues lacking here, such as the bishops *sacra potestas*. No distinctions are made concerning the bishop's *munera* and *potestates*, or the tasks and functions, the mission, of his office. Similarly, there is confusion about the question of episcopal jurisdiction, as there is concerning an "interventionist pope" (Paul VI was supposedly such, as a result of suggestions made by Archbishop Samoré [of the Vatican Secretariat of State], and pressed further by Bishop Carli and Cardinal Siri—see p. 191). Further subjects discussed here include the episcopal conferences (comprising the structures for collegiality), and their relationships with the papal nuncios (subservient to their "control").

But for Routhier all this impeded the progress of the Council. "It is necessary to admit," he writes, "that it was in the commissions and not in the *aula* that the fate of the various *schemata* was decided...It had also become clear that one's objectives could be achieved by exerting pressure on the pope; nor did the adversaries of various *schemata* fail to make use of this avenue." This was perhaps not the case for the supporters of the *schemata* as well? The author continues: "The pontiff was preoccupied with the unity of the Church, and hence he aimed at unanimity whatever the cost, even if the support he obtained thereby was counterproductive. His concessions had the further disadvantage of raising the stakes. Since it had proved possible to influence him once, nobody was going to worry about trying to influence him again with increased pressure" (p. 192). In any case, the Fathers were already "prisoners of a universalist perspective, with the bishop seen as occupying a place in the universal Church structure more than as heading up his own diocese" (p. 193). The conclusion to which all this was leading turns out badly. Routhier goes on: "Paul VI more than anything else was the victim of the defective assimilation of the doctrine of collegiality by the Council Fathers themselves; they ended up considering him an arbiter superior to the Council itself" (p. 194). But is not that in fact the case? Routhier continues: Paul VI "was also the victim of his temperament and of his acute consciousness of the demands of his role…he was thus exposed to tremendous pressures coming from persons with few scruples, some of whom belonged to his own inner circle, and who, in many cases, were unconcerned about his image…Thus, the Fourth Session posed very concretely the problem of the collegial system of the Catholic Church and its relation to the primatial activity of the pope in a collegial context" (p. 194).

The other problem that emerged from these debates was the question of sacred Tradition. For many this proved to be both cumulative and repetitive. According to Routhier, "the Fourth Session quite eloquently posed the question of the Church's traditional interpretive role" (*Ibid.*). In the end, it was the whole question of the development of doctrine that was brought out by the conciliar debates. While I was preparing this review, I happened to read an interview in which Florence Delay interviewed Jean Guitton on the subject of Newman's theory of the development of doctrine (see *La Documentation Catholique*, January 6, 2002, p. 36). It seems to me, therefore, that Routhier becomes exercised here against what can only be styled a caricature of authentic Tradition. However, for [the Methodist observer] Dr.

Albert C. Outler, whose opinion is reported in Routhier's conclusion, the months of September-November 1965, could be considered a new "Reformation Day for the Catholic Church"—but it was a "Roman-style Reformation." And what indeed could be more appropriate than that it should be that? "In any case," Routhier concludes, "something important had gotten changed" (p. 195).

M. Velati, in Chapter III, deals with the topic of "The Completion of the Conciliar Agenda." According to him, the Council ended "in a climate characterized by a mixture of frenzy and weariness." This theme of weariness, of apathy, is a note that is carried too far here (pp. 197, 204, 208, 222, 245, 270, and 277). This is also true of the chapters which follow (see pp. 287ff., 306, 329, and 420), and, although there is some truth in it, we would not like to credit the idea that the Fathers were prepared to "swallow" anything in order to bring things to a conclusion. This would be to diminish their responsibility and freedom, in a period that was particularly rich in decisions being voted on. As a consequence, the result would be—wrongly—to devalue the approved texts, as, for that matter, some wished to do. The style of the presentation here is smooth, and the various "orators" are well presented. The subjects covered include the renewal of the religious life, the formation of priests, and Catholic education. There were some difficulties here regarding both the "definition" of obedience and on the question of priestly celibacy. On the latter subject, Paul VI "cut off the debate" (pp. 244-249). Such judgments rendered by this author are really questionable, however. There were further difficulties concerning the role of the philosophy of St. Thomas Aquinas. Once again the key functions of the Council's Secretary General, Archbishop Felici, are covered (p. 221).

The topic next taken up is the *schema* that became the Council's Declaration on the Relation of the Church to Non-Christian Religions. The author speaks about "traditionalist" bishops (pp. 223ff., 232, and 242) when he should have simply said "traditional" bishops. He mostly means the members at the *Coetus Internationalis Patrum* (pp. 224, 226, and 232). Moreover, he uses inappropriate language in their regard, for example, "anti-Semitism" (pp. 226, 229, and 242). He speaks of a Father Cocq when he means Father J. Cuoq (p. 226). Velati fails to pose the question properly between what he calls "the conscience and the opportunity" of the Council Fathers (p. 230). He also deals with the question of what he calls "the suppression of a clear condemnation of the notion of a 'Deicide' people" (pp. 228ff. and 231). With regard to the seventh public meeting held on October 28, 1965, he describes the pope as "at the center of a series of appeals and maneuvers" (p. 235), yet with varying results obtained in each case. The author sees this situation as "degrading the climate of the meeting and altering nearly every regular procedure" (p. 238).

It is at this point that Velati reports various criticisms of some of the approved documents. We are obliged to ask once again how the texts of a general council of the Church can possibly be received in such a negative and pessimistic spirit. By contrast, he reports good and sound considerations with respect to the non-Christian Declaration *Nostra Aetate* (p. 242).

In the meantime, the conciliar debate went on, varying between "nostalgia for the past and a sense of the present crisis." There are many things we could say in criticism of the author's presentation here, but we would enter thereby into a maze of details when it is probably enough simply to have cautioned the reader. The author goes on to discuss "the work done by the commissions," and he notes that everything was being "done in haste" (p. 260). Everywhere, one of the author's principal guides seems to be the diary of Yves Congar (see Chapter 45 of this book for my view of Congar's vision of the Council). Following on, that author considers the *schemata* more in terms of the differences with earlier drafts rather than in terms of any possible continuity achieved. Then there is the intervention of the pope presenting his amendments; for the author, these are "of small relevance" or else they are simply considered "papal opinions" (p. 266). He actually sees them as "a mode of participation by the pope in the debates on the floor" (*Ibid.*). He also characterizes them as "undoubtedly late in the game." Once this was made clear, what the author styles "the non-authoritative character of the papal intervention resulted in placing these amendments among the many amendments offered by the bishops during the voting in the *aula*. And thus the pope's effort inexorably failed to add anything substantial to the text already approved by the Council" (p. 267).

As a former nuncio in Belarus, I find it strange that St. Josaphat is considered a missionary and a martyr in Ukraine, but [Protestant observer Douglas] Horton compared him instead to Martin Luther, and, meanwhile, the latter is described as "courageous" by the author (p. 267, n. 197). In any case the final vote on the [ministry and life of priests] document proved to be "almost plebiscitary" (p. 275). The author concludes that much progress has been made in rethinking the theology of the priesthood in a missionary and pastoral mode; but he notes that "the incomplete character of the definitive *schema* was recognized" and thus "it is possible to speak only of a partial overcoming of the traditional scholastic theology of the priesthood"— this is the thesis of C. Duquoc—"or else of a fundamental lack of sufficient and proper reflection"—the position of Father Dossetti— "on the theology of the local Church" (*Ibid.*).

The final subject tackled by Velati is entitled "The Laity: Protagonists in the Church?" The low number of *non placet* votes on the individual parts of the *schema* indicated that there was a general consensus that was favorable. But here again there were amendments requested by the pope which, for the most part, revealed a preoccupation with seeing that the role of legitimate authority in the Church was given proper emphasis. It was Routhier who noted that "in the debate no scruples emerged indicating that obedience was thought owed to the decisions of the pope as such. On the contrary, the amendments were discussed and weighed only in the light of the general thrust of the text." Velati, however, speaks instead of "rejection," "refusal," and "failure" of the pope's initiative here. And it seems to us that he takes more than a little pleasure in the use of such words...Yet the Council was faced here with what the author calls "an absolute novelty," since this was the first document in which a general council even treated the subject of the laity." And here, beyond the value of the effort itself, there could be seen "the limits of a *schema* which opened up such vast new spaces, even while remaining linked to the theological and pastoral views of the preceding epoch" (p. 284). But should not that alone have said something to this author?

"The Church under the Word of God" is the title of chapter IV contributed by C. Theobald. His title is apt if we take into consideration the balanced vision of *Dei Verbum* itself with regard to the trinomial of sacred Scripture, sacred Tradition, and the Magisterium of the Church. In the text of this author, however, significantly, he grants an initial capital letter only to Scripture. Both Tradition and the Magisterium are spelled only with small initial letters. However, this is not an insignificant or trifling matter, as, for example, the noted scholar Father A. Vanhoye has shown.[1] Theobald gives extensive space to the diary of Monsignor Albert Prignon (as he does to that of Father Umberto Betti). He speaks, for example, of "a day of deceit" (p. 287) and he also mentions what he calls "a new 'Black Week'" (p. 339, n. 269). Theobald, naturally, does *not* give the same kind of space to the *Acta Synodalia*, and, even where needed, to the excellent Father Giovanni Caprile, S. J., who did not supply "the official version of the facts" (pp. 336 and 344), as the latter himself conceded.

Theobald begins by speaking of "an irreducible doctrinal conflict." The expression itself is significant, and he supplies sixteen notes in order to indicate where "the zones of turbulence" in the *schema* are to be found. Theobald finds it strange that sectors of the assembly generally far apart from each other converge in the case of this *schema* (pp. 296 and 315, n. 159); but this merely indicates how much, both in the past and in essence, they were in fact always closer to one another than was sometimes judged to be the case; and this was surely confirmed by the results of the voting, which proved to be close to unanimous (p. 349). There were, in fact, 2115 votes in favor, only 27 *non placet*. Nevertheless the author speaks of a "Roman-Florentine-Belgian axis" (p. 300), and he speaks also of the great question of "the constitutive

---

[1] See "*La Parola di Dio nella vita della Chiesa: La recezione della 'Dei Verbum,'*" [The Word of God in the life of the Church: The Reception of *Dei Verbum*], in Various Authors, *Il Concilio Vaticano II. Ricezione e attualità alla luce del Giubileo* [Vatican Council II: Reception and Actuality in the Light of the Jubilee], Saint Paul Editions, Vatican City, 2000, pp. 29-45.

nature of tradition as one of the sources of revelation" (pp. 299 and 335ff.). The well-known theme of the *veritas salutaris*, the truth that saves, also emerges (pp. 303, 321-323, 332ff., 339ff., 342ff., and 357), as does also the theme of the historicity of the Gospels (see pp. 323-326, 340, 342, and 344); these topics remain with us all the way to the end of Theobald's study (and with regard to the important theme of the *veritas salutaris*, see my *scholium*, or explanatory note, in Chapter 30 of this book). The climate presented by this author is hardly idyllic, but the colors in which he paints things seem to be quite forced in the direction of "dark." Thus he speaks of "a sort of blackmail" of the pope on the part of "some of the members of the minority" (p. 304). He does notice that perhaps this was an instance related to the personal positions and preoccupations of the pope (see p. 312). He speaks of the formation of "a third party," divisive in its turn (pp. 305, 311ff., 328 and 341). It was this party that "won," according to him, but does not this characterization itself connote divisions? Again, there were "impasses in the Theological Commission," but also the desire "to safeguard the 'economic' approach to revelation" (p. 307).

The author goes on to explain briefly the text of the *schema* and the various attempts at solutions for the most outstanding questions. And it turns out that even Monsignor Gérard Philips manifested "a crumb of ingenuity here" (p. 319), yet at other times this theologian made wreckage (p. 320). Then came "the intervention of higher authority," where several "particular" judgments of Monsignor Prignon are cited (p. 329). There is even a direct reproach aimed at Congar who "did not seem to realize the ambiguity of the *modus* 40D which added the word *directe*" (p. 331, n. 230). The words of Paul VI are much criticized, especially his use of the title, "Vicar of Christ" (p. 341). Actually, his words were both clarifying and significant (p. 338ff.): "Our duty," he declared, "is to seek a doctrinal certainty that will allow us to associate our approval with the decisions of the Council Fathers" (p. 338). The intervention of Cardinal Bea proved decisive (p. 343): "Thus it comes about that the Church does not draw her certainty about all revealed truths from the Holy Scriptures alone" (DV 9). But this created some surprise, and there were accusations of "abuse of authority" (p. 345).

The author gives the results of the voting and then comes back to what he calls the "significance of the 'doctrinal compromise' and its reception" (p. 350) in the case of *Dei Verbum*. He interprets the text in his own way.

We do not need to go back over all of this, but, yes, let us consider the question of "the permanence of doctrinal conflict" (p. 355), as well as the idea of a "doctrinal compromise." Theobald underlines the "violence" of the discussions that took place (on page 358 he mentions "debates of rare violence"). He also discusses the various "camps" involved in the conflict, unfortunately from our point of view associating Father Karl Rahner with Pope John XXIII (p. 357). That "Paul VI first wanted to suppress the formula *'veritas salutaris'* and then in the end accepted it—gritting his teeth," this constituted, for Theobald, "a choice at the last moment that was objectively equivalent to what had been decided at the first moment" (p. 357ff.). This does not seem exact, even if we were to say something like this ourselves—but it would not be in the same sense as understood by Theobald and Rahner.

One of the particularly important mistakes of this author is his position on "the historical foundation of the Church." Even if it means increasing the length of our discourse here, it is important to report exactly what the author says so that the reader will not be in any doubt about the validity of our critique. Thus, then, Theobald himself: "The neo-scholastic image of the foundation of the Church always consisted of a sort of a-historical projection, indeed an ideological one, reflecting the current hierarchical structure and doctrinal make-up of the Church as it has existed from time immemorial. But this account had suddenly become uncertain. *Strictu* [sic!] *sensu*, one cannot speak here of any 'doctrinal compromise,' because the divisions existing between *Lumen Gentium* and *Dei Verbum* were never discussed as such, either in the conciliar commissions or in the *aula* of St. Peter. But the tacit elimination of a problem is also a way of leaving out 'grey areas' and, in effect, deferring any decision in the matter to the future." Thus, this author concludes his account by expatiating on the authority of the Council's two dogmatic constitutions, which, although both are properly recognized as "Christocentric," are supposedly based on two different theologies.

What follows in the text are his conclusions on the Decree on the Apostolate of the Laity. Is the question of the mandate "juridical"? (p. 366). He also covers the public meeting of November 18, 1965, when "Paul VI offered his views on the post-conciliar period. There were to be institutional reforms. The author discusses whether the reception of the Council should be "official" or "kerygmatic"—this latter adjective does not even apply as far as we are concerned. But a new period had nevertheless begun: "The discussions are over; comprehension of them has begun. To the plowing that has torn up the ground succeeds the ordinary and positive cultivation." (These were actually the words of Paul VI, but, for this author, they signaled the reduction to nothing of the conciliar spirit. For him the conciliar spirit seems to consist of perpetual discussion and debate but never with any conclusion or application.) "It was in this atmosphere," Theobald reports, "that Pope Paul VI announced his intention of opening up the process of beatification for his two predecessors" (p. 369). The author remarks that the pope thereby eliminated the possibility of beatification by acclamation. By this time, though, both Pius XII and John XXIII had become associated with Roman continuity and were to be pressed into service in support of the renewal and *aggiornamento* as now seen by Paul VI. His view of these things would be a "synthesis" of John XXIII and Pius XII. He reminds us that the text he is covering (*Dei Verbum*) will be placed in the line of decisions from both Trent and Vatican I. But is it not the case, we are obliged to ask, that this text is already in the line of these previous Councils? The comment of Father Yves Congar on this same subject is even worse than Theobald's (p. 370).

Chapter V, "The Last Weeks of the Council," was given over to the pen of P. Huenermann, who has made very few notes. He relies on the *Relationes* of Father Sebastian Tromp, and rightly, for though it is in pure diary form, it is detailed and precise to the hour and to the minute. He also relies on the diary of Father Otto Semmelroth, with less reason, since this diary is hard, bitter, and skeptical; also on that of

Father Yves Congar, which is rather unpredictable and exhibits much nervousness and sensitivity; and, finally, on that of Monsignor Albert Prignon, which is biased and I could say tendentious. This chapter is well done in its own way, though it is quite ideological. He begins descriptively, speaking of "restless activity" at the Council. Things are difficult, and he is very critical of Paul VI, who in his discourse of November 20 used citations from Pius XII alone (p. 374). But was not this same pope the most cited single authority in the conciliar texts themselves? Paul VI provided "an image of a Church that was totally hierarchical," with no "differentiation between the juridical Church and the Church of love." But did not the Council itself proceed in exactly the same way? On the basis of such premises as these, the author goes on to speak of the promulgation of the conciliar documents "on religious liberty, on the missionary activity of the Church, on the life and ministry of priests, and on the Church in the modern world." He treats "the conciliar commissions as a decisive factor in the final work of the Council," and he describes their methods of work.

It is worth recalling that Paul VI "had an extraordinary interest in the success of *Schema* XIII" (p. 379), and he had "placed the commission in a position of strength" (p. 380). "In the final revision phase, Paul VI was in close contact with Archbishop Gabriel Garrone, and he buttressed and supported the work in a decisive manner" (pp. 381, 395, and 430). At the same time, Paul VI placed himself quite openly above the conciliar process…he assumed the right to intervene directly as the one finally responsible for the orthodoxy of the result" (*Ibid.*). It is even possible for him to ask "if any of the documents would have seen the light of day without the diligence of Paul VI" (p. 383). This seems to us to be the case.

Thus, one can understand the pope's "delaying tactics" with regard to certain amendments which he had proposed for the action of the commission, though not in a way that made them binding upon the bishops "who were the true members of the commission" (p. 383). Finally, this last fact is brought out! At that point, the author says, "the theologians were decisive in the formation of opinions on these matters." They were "men of great sacrifices." The author offers a further interpretation of his own: "The state of theology today would require a different way of proceeding, not to speak of the different themes that would have to be broached today—by both men and women theologians" (p. 385). This is an interesting perspective, to say the least. Huenermann concludes: "It was a great grace that the commissions represented, at least in some measure, the various groupings and diverse tendencies present at the Council. In this way various compromise formulas had to be worked out, and thus the actual texts produced by the commissions in no uncommon measure corresponded to the actual opinions of the Council Fathers" (p. 386).

There comes then a discussion of "indulgences." This topic was significant for the author, since it brought out how "a traditional ecclesiology of a juridical type, along with various Counter-Reformation practices, became significantly modified when introduced into a new theological situation—almost as if these practices were the stones and boulders in the detritus of a moraine" (p. 387). It is too bad that Huenermann does not see fit to cite the *Acta Synodalia* on this subject (AS, Vol. 4, pp. 521ff., 543ff., 556, 609, 611ff., 638, 663ff., 676ff., and 786). The author commends in this regard the "temperamental" position taken by the Melchite Patriarch Maximos IV Saigh and some others, even though it was critical; he speaks of the "dismay" of some, especially among our Lutheran brothers; but this would not have been right, because it was not in accord with the practice of the ancient Church. Moreover, there was no further display of "dismay" after the opening of the Holy Year door at the Basilica of St. Paul outside the Walls on January 8, 2000.

There comes then the beginning of the dialogue with the modern world, involving the final work on what became the Pastoral Constitution on the Church in the Modern World, *Gaudium et Spes*. For the author this constitutes "the apex of the significance of the Council" (p. 395). But there are still exaggerations or errors of perspective evident here, such as the following: "In the background, there was the question of the development of the social doctrine of the Church oriented towards the natural law, or, alternatively, an attempt to propose a theological interpretation of the historical situation" (p. 397

and also pp. 406, 411, 430, and 434ff.). The same kind of thing can be said for other similar expressions of his, which are often disjointed" (pp. 397ff.). For the author, there were on the table essential questions for the renewal of theology and for the development of a new vision of the Church. He refers to Father Chenu who, as we ourselves can attest, did not even want to hear about any social doctrine of the Church, showing where Huenermann is coming from. He also deals with "Paul VI at the UN" as a "conciliar event," and he further discusses general tendencies in the amendment process. According to him, around 30 percent of the texts resulted from the amendments that were adopted (p. 404). Such are the *desiderata* of Huenermann, who treats the work of Christ in the Church from the standpoint of "the history of sin in the Church" (p. 405).

The author then moves on to deal with atheism and its condemnation, the social responsibilities of property ownership, the ends of marriage, birth control, war and peace, and the international community of peoples. He records that to the great surprise of the minority—and to actual "irritation in conservative circles"—"all of the various parts of *Schema* XIII obtained a majority greater than two-thirds" (p. 414). On the much debated question of whether or not Communism should be condemned, the author finds that the Council "was grossly manipulated" (p. 416).

Another very difficult problem treated is that of marriage, and of the amendments required by Pope Paul VI on this subject. There are a fair number of pages here (pp. 420-427) where it would be necessary to make constant corrections and distinctions; the same thing is true of the pages where the author discusses the possible banning of war. But we will spare the reader the details of all this. Surely the customary "passionate taking of positions" is by now well understood, as is the regular "disappointments" expressed concerning the pope. The author concludes that "a majority of the mixed commission wished to leave open the question of the ends of marriage, as it did the question of any new condemnation of birth control" (p. 424). On the general subject of the Church in the modern world, there was to be "a system of open relations" (p. 431); and the author believes that there were "no great ecclesial controversies in the post-conciliar era that were not strictly linked with the affirmations of *Gaudium et Spes*" (p. 432). We would not say this at all. The author affirms further that "the inspiration of the document corresponded to its structure." He speaks of "tones which had never been previously heard" (p. 433). He describes "a concept of the goods and finality of marriage which had been dominant up to that time, but which came from the Stoics and emphasized the great importance of the procreation and education of children; this was *opposed to* a personalist concept of marriage and the family" (*Ibid.*; emphasis added by us). But there are limits here, and problems left unresolved. The author's language, however, grows heavier yet: "The Council had a clear consciousness of its initial effort to establish new terms to describe the relationship between the Church and the world; this was certainly understandable after four centuries of estrangement." We ask: "four centuries of estrangement" from *what*?

The next topic taken up by this author is that of *de Propaganda Fide*, or the evangelization of the peoples. The treatment proves to be rather disjointed, and deals with a new *schema* "essentially developed by Yves Congar." I will not go into the "laments" and the other frustrations expressed by Congar himself regarding this *schema*. These were supposedly "brought out by the radical reform of the Roman Congregation for *de Propaganda Fide*"—but it was never within the competence of the Council to decide on the organization of a Discastery of the Roman Curia, as Cardinal Francesco Roberti pointed out (p. 436; see also p. 450, however). But it is in this context that the author delivers himself of a rather strange discourse, including the following: "already at the beginning of the 1960s the question [of evangelization] often got linked up with the question of secularization. God effects his salvation in the profane world as well as in the sacred world. Historically the missions have had a collaborative role in the construction of a society aiming at the perfection of men. The mission given by Jesus to spread the good news got moved into the background, as did the idea of conversions. The new dialogue with other religions and cultures was then moved into the foreground. The mission no longer was one of *plantatio ecclesiae*. These new issues were first opened up in missionary circles, but they quickly became assimilated in Catholic theology" (p. 437). Let the reader himself judge concerning a passage such as this! There follows in the text a critique of the *schema*. And even though "the structure and the title give no indication of anything new," the author discovers "a new conception of the Church here" (pp. 438ff., 447, 451, 454, 456, and 469). The critique follows from here.

The discussion in the *aula* is then presented; the principal points of the debate are passed in review following the *Acta Synodalia* but with a selection of speakers chosen *ad usum delphini*, according to preference. The presentation of the *schema* itself continues with "the revisions made by the commission and the final vote." Thus the text criticized by Cardinal Roberti was replaced (p. 453), and other considerations were also brought up, resulting in changes. The final vote came to 2162 *placet* votes and only eighteen *non placet*. The author concludes by speaking of the limitations of the document. We are not at all in agreement with him about this (pp. 454ff.). In the end, the principal lines of the theology of missions is laid out and the author declares the finished product to be "an essential contribution to the consolidation and, indeed, the creation of a new orientation for the Catholic Church's theology of missions at the end of the twentieth century" (p. 459). In truth, though, "consolidation" and "creation" seem to us to be fundamentally disjointed.

At this point the document that became the Church's Declaration on Religious Liberty, *Dignitatis Humanae*, is taken up. According to the author, it was "first discussed with great obstinacy and tenacity but then finally accepted by a crushing majority...it was a document that was decisive for the history of humanity" (p. 459). But the author then abruptly changes course and treats the document as "a juridical elaboration of liberty within the Church," that is, in relation to "the exercise of authority within the Church." He admits, however, that, "this application is not found in the document itself." This is an honest admission. But he nevertheless thinks it can be "deduced from the principles that are developed in the document as well as in the light of the conceptual clarifications found there" (see also p. 465). Sadly, this kind of approach accords with the way the post-conciliar period is too often interpreted. And we can only register very serious doubts about this way of proceeding, as we must also register them with regard to what the author says about "state Churches" (p. 460). But it is, of course, true that religious liberty is based on the dignity of the human person. [As *Dignitatis Humanae* teaches] religious liberty "has to do with freedom from coercion in civil society," and "leaves intact the traditional Catholic teaching on the moral duty of individuals and societies towards the true religion and the one Church of Christ" (DH 1; p. 463). This, finally, is stated plainly.

Still to follow in the chapter is the treatment of the document that became the Decree on the Ministry and Life of Priests, *Presbyterorum Ordinis*, which this author describes as a "reform carried out with little enthusiasm," "one of the step-children of the Council" (p. 465), he calls it. The treatment of this topic alone suffices to justify our negative critique of this author's work. Still, may we be allowed a further question: on what basis does he become qualified to go from one document to the next, giving out certificates of merit or blame as he sees fit? Perhaps there is lacking here, as he himself writes, "a theological definition adequate to the definition of a priest" (p. 465).

This is the kind of interpretation that, for a long time now, we have judged to be "ideological" in the matter of conciliar hermeneutics (see pp. 466ff.). The conciliar text is faulted for ambivalence or such questions as the hierarchy, etc.; it supposedly consists of a "tangle" of diverse approaches (p. 469), and is even said to exhibit "an Old Testament model of the priesthood" (*Ibid.*). Then there is the critique of Semmelroth concerning the Holy See's "costly tribunals" and the "papal throne." Further criticisms are lodged against Paul VI's closing discourse of December 7, 1965 (p. 485). Viewed from the perspective of today, this speech is not considered "historic." In the final pages of Huenermann's contribution, especially pages 488 and 489ff., the critical spirit remains dominant. Writing of Paul VI speaking on the subject of ecumenism, the author finds the pope's "voice and attitude to be that of Pius XII rather than that of the Council and of John

XXIII. It is difficult to frame within the same picture," the author goes on to write, "the appearance of Paul VI at the United Nations on the one hand...and, on the other hand, this closing papal discourse to the Council: there are two different papal faces exhibited here. They are the two faces of a Church in transition in fact" (p. 491).

Chapter VI, on the subject of "The Council as an Event in the Ecumenical Movement," is the work of L. Vischer. It is an interesting and useful contribution. The author identifies three instances where the observers at the Council influenced the conciliar texts issued: with respect to *Gaudium et Spes* (p. 506); to *Unitatis Redintegratio* (p. 507); and to religious liberty (p. 514). Vischer proceeds by presenting the conciliar developments according to "world confessional families" (pp. 516-545). He concludes that "in almost all the Churches new discussions arose as to how to give a more credible expression to the *communion* of the Churches, including at the universal level. The discussions on this subject still remain open today" (p. 546).

At this point Professor Giuseppe Alberigo contributes a "Conclusion," which covers what he calls "the first experiences of the reception" of the Council. He begins with three densely packed summary pages in which his usual themes recur, including a revisit to the initial period of preparation (p. 548). The author reprises here his typical points of view, already criticized by us many times. I refer in particular to his placing Paul VI in opposition to John XXIII (pp. 549 and 561); and to the question of modernity and what it means and the passage from that to what he calls "humanity." (p. 551). I refer also to his moving and displacing the center of gravity of the Council from the conciliar assembly itself (along with the *Acta Synodalia* as its proper record) and moving to the commissions and the private diaries of some participants. I deplore his tendency to label as "new" *schemata* which were not new (p. 552); his characterization of the Council as "headless" (*Ibid.*); and his biased and partisan position on the subject of religious liberty (he thinks that at the Council "personal conscience finally found solemn and unequivocal recognition"). I also must make reference to his reductive understanding of the *Synodus Episcoporum*, which he appears to see as a centralized collegial organ sharing the *plenitudo potestatis* in the universal Church with the bishop of Rome. Nor can I agree with his view of "the disparity between the various approved acts of the Council...their levels of elaboration and their correspondence to the fundamental line of Vatican II are quite visibly uneven and irregular" (*Ibid.*). But who is the judge of such things, and on what basis? The author writes that "the conciliar machine and the various lobbies kept going on with these texts all the way up to their final approval, in spite of the fact that many of them were in part insufficiently developed and in part simply redundant." Among other areas of disagreement, I must cite also Alberigo's downgrading and undervaluing of the votes of the Council Fathers (p. 557). Similarly, there is his depreciation of the Code of Canon Law and, by contrast, his liking for "abridged laws" (p. 559). And, once again, I am obliged to disapprove of his typical characterization of so-called "Black Week" as precisely that (p. 560). It was not at all "black," as a matter of fact, but was importantly clarifying. Then there is his disapproval of the *Nota Explicativa Praevia* (which was supposedly a hermeneutical norm issued in advance), and his criticism of the supposed "long wait" between the decisions made by the Council and their implementation (p. 566); this latter period of time supposedly justified the "spontaneous unrest" that occurred. His views on the reform of the Roman Curia (p. 567) are similarly not at all well taken; supposedly there were "no appreciable structural results" stemming from these reforms. His anti-centralizing ecclesiology—"incoherent in the light of Vatican II"—is also mistaken. So is his view concerning the "silence" of the Council on various subjects (p. 567) [where he thought it should have spoken out] such as marriage, responsible procreation, and priestly celibacy. He speaks of "the trauma stirred up all over the Christian world by the encyclical *Humanae Vitae*" (p. 568). He calls for the necessity of new criteria of interpretation for the Council (pp. 570ff.). In the same way, he speaks of the need for the Council to have itself canonized Pope John XXIII (p. 571). Then there is his systematic devaluation of the documents of Vatican II by comparison with his interpretation of the Council as primarily an "event" (p. 572). Similarly, Professor Alberigo criticized the official edition of the Council documents, and through the interposition of others, he has also been critical of the *Acta Synodalia* prepared by Monsignor Vincenzo Carbone (p. 572, n. 70).

There is yet a further chapter in the book, also by Professor Alberigo, entitled "Epochal Transition," which is affirmed as precisely that. In this chapter, the thought of the author is a bit less drastic and his style is a bit more polished than earlier, and some of his affirmations even turn out to be both right and apt. For example: "There never was a Council of the 'majority,' or one of the 'minority'; even less was there a Council of either victors or vanquished. Vatican II was rather the product of all of the factors that went into it" (p. 606). We take note of this statement with great pleasure, especially considering all the instances in the preceding volumes where an "anti-conciliar minority" is spoken about. In the light of this statement, however, all these five volumes surely now have to be redone! But, in fact, even in this final chapter, the author continues to expound his well-known point of view, which also continues to merit criticism because of its ideological character. Questions therefore remain such as that of the representative nature of the Council, concerning which the author describes "the mortification stemming from the fact that the assembly was almost exclusively composed of clerics, while the feminine universe was totally absent" (p. 606). The author similarly deprecates what he calls the Roman attitude "of superiority over everyone"; indeed, he speaks of Roman "arrogance" (p. 606), while he lauds the vision of the theologians who "intervened" so effectively; he includes Father Dossetti among the "great" theologians (for his perception of procedural programs). Moreover, the author still regards Vatican II as, first of all, an "event," and only secondarily as "the corpus of its decisions" (pp. 538 and 632). Our opposition to such a prioritizing goes without saying; these two realities go together and mutually validate each other. Furthermore, if he understands an "event" in the way that current secular history tends to see events, that is, as a break with the past, then we cannot go along with this interpretation of his at all. (For our review of the 1997 work *L'Evento e le decisioni* ["The Event and the Decisions"], see Chapter 23 in the present work.)

The event of which Alberigo makes of much is correctly tied to *aggiornamento*, but it has also been filtered through the screen of Father M. D. Chenu, O. P., with whom we disagree, beginning with this reading of "the signs of the times" (see p. 640); these signs need to be interpreted "in the light of the Gospel" (GS 4). Again, the event in question is rightly characterized as "pastoral" (p. 585), but also here recourse is again had to Chenu, and mention is made of a presumed contrariety between his "method of research" and that of the late, lamented Monsignor Maccarrone, for whom the Council was "supposed to have exercised a judicial function and one that was conclusive." Professor Alberigo does not cite a source for this idea of Maccarrone's, of which he is nevertheless so critical. For him, "pastorality" and *aggiornamento* "together laid down the premises for overcoming the hegemony of 'theology,' understood as isolating the doctrinal dimension from the faith and transforming it into an abstract, 'juridical' concept" (p. 588, and then pp. 633ff.). Serious consequences follow from this new way of viewing things: "The faith and the Church are no longer co-extensive with Catholic doctrine; indeed the latter is not their most important dimension...Adhesion to doctrine, and, especially, to a single given doctrinal formulation, can no longer be the final criterion for determining whether one belongs to the *Unam Sanctam*" (p. 634). Thus, "pastorality," or focusing on the pastoral nature of the Church, "raises questions concerning the 'doctrinal' dimension of ecumenism as well, and calls for an all-inclusive search for unity" (p. 589).

However, precisely as regards ecumenism, Alberigo attempts to maintain that the non-Catholic observers at the Council, "were themselves substantially members of the Council, even if in their own special ('informal') way" (p. 590). For him there was a kind of *communicatio in sacris*, in other words, even if it was an imperfect one (p. 590). The author then goes on: "In this way, there emerged at

Vatican II a new pastoral-sacramental conception of Christianity and of the Church that could supersede or replace the previous 'doctrinal-disciplinary' conception" (p. 591; see also, pp. 608ff., concerning the doctrinal question and the proper hermeneutic of the meaning of the Council, and p. 634). But, we ask, how can anyone speak of "substitution" here? The author goes on: "At a Council rigorously inspired by 'doctrine,' and thus oriented towards rendering judgments concerning truths, the participation of non-Catholics could never have been anything but *affective*, and, in the end, purely decorative" (*Ibid.*). However that may be, looking back now at the pre-conciliar situation can only be "sensational"; "an authentic transformation or overturning has in fact taken place" (p. 592).

There follows in this chapter another section which is entitled "Physiognomy of the Church and Dialogue with the World." There is some equivocation in the use of terms here, especially on the subject of a differentiation between Pope John XXIII and Pope Paul VI. The latter was supposedly motivated by "a sympathetic evaluation of the modern world, but was still critical concerning our actual times. However, dialogue required a greater degree of availability, though not necessarily agreement or fraternity" (p. 594; see, however, pp. 638ff.). There were differences between the two popes with regard to their views of Vatican Council I. "Thus Pope Paul VI insisted upon the 'hierarchical constitution' of the Church to the point of introducing the idea of a 'hierarchical communion.' From this there arose difficulties impeding full agreement with the conciliar majority, which would have preferred not to have to carry on with the concept of the 'mystical body.' These difficulties eventually resulted in the *Nota Explicativa Praevia* appended to the third chapter of *Lumen Gentium*" (p. 595). Thus, this author makes some rather long jumps, here and elsewhere, in order to differentiate the two popes from one another (see pp. 602ff., 624, and 635 on the *Mystici Corporis*).

Another burning question is treated under the subtitle "Vatican II and Tradition." In this regard, Alberigo, now able to compare preparatory and final texts, sees "substantial continuity"; but for him there is "discontinuity with regard to the Catholicism of the centuries of medieval Christianity and post-Tridentine eras. It is not that substantial novelties emerge but rather that an effort [is made]...to reformulate the ancient faith in terms comprehensible to contemporary man" (*Ibid.*; but see, however, p. 639). Yet shortly after the occurrence of this statement, there reappears the old distinction between Church and Kingdom of God (the former term is treated in such a way that it is not seen as "the seed and the beginning" of the latter [as *Lumen Gentium* 5 teaches]). Rather, the premises are laid out "for going beyond or overcoming 'ecclesiocentrism' and therefore relativizing ecclesiology...by means of a re-centering of Christian thought" (p. 599; but see, however, pp. 616 and 636).

The author thus introduces a vision of "a parallelism of forces, including episcopacy, papacy, curia, and public opinion." He exhibits great indulgence for a certain kind of psychologism, and regularly uses terms such as "fear," "weariness," "apathy," and "marginalization" (p. 600). He calls to witness bishops' conferences that did not even exist; they are creations of his imagination based on secular models such as the parliamentary-style "lobbies" which he equates with the "nations" at the late medieval councils. He refers to the warning of Paul VI against the organization of groups within the Council—the pope was not referring to the *Coetus* alone—and he believes that jealousies or rivalries "hampered the work of nearly all the conciliar commissions" (p. 601). His treatment of the Roman Curia is, again, typical for him. He believes there was a curial "hegemony...in both the ante-preparatory phase and the preparatory phase of the Council." The Curia constituted "a pillar throughout the entire life of the Council...[it] had its own vision of the Church and was very jealous in guarding this vision" (p. 603). The author continues in the same vein: "The presence within the Curia of various positions, some loyal to the Council, did not change the basic structural fact that the Curia always remained a powerful and authoritative ecclesiastical pillar, which pursued its aims even when they diverged from the wishes of the conciliar majority." The author goes on here to mention the names of Cardinal Ottaviani, Archbishop Felici, and the Secretaries of State, all of whom "had a powerful influence on the Council, whether directly or working through the pope" (p. 604). Alberigo does not seem to recognize that these prelates were [through their offices] necessarily the closest collaborators of the pope, his *longa manus.*

He continues: "The greatest incidence of curial influence was above all found in the weight that the original preparatory *schemata* continued to exert virtually up until the end of the work of the Council... the survival of this material was tenacious" (*Ibid.,* and p. 612). A basic misunderstanding persists here: the original *schemata* were not curial, and they expressly did provide continuity with the past, while attempting also to deal with *aggiornamento* and renewal. The Catholic Church, after all, cannot leave Tradition out of account. From the very beginning, in the reworking of the original preparatory *schemata,* the Curia always had to take into account what it had to contribute insofar as that was possible. This was not merely a preoccupation of Cardinal Cicognani, for example; it was true of Cardinal Suenens as well, as it was of Monsignor Philips. We are also far from the author, later, saying that "the first order is the action of the Holy Spirit, and not of the pope or of the Church and her doctrinal universe" (p. 610). He has similar thoughts as far as the Council is concerned on the subject of the social doctrine of the Church; and on the idea of a "guided Council"—but could the Council have operated by itself? He has yet more similar thoughts on the methods followed—was it not possible, he wonders, to go beyond the traditional, "deductive" method, even if only partially? (*Ibid.*). He raises the same questions when coming up against modern, "profane" science (*Ibid.*), concerning theological reflection with regard to Protestantism, and also concerning what he calls "the acceptance of history"—"in the context of the divine plan for salvation within which, and not is spite of which, the Christian fact unfolds," he writes. According to him, there would be, in the relationship of the Church with the world, "a macroscopic inversion of the tendencies present in Catholicism for at least four centuries" (p. 614). "Friendship and acceptance of human history characterize the conciliar turn" (p. 638). There is an "organic relationship between history and salvation" (p. 640). This relationship "supersedes the old dichotomy between sacred history and profane history" (p. 641). "And thus, history comes to be recognized as a 'theological locus'" (*Ibid.*). The author offers further thoughts on the subject of the rigorous use of the historico-critical method and on Vatican II's being weighted down with "a certain number of decrees of a pre-conciliar inspiration" (p. 615). He concedes, however, that "the Council for the most part transcended expectations."

Our critique, however, is again directed at his concept of the newness or novelty of the Council (see also p. 585ff.). Quite apart from what is said about the legitimate diversity of previous councils, what is attested here about "pastorality," or "pastoral practice," along with what is said about *aggiornamento*, is that these characteristics were "for a long time unusual, not to say alien, to Catholicism" (p. 615). The author concedes that the juridical aspect of the Church nevertheless remains a constitutive expression of the institution (p. 616). At the same time, Alberigo retains his conviction that the Council documents are merely "orientative and not prescriptive" (*Ibid.*). Institutionally speaking, this means, he believes—erroneously—, "a reversal or overturning of [the Church's] priorities." He believes this amounts to an "abandonment of having recourse to ecclesiastical institutions, to their authority and their effectiveness, as the center and measure of the faith and of the Church." This is a very grave affirmation, and one recalls that this same author has previously asserted that "the hegemony of the institutional system on Christian life...reached its apex with the dogmatic definition of the primacy and magisterial infallibility of the bishop of Rome" (p. 587, but see, however, p. 637). "All the Churches and their bishops should be seen as equal"— including the bishop of Rome? "Faith, communion, and availability to perform service—these are what constitute the Church. They are the values-guides according to which the evangelical inadequacy of the structure and behavior of the institution can be measured. To rethink and re-order the Church's priorities entails recognizing the ecclesial criteria of the *sensus fidei* and of 'the signs of the times' in place of the internal logic of the institution itself, too often guided by questions of power rather than by *exousia*" (p. 616 and also p. 626). But we ask: why place these things in opposition? From where does one draw the conclusion that "the reception of Vatican Council II—perhaps even the understanding of it—still remain uncertain and in an embryonic stage" (*Ibid.*)? We would not be nearly so radical on this score, and, in any case, Alberigo should not imagine that he can point to the Extraordinary Synod of 1985 in support of his thesis; that Synod was opposed to hermeneutics such as his. And can he, in any case, condemn a presumed ecclesial leveling of institutions at their time as he continues to promote a democratization of the Church?

Could the Council have done more? "The question is embarrassing and the answer doubtful," Alberigo says. Yet he answers it anyway, revealing thereby delusions of his own. The author claims that, in a strict sense, Vatican II was not even "ecumenical" (p. 642). One has to ask why; he does not say. But he affirms that the Council "left the Catholic Church in a very different state than the one in which the Church launched the Council" (pp. 617ff., and 624; but see, however, p. 643). In support of this proposition, he cites as "consultants" Jedin, Rahner, Chenu, Pesch, Vilanova, and Dossetti; they introduce us to "the third great epoch in the history of the Church" (Pesch). The author himself speaks of "epochal changes," an "epochal transition," and of a place "between the end of the ideological era and the beginning of the post-modern era...On the one hand, it is a new point of arrival and the end of the post-Tridentine era characterized by so many controversies—and perhaps it is even the end of the many centuries of the Constantinian era. On the other hand, it represents an anticipation and a starting-point of a new historical cycle (pp. 631 and 645).

What should we say about all of this? First, let us state again that we do not accept the method of detaching conciliar decisions from the conciliar "event" in the course of which they were decided. And we must say also that, for us, Vatican Council II was indeed a great event, but it was in no way a break, a revolution, or the creation of a new Church, now somehow divorced from the great Tridentine Council or from Vatican Council I (or from any of the other ecumenical councils that preceded it). Certain "turns" were indeed taken at Vatican II, but—carrying on with the image of traversing "streets"—there were not, in fact, any "U-turns." There was indeed an *aggiornamento*, or updating, and this Italian word actually describes very well the nature of the "event" that Vatican II was (see my essay, "Tradition and Renewal Together: The Second Vatican Council," originally printed in *Bailamme* for December-June, 2000. It is reprinted in Chapter 50 of the present volume). Within the Council there is a "co-presence" of *nova et vetera*, at the same time as there is fidelity *and* openness. The texts approved by the Council demonstrate this—*all* the texts.

This famous "event" thus *was* "an ecumenical council."[2] We should not consider ourselves in any way biased in treating it as such. This is what it is for the Catholic faith; it has its own recognizable characteristics, which cannot in any way contradict what other ecumenical councils have decided. It was an event signifying unity, consensus. The Church has always been the friend of humanity, even though that does not mean she has been the friend of modernity as such. In what sense, indeed, could she be the friend of modernity?

Alberigo is inclined to think that "the elements showing continuity with the conciliar tradition are considerable, and even the new elements are relevant and perhaps even more than that" (p. 646). We are not concerned with questions of quantity, however, but with those of quality, we are concerned with questions of faithful development, not with those of a subversive or revolutionary character. It will have to be history itself which tells us whether or not Vatican II, in fact, represented an "epochal transition" or made an "epochal turn." There remains for all of us the task of waiting and working for a correct, true, and authentic "reception" of this great Council, not just because of the new things that it brought forward, but also because of its continuity with the great Christian Tradition—the ecclesial and Catholic Tradition!

---

[2] V. M. Deneken, *"L'engagement oecumenique de Jean XXIII* [The Ecumenical Commitment of John XXIII], in *Revue des Sciences Religieuses*, 2001, pp. 82-86

We conclude with an expression of appreciation for the talents that the various authors of this book reveal in the course of their presentations; but these talents could have been worthy of serving a greater cause, the cause of seeking the actual historical truth of Vatican Council II.

15

Faces at the End of the Council

Doré J. and Melloni A., eds., S*tudi di storia e teologia sulla conclusione del Vaticano II* [Studies of the History and Theology on the Conclusion of the Second Vatican Council], Proceedings of the 1999 Klingenthal Colloquium in Strasbourg, Il Mulino, Urbino 2000, 445 pages.

This volume opens with a fresco painted in beautiful brush strokes by A. Melloni, though perhaps we should speak more properly of a painting with the colors daubed on with a palette knife. However that may be, the author brings out his well-known points of view on the subject of Pope Paul VI and the Roman Curia. We find ourselves in the mainstream of psycho-history here, with all the worth and merit that this sort of history typically commands (see pp. 191ff.). The study covers the diverse subjects treated by the Council; they recover their individual autonomy here, and exhibit the ties and even the antagonisms created during and after the Council. The study is divided into three sections, including the Council itself, contemporary theological evaluations of it, and the programs, hopes, and preoccupations of the post-conciliar era.

For Melloni all these things are summed up in the completion of the five-volume *History of Vatican Council II* directed by Professor G. Alberigo, along with the attention in it given to "the reciprocal reception of it" (whatever that means). He emphasizes the "pastoral" character of the work and believes it expresses new acquisitions and a new fecundity inherent in a language...of compromise" (p. 9). Yet Melloni does record that the Council was "the greatest international legislative assembly with powers extending to the whole world ever assembled" (p. 10, n. 8). However, this is not really the proper kind of language that should be used to describe the Council.

At the end of the Council, there was supposed to have been a "sense of liberation," of "relief," both individually and institutionally, that the Council was finally over, and that the pope was returning once again to his "princely solitude" (p. 12; see also p. 22). The new Synod of Bishops was considered to be, "objectively, an unaccustomed encumbrance." Other views of the pope saw him as a "prince-reformer," now returned to his "Hamlet-like uncertainty" (p. 12), with no longer any "leftist-rightist division" for which he might be the mediator. As for the Roman Curia, it was "unfortunate for the Council when Pope John XXIII gave to the Curia the keys to its entire preparation" (*Ibid.*). The Curia, with no distinctions made concerning its composition and staffing, supposedly exercised "passive resistance," *concilio sedente.* The end of the Council "was viewed by the highest ranking officials of the Curia as if it were a recovery from an illness" (*Ibid.*).

Even the mention made here of the reform of the Curia, like that made of the Curia's ties with the conciliar minority, "obsessed with papal authority," are not well realized (see pp. 12ff.). "For the Curia, it was a return to the typical *heri dicebamus* of a bureaucratic priest" (p. 13). However, the author does finally recognize that "the Secretariat of State, thanks to the ability of Cardinal Cicognani, was the highest authority for the Council and the mediator of conciliar tensions" (p. 14). As often as not, the author speaks of the *papal* Secretariat of State. However, Melloni does not recognize that the Secretary of State "was the true spokesman for the heads of the curial dicasteries...and the logical meeting point for the relations between the episcopate, the curia, the pope, and the Council itself" (*Ibid.*). Rather, he sees the Secretary of State as simply a spokesman for the pope.

However, for this same author, by the end of the Council, even the episcopal conferences had begun to acquire weight, "trying to carry out the henceforth daily task of collegiality for all" (p. 15).

The other dominant sentiment besides "relief" at the end of the Council was "hope" (p. 16). "For the pope, the source of hope was the realization that, everything considered, he had emerged unscathed from the conciliar process" (*Ibid.*). "The Council did not signal any victory for conservatism...nor did the typical self-referential attitude of past Catholicism prevail." Now there was actually some hope that a positive relationship could be forged "with modernity" (p. 17). "The experience of the observers as virtual members of the Council, even with their *titulo proprio*, constituted a challenge for the ecumenical quest" (p. 18). But it should have been asked what these observers themselves thought of such a "membership." Hopes for the poor were also aroused, although "without the possibility that the network of nunciatures might find a way of operating that would be sensitive to the tragedy of Churches and peoples" (pp. 18-19).

The third prevailing sentiment after relief and hope, was "disillusionment." This was the feeling of those who believed they had lost out at the Council. Here the author exaggerates greatly, and, as we have said, gets deep into psycho-history, making no distinctions with regard to the conciliar minority. At bottom he does not really take into account the papal commitment to bringing the majority and the minority together in a consensus, a "conciliar" approach *par excellence*. However, Melloni does make mention of those who were not necessarily opposed to the direction in which the Council was heading, but were only concerned at the speed with which it was traveling; these elements were not saying that the process needed to turn around and go back, but only that there should be careful attention given to the curves in the road. "To be against excesses was not to be against the Council itself" (p. 20). However, it was not a happy comparison for the author to be identifying this tendency with the founding, a little while later, of the review *Communio*—which was created in opposition to the journal *Concilium*.

For Melloni, this particular "vein of intellectual pessimism"—or was it realism?—"attracted those who, like Jacques Maritain, had experienced the pains of the first stages of the reform of the liturgy" (p. 21). A different kind of bitterness, though it definitely was bitterness, afflicted those on the extreme fringes of the majority itself, who thought instead of "lost opportunities." In this category the author places Dossetti, Küng, and Schillebeeckx, all of whom had the habit of invoking "the spirit of the Council." These elements, Melloni observed, "would not be slow in exhibiting impatience for a Church that was still too authoritarian" (p. 22).

For all this, the author sees a kind of "precarious equilibrium" for the *semina receptionis* at the time of conclusion of the Council (*Ibid.*). This was the case because "among the theologians, a pluralism was coming about that would result in fractures and clashes destined to go on for decades" (*Ibid.*). Among the considerations lending support to this point of view, the author notes "that Vatican II closed without any 'conciliar party' having been organized" (p. 23). At key points leaders were lacking who could have brought together and melded the appropriate elements for this. Yet it does not seem to us that this would have been the way to go, that is, apart from the "leader," *par excellence*, that is, the current incumbent at the head of the Holy See. There is a full page of this kind of writing (p. 23) that needs to be read and meditated upon in order to understand why Melloni deserves at virtually every turn the severe critique we are obliged to accord to him. He is not, however, a pure "pessimist' in the mode of Dossetti in thinking that "lacking all at once was a party of the clerical profession, a party of ideas, a regional party, a conciliar party, and even a party, properly speaking, of the pope" (p. 24). What does this even mean? Something is seriously lacking in an author who was himself only born in 1965, and yet is able to write that "the time of enthusiasm was over by the end of 1963; 1964 would be a year of clashes, and both the Council Fathers and the theologians would find themselves constrained by fatigue and obliged to preserve what had been gained and then to try to reach some actual conclusions. Hence the most fruitful period of Vatican II from the point of view of the decisions taken, as well as the period when the most important questions would be resolved, was the period when the Fathers were most under the pressures of time, and of the fragmentation of the positions that had been taken earlier" (p. 24).

We have spent a good while dwelling on Melloni's introduction to this volume. This was useful because it helps us to understand the thrust of the whole book. At this point, though, we need to move more rapidly as we look in Part I of the book at the contribution by J. Famerée. He examines the questions of the responsibility of the episcopal conferences, and of the concession of various faculties to the bishops, and he asks if these developments were "signs of decentralization."

After having described his method of proceeding (p. 27), he chooses well, we would say, the main points of his research (these points are found especially on pp. 29, 30, 33, 35 n. 15, 37 n. 23, 41, 44, and 51; he makes a distinction with regard to collegiality, viewing it in both a wider and a narrower sense; and in this he is much indebted to Father Wilhelm Bertrams, S. J.). He goes on to conclude—and here we allow him full "responsibility" for his own words, since he himself is writing about "responsibility"—: "Following the end of the Council, the Roman Curia moved quickly to take things in hand, even though it had to contend with the resistance of certain episcopates as well as with the freedom of speech being exercised by certain bishops. After Vatican II things could no longer be as they had been before; the Council had affirmed the college of bishops; it had supported the development of 'collegial sentiment' and collaboration among the bishops. But so long as this new collegial spirit was not guaranteed by institutions enjoying a true autonomy in communion in relation to the pope—and, especially, in relation to the control that continued to be exercised by the Roman Curia—nothing was going to be fundamentally changed: we would remain, for the most part, in a situation of hierarchical and vertical dependency for the bishops with respect to the pope, and, what was even more abnormal, with respect to the Curia. Decentralization had not been achieved by the end of the Council, in other words; nor has it been achieved yet, in conditions that are much more difficult today because the conciliar euphoria is now long gone. This does not mean that the conciliar advancement that has been achieved should be minimized, nor that conciliar innovations should not be put into operation, as some already have been, on the diocesan, regional, national, and even continental levels. But in order that such conciliar innovations should work effectively, it is necessary that there should be an appropriate autonomy that is recognized by the Roman primacy. More exactly, this means a transformation of the function of the primacy and the way it operates. Such a realization probably would require a new general council of the Catholic Church to effect, and one, moreover, carried out in strict collaboration with other Christians" (p. 52).

The contribution to this book of S. Scatena deals with what is called "the philology of the conciliar decisions," and it covers this topic from the votes in the assembly through the issuance of the final *Editio typica*. After mentioning the huge problems of the language of the Council (pp. 52ff.), and after having examined, perfunctorily, the alphabetical-analytical index of the conciliar texts (which is of a private character), the author analyzes the differences between the successive versions of the texts up to and including the final versions. Apropos of the index, by the way, it is obvious that the term *collegialitas* lacks references in *Lumen Gentium* because it is the abstract noun (see p. 57, n. 12). One of the most prominent issues that arises is that of the *Nota Explicativa Praevia*. The author notes that "it was included by the Secretary General even though it had not been sanctioned by a conciliar vote" (p. 62). We would add, however, that the conciliar vote was taken in full awareness of the *Nota* and its contents; we need only recall what Congar said on this score. The author underlines the differences relative to *Dei Verbum*; there was a *passim*, an *eis dona divina communicantes,* referring to the apostles, and the famous *Deus nostra salutis causa.* She also makes mention of the substitution in *Gaudium et Spes* of the phrase *doctrinam de societate* for the expression *doctrinam socialem.* These are not minor or trivial questions.

The author explains this latter change while exhibiting a propensity against the traditional usage, namely, "social doctrine" (or "teaching"), which, however, finally prevailed. A great deal of space is nevertheless given to the viewpoint of M. D. Chenu, who was notoriously and viscerally against "social doctrine" because what he saw in the term was "a Christian civilization needing to be restored in the face of the evils of our time" (p. 86). The question was finally settled by a petition of Cardinal Cento requesting that, in the printing of the "typical edition," the expression *"socialem suam doctrinam docere"* should be reinstated (p. 95).

The subject of "The Closing Messages of the Council" was assigned to C. Soetens. These Messages were the pope's idea; he aimed thereby to make *Gaudium et Spes* effective in a very concrete way. The Messages were gestures that were characteristic of the personality of Pope Paul VI. For the author, they "were conciliar acts, without being so really" (p. 111). Nevertheless he recognizes that they represented "a pastoral gesture which committed the Church" (p. 112).

The second part of the book, entitled "A Theological Evaluation," opens with a study by J. A. Komonchak. It is an interesting study, even though we cannot agree with several of its points. And then, in his heading, he invents the order of the authors discussed, as follows: "The Evaluation of *Gaudium et Spes*: Chenu, Dossetti, Ratzinger." In the text, however, although we find Chenu in the first place, he is followed by Ratzinger and then by Dossetti.

From the outset and in his own way, the author takes note of what he calls "one of the most surprising developments in the decade following the closure of Vatican Council II," namely, "the breaking up of the solid front of those theologians who, after having contributed in the First Session to breaking down the hegemony of those who had controlled the preparation process of the Council, then played a decisive role in the debates of the subsequent Sessions" (p. 115). Symbolic expressions of these same developments could be located in the founding of the two theological reviews: *Concilium* and *Communio.*

These developments call for a study, in the opinion of this author, of the theological dynamics of Vatican II. This study would employ a heuristic model capable of a wider interpretation than that employed by Giuseppe Alberigo. Re-echoing Joseph Ratzinger, the author critiques as crude and elementary the opposition so often posited between the curial line and the progressive line (pp. 115ff.). There were "two tendencies in modern theology"—to echo the title of an important composition by Monsignor G. Philips. For Komonchak, however, this kind of approach is not sufficiently critical.

The author begins with an analysis of *Schema* XIII, *sui generis*, at the Fourth Session. He records various opinions on this *schema*. From these there emerges an approach that is both "more radical and more evangelical," especially with respect to "the very difficult problem of war and peace." This is a problem much studied by the Bolognese group, which is expanded upon by Father Dossetti to an undue and even excessive degree, in our opinion. Then the views of Father M. D. Chenu are presented in the way that many wanted to "introduce" him into the Council proceedings, although he was merely the *peritus* of a Malagasy bishop, and thereby increase his influence on the outcome finally enshrined in the text of *Gaudium et Spes* (in confirmation of this, see the considerations mentioned by G. Ruggieri on p. 195, n. 5). The main points of the thought of this noted theologian [Chenu] are well known to those who have been involved with this question, and consequently we will not repeat them all here—as we will not repeat those of Father Ratzinger either, even though the latter are very apropos, and would become notable within a year or so after the closure of the Council.

In his final "theological synthesis," the author labors to reconcile the views of his three commentators, but in vain; what he succeeds in doing is delineating the diversity of the three approaches. From this analysis there emerges an emphasis on the views of Dossetti, "who alone shared the vision of Pope John XXIII" (p. 148). "The disagreement of Father Dossetti with the general program and tactics at the Council represented a theological and religious commitment for him; this disagreement, as soon became clear, and isolated him not only from the intransigent minority, but even from many bishops in the progressive majority." "New views" such as these—as they seem new to us—continue to be provided by the author in the final pages of this essay (pp. 150-153), especially as regards *la nouvelle théologie* (employed in the singular), *ressourcement* (from diverse sources), Thomism, and the future.

But the viewpoint which seems to us emblematic in characterizing the problems of the position of Komonchak is expressed in the following sentence: "It would seem that Dossetti and Ratzinger were the ones who gained the victory for a post-modern orientation. We suspect, however, that Chenu would have asked whether their approach remained faithful to the results of Vatican II" (p. 153). Once again everything gets turned upside down here.

The years 1966 and 1967 are covered from a theological point of view by P. Huenermann. His contribution in not easy reading. He goes back to Kant, and also discusses modern philosophy and theology in the works of such thinkers as Heidegger, Habermas, and Luhmann.

Except for the hermeneutic for *Gaudium et Spes*, the author sees the two years he surveys as a time of positive reception for the conciliar documents. We would agree in the case of a simple reading of all the documents in question, but we disagree that *Gaudium et Spes* should have been left out (see p. 218 of the study by Ruggieri). This Pastoral Constitution possesses its own specific characteristics, and in some ways it is really the key document expressive of the meaning of Vatican II. Then there is the usual question of the meaning of the Council as an "event."

In any case, however, it is useful for various authors to go back to the immediate post-conciliar period, even if the accounts of some of the groups and categories presented sometimes seem forced. However, the main point here is that of the *societas perfecta*, which was identified with the key concept of the "Counter-Reformation," but which was then abandoned by Vatican II, since the latter saw the Church as mystery, sacrament, and people of God (the text calls this concept a *schema*: "*Das Schema ist so eine Regelanschaung gemäss einem gewissen Begriff*" [Tbe *schema* is thus a view of the rule in accordance with a certain idea]). However, the author "concedes" that there is a continuity in the texts with those of Vatican I and Trent (p. 163). Yet it is the model of a Church that changes in a way that goes beyond the pastoral finality of Vatican II; but this is what has gotten contracted and diminished here; and this would have been the case even if the idea of a *societas perfecta* had never gotten dogmatized. It is strange, although not too strange, that there does not seem to be any idea of *communion* in the thought of Huenermann; this idea was fundamental for Vatican II, of course, and is quite capable of marrying institution and sacrament. Nor does the author seem to take into account the other aspects of *societas perfecta* which have in no way disappeared from the conciliar texts concerning the nature of the Church, even if it must now be conceded that the *societas perfecta* of Bellarmine must be understood in the context of its own time and tradition.

What the new identity of the Church posited by the author really consists of can be gathered from various passages in *Dei Verbum, Lumen Gentium,* and *Sacrosanctum Concilium.* In the various authors brought together here, there are not lacking comments that are quite simply unfortunate on this subject. What is called for is to ponder, rather, the fact that if we remove the "counter" from the word "Counter-Reformation," we arrive at a concept of the Church that has in fact been underlined by some of the noted historians of the Council of Trent, namely, that following that council and as a result of it, there *was* a true *"Catholic Reform."*

There follows here in this text an excursus on the encyclical *Ecclesiam Suam* [of Paul VI] and also on *Gaudium et Spes.* Its conclusion turns out to be favorable to the changes in the *schema* on the Church.

"Disillusionment at the End of the Council" is the title of an essay by G. Ruggieri on the attitudes that emerged in the French Catholic milieu. It is illuminating for both the conciliar and the post-conciliar periods. We learn a number of interesting things, some of them unpublished elsewhere, about Henri de Lubac, Jacques Maritain, and Étienne Gilson. Various rather precise points are made about these three illustrious personages, not a few of which are certainly debatable; some of them amount to virtual gibes or taunts which leave no doubt about what the author's "thumbs down" means. Are these legitimate judgments? It seems to us that the author goes beyond what is called for by respect for historical objectivity, or at least what is required if one is to strive for such objectivity. One of the first arrows launched by him is the one directed against the social doctrine of the Church (pp. 194ff.); the attitude revealed here is illegitimately extended to the *Coetus Internationalis Patrum*. Another arrow is launched against the opinion of Father de Lubac on the magma that eventually became *Gaudium et Spes* and some other conciliar texts (viewed in relation to the thought of certain theologians). There is evidenced, however, an attitude of enthusiasm for Cardinal Wojtyla, and for a true *aggiornamento* rather than for mere worldliness and secularization (the latter described as "miserable").

And with respect to what is reported about Maritain's thought, this is worthy of great attention; nor should it merely be catalogued and treated like a kind of *apologia pro vita sua*; that it is, however, repeated and placed in evidence (p. 200). This is more important if, as the author himself thinks, for that matter, this self-designated "Peasant of the Garonne" wrote a book "not against the Council but against a neo-modernist interpretation of it" (p. 201). Thus, it cannot be maintained that Maritain produced a devaluation of the Council as such (p. 202). The interpretation given to Gilson here is also forced. There is a lack of balance in the treatment of the continuity—indeed the very presence—of "the perennially valid philosophical patrimony" at the Council and in a widened context (pp. 204ff.).

The pages devoted to "the spectra of the post-conciliar period" make interesting reading. It is here that the thought of Father Jean Daniélou, S. J., comes into consideration. His thought squares with that of his colleague, who is also theologically close to him, Father Henri de Lubac, S. J. Father Daniélou's fears bring out a problem that is very real for us as well, namely, "the equilibrium of the *aggiornamento* itself" (p. 222). Similar warnings were voiced by the German theologians, Bishop Hermann Volk and Father Joseph Ratzinger, and by others as well. In order to deal with the kinds of problems being raised here, Ruggieri recommends a hermeneutic of the Council as a whole, one which does not "locate the total meaning and significance of the Council in the recent history of the Church, but rather defines its role both in relation to the past and to the future" (pp. 223ff.).

If the true relation to the great Tradition spoken about here were being respected when evaluating the renewal (that is, the *aggiornamento*), we would certainly be in agreement with this author; but when we see how, later, he treats the post-conciliar work of both de Lubac and Daniélou, we are not encouraged thereby to go along with him. According to him, both men simply placed the Council between brackets and took from it only what they thought might contribute to their own personal theological reflections. He does not fail to cast his stones, in other words, even if he then adds: "But this is a judgment that needs to be verified" (p. 224).

"The Council as Seen by the Observers from Other Christian Traditions" is the topic covered by A. Birmelé. The author means "observers" in both the broad and strict senses. The resultant essay is very instructive because it can help Catholics be more cautious and circumspect in their synodal hermeneutics. We refer, for example, to the always vexed question of the *"subsistit in"* [found in *Lumen Gentium* 8] which has caused such proverbial rivers of ink to flow (see pp. 244ff. and 254); and to the obvious fact that the Catholic Church had to remain faithful to herself even during the Second Vatican Council (pp. 254ff. and 261). We also welcome the discussion concerning the prevalent practice of adding the adjective "Roman" to "Catholic" to indicate being in communion with the bishop of Rome (p. 225, n. 1); this issue is properly laid out here, but it still remains a highly problematical question. I believe that, to be consistent, this author and others of like mind should drop this practice as erroneous since, after all, in the ecumenical context, we have long agreed to accord to each Church and ecclesial Community the name it chooses to give to itself.

A number of well-known observers are mentioned and quoted in this fine essay. We would like to encourage our readers to take up this particular essay, in fact. We note especially in the names of Cullmann, Schlink, Vajta, Vischer, Aldenhoven, Skydsgaard, Roux,

Lindbeck, Scrima, Nissiotis, Clément, and, finally, Barth, who carried the ball for the Protestants at the Council (in this case, we ask pardon for employing a sports metaphor). The phrase "among us" was repeatedly heard (p. 264) referring to the new kinds of relationships being established with the Catholic Church.

One final observation: this author seems to exaggerate the role and influence of the observers at the Council. For a more balanced treatment we think of the careful work of Velati.

The third part of the volume, entitled "Hopes and Programs," begins with an essay by P. C. Noël bearing the subtitle "Post-conciliar Work: Expectations of the *Domus Mariae* Group and the Organization of the Post-conciliar Period." The author bases his work on the fact that in many places in the *Acts* of the great Synod the post-conciliar period is explicitly referred to. He explains first of all what Paul VI said apropos of this, comparatively speaking; and he describes the "initiatives" of the group of representatives of the various bishops' conferences which adopted the name of the place where they held their meetings, namely, the *Domus Mariae* (pp. 270-308). In this essay, there are not lacking various unjustified conclusions made by Noël himself; they are, however, instructive (see pp. 271ff., 276, 280, 286, 294ff., 298, 301 and 308). The major point of confusion here came about during the Council itself when, these representatives of the bishops' conferences began meeting. The author describes them, erroneously, as "pre-Synodal," referring to the *Synodus Episcoporum*, and, for Noël, they are linked to the basic theme of the necessity for a reform of the Roman Curia. This attitude would finally lead to a diminishing of interest in the *Domus Mariae* group itself (see p. 303); and the establishment of the post-conciliar commissions instead. Some life remained in the *Domus Mariae* group, however.

Then comes G. Routhier, addressing a particular case, that of Quebec. He speaks of a "Kerygmatic Reception of Vatican II in its First Stage." We do not agree with this characterization. We state this at the outset. Father Alois Grillmeier, S. J., used the term "Kerygmatic reception" when speaking of the Council of Chalcedon. The meaning of the expression can certainly be understood, but as far as we are concerned, it does not apply in the case of Vatican II. It would have been better to use the terminology proposed by Hermann J. Pottmeyer (p. 310), namely, an "official interpretation." This would have been clear and acceptable to everybody. We will not go deeply into the particular case of Quebec. Our interest in the Council is both more general and more specific, but we cannot neglect to note that Routhier himself found the results of his research to be disappointing. He felt that, in the future, it ought to be "more persevering, more lengthy, and more detailed and meticulous," especially since it was based on sources that were both fragmentary and not easily accessible. In any case, to justify "liturgical excesses" because of the delays and "slowness" of the official reforms (p. 354) contradicts what the author himself said earlier about the objectivity of facts and the rhythm of their application.

Another particular case, this one expanded to an entire continent, Latin America, is next presented by O. J. Beozzo. His contribution is entitled "Medellin: Inspiration and Roots." Among other things, there are not lacking misprints which spoil the Portuguese. The rather free and easy way, ideologically speaking, in which this author proceeds will not surprise those who know him. His *reductio ad unum* quite naturally issues in a "Church of the poor" (pp. 362, 375ff., and 381). He also takes for granted "the fight against the Curia," though always in communion with the pope (pp. 361ff., 371 and 380). He speaks of a "theology of the signs of the times" (pp. 367 and 373), and of collegiality but without the necessary distinctions" (pp. 361, 368, 370ff., 372, and 393). He would expand collegiality to the whole Church; everyone would vote on pastoral themes. He continues with the idea of the Council as an "event" (p. 369), restrictive and "poor" in its theology (p. 369), he thinks. Yet this author was inspired by Father Congar! How different was the "concept" of Bishop Jan Willebrands! (*Ibid.*)

According to Beozzo, again, the reception of Vatican II at Medellin was "faithful—pastoral, especially—creative, critical, and selective" (pp. 368-385). The perspective here is in accordance with what the author defines as "the ecclesiastical revolution that was Vatican II" (p. 372). There follows an analysis of the reception of the teachings of the papal Magisterium, as well as of the "gaps" at Medellin, among which the author lists "an absence of any historical vision of reality" (pp. 387ff.). The author concludes, however, on a positive note (pp. 392ff.).

Professor Giuseppe Alberigo also contributes to this work with an essay entitled "Vatican Council II: From Expectations to Results: A 'Turn'?" He replies affirmatively to this question, defining the "turn" as "profound" (p. 395), "sometimes questioned but now irreversible" (p. 414). It was, he says, "more profound and organic than anything that had been thought on the eve of the Council, or that the latter had been far-sighted or courageous enough to foresee or to hope for" (p. 415). Vatican II was thus a "new" Council, according to this author, fundamentally different from the councils of the tradition that preceded it" (*Ibid.*). The Council was committed "to respond positively...to humanity today in accordance with the criteria of 'pastorality' and *'aggiornamento'*" (*Ibid.*). These criteria, according to him, were "unusual, indeed, alien, to Catholicism" (*Ibid.*). There was a "qualitative jump that can be seen by comparing the preparatory material for the Council with the final texts; and, more than that, by comparing the climate of Christianity in the 1950s with the climate that prevailed after Vatican II" (p. 416).

Nevertheless, in a tone less radical than he usually exhibits, the author, to prove his points, offers his usual critique, referencing earlier publications, by him and by others. On the opinions of this author, we have already amply offered our grave reservations, which we will not repeat here. However, even remaining at the level of the author, while carrying on with this metaphor of "going down the street," we can surely reaffirm that the "turn" he mentions was in no way a "U turn"—this would not have been at all characteristic of Catholicism in its essence.

The conclusion of this work was confided to J. Doré. He is necessarily taken up with an effort of synthesis and bringing together—from which some of his collaborators seem to be far removed. The very title given to his contribution, "That Which Can No Longer Be the Way It Was Before," is one that nobody could disagree with (see p. 433). This is obvious. But it remains to be seen what the author is talking about. He tries to clarify this. There are certain important affirmations that have to be made here, first of all, we are really dealing with an "authentic ecumenical Council" (p. 421)—a Council which manifests "the conscious will to deliver a teaching, to impart a spirit, and, meanwhile, not forget to be concerned with institutions" (*Ibid.*). This concern with institutional questions is confirmed later (p. 422) with the affirmation that "the doctrinal *is* 'pastoral'"—there is no need, he says, to have recourse to "the illusory flight into ideology and into a contestation of the Church's Magisterium, which is always suicidal" (*Ibid.*).

This analysis, always interesting, becomes concrete in the discussion which is entitled "From the Event to the Teaching." All this is in the context of "the mystery of communion." It is stated that "it would not be the Church if there were not on the one hand, the juridical and institutional, and, on the other hand, the humanitarianism and the commitment to the needs of others, in service to the pneumatic and the spiritual" (p. 424). Reference is also made to "the revelation of God and to the liturgy of the Church" (*Ibid.*). And—we repeat—attention is given also to the institutional, organizational side of the Church as well as to its hierarchical structure. This is understood to be "the place where the life of the Church is manifested as such" (p. 425).

There was also, according to this author, a significant change in the understanding and carrying out of the reciprocal relations between the Church and the world" (p. 427). This was styled "From Communism to Communication" (*Ibid.*). But in all cases "it is necessary to follow the evangelical charge to do one thing without omitting other things" (p. 428). This means that "in turning towards the world in order to honor it for what it is, the cross should not be abandoned; nor should proper discernment be renounced, or the sense of sin" (*Ibid.* and pp. 430ff.).

We harbor certain reservations here concerning the interpretation of the *societas prefecta*. However, in those circles marked most definitely with a change of attitude towards others brought about by Vatican II, the new ecumenism among the various Christian Churches must be placed in the first rank" (*Ibid.*). But this should not indicate any downgrading of Catholicism. Moreover, the Vatican II changes were "even more spectacular with regard to other religions" (p. 429). However, the author repeats the call for "a Catholic theology worthy of the name": by this he means "fidelity to the riches of the ecclesial tradition while facing up to the inevitable challenges of the modern world" (p. 433).

Naturally, we can add to all this: it gets back to the question of the proper "dosage," but this can also lead back to the "ideological." Better than that, it is a question of applying the proper conciliar hermeneutic, according to which the Council was "a blessing, coming at the turn of the millennium." It will prove to be a blessing, however, "in the exact measure in which it has been and will be received in the same spirit in which it was opened, conducted, and concluded, that is, in the Holy Spirit of the living God" (pp. 433ff.). This implicit appeal from one of our confreres in the episcopate cannot but find us in agreement, if, however, we are also permitted to add "and in the acceptance of the conciliar documents as they are written." They represent the fruit of a constant search for consensus, and this itself was the work of the Holy Spirit; and hence it is an authentic expression of both Catholicity and unity—in an embrace between both Tradition and renewal.

IV

OTHER HISTORIES
OF THE COUNCIL
AND OF
THE POPES OF THE
COUNCIL

16

The Church of Vatican II
(First and Second Parts)

Guasco Maurilio, Guerriero Elio, and Traniello Fracesco, Eds., *La Chiesa del Vaticano II* (1958-1978) [The Church of Vatican II-1958-1978], Part I, Editions San Paolo, Cinisello Balsamo, 1994, 594 pages. (Volume XXVI of the Fliche-Martin *History of the Church*).

First Part

The arduous enterprise of a "complete" investigation of the great conciliar event which stands at the center of the history of the Church at the end of the millennium has begun in earnest. This history, although still provisory and carried out in haste to some extent, is in the form of a narrative synthesis. Some risks have not been lacking in the enterprise, particularly since the authors remain too wedded to their particular visions of the Council. Producing research that is truly scholarly has also proved difficult, since a long and patient assimilation of the sources is similarly required, including especially proper control over some of the "chronicles" of the Council (see p. 15), in particular those of Caprile, Wenger, Laurentin, La Valle, Congar, Rynne, and Kloppenburg (we would add Villot; La Valle's chronicle is mentioned here as "the most complete"). Proper control is also required over how the contemporary journalistic accounts of the Council are used; it is too easy simply to repeat them, and this sometimes occurs in the present work. Supposedly they are cited in the light of the official *Acta Synodalia.* Again, though, it is easy to cite these as bibliographical references; but to go deeply into them and draw the appropriate critical and comparative consequences from what they contain is something else.

However, the effort of the editors and contributors to this First Part of the work reviewed here is praiseworthy. They say they "want above all to offer the history of the conciliar journey pursued by the community of believers in the light of the new model of the Church offered by the Council" (p. 5). And the Council is indeed presented at the center here along with its various events, and also with the men who participated in it as protagonists and with the content of the documents it enacted.

In general, we note that the volume is lacking with regard to any critical apparatus, especially in the chapter devoted to the pontificate of Paul VI. The citations in this text of Roger Aubert do not indicate any sources at the bottom of the page. Did Aubert himself in fact supply these citations? Another deficiency in the study is the constant recourse to such categories as "conservatives," "progressives," "moderates," "reactionaries," "leftist," "center-left," and the "Roman school" (the latter mentioned without further specification). More careful consideration should have been given to the mode of expression, which is too often journalistic. the unnuanced judgments and the general references without any concrete details provided that are directed at the Roman Curia. The various tendencies at the Council should be treated by the historian in good faith, without qualifying them with partisan terms. They should be described on the basis of what they affirm, propose, and defend—unless there is proof to the contrary about this (see the judgment of the late, lamented Father Giovanni Caprile, S. J., reported by Aubert himself). The historian should not be a partisan, even if he does have his own personal preferences and limits. Thus, to speak simply in terms of majorities and minorities— but not as "ideological tendencies" (see p. 174)—seems to us to be more consonant with the neutrality that the historical method calls for. This is true even if there are shifts and changes within the "majority" and the "minority."

Following the bibliography, the first section of this First Part of *The Church of Vatican II* opens by treating the subject of "The Papacy." Three chapters are devoted to this subject. The first one is devoted to "The Pontificate of John XXIII" (pp. 15-51). Its author is Professor Giuseppe Alberigo, whose personal historiographic criteria are well-known. In the past we have maintained our distance from his kind of approach. In this case, the author practically treats John XXIII as a "myth" (see especially pp. 47-51). Adopting a saying from the historian Fustel de Coulanges on the subject of patriotism, we too can affirm that "devotion is a virtue, but history is a science; they should not be confused." Then there is the case of the care taken by Angelo Roncalli to avoid a transfer to Rome to head up the Consistorial; as reported here, this supposedly shows that the future pope treated his motto *oboedientia et pax* with a grain of salt. Similarly, to attribute to Pope Pius XII "a Manichaean optic" (p. 17) is totally off base, as is the author's judgment concerning the supposed "weighty and serious dissent" of Cardinal Domenico Tardini towards holding the Council itself (see also p. 4). It is possible, on the contrary, to document the cardinal's actual enthusiasm for the bold initiative of John XXIII. To hold that John XXIII "was not committed, perhaps on account of the foreseeable brevity of his pontificate, to name men loyal to him to the curial apparatus" (p. 27, n. 30) is to betray the Johannine "spirit" in a fundamental way. This "spirit" was solidly confirmed by Pope John's first and closest collaborator, Cardinal Tardini, in fact (see also p. 32). Again, the author's negative judgment concerning the Roman Synod is deficient because of the author's evident bias, it seems to us, especially after one reads the volume by M. Manzo cited here, *Papa Giovanni, Vescovo di Roma* [Pope John, Bishop of Rome]. We are also obliged to disagree with the very narrow and one-sided interpretation given to the "excommunication" lodged by the Holy Office "against those who voted for the Communist party list" (p. 25, n. 25). The same thing is true of the supposed "maneuvers" of the by then Papal Nuncio in Paris [Roncalli] in favor of the election of Athenagoras as the new Patriarch of Constantinople. [Roncalli] supposedly urged Ambassador Taylor to go to Constantinople to seek this goal through "Turkish and English influence." The Turkish government was described as "an important element in the process by any standard." None of this establishes that the author's assertions here are even true, however. And is it really possible to describe the traditional social teaching of the Church up to the time of John XXIII as exhibiting "its usual moralistic tone" (see p. 31)? Again, is it really possible to characterize John XXIII's own encyclical *Pacem in Terris* as contributing to establishing peace as an absolute feature of the kingdom of God and hence as an unavoidable obligation on the part of the Church? And is it really possible to describe John XXIII himself as constantly falling back on things that undermined his own general line? Is the author perhaps thinking of *Veterum Sapientia* here? Pope John XXIII certainly was a man "of the transition," but he was also profoundly traditional, and, moreover, he was a lover of the Latin language.

The second chapter of the section of the book is devoted to the popes and starts with "The Pontificate of Paul VI" by Antonio Acerbi. He treats his subject in a narrative mode, quite briefly, but also satisfactorily and without introducing any novel theses for this addition to the already notable number of studies devoted to Montini. One thing we would have liked to see at least mentioned is the historical credentials of the Brescian pope himself (see, however, p. 494, n. 36), along with the latter's own great historical sensitivity, which helped him so markedly in conducting the Council itself. Here we agree with the author that the great conciliar assembly "rapidly became the Council of Paul VI" (p. 59). We do not, however, agree with formulations sanctioned by this author such as the following, namely, that "Paul VI desired to safeguard at all costs the total monarchical power" [of the papacy] (this is a citation from J. Grootaers, taken up by Acerbi; see p. 61 and also p. 97).

We did find some of the observations of this author particularly pertinent, however. For example: "The positions taken by Paul VI ended up establishing a line of demarcation within the conciliar majority itself, between a radical wing and a more moderate wing—

the former reluctant but the latter inclined to adopt the points of view delineated by the pope. This division was covered up by the general fear of giving the minority more room to maneuver and thus possibly compromise the approval of the more innovative documents. But the overall climate of trust was thereby spoiled, at least as far as some of the bishops and theologians were concerned. The disagreements that were covered over at that point, however, later on, within a few years, along with other elements that had meanwhile entered in, resulted in open challenges to the authority and even the person of the pope himself" (p. 62).

After treating "Paul VI and the Council," the author goes on to "The Years of Reforms (1963-1968)" as not subversive but gradual. He offers a rather acute interpretation of them, as follows: "The Council was the fruit of particular dynamisms, both converging and diverging. A certain point of equilibrium was achieved in the documents themselves, but the dynamisms driving the whole were not exhausted in the documents themselves, but continued to inspire action even after the end of the Council" (p. 65). Following the analysis of the ecumenism of Pope Montini and his dialogic relationship with the contemporary world, the author then presents what he calls "the first skirmishes of the crisis." After that comes "the Post-conciliar Crisis (1968-1973)" itself. He explains it correctly as a new phenomenon in the history of the contemporary papacy, consisting of challenges to the pope from within the Catholic community itself" (p. 86). We would add that this polarization within the Church also extended to the interpretation of the conciliar texts.

The author's presentation of "The Final Years of the Pontificate (1973-1978)" provides the occasion for a very brief and apt synthesis of the pontificate itself: "The great discourses had become diminished long since, the dramatic voyages were over, public opinion had become detached from the papal fortunes, and the pontiff's health was declining. Suffering from both indifference and often open disapproval, the pontificate of Paul VI, from 1970 on, seemed in irreversible decline. But then the pope surprised the world and cut through the atmosphere of resignation, mistrust, and lack of confidence with two new initiatives: they were the Holy Year of 1975 and the pope's apostolic exhortation *Evangelii Nuntiandi* on evangelization in the modern world. And then, also in 1975, there was the pope's own reflection on Christian joy, *Gaudete in Domino*—a strongly personal statement." It was clear that the pope himself was reconciled and peaceful. "My state of mind?" he asked. "Am I Hamlet? Don Quixote? Am I on the right or the left? I cannot even guess. Two sentiments predominate in me: *superabundo gaudio.* I am full of consolation, and I rejoice in our every tribulation..." And the author, Acerbi, with a deep and apt intuition, attests that "the human spirit, when pushed to its extreme limits, either becomes paralyzed or turns itself around. Paul VI found within himself the strength to turn himself around. Thus, his final years were illuminated with a hope that was echoed in his words announcing unexpected confidence in God and in man" (p. 94).

It was in this way that Paul VI revived the image of the papacy, a work that had commenced with John XXIII. This is something to take note of when we think about the importance of the "image" in today's world, and also when we recall that the pope's governance of the Church was criticized not only for what it represented substantively, but also for the hesitancy and irresolution with which he sometimes governed (p. 98). It would be worthwhile quoting the fine and apt response of this author to these kinds of criticisms. We shall limit ourselves, however, to quoting just one single passage: "Patience was the virtue exhibited by the governance of this pope when he was confronted with the objective difficulties arising out of the contrasting thrusts he encountered. But he also exhibited firmness when circumstances threatened to obscure one of the two poles" (*Ibid.*). For Acerbi, Paul VI was definitely a modern pope "if by modernity we understand an awareness of the complexity of what is real, a perception of opposing potentialities in man, a sense of interior wounds with an aspiration towards healing and reconciliation...[Again] if modernity means a sense of historicity, then he definitely was a modern man. His passion for the truth was joined with his sense of relativity...[But then] how far could the historicity of the Christian message be pushed?...In this resided the drama of the pontificate of Pope Paul VI" (p. 99). And as for "the historicity of the papacy" itself (*Ibid.*), Paul VI certainly posed the problem and provided his answer to it. Perhaps his answer must be judged as only a beginning, but the fact that he had an answer was not the slightest of the merits of his pontificate" (*Ibid.*). We tend to agree with a judgment as well stated as this one.

In Chapter Three it is A. Acerbi again who presents "Pope John Paul I" (pp. 101-117). He writes of Albino Luciani's formation, with mention of his serious health crises. He covers his time as bishop of Vittorio Veneto (1959-1969) as well as his Venetian years (1970-1978). What comes through is the essential simplicity of the man's character, his humble and accessible style, and his interest in ordinary people; but the author also finds in him an "anxious spirit, which is the interpretative key to some of his rather radical interventions...He was distressed by theological and pastoral experimentation (concerning such questions, for example, as the worker-priest initiative). He was capable of issuing a devastating polemic on the referendum for repealing Italy's divorce law. Another issue which concerned him was, precisely, the Roman papacy. Looking at his 'programmatic' discourse after he was elected pope, one can discern a number of statements that seem a bit out of focus" (pp. 116-117). Because of his sudden death, however—the death of "one of us"—the author's comments seem quite appropriate in the case of Pope John Paul I.

The second section of this First Part of the *Church of Vatican II*, following the first three chapters on the popes, consists of seven chapters dedicated to the Council. These chapters are preceded, however, by a "Premise" written by Roger Aubert in which he discusses the major sources and studies available on the subject of the great conciliar Synod and provides an outline of the general subject. He then contributes four of the seven chapters devoted to the Council. This noted Belgian historian thus takes on the lion's share of the writing of this part of the book.

Chapter IV, "The Preparation" (pp. 129-157), consists of an analysis of the announcing of the Council and its ante-preparatory phase. He hazards an opinion on Cardinal Tardini: "It seems that the enthusiasm of Tardini was in fact rather nuanced: once he realized that the pope had in fact made his decision in the matter, he judged it opportune to lend his support rather than try to impede what he could not prevent." However that may be, this is not established merely by citing the fact that the cardinal had "observed to the pope concerning the latter's belief that two years constituted the required time to prepare for the convocation of a council that Vatican Council I in 1870 had in fact required six years' preparation" (p. 132). This unfavorable judgment recurs later on (p. 136) and is extended to the entire Roman Curia, which is described as "fearfully on the defensive" (pp. 138, 144, and 151). Not even legitimate distinctions are made with regard to the preparatory phase, although in the next chapter it is stated that "it would be a mistake to consider the Roman Curia as a bloc in league with the conciliar minority...because it was composed of a number of 'curial elements.'" Nevertheless an unfavorable judgment of the Curia is encountered at various points in the text, and it seems to us that this is an excessive degree (pp. 184, 185, 201, 202, 203, 231, n. 12, 270, n. 39, 312, and 383). [Another thing]: It cannot be said that the liturgical reform suffered from a "slow" implementation procedure (p. 388, n. 11). Certainly, their was no justification for free and easy liturgical experimentation.

In the course of Chapter V entitled "Organization and Functioning of the Assembly" (pp. 159-226), Roger Aubert exhibits his "world sense," passing in review "the national groups" at the Council ("from a geographical point of view for the first time in history"). He describes the pressures and tendencies involved, as well as the experts and observers. He is a bit heavy-handed here, issuing judgments that are rather too weighty. This is true of his comments on the Italian episcopate; according to him, "most of the Italian bishops exhibited an orientation that was too 'anti-modern'" (p. 162). His attitude becomes more positive a little farther on, and he even has a good word to say, for example, for Cardinal Ruffini, "whose criticisms more than once obliged those presenting *schemata* to express themselves with greater rigor" (p. 163). He gives several examples. Also his opinion on the role of the French episcopate seems not right if we look with his text the note 77 on page 176. This Belgian's method of measuring seems a bit diffuse to us. We need only mention his judgment on Archbishop Thomas Roberts, whom he describes as "a Jesuit who was not afraid to sate unpleasant truths" (p. 170). Perhaps it should be asked if all the Jesuit archbishop's statements were, in fact, "truths"; one might add, smiling, that not even the Supreme Pontiff enjoyed such an ample degree of infallibility as Archbishop Roberts tended to claim.

The author goes on to examine the conciliar Regulation. Here again we are obliged to distance ourselves from his assertions in a number of cases, including the question of "progress" for the Council in the elections to the Conciliar Commissions (23 members were named by the pope). This is the case given that, at Vatican Council I in 1870, all such commission members were elected by the assembly. But did not the pope select his nominees from among those not elected? (see p. 189, n. 8; also p. 203); the author sees this as another abuse by what he calls "the pontifical monarchy." He evinces the same kind of sarcasm in speaking of the role and person of the Secretary General of the Council; he does so in the context of the conciliar "directive organs" (pp. 197, 199, 200-202; but also p. 344), which are judged to be "a bit dictatorial at times." This treatment is not without its nuances, however, although "Greeks and Trojans" are regularly found incorporated into his text. In this connection, we wonder if the author did not simply hazard a guess in adopting the opinion of Cardinal Suenens according to which the selection of Archbishop Felici as Secretary General "was not the personal choice of the Supreme Pontiff" (p. 200). The conciliar commissions themselves are then passed in review; "the role of the popes" is also described as one of "careful discretion," which still, for the most part, "awaits any proper description." Yet both John XXIII and Paul VI are said to have "intervened regularly and on diverse occasions in order to put their stamp on the unfolding of the conciliar activity or to influence the work of certain commissions" (p. 210). The saying of Paul VI that "the pope is not merely the notary of the Council" was correct; he was, in fact, the supreme arbiter between the various tendencies, all legitimate, that nevertheless contended with each other. In fact, it was truly a marvel that such a nearly unanimous consensus was reached within the entire assembly so often as a result of the pope's profound efforts at clarification. This pope truly was "a prudent reformer" (p. 212). There then follows a presentation of "the daily activity of the assembly," both in the *aula* and apart from it—which illustrates the difficulties of acquiring proper information.

"The Unfolding of the Council" is the theme of Chapter VI (pp. 227-345). This chapter reviews the Four Sessions and the three "intersessions." This text is a valid and concise compendium of the "history" of the Council as it has emerged up to now; it covers the conciliar discussions in the broad sense, rightly giving particular attention to the *schema* on the Church—including two of the subjects that brought out such vivid contrasts, namely, the episcopate and the revival of the permanent diaconate. Among much that is valid here we have nevertheless found several points that need to be criticized. The idea of the *potestas ordinis* of the bishops deriving from their sacramental ordination (their episcopal consecration), while their *potestas iurisdictionis* is conferred on them by the pope—so that "their ministry is carried out not merely *cum Petro* but also *sub Petro*"—this idea is in no way based on "recent theological thought, widely diffused in the Roman School" (p. 257, but see also pp. 258 and 287, n. 17). Coupling this idea with the Petrine formula just referred to is seriously misleading in any case, since the conciliar expression *cum Petro et sub Petro* applies and is valid for all schools of thought that are "Catholic," quite independently of any reference to the origin of the *sacra potestas*. There is, however, the question, which is quite properly raised by Aubert, of the lack of any adequate juridical formulation of the fact of episcopal collegiality. Worthy of mention here also is the treatment of the famous "five questions" (pp. 259-260), in which the role of Father G. Dossetti comes out, initially, and then, later, is "retrenched" or reprised: "Questions were reformulated for the third time." It was the beginning of a descending parabola for the "role" of the Moderators. May we also be permitted an observation here apropos of Cardinal Ottaviani? According to Cardinal Suenens, he made the statement that "it belonged to the Theological Commission alone"—which, according to this account, was supposedly "his" commission—"to formulate questions in the theological order." Yet, shortly afterwards, a decision was approved by that same Theological Commission based on a proposal by Cardinal Suenens; and it was approved in spite of the opposition of Cardinal Ottaviani" (p. 267). And as for the question of the Blessed Virgin Mary and the insertion of the *schema* concerning her into the *schema* on the Church, it is simply not true or exact to state that treating her separately amounted to "placing her in opposition to the rest of the Church" (p. 263). Rather, this was meant to lend distinction to her.

The topic entitled "Concerning Paul VI and the Council" (pp. 273-276) contains a very unbalanced judgment according to which the many amendments proposed by Paul VI to the Doctrinal Commission represented a papal intention aiming "to attenuate in some degree episcopal collegiality as it related to the papal primacy." Rather, the pope's aim was to harmonize the co-existence of the two realities [of primacy and collegiality] without inflicting damage. This, in fact, is recognized in note 4 on page 284, in which, however, Giuseppe Alberigo defines the minority as "always inflexibly opposed to the ecclesiology of Communion." In point of fact, Montini himself clearly stated his aim, adding to "communion" the adjective "hierarchical" which, in our opinion, succeeded in joining together, in a most happy communion, the Church of the first and of the second millennia. This was the way in which consensus was achieved, in fact. We find that Roger Aubert's own final comment on this subject, which place Paul VI "entirely in the line traced by John XXIII" (p. 276), corresponds to the truth.

Then we come not only to "Black Week" but to "Black Thursday." Again we state our preference for a less partisan and less journalistic expression to designate the week in question. Could one perhaps speak rather of a "crucial week"? In passing, we note that Bishop Lamont was a bishop in then Southern Rhodesia, *not* Northern Rhodesia (p. 301). While Exhibiting an excessive degree of consideration for the views of the School of Bologna and the positions of Grootaers, the author does nevertheless avoid running into both Scylla and Charybdis here by means of an exceptional stretching of the rules (see, for example, p. 310, n. 97, in relation to the text on p. 309). In fact, he also does present the historical events of those days with a genuineness that is quite mature. His deference to the positions of Grootaers, however, amounts to undue respect for someone who, like Dossetti, and Alberigo himself for that matter, is simply an extremist on the question of the *Nota Praevia*. Grootaers does not accept the judgment of G. Philips, for whom there is no contradiction between the *Nota* and what the Council itself decreed. Also, we cannot share the judgment of Roger Aubert on Father Wilhelm Bertrams, S. J., who is described as "favorable to episcopal collegiality but on a drastically reduced scale" (p. 306, n. 81). On the contrary, he contributed greatly to the drafting of the definitive text of the *Nota Explicativa Praevia*.

Chapter VII (pp. 347-388) examines the conciliar texts themselves. Aubert gives a very brief history of each one, following a summary in which he lays out both the merits and loopholes of the texts in question, its lights and shadows, according to the opinions of various authors. He then gives a final judgment of his own. We do not think at this juncture that we can go point by point providing comments, critical or otherwise, on this treatment; that would take us too far afield. We would like to make the point, however, apart from any other comments or observations, that we are dealing here with *conciliar* documents; their "theological merit" ought always to be kept prominently in mind, especially in view of the "reception" of them that everybody claims to want, beyond any partiality. Or, if possible deficiencies are underlined, we ask if room is also being left for the acceptance of the Church's "doctrinal magisterium in a pastoral context"—which is what Vatican II, after all, emphatically called for. This is a general problem, and one of the difficulties of the present day is that, even if, of course, "the force and authority of the documents have to be judged on the basis of their literary *genre*, on obligatory criteria of engagement, or on the nature of the subjects covered in them" (p. 348).

Always on the same subject of conciliar "exegesis," we ask if it is really appropriate to assert that "numerous ambiguities remain in the text, where traditional statements are melded with innovative ones; they are simply juxtaposed with each other rather than being truly integrated." Or again: "Such a lack of coherence often produces divergent interpretations, with the result that some passages come to be unilaterally insisted upon more than other passages. In this situation, a historical study serenely carried out can decide to try to ascertain the deeper intentions of the great majority of the assembly—beyond the efforts that were exerted to obtain a broader consensus" (p. 348). Yet later on (p. 384), the approach is different, though here too the author tends to oscillate between two points that are not successfully fused (but see, however, pp. 386-388, including n. 11 in this regard). We are in agreement with the author that a deepening of historical investigations is important (yet see, however, p. 387, where he states that "even though theologians tend to take into consideration only the texts that are approved, historians know that a council is also very much a historical event in itself"). But we do not agree that one can arrive at the "real" conciliar thought *qua talis*, while prescinding from the preoccupations that made a search for a consensus necessary. Arriving at a consensus is, in fact, a characteristic of any council; such a consensus is not sought merely for its own sake, but in order to remain faithful to Tradition and to bring about *aggiornamento* at the same time. Only the definitive texts approved by the Council and promulgated by the Supreme Pastor *are* the conciliar texts. Otherwise, everyone would simply "receive" the Council in his own fashion, and in accordance with his own preferences, both personal and theological (or according to the "school" to which he happens to belong). Instead, the reception should be an extension of communion, an occasion for the new and the old to kiss and fecundate each other. This process illustrates how the new and the permanent come together in the Catholic Church; from her deposit the Church draws out both *nova et vetera*, which in this case we view with a theological eye. Conciliar "exegesis" needs to take all these things into account if it aspires to be properly theological and historical, and not partisan or ideological.

With regard to the presentation of the Dogmatic Constitution on the Church, *Lumen Gentium*, which is of great interest to us, for obvious reasons, we are again obliged to put forward some reservations, especially as regards the question of episcopal jurisdiction (p. 349). There is no reference made to the distinction between the bishop's *munera* or offices, and his *potestates* (powers); nor is there any mention of the liberty of thought and research which still subsists in various "schools" concerning the power of jurisdiction and its derivation. In addition, a statement about the "episcopal college" and the presumed restrictions about collegiality "which were introduced into the text in order to tranquilize the fears of some of the Fathers, and also of Pope Paul VI himself" (p. 350), is simply not satisfactory, as far as we are concerned. Similarly, to speak of "strata of the old ecclesiology" and the "not always perceived articulations of different ecclesiologies—those of juridical inspiration and those centered on the idea of communion"—, to speak of these notions as present in the actual Council documents, amounts to a hypothesis in need of much more examination. What is vital for us here, as we mentioned above, is the difference in the broad sense between the first and the second millennium, which the Council did manage to reconcile in spite of everything. And it was of the highest importance to meld these two millenary ecclesiologies.

Besides, the author affirms in the end—even though he also includes one of his notes on which a much more balanced judgment was called for—that "the fulfillment of the conciliar dispositions" (as he titled one of his subchapters) was summed up in the "prime reactions," that consisted of, first, euphoria, and later, disillusionment.

The following passage needs to be placed on the record: "In formulating a complete judgment on Vatican II, it is necessary...to recognize...that the Council was able to set in motion in a whole series of fundamental areas a profound renewal based on a return to an authentic tradition that was able to go beyond the positions inherited from the Counter-Reformation. This renewal included a will to equip the Catholic Church to deal with the transformations of the modern world, and to recognize the legitimacy of diversity within the local

Churches and the various cultures that the post-Tridentine monolithic structure had largely suffocated. The fecund inspiration that animated the leaders of the Council, supported by a great majority within the Council, along with the new climate that has undeniably been brought about in the Catholic Church (notwithstanding numerous efforts at 'restoration'), appears with the passage of time to be a much more important result than the documents promulgated by the Council, however rich and interesting the latter may be. Thus, even though not all the premises of the Council may have been maintained, it has nevertheless represented a wholly decisive turn..." We break into the author's narrative here to note that the promulgation of the Council's documents was made by the pope. Also, which of the "renewal movements" maintained all of its "premises"? The author goes on to state that the Council "certainly did not impede the crisis that followed in subsequent decades. Indeed, without falling into an affirmation of the simplistic model of the Church to which so many people have been committed, we can grant that the Council perhaps even contributed to a certain amount of the destabilization that occurred. At the same time, however—and this is very important— the Council also contributed at least in part to the attenuation of some of the unfortunate consequences of the crisis. The Council did this by committing the Church resolutely to remaining on the road leading to the future, meanwhile providing a renewed impetus on the pastoral, spiritual, and intellectual planes" (p. 388).

Chapter VIII of the book was confided to Jan Grootaers and is entitled "Protagonists at the Council" (pp. 389-515). His text, including a presentation of the two principal actors, namely John XXIII and Paul VI, had already been published earlier by the St. Paul Editions, publishers of the present book. Following the treatment of the two popes, snapshot presentations of some of the major Council Fathers are paraded past us, in alphabetical order, along with a *curriculum vitae* and a sampling of their conciliar *gesta*, or acts. Their strong or weak points are indicated, along with some of their major interventions. The "protagonists" in question include: Augustin Bea, Carlo Colombo,

Julius Döpfner, Pericle Felici, Gabriel-Marie Garrone, Franziskus König, Giacomo Lercaro, Maximos IV Saigh, Mark McGrath, Alfredo Ottaviani, Pietro Parente, Ernesto Ruffini, Léon-Joseph Suenens, and Stefan Wyszyński. All of this is preceded by an account of some of the confrontations between them—along the lines of Plutarch's "parallel lives." The author defends this way of proceeding by noting that "we simply wanted to show some of the relationships between some of our 'illustrious men' who were prominent at Vatican." Thus, there are encounters described between Suenens and Döpfner, Lercaro and Suenens, Maximos IV and Bea and one showing König as closer to Lercaro than to Suenens. These are all interesting encounters. So is the conclusion which the author derives from it all: "All this demonstrates that in an assembly such as the Council, the idea of a 'group' or of a 'party' must be used with great prudence and caution and never in any absolute way" (p. 394).

We may be permitted to report that among the "portraits" of those listed immediately above—the more unhappy (and we are playing on the word) —the one depicting the Secretary General, Archbishop Felici, even though some positive characteristics of his are mentioned, is a most unfortunate one. Here are some of the negative traits about him that are included: "With regard to his characteristics, he was basically at the antipodes of the major tendencies of Vatican II: he represented Roman centralism, and an apologetical attitude [towards the faith]; he was opposed to any expression of 'public opinion' within the Church; he had an aversion towards the idea of the Church as a mystery or sacrament. His innate 'juridicism' and his negative attitude towards any doctrinal development were elements which constituted definite obstacles within the Council as it proceeded to move towards its conclusion. The conception that Archbishop Felici had about the Council and what it was aiming at corresponded to the most conservative of all the visions present in the conciliar minority" (p. 436).

It should not be a surprise that in the gallery that Grootaers thus presents, the most prominent protagonist at the Council was Cardinal

Giacomo Lercaro of Bologna, who, according to him, "represented...
the highest religious and moral authority in the assembly." And again:
"The interventions of Cardinal Lercaro were the 'masterpieces' of
Vatican Council II" (p. 459).

Some mention might also perhaps be made of the "sensitive
question" of the *Nota Explicativa Praevia* which this author deals with
in connection with the presentation of Pietro Parente (see pp. 45ff.);
this latter presentation, however, was treated by Grootaers himself in
the volume *Primauté et Collegialité: Le dossier de G. Philips sur la
Nota Explicativa Praevia* [Primacy and Collegiality: the Dossier of G.
Philips on the *Nota Explicativa Praevia*], (Louvain, 1986). However,
we shall pass on this here, since we have already had the occasion to
review the book in question (reprinted as Chapter 28 of this present
book).

"Vatican II and the Means of Social Communication" is the title of
Chapter IX of the book under review here (pp. 517-549). It is divided
up into the following sections: *ad intra* and *ad extra*, Rome and public
opinion (January 24, 1959-October 11, 1962); the principal historical
lines (October 11, 1962-June 3, 1963); conciliation and authority (June
3, 1963-August-September, 1968); the reception of Vatican II (1968-
1978). In this last section are found echoes of the press on various
related conciliar and post-conciliar subjects; these echoes followed
the initial difficulties [the Church had] in locating a proper channel for
handling questions of public relations, and in dealing with questions
of public opinion generally, especially given the importance of the
subject matter and the Church's lived experience of it with the Council.
Many themes "required secrecy," however (p. 523). Then there was
the question of the language of the Council (p. 526).

The final chapter of this volume comprising the First Part of *The
Church of Vatican II*, was entrusted to Gian Piero Milano. Its title is
"The Synod of Bishops and the Reform of the Roman Curia" (pp. 551-
563). The treatment is quite precise overall, and includes explanations

of the nature and aims of Synod, as well as the type of assembly it is supposed to be; its directive organs and operating procedures are also discussed. From all this the author draws a number of conclusions concerning the *Synodus Episcoporum*. With regard to the reform of the Roman Curia, a brief analysis is included of the apostolic constitution *Regimini Ecclesiae universae* (which came out within two years of the end of Vatican II). According to Father Yves Congar, it gave rise to a *new centralization*. Milano ascribes this to the document's "reinforcement—thanks to the central and superintending position given to the Secretariat of State—of the pope's authority over the Congregations. In doing this it failed to carry out conciliar expectations for a more definite decentralization of some of the papal functions and prerogatives in favor of more activity by the local bishops. Yet, in spite of this, the conciliar origin of *Regimini* is quite evident and hence its relevance to ecumenical meetings remains" (p. 559). Mention is also made of the restructuring of the former Congregation of the Holy Office, with its new name, the Congregation for the Doctrine of the Faith. Important also was the *motu proprio* entitled *Ingravescentem aetatem* by which members of the College of Cardinals over eighty no longer participate in conclaves to elect a new pope.

The volume concludes with an analytical index (pp. 565-586) as well as indices of both illustrations and iconographic references, and, finally, a general index (pp. 589-594).

Second Part

Guasco Maurilio, Guerriero Elio, and Traniello Francesco, Eds., *La Chiesa del Vaticano II* (1958-1978) [The Church of Vatican II (1958-1978)], Part II, Editions San Paolo, Pioltello (Milan), 727 pages. (Volume XXV/2 of the Fliche-Martin *History of the Church*)

In our introduction to Part I of this work, we defined it as "an arduous enterprise of a 'complete' investigation of the great conciliar event." We also noted that it was "provisory and carried out in haste to some extent," but that it remained "at the center of the history of the Church at the end of the millennium." We further remarked on the risks incurred by authors "wedded to their particular visions of the Council," and also on the difficulty of achieving "research that is truly scholarly" without a long and patient commitment to assimilate and control the various "chronicles" of the Council in the light of the official *Acta Synodalia.* Simply to cite these latter, in general, in a study, is easy. But to read them correctly, get to the heart of them, and draw the appropriate critical and comparative consequences from them, without falling into partisan and one-sided interpretations, is something else again. Thus it seems right to repeat these observations in substance here in relation to this Second Part, even while recognizing that the risks about which we have spoken above are less serious here, it seems to us.

This volume begins with the third section of the overall work. It bears the title, "The People of God," but its first chapter (the eleventh in the work as a whole) is dedicated to the "Episcopal Conferences" (pp. 7-16) and it comes from the pen of an acknowledged expert in the matter, Giorgio Feliciani. Nevertheless, in our opinion, some of the expressions in the text (pp. 15-16) could have been a little less fanciful, if we are to recognize correctly the true problems and prospects arising in connection with the bishops' conferences.

There follows, in Chapter XII (pp. 17-27), the work of Juan Ignacio Arrrieta which consists of a precise explanation of the canonical regulations regarding "Diocesan and Parochial Councils." Following this, there is a study by Maurilio Guasco on the subject of "Seminaries, Clergy, and Religious Congregations" (pp. 29-80). This, again, is a good and precise documentary presentation of the current ecclesial discipline erected in response to the problems that have emerged in these areas. We noted a somewhat unfinished quality in the author's treatment of the *ratio studiorum* (p. 44), of the "national paths" for the clergy, and of the nature and identity of the religious life as delineated by the Council (p. 63)—and also of the crisis of our day as reflected in the life of the Church and the priesthood (p. 79).

"The Laity in the Life of the Church" (pp. 81-118) is the title of

Chapter XIV, which was entrusted to Giorgio Vecchio. His research pertains mostly to Italy, and he frankly recognizes the limitations of his study, which he says "has not yet resulted in a satisfactory synthesis." His exposition is valid, and he covers the essential and does not neglect any really important aspect, even if he does evidence some perplexity concerning developments at the end of the pontificate of Paul VI, where his position does not seem to be completely balanced, precisely with regard to the Council and to some of the ideas of the School of Bologna.

The fourth section, "A Church on the Road," begins with Chapter XV by Luigi Dalla Torre, who deals with "The Liturgical Experience: Prayer, Liturgy, New Devotions" (pp. 121-165). He covers the long road that has been traveled, and, partly because it has been so long, the author's lack of serenity in his presentation is rather surprising (see p. 122, n. 5, and pp. 123, 135, 148, 155, n. 80 and n. 81, 157, and 161-162). His final conclusions, however, are not lacking in either depth or acuteness; he lays them out under the title, "An Evaluation of the Past and a Look at the Future."

"The Biblical Renewal" is the subject of Chapter XVI (pp. 167-216). It is expounded by Mauro Pesce who has ventured upon this theme before. He lays out the principal issues with precision, and explains how he plans to approach them. His major focus is Bible studies within Catholicism and the encouragement of them by the central organs of the Church, and by Vatican Council II in particular, which wished to see a greater use of the Bible in the life of the Church. He also describes how effective these initiatives have been. His treatment is exhaustive, even if we cannot agree with all of his judgments, for example, with his view that Pope John XXIII's "biblical theology was not adequate in order to allow him to understand recent biblical studies. More than that, it seems that this pope was not able to control the Curia in the matter" (p. 185, and also p. 196, n. 114). We also lament the author's failure to describe the amendments to *Dei Verbum* introduced at the Council at the behest of Paul VI (see p.

196). This would have allowed the reader to view the position of the "conservatives" in a rather different light. It does please us, however, to be able to report the following conclusion of this author: "The faith life of believers, in conjunction with the new liturgy, the new 'biblical' style of preaching, and the biblical content of the *Catechism* have all come to be heavily based on the Bible. And this has in turn brought about a reformulation of Catholic theology itself, of priestly formation, and of the curricula in theology faculties and seminaries. All this has represented a turn of truly epochal dimensions. An evaluation of the turn in question, however, is not yet possible, since for a project of such ample dimensions, the past twenty-five years have constituted only a beginning" (p. 205).

"The Progress of Theology," Chapter XVII (pp. 217-247), was entrusted to the expert hand of Rosino Gibellini, literary director of the *Queriniana* publishers. He emphasizes, first of all, the situation preceding the twenty-year period (1958-1978) considered in this book. He pays particular attention to neo-scholastic theology and to what is commonly referred to today as *la nouvelle théologie*. His narrative is sustained by two guiding ideas, namely, the return to biblical, patristic, spiritual, and liturgical sources, and a dialogue relationship with modern thought and culture which is not adversarial. He then analyzes the renewal in contemporary theological investigation from the perspective of the history of salvation, developments in ecclesiology, the movement from the theory of the development of doctrine to a hermeneutical theology, the Catholic debate on secularization, the anthropological turn in theology, the new political theology, and the emergence of the theology of liberation in Latin America. Concerning his treatment of this last subject, the author seems to go down a road of his own, which is less than satisfactory; he introduces a number of judgments concerning Vatican Council II that we are unable to share (see pp. 234-236). We also have reservations concerning a subchapter that follows on the subject of "The First Steps of a Theology of the Third World." It is not convenient this kind of analysis that we would describe as ahistorical. He also seems to regard Asia according to his own way of thinking.

His treatment of "The Hour of Women" is quite good, however, as is his conclusion, styled "Dislocations." "This brief history of theology over two decades," he writes, "confirms the interpretation of the great influence Vatican II had on theology" (p. 247).

In Chapter XVII (pp. 249-270), Étienne Fouilloux deals with the theme of "Ecumenism from John XXIII to John Paul II." He writes in continuity with his treatment of this topic in Volume XXIII of the Fliche-Martin *History*. There he covered the subject up to the year 1958. But we must report immediately that here he goes beyond the limits of the time assigned to him. "Towards 1980," he writes, "ecumenism was more a victim of its own success that stopped in any actual way. It did not badly overcome the crisis of 1968, but it did do so well with regard to the identity crisis that occurred in the 1970s. By the end of the 1980s, it was not doing so well in the climate of the political-religious nationalisms that were breaking out anew after having remained stable for nearly forty years" (p. 270). Following his initial consideration of the topic, the author speaks about the general problem of writing a history of ecumenism today: "Submerged in the sheer mass of various confessionalisms, and lacking any studies of a true scientific character, the historian of ecumenism must take note of the change of focus for his inquiries that followed upon the great expansion of his general subject at the beginning of the 1960s...More than any synthesis, however, which would be premature given the present state of research, the following pages represent, rather, an essay which simply attempts to delineate some of today's perspectives in a form that is dear to historians, one resulting in a chronological division of developments that remains hypothetical" (p. 249). The essay is divided up among a number of topics: "a dramatic official recognition," "euphoria," "challenges and controversies," and "falling back on confessional identities." Another element to keep in mind is that the author's interest here is only in ecumenism as such; he is not interested in the possible acceptance of the "Catholic claims." Moreover, in the course of his treatment, there occur instances of language that we would have preferred to be more precise and less "journalistic," that is, more "historical," capable of dealing with the continuity underlying all the current innovations (see pp. 252 and 253). The author observes: "One comes to understand better how it was that the Council overall was the fruit of a conflict of different orientations and hence represented a compromise between transalpine reformism and Roman tradition." This was aided, the author writes, "by the interventions of Pope Paul VI aiming for a unanimous result" (p. 264). We cannot but harbor reservations concerning the author's characterizations of "the neo-conservative line of *Communio*" (p. 265), "the Vatican's *Ostpolitik*" (p. 268), and "Pope Montini's tendency…to favor the diplomatic route" (p. 269).

"New Themes in Morality" is the subject of Chapter XIX (pp. 271-303). It offers the occasion to go into some of the sensitive post-conciliar developments under the guidance of Giannino Piana. Evident here is an effort to realize a true general renewal, both in method and content; the author has been stimulated by the Council as well as by developments in science and technology, and also by the rapid changes that have taken place in modern society. Piana therefore offers a rapid review of the most significant stages in recent developments which illustrate the main lines that have emerged. The study seems less attentive to the continuity of moral teaching, however. The author writes: "The Word of God does not in fact provide us with an organic doctrinal system, nor even with a precise framework of values and norms that are established once and for all" (p. 284). And again: "It is urgent…to effect a critical revision of certain traditional moral principles such as absolute norms, *intrinsice malum*, the principle of double effect, etc." (p. 285). This lack of continuity with traditional moral teaching of the Church becomes rather obvious when scanning the various subtitles of the issues treated by the author: "the contribution of the Council," "methodological renewal," "the question of the 'specific,'" "searching for a model," "from a hermeneutic to the problem of language," "towards a systematic exposition," and "the ethics of sexuality and marriage." Concerning this last topic and the issue of the encyclical *Humanae Vitae*, the author should have cited, at the very least, in addition to Bernard Häring and Dietrich von Hildebrand, Father Gustave Martelet, S. J., especially in view of the latter's presentation of the encyclical in the *Nouvelle Revue Théologique*. Further issues treated include the issue the author subtitles as "the centrality of the social question," of which we are quite frankly obliged to be seriously critical, since it appears to break with a teaching nevertheless issued "in the light of faith and authentic Church tradition." We are reminded here of the lessons taught by the late, lamented Pietro Pavan. The author concludes this chapter with treatments of "bioethics: a new chapter" and "critical themes and prospects."

Happily, on the subject of "Christian Social Teaching and the Challenges of the New Economy," Silvio Berretta and Stefano Zamagni follow upon Piana's presentation with a praiseworthy contribution of their own in Chapter XX (pp. 305-337). Meanwhile, in Chapter XXI (pp. 340-374), Francesco Traniello gives an essay on "The Church and Politics" which is, rather, practically a prolongation of Piana's deficient treatment. Traniello sees in John XXIII's encyclical *Pacem et Terris* a "turning point"; he then goes on to deal with the political themes addressed by the Council in *Gaudium et Spes* and *Dignitatis Humanae*. The author continues with an analysis of the crisis of the political culture of the Occident, including subtitles on "contradictory post-conciliar ferments," "Paul VI and Politics," "the expansion and diversification of the episcopal magisterium in political matters," and "the Catholic Church and politics in the 1970s." Naturally, our views do not always coincide with those of this author. See, for example, pages 349ff. on the subject of regimes with papal concordats; page 358 on the supposed "activism" of Vatican diplomacy; page 367 on the political role of the papacy; and pages 373-374 on the double significance of secularization (labelled non-conciliar). Here are the author's exact words concerning this last point: there has supposedly been "a tendentious deformation of the principal cultural referents which, not without difficulty, had been systematized in the conciliar texts dealing with the political sphere and with the problems of politics." This "deformation" is attributed to the movement Communion and

Liberation. On the same subject, and even more strongly, the author adds that "the strength of the attraction of this movement [CL] in many Catholic areas...depended not least on a new viewpoint which combined a negative perception of politics with one of modernity, as well, thus returning to a position deeply rooted in the history and traditions of Catholicism." Such a serious and all-embracing statement would have been worth more if it had taken into account the judgment which followed it belonging to one who is, after all, a well-known historian (see p. 404).

The fifth section of *The Church of Vatican II (1958-1978)*, which is the last one coming before the book's Postface, consists of seven chapters. The first two are devoted to Western Europe (pp. 377-410) and to Eastern Europe (p. 411-442) respectively. These two chapters were written by Andrea Riccardi, who is not new to these areas. In a divided Europe there is presented the structure of a "European Church," along with the crisis that currently characterizes it, a crisis of the clergy in particular. Then, there are the new models that have been developed; the other causes and a renewed episcopate; the existing polarization; and a new profile of Catholicism (this last is a good synthesis, positive, in fact). As a final topic, the author deals with "pluralism, unity, and evangelization." His treatment is discursive, straightforward, serene, and well-informed. This contributes to smooth reading and reasonable judgments. We limit ourselves to remarking that the use of the term "national Churches" is not appropriate (see pp. 383, 386, and 392). Nor are we convinced by the case made here for Cardinal Lercaro. We do appreciate, however, in the midst of a number of rather hasty judgments made by the authors, the prudence with which he judges the impact of Vatican Council II on the European Churches. We will not attempt to summarize them here, however (see also p. 403). We believe Riccardi correctly identifies the major role of the press in mediating the conciliar texts to the Catholic masses. The whole business amounts to a lengthy discourse! We find ourselves viewing favorably the author's attempt to demythologize the current categories based on politicized models of "progressives" and "conservatives"; among other deficiencies, these categories cover a whole range of different positions; we need think only of such cases in this connection as those of Jean Daniélou and Henri de Lubac, for example (see pp. 392-394). More than that, they bring about an undue simplification. Also worthy of praise is the author's attempt to analyze the post-conciliar crisis in the Church, the roots of which go back before the Council (p. 396) and which are related to the new secular horizons in society at large. Riccardi concedes that "the impact of the Council...provoked an acceleration in the processes of change. The crisis of modern society inevitably involved the Church as well" (*Ibid.*). Along the same meritorious lines is the author's treatment of the organizations and parties based on Christian inspiration which grew up in Europe during the period (see p. 402) and also of the encouragement given to the study of pious movements and sanctuaries in the post-conciliar era (p. 406); these latter surely represent a position consistent with the lived experience of European Catholicism (*Ibid.*).

With regard to Eastern Europe, no novelties are encountered. The "turn" of John XXIII is explained as well as the Vatican's policy towards Eastern Europe (We greatly prefer that the term *Ostpolitik* not be used). The serious difficulties of the Vatican's policy are covered. We also note in passing and with satisfaction that "it is not possible to speak of the reception of Vatican Council II in the Eastern European countries in the same way this is spoken of in Western Europe" (p. 432). We further call attention to the author's effort to sketch out the reception situation in Poland in particular. He concludes, however, "that Polish religiousness...remains an area that requires further study" (p. 435).

It remains only too true, however, that the post-conciliar situation was a very difficult one in Yugoslavia, Czechoslovakia, Romania, and Bulgaria, not to speak of Albania. But there was no possible alternative for the policy of the Holy See towards Eastern Europe, even though the situation was "stagnant." But the pope did not harbor any illusions about it.

Chapter XXIV (pages 443-495) deals with North America. It is divided into two parts dealing with the United States and Canada, entrusted, respectively, to Gerald P. Fogarty and Paul Crunican. The first of these authors gives his attention especially to subjects of particular interest in the United States (the question of religious liberty, for example). But one of the aspects that Father Fogarty treats is that of the "leadership" of both the apostolic delegates in America—where one would have liked to have seen judgments less partisan and one-sided—and of the American cardinals themselves. This study seems to us rather too polarized and it evidences distinct animosity in some of its language which is displeasing. Paul Crunican writes in much the same vein as regards Canada, and again makes clear his irritation with things in general. He devotes two full pages of the ten ones allotted to him to the Canadian response to the encyclical *Humanae Vitae*. There is no question about his marked partiality.

Chapter XXV on Latin America (pp. 497-534) by Eduardo Cárdenas is satisfactory, beginning with its methodological premises, in which the difficulty of achieving a historical synthesis for this continent is recognized. Latin America is too fragmented and diversified, even if there are common elements and similar tendencies corresponding to the historical identity of Ibero-American Catholicism. The author briefly analyzes in a general overview the social and political aspects of this Ibero-American Catholicism; he then looks at the life of the Church and her structures, giving particular attention to Medellin, which brought about a great change in pastoral vision. There follows a reminder of some of the significant characteristics of the 1968-1978 decade, with particular attention paid to Cuba, Chile, and Nicaragua (but we would not use the word *"cricca"* [three in a deck of cards] here to describe this threesome). It is noteworthy that Msgr C. Zacchi was for many years the acting representative of the Holy See in Cuba; and that the number of Catholics indicated for the year 1978 was an estimate. Particular attention is also given to Christians opting for Socialism, to the theology of liberation, to Protestant sectarianism, to the educational apostolate, and to religious communities and "base communities." The chapter concludes with a section on the subject "towards Puebla."

The synthesis for Africa in Chapter XXVI (pp. 534-578) is quite good. It is written by Jacques Gadille. He presents a twofold conscientious political and Christian position related to the two decades, 1958-1978, that have been under consideration in this book. One is that of John XXIII, and concerns the role of the African bishops at the Council; the other is that of Paul VI, and consists of a description of two lines of action, namely the development of a less centralized ecclesiology and the search for more adequate conditions in which to carry out the evangelization of the culture. The author writes of the difficult process of negotiation of the relationship of the Catholic Church with the young African states and also of the obligation of evangelization. This latter question also brings to the fore the issues of ministry, the current problems of society, and also the character of African Catholicism. May we be permitted, however, to register a critical remark or two, and precisely on the question of the "imposing" of the conditions of both monogamy and celibacy (p. 566). Paul VI was said to have been "open" at one point to a "development" in very precisely defined cases (p. 573). There is also the question of the use of the word "*abate*" (French *abbé*, "father", a priest) which, in Italian, has a very precise meaning rather than a more general one, as in French. There is also a question of the symbolic importance of the personal position of Bishop J. D. Sangu: "he had called for a genuine overturning of practices typical of Roman centralization" (p. 578).

In Chapter XXVII (pp. 579-607), Giuseppe M. Croce explains the situation of the Church in the Middle East. There Catholics are a "minority within the minority." This fact is confirmed by a statistical or geographical profile of the countries involved, as well as of the various patriarchates: of the Coptics in Alexandria, the Melchites of Antioch, Syrian Catholics, Armenians in Cilicia, the Chaldeans of Babylon, not to speak of the Maronites of Lebanon. The author covers the Eastern presence and actions at Vatican II, as well as relations with the Eastern Orthodox and the Islamic world.

The treatment of Asia in this work, in Chapter XXVIII (pp. 609-665), was entrusted to Arnulf Camps. In his contribution he reveals himself as a scholar who is both biased and partial. He focuses on subjects pertaining to three historical moments, namely: the situation prior to Vatican Council II, the changes brought about by the Council, and the situation at the end of the pontificate of Paul VI. His treatment introduces "important facts, problems, and tendencies"; however, he has no intention of trying to outline a history of the local Churches in the various countries or regions in such a vast continent as Asia. There is the basic question of these "local Churches in Asia" (not all in Asia!). With them what the author calls "a third reform" or, indeed, an "ecclesiastical revolution" (p. 611) has taken place. According to him, they now represent an approach based on seven (7) theses which, in due course, he explains.

The situation in Asia prior to Vatican II is divided into several subtopics: religious liberty, India, Malaysia, China, regional Catholic institutions, and Asia as a land of religious people. Changes that have come about are described with respect to India, and also with respect to Sri Lanka and Hong Kong. Near the end of the pontificate of Paul VI, reference is made to the "Episcopal Conference of India" concerning new lifestyles in India and in the Philippines and also to the experience of the laity in Indonesia. All of this supposedly points toward "conclusive observations" by the author. But we must be permitted to say here that we always find ourselves in great difficulty—the case is the same for the author—when confronted by categorical declarations such as the following: "One cannot transplant a Church. The point of departure must be a local Church with roots in a particular place; in Asia this means poverty, religiousness, cultural richness, and pluralism" (pp. 611ff.). Or again: "The future belongs to an attitude of double fidelity (fidelity to one's own religious culture but to the Christian creed as well)...thus, any choice that does not recognize this requires a theological position that is radically new" (p. 612). The author goes one: "It is certain that excommunication for the 'autonomous' Chinese bishops was never contemplated" (p. 617). "Pope John employed the word 'schism,' but not long after that he promised never to use the word again" (*Ibid.*). Yet even his typical judgments on missionaries here lack the nuances that are otherwise typical (p. 620). The result became a widespread conviction that "salvation is possible only in and through the Catholic Church" (p. 621).

This volume concludes with a Postface (pp. 667-689). It bears the title "The Council, Challenge to the Pontificate of Pope John Paul II." The author is Jan Grootaers. He describes his task as a "particularly risky one, and one not free of snares or traps which arise out of the necessity of describing a phenomenon which is contemporary to us and yet not completed; it is a task which entails the temptation of making judgments about an event which is still going on and hence can only be captured in an 'arbitrary' moment of its on-going development" (p. 669). Precisely for the reasons he describes, we disagree with whoever decided that this Postface was necessary. The author rightly presents Pope John Paul II primarily as a pastor, and recognizes in him his firm will to promote both the spirit and the letter of Vatican Council II—although "properly understood and interpreted," the author adds.

And it is on this point, the interpretation of the Council, that Grootaers has already formed his opinions, as is well known. They are opinions that we cannot generally share. Perhaps the most fundamental one concerns the question of continuity with the Church's past, with the Catholic Tradition, in other words. This is a factor which constantly forms the vision of John Paul II, for example, who always treats the present in continuity with the past. The author falsely attributes this constant vision to the pope's Polish origin and experience—to the Eastern European background of the bishop of Rome (see pp. 671ff.). [In adopting this explanation], the author fails to see that continuity with Tradition is the principal characteristic of Vatican II itself, as it has been of all of the Church councils. This author is not alone in taking this position, of course. In Italy the same line of thought is basically maintained by Giuseppe Alberigo, who is quoted as complaining: "The reception of the Council would then have as its principal criterion its organic homogeneity with Post-Tridentine Catholicism" (see p. 672). But did not the much praised by such as

Alberigo and Grootaers Pope John XXIII himself speak rather of *aggiornamento*? Yet what would that be if it did not continue in the line of Tradition rather than breaking with it? Alberigo is quoted further as observing, however, that "it would seem that Vatican II is being seen as a kind of definitive synthesis of modern Catholicism rather than as an invitation addressed to the Church to renew herself through the action of the Holy Spirit." Can it really be said, as Alberigo does say, that "the post-conciliar crisis of the Church can be attributed to fears and delays in the implementation of the Council" (*Ibid.*)?

We do not wish to comment on every opinion of Grootaers, or of those who share and sustain him in his opinions, as we could and perhaps even should. Instead, we shall confine our remarks to some of the "personal" criticisms he makes about the pope now guiding the bark of Peter [Pope John Paul II]. There is in this pope supposedly a significant lack which entails a "tendency to neglect the historical dimension of events in general and that of Vatican II in particular" (p. 673). He is described as more a philosopher than a theologian, and his phenomenological philosophy supposedly liberates him from history. Grootaers concludes from this that "he loves to underline the *continuity* which brings the past nearer, while he seems to undervalue *change*; history thus seems for him to accentuate the distance of the past from the present" (*Ibid.*). But does the author not understand that among historians there are those that legitimately favor the continuity aspect rather than the change or novelty aspect? In any case, where the Catholic Church is concerned, and speaking in theological terms, there must always co-exist a double fidelity both to Tradition and to its incarnation in the present viewed in the light of the signs of the times illuminated by the Word of God. But then the idea is floated by Grootaers that Scripture does not really have great importance in the thought of this pope because he studied at the *Angelicum* in the old days; this idea is instantly contradicted, of course, by the great and very personal regular use of Scripture by John Paul II, for example, in the encyclicals of his pontificate.

But we need to get back to the question of history, since it is foundational for the correct interpretation of the Council. Back in 1965 the then Archbishop Wojtyla insisted on the fact that what counted for the Council was the "totality" of its acts; once the Council had acted definitively, "the interventions made in the course of the conciliar debate were no longer important"; nor was the labor which had brought about this finished result any longer important. What was necessary was to produce the definitive texts themselves. These alone constituted what "seemed good to the Holy Spirit and to us" (Acts 15: 28). In them too was found the *consenso*, the fruit of the Council. That there was a "personal" difference in the formations of Pope Montini and Pope Wojtyla, respectively, no one can deny. But what difference does it make? Pope Paul VI certainly did intervene in the conciliar process, sometimes forcefully, but he did so in order to enrich the final conciliar texts by drawing from the treasures of the Tradition; his mediation served to improve the Church's communion with her own past as well as opening herself out to the modern world. Alberigo when invoking "historical conscience" seems to us to be incredible, especially when coming from an author who himself has a strong tendency to do history in his own fashion, as we have shown in these pages.

As for the Extraordinary Synod of 1985 called to evaluate Vatican Council II, we do need to offer a gloss or two. The language employed by the author here is biased and partisan and evidences a basic incomprehension of the significance of the conciliar event. In addition, he registers unfavorable judgments on various ecclesiastical personalities; we need think here only of Archbishop Jan Schotte, now a cardinal. The same thing can be said about his account of the case of Archbishop Lefebvre—and can Cardinal Edouard Gagnon really be classed as an "ultraconservative"? All this offers an occasion for the author to speak about the Roman Curia, which is scarcely surprising; but he does it under the rubric of a subtitle, which he places in the interrogative: "Are We Distancing Ourselves from the Council?" This is a question that automatically signals a simplification, and this is how Grootaers expresses it further: "The process of the centralization of power carried out by the Secretariat of State was already operative under Paul VI and was reinforced by John Paul II; it represented something so far from the conciliar ecclesiology of Vatican II that nobody could have any illusions about where it was finally heading." But was it not the case that Paul VI wished to strengthen the Secretariat of State precisely in order to remain in control of the Curia?

This Postface concludes, logically, with a discussion of "the dilemma of being the pope"—supreme Pastor, and therefore "responsible" for the various Roman "institutions." The author observes that "the pontifical charge remains a crushing task," and he even asks if this function is "humanly realizable," referring to the many institutional interests and the dysfunctions of the curial administration. The author then moves on from the question of doctrinal continuity to that of structural continuity, and speaks of the dilemma that supposedly exists between "spiritual leadership and organizational authority" (p. 688). Grootaers goes on: "If the pope speaks of a great spiritual transformation, he alarms the bureaucracy; for the bureaucrats, any decision which threatens the continuity of existing church structures must be neutralized or fended off. But if the pope fails to institute necessary changes, then he risks alienating those for whom the Church founded by Christ demonstrated her vitality most effectively, that is, when accepting necessary changes. These changes are for the sake of the spiritual good of the members of the Church...Thus fundamental changes in the carrying out of the 'crushing task' of the Roman pontiff must be brought about." The author continues on rather dramatically, exaggerating as he goes along: "A tension between these opposing roles has been present in the case of earlier popes, but it seems to have become much stronger with Pope John Paul II. The theology of the primacy as it is lived and legitimized today in Rome risks becoming even more particularistic today; it even seems to be in contradiction with the model of the pope as the guarantor of the universal faith... And today the dilemma extends beyond the personal characteristics of whoever is carrying out the charge. It is possible that the exceptional merits of the strong personality of John Paul II can come to be not only attenuated by the qualities and limitations of the man Karol Wojtyla, but that his charisms too can be endangered by the current structures of the papacy and by the way they are organized" (p. 689).

This phraseology, "seems to be in contradiction with the model of the pope as the guarantor of the universal faith," is surely the most objectionable thing said here, as it is also at the same time the least well founded. It is a pure Philippic. To mix up and confuse Church discipline, Church structures, and features such as centralization and de-centralization with questions of *faith*—and I would add, of morals as well—evidences undue confusion and even frivolity in a very serious matter.

There follow the indices in the book (pp. 691-727): an analytical index, a list of illustrations, an iconographic index, and a general index.

And we may summarize the *errata* in this volume as follows: p. 26- *compentenza* should be *competenza;* p. 115-*Schonstatt* should be *Schönstatt*; p. 138-*praesse* should be *praeesse:* p.168 -*Biblischen* should be *biblischen*; p. 252-Leuven 1922 should be Leuven 1992; p. 344-Giovani XXIII should be Giovanni XXIII; p. 367-*alto verso* should be *altro verso;* p. 461, etc.-*ausiliaro* should be *ausiliare*; p. 466-*gesuita* should be *dei gesuiti*; p. 503-*aggregaziome* should be *aggregazione*; p. 526, n.35-Vanzane should be Vanzan; p. 556-557-*Resendé* should be *Resende*; p. 557-*e il piu stretto* should be *è il piu stretto*; p. 558 *oblate* should be *oblato*; p. 561-Constantine should be Costantina; p. 561-*dal 1982* should be *per molto tempo*; p. 567 Rulenga should be Rulenge; p. 567-*ujmaa* should be *ujama*; p. 568- *evangalizzazione* should be *evangelizzazione*; p. 662-*un liturgia* should be *una liturgia*; p. 664-*l'ordine della messa* should be *l'ordinario della messa*; p. 680-Levebvre should be Lefebvre.

17

Concerning the "Dossier" on "Two Thousand Years of Christianity"

Giovanni XXIII e il Concilio [John XXIII and the Council], Dossier No. 12, Volume 3 of the Series *Duemila anni di Cristianesimo: Dall' Illuminismo al Terzo Millennio* [Two Thousand Years of Christianity: From Illuminism to the Third Millennium], published by the journal *Famiglia Cristiana* [Christian Family].

Christian Family magazine undertook a really fine initiative when it decided to make available to its many readers a popularized "History of the Church" in installments. Entitled *Two Thousand years of Christianity*, the series has been well written and illustrated. Such a series could not but be welcomed by historians, and not only by historians. Unfortunately, however, we have the impression that there has been a decline in the scholarly quality of the series as we approach the contemporary period in the Church's history, where a rather evident partiality of the authors of the series becomes visible. This stems, I believe, from the ideological bias of the authors. A very clear example of what I am talking about as unsatisfactory can be found in the number or "dossier" in the series entitled *John XXIII and the Council*.

In defense of this judgment, which I state quite frankly here—and quite painfully too as a pastor rather than as a scholar, thinking of the kind of material being disseminated among the simplest members of the People of God—[I feel obliged to protest], especially since the subject matter concerns the Church's greatest expression of her communion, namely, a Council. I limit myself to reproducing, as a simple reader, the text of the first page of the dossier in question, which contains the salient points in a way that is unmistakable. Here is the text I am referring to:

"The election of Angelo Roncalli as the successor of Pope Pius XII prompted many observers to conclude that the cardinals assembled in the conclave had decided upon 'a transitional papacy.' In fact, it required only a few months before John XXIII opted for an initiative that would decisively affect the life of the Church. The convoking of Vatican Council II would set in motion a process of renewal in the Church that is going on still. In the course of the work of the Council, which was completed only with the pontificate of Pope Paul VI, the diocesan bishops and the other Council Fathers *affirmed their autonomy as against the Vatican Curia*, which had attempted to guide and control the sessions of the Council. Many theologians also found in Vatican II the occasion to develop their own reflections and initiate discussions that have borne rich fruit. Among the more prominent names of the latter were many French theologians, among whom can be mentioned *Chenu, Congar, Daniélou,* and *de Lubac.* In the sixteen documents issued by the Council, many of their ideas and observations are to be found."

This first page reflects the monochord or one-stringed character of the work as a whole. It is mentioned that the authors worked in collaboration with and under the patronage of the Catholic University of the Sacred Heart in Milan. In our view, this page evidences an acceptance of a conciliar hermeneutic that is partial and one-sided and even "Manichaean" at bottom in its use of unfounded journalistic common-places and *clichés.* In short, it in no way reflects the complexity of the conciliar synthesis as a whole.

In order to realize this, it suffices to recall the Extraordinary Meeting of the *Synodus Episcoporum* in 1985. The results of this meeting are found in the recent volume, *Il Concilio Vaticano II: Ricezione e attualitá alla luce del Giubileo* [Vatican Council II: Reception and Actuality in the Light of the Jubilee], edited by R. Fisichella, Editions San Paolo, 2000. [These results can also be garnered] from the article I myself wrote in the journal *Bailamme* (the review in honour of Father Giuseppe De Luca) for June-December, 2000, pages 51-64. This article of mine is entitled *"Tradizione e rinnovamento si sono abbracciati: Il Concilio Vaticano II"* [Tradition and Renewal Together: The Second Vatican Council] (This article is reprinted as Chapter 50 of the present volume.)

Those who continue to pit the Council Fathers against each other now that we have the definitive texts created by the Council do not respect history, objectively speaking, and precisely in what is specifically Catholic in history. These conciliar texts were developed through dialogue and discussion, and the comparing of contrasting views and opinions; they reflect the idea of the *consenso conciliare* that developed out of the conciliar process, owing especially to the efforts of Pope Paul VI (a "martyr of the Council," Cardinal König called him). "Innovators" and "Conservatives"—as they are commonly styled by so many people—through and with the Holy Spirit—made the Council what it was by *working together*. Each tendency contributed, acting out of its own theological *forma mentis*, its own experiences, its sensitivities, and its various "schools"—not to speak of the human and ecclesial preoccupations, both local and universal, of all involved.

We are wholly convinced that those who today focus instead on the things that divided the Council Fathers and suggest that there was an impassable gulf between them—as if they were not all members and pastors of the same Church—do not serve the good of the post-conciliar Church. To divide up and oppose the Council Fathers to each other in this way, along with the theologians in their special role, as well, characterizing them all as "good" or "bad"—this is to demonstrate the kinds of choices which I have designated as "ideological."

Among the theologians, however, there was one who exemplified a salutary will to overcome and move beyond this ideological tendency so prevalent at the Council. This was Monsignor Gérard Philips, [a Belgian] whose name is not even mentioned by these authors. Yet he was the key man involved in the preparation of some of the principal conciliar documents. He was willing out of conviction to serve as a "theological scapegoat," and he thus exemplified the *acceptio rerum* (by analogy with sacred Scripture) of the Council. He accepted and respected the conciliar preparation process as the basis for further action; this included the original *schemata* produced in the course of the conciliar preparations; but he was also willing to change and improve them as a result of the debates and discussions in the *aula* and then to offer them back to the Council Fathers for their final judgment.

Monsignor Philips had occasion to say, in a statement that illuminates the entire conciliar process, that the text of what eventually became *Lumen Gentium*, revised and then revised again under his shrewd and patient efforts, retained 60 percent of the original *schema*. Certainly such a figure must be taken as an approximation, but it is significant that some practitioners of conciliar hermeneutics have deplored the fact that, unfortunately, in the successive drafts, so much was retained of what was originally proposed. Moreover, the decision to retain as much as possible of the original texts prepared, in the course of their revision, was not just a plan of the Roman Curia, which was and is of mixed composition that includes various components. In no way was it or is it "monolithic," as this "dossier," unfortunately, makes it appear; in this connection, we need consider only the attitude of Cardinal Suenens himself, who guided Monsignor Philips in his patient task of serving as a weaver, synthesizer, and mender.

The text of this "dossier" under review here, then, seems to have adopted its method of conciliar exegesis from the extreme fringe elements of the majority, already present during the Council, who did not accept the necessity, exemplified by Pope Paul VI in particular, of maintaining both dimensions of authentic Catholicism together, namely, Tradition *and* renewal. This was necessary, in a word, to achieve true *aggiornamento*. The conciliar "turn," adopting the language of "the road," was well chosen since the very word "synod" means, originally, "together on the road"; but the "turn" in question was in no way a U-turn, and hence those who attempt to raise up a wall or barrier between renewal and *aggiornamento*, as against Tradition, have manifestly gone *off the road*!

If we were to conclude with an appeal to the excellent apostolic letter of John Paul II, *Novo Millennio Ineunte*, in the context of Vatican II as it is described above, it seems to us that the pontifical invitation to commit ourselves, both at the level of the universal Church, and that of the local Churches, to a communion of spirituality (n. 42) in order to make of the Church a home and a school of communion, none of this would be facilitated, as part of the legacy of Vatican II, by the kind of "polarization" that we find in the "dossier" under review here.

The proper mentality, seeking for that which unites rather than for that which divides, looking for what is positive—and then accepting and appreciating it as a gift of God—was one of the components, we should recall, of the spirituality of Pope John XXIII; all of this should be evaluated, therefore, not only as something *ad extra* to the Church, but as something *ad intra*, especially with respect to legitimate theological visions as well as to very understandable sensitivities. The logic of parties and of pressure groups, even "hermeneutical" ones, does not offer—we are certain of this—ecclesial paradigms such as might resolve the conflicts that do arise today, even in the Church that guarantees communion.

18

Vatican II Viewed from Moscow

Melloni A., Ed., *Vatican II in Moscow (1959-1965)*, Leuven, 1997, 352 pages.

The "Acts" of a Colloquium on the history of the Second Vatican Council that took place in Moscow from March 30 to April 2, 1995, have now been published in Italian, English, French, and German. The exact title of the Colloquium in question is: "Vatican Council II: The View from Russia."

The editor, A. Melloni, introduces the volume. He writes in the context of the research that has been done to date. His title is: "Sister Churches, Adversarial Diplomacy: Vatican II in Moscow Amidst Propaganda, *Ostpolitik*, and Ecumenism." He thus synthesizes the work that characterized the encounter represented by this Colloquium. He writes that "Russian participation at Vatican II constitutes an integral part of that assembly which constituted the principal event of Catholicism in the course of the twentieth century. The principal questions include: the way in which the Church of Rome looked on the Soviet State, and the way in which the Russian Church looked upon this solemn meeting with Latin Christianity in the ecumenism of the years 1959-1962 (the years of the preparation for the Council), and then, later, of the years 1962-1965 (the ones of the Council's effective actions). All this represented a fitting series of approaches, rethinkings, and re-interpretations of all of this subject matter, concerning which, up until a few years ago, very little was known. Soviet diplomacy disliked speaking about what the attitude of the U. S. S. R. was in those years; and, on the other hand, from the standpoint of the Moscow patriarchate, minimal conditions were lacking to allow the period in question to be considered with the necessary liberty. The attitude of reserve of he Secretariat of State similarly made it impossible to judge what steps had been completed or even what talks had actually taken place. For these reasons, these studies, of diverse historiographical value, pass quite rapidly over the theme of Vatican II and Moscow" (p. 1). But then the Russian archives were opened up.

The exaggerated emphasis placed by Melloni on Russian participation at the Council as the "integral part of that assembly" which he claims it was does not diminish the fact that there are elements of very great interest here. More than that, the Colloquium in question furnished the occasion to raise some other questions, even if only fleetingly, in some other areas of research that are quite sensitive; among these are the Italian politics and policies of the period and their influence on things pertaining to the Church. In addition, beyond the events of the Council itself, there is the question of Soviet religious politics and policies, which can throw light on the history of those years of sometimes fierce and even violent events.

Melloni lays out the boundaries of the study up to 1978. He explains from his own perspective recent contributions and prospects for research, and he also mentions some names, including Stehle, Wenger, and Riccardi, whom he describes as "pioneers" in the matter; he criticizes as "ideological," however, the work of A. Tamborra and S. Trasatti (the latter having passed away prematurely). He is critical also of the efforts at dialogue undertaken by Cardinal Giuseppe Siri, to whom several qualified Soviet interlocutors had turned on their own initiative (see p. 10).

This editor then goes on to indicate both the limits of study and the various hypotheses on the whole Soviet situation, including a rather strict analysis of the Moscow patriarchate, Soviet policy, and a vision that we would call ecclesial and ecumenical (see pp. 8-9, esp. n. 27). He concludes by speaking of an "unexpected confluence...objectively paradoxical" which "brought together elements of the Roman Curia with officials of the Communist Party of the Soviet Union: both were very interested in the question of any condemnation of Communism—or lack of such a condemnation—by the Second Vatican Council" (p. 10). Making this connection, it seems to us, is an indication of where Melloni himself stands.

However that may be, he reverts to his traditional position regarding the Roman Curia. After the treatment of the Colloquium talks, he speaks of the decision of the Moscow patriarchate, which he judges to be "political" and "forced (by the CPSU)." The conclusions of some others, including Roccucci, whose views we will be touching upon shortly, are much more nuanced and balanced; and, at the same time, as other scholars mention, they are more in line with the policy of maintaining independence and a proper distance vis-à-vis Constantinople.

The material contained in this book is divided into four parts: "International Relations," "Ecumenism," "Topics and Controversies," and "Testimonials." These four sections are introduced by a good preface by A. O. Tchoubarian, who focuses on the underlying problems.

The first "intervention" is by V. Gaitduk and is entitled: "Vatican and Kremlin: Becoming Aware of the Opening of the Nuclear Age: Apocalyptic Watershed of History." It becomes quite evident here that there are instances of simple incomprehension between the Holy See and "revolutionaries" on such subjects as: the origins of the revolutionary process; the status of *L'Osservatore Romano* (considered an "official" journal); and the position of the "occidental" Holy See ("The precipitous erosion of the international situation and the appearance on the horizon of the real menace of a nuclear holocaust permits [the Holy See] to adopt openly the principle of peaceful co-existence in the environment of today's bi-polar world"—p. 18). The roots of a more "open" position on the part of the Holy See is actually traced back to—we should take careful note of this—Pius XII, who grounded the international position of the Apostolic See in its "independence, impartiality, and mediating role" (*Ibid.*). [The TASS News Service reporter], A. Krassikov, whom we shall consider farther on, rendered this same judgment as regards Pius XII (p. 317). The author here believes that this pope's "apostolic letter to the people of Russia," issued in 1952, constituted "an important stage on the road in the Vatican's increasingly open attitude towards the Kremlin." The author then outlines the development of Vatican-Kremlin relations after Stalin. We note one discrepancy concerning the role of Pope John XXIII with regard to the Cuban missile crisis, as confirmed from the American side by Father G. Fogarty. In concluding here, we would like to cite one saying of this author to the effect that "as time goes by the historical laws of 'simplification' become operative." However, we believe it is rather imperative that this be avoided, as a matter of fact!

V. P. Ljubin then covers the topic of "Scholarly Study in the U. S. S. R." It is on the whole subject of the Second Vatican Council. It is interesting to go back to this atheistic past and to the narrow judgments of those who were closed up in their preconceptions and ideological visions. It also allows the verification of what the sources of information and disinformation were for Soviet citizens during the long winter when they were deprived of the sun of liberty. However, this situation did not finally prevent the recognition that the *aggiornamento* of the Catholic Church was taking place and that there was a definite change in "Vatican politics."

The contribution of A. Roccucci that comes next is both substantive and decisive, thanks to the ability of this author to consult the proper documentation related to his subject matter. His title is: "The Russian Observers at Vatican II." He covers both the Council for External Affairs of the Russian Orthodox Church and the Patriarchate of Moscow caught between Soviet anti-religious policies and the Kremlin's international strategies. Following the "unwritten concordat" between Church and State concluded by Stalin during the Second World War, Nikita S. Khrushchev initiated a new anti-religious policy in 1957; and he did so without any hesitation. This resulted in changes within various entities under the control of the Moscow patriarchate. In effect, "patriotism" was abandoned as the keystone of the solution to the difficulties between Church and state; also, there was the removal of G. G. Karpov. Of particular interest here are the conclusions recorded by the author concerning the idea of the "Vatican," favored by the Patriarch Athenagoras of Constantinople—who was considered a "creature of the Americans" on account of his anti-Soviet stand (pp. 52-53). But then Bishop Nikodim Rotov came upon the scene. He was considered "a partner of the Soviet regime but was more independent than his predecessors" (p. 56). He was determined to reinforce the prestige of his Church internationally in order to fend off new and possibly devastating persecutions by the Soviet state" (pp. 57ff.). It was in this context that a change of position was brought about, moving from the earlier *non possumus* to a willingness to participate, following the invitation to the Holy See to send observers to the Council (pp. 58-69). All this took place also in the course of the "battle for influence" with regard to Constantinople—and as the aims and scope of the Council also became clearer as a result of various signs, encounters, and new information. It appeared that "political positions" in any strict sense really were going to be excluded, given the pastoral aims of the Council. There was, however, "no formal accord to this effect" (p. 65; see then p. 158). The sentiments, calculations, and strategies of Bishop Nikodim (and of the Archpriest Vitaly Borovoy) were thus finally adopted by the Soviet authorities, who decided to permit a Russian Orthodox presence at the Council, "since the strategy of an opening promoted by Nikodim could then coincide with Soviet interests" (p. 64).

It can be said, in conclusion, that both the Council for External Affairs of the Russian Orthodox Church and the Moscow Patriarchate changed their once firm opposition to Russian participation at the Council (pp. 68-69); and the Soviet Politburo then approved the proposal to send such Russian Orthodox observers (Resolution 5830 of October 10).

The part of the book labeled "Ecumenism" is introduced by Vitaly Borovoy himself, who, as is well known, was the most prominent person in view among the Russian Orthodox observers at the Council.

His title is: "The Significance of Vatican Council II for the Russian Orthodox Church." His intervention is of great interest because, quite independently of the objectivity or lack of it, of his various assertions, or of his judgments—which we shall not undertake to discuss here— there comes through the viewpoint of the Council common among our Russian Orthodox brothers and sisters. This proves to be the case even though this viewpoint is being transmitted through the filter of this particular observer. We shall limit ourselves to mentioning the various divisions of the author's contribution, from which it is possible to at least sample what is contained in his complete text. [His headings, then, are as follows]: "The Council of Great Hopes"; "The Revolution of Pope John XXIII"; "The *Ostpolitik* of Pope Paul VI"; "Paul VI Continuator of John XXIII"; and then there are "Some Observations concerning the Importance of Vatican Council II for the Russian Orthodox Church at the Present Time." We permit ourselves to report here only that this text testifies to the evident importance of the Council for these brothers not yet in full communion with us, as well as indicating their great sympathy and even 'compassion' for Pope Paul VI ("We always saw, understood, and shared fully in the solicitude of this pope to maintain unity and promote conciliation within the Church...while preserving full liberty of discussion...and the possibility of arriving at agreed-upon decisions...among the diverse tendencies at the Council" (p. 87). Or again: "The experience of Vatican Council II for the Catholic Church was a veritable laboratory for conciliar action and conciliation in the Church" (*Ibid.*).

The subject of "The Russian Orthodox Church: Between Geneva and Rome during the Years of Vatican Council II" is treated next by M. Velati. The author covers first of all the various stages of the rapprochement between Geneva and Moscow in the post-war years up to the eve of the Council. This contribution is in narrative form, is precise and well-done, and eventually the author arrives at "the clarifications exchanged between Rome and Moscow" and "the crises and difficulties during the years of the Council." In general he deals with things already pretty well known. The outline he presents of the various ecumenical strategies being pursued in those years, in Geneva, Rome, and Constantinople, is outstanding. He notes the eventual adoption by the central committee of the World of Council of Churches that the latter body "could not interfere in the bilateral relationships among the various Churches, leaving to each Church-member of the World Council responsibility for dialogue with Rome" (p. 109). This was quite a change, considering the previous obsession in a contrary vein of [WCC Secretary General] W. A. Visser't Hooft.

Dom E. Lanne was called upon to describe "The Perception in the Occident of the Participation of the Moscow Patriarchate at Vatican II." From this account there emerges an item of particular importance, namely, the meeting of Cardinal Eugène Tisserant with Bishop Nikodim in Metz. Of interest also are the pages dedicated to "the presence of the observers from Moscow along with the Ukrainian Catholics at the Council"—not to speak of those same observers in relation to the Russian Orthodox theologians of the St. Sergius Institute in Paris, including Nicholas Afanassief, Nicholas Koulomzine, John Meyendorff, and Alexander Schmemann, who, in 1960, published their book *The Primacy of Peter*, briefly characterized by Dom Lanne.

A. Cavazza contributes a good essay entitled "The Idea of *Sobornost'* according to A. S. Chomjakov at Vatican Council II: Focusing on the Problem." The conclusion of the author is that there is a connection, although an indirect one, between reflection on *sobornost'* in Russia in the nineteenth century, and the Second Vatican Council; his conclusion here is particularly valid with regard to the underlying aspects which can provide help in understanding the difficult dialogue between Rome and Moscow.

The third part of these "Acts," labelled "Topics and Controversies," opens with a contribution of G. Turbanti entitled "The Problem of Communism at Vatican II." Fundamentally, it is a good piece of work, in which the author demonstrates that he knows how to utilize sources in the way indicated by the pioneering article of Monsignor Vincenzo Carbone that appeared in the *Rivista di Storia della Chiesa in Italia* [Review of the History of the Church in Italy] in 1990. Thus, in this contribution, the basic "historical-cultural context" is properly provided, even if we have to register reservations about some of the author's judgments concerning the "summary report" and "final synthesis," referring to the advice and suggestions that came in from all over the world in view of the coming Council (see p. 150). Clearly unfortunate, however, is what comes under a subtitle, "The Preparatory Phase: The Council of the Curia and the Council of John XXIII." Here the author supplies various articulations and differentiations related to the Curia internally, and analyzes a number of private sources with less precise and sometimes erroneous language (see pp. 152 and 160, esp. with regard to M. D. Chenu).

For this author, following the First Session, the theme of Communism seemed to have disappeared almost entirely from the horizon of the Council. But it re-appeared in connection with the "dialogue" of Pope Paul VI. Opinions on the subject of one Council Father, namely, Archbishop Karol Wojtyla, are given (pp. 165 and 170ff.). The subject was raised again in the "negotiations on the subject of atheistic Humanism" and again in what is styled "the last battle for a direct condemnation" [of Communism], which strangely refers back to Pius XII (p. 176). Mention is made of the Secretary General of the Council, who is said to have "known how to maneuver adroitly" and, afterwards, to have "played well" (p. 183). All this obliged the commission to accept a substantial compromise with the conciliar minority (p. 179). Finally, the admonition to Father Glorieux [for involuntarily not properly forwarding a minority appeal] is noted along with the appeal itself of Bishop Carli [to secure an express condemnation of Communism] (p. 180).

The withdrawal of this just appeal by the latter was "rewarded... by means of an insertion into the text of footnote references to the condemnations of Communism already made by previous popes," along with another insertion at the beginning of paragraph 21 referring to these added footnoted references expressly condemning

Communism" (see p. 184ff.). Turbanti's conclusions concerning all this are balanced (p. 186ff.), although his last two paragraphs reveal some uncertainty, especially in his criticisms of Father Jean-Yves Calvez, S. J., and in his acceptance of the concept of "negotiation" with Communism (p. 187).

The very difficult subject of "The Italian Communist Party and the Church in the Years of Vatican Council II" is treated by R. Burigana. He relies on some unpublished sources, and, in any case, the volume of Hans Jakob Stehle which he uses is not only out of date but is also biased and partial. He also refers to the diary of Pope John XXIII during the period of the latter's pontificate; but this diary is not yet in the public domain. The temptation here is to go into great detail with what one has while neglecting the rest.

We are not able to follow this author in his passage through such topics as what a council is; subterranean diplomacy and public messages; "the Council of peace"; a new pope at an old Council; and Marxism and Christianity. It is true that his treatment is not lacking in interest. We can, however, mention a number of points we consider weak, especially from the point of view cited above in the pioneer work by Monsignor Vincenzo Carbone speaking of "considerations which are not of historical value but which are interesting as indicating the attitudes of some Council Fathers" (p. 205, n. 54). These weak points include the reference to the "implicit agreement" between Rome and Moscow not to issue a conciliar condemnation of Communism as such (p. 205; see, however, p. 258 of the "Acts"); the author's judgment concerning the Cuban Missile Crisis (p. 206); and his view of a presumed dissociation of the Secretariat of State from the conduct of Pope John XXIII in the matter of the liberation of [Ukrainian Church Archbishop Josyf] Slipyj (p. 208, n. 69). Reservations are also called for in the matter of the supposed opposition "in every way" on the part of the Roman Curia to Pope John's meeting with [Krushchev's son-in-law Alexei] Adjubei (p. 209, n. 76); in that of the so-called "schemes of Cardinal Ottaviani" (p. 210); in that of supposed "curial maneuvers against collegiality" (p. 217); and, finally, in that surrounding the interpretation of the *Nota Explicativa Praevia* (p. 218). On the other hand, this study of Burigana allows us to follow the evolution of the "politics" and the "judgments" of the Italian Communist Party concerning the Church, which, later, in the time of Pope Paul VI, adopted the supposedly beneficial line of "a rapprochement with Catholic exponents of dissent from and criticisms of the magisterium of Pope Paul VI" (p. 219; see also p. 233ff. and n. 128). The weakness of such a position, and of the analysis of the Council based on it—both tendentious and partial—is quite evident in the work of this author (see esp. p. 222ff.). This is true of the following judgment of his as well: "The position of the Italian Communist Party became fixed on account of the repercussions that the Council could have within the Italian and international political frameworks. The theological debates, the theme of fidelity to the Roncallian line, the interventions of Paul VI, the emergence of clear lines between the conciliar majority and minority among the bishops—all these elements could be utilized to demonstrate the validity of the line adopted by the Italian Communist Party. There was a realization that a dialogue between Communists and Catholics could inspire a new political majority in Italy, in such a way as to splinter the hegemony of the Christian Democratic party and of the favored capitalistic model of the Occident" (p. 225ff.).

One final point to be noted, bearing in mind previous triumphalist evaluations of the actions of Monsignor Lardone: the judgment of Burigana according to which "the negotiations got off to a good start but then ultimately did not result in anything tangible" (see also in the "Acts," p. 296). Important in this regard is what the [Soviet TASS correspondent] Krassikov asserts (p. 323), which touches upon the work of the pontifical representative, who was supposed to have furnished "another version" of the Soviet response to the solicitude of the pope, without mentioning the reservations which his colleague, N. S. Ryzhkov, is supposed to have had. The lack of success in the end was evident.

In his contribution "Anti-Sovietism and *Ostpolitik* of the Holy See," A. Riccardi provides a good and balanced synthesis (except for his improper use of the now general term, *Ostpolitik* [Vatican policy towards the East]). His treatment is accompanied with at times acute intuitions, anticipating and in part taking up again the themes of his well-known study. "The Vatican and Moscow 1940–1990." He divides the work up among the following topics: "Benedict XV and the Bolshevik Revolution"; "the years of Pius XI"; "contrasts and antitheses"; "war and postwar periods": "confronting the new Islam"; "the 'turn' of Pope John XXIII"; "the Eastern policy of Pope Paul VI"; and, finally, "what alternative?"

Of particular weightiness are pages 244-245, which we recommend to be read in particular, although it seems to us that too much is said about the "involvement" in the election of Athenagoras as the Ecumenical Patriarch, of "responsible Vatican officials," of the papal nuncio in Istanbul, Angelo Roncalli, and of President Truman's personal representative to Pius XII, Myron Taylor (see p. 245). One item to file away for future reference, however, is the analysis of the participation of the Holy See in the Helsinki Conference (p. 264ff.).

The work of V. Martano is also quite well done. His title is "Constantinople and Moscow: Alexei and Athenagoras." He focuses, in other words, on the two principal figures in Eastern Orthodoxy, Byzantine and Slavic, during the Vatican II years of 1959 through 1962. This topic fits well within the framework of the Moscow Colloquium. The principal question at issue appears to be the "primatial" position of Constantinople. In this connection, it is interesting that Moscow had no intention of being linked with the ecumenical patriarch as far as negotiations with Rome were concerned (see p. 278, 280, 283, 287ff., and 291). Martano, however, concludes his treatment in an irenic vein (p. 292).

The final part of the book is given over to the "testimonials" that were delivered at the Moscow Colloquium. The first of these, by Ambassador J. E. Karlov, is very useful in providing the background for the momentary willingness to dialogue of Nikita Krushchev, as he was urged to do by the Italian Communist Party and by other Italians as well. We learn about this later in the volume (p. 318). The Soviet leader wanted to involve the Holy See in Soviet foreign policy (p. 295, and also p. 317), although his knowledge of the Holy See was gravely deficient, as can be gathered from his practice of speaking always of "the Vatican" (see also p. 309). More or less "ideological" always, he was simply ignorant of the religious motivations which inspired the Holy See in its positions and its solicitude for the situation of believers in the U. S. S. R. (pp. 296 and 300). The Soviet aim was always to expand the base and the influence of the international Communist movement (p. 298).

The topic of "The Vatican and Its Role in the History of the Twentieth Century" is "defended" by N. A. Kovalskij. Although it evidences a lack of vision and of understanding of the Holy See, also here again simply considering it "another entity in international relations" (p. 303), this contribution is pleasantly surprising in its grasp of continuity and renewal on the part of the Catholic Church, especially with regard to the Church's social teaching (pp. 304 and 311). For the author, this translates into a policy of "peace" towards the Soviet Union.

The contribution of A. Krassikov, entitled "The Second Vatican Council in the Context of the Relations between the U. S. S. R. and the Holy See," is of great interest. It succeeds in suggesting satisfactory replies to some fundamental questions that have been in suspense and it gives the lie to certain provisional "historical" solutions that have been offered. We recommend this text to the patient reader since our own reflections on it would be too lengthy. However that may be, it would appear that the Soviet TASS news agency, of which this author was a correspondent, played an important role in the creation of a new climate in the relations between the Holy See and the Kremlin.

The final testimonial here is that of Cardinal Johannes Willebrands. The special value of his contribution is to confirm a number of the aspects that emerged in the course of reading this volume, particularly with regard to the initial contacts with the Patriarchate of Moscow aiming at insuring the presence of Russian Orthodox observers at the Council. The testimony of a major protagonist always contributes to historical research and provides a firm foothold for the historian. One result is how well the fine and frank personality of Bishop Nikodim is sketched here. He was a key figure. No guarantee was given to him—on the evidence of this text—that the Council's treatment of "the question of atheism" would not get transformed into a "condemnation of Communism."

An Index of proper names concludes the volume.

19

John XXIII: "The Good Pope"

Alberigo Giuseppe, *Papa Giovanni* (1881-1963) [Pope John (1881-1963)], EDB, Bologna, 2000, 221 pages.

There has appeared in the bookstores under the title indicated above this rather light publication which now assumes its place in line among the biographies of Pope John XXIII behind those of Algisi, Balducci, Chaigne, Dreyfus, Gorresio, Hebblethwaite, and Zizola, to name only the most notable of the books already dedicated to the life of John XXIII. This work joins yet other new works in the wake of the great editorial interest aroused by the announcement of the beatification of John XXIII. Limiting ourselves to Italy alone, we note a number of new publications dedicated to his life and illustrative of his message. Among publishers, the Mondadori house has just published *Il papa buono. La Vita di Giovanni XXIII* [The Good Pope: The Life of John XXIII] by R. Allegri as well as *Giovanni XXIII. Una vita di santità* [John XXIII: A Life of Sanctity] by S. Gaeta. Meanwhile, the San Paolo house has put into the hands of readers a definitive edition of his *Giornale dell'anima* [Journal of a Soul] along with other pious writings, as well as an "official biography" written by M. Benigni and G. Zanchi, along with a preface by Archbishop Loris Capovilla (who was the private secretary and literary executor of the pope). The Paoline publishers have similarly put on the market a book entitled *Saggezza del cuore, primavera della Chiesa* [Wisdom of the Heart, Springtime of the Church] by M. Sgarbossa. The Borla house too has come upon the scene with *Papa Giovanni: La parola agli atti processuali* [Pope John: The Word to the Acts of the beatification Process] by A. L'Arco.

347

At the same time, the Gribaudi publishers have issued *Giovanni XXIII: Vita di un padre santo* [John XXIII: Life of a Saintly Father]. This last volume was written by A. Tornielli. Yet another biography is supposed to be coming out from the Rizzoli publishers (in the BUR series) with the title, simply, of *Giovanni XXIII*, which is outlined by M. Garzonio, followed by *Un santo di nome Giovanni* [A Saint by the Name of John] from the pen of V. Sansonetti. Along with this brief summary of ours, we also cannot forget the city of the lagoons, so dear to the heart of this pope, where the Studium Cattolico Veneziano, along with the Canal Printers, has now published *Giovanni XXIII. La mia Venezia* [John XXIII: My Venice], with an introduction by the current Patriarch of Venice, Marco Cé, and one by Archbishop Loris Capovilla as well.

Among all this copious harvest of publications we have elected to present this small volume by Giuseppe Alberigo. It is rich in quotations from the pope himself, and its principal value—for, in fact, it is again a "one-stringed" work—is its focus on Vatican Council II and its link with Pope John XXIII. In fact, six of the sixteen chapters which constitute the book are devoted to this subject. Unfortunately, there is no index (which would have helped for those engaged in scholarly research). In our examination of this book, we shall look principally at the chapters devoted to John XXIII and the Council, but we will also consider the remainder of the book in that same perspective.

We must state at the outset that, unfortunately, in the present inquiry, we find the usual parameters containing subjective judgments on the part of this author, judgments often not based on solid foundations. The author indubitably has great sympathy for the "person" of John XXIII; more than that, he is taken up with the "image" he himself has constructed of this pope. But precisely because of his passionate advocacy of his particular positions, he should have labored to achieve a more critical use of the tools of historical inquiry. In effect, he seems to assume that serious historical problems have, in fact, been solved where John XXIII is concerned. But it is not at all here a question of the possible sanctity of this pope. In fact, precisely because some of the historical sources in this case are not accessible, the whole problem must be approached with great prudence and care, as "history"—precisely. It suffices in this connection to quote the author himself with regard to the archives of the Secretariat of State (see p. 105, n. 11)—not to speak of the question that we ourselves have often raised, namely, how the various "reports" on the period covered are to be evaluated. How is the link, or lack of any such link, with the "sanctity" of the pope of any of the drafts or signs in a given document to be evaluated?

In the present case, let us begin by looking at the constant tendency of this author to differentiate or distinguish between Pope John XXIII and his predecessors. The author does this up to the point of exasperating anyone trying to follow him (see pp. 143, 161, 189, and 198). He does the same thing with regard to the differences between the pope and the college of cardinals (p. 119); between him and his vicar for the diocese of Rome (p. 152); between him and the Roman Curia (pp. 145, 177ff., 195ff.); between him and the Holy Office (pp. 157, 166, 177, 196); and, finally, between him and his closest collaborators (with a few exceptions); see p. 168, esp. n. 9, on the "threats" of Cardinal Tardini; but see also p. 177ff. on the subject of the Regulation of the Council, and also pp. 189, 199, and 202). In this regard, let us also recall the *Documented Biography* edited by Alberigo and Melloni themselves. In Part IV (2665-3459), the "benevolent" and "consoling" comments are passed over on the subject of the famous agenda of Pope John XXIII of January 4-13, 1961, on the occasion of his visits to the various Roman dicasteries. A distinction is also made between John XXIII and the bishops (with regard to the preparatory phase of the Council: pp. 169, 171 and 200). Prior to that, a distinction is similarly made between the patriarch of Venice and the Venetian bishops [of the Venetian ecclesiastical province] (p. 130 ff.).

Our criticism here reflects some of the ones to this author, Giuseppe Alberigo, that we have offered in connection with his view of Vatican Council II. He considers the Council as "innovative" and "progressive," as a revolutionary event, in fact, without sufficiently connecting the Council with the Tradition; he sees it as opposed to the past, in effect. In offering these criticisms here, however, certainly, we do not intend to criticize or diminish in any way characteristics of Pope John himself such as: his welcoming stance towards "new things" (p. 11); his "optimism," if one may express oneself thus (pp. 161; 189, and before that, pp. 82, 117, and 120); the special love this pope nurtured toward sacred Scripture (pp. 45, 95, 121ff., with some distinctions on our part, and then p. 124); his desire to realize the *Imitatio Christi* (p. 21); his indefatigable quest for "poverty and humility" (pp. 44, 118ff., and, on his "career," pp. 58ff., 63, 71, 205, and 216); and, finally, his mercy and gentleness (p. 51ff. and p. 60) in fidelity to the pope (p. 43). Our criticism here, however, is based upon considerations of the complexity of the personage of Angelo Roncalli, even though he was at bottom a simple man and a great lover of Tradition—but then see this author's disputable "Tridentine interpretation" (pp. 131, and esp. his other interpretation on p. 190). Still, along with others, this pope loved Tradition at the same time as he remained open and desirous of achieving *aggiornamento*. However, Alberigo cannot save himself here with a "kick to the corner" (though I will abstain further from any such football language!) merely by writing that Roncalli was "a man of the Tradition in the highest sense" (p. 217). For what the author seems to be really aiming at is to isolate him from Tradition in a strictly ecclesiastical sense.

However, Alberigo himself, in the synthesis he provides, allows the weakness of his own one-dimensional interpretation to become visible (see esp. p. 170); he speaks euphemistically of "other pontifical decisions more difficult to interpret." Naturally, these difficulties arise for him from the fact that they contradict his fundamental thinking about the subject of his research. The "Roncallian exceptionalism" which he describes, for us, arose from a wholly different source than he thinks; it arose, precisely, from the source of sanctity (p. 10). It was a sanctity directed towards evangelism, though, and as the author correctly notes, it was characterized by "ordinariness" (pp. 9 and 216ff.) and by "pastoralism" (pp. 78, 82ff., 94, 107, 111, 147, and 190). Nevertheless, we would add, it was a heroic sanctity. As the author further notes, John XXIII was truly dedicated to the cause of the unity of Christians, which was the will of the blessed Christ (pp. 67ff., 73). It is too easy to find solutions to the difficulties encountered merely by citing the language used by Roncalli himself (pp. 77ff., 79ff, 87ff., 156, 191, and 203) on his love, for example, for Catholicity, as against any exaggerated nationalism (p. 77ff.). Finally, there was assuredly his acute historical sense (pp. 41ff., 67, 96f.) and his appreciation of "the signs of the times" (p. 160ff.). This same attitude applied to his views on the relationship of Church and State and those of the Church and political parties, always, however, observing due distinctions (pp. 154, 167ff., 183ff., and, before that, pp. 78, 94, 114, 120, 124f., and 128ff.). On this last point, we would agree with Alberigo, although it would be necessary to discuss Pope John's use of the category of "prophecy" (p. 9).

However, we are quite convinced that we cannot share the opinion of the author concerning the position of Roncalli, before and following his election to the supreme pontificate, with regard to what the author calls the "common," prevailing ecclesiology of his time—"at least on the official level," Alberigo adds (pp. 63, 77, 80, 96, 109, 113ff., 125, 131, 145, 155, 190, 203, and 207). The same thing is true of John XXIII's views on Modernism (pp. 163, 191, 203, and before that, pp. 31, 34, 41, 46ff., and 123); on worker priests (pp. 105 and 157); on Fascism (pp. 65 and 93); on dealing with Franz von Papen (pp. 92ff.; to his credit he acted with charity also after the war); and on the Jews (pp. 86ff, and 97). John XXIII was supposedly "particularly reticent" on this last subject it is said incorrectly with regard to the series *Acts and Documents of the Holy See relative to the Second World War* (see also p. 64). All of these subjects, however, need to be examined more carefully in the course of conducting solid historical research. There was no call to get into the kinds of facile solutions that this author presents here.

On the subject of accuracy, we may cite two examples. The first has reference to the Pontifical Biblical Commission, and to the "uneasiness" and "anxiety" that John XXIII supposedly had on the subject of Catholic biblical scholarship (pp. 163, 178, and 183). But although he expressed an opinion on the loosening of standards, John XXIII otherwise maintained as a habit the silence of the Patriarch Jacob when conversing with interested parties on this subject, and this because he may have had mixed feelings about it. He maintained the same attitude of reserve, again, in the manner of Jacob, in other circumstances as well (see p. 183). Alberigo, however, having singled out a Johannine phrase referring to "the divine books...containing the apostolic tradition on which the holy Church of Christ is based," simply eliminates the contextual focus that would even allow a judgment on the use of such a phrase. The same thing is true of our second example here. In this case, Pius XII, was "greatly preoccupied" when speaking with Archbishop Roncalli "on the subject of Nazi atrocities"—this is the way the author describes the case. But what Archbishop Roncalli wrote was merely that "Pius XII wondered whether his silence on Nazi behavior might not be judged unfavorably." The case was thus actually quite different. Alberigo insinuated that the pope knew all about the "Nazi atrocities" at the time. He similarly speaks about the diagnosis of Pope John's cancer (p. 187) when it is not clear that the pope had even been informed of such a diagnosis as yet. And we may add further that his treatment of the important papal discourse entitled "The Church Rejoices" does not take into account the pertinent and indeed definitive clarifications about this discourse found in Monsignor Vincenzo Carbone's book *Il Concilio Vaticano II. Preparazione della Chiesa al III Millenio* [Vatican Council II: Preparations of the Church for the Third Millenium], published in Vatican City in 1998 (pp. 36-39). Our review of this important book is reprinted as Chapter 48 of the present work. But this research of Carbone is not utilized at all by Alberigo (or Melloni).

However that may be, we must take into account the fact that Pope John XXIII was certainly a child of his own time, and thus it is necessary to place his views and attitudes in their proper historical context and not "mythologize" him or them. We are dealing here with a "blessed," a saint, a man of the deepest kind of faith and courage; and hence everything about him must be treated in order to bring out the real qualities of his own beloved person and not some subjective idea of our own about him in conformity with our own choices, priorities, and desires. This is especially true of the time after he fell sick and became aware that someone else would have to finish the work of the Council which he had started. All this also applies especially to the now very real process of his canonization—"a slow and fatiguing process" (p. 7), the author remarks. It does not appear to us, however, that any such process was "blocked at the Council" (*Ibid.*). Rather, it was decided by the assembly to follow the "ordinary" way. And this was the attitude of Cardinal Lercaro as well.

A bird's eye view of the other chapters in this book, which are thematic, at least in part, reveals aspects which we have already noted in our view of the whole. The author proceeds in a linear direction, revealing an underlying and, for him, typical point of view. He is introducing, in effect, his overall view of the Council also in this book. But he goes astray, for example, when he speaks of the "persecution" of Angelo Roncalli, or of him being passed over or being otherwise afflicted with "institutional humiliations" (pp. 70, 77, and 83); or about his "disappointing promotion after his exile in Bulgaria" (pp. 84, 94, and 96); or about his being "held apart from the heart of the Church, pastoral activity, and the [Church's] historic center" (pp. 101ff. and 109, n. 22). All these things Roncalli supposedly suffered at the hands of his superiors and the Roman Curia. Certainly he had his share of misunderstandings and incomprehensions (see pp. 74 and 93); he had his crosses to bear. But how many, whether in the diplomatic service of the Holy See or in the ministries in which he served, were treated likewise without any special mistreatment or actual discrimination? The same question can be asked of anyone operating in this wide world, where misfortunes, even apparent "abandonment," do occur. They are part of life—especially the life of a priest, and, most especially, the life of a bishop! Who is moving up, and who is being left behind? Who is at the head of the line, while others are falling back? The circumstances of one's life, favorable or not, count for a great deal here. But we are quite convinced that, as far as good Pope John was concerned, what was always important were the words of his chose motto: *oboedientia et pax*!

It was precisely this kind of supernatural vision of things, of events, that constitutes "Christian wisdom" (beginning with "God is everything, I am nothing"). We know this from the pope's own *Journal of a Soul*. It was what made Roncalli great. This greatness comes through in the last chapter, the best chapter in this book—written by a man, Alberigo, who professes himself to be "enraptured" by Pope John XXIII. He has managed to capture the pope's spiritual physiognomy here. We ourselves can even subscribe to the account contained in the last chapter, with two exceptions. The first has to do with the identifying of Pope John XXIII in death with St. Francis of Assisi (p. 209), and the second concerns the assertion made by the author that it is impossible to admire Pope John today "without sincerely accepting and trying to understand in depth his essential intentions, both with regard to Church governance and to his ecclesial and historical magisterium" (p. 211). To this last point we would have to add: But not as Professor Alberigo himself understands the pope's intentions! Then there is the question of the Johannine vocabulary which the author finds "simple and free of affectation" (p. 216). In general, this does not seem to us to be the case, since in our estimation, his vocabulary often appears to be rather courtly. However, we do hold that the sanctity of Pope John XXIII manifested itself especially in his exceptionally profound faith and charity, and in his personal communion with God. In the course of his life, he succeeded, always and everywhere, in transforming everything into prayer. His *Journal of a Soul,* of this his "agenda," constitutes an ardent and very attractive testimonial. In his long and consistent life, the pope knew how to transform into prayer all that happened to him, whether it was personal, familial, ecclesial, diplomatic, religious, or merely human. To be convinced of this, it suffices to look at his personal experience, and to note how he treated and judged all of his collaborators.

20

Unpublished Writings of
John XXIII on Conciliar Subjects

Giovanni [John] XXIII, *Nostra Pace è la volonta di Dio* [Our Peace is the Will of God], Unpublished Notebooks edited by Marco Roncalli, Edizioni San Paolo, Alba (Cuneo) 2001, 263 pages.

I am always amazed when I think of Kierkegaard, who virtually as a twenty year old, began recording his thoughts and the things he wanted to keep in mind concerning his life and his studies; he recorded these things in notebooks labeled on the front NB (*Nota Bene*) and continued to do so, with fidelity and patience, up to the time of his death. It was a marvelous example of perseverance; he filled 36 notebooks with a total of 7600 pages, with points and counterpoints, recording thereby one of the best "documented" lives of modern times.

Recalling Kierkegaard in this fashion seems to me a suitable preamble to the presentation of these seven notebooks of Pope John XXIII (Q1-Q7) edited by another Roncalli, who recently offered us another fundamental work which allows us to become better acquainted with the former patriarch of Venice who became (along with Paul VI) the pope of the Second Vatican Council (see Marco Roncalli, *Giovanni XXIII, la mia Venezia* [John XXIII, My Venice], published by the Studium Cattolico Veneziano in 2000).

In the Preface to this book, the man who was the diligent and beloved private secretary of the pope and the executor of his papers, Archbishop Loris Capovilla, tells us how the pope thought that, after his death, "his notes and reflections and documentation concerning his service, from the days of his work as the secretary of a bishop, to those of his tenure as supreme pontiff, might be helpful to historians." In this the pope confirmed the fact that he himself was a historian; he taught ecclesiastical history, patristics, and apologetics, and he published some notable works of a historical character.

Following his *Journal of a Soul*, his *Letters* and his diaristic *Agendas*—these latter published in connection with his cause for beatification—the notebooks here which constitute a self-contained collection, and which preceded the material already published, "a testimonial of the author's attention to sudden inspirations and to the signs of the times; they reveal the feelings of a soul always permanently abandoned to God." Hence the title of this little book.

In his Introduction, the editor explains his sources, which he describes as "a collection of texts in [the pope's] own handwriting, mostly relating to his years at the nunciature in Paris and the patriarchate in Venice, and, especially, to those of this pontificate; they cover various themes and some come with notes attached" (p. 9). Thus, this collection is a sort of spiritual miscellany; but it is also an ideal prolongation of the pope's *Journal of a Soul*; it includes "brief meditations, hastily jotted notes, ideas for homilies or *schemata*, outlines for retreats, underlinings, diaristic-type notes on Vatican II, memo books recording meetings and visits, scholarly reminiscences, and transcriptions" (*Ibid.*).

The very markings and underlinings here of these "sparse notes" confirm for us the youthful Johannine *pietas* already familiar to us from his pastoral service during which he practiced prayer and contemplation, *ruminatio* on the Word of God, total confidence in Providence, and daily fidelity to both Book and Chalice.

The editor, as appropriate, becomes more technical when presenting a brief critical apparatus to go along with the text, but this is not a "critical edition." We do find, however, some of the necessary information for the "more demanding reader." We know that the order followed in the transcription of the material being published represents choices made by the editor when referring back to the original texts; the latter show a diverse ordering of extracts, some undated or datable, but which do not follow any chronological order. It seems to us, however, that the context of these notebooks does represent a kind of supplement or extension of the pope's *Agendas.*

One obvious example of this, related to the Vatican II situation, would be the very significant pages devoted to "the Personal Visit of the Holy Father to the Offices of Each of the Roman Congregations" (p. 16ff.). This publication reproduces the papal notes (pp. 103-134) which illuminate the true facts about the relationship of Pope John with the Roman Curia in general. These visits were carried out to the great satisfaction of the pope and include praise for everyone involved, with the unique exception of Monsignor Zerba (p. 106).

Always in the context of the Council, which is particularly interesting for us, it is worthwhile recording what John XXIII himself wrote apropos of his visit to the Council's Central Preparatory Commission: "I was welcomed by His Excellency Archbishop Pericle Felici, along with his collaborators…I was very happy to make their acquaintance; they are deserving of great merit for the work they have accomplished under Archbishop Felici's direction. I was happy to encourage them" (p. 108).

In confirmation of what has been stated with regard to how this collection supplements the pope's already published *Agendas,* I note that the texts referring to various dicasteries are much more developed, detailed, and accurate than some of the material in the *Agendas.* (This latter material, by the way, was not "strangely" published there in connection with the cause for beatification of Pope John; on this, see my review of Professor Giuseppe Alberigo's biography, *Pope John (1881-1963),* which originally appeared in the journal *Nuova Storia Contemporanea* and is reprinted as Chapter 19 of the present volume.)

Still on the subject of the Council, though, let us record that various ones of these diaristic notes, especially those related to the preparation for the great conciliar event during the period 1959-1962, the editor has made use of a 1959 "Agenda" notebook, chestnut brown in color. As an indicator of the great pope's concern for historical accuracy, we would like to quote what he himself wrote in this notebook: "*Nota*

Bene: this register carries the date 1959, but in fact it is a miscellany of different texts and notes that refer less to the year 1959 than to other years. It is rather in the years following 1959, for which there are notes that are better followed in other diaries. Here in random order there is mention of various factors, especially those related to the preparation of Vatican II; to avoid confusion when reading through these notes, one should in each case look at the date when it was signed" (p. 18).

For the convenience of the reader interested in Vatican II in particular, beyond what is already mentioned above, we may indicate yet others, especially those that refer to the responses (or non-responses) of bishops to the famous letter of Cardinal Tardini asking for proposals, for example: "I have read the first notes summarizing the responses from the bishops of Italy concerning the desires of the clergy and people with regard to how the liturgy and the pastoral ministry are to be treated by the Council; they are serious and worthy of respect" (p. 94). And then there is this example: "Archbishop Felici, who at my request through Cardinal Tardini was put in touch with Msgr. Loris Capovilla—in order to expedite the channel of communications between the pope and Cardinal Tardini—Archbishop Felici, I say, has begun to send recapitulations of various responses and proposals from the bishops from all over the world which will form the elements of documents that will be the first drafts of the conciliar constitutions that will be presented and eventually decided. Under today's date, February 19, 1960, I myself have personally examined the complex of summary notes of the various letters from the bishops of Italy. This initial and successful clarification of the prospects constitutes a preparation in the spirit of the work that will be carried out day by day" (p. 94ff.).

Following this we read: "In the Vatican gardens with Monsignor Capovilla: a reading of the proposals of the bishops of France. We can combine them in summary with those from the Italian bishops, and we find a happy convergence of agreement on the principal points which correspond to the exigencies of the circumstances of today" (p. 95).

Following the perusal together of the proposals of the bishops from Belgium, Denmark, Finland, England and Malta, Ireland, Iceland, Luxembourg, Norway, Holland, and Sweden, the pope notes: "There is much discretion exhibited here, but also some bizarre results owing to differences in climate, education, and particular circumstances." Then, the next day, Pope John describes as "most interesting" his perusal of the proposals of the bishops of the Eastern rite in Greece and Asia Minor for the coming ecumenical Council, and he adds: "Naturally, this variety of attitudes and colors can be explained by the historical experiences of the various countries and diverse races. The harmony concerning the fundamental principles of creed and cult according to the different liturgical rites is just perfect and a very happy result" (p. 96). It is worth quoting yet another significant passage on the conciliar preparation as well as on the prospects for the length of time required for the Council. Apropos of this, the pope wrote: "The thinking of many bishops concerning the various questions of doctrine and discipline is displayed in orderly and attractive ways. Who knows? The Council could easily be concluded in the course of 1961 and 1962. I have no anxiety on this score, nor do I wish to dictate to the Council what its conclusions should be. What the Lord requires of me in this connection is that I should lay aside my own *amour propre*, sacrifice my own life; all this should prepare me for the resulting blessing" (p. 98ff.).

A memorandum from the Central Preparatory Commission brought out a papal reaction to the effect that "[these are] excellent proposals... both for the doctrine which clarifies and the encouragement which makes one happy" (p. 99). *"Omnia in bonum et utile"* was the pope's Latin comment after reading the proposals from the Congregation responsible for the sacraments as well as from the one responsible for seminaries (*Ibid.*).

Leaving aside other mentions pertaining to the Council, we find it worthwhile to make mention of what the pope described as "a long meeting with Cardinal Amleto [Cicognani] aimed at systematizing and ordering the various conciliar assemblies" (pp. 149-151); there were significant readings on the Council of Trent and Vatican I undertaken in preparation for Vatican II (pp. 83, 96ff. 147, 202ff., and 241).

A judgment on Archbishop Pericle Felici is also worth noting: "He is a priest of some distinction with whom I will find it easy to work in preparation for the great event. The outside world knows nothing and understands nothing" (p. 98; see also p. 151, n. 13). There is an interpretation here that does not seem to me well set forth; perhaps it refers to the desire of the secretary general to have effective collaborators within the Secretariat itself rather than to have archbishop-undersecretaries.

And as for what concerns the hierarchy generally, I recommend also a number of other "Johannine" thoughts on the papacy found in these pages (pp. 44, 167ff., 172ff., 178ff., and 243ff.); on the patriarchs (pp. 55, 66ff., and 90); and on the cardinalate (pp. 142ff., 169, and 246).

Of great interest for us are the mentions by the pope of the formula in his encyclical *Mater et Magistra* as applied to the Church (pp. 218, 232, 234, and 248) and which the use of the Pseudo-Isidorian Decretals contributed to extend. We note also mention of another medieval forgery, namely, the prophecies of Malachy (pp. 216, 235, and 237ff.).

We would not like to leave the wrong impression that these notebooks contain only conciliar themes and those of Church business. On the contrary, the subjects mentioned touching upon the spiritual life are abundant. We need think, for example, only of the number of times the pope mentions the reading of his breviary, in which he encounters and appreciates beauties and sweetnesses (p. 213), the poetry of the psalms (pp. 228ff., 232ff., etc.), and, frequently, the consolations of sacred Scripture.

To conclude this delightful cavalcade in the spiritual fields of Pope John XXIII, we would like to make mention of his sanctification of "the ordinary," as we may call it; for that was *his* view of the matter, in fact. We would like to include two citations illustrative of this; they are found, significantly, at the end of the book (p. 250). One is from St. Thomas, according to whom "it is heroic to persevere to the death in the exercise of the common virtues." The other one we will transcribe in Latin; it has reference to the cause for sainthood of Bishop A. M. Gianelli, bishop of Bobbio, about whom it attests to the perfection which he had achieved: *"In una dumtaxat, fideli, jugi et constante proprii status munerum et officiorum perfunctione."* We may translate this as follows for the many who do not know Latin today: this bishop was outstanding "in the faithful, constant, and inexhaustible carrying out of the duties and tasks of his particular status."

21

John XXIII and the Council

Garzaniga Gianni, Ed., *Giovanni XXIII e il Vaticano II. Atti degli Incontri svoltisi presso il Seminario Vescovile di Bergamo 1998-2001* [John XXIII and Vatican II: Acts of the Meetings Held at the Diocesan Seminary in Bergamo 1998-2001], Edizioni San Paolo, Cinisello Balsamo 2003. 109 pages.

The *Works* of John XXIII being published by the Pope John XXIII Foundation at the Radini-Tedeschi Studies Center in Bergamo is enriched by the appearance of this slim volume which contains reflections of Acerbi, Bertuletti, Lafont, Monticone, and Zanchi. These reflections are basically on the subject of the convocation of the Second Vatican Ecumenical Council.

Professor Monticone first situates the Johannine pontificate in the Italy of the 1950s; he reviews the various international changes that followed one another, giving some emphasis to the pontificate of Pope Pius XII. For this author "there were great ecclesial and social ferments going on in the course of the 1950s" (p. 11). There was also "the development of the Italian laity" (p. 12). For Monticone, Roncalli was a "Tridentine bishop" (p. 14), though he was "pastoral" and prepared to dialogue. G. Zanchi, for his part, underlines the diverse "modalities of Pius XII and John XXIII in developing the papal ministry." This seems rather obvious, but for us some of this author's judgments seem somewhat questionable (see pp. 27ff., 30, 34, 36, 43, 45, 46, and 50).

It is a pleasant surprise, however, to read the essay of Antonio Acerbi bearing the title, "The Magisterium of John XXIII and the Conciliar 'Turn.'" This article exhibits an initial recognition that the

Council was a "complex occurrence" with an "institutional stamp" (p. 51). Beyond the question of the magisterium, however, there is the person of John XXIII who represents "a great and irresolvable datum" (*Ibid*.), and who introduces "a *novum*, a novelty or new thing, which for the historian represents a great problem" (*Ibid*.).

We can follow what the author says also on "the other problematical aspect," namely, "the question of "the 'turn' of Vatican II. The very idea of such a 'turn' implies both a break and continuity," he says. We would not always characterize it as definitely a "break," however. The author goes on: "A road which turns is still the same road…it simply changes direction." We would add, while maintaining this same metaphor, that a turn is not necessarily a U-turn. The author concludes from this that "in speaking of a 'turn,' we have in a certain sense, rejected the idea that Vatican Council II represented a 'simple beginning' " (p. 52).

Thus does the reason for our "pleasant surprise" because here, finally, we find actually stated, clearly and directly, a rejection of the interpretation of Professor Giuseppe Alberigo for whom is dominant the idea of a simple beginning." Acerbi continues on this subject: "Some of you will have seen the first volumes of [Alberigo's] *History of Vatican II* and may have noted with astonishment that he begins this history with the pope's decision to convoke the Council." At this point, Acerbi compares this approach with Hubert Jedin's masterful *History of the Council of Trent*. Jedin devoted his first volume ("the best one") to the preparations for the Council. Now Alberigo, who was Jedin's student, is much too clever to imagine—Acerbi goes on—that anyone could think he has have "forgotten to cover the hundred years from Vatican I to Vatican II…Evidently this was a methodological choice" by Alberigo. We have always maintained that it was an *ideological* choice, corresponding to the idea of absolute newness or novelty associated with the personality of John XXIII. We are entirely in accord with Acerbi about this. He writes that "Alberigo's criterion is one of *post tenebras lux*, that is, the light came after the darkness, John XXIII being the light. But then there is *deinde tenebrae*, afterwards the darkness returned." In point of fact, for Alberigo, "Pope Paul VI reorganized the Vatican II tendencies to the point of betraying them." Finally, someone has pointed this out about Alberigo! I am not the only one to have to say it, clearly, and in the face of contrary winds and tides! This is what was such a pleasant surprise for us here!

Acerbi's essay is well worth reading, for he has written some other interesting things, whether for the historian, the theologian or the philosopher. He has written that the Council represents a time "when the Church of the periphery moves to the center" (p. 55). He finds that the Roman Curia operates in accordance with "a normal institutional dialectic"; he does not represent "Western-style historical reconstruction." The author adds in this connection: "Certain historical reconstructions trouble me; they are presented in black and white... Alberigo is the master of this method." So Acerbi rightly recognizes that "the minority played an indispensable role at the Council and not necessarily a negative one" (p. 57). He advances the idea that for John XXIII the fact of not governing heavy-handedly proceeded "from a very elevated spiritual conception" (*Ibid.*). Acerbi concludes that this "differentiated him from Paul VI. What happened here was the same thing that happened between Pope Pius X and Pope Benedict XV." One cannot, however, simply say, as the author does say, that "John XXIII did not intervene in the case of the initial preparatory documents."

One of the few subjects on which Acerbi is in agreement with Professor Alberigo of Bologna is his conception of a Council till Vatican II as an extraordinary arena, a kind of "supreme tribunal, or place to settle disputes and make decisions concerning internal Church controversies" (p. 58; see also p. 60 and 66ff.). According to Acerbi, John XXIII had a "mystical" vision of the great Synod.

Another one of his judgments merits mention, namely, on the subject of G. Philips, whom he considers a wise scholar but not a theologian; he came out with "many ideas because he did not have any of his own"—or, rather, "he was not a great theologian; great theologians are dangerous men; they are like great artists" (p. 60). There is some truth in this judgment. We too consider Philips to have been more of a mediator; he did not have a theory or represent a school of his own. Acerbi delineates a number of the characteristics of the great conciliar event, taking his cues from Pope John's Opening Address to the Council. We note in particular his treatment of the question of the "pastoral" nature of the Council, which he considers an "element not too clearly spelled out...no sooner was it launched than it began to be contrasted with or opposed to doctrine and truth. And that was never the intention of the pope" (p. 63). We shall not go on to describe what follows from this view for this author, except to say that he believes that the "pastorality" of the Council introduced its "historicity." This, of course, is true, and it should have been better illustrated and explained by the author in the pages that followed, in order to clarify the relationship between the Church and the modern world. In fact, however, the author does not do this.

A. Bertuletti takes up next the subject of what he titles "John XXIII and the Council." He treats of the Council's "pastoral form" and he explains "the reciprocal relationship between the pastoral and the dogmatic which constitute the substance of Christian truth" (p. 77), particularly in the context of the Pastoral Constitution on the Church in the Modern World, *Gaudium et Spes*.

Bertuletti also concludes his essay by underlining the "spiritual" quality of the intuitions of Pope John XXIII. In our opinion, however, his treatment is characterized both by imprecision and by exaggeration (see p. 82 in particular).

Along the same "spiritual" line is the essay by G. Lafont entitled "Tradition and Prophecy in John XXIII: Blessed Pope John, a Doctor of the Church." He reveals his weakness as a historian, however, in his supine acceptance, minus any critical spirit, of the distinction proposed by Delumeau between the Catholic Reform and the Counter-Reformation with regard to the Council of Trent. He similarly accepts the work directed by Alberigo on Vatican II.

For us, in effect, Roncalli certainly was a priest, as Lafont attests. He was also a bishop; and he was a pope whom we can label "Tridentine" in the sense of maintaining continuity with the Catholic Reform; this tied him to Vatican II as well, in fact. A sound conciliar hermeneutic tells us that, in the course of the Church's history, there is no sudden "U-turn" between one council and another; rather, we repeat, there is development and enrichment in continuity *in rebus fidei et moribus*. "John XXIII, the purest fruit of the Catholic Reform" (p. 86), certainly represented this, also in the way in which he appreciated the ideal Tridentine sacerdotal figure, Pope Pius IX. He would equally have appreciated the great Jubilee proclaimed by Pope John Paul II, the *Catechism of the Catholic Church*, and so on, as Lafont attests. Even though the contemporary polemical approach to the Tridentine *Sitz im Leben* has since come about, it remains necessary to preserve the links with the Tridentine Council for the sake of the Catholic Tradition. Pope John XXIII was not an exception in this regard, especially in view of "his charism for universal charity" (p. 95ff.), as Lafont characterizes it. He sums up John's position in three points, as follows: "In the first place, there was his great hope for the salvation of all; then there was the replacing of the primacy of truth by the primacy of charity; and, finally, there was his valuing of dialogue as a place for the germination of charity" (p. 98). Lafont concludes his essay by associating John XXIII with St. Therese of Lisieux: he holds that he was a "doctor of the Church in the same way that Saint Therese of the Child Jesus was" (p. 108).

Lafont does not end up quite as happily, however, since he goes beyond both John XXIII and his own earlier judgment by saying that "although he was not entirely conscious of it, John XXIII surpassed not only the Counter-Reformation but the Catholic Reform itself in putting his stamp on his own epoch in the history of the Church" (*Ibid.*). The author's final words describe the present day in rather negative terms with respect to the Church's Magisterium, which he claims "wants to maintain the new things introduced by Pope John XXIII at the same time as it wants to preserve intact the Tridentine Church" (*Ibid.*).

22

Paul VI,
the Pope Who Kissed the Ground

Acerbi Antonio, *Paolo VI, il papa che baciò la terra* [Paul VI, the Pope Who Kissed the Ground], Edizioni San Paolo, Alba (Cuneo) 1997, 164 pages.

This fine small book on Pope Paul VI arrived in the bookstores, almost co-incidentally, with the September 26, 100th anniversary of the birth of Giovanni Batista Montini. Its author is the historian Antonio Acerbi, who has already provided his credentials on his subject with his contribution to the volume *I cattolici nel mondo contemporaneo (1922-1958)* [Catholics in the Contemporary World (1922-1958)]. This earlier contribution of his was entitled "G. B. Montini, Archbishop of Milan." The author has written elsewhere on the same subject as well.

In his "Premise," the Ascerbi very humbly describes this book as "a biographical sketch," and he states that his aim is to "help overcome the barriers of misunderstanding." We too believe that one of the tasks of the historian is to help overcome misunderstandings. However, there is no question here of this being an "apologetical" work; nor is it a work of either adulation or denigration. He adds the following comment to verify this: "It does not aim to show that Paul VI was always in the right. That is not the task of the historian, but of God, in the valley of Jehoshaphat." Besides, the author adds, Paul VI's "personality was too complex and nuanced not to be betrayed by too easy, pat, and clear-cut judgments about him." Acerbi concludes that "the effort to capture the reasons behind a great spirit is actually a gesture of *pietas*, the only one given to the historian to accomplish; it is the latter's means of becoming reconciled to a past which is still too near to permit complete equanimity in one's judgments."

The study begins with "The Years of Formation (1897-1922)." There is a well-conceived though brief description in this chapter of the future pope's "master," Father Giulio Bevilacqua, as well as of the general background [of the future pope's life] in Brescia. As has been the case, we find it necessary to note that the *curriculum studiorum* of Montini presented by Acerbi here (see p. 9ff.) contains several inexactitudes and contradictions. Nor does it appear that Montini's vocation as a "historian" came about and was partly realized, in the first months after his priestly ordination. We have dealt with this issue before: see the introduction to the work of N. Vian, *Lettere a casa 1915-1943 G. B. Montini, Paolo VI* [Letters Home—1915-1942—of G. B. Montini, Pope Paul VI], Edizioni Rusconi, Milan 1987 (p. 9); see also the two "Notes" of ours in *Apollinaris*, in 1989 and 1990, on pages 243-252 and 869-883. These "Notes" were entitled, in fact, "Was Giovanni Batista a Historian?" What the author reports about Montini's favorable encounter with French culture (pp. 10-11) is very important, however, as is the fact of Montini's "regret at not having been able to cultivate properly his own intellectual inclinations" (p. 11). The reader must realize the seriousness of Montini's health problems at the time when he was in Warsaw; they were much more serious than Acerbi's text indicates.

Also valuable here is the description of "The Years of FUCI" [*Federazione Universitari Cattolici Italiani*=Federation of Catholic University Students]. The "spiritual Augustinianism" of the future pope is mentioned here—but see also the reference to his adherence to "Thomism," described as "not the reflexive doctrine of authoritarian politicians that was in vogue at that time in certain circles, but rather the doctrine that lay at the foundation of Christian Humanism and was in equilibrium with the natural and the supernatural, culture and faith" (p. 18). Also discussed here is the future pope's unyielding attitude towards theological Modernism, for which he did not have even tacit sympathy—in contrast to his open attitude towards the modern world, to which the author shows that he was very attentive (p. 17 and esp. pp. 18-21; then p. 99ff, 130, and 145). It seems to me that Acerbi is inspired here by the fine volume in French, *Paul VI et la modernité dans l'Église* [Paul VI and Modernity in the Church], published in Rome in 1984. He certainly makes the necessary clear distinctions here between modernity and Modernism (see p. 145). The treatment also brings out Montini's "spiritual approach" to youth and deals as well with his resignation [as the FUCI national chaplain].

The chapter entitled "In the Secretariat of State" (1925-1954) opens with an assertion that needs to be interpreted by overcoming a certain "Semitic"-type mentality which tends to eliminate the idea of "more or less." The author claims that "Montini did not enjoy his work in the Secretariat of State" (p. 27). This is not true, although to the "poor cards" that had been dealt him in this connection, he did prefer "spiritual contacts and intellectual debates" (*Ibid.*).

The approach of the chapter entitled "Montini and Italian Issues" is particularly important in setting forth his relationships with Alcide De Gasperi (pp. 36ff.), and also his relationship to his nomination as archbishop of Milan. It seems that this had something to do with the crisis of Catholic Action, but it is too soon to be able to affirm this with assurance.

"In Milan (1955-1963)" is the title of the chapter that follows. There is a good treatment of the archbishop's attitude to the famous "opening to the left" and to Communism [of the Christian Democrats]. It seems to us that Acerbi has succeeded better than others in his attempt to disentangle the Montinian approach to this question. And we are also with him in the case of the chapter on "The Coming of the Council (1959-1963)," where the author explains the ante-preparatory *votum* of the archbishop, which did not distinguish him that much from the *vota* of his fellow bishops around the world. His conciliar "maturity" had not yet been developed, though it would develop very soon, and, indeed, it becomes evident already in this chapter. The author notes that "Montini, perhaps without any definite or precise intention, already prefigured the mediating role between advanced theological positions and the established theological patrimony handed down in the Church; he was alert to validate and to avoid the elimination of whatever was valuable from either source" (p. 56). This is well said.

But in due course this archbishop of Milan was elected to sit "On the Chair of Peter" (1963). This is the title of the next chapter. The description of this great changeover in his life is regular and balanced, even if it is a bit "indulgent," especially in view of what followed, and also in the use of the word "reform." This was the case even where the papal text spoke of "new things" (that is, sentiments, proposals, customs, and spiritual benefits, in every sense of the word). And to think that the first "magic" word here was *aggiornamento*! However that may be, the author concludes that "a renewal of fidelity to the will of Christ and in fostering the vital continuity of the Church was the perspective in which Paul VI prepared himself to face up to his new task of being the universal pastor" (p. 69).

The following theme is that of the chapter "Paul VI and the Council (1963-1965)" with indications of how the Council would become his Council (p. 72). This is a point to underline while others were still calling it "the Council of Pope John XXIII." Certainly it was up to each person to interpret in his own way, apart from adopting any sectarian or ideological interpretations. In this perspective, the author does a good job describing the relationship of the bishop of Rome with the members of "the conciliar majority." "The basic agreement that obtained would not have eliminated moments of confusion and even of tension" (p. 72). "In fact," the Ascerbi continues, "when Paul VI indicated that there was a certain distance between him and certain opinions maintained within the ranks of the conciliar majority, this was not merely a tactical move; it corresponded to reservations of principle of his" (p. 73). We are in agreement with this conclusion, but not necessarily with everything else that is said in this same connection, for example, that Paul VI "was not a speculative theologian...nor was he a canonist. He was a practiced diplomat, and, at bottom, in his heart, a very literate priest, a 'spiritual director of souls,' and a man always looking into 'the drama of human existence.'" For us, however, he *was* a theologian, just as he was a canonist as well; more than that, he was a practiced diplomat and a pastor too—but yet more than that, he was a "historian"! And he complained, in fact, above all that the Italian bishops at the Council were not very well acquainted with the history of theology. And with regard to history, it just does not seem plausible to us that there was a "combine" called "Ottaviani and Felici" (p. 74). The latter was the spiritual father of the Roman Seminary; he was chosen by Pope John XXIII himself precisely because he was not a member of the well known groupings in the Roman Curia. To contrast Felici with Cardinal Montini and to put him in league with Cardinal Ottaviani does not appear to be very "historical" to us. Here again, time, and honest research—we firmly believe it—should be able to establish the real facts. Meanwhile, a phrase such as "total monarchical power" (*Ibid.*), meaning the power enjoyed by the pope, is a most unfortunate phrase. It has to be said the power personally excercised by him. Similarly, any judgment on his concept of collegiality (p. 75) cannot be justified with reference to the Regulation of the Synod of Bishops. However, the "challenge to the authority and indeed to the person of Paul VI" was not verified on the episcopal level (*Ibid.*). This is the case even though "the positions adopted by Paul VI will finally establish a line of demarcation within the conciliar majority, between a radical wing and a moderate one, the first reluctant, the latter inclined to accept the pope's point of view. This division was covered over out of a fear of giving encouragement to the conciliar minority and thereby jeopardizing the approval of the very innovative Council documents" (*Ibid.*). We would add that this was not the only effect of the pope's taking particular positions. And certainly the documents "would not have been able to come safely into port without the support of the pope. The renewal of the Church enjoyed the seal of approval of Paul VI. He was the guarantor in that moment of the general movement of transformation within the Church that had been launched by the convoking of the conciliar event" (p. 76). This is well and clearly stated and we congratulate the author. More than that, "the consensus that formed around Paul VI was enhanced by the journeys he undertook alongside the Council but very much in its spirit...with his two journeys to Bombay and to the United Nations, the pope inaugurated in a grand style the process of dialogue of the Church with the modern world, focusing on two main themes, peace and development; he could never have allowed these two themes to remain apart" (*Ibid.*).

The chapter that follows is entitled "The Years of Reform (1963-1968)." The author gives a certain emphasis to papal decisions indicating the pope's desire "to clarify the fact that the Roman papacy had abolished the residual features of the old papal states" (p. 77). But we must not forget that the state of Vatican City remains, almost as a confirmation of the papacy's need for territorial sovereignty, even if only on a postage-stamp plot of land, in order that the Petrine ministry might be freely exercised. In any case, there were reforms "in continuity with the profound meaning of the ecclesial tradition... but without any diminution of the sacred authority" (p. 78). There were reforms, then, but they were not imprudent ones. However, the considerations discussed and the contrasts made on page 79 concerning Pope John XXIII leave us perplexed, because it seems that the latter had come around to deciding to provide a greater direction to the Council, following criticisms of the "*laisser faire*" policy he had adopted during the First Session. The author made Montini a comparison between the period of the Council itself and the period to follow, the first being a time of discussion and the second one of understanding what had been discussed: "The period of plowing up the field is followed by the period of cultivating and bringing the crops to fruition" (*Ibid.*). On the other hand, the idea that "the post-conciliar period would be free of problems could never be more than a wish, not a realistic vision, of the way things would be" (p. 80). The author wisely reports in this connection: "The Council was the fruit of various dynamisms, both diverging and converging, which found a certain equilibrium in the conciliar documents; but these dynamisms were by no means exhausted thereby; they would continue to be operative after the Council. But there were two areas where Paul VI could apply his criteria, though not without resistance; these two areas were the reforms of the liturgy and of the Roman Curia" (*Ibid.*). To explain all this, the author moves ahead with great confidence—if not, in our opinion, a little nonchalance in his judgments. The same thing is true of his remarks on collegiality (employing the word "affective" instead of "effective" in one place—p. 86). According to him, the Pauline vision here was due to "a precise historical situation." For us, however, it grew out of a theological conviction.

The chapter that follows is entitled "The Ecumenism of Paul VI." This subject is treated in linear fashion. However, there is not, as the author asserts, any renunciation of the idea of the Roman Church as the *mater et caput omnium ecclesiarum* (p. 91). This is especially the case given that this formula must be applied with special significance to the Church in the Occident. We may note one small mistake here too in the author's reference to the Church of Rome "as the only apostolic see" (p. 93). Once again, this is true as far as the Occident is concerned, where Rome is the only "apostolic see"—and is doubly apostolic, in fact, by virtue of the martyrdom of both of the two apostles, Peter and Paul.

Of particular interest today is the chapter on "The Dialogue of Paul VI with the Modern World." We have made mention of this above already. In it there is described the pope's attitude "recognizing the autonomy of the worldly reality of the day, in the first place the reality of the state." We would add the adjective "just" before the word "autonomy" here. The author continues on: "The Church must renounce all worldly power and pretexts, exerting influence only by way of moral conviction; she cannot renounce her own identity nor her own mission, however; nor can she uncritically adopt the mentality and opinions that prevail in modern society" (p. 99). She has a role in fostering "Christian culture," and in promoting the social teaching of the Church as the foundation of any social construction which takes man into account with the totality of the truth about him. There is a certain lack of realism in some of the author's judgments concerning, for example, the existence of Marxist-type ideological underpinnings in some of the Latin American "theologies of liberation"; and, again, concerning Vatican diplomacy ("barely touched by reforms," Acerbi thinks, though for us it was "revolutionary" to the extent that it had become "pastoral"). This lack of realism of the author extends to his comments on the Helsinki Conference, which he considers a "first" for the Holy See, although the latter has been involved in international diplomacy for centuries. There is also a mistake here regarding Spain, where Acerbi writes January 1976 instead of 1979 (p. 105). There is not much profit to be derived from the reading of these particular pages, nor of those in the chapter that follows covering "The Italian Church"—again, we would prefer to say "the Church in Italy." This remains true of the author's treatment of the "new" Catholic Action as well.

In this connection, we shall limit ourselves to making three points. First, we would delete "collective" before "co-responsibility" here, or else we would leave it as it is in the papal text, namely, as "collective responsibility" (p. 109). Then, next, we would add to the phrase "lay action" the adjective "specific"; that would correspond to "the organic link between the hierarchy and the laity"—which is proper to Catholic Action (p. 112). Finally, we do not believe that one can properly write that "the fact that the Christian Democrats possessed their own autonomous political culture with respect to ethical-religious motivations which stemmed from their very foundation as a party was something that escaped Paul VI" (p. 115). For this author, "a non-institutional factor, though a very powerful one, namely, the dialectic of social forces...always eluded Pope Paul VI" (p. 116). There is some truth in this, as there is in the further consideration that the Church was affected by the strong currents that "in the tumultuous post-conciliar era swept through both society and the Church." But these currents, of course, were factors that went beyond the confines of Italy and applied to the whole Church.

At this point we find ourselves faced with a chapter entitled "The First Skirmishes of the Crisis." These are well-described. With regard to the 1971 Synod of Bishops, while admitting "professional and even political commitments applied to the clergy," we would nevertheless have to add: "But only in a restricted context." And we would also have to take careful note as well of the fact that "the discipline of celibacy was maintained," thus "eliminating the possibility left open by Paul VI in his letter to Cardinal Villot." Also, on various points, the author's presentation of the thought of Paul VI in the encyclical *Humanae Vitae* is quite inadequate; for example where it is said that Paul VI was not dealing with the subjective aspect of this question (p. 121). However, for Acerbi, "the historical question remained in suspense." Yet he does recognize in the sentence that follows that "this was an entirely new phenomenon in the history of the contemporary papacy, namely, a direct challenge to the authority of the pope coming from inside the Catholic community" (p. 122).

Then comes "The Post-Conciliar Crisis (1968-1973)." This means the crisis in its fullness. In this connection, it is worthwhile both making an observation and adding a clarification. The observation relates to "some old friends of the pope (de Lubac, Daniélou...)" (p. 125) who supposedly themselves "also assumed a critical attitude going against the conciliar event." We would say, rather, against certain post-conciliar developments. As for the clarification, we can agree on the need to wait for the opening of the archives before writing about the "collaborators" of the pope (p. 129) and about their "responsibility" for "acting in an authoritarian way towards local Churches"—and therefore for projecting a false image of Christ the Lord, to employ Roncallian language. Nevertheless, we insist that Paul VI was not the kind of man to be led by others, rather, he had a steady record of conducting the affairs of the Church as if he were still "the 'substitute' [deputy] of the Secretary of State," which at one time he had been. And his own "substitute" of the Secretariat of State, Giovanni Benelli, had been his secretary. Nevertheless, the account here of the very unfortunate conflict with the ACLI [the Catholic labor union] is well described as "a drama" (p. 132); the same thing is true of the introduction of divorce into Italy. With regard to this latter issue, we would not say that there was any "alternative, according to which there were two options or choices between two profoundly different images of the Church," between "turning the defense of Christian values over to the laws of the state or to the witness of the faithful" (p. 133). Nor does it appear to us that "the defeat of the referendum on divorce, and then that on abortion as well, set in motion a process within Italian Catholicism of reaffirming the Church's Catholic identity and rallying around the hierarchy, the results of which would become visible in the 1980s" (p. 133ff.).

There comes, at the end, the chapter on "The Final Years of the Pontificate (1973-1978)," in which the 1975 Holy Year was supposedly "celebrated in a minor key and without any particular resonance in the dioceses" (p. 136). That depends. We have vivid memories of some of the Holy Year celebrations that were well prepared and drew substantial participation, in Cuba, for example. There was the further example in 1975 of the outstanding and beautiful apostolic exhortation of Paul VI, *Evangelii Nuntiandi* [on Evangelization in the Modern World]. There was the evidence of Paul VI's experience of the Holy Spirit operating in the renewal of the Church as well as in the renewal of his own intimate personal life. He wrote: "My state of mind? Am I Hamlet? Don Quixote? Am I on the right or the left? I cannot even guess. Two sentiments predominate in me: *superabundo gaudio*" (p. 138ff.). At the conclusion there is mention of Paul VI's letter to the Red Brigades and his celebration at St. John Lateran of the funeral of Aldo Moro after the tragic death of the latter. According to the author, these efforts of the pope "revealed the humanity of Giovan Battista Montini, never very well known to the grand public at large, and often distorted because of polemics and the uncommunicativeness of the pope himself as far as the great masses were concerned" (p. 140).

Along with a very useful chronology, there is in this volume a complete and essential bibliography, as well as an index of names and books. The author provides a conclusion as well. Although we agree with some of his points, we think it is fair to formulate several critical observations as well. We will begin with the author's characterization of Montini as "a reforming pope"—he was "explicitly conscious of being such" (p. 141), Acerbi adds. He goes on to say: "He renewed the image of what a pope is. John XXIII had begun the same process." Yes, in one sense we can say that, just as we can also say: "In Catholicism the symbolical value of the papacy plays a very important role in the self-knowledge of the community. To become part of this symbol is already to effect a change which can be felt throughout the whole Church" (p. 142). Paul VI's aim was to present a Church which was "humble, missionary, and fraternal—and was all of these things out of fidelity to Christ" (*Ibid.*).

With regard to what was inherent in collegiality, we refer back to what we have already said above, even if, "the conditioning of the ecclesial climate" appears to have been completed by a correct and appropriate consideration of "theological divergences on the primacy which the pope did not want to see touched in any way by the discussions and divisions in orientation of the episcopate or by the pressures tending towards autonomy in the local Churches" (p. 143). Some good things are said here also on the relationship of the Church with the modern world; but these things all supposed "a clear identity on the part of the Church"; some of them dealt with the Church's "hesitations and irresolution."

For the solution to the difficulties the author relies on the dominant psychology of Paul VI. This did not consist of an inability to decide, but rather "the firm will not to abandon either of the two poles of the questions at issue; there were diverse exigencies that could not be neglected or renounced; historically, they had often been realized in opposition to each other." The many dichotomies included "truth-charity, historicity-permanence, liberty-authority, power-fraternity, superiority-humility, separation from the world-unity with the world..." Paul VI could not abandon these issues, "even when, at least in the short run, they could not be reconciled" (p. 144). Thus, "The pope firmly pursued the program of the renewal of the Church." At the same time, "he gave equal weight to the preservation of tradition when it seemed to him that it was threatened in any way—without, however, adopting a line of march that entailed pure preservation" (p. 145).

As regards the "modernity" of the pope, which the author labels a "very ambiguous notion," he asks: Was Paul VI a "modern pope"?

Acerbi replies basically positively to this question, but he also poses another question: "Was the pope evangelical?" This question did not have reference to the personal sanctity of Giovan Battista Montini; rather, it had reference to "the way in which he understood the papacy and how he aimed to carry out the papal ministry in practice" (p. 146). Posing the question this way makes the reply even more difficult, but the author extricates himself from the difficulty with both skill and wisdom by writing: "I limit myself to saying that Paul VI wished that the image of his pontificate would be evangelical." For him the Gospels were put forth as "the fundamental criteria of renewal."

Coming down to the present, the author concludes as follows: "Only Pope John Paul II could have effectively placed this kind of problem on the agenda in the way that he did with his encyclical *Ut Unum Sint*, when he invited followers of Christ everywhere to reflect with him on a possible new form of the exercise of the Petrine ministry." It is worth adding that for Paul VI's successor, as for him, there was not only the Gospels that had to be considered, but also the historical developments which trace their origins back to these same Gospels, giving special attention to the first Christian millennium and to the then still undivided Church.

23

The "Event" and the "Decisions": concerning a "Thesis"

Fattori Maria Theresa, and Melloni Alberto, Eds., *L'Evento e le decisioni. Studi sulle dinamiche del Concilo Vaticano II* [The Event and the Decisions: Studies on the Dynamics of Vatican Council II], Il Mulino, Imola 1997, 534 pages.

On the occasion of the publication of a "manifesto"

Anyone who follows with attention the studies that have come out on the Second Vatican Council cannot but have experienced the sensation of a certain dispersion of efforts, a splitting into a number of small rivulets separate from the main stream; there has been a dissection and a laying bare by peeling off the layers of this fundamental event in the history of the Catholic Church—and not merely her history in this century. The danger inherent in this situation is indicated in the Introduction to this volume which we have under review here; it involves a "risk of sliding into a history which consists of mere fragments, and which thus amounts to no more than a simple chronicle" (p. 12)—or perhaps into producing a kind of "encyclopedia," we would add. Underlying this fragmentation, in many cases, is the aim of diminishing or removing the importance of the Council's actual documents in order to substitute an interpretation of the event which from the start we have defined as "ideological."

What this amounts to, generally speaking, is evident in this publication, which aims, in the manner we have just indicated, to "recover" *ad usum delphini* a historiographical tendency which focuses on the event itself, its discontinuity, indeed its character of drastic change, in contrast to what came before it; this contrast, in fact, is antithetical to the idea of the famous historical "Annales" which cover long periods of time, giving emphasis to historical continuity. (For F. Braudel, for example, history is supposed to be an "applied social science which brings out structures, systems, and perennial models which at first sight were invisible" (p. 58). Often it is not perceived, nor is it widely realized, that treating a historical event, that is "worthy of notice" (see p. 417), as some kind of a breaking point, or rupture with the past (see pp. 418ff.), represents novelty in the writing of history. In the present case, it means treating it almost as the birth of a new Church, a Copernican revolution, the passage from one type of Catholicism to another and different one. This way of proceeding cannot and must not be accepted, certainly not as regards Catholicism. A true history must take into account its specific character and its continuity with its own past which must be preserved in the interpretation of the events and documents that pertain to the Catholic reality.

In this regard, reading the contributions to historical research published in this volume, one is truly surprised at the radical criticisms leveled at the thought of three figures as eminent as Hubert Jedin (pp. 459-462), Joseph Ratzinger (p. 66 and 420ff.), and Walter Kasper, this last figure with his four hermeneutical rules, to which we fully adhere (p. 67ff.). Here these rules are considered "abstract," however, and thus they are left out, even for the purpose of underlining the differences between Vatican Council I and Vatican Council II. This judgment of insufficiency with regard to Kasper is expressed by G. Alberigo (p. 520) and even to E. Poulat (pp. 61-62 and 421 and 433); its aim is apparently to validate the idea of the Council as an "event," understood in a particular way—and always with the "ideological" purpose indicated above. However, it is probably just as well that this way of proceeding can so clearly be seen here as a strategy of what we have called "the School of Bologna."

It should be realized that what was considered to be an extreme position at Vatican II, even among the so-called "majority," has succeeded after the Council in monopolizing up until now the interpretation of the Council, rejecting every other approach as contrary to the Council itself. We would certainly characterize this position as extremist; it is at odds with what at the Council was a constant and active search for a *consensus*, accepted by those desirous of reaching agreement. Father Joseph Komonchak even mentions this here, as a matter of fact (p. 435ff.). This Bologna school has always aimed to impose its own point of view, and it has simply been deaf to any calls to the contrary, just as it has been dismissive of the careful work of "mending" carried out by Paul VI (see, for example, pp. 360-368).

The reader may stop right here, if he so desires, because the basic problem with this book is already quite clearly laid out and delineated. But those who wish to dig deeper and understand more fundamentally what is at stake can follow us in examining at some length the problem already indicated in the Introduction by the editors. The work presented here is illustrative of what has been announced for the forthcoming third volume of the *History of Vatican Council II*, the Italian edition of which is pretty much the work of the same people to be met with here. "We have been questioned," they write—we know they have been so questioned because we ourselves have been among the questioners—"we have been questioned on the subject of the Council as an event and on the relationships which exist between one level, that of the actual experience of the international context in which the Council actually lived and breathed, and the other level of the acts produced by it as well as of the dynamic which launched it. To do justice to the whole question, then, we have asked scholars of parliamentary assemblies, theologians, historians of institutions and of doctrine, and experts in the historiography and textual criticism of the Council to address themselves in this inquiry to textual questions which are both complex and delicate" (pp. 8-9). Well, the results of this inquiry of theirs are here collected in this volume, which we may note is divided into three parts.

In the first place, there is presented an examination of the hermeneutical categories and historiographical questions "linked to the dimensions of an event characteristic of legislative, constituent, or conciliar assemblies." Recent political historiography is instanced as providing an appropriate approach, without taking into account what is specific to an ecclesial council—which is in no way either "political" or "democratic" in the way these terms are generally understood.

But it is nevertheless along these lines that the first author, P. Pombeni, proceeds in a difficult essay which is entitled "Parliaments and Constituent Assemblies." For this author, "political-type parliamentarianism, in its origins, is entirely dependent on the Christian idea of the *ecclesia*, or assembly" (p. 17). To validate this position, he cites the "Dossetti case." Father Dossetti "had the good fortune to be a key and decisive person on two occasions in which he was involved, one pertaining to the great history of occidental parliamentarianism, the other to the history of religious assemblies, namely Vatican Council II." He thereby assumed "the double robes both of the political reformer and of the religious reformer" (p. 18; see especially p. 8, the thesis of which, however, has already been superseded by later research, particularly with respect to Father Dosetti's supposed contribution to drawing up the Regulation for the Council). We believe that the *punctum dolens* of the entire question is brought out here in this focusing upon an individual person. Father Komonchak discreetly mentions the same thing (p. 436). And we are not talking about a political or even a "spiritual" point of view, but very plainly about religious thought. We ardently hope to be understood about all this, because in the two fields there are very different "liberty of maneuver" and about interventions (in this regard, the truly "extremist" approach can be found expressed in the book by Father Giuseppe Dossetti, *Il Vaticano II. Frammenti di una riflessione* [Vatican II: Fragments of a Reflection], Il Mulino, Bologna 1996; pp. 23-102). Confirmation of the need and the desirability of making the proper distinctions here is very quickly seen once Pombeni gets to what he calls "conservative theology."

For our part, we cannot follow this author in the approach he takes, not even with regard to his categories of "critical event" ("constituent") and "decisions," and this applies particularly with regard to Vatican Council II. It applies even more particularly when, with a show of humility, the author describes himself as only a "non-expert and external observer" of the Council (p. 48).

The true underpinnings of the theme of the Second Vatican Council as an "event" is delineated by Étienne Fouilloux in his study, "The Category of 'Event' in Recent French Historiography." By "recent" he means about a half century. He mentions its "return" thanks to E. Morin; and he rightly does not fail to deal with the strict link between the actual historical existence of an event and the way it has been mediated. In this connection, he cites P. Nora to the effect that "in order there be an event, it is necessary it should become known." The author then adds: "Vatican II responds very well to this 'mediated' definition of what constitutes an event" (p. 58; but then, however, see p. 419 and, especially, the *Addendum* on p. 438ff.).

P. Hünermann completes the first part of this volume with a contribution which underlines the importance of the hermeneutical criteria proposed by Professor Giuseppe Alberigo. We, of course, have criticized these criteria on various occasions. Hünermann also recommends the method of Georg Gadamer with a number of good, though complicated, themes and final conclusions (pp. 87-92). There would be much that could be said about each one of these conclusions, especially the final ones, but it would obviously be impossible to do all that here. These conclusions are nevertheless taken for granted by the author, particularly when he states that "the event of the Council can be understood as the formation of the practice that can be expressed conceptually as 'subject dialectics' (and described in the language of the *Philosophical Investigations* of Ludwig Wittgenstein). This 'subject dialectics,' which make possible a *consensus*, constitutes in a radicalized and renewed form the foundation of the Council; it consists of a unitary movement which has closely tied together innumerable individual activities, inserting them into a flux which then produced as its fruit and result the new vision of the Church and of divine Revelation which are now to be found embedded in the various texts of the Council."

The second part of the volume deals with "Episcopates and Other Groups: Sources and Problems pertaining to Participation in the Event." Here are brought together the contributions on the subject of the groups and collective organs that participated in the Council. Then there are those groups that, while they did not, strictly speaking, participate in the Council as such, were nevertheless present within the framework of the overall event: groupings of the Council Fathers themselves or of their *periti*, organizations from which the observers were drawn, groups related in various ways to the conciliar majority and minority, and regional or continental conferences (p. 10). These groupings are not, in reality, presented here for the first time.

The treatment of these diverse groupings begins with a study by P. C. Noël on the formation of episcopal Conferences. He investigates this topic in particular by means of the archives of M. Baudoux and E. Primeau. In this regard, the group of the *Domus Mariae*, also called the "Interconference" or the "Conference of 22," was particularly interested in the matter and in the quesion of the Synod of Bishops and the reform of the Roman Curia. The author concludes his presentation by recognizing that his presentation of the activities related to the groups involved with the formation of the episcopal Conferences, "set forth here sometimes according to a dialectic of cause and effect, does not guarantee in and of itself the correctness of the interpretation" (p. 131). "Naturally," he adds, "the group of the *Domus Mariae* was not the only group involved. To attribute to it the exclusive paternity of the successes reported by the episcopal conferences—on the basis of this research alone—would be to circumscribe what was considerably broader activity than that of this group alone, thereby falsifying the complexity of the total reality of the matter" (*Ibid.*). Along with this candid and honest declaration, Noël poses at the end of his contribution a number of questions in order to stimulate future research on this matter (cf. p. 132ff.).

Bishop Mark McGrath follows up at this point with "The Creation of the Conscience of a Latin American People: CELAM and the Second Vatican Council." He relates here the history of the progressive formation of a continent-wide unity. He testifies to the fact that "Vatican Council II without doubt left its imprint on the Church throughout the continent and it increasingly became a determining factor in the life and history of our peoples, with social consequences that coincide with the collective interests of the Latin American community" (p. 137).

Then comes the fine study of Claude Soetens on "The 'Belgian Team' within the Conciliar Majority." According to this author, this majority was "not a monolithic bloc" (p. 143). He first describes the situation of the Church in Belgium, where, according to him, there was a "modernized system of Christianity" (p. 145). He then treats the activities of the Belgian bishops and theologians, who played an important role in the preparation and the first phases of the Council. He makes an effort to describe the characteristics of this group and of the way in which those who belonged to it understood themselves. After that he provides some examples of their role within the conciliar majority after the Council itself "had achieved its maturity," that is, after the Second Session. The line they followed was based on realism in the development of solutions that could command a conciliar majority.

Indicative of the general theme is the following thought of Monsignor Gérard Philips, who was especially criticized by Dossetti on account of his conciliation efforts" (p. 154). According to Philips, "it is not a situation where we are trying to see our own personal ideas prevail; rather, it is one of arriving at a *consensus* on what the entire Church can accept today as the expression of her common faith," without, however, "any compromises on fundamental principles" (*Ibid.*).

With this aim in mind, Philips sought "to safeguard to the extent possible the original *schemata*" (p. 152; see, however, p. 162 and the p. 340). This was the case, for example, with the *schema* on the Church.

The author cites other examples where the Belgian intervention was not crowned with success (pp. 152ff. and pp. 165ff. on "the question of the 5 votes"). Some of these examples, however, are not well described by the author. With regard to the role of Cardinal Suenens as part of this "Belgian team," in which personal factors played a part (p. 161, n. 40), Soetens shows himself to be a rather dispassionate observer; he includes a critical judgment of the bishop of Tournai concerning the conciliar "Memoirs" of the Belgian cardinal (p. 160, n. 39); and he includes the judgment rendered by Yves Congar as well (p. 164).

There follows the treatment of the *Coetus Internationalis Patrum* and the conciliar minority. This is handled by L. Perrin. It is difficult to evaluate because it does not rest upon any archival source. Moreover, the author concedes that the preservation of pertinent documents is "unequal, indeed mediocre" (p. 172). The *Coetus* came into being relatively late in the game, and its origins were obscure. Very quickly, though, it was found making "demands" through its "Roman confederates," and this certainly was a tactic adopted at the end (p. 179). Its organizational structure, however, was minimal and it disposed of few means; the author describes them as "ranging from extreme indigence to bare modesty" (p. 180).

"For the most part," the author writes, "it was at Solesmes that the theological bread of the *Coetus* was baked" (*Ibid.*). It was "a group with indistinct outlines" (p. 181), in which there was "considerable movement but little direction" (*Ibid.*). Moreover, there exists nowhere an accurate list of the members or sympathizers of the *Coetus*. Perrin's conclusions, however, are of great interest (pp. 185ff.). He testifies correctly to the "convergences coming from variable geometric points" (p. 185), and also accurately notes "the complexity of the curial world" (*Ibid.*; but then see p. 341). He establishes differences between John XXIII and Paul VI (p. 186). Moreover, the influence of the group is shown in connection with "the Belgian choice to preserve the original *schemata* as the basis of the conciliar work" (p. 187).

The role of "The Observers of the World Council of Churches at Vatican II" is treated in the longest essay in the volume, and is quite well treated, in linear fashion, by M. Velati. However, it seems to us that he exaggerates the influence of these observers, although he is well aware that only future historical research can allow us "to appreciate fully the depth of this presence and its ramifications in a context wider than that of the conciliar assembly itself" (p. 190). In his treatment, the author relies mainly on the documentation preserved in Geneva by the World Council itself, making particular use of the reports sent there by some of the observers; notable among these were those of L. Vischer and the Greek theologian, N. Nissiotis (cfr. p. 190).

With respect to the judgments of Velati—we are not going to get into those of the observers themselves—it seems to us that his opinion on the views of the Council expressed by W. A. Visser't Hooft is not entirely correct (p. 196; cfr. pp. 219 and 225), and we also believe that the idea of a "second preparation" of the Council is to be entirely excluded (p. 203). We think the same regarding the so-called "Black Week," mentioned in several places. Two subjects, however, are important with respect to the ecumenical dimension: namely, ecclesiology, "the source of all the differences," and, naturally, the conciliar debate itself on the subject of ecumenism.

In the end, Velati takes up the cause of attempting to represent the thinking of the observers as favoring the idea of the Council as an "event," a "fact," or even a "secret synod," adding that "it was not possible...to deny the depth of the impressions made upon the observers by the conciliar decisions" (p. 253). In this connection, however, the author can, on the other hand, claim that "there were direct connections between the positions of the observers and the interventions of some of the bishops"—although the author admits that "these are not easy to document." He further mentions in the case of Vischer, the latter's constant contact with the work of some of the commissions where a number of proposals and suggestions were being made, usually through the mediation of the Secretariat, on a number of rather disparate subjects. It "probably remains necessary, however, to verify the actual incidence of such initiatives in the course of the complicated process of the drafting of the conciliar documents" (p. 253). We can surely excise the "probably" here. It is not an unpleasant thought that we should finish up on the subject of this particular topic—as Velati himself does, as a matter of fact—by recalling the very important "conciliar presence" of Oscar Cullmann, "who incarnated an attitude that was very pragmatic, yet who strived to underline his respect for theological tradition and for the 'genius' of Catholicism" (p. 257). It is not unpleasant to record this because, in the ecumenical sphere, this attitude of his can be very useful.

"The Sources for the Participation of the Orthodox at the Council" is the topic presented by M. Brun. He divides his work up among the following sections, preceded by a "premise": "Problems of the Context"; "The Observers at the Council: A Challenge to the Church"; "The Ecclesiastical Politics behind the Question of the Observers"; "The Solution to the Problem" (in the end, each Orthodox Church was free to act on its own in responding to the invitation); and, finally, "The Orthodox Observers at the Council."

In continuity with what preceded it, there follows the contribution of A. Roccucci, who had already demonstrated a good knowledge of what the Russian sources ultimately turned out to contain when they were made available for historical research. This essay is limited to the First Session, however, and bears the title: "The Conciliar Event according to the Analysis of the Russian Orthodox Observers and the Council for the Affairs of the Russian Orthodox Church." The research here unfolds amidst the meanderings of what was a very complex reality, not only as regards Church questions, but also those pertaining to the Soviet Union of that day. In the beginning, acceptance of the invitation to attend the Council was favored. Then, there were "two different but converging requirements, namely, the 'direction' provided by the Soviet state and the relationship of the Russian Orthodox with Constantinople" (pp. 298ff. and 319).

We will not go into the thinking of the Archpriest Borovoy reported on by Roccucci. Borovoy did not forget, in his reports sent back to Moscow, the "socio-political significance" of the Council (see p. 309ff.). The same thing was true of the twists and turns of the policy towards the Ukrainian Catholic Church—not to speak, in this regard, of the case of Archbishop Josyf Slïpyj. We need only recall here that the experience of the Council motivated the Council for the Affairs of the Russian Orthodox Church to recommend to the Central Committee of the Communist Party of the Soviet Union that the Russian Church should continue to maintain the contacts of the Russian Church with the Holy See (called, naturally, "the Vatican"); should send observers for the Second Session; and should even grant the wish that the Orthodox Churches of Bulgaria, Romania, Czechoslovakia and Poland might also become involved with the Council. Further recommendations were to extend the initiatives finalized for the Council to include the Christian peace movement involving the Vatican in Prague; and, finally, to organize in Warsaw a meeting of all those responsible for religious affairs in the Communist countries in order to coordinate a response to the actions emanating from the Council.

At this point J. Famerée comes upon the scene making "comparative use," as he calls it, of the veritable forest of private conciliar diaries and memoirs. He examines the work of the Council during the period of 5 to 15 November, 1963, in the light of these private conciliar sources as exemplifying how they may be taken into consideration. We have already stated elsewhere that we agree that such sources may be used alongside the official conciliar sources, but not as alternative primary sources, even with valid critical comparisons. Even when speaking "psychologically", they lack depth.

The author, however, makes use of the conciliar diaries of Archbishop Neophytos Edelby as well as those of Father Y. Congar and P. Dupont. He also utilises the "chronicle" of Father B. Olivier, as he does the "notebooks" of Father C. Moeller and the "notes" of Monsignor A. Prignon. Merely from this listing, it can be seen that there is a very different typology involved here, where the writings and the intentions of the various authors may differ considerably. Interested readers can judge for themselves, personally, just how much this kind of writing really contributes to the "greater" overall history of the Council itself. What we get here are partisan treatments of such incidents as "the Frings-Ottaviani clash" or the "attack of Ruffini on Maximos IV."

"Paul VI and the Council in 1964" is the title of the essay contributed by L. A. Tagle. It deals with a particularly difficult conciliar period, namely the very last days of the Third Session, when the "scrupulous" and "exacting" figure of the pope stood out. Some of the pope's decisions resulted in the creation of much uneasiness and many anxieties in not a few Council participants. "How and why did Paul VI act as he did?" the author asks. He replies to this question by offering the opinion that the pope during this Third Session was acting in accordance "with his understanding and interpretation of the theology contained in *Lumen Gentium*, but with special reference to the difficulties of safeguarding the papal prerogatives included there...Without discounting the very real influences of his own temperament, of the formation he had received, and of his own personal predispositions towards the events of 1964, I believe it can be said," the author testifies, "that his acts simply reflected the dynamic tensions and the hesitations inherent in the teaching of the Council itself on the subject of the episcopal college and of the head of the college" (p. 357ff.). The author proves this; in this connection, see pages 360ff. in particular. However, the author's judgment on the subject of "the sacramental conferring of the power of jurisdiction along with the power of orders" (p. 361) needs to be refined. The author concludes, however, that "nobody suffered a defeat on this; all ended up convinced" (p. 368).

"The Synergies and Conflicts of Vatican II" is the topic taken up by J. Grootaers. He deals with what he calls "the two sides of the actions of the 'adversaries' of renewal (October 1962—October 1964)." This author employs language in this text, however, that is not always correct; we have stated this before about him. If he would use less partisan language, he might be able to speak more respectfully of everybody involved, including both the "conservatives" dealing with the situation before them, and the "innovators," also faced with the same situation, such as it was. The last ones may well have wished to return to an older tradition. But in this author's account, he speaks both imprecisely and confusedly of traditional Catholics, traditionalist Catholics, "integrists," and progressives (see pp. 420 and 426). Even among these last, however, there were certainly extremists, just as there were extremists among the "conservatives." The case of Archbishop Lefebvre amply demonstrated this last fact.

We have to say from the outset that we are unable to follow this author in all of his "mental constructs," which even he himself styles as "working hypotheses" (p. 372) and taking "risks." He notes, however: "We have risked talking about the 'two sides'..." (p. 412). Clarifications and corrections are required on practically every page of this text. Nevertheless, research that is authentically historical has its own rules and they are not suspended simply because the author says "in my opinion" (see esp. p. 382). We limit ourselves here to rejecting again the category of any "second preparation" of the Council—the term "change in the Council" is also used. Grootaers even speaks of a supposed "third preparation" (p. 413). He issues summary judgments on such things as what he calls "the Cicognani-Felici *team*," on the supposed "indulgence" in the "Dossetti case," and on the value of the "Döpfner plan." And what can be said about his gratuitous suggestion of an "accord" that was supposedly concluded for the papal election? Grootaers actually writes that "it is possible to imagine that the candidate Montini...," etc. (p. 401, n. 51). Such an accord could never be anything but a "phantom accord."

In the third and final part of the volume, Father J. A. Komonchak contributes his "Historiographical Reflections on Vatican II as an Event." This comes in a section entitled "'Event' and 'Decisions' in the Dynamics of Vatican II." This opens up a problematic without end. It is thus impossible here in a chapter that is already too long even to sketch out the nature and scope of this problematic. It suffices to mention the divisions into which this author divides his topic in order to invite the patient reader to go back to its roots. He speaks of

"The final Documents"; these, he says, "possess an objectivity and a continuing existence which mere experience cannot claim" (p. 417). "The sixteen documents of Vatican II represent what the Council, for better or worse, was able to agree upon saying, and they are rightly instanced as expressing its intentions and decisions" (p. 421ff.). The author further covers the subjects of "The Experience of the Council"; "Experience and the Event for Historians"; "An Event as an Episode within the Whole Picture"; and "How Will the Story End?" He writes concerning this last question: "The documents are *final* only with respect to a temporal horizon and within only one of the many possible pictures" (p. 435).

Let us add that among "the types of interpretation of the Council... roughly speaking" for this author, there was lacking one that would enable it to be considered a "great happening" and thus in this sense an "event." But as "Catholic," it was capable of combining *nova et vetera* evangelically. Could we say, then, that this is a "type" we could agree on? Let us take an example in order to understand better what is involved. Concerning the Constitution on Divine Revelation, *Dei Verbum*, Komonchak notes that the final text "certainly was intended to express something else besides a 'simple re-confirmation of the continuity of Catholicism'" (p. 424). It is evident that the word "simple" is introduced here wrongly because another word is lacking that ought to be here, namely, *aggiornamento*; note, however, that the author attempts to recover from this misstep by saying that "the two camps...perhaps had much more in common than seemed to be the case at first sight" (p. 434); note, also, what Komonchak says in his later contribution (pp. 443 and 450). The various aspects go together, and this applies also for page 426.

"Times for Debate, Time of the Council" is the title of the next contribution by G. Ruggieri. We find this to be something of a confused "hodge-podge". Fortunately, however, this author is "less sure" about it all, and he is also much more conscious of the complexity of the problems than has generally been admitted. In "The Council's Time"—"time" that he later says "suspended"—the author faces the central question of the Council as an "event," and for him both this "time" and this "event" mean the same thing (p. 457). He accepts the thinking of Alberigo completely in this regard; and this is something that, obviously, we cannot accept for reasons that we have already indicated. But it is on this path that Ruggieri gives his definition of the "Council's time." He contrasts the positions of John XXIII with those of Paul VI. Again, we cannot agree with him. It suffices to look at the critique this author makes of the work of Hubert Jedin—for having defended the "continuity" of Vatican II with the Tridentine era. Jedin called Vatican II "not a revision but a completion" (see pp. 459-462) The author's critique of Jedin on this shows how unbalanced he is in his judgment.

Riding on the enormous wave of thought holding the Council's time "suspended," there comes next the contribution of G. Routhier. His title is: "Orientation for the Study of Vatican II's Reception." This is a theme upon which much has been said over the last twenty years, a fact, the author believes, which may have led to "the neglect of analyzing the processes of reception which were already operative within the Council" (p. 466). This indicates the basic path followed by this author in the case of this present historical research. The reception of the Scriptures, the Creed, previous councils, the teaching of the ordinary Magisterium, customs, and the life of the Church herself— all these topics are covered, but the author nevertheless asks: "Are not the Churches themselves, and not simply the bishops, really the proper subject of the Council?" (p. 480). Other subjects covered include: culture (but with the idea of "democratic culture" brought in—see p. 484) and then what the author styles "the negative reception exercised by the Council itself." This latter subject supposedly includes what the Council did not wish to receive by applying it wrongly (p. 484 ff.). Then there comes the question of the "internal reception," consisting of the affirmation of what was contained in the documents of previous councils. The author gives some examples but demonstrates thereby his own incomprehension of the basic conciliar theme—indeed, the keys to the Council as far as we are concerned—namely, "adaptation" and "*instauratio*" (we give this latter term in Latin in order to avoid any misunderstanding). The author concludes with "The Reception of Vatican II in the Life of the Church during the Conciliar Process."

Giuseppe Alberigo concludes the volume with a contribution entitled "Lights and Shadows between the Dynamics of the Assembly and the Conclusions of the Council." He proceeds with his exposition in response to the following question: "Is there any proportionality between the conciliar event and the Council's decisions?" For this author there is a huge "defect" here because the "fact" of the Council is neither exhausted, nor is it completely expressed, in the decisions it produced [in its documents], and also with respect to its proper "physiognomy," which was "pastoral." In a word, according to Alberigo: "The history of the Council does not coincide—far from it—with the simple reconstruction of the formation of its actual decisions" (p. 502). This, of course, is the well-known "thesis" of this Bologna professor, and not of him alone. There is a large *gap* here [the word "gap" is given in English in the original]; this is "not merely quantitative" but is also "qualitative" (p. 503). Alberigo repeats in this contribution to this conciliar research certain points that he has made at various times and in various ways; these are brought together here by means of various "typical cases," which he cites (p. 504).

Having examined these cases, we can say that they have had reverberations or have included elements involved with the conciliar texts (if they were not rejected or laid aside by the assembly—for example, "the Döpfner plan" mentioned on page 509). But the author's argument falls to the ground, since it is based more on what he wished the Council had done than it is on what actually happened at the Council. It is sufficient in this connection to look at the author's hope for "an organ of collaboration and co-governance with the pope in directing the orientation of the universal Church" (p. 507ff.). Alberigo himself testifies that "the conciliar majority aligned itself with the suggestion of Cardinal Lercaro to leave to the Holy Father himself any decision in this regard, as was also the case regarding proposals for the reform of the Roman Curia" (p. 508). Similarly, it is sufficient to recall the criticisms leveled at the conciliar Regulation—although it truly was a Regulation—and "the recurring weaknesses in the directive organs of the Council" (p. 509).

On the question of the participation of the observers in the great synodal "event," the author sees them as true and proper members of the Council itself, "in some sense," he specifies, *"de facto* if not *de jure"* (p. 511). But what did the observers themselves think about this, especially the Eastern Orthodox? Alberigo also goes back to the proposal "that the Council should have solemnly affirmed the sanctity of John XXIII by canonizing him" (p. 510). Yet it was Cardinal Suenens himself who blocked this (p. 510). The author mentions it. So what is he really driving at? It is true enough that such a proposal was made at the Council, but does this mean it was properly a conciliar matter? In fact, it was not accepted by the Council. Carrying on with his own line of thought, though, Alberigo asks if the whole thing should not have been approved at least "figuratively" (p. 511). Moreover he asks if "there did not emerge at Vatican II a new pastoral-sacramental conception of Christianity and of the Church to replace the previous doctrinal-disciplinary conception which, in the modern era, has done great harm to the Christian tradition across the board" (*Ibid.*; see also p. 520). But how can one oppose—and the author says "replace"—the "pastoral-sacramental" to the "doctrinal-disciplinary"?

Then there is his idea of a "broad Council" (p. 514), one with what he calls a "subversive conciliar density" (*Ibid.*). These ideas confirm our judgment with regard to the finalization of everything, but what is "broad" factually applied to the texts that the Council produced in the end? These represent the only authentic criteria for judging how "conciliar" any group or movement actually was, whether this means any degree of "density" or not.

The search for *consensus*, moreover, did *not* "diminish the scope of the event" (*Ibid.*). Rather, it was precisely what made it truly conciliar. One cannot try now to evade the perceived "narrowness" of what was decided by appealing, as the author does, to the supposed lack of coherence within the Council.

On this point, Alberigo's claim of a special conciliar liberty, of what he calls the Council's "rediscovery of the liberty of the Christian and of liberty within the Church" (p. 517), and it cannot sound like anything but a direct challenge to the conciliar texts as they were approved by the Council. And this is just not right. In this connection, to continue to speak about "the new Pentecost" with a Johannine reference in mind in order to indicate the uniqueness of Vatican II—unique in the sense that "the action of the Spirit comes first, not that of the pope and the Church" (p. 518)—does not appear to us to accord with the thinking even of Pope John XXIII himself. Sacred Scripture declares that "it has seemed good to the Holy Spirit and to us" (Acts 15:28) in describing the decisions of the primitive "Council" of Jerusalem. But the same thing applies to *every* Council of the Church.

The fact that the author says he realizes that his "hermeneutical choice...entails certain risks and costs" (p. 519), and that it results in "a vision that is somewhat fragmentary and individualistic" (*Ibid.*), in no way removes from him the responsibility he has incurred in taking the path he has chosen.

And, in any case, the ultimate hermeneutical criterion, that is, applying to the documents of the Council the "hierarchy of truths," does not resolve the fundamental problem here because the author refers instead to "the will of the Council as it emerged out of the totality of the conciliar event itself" (p. 520). This approach issues in a vicious circle and creates a short-circuit since the author writes that "the final documents express an overall point of view that contradicts the sentiment that was present in the assembly" (p. 521). For us, what the documents actually say cannot and must not be separated from any supposed contrary sentiment presumed present in the assembly.

The thinking of this author overall obviously follows from the premises he has adopted from the outset—ideas such as "getting beyond a purely 'deductive' culture," the "relativization" of many "certitudes," the rediscovery of "the historical dimension of the faith and of the Christian experience," "the signs of the times," certain "theological *loci*," and so on. Relying on such ideas, the author believes that he has discovered "conclusions coming out of Vatican

II" that are both "more creative and even more explosive" than conventionally believed, even if they are more "hidden" (p. 521). Does Professor Alberigo not realize that he is really seeking to find his own opinions and convictions being expressed by the Council rather than recognizing what the Council actually did say?

The volume includes an Index of Names at the end.

24

Vatican II and the
Prospects for "Modernization"

Kaufmann Franz-Xaver and Zingerle Arnold, Eds., *Vatikanum II und Modernisierung. Historische, theologische und soziologische Perspektive* [Vatican II and Modernization: Historical, Theological, and Sociological Perspectives], F. Schöningh, Paderborn 1996, 423 pages.

Following the Table of Contents, the sociologist F. X. Kaufmann explains in his Introduction the nature of this work. It represents the fruit of a common (?) effort by theologians, historians, and sociologists, Catholic and non-Catholic alike. The basic theme is "Catholicism," but this term then turns out to be somewhat ambiguous (see pp. 13 and 68, for example). A number of other themes emerge as well in reading through these studies: for example, the theme of Catholic "cultures" and "sub-cultures" (p. 76). We would prefer to say "specific culture" rather than "subculture," by the way. Another theme that appears is "Ultramontanism" and even "neo-Ultramontanism" (e. g., pp. 13, 15 and 135). Kaufmann speaks of a Catholic "hierarchy" (p. 13) as well as of a Catholic *milieu* (p. 68). The risk of misunderstanding derives, however, from the diverse "methodologies" of the different disciplines which are linked together here. The interdisciplinary project attempted in this publication is not to be undervalued, however, even though one is conscious of the risks that are involved. This is the case because its interdisciplinary character and, possibly, its internationalization as well, is something that should henceforth be aimed at in every effort of "scholarly collaboration" of this kind.

The focus of the research, as the book's title indicates, is the Second Vatican Council, or perhaps better, the new coinage of "Catholicism" which the Council supposedly coined, as seen by several institutions which have been particularly occupied with the whole question, two of them in Italy and one is Germany. Of particular interest to them are the typical cultural transformations of the present day, which generally go by the name of "modernization." And the "post-modern" as far as Catholicism is concerned? It apparently amounts to the same thing (pp. 15 and 104). The tone is set, then, and the choice that has been made is at least clear. The perspective is wholly European, however, and we would even say that it belongs to a certain "special" Europe, with opposition or divergence unjustified, especially as far as the previous synod, Vatican Council I, is concerned (see p. 13 in this connection and, especially, see the study by Hermann Pottmeyer included in this volume).

There follows, connected with the Introduction itself, a further contribution by Kaufmann himself discussing the problem of evaluating that earlier council, Vatican I. For the "development" of that evaluation, the author avers, "the Church employed the better part of an entire century" (B. Kötting). The path that was generally followed was that of the modernization of society, for example, with regard to agriculture, and industry, where new methods of rational productivity were applied; and also with regard to culture and social structures, where factors such as "functional differentiation" and "individualization" applied. Yet other factors included pluralism, autonomy (of the world), and "liberty"—Gregory VII's call for this last being happily mentioned here (p. 22).

Kaufmann then presents briefly the various studies of the authors included here in this volume. They are classified and placed into three categories, beginning with those concerned with the preparatory phase of the Council (especially in Germany). Then there are those concerned with the treatment (a sketch) of the various aspects which can be seen as responses to current modernizing tendencies. Finally, there is the category of post-conciliar Catholicism in various countries, which is treated by several authors.

For the analysis of the preparatory phase of the Council, we have the study of W. Lot, a historian, who deals with political Catholicism in Germany from its beginnings to its eventual demise—but was it the case? It is true that this author covers "politics," but he does so in a fashion that is quite simplistic, and linked, we would say, with Ultramontanism (p. 35ff.). One question which exemplifies all the difficulties inherent here needs to be asked, and it is this: can it really be said that the parish communities faced with the changes leading into the twentieth century constituted some kind of parallel "Ultramontane" structure characteristic of modern individual society? (p. 46).

Another historian, H Hürten, treats "German Catholicism under Pius XII: Stagnation or Renewal"? A sociologist, K. Gabriel analyzes quite well the topic of "Catholicism and the Catholic Milieu during the Fifty years of the Federal Republic: Restoration, Modernization, and the Beginnings of Decomposition." As can be gathered from their titles, both authors thus deal with German Catholicism, particularly in the 1950s; and they are concerned with the relationship between restoration and modernization (sometimes "continuity" is mentioned instead of "restoration"). Supposedly there was, in effect, an "alliance" between the German episcopate and the economic modernization promoted by the Christian Democrats (p. 26); and this supposedly "covered" the growing tensions between structural and cultural modernization (where the Catholics were "behind" with respect to the latter).

The historian K. Wittstadt treats "The Prospects for Church Renewal: The German Episcopacy during the Preparatory Phase for Vatican II." He claims to be aware of the fact that, at that time, "the existing ecclesiastical structures, and the responses required by the new situation of contemporary man, were no longer adequate" (p. 260). Change was therefore necessary, as was demonstrated by Church developments in the pre-conciliar period; these latter are analyzed here in a manner that does not go into any depth, although the thinking of many authors on the subject is cited. Wittstadt also evinces the familiar anti-curial sentiment (p. 90) in a way that does not take into account the variety existing within the Curia itself, even in that day. The author also presents an account of the *Consilia et Vota* sent in by the German bishops in view of the coming Council (pp. 91-101). And he also discusses "The Church of John XXIII" (p. 101ff.). All these things are quite well known.

V. Conzemius, however, also takes up "The Problematic of Modernization in the Recommendations sent in by the European Episcopacies." Again, this is a well-studied topic, and the author is well aware of this in view of the number of studies he cites of various authors" (p. 108). He speaks too frequently about "obsessions" (of the "sacristy," for example), and his presentation on the subject of Italy is too negative. Indeed, this is true of the point of view of this author generally, as is confirmed by what he says about pre-conciliar England. His analysis of the German situation is much better developed (pp. 116-122). In his final reckoning, however, Conzemius distances himself from the judgments of Roger Aubert and Giuseppe Alberigo, for whom the *vota* sent in beforehand by the bishops, as mentioned above, were very misleading with respect to what the Council would eventually decide. On that subject, much more could be said, especially if one makes the proper distinctions.

But what can be said of the effort of H. Pottmeyer to distinguish between the two Vatican Councils? He affirms that "Vatican II cannot be understood without reference to Vatican I." Still, the former was the sequel to and was corrective of the latter in some respects (p. 132). However, the text of this author leaves much to be desired, in our opinion; this certainly applies with respect to the evident confusion he suffers between explaining tradition as such and neo-Ultramontane theology (see esp. pp. 135-139). This essay deals with the modernization of the Catholic Church, and starts with the question of the reception of the two Councils. But the term "modern," as he employs it, is not clear, while the post-conciliar conflicts he discusses are seen as a sign of disappointment concerning the basic hopes aroused by the Council (p. 145). The same thing is true of his treatment of the centralization and bureaucratization of the Church: the discussion is not clear.

The study of J. A. Komonchak, "Vatican II and the Disputes between Catholicism and Liberalism," is quite good. In its presentation of the vision of John Courtney Murray, it makes a distinction between American liberalism and European liberalism; the latter is ideological and is accused here of both relativism and indifferentism (see esp. the author's conclusions on p. 167ff.) This distinction [between the two liberalisms] helps us to understand why it is necessary to proceed with "historical" caution in analyzing related ecclesiastical positions. We note in this connection the battle of the Church against the "privatization of religion," for example, as well as against "idolatry towards the democratic process" (p. 166). The same thing applies to the "magic" of "modernity." For this author, there is no "capitulation" on the part of Vatican II towards classical doctrinal liberalism, nor even any "concession" (see esp. pp. 157 and 164). The same thing applies to modernity as understood in a certain sense (see n. 26 and pp. 166-169), and, indeed, is the case with religious liberty as well, and rightly so. Thus, the liberal political structures of modern democracies must be distinguished from the ideology of Liberalism, which, however, was the thing that often legitimatized these structures (p. 168). Still and always, we would add, it is necessary to distinguish, but this is something the author does not do in the end, that is, he does not treat continuity in connection with the "decisive change" he says was "marked" by the Council (see n. 31).

The theologian E. Klinger then provides an *apologia* for the Council's Pastoral Constitution on the Church in the Modern World *Gaudium et Spes*. His title is "The *Aggiornamento* of the Pastoral Constitution." For him, everything has been changed with and by this document; and the change in question is new, revolutionary, and, indeed, epochal; he cites Cardinal Suenens in this regard (pp. 180 and 184). *Gaudium et Spes*, according to him, is the most important of all the documents produced by Vatican II (p. 172). This is the case, he thinks, because it describes what *aggiornamento* consists of and incorporates it into its program. Klinger adopts the typical anti-curial language without making any distinctions within the Curia. He briefly describes the history of the text of *Gaudium et Spes*, and he then attempts to analyze the consequences of the modernization of the Church, whether in the pastoral field, or in the dogmatic, anthropological, ecclesial, or other fields. He makes references to both Modernism and Traditionalism (p. 181ff.).

As is well known, exaggerations are not conducive to good history, just as excessive partisanship sometimes tends to bring out its opposite. How can Klinger simply assert that "the future of the Church does not depend upon tradition and not at all on Traditionalism, but rather on modernization"? (p. 184.) This work of Klinger's concludes with a subchapter, on "Sociology and Pastoral Practice." The conciliar citations with regard to this discipline are one thing, and we can accept sociology as a "maidservant" of evangelization and pastoral practice, but in no sense is it the "mistress" of them. The case of Liberation Theology, mentioned by the author as exemplary, instead becomes very problematic, we would judge (p. 186). This approach is illustrative of the underlying problem that the author calls the sociological "turn" in theology (p. 187). He, however, invokes an ulterior "Illuminsm" for this (*Ibid.*).

The co-editor of this volume, A. Zingerle, a sociologist, contributes the essay "The Council Seen from the Standpoint of the Sociological Theory of 'Charisma.'" He thus treats the theme of the relationship of the institutional and the extraordinary, with particular reference to the thought of Max Weber. He treats this theme as it applies to the vision of the great Vatican Synod, and as a "moment of modernization for the Church." He keeps in mind the concept of "charismatic institutions," which link the institutional and the charismatic together. He focuses particularly on the charismatic dimensions of Vatican II, namely, secularization, religious liberty, human rights, and the relations of the Church with the world. He exhibits a number of "understandable" misunderstandings—understandable, that is, for a sociologist (we like to juxtapose these two terms) (see p. 196). He also examines the authenticity of various charisms (he speaks of the concepts of "secondary charismatization," for instance), as well as that of the permanence of various charisms ("do not stifle the Spirit!"). And so on. In the end, though, Professor Zingerle considers that Vatican II, besides being a "charismatic" phenomenon, also represented a sharp break in the history of the Church with respect to her past. In this we are unable to follow him, and we find ourselves in good company in declining to do so. It suffices to think of the example of the great Hubert Jedin—who, however, is cited by the author in support of his, the author's position, going back to "words" of Jedin's dating from 1959 in order to do so (p. 205ff.). But what we remember are rather Jedin's words later on affirming the "continuity" between the Council of Trent and Vatican Council II.

It is at this point in the book that begin the sociological analyses relating to European Catholics and to the "Catholic Churches" in the period following the Council. This section begins with a general view of the work of K. Dobbeläre and L. Voyé. Before getting into any empirical type analysis—such as using an "instrument" to ascertain the truth about questions such as Mass attendance and the like, these authors move from some initial "theoretical reflections"—such as "the functional differentiations" that have led to the secularization of society—to the formulation of concrete hypotheses, e.g., concerning "individualization."

There follow a series of analyses, always written from a sociological standpoint, of the situation in a number of countries, beginning with British and Irish Catholicism contributed by M. P. Hornsby-Smith; Catholicism in the Low Countries written by L. Laeyendecker; in Italy by F. Demarchi and G. Capraro; and in Hungary by M. Tomka. This last case is considered exemplary for East Central Europe. We are not sociologists, and hence we cannot judge these contributions critically.

Nevertheless, there are perhaps a number of things we should say, at least as regards the one-dimensional interpretations that are included here, and, as we see it, the arbitrary decisions that are offered as far as the Council is concerned.

But it is at this point in the volume that we encounter a study which is both well done and interesting. It is a different type of study and concerns both "popular culture" and "cult," or worship. G. Korff is the author. He asks whether cult is "dynamic" or "differentiated." He writes of devotion to Saint Roch and Saint Sebastian in Germany in the nineteenth and twentieth centuries. He notes the shock that was produced in Germany by the new Roman Calendar.

We have many reservations concerning the article of the historian M. Klöcker, about his rather negative judgments on Catholic education and formation in Germany in this century, but especially in the post-conciliar period. We would even term his approach "ideological." He oversteps proper boundaries and renders judgments that are truly defective both as regards morality and as regards catechesis; the latter is true even with respect to the *Catechism of the Catholic Church*. Given the bias and even the frank partisanship of this author, we shall not venture further into any kind of critical reading of his contribution.

More or less along the same lines, unfortunately, is the contribution of the sociologist H. Tyrell. His topic is: "The Rhetoric of Vatican II concerning Marriage and the Family." He sees it as signalling the de-institutionalization of the family. Both on this subject and on many others, this author's views regularly call for correction and even outright refutation, for instance, on the subject of the encyclical *Humanae Vitae*. To cover all this would require a separate review within this review! But the length of our presentation already precludes any such thing. We will note only that the author does see this subject, significantly, as part of "the third Modernist crisis," a concept he has borrowed from P. Hünermann. He applies it to the *Kirchenvolk*, (people of the Church) [. He speaks] with application quite uncritically to "the privatization of morality," and he accuses anyone who does not agree with him as guilty of "fundamentalism."

"The Erosion of the 'Institution of Grace' [the Church]" deals with the on-going process of the de-institutionalization of Catholicism and is handled by the sociologist M. N. Ebertz. He takes as his point of departure both the Catholic and Protestant understandings of the Church as an institution, and he finally arrives at his own conclusions concerning the Church after covering also the views of Max Weber. Here again we encounter the idea of a supposed growing Catholic "fundamentalism," but the author's views on this subject are simply erroneous (p. 393). It becomes increasingly clear to us that some writers have taken up the use of this term simply to disqualify the thought of anyone who thinks differently than they do in their manner of judging.

Before we finally arrive at the Table of Contents, and the Index of the Names of the authors (listed without their scholarly affiliations), located at the end of the volume, the book concludes with the contribution of the theologian G. Fuchs. His topic is: "Discernment of Spirits: Notes for a Conciliar Hermeneutic." These notes are brief but profound—though they are also quite problematical. They begin with this initial affirmation: "Vatican II can be understood as an expression of the Modernist crisis which arose at the beginning of the century. In a sense Vatican II was a response to this crisis. [This is seen in its dual character that was both] conflicting and consensual...espousing both Modernist and anti-Modernist positions...a problematical distinction between its (of the council) letter and its spirit" (p. 401). What follows from this, according to the author, is an inner conflict that is necessarily involved in any conciliar hermeneutic. The study is divided into several sections derived from the way the author has described its meaning. These include, first of all: "The Church as an Event in the Dialogue" (expressed in the opening to the world evident in *Lumen Gentium* and *Gaudium et Spes*, and protected theologically in *Dei Verbum*). The second section is entitled: "Theodramatic Concentration" (this refers to and deals with the Trinitarian mystery and the "consequences" that flow from it). The third section is entitled: "The Faith in Practice: Dogma and Existence" (this covers the life and teaching of the Church, the truth of faith, and ecclesial practices). Then comes the *"Anschauung* of Power" (this deals with how power is viewed, and with a living community of unity and diversity; also, the consequences of this conciliar hermeneutic are brought out here). After this there comes "The Church Dying and Rising" (here the importance of "lunar" and "solar" ecclesiologies is brought out). We would add that this last notion represents a kind of symbolism derived from the Fathers, which was applied by theologians in early times; it is this author who adopts such ideas today in order to describe the conciliar process in which, he says we are "involved" today.

25

Vatican II as Seen by
Roger Aubert and Claude Soetens

Mayeur Jean-Marie, Ed., *Crise et Renouveau—de 1958 à nos jours* [Crisis and Renewal—from 1958 to our Days], Lonrai, Desclée 2000, 794 pages. Volume 13 of the *Histoire du Christianisme* [History of Christianity]

Because of our special interest in the Church's most recent ecumenical Council, we wanted to look at this volume of a larger *History of Christianity*. In fact, the first part of the book, entitled "A Time of *Aggiornamento*" (p. 15-122), is dedicated to the Council. The last three pages of this part also contain an excellent summary bibliography on the subject of the Council, although it exhibits a pronounced bias in favor of what today is the main current of thought in conciliar studies, a current we have elsewhere judged to be "monopolistic" in the matter of conciliar hermeneutics (see A. H. P. XXXVIII-2000, pp. 275-286).

It is the editor, J.- M. Mayeur himself, who gives us "The Orientations of John XXIII" as a kind of introduction to the whole subject. We would have liked to see more shadings and gradations in his treatment of such topics as the "conservative" image of Roncalli in Venice (p. 16); "future structures"; "institutional solitude"; Italian affairs generally; the Italian Episcopal Conference; the pope's encyclical *Mater et Magistra* (p. 18) and so on. These are all topics treated by the author. In any case, though, we agree with the following conclusion of this author's: "John XXIII was not a reformer; he sincerely wanted, by means of the Council, to invite the Church to an

411

aggiornamento, that is, to a renewal, based on a return to the sources of the tradition" (p. 20).

Beginning with Chapter I entitled "The Preparations for and the Opening of the Council," we encounter a collaboration between Roger Aubert and Claude Soetens. Much of this same material was covered by Aubert alone in his contribution to the corresponding (1994) volume in the Fliche-Martin *History of the Church* (reviewed in Chapter 16 of the present volume; this review was originally published in *Apollinaris LXVIII* in 1995, pp. 412-421). In the interim, not much progress in the correct interpretation of the Council seems evident, although the tone here is much less radical than that maintained by the School of Bologna generally in the conciliar histories it has orchestrated.

On two fundamental points, in fact, there is a notable difference between this account and the earlier one. These two points concern the issue of continuity in the guidance provided to the Council by Pope Paul VI as compared with that provided by John XXIII; and the issue of the Roman Curia, which had undergone some diversification, though this was not complete. Moreover, there is a slightly different attitude towards the Council's Secretary General, Archbishop Pericle Felici (see p. 41). Judgments on the question of the conciliar documents, however, coincide more closely. Similarly, the "myth" of the "new"—thus we label it "myth," and we do not mean this in any positive way—is very much evident in this volume. Rather, the *novum* is treated here as if it were in and of itself the *bonum*! The "new" is the ideal, while whatever is still linked with the past is considered to be dead water in the wake of the ship—or simply encumbrances not yet cast-off, residue from the past that needs to be cleared away. There is no suggestion here that the Catholic Church, in particular, might be obliged to maintain fidelity to her tradition, while seeking to make appropriate adaptations to the present; that she might naturally try to avoid revolution or a sudden break with the past, moving ahead under the guidance of her Magisterium; that she would carefully sift and examine any *acceptio rerum*, theologically speaking; and that she would read the signs of the times in the light of her sacred Revelation

(Scripture and Tradition). Certainly, she would always aim to be up to date with "God's today," which is not the same thing as, and does not coincide with, the "today" of the world. Everything got started with what is termed here "slowly getting underway." However, it must be said that Cardinal Tardini did *not* try to discourage the pope with regard to the Council; on the contrary, he was surely almost enthusiastic about it, although some of his words may not have been clear about this (see p. 21). Words may be interpreted differently, but not necessarily more accurately (see pp. 21, no. 1, and 23). Sometimes things can be embellished more than is necessary too. What is meant by "Roman" here, for example? (p. 24.) The narrative proceeds, describing "the work of the preparatory commissions"; various judgments are offered, some are definitely matters of opinion, such as the one on Cardinal Bea describing him as "rather conservative" (p. 25, n. 1). Two distinct principal tendencies are identified and described here: one, that the Council was "open to the world and open also to a collegial manner of operating"; the other, that it was "defensive to a degree that was almost chilling, and it often confused its own routines and ways of operating with the 'authentic Catholic Tradition'" (see p. 26).

However, the authors do show here three negative tendencies in the documents with which the preparatory commissions had to deal (although John XXIII was on the whole "very satisfied" with them). These three tendencies included a lack of any ecumenical spirit, a similar lack of any openness to the modern world, and a scattering or an excessive number of subjects taken up (see p. 27). "The pope preferred...to leave to the body of bishops the liberty to act as they saw fit, but he was also influenced by the suggestions of Cardinal Suenens," as is clear from his address of September 11, 1962 (*Ibid.*).

With regard to the beginning of the Council, again, we note also (p. 28) elements of moderation with respect to points of view which, today, are greatly exaggerated. It is incorrect, for example, to speak of a single list of the members of the conciliar commissions which the Roman Curia wished to "impose" on the Council (p. 28). It is equally incorrect to speak of a plot or conspiracy supposedly organized by Cardinal Liénart of Lille [to place different members on the commissions] (*Ibid.*). Similarly, the "victory" declared by some [in the matter of the election of commission members] was almost certainly a less clear-cut thing. Also, the account given here of the Council's initial "Message to the World" really needs to be redone.

Chapter II deals with "The Assembly and Its Functioning." It begins with an explanation of the Council as a "worldwide assembly"; it is characterized as the first in the history of the world. The authors describe the participants as divided into different nationalities. We also think they typically simplify things in their descriptions of the "majority" and the "minority," assigning various "leaders" to each camp. They do correctly recognize that "it would be an error to consider the Roman Curia as the motor element of the minority" (p. 37). And they add, correctly: "The persistent action of the minority was often rather severely judged. In reality, however, in addition to the fact that it was a question of conscience for some of the Council Fathers, it is also necessary to recognize, objectively, that the minority members really obliged the majority members to examine their texts much more carefully and hence to improve them" (*Ibid*). Too often, however, the various maneuvers employed resulted in "the adoption of compromise formulas which were sometimes ambiguous and which definitely lowered the quality of the texts adopted" (p. 37). In our view, this last statement is too much of a generalization.

The subchapter entitled "Experts, Observers, and Auditors" enables the authors to present some of the important people connected with the Council. They go on to treat, not always happily, the conciliar Regulation and various "organs" of the Council. Even though their final judgments about these things seem to be positive (p. 41), the references they make to the very negative opinions of P. Levillain and J. Grootaers create some uncertainty as to their true opinions, particularly as regards Archbishop Felici.

The tone they adopt on the subject of "information" is somewhat equivocal. Still, what is dealt with here is the important role of the commentators, who turned themselves into a pressure group (p. 43). Aubert and Soetens do not take any position on the merits of the case supported by the journalists, but they do recognize the importance of the whole issue.

Chapter III deals with the unfolding of the Council itself. The authors begin with a discussion of the *schemata* on the liturgy and on divine revelation. They then go on to discuss the revisions of the Council's schedule brought about by the interventions of Cardinals Suenens and Montini and the tasks set for the "intersession" between the First and Second Sessions. Here, however, they speak quite inappropriately of further conciliar "preparations" (pp. 50-51). There was only one preparation period. At this point we are well into the Council itself.

The way of proceeding of the two authors is not always clear and impartial. Nevertheless, they arrive at the topic of "The Election of Paul VI," whom they describe as a "moderate progressive." This topic is given to J.-M. Mayeur himself, who also prepared a subchapter entitled "From John XXIII to Paul VI." It is significant that Paul VI is viewed positively here in spite of judgments concerning his character that seem to us rather ponderous (p. 57). The authors are correct, though, in judging that Paul VI was "faithful to the spirit of John XXIII" (see also p. 58), but was at the same time "more intellectually rigorous; he watched more carefully for signs of abuse and error that might result from too broad an interpretation of texts that were ambiguous" (p. 57). The pope thus exercised "the role of supreme arbiter concerning tendencies that were legitimate in their own way" (*Ibid.*). He desired *consensus*, and he also did not want to "humiliate" the minority. He was also preoccupied with "doctrinal precision." However, "it cannot be said that Paul VI really allowed himself to be maneuvered by the minority" (p. 58). "Essentially his position was definitely but prudently reformist, and he succeeded, along with the episcopal college, in bringing about the triumph of a liberalized theology freed from the old 'manuals' and established administrative routines" (*Ibid.*).

The authors then continue their examination, taking up the Second Session of the Council. They begin with a discussion of the *schema* on the Church. It was the subject of "lively controversies" concerning two major themes in particular, namely: the episcopacy, which is described as "the most important part of the *schema*, if not the dorsal spine of the entire Council" (U. Betti); and the restoration of the diaconate as an autonomous component of the sacrament of Holy Orders, and not just as a transition phase on the way to the priesthood" (p. 59). With regard to the episcopacy, the major questions concerned its sacramental nature and episcopal collegiality. It is necessary to clarify immediately the idea shared by these authors, who repeat it often, namely, to consider "against" collegiality those who did not fully understand the idea or who were actually opposed to an imperfect version of it. For the fact is that, after making the explanations and clarifications that were contained in the *Nota Explicativa Praevia*, particularly with regard to the relationship of episcopal collegiality to papal primacy, the promoters of the *schema* gained almost unanimous approval for it from the Fathers.

In this connection, there are not a few inexact or even erroneous assertions made by these authors (see p. 60ff.). These include their treatment of the concept of "the people of God"; and also the position of the chapter on this subject in the *schema* itself. The latter was a question of "logic," as the Central Coordinating Commission determined. However, the vision of the "local Church" that is encountered here suggests some wisdom after the fact (see p. 61). And the authors are also guilty of conciliar "utilitarianism" when they speak of the Decree on the Means of Social Communication, *Inter Mirifica* as "anodyne"; it was a text that was "duly discussed and duly approved" (see p. 63). The Constitution on the Sacred Liturgy, *Sacrosanctum Concilium*, is styled "remarkable," and is held to mark "the end of the Counter-Reformation." But is not, rather, "Catholic Reform" the correct designation for the historical period in question here?

The "intersession" of 1963-64 between the Second and Third Sessions saw an effort to recast and reorganize the various *schemata*. One need think only of the famous "Döpfner plan" in this regard (p. 64ff.) or of "the diplomatic and theological qualities of the new adjunct secretary, Monsignor Gérard Philips" (p. 65), who was the key person in all of the pain and labor surrounding the drafting of the conciliar texts (in place of Father Carolus Balić, whose name these authors spell as Balié). There is, however, a fine synthesis in this text treating the preoccupations of the minority; this introduces a subchapter entitled "Paul VI and the Council" (see p. 67). The treatment given suggests several reflections to us.

Then we arrive at the Third Session, where the *schemata* on the Church and the Bishops are taken up again and in contrast with those on religious liberty and on the Jews. There are not a few exaggerations and points stretched here, particularly if we think about how many wished to see put on the record in connection with the first of these two themes, continuity in the attitude of the Magisterium, taking especially into account the ideological tendency represented by European liberalism. In the end, this was the thesis that prevailed, and, in that respect, it resembled some of the positions set forth in *Dei Verbum* that in the beginning were not considered likely to make the grade (see p. 70).

Without getting into all the twists and turns exhibited by these authors, we do need to make mention of their biased judgments on the *schemata* on the missions and on the religious life (for Cardinal Agagianian and some of the religious Bishops, this was a very personal matter—p. 71). And, once again, we come upon that famous expression, "Black Week." It is placed within the usual "prophylactic" quotation marks, but that simply points to the dependence of the authors here on popular journalism. The historical accounts common in it, of course, have characterized the week in question as manifesting great disappointments on the part of both the Council Fathers and public opinion generally as to how the Council was going at that point. We, however, would call the prophetic week in question not "black" but a "moment of truth." It has been solidly established, in fact, that the week some call "black" was almost wholly "beneficial" (p. 73), and served to clarify many things quite considerably: "In spite of the seemingly dark clouds that accompanied it, the final outcome of the week was largely positive" (p. 73).

The authors continue their negative treatment of the conciliar texts, raising the question that we consider to be at the heart of the matter, namely, what are the criteria that lead them to make the negative judgments they make? It seems to come down at bottom to the question of the "reception" of the conciliar documents, or perhaps only to the partial acceptance of them, based on personal criteria which are themselves vulnerable to criticism. It seems to us that a principal criterion here is that of the so-called "great turn" (p. 73) that was supposedly made by the Council, with emphasis being placed upon its "novelty" or uniqueness. The reality, however, is that in order to be Catholic, and to achieve any authentic *aggiornamento*, the Council had to embrace both *nova et vetera*, both Tradition and renewal (on this subject, the reader is referred to Chapter 50 of the present volume).

However, the authors have nothing but praise for *Lumen Gentium*, which they greatly appreciate (see p. 74). Once again, though, they speak of passing from "the era of the Counter-Reformation to the era of ecumenism" (p. 74). We would not reduce things in this way.

The final "intersession" between the Third and Fourth Sessions focused on questions such as the liberty of conscience and on the "obstructionism" that was supposedly encountered (see p. 27). This led into the Fourth Session, which dealt with the theme of religious liberty. But it is not correct to speak of a nostalgic obscuring or diminishing of things on the part of some because that was not the case (p. 77). For there were, after all, the final positive votes and the issuing of the documents themselves. The authors always judge these things in terms of whether or not they represent the "new" (which they approve of). They toss out indiscriminately references to [the encyclical of Pius XI] *Casti Connubii*; atomic weapons; ecumenism; the conciliar decrees *Ad Gentes* and *Presbyterorum Ordinis*; the conciliar declaration *Dignitatis Humanae*; and the Council's Pastoral Constitution on the Church in the Modern World, *Gaudium et Spes*. There is a veritable blizzard of opinions thrown out on these topics, in fact, concerning which, we repeat, the ideal is always whether or not they are "new" with regard to the positions they adopt. The authors could perhaps conclude, as a result of this approach, that "the post-conciliar era, with its particular problems, was about to begin" (see p. 82). With assumptions such as theirs, certainly, serious problems were not likely to be lacking.

Chapter IV is dedicated to "The Council and the Ecumenical Movement." The importance of the presence of the observers at the Council is stressed, even though the authors admit that their "influence is not easily measurable" (see p. 85). In fact, as far as we are concerned, even though we have great respect for the observers and affirm that their presence *was* important, we can in no way agree that they played a role that amounted to "a quasi-participation" at the Council (see p. 86, n. 13). In the end, the authors ask if Vatican II represented a decisive stage in the progress of ecumenism, and they correctly reply: "It represented a very important stage without any doubt" (see p. 87).

"The Results" form the body of the fifth and last chapter in the book. Obviously, what these results amounted to depend upon the ideological point of view of the authors. First of all, the authors do look at the content of the conciliar and post-conciliar documents. But they offer so many criticism of them (e. g., pp. 91, 92, 93, 94, 95, 97, 98, 99, 101, 102, 104, 105, 107, 108, 110 and 111) that it is hard to see how in their case there could be any favorable "reception" of the Council at all, that is, of the whole Council. And this seems to me to be a huge and very serious problem in and for the Church. The authors certainly do recognize that with the Council we are dealing with "a doctrinal magisterium framed in a pastoral perspective." This is obvious, in fact. But then in their interpretations, they go off on their own, speaking of "juxtapositions" (here the "two ecclesiologies" raise their heads) and of a "lack of coherence." What is this lack? This kind of thing is offered in the name of what they specify as "the results"; they speak of "a true and profound intention on the part of a great majority of the assembly to try to get beyond the preoccupation of attempting to achieve as broad a consensus as possible" (see

p. 90). We cannot agree with this viewpoint. The Council represented precisely that, namely, a "consensus" arrived at by the participants.

Once again, we shall not follow these authors in their detailed critique of the conciliar texts. If their ideal is indeed always "newness" or "novelty" (or a "revolutionary" turn or character) in the positions adopted by the Council, then they have simply gone off the tracks. The same thing must be said about those texts approved as, in effect, "master laws," the implementation of which was to be relegated to the action of "post-conciliar organisms" (p. 112). Supposedly the characteristic of such documents is "the systematic slowness" of the implementation of the various reforms called for; this "systematic slowness" supposedly provided a justification for by-passing the official processes and, in effect, condoning abuses. This was a very serious matter, particularly as regards the reform of the liturgy. The results have been only too visible and fraught with consequences.

Under the subtitle, "First Reactions," the authors assert that "the Churches of the Third World" were not "interested" in "receiving" the Council properly. This seems to us both a gratuitous and a distorted statement (see p. 115ff.). The authors nevertheless go on nonchalantly speaking of "disappointments," "restrictions," the "negative views of the lower clergy," the "much more radical *aggiornamento* that was desired," "improvised reforms," "drifting," and so on (see p. 116). This kind of treatment leads to the assertion that "those who had been against the Council all along" now suddenly had "found a wider audience" consisting of those who were "denouncing the post-conciliar abuses" (see p. 117).

These denunciations and accusations are here repeated to the point where the question is raised of whether or not there should now be a Vatican Council III. Evidently, or so the authors conclude, "Vatican II had its limits," and thus "the solutions adopted were half-way measures and ambiguity was actually cultivated in order to avoid unacceptable opposition" (see p. 117). More than that, the authors claim that "the preoccupation of Pope Paul VI with reaching a consensus that was practically unanimous led him more than once to introduce into doctrinal texts modifications inspired by a different theological system entirely; these modifications tended to distort the coherence of the text to the point where it sometimes almost became a "puzzle" (see p. 118). Let us stop here, though, since the informed reader can see by now where these authors are tending. In the end, they speak of a Council "in transition," almost as if, by girding up one's loins, the more "active" Council they favor could somehow be conjured into being (see p. 118). What they consider the true Council is consistently identified with "innovation" and "new positions" (but then it sometimes turns out that they "were often traditional positions that had been forgotten for centuries").

In the book's final paragraph, they reveal the true character of the Council as an "event." As we have several times put on the record, this is an interpretation which is simply unacceptable, as far as we are concerned (see our review of the volume *The "Event" and the "Decisions"* in Chapter 23 of the present volume—reprinted from *Apollinaris LXXI*, 1998, pp. 131-142). It becomes particularly unacceptable when we see how these authors consider this "event" to be a "more important phenomenon than the texts produced by the Council, however great the interest or the richness of the latter" (see p. 119). The so-called "turn" the Council is considered to have taken is supposedly "decisive" in the matter (*Ibid.*); but as we have already said elsewhere, the "turn" taken by the Council was in no sense a "U-turn," if we may continue to use the same figurative language employed by these authors.

26

Vatican II as Seen by Joseph Thomas

Various Authors, *I Concili Ecumenici* [the Ecumenical Councils], Queriniana, Brescia, 2001, 475 pages.

Section III of the above-listed volume is dedicated to Vatican Council II and was written by Father Joseph Thomas, S. J., a teacher at the Sèvres Center in Paris and the editor of the journal *Études*. In view of our continuing interest in the great synod that was Vatican II, we examine this work here, offering as our initial impression that although this essay is not as radical as some of the other things written about the Council, it is still not as sufficiently balanced and impartial as it should be. It exhibits a ponderousness in its judgments and includes not a few rather far-fetched *clichés*. The style of the presentation is simple and discursive, but also rather popular and pedagogical. The author provides lists and explanations of things which others might have thought could be taken for granted, although that is not actually the case.

The author declares his "ambitious" objective of wishing "to explicate the fundamental ideas which unify documents that at first sight seem to be so different." He attempts to do this by going back to the beginning of the Council which produced them all.

The first of the three major parts into which the work is divided bears the title "The Event," and we already know the ambiguity inherent in the use of this term in this way. It is worth noting that it would necessarily be understood as a great and important event. Following the typical historiography of the day, however, it would also be one that revolutionized or overturned the history with which it deals. We can naturally not accept the use of the term in this sense, particularly since we are conscious of the continuity that is implicit in the fidelity of the Council documents to the great Tradition of the Church.

From the very first page, the author reveals his commitment to treat the decisions of the Council differently than others have treated them. That is all very well, but he does not succeed completely in detaching himself from those others. For him John XXIII is "the pope of the Council," even though "Paul VI understood himself to be the heir of his predecessor, continuing his work." "The majority of the cardinals of the Curia had reservations concerning any such adventure" [as a council]. The idea of a council, however, "reappeared periodically," adding a Johannine stamp to what had appeared to be "a sudden inspiration from God." But the author also notes that "the idea of a council may have occupied the mind of John XXIII for some time" (p. 376).

He goes on to deal with "the preparation," mentioning a questionnaire that was in fact never sent out, and he covers "the unfolding" of the Council with a somewhat critical mention of the role of journalists. At this point, Archbishop Pericle Felici appears on the scene; his influence was supposedly "excessive," in the absence of any "firm and unified guidance" for the Council (p. 379). The Council supposedly lacked proper coordination.

Another difficulty with the Council was "the fullness of the task which awaited it" (p. 379) and also the decisive role of the conciliar commissions which "possessed powers that were perhaps excessive." That was true, in many cases. The author then follows up with a rather succinct sketch of the action of Pope Paul VI which is quite well done. This pope was preoccupied with the concern "that the continuity of the Church's teaching should appear with clarity. He was faithful to the spirit of John XXIII, but he was more rigorous intellectually. He was also more watchful concerning the risks of possible abuses and concerning the errors that might arise from too wide an interpretation of texts that were ambiguous" (p. 381).

The author then goes on to examine, always quite briefly, the question of the "reception" of the great Council. He examines questions from a point of view favorable to the bishops; yet he correctly recognizes also that "the reforms...were carried out too quickly, perhaps, at least in some countries" (p. 382). In any case, "a practical unanimity was realized during the Council, and there continued to be at least a moral unanimity, as the affirmative votes taken in the presence of the pope proved...At the same time, no one doubted that the Council was a place where serious clashes occurred between what we may call a majority and a minority. These two tendencies manifested themselves more rigorously as time went on." (*Ibid.*)

I do not believe, however, that it is sufficient simply to put matters this way. For within each of the tendencies we identify a process of radicalization was going on at the two extremes; this process eventually issued in the schism of the traditionalists on the one hand. On the other hand, the result was that the *consensus* that had been achieved during the Council with an acceptance of the spirit of truth which was present in the minority was *not* accepted by the extreme liberals on the other side. Paul VI had always been very conscious of the views of the minority, and he took pains to see balanced the twin fundamental characteristics of Catholicism, namely, continuity and *aggiornamento*, the legitimate realizations of the present and the prospects for such realizations in the future. We do not find that the deep conviction we have about all this is really understood or expressed by this author (p. 385). For us the danger has not come solely from the reactions of the "integralists."

In the same way, the author's judgments on the *Coetus Episcopalis Internationalis* are not very balanced, nor is it really exact to consider only "progressives" and "conservatives." Much better terminology would be "reformers" and "anti-reformers" (or "immobile," as the author styles the latter). However that may be, Thomas always extends to the former a very considerable benefit of the doubt (p. 384ff.). This shows where his sympathies lie. He declares, however, that in the context of "an absolutely unprecedented crisis of civilization," the Council "fell back into the shadows and went largely unheeded."

Here we need to be very clear in our understanding, even while the author helps us in this regard by statements such as the following: "Catholics are often content to appeal to the 'spirit' [of the Council] without taking the trouble to give a closer reading to the letter. Faced with those who were against the Council to begin with, many adopted instead a conscious post-conciliar outlook, which only served to harden to a greater degree the opposition some already had to either a 'pre-conciliar' or to a 'post-conciliar' Church. Those who opposed the 'post-conciliar' Church were simply to be left out of consideration, while those who rejected the 'pre-conciliar' Church were supposed to be always open to new things. And just as was the case after Vatican Council I, when what resulted was an inflation of the role of the pope, so after Vatican Council II, what resulted was just the opposite, a diminution or a downgrading of the role of the pope...What then followed was a feverish period when the Council was invoked or referred to in order to justify every innovation and every conceivable type of experience."

This analysis obviously does not lack a certain foundation, as the following statement attests: "We had to await the convocation of the Extraordinary Synod of Bishops...in 1985 in order to discover, at least as far as the conciliar documents were concerned, an almost unanimous affirmation of the decisive contribution of Vatican II to the life of the Church. Between the integralists and the progressives, the true path of the Council was finally delineated and confirmed by the pope and the delegates of the world episcopacy" (p. 386).

With the next subtitle, "Continuity and Newness," the author develops as a binomial pair of tendencies what is in fact a single thrust, namely, a Catholicism that both provided the key to the *aggiornamento* that John XXIII wanted, and constituted a link with the Councils of Trent and Vatican I. John XXIII did want, precisely, "a renewal of the Church by means of a *clearer* realization of her basic character brought about in order to allow her to bring the Gospel more effectively to the world of today" (p. 388). This was actually demonstrated by the "new subjects" that were raised and debated at the Council—subjects that had "never before been objects considered at a Council" (p. 389ff.). Even the "style" of this Council was "new" for this author: it was more biblical than juridical, with "breaks" with tradition, and "sometimes with the juxtaposition of theological perspectives very imperfectly joined together, and perhaps not even reconcilable in fact" (p. 392). We cannot follow Thomas down this road, certainly not in the final part of his summary here, where he sees an "overturning" of the "canon." He does add, wisely, though: "With regard to the controversial points outstanding between the two schools of theology, Vatican II decided not to take a decisive position" (p. 392).

The second major part of this study takes up the subject of "The Work." The author sets the tone in his discussion of "the nature, structure, and mission of the Church," which represented for him the rather diffuse framework within which the Council was able to arrive at a more traditional vision compared to that set forth in the manuals of the theology" (p. 396). The "nature, structure, and mission" of the Church represented "the fundamental axes of the conciliar concerns." These three dimensions of the Church are discussed and explained by the author. He begins with the nature of the Church, speaks of the danger of schisms, and goes on to discuss the opposition, for "many believers" between a "spiritual Church and a juridical Church" (p. 397; see also p. 403). The author thinks about how the media convey to public opinion "the image of a Church analogous to a multinational society whose headquarters happens to be in Rome and whose president regularly visits its branches located throughout the world" (p. 398). There follows then presentations of the Church as a "perfect society," as a sacrament, as a mystery, and as a people of God and body of Christ, with access to the sources of grace.

The author then rather hastily attempts to sketch out the main lines of the Constitution on Divine Revelation, *Dei Verbum*. He does not do this very adequately, as a matter of fact; this is the case also with all that he has dealt with up to this point. For example, he makes no mention of the Magisterium of the Church, although he mentions that revelation "comes to us thanks to Scripture read in the Church, received by the Church, and transmitted in her Tradition" (p. 401).

He then addresses the Council's document on the liturgy, and also the theme of the boundaries of the Church, not always with the sharpest pointed pencil, however. He falters on the subject of *"subsistit in"*, for example (p. 403). We are also not satisfied with his vision of the Church as "a communion of Churches," even when he speaks of "communion especially with the Roman Church" (p. 404). We are then introduced to the question of ecumenism and "the paths of renewal." He casts a few critical glances here and there but this is no systematic critical study (see p. 408).

Following "Mary, Figure of the Church" (p. 409), the author arrives at: "The structure of the Church: Hierarchical Communion" (p. 409). This general topic is divided up into subtopics, including "clergy and Laity"; "the Church as Communion"; "the laity"; "the hierarchy"; "sacramentality"; "collegiality"; and "the religious life." As the pages succeed one another, our difficulty in following the author increases. For example, he says, that "the Church is entirely hierarchical" (pp. 416ff. and 419). But then he expresses other viewpoints as well (p. 425), especially when we look at his explanation of collegiality (pp. 419-424), because he incorrectly expands the meaning of "college" (see p. 422). Yet he does so without making proper distinctions—in either "a strict or a broad sense"—which might have helped us understand the texts. To the many "yeses" we have mentally uttered as we read along, we were adding many "buts".

Thomas' third great distinction on the mission of the Church is entitled: "The Mission of the Church: Church and Society." In this section, we find it less difficult to approve of the author's general line of thought. We can cite a couple of phrases in this connection: "Once more the Council charted a path equidistant from the two temptations of confusion and separation... The Church is in the world but not of the world—but she is certainly also *for* the world" (p. 430). We take note of something else the author says which attracted our attention, as follows: "Many people especially in the mass media, have translated 'dialogue' as meaning simply 'open to the world.' But this is a very ambiguous word, one never adopted by the Council as such. It has aroused the enthusiasm of some people only because of its obvious character as a 'general' term; but it has also provoked irritation in others, such as Jacques Maritain in his book *Peasant of the Garonne*" (p. 435).

Following the treatment of the topic styled "Beyond the Frontiers," we find once again reasons to harbor serious reservations, in particular, concerning the author's treatment of religious liberty. He explains quite poorly the correct development of the Council's doctrine on this subject, which in continuity with the authentic tradition of the Church the Council definitely wished to uphold (see p. 439ff.). Thomas also goes unhappily astray in treating both the number of the sacraments and the question of papal primacy (p. 440).

We then come to the third major part of the study. The title here is: "The Future of the Council." The author starts out well by observing that "the institutional transfer of the various conciliar options was well realized, indeed fulfilled" (p. 445). Among so many critical remarks, this is a statement worth noting. But the author then asks: "What will remain of this Council"? This question is correctly posed, considering that it is followed by another asking whether the Catholic Church will be "marked by this Council for a long period of time. Will she therefore guard its legacy? In order to designate the nearly four centuries that separate us from the Council of Trent we speak of the post-Tridentine era. Will an equally lengthy period bear the name of the post-Vatican II era"? To ask such questions was almost to break a kind of taboo, it seems to us; but then we were disappointed by what followed in the author's narrative. Still, the questions were asked: what *will* remain of this Council? In this regard, we cannot do anything else but...await the verdict of history. Nevertheless, we must strive to receive and carry out the Council in its full and correct meaning, not merely in some of its aspects that happened to be "new."

With respect to the conciliar texts, the author generally says the right thing, particularly if we bear in mind what we said earlier concerning *aggiornamento*. Thomas invites us to re-read them: "In the end," he says, "it is the texts that were produced that will allow future generations to appropriate the legacy of Vatican II—on the condition that they will consent to read them" (p. 446). Fidelity and renewal were embraced mutually at the Council, and they must continue on together, arm in arm, out of sheer Catholic necessity. Yet it does not seem to us that the author's final pages are always in accord with this necessity. We may look, for example, at the themes of what the author calls "the 'relativization' of the Church, as well as at what he says about the Church's supposed "monolithic administration"—and also about the "spirit of the Council." Regarding this, he affirms that "we must above all remain faithful to the spirit of the Council," as if this spirit were somehow independent of the acts of the Council that the author claims were "not just those written down" (p. 447).

The permanent and authentic meaning of renewal, which Thomas says is what he aims at, does not square with his strong criticism of Joseph Ratzinger, who vigorously (and correctly) denied that Vatican II represented any break with what had preceded it (see p. 449). For the author, though, this position "undermines the opening represented by the Council in the history of the Church, and is equivalent to an invitation to a regression. All of those who are nostalgic for the past, discoverable as they are in the various traditionalist currents, are ready to subscribe to a similar affirmation" (*Ibid.*). It is not clear, however, whether the author distinguishes here between "traditionalists" (extremists) and those who are simply traditionally minded Catholics (see p. 450). Nor is it clear he understands that the idea of the Council as representing a clear break with the past is an idea that has been denounced by none other than Pope John Paul II himself—and John Paul is no "traditionalist," according to Thomas himself. Also, to assert that "the spirit of the Council definitely coincides with the call to a permanent reform" (p. 450) seems at the very least both reductive and partial; if we are to go by what most people understand by the term *aggiornamento*.

With both "A Query" and "A Risk," Thomas reveals his own preoccupations with regard to the future of the Council. He is uncertain where such factors as "restoration," "integralism," and "Vaticanolatry" (as he calls it) are going to lead. Yet "Vatican II...ought to be read in the light of the councils that preceded it." This is correct, but then he himself adds a qualification: "To pretend that one can interpret a council in the light of preceding councils risks eliminating everything produced that was new" (p. 452). But is this really true? The author continues in the same vein: "The Second Vatican Council was a council like the others and thus its teaching is necessarily incomplete. At the Extraordinary Synod of Bishops in 1985 it was possible to discern some rather eloquent backsliding on this point" (*Ibid.*). Is this really the case? If so, in what sense? Yet the author goes on with his critique here, reproaching those "obsessed" with affirming an authentic Christian identity. He concludes as follows: "The margin here is narrow. There is more than first appears among those who reject any reception of the Council, and those who affirm this...There were distinct Roman reactions to the pastoral practice decided upon at Medellin and Puebla by the Latin American episcopate" (p. 454). It does not seem to me, however, that this is a very good conclusion to draw. However, it is indicative of the author's belief in an alternative that does not exist for the authentic vision of Vatican Council II and for hierarchical communion.

V

PARTICULAR THEMES
AND QUESTIONS

27

Italian Catholic "Traditionalism"

Buonasorte Nicla, *Tra Roma e Lefebvre. Il tradizionalismo cattolico italiano e il Concilio Vaticano II* [Between Rome and Lefebvre: Italian Catholic Traditionalism and Vatican Council II], Edizioni Studium, Roma 2003, 177 pages.

As Roberto Morozzo della Rocca observes in the preface to this work, "it is not easy to write about Catholic traditionalism in accordance with any established scholarly criteria. The subject does not stand out as a distinct thing. Above all, it is necessary to distinguish between tradition and traditionalism. The Catholic Church is impregnated with tradition, as, in varying degrees, are all other Christian Churches and denominations" (p. 11). We have to state at the outset that this author, N. Buonasorte, does not always succeed in making the proper distinctions, since she proves unable to distinguish between "traditional" bishops and "traditionalist" bishops. This represents an "original sin" of hers that serves to falsify her scholarly work and continually provides reasons for dissatisfaction for anyone reading this work. Besides, within both the majority and minority groups at the Council, there were extremists who only revealed themselves after the Council, either in the interpretations they then made of it, or in the harsh criticisms they then leveled at its documents. Some of these ended up thereby on the extreme fringe of what had been the conciliar minority, and only these could therefore be truly called "traditionalists" in the full sense of the word.

In the case of these traditionalists, it was a question of "an incomplete and contradictory notion of tradition...which they opposed to the Magisterium of the Church, the one of the Bishop of Rome and of the body of the Bishops in communion with him. It is not possible to remain faithful to tradition when the ecclesial link is broken with the one whom Christ himself, in the person of the Apostle Peter, charged with the ministry of unity in his Church" (Pope John Paul II, *Litterae Apostolicae Ecclesia Dei*, July 2, 1988). It is here that the root of the error of traditionalism is to be found.

And thus, as far as we are concerned, it is not proper to speak simply of "traditionalism," *tout court*, as applying to the Council Fathers belonging to the minority. The author admits this, but then gets lost along the way. We need think only of the Italian episcopate in this regard. Most of the Italian bishops belonged to the minority at the Council itself, but subsequently they were to be found accepting of its final documents and they continued in obedient communion with the Roman Pontiff, who was the great guiding spirit involved in securing a correct reception of the conciliar documents.

Buonasorte begins her study by asking, "Which Traditionalism"? She discusses the whole question in terms of some of the themes related to the Church and modernity. For us these themes are not so clearly identifiable, particularly in terms of what the author calls "the fundamental turn of the Council in redefining what it means to be the Catholic Church" (p. 19). Our dissatisfaction continues with regard to her "note on the definition of terms" in which she claims that, given "the present state of existing studies," and "the traditionalist humus in the Council's minority," she is able to treat the situation mostly in relation to Cardinals Siri and Ruffini and Bishop Carli, along with their "political followers."

Certainly, as we have already noted, Buonasorte admits that "the conciliar minority cannot be identified in any absolute sense with traditionalism" (p. 48); but for her, it is nevertheless equally certain that the traditionalist phenomenon, as it manifested itself following the Council, had roots in the particular mixture of opinions found among the members of the conciliar minority" (*Ibid.*). At this point in the text, she presents some of the major themes on which this kind of conservatism was based (see pp. 51-78). Unfortunately, in this presentation we do not find the kind of careful exactitude that is necessary in dealing with the sensitive subjects involved (see pp. 60, 62ff., 65ff., 69, 71ff., 75, n. 75, 77ff., 84ff., and then 108). Buonasorte's pen seems insufficiently refined to be able to deal correctly with all of the distinctions that are necessarily involved here.

In the third part of her study, the author takes up the subject of the "post-conciliar traditionalist." This subject provides terrain a little easier to walk on for the obvious reasons already indicated above. Nevertheless, ambiguities are not lacking here as well (see pp. 87ff., 90ff., and 93ff.). Here Buonasorte seeks to "furnish a description of the geography and some of the examples of Italian conservative Catholicism; it is in this wide sea that outbursts of traditionalism again become manifest" (p. 94). She only complicates matters, however, when she brings in politics as well (see p. 158); the same thing is true of her use of the term "ultraconservative."

The author then examines the paths followed by Cardinals Siri and Ruffini and Bishop Carli. According to her, these prelates represented "examples of an orientation which entailed formal adhesion to the Council but internal opposition to it which was not always completely hidden" (p. 99).

Much better is the treatment by Buonasorte of what she titles "The Rejection by Archbishop Lefebvre and His Followers" (see pp. 110-128) and "The Sedevacantist Movement" (pp. 128-135). She also treats what she calls "traditionalists who are more anti-Roman," and she does supply some facts and evaluations of that particular "traditionalist archipelago" (pp. 135-168). The material in this section, however, should have been more carefully sifted, since she deals with figures who are not traditionalist at all (I am thinking, for example, of A. Del Noce and Cornelio Fabro).

In any case, the author realizes that "the critics of the Council never made up a compact and organized front" (p. 135). Moreover, the ultras or extremists were not to be found only in the minority; there were some in the majority as well, about whom this author breathes not a word. But she does not fail to note "the undeniable existence of convergences in the common objectives to be attained on the part of

"Italian conservatives and traditionalists" *and* Archbishop Lefebvre himself. All this, however, "was not sufficient to maintain such alliances intact when Lefebvre called into question, not only in theory but also in practice, the role of Rome and the papacy" (p. 121). For our part, we would be extremely cautious about asserting that there were very many "convergences in the common objectives to be attained."

Before coming to her conclusions, Buonasorte explains "the strategies followed by the Holy See in dealing with the traditionalists" (pp. 158-168; on p. 161, by the way, it is necessary to use the term "licitly," not "validly"). The author concludes her study by saying: " '*Romanitas*,' besides being a point of reference which could bring together many different traditionalist currents in Italian Catholicism, also served to blunt the more extreme points raised in the contestation, and hence it worked to safeguard the unity of Italian Catholicism" (p. 172). But this conclusion seems to go against the idea of traditionalism as defined in John Paul II's *Litterae Apostolicae Ecclesia Dei* which was quoted above.

28

Primacy and Collegiality
(According to the *Nota Explicativa Praevia*)

Grootaers Jan, Ed., *Primauté et Collégialité. Le dossier de Gérard Philips sur la* Nota Explicativa Praevia [Primacy and Collegiality: The Dossier of Gérard Philips on the *Nota Explicativa Praevia*]. Edited with a historical introduction, annotations, and annexes by J. Grootaers, Leuven 1986 (Bibliotheca Ephemeridum Theologicarum Lovaniensum LXXII), 222 pages.

This publication is of very great interest for the study of the doctrinal element underlying the structure of hierarchical communion in the Church as well as the whole question of collegiality. G. Thils underlines the importance of these points in his preface. Thanks to this publication we get back into lively contact with the human protagonists who dealt with the hierarchical communion and collegiality of the Council itself: Pope Paul VI, Cardinals Suenens, Browne, and Cicognani, Archbishop Felici, Bishop Colombo, Father Tromp, Fathers Ciappi, Gagnebet, and Bertrams—and Msgr. Philips. All the tendencies touching upon the important themes of primacy and collegiality are represented here. That this whole business was of fundamental importance for papal-primatial and episcopal relations was certainly the conclusion of the Extraordinary Synod of Bishops convened twenty years after the end of Vatican Council II.

This collection is composed of three categories of documents. First of all, there is a study of the genesis and the repercussions of the famous *Nota Explicativa Praevia* that was inserted into Chapter III of the Dogmatic Constitution on the Church, *Lumen Gentium,* in

November, 1964 [at the behest of Paul VI]. The author of this study is J. Grootaers himself.

There follows a complete dossier of related unpublished documents taken from those left by Msgr. Philips, specifically, his own notes, which he put together as a service to history in 1969, along with 11 enclosures as supporting documentation; all these documents were chosen by Msgr. Philips himself, who was the adjunct secretary of the Doctrinal Commission at Vatican II. Grootaers as editor has taken from the archives four documents regarding suggestions by Pope Paul VI on the subject; they were transmitted on May 19, 1964, to the Doctrinal Commission. These latter documents "constituted a premonitory sign of the difficulties that would ensue in November, 1964." Then there are five further working documents to which Msgr. Philips alluded in his memoir on the subject.

There are also extracts here from the "chronicle" of Father Sebastian Tromp, who was the secretary of the Council's Doctrinal Commission that we have already mentioned. There is also a synopsis of the modifications introduced in the course of the development of the definitive text of the *Nota Praevia*. Finally, in an appendix, there are three "articles" by Msgr. Philips related to the events and subjects covered in his confidential dossier.

In reading this volume, we are happy to report, one notes that, beyond the importance of the valuable documentation made available to scholars here, there is the further notable fact that there are important differences between the analysis and judgments of Grootaers and those of Philips. One indication of this can be seen in the question mark added by the former to Chapter I's title: "The Pope, Vicar of Christ and Head of the College of Bishops?" It is also evident from the note the author supplies here. Another indication, in our opinion, is his use of the adjective "monarchical" in opposition to the collegial exercise of the *potestas plena et suprema* in the Church (pp. 28, 32, 42, 54, 56, and 84), as is the author's judgment on the thought of Pope Paul VI (pp. 32, 38, 40, 77, 83, 192, and 202), and on his conclusions concerning the publication of this *dossier* itself (pp. 27, 37, 41, 46, 49, 51, 54, 56, 84, 192-193, 203, 213, and 216). Msgr. Philips himself was convinced that the *Nota Praevia* did not weaken the conciliar text that had been voted by the Fathers.

The convictions of Grootaers on the *communio hierarchica* are also revealing; he calls Father Gianfranco Ghirlanda's treatment of this topic "exorbitant" (p. 52). He also instances the interpretations by a number of post-conciliar writers such as Lanne, Alberigo, Acerbi, Pottmeyer, Holstein, Dejaifve, and Tillard. He ends up stating that "Msgr. Philips, in November of 1964, could not have foreseen how certain Roman elements would seek to exploit the *Nota Praevia* in a major effort to evacuate episcopal collegiality of any substance" (p. 59). Still today collegiality is hardly alive (see C. Butler and J. Tillard: p. 60).

As the counterpoint to these tendencies, we greatly admire the efforts of Msgr. Philips, whose objectivity was outstanding, and whose detachment from his own task in working to support the correct interpretation of history in the matter of the *Nota Praevia* was exemplary. Similarly, there was his honesty and balance, and also the maturity of his judgment, concerning an issue that has still aroused passions right up to the present day. The importance of the issue of papal primacy and its relation to episcopal collegiality at the Council can only now be fully grasped in connection with the tensions we experience today between the universal Church and the local Churches.

May we be permitted, however, to make reference to two items in the appendix, where Msgr. Philips demonstrated that he was no expert in understanding the proper function of canon law. The items in question concern the concept of jurisdiction that he exhibits (p. 194) and the comparison he made between the ancient patriarchates and the present-day episcopal conferences, even though he says that "their concrete forms differ" (p. 195, and also p. 215).

29

The conciliar Constitution
Lumen Gentium

"A Brief History of the Document and its Ecclesiology with Special Attention to the Subject of the Laity." A lecture delivered on October 21, 2000, to the Roman M. E. I C. in the Paul VI Hall of the PUL for the opening of the 2000-2001 year of activities. The general subject of the gathering was "One Faith and One Church."

I do not believe that I have to convince any of you about the importance and of the doctrinal, spiritual, and pastoral value of Vatican Council II, nor of the central place occupied by *Lumen Gentium* in the work of the Council (along with the Council's other three Constitutions). The name of this particular Constitution alone, however, evidences both its importance and its uniqueness. As for the Council, I could define this most recent of the general councils of the Catholic Church as a kind of icon of the Catholic Church herself, that is, of what constitutes Catholicism in particular: her communion with the past and with her own origins, the maintenance of her identity in the course of her long history and development, and her fidelity to all of this when renewing herself—a leafy tree sprung from a humble seed buried in tears and darkness two millennia ago by the redemptive death of Jesus Christ, but bursting forth in a perpetual springtime through the Lord's resurrection: it is the vine of the Lord himself, which has extended its roots throughout the world. One testimonial to all this, to give an example, I myself have found in the presentation of the Catholic Church that is made in the book *Le Chiese cristiane del Duemila* [The Christian Churches of the Year Two Thousand], published by J. A. Moehler Institute in Brescia in 1998. This account stresses the link with the Bishop of Rome and the Tradition of the Church; in it is cited a phrase of Klaus Schatz, who says that "thanks to the structure of the primacy, the Catholic Church has the ability to link together both stability and Tradition, on the one hand, and dynamism and innovation on the other (see the study *Papato ed ecumenismo: Il ministero petrino al servizio dell'unità* [Papacy and Ecumenism: The Petrine Ministry and the Service of Unity], edited by P. Huenermann and published in Bologna in 1999[-]p. 26).

The conciliar event was a great one and many of you may remember it still, some from having seen it unfolding before your own eyes. Some 3068 Council Fathers participated, coming from practically all of the countries in the world. Its four annual sessions went from October 11, 1962, through December 8, 1965. There were 168 "general congregations" held and 10 "public sessions." The Council issued 16 documents, including 4 constitutions, along with 9 decrees and 3 declarations.

I would add, in order to convey some idea of the vastness of the whole enterprise, that if one takes only the official acts of the great Synod, I can see, lined up on my bookshelves, no less than 62 large volumes bound in red leather. Then, there are the various memoirs and diaries of other well-known figures connected with the Council or others who participated in it in some degree. Naturally, these latter accounts need to be subjected to careful critical scrutiny in order to see their value validated, and this no doubt always involves a long and difficult process. Still, these accounts too provide flavor and personal ingredients to the overall history (though they certainly must be read in the light of the official *Acts* [facts] of the Council).

Today there is a great risk of slipping into a kind of fragmentary history of the Council, which in truth could not then escape from being a simple chronicle of events. And underlying that tendency is the intention of many to try to diminish the importance of the conciliar documents. I will look at one of these today. But these documents actually do represent a synthesis of *aggiornamento* and tradition. Those who try to obscure or deny this are acting on the basis of convictions that I have consistently labeled "ideological." Such convictions aim at bringing out only the innovative aspects of the Council—aspects which continued to manifest themselves after the Council. Such convictions point to a discontinuity, if not to an open break, with the authentic Catholic tradition. One prominent example of this way of viewing things is the volume entitled *The Event and the Decisions: Studies on the Dynamics of Vatican Council II*, edited by Maria Teresa Fattori and Alberto Melloni and published in Imola in 1997 (see Chapter 23 of the present volume). In this book, one encounters the contemporary tendency in historiography which places the emphasis on the "event" and its discontinuity with what has gone before, indeed, its "changes," and even its "traumatic mutations," from what was there earlier. This kind of interpretation is supposed to provide a counterpoint to the way the famous "Annales" used to treat history by viewing long periods together while underlining their historical continuity. F. Braudel, for example, believes that history is "an applied social science that brings to light systems and perennial models which at first sight were invisible."

Here it must be noted that, by "event," according to this ideological theory, is meant not just "a happening worthy of note," but instead what is meant involves a break with the past, what is reported is considered an absolute novelty, the coming into being of a new Church, or at least a kind of "Copernican Revolution" in the Church, moving from one type of Catholicism to another—which do not retain the unmistakable characteristic of "being Catholic." But such a perspective cannot and must not be accepted, certainly not as far as the Catholic Church is concerned. Any history which takes into account the specific character of the Church, and the preservation of continuity in her own mysterious reality, must see these factors reflected in the kind of historical interpretations this history provides.

In this regard, reading over the contributions to the Fattori-

Melloni work mentioned above, one cannot but be truly surprised by the radical critiques encountered there leveled against such notable subjects as Jedin, Ratzinger, and Kasper (with his four hermeneutical rules), and also against Poulat. The result of this approach is that a position within the majority that would have been considered extreme during the Council itself succeeded after the Council in virtually monopolizing henceforth the interpretation of the entire "event," meanwhile rejecting any other possible interpretation and even stigmatizing such as "anti-conciliar." For my part, of course, I would consider such an approach to be itself extremist, and opposed to the consistent and factual search in the course of the Council for a true "consensus," for always balancing *aggiornamento* with authentic tradition (those opposed to doing this were also deaf to any appeals to proceed in that direction, just as they were opposed to the very important work of "mending" carried out at the Council by Pope Paul VI).

But P. Huenermann, in the volume cited above, invoking the method of G. Gadamer, believes that "the event of the Council can be understood as the formation of Church practice that can be expressed conceptually as 'dialectic'" (as understood in the *Philosophical Investigations* of Ludwig Wittgenstein). This "topic", which ultimately makes possible a *consensus*, constitutes in a radically renewed form the fundamental movement made by the Council. It was a unitary movement, which tied together the innumerable single activities of the Council, inserting them into a flux which then produced as its result and fruit a new vision of the Church and of revelation. This new vision is a sediment in the Council documents themselves.

In this regard, I find that my thoughts on all this are confirmed by the Eastern Orthodox theologian Nico Nissiotis. I mention this before we go on to examine the development of *Lumen Gentium* itself. In the Vatican II volume edited by R. Fisichella, published under the auspices of the Central Committee of the Great Jubilee, one of the contributors, Y. Spiteris, notes that Nicos Nissiotis "made the point that the well-attested co-existence at the Council between the progressive and conservative tendencies made it possible for the Catholic Church to take great steps forward without undue shocks and traumatic injuries, and without excluding anyone from her communion. We find this very necessary kind of dialectic present in the principal conciliar documents such as *Lumen Gentium, Gaudium et Spes,* and *Unitatis Redintegratio.*" Personally, I see in the co-existence of the two major tendencies at the Council much more than just a simple juxtaposition of contraries; rather, in spite of all the differences, I see the dynamics of the dialectic and the dialogue that actually took place.

I add a further consideration coming from the same Orthodox theologian, and which can also be very useful for us, namely: "20 years later"—his comments were published in 1987—"the World Council of Churches, among others, has become very critical of the Vatican...They are disappointed because they expected from the Council a recognition of their Churches and priesthoods. But this recognition did not come about...Everybody went on evaluating the Council according to his own views and interests. Thus, evaluations that were made were limited to various aspects of the Council and generally failed to take in the whole. For in the case of the Council, we are dealing with an event that *was* very complex, and in which all of the various tendencies within Catholicism were obliged to co-exist." I cannot not agree with this! The complexity was also seen in the case of the Holy See's recent Declaration *Dominus Iesus.*

However that may be, in order to consider a brief history of *Lumen Gentium* and extend one's knowledge of it, I recommend, first of all, the concise summary volume of Annibale Zambarbieri entitled *The Vatican Councils* published in 1995 by the San Paolo Editions in Cinisello Balsamo (A review of this book is included in Chapter 4 of the present volume). From the beginning of the Council up to December 7, 1962 [the end of the First Session], what came to be called *Lumen Gentium* was the *schema* entitled *De Ecclesia,* which attracted much attention, both within the Council and outside. This *schema* consisted of 11 chapters, according to the document's *relator* (reporter), Bishop Franjo Franić. In reworking the *schema,* the Doctrinal Commission did not see itself as composing a complete treatise on the Church. Criticisms of the effort were not lacking, in fact, as was natural at a Council. It was widely considered that the original draft was too abstract and scholastic, and was lacking in the pastoral, universalist, and ecumenical spirit desired by Pope John XXIII when he convoked the Council. This original draft was quite reticent on the subject of episcopal collegiality as well. It was Cardinal Döpfner, followed by Cardinal Suenens, and then Archbishop Jaeger and even Archbishop Wojtyla, who urged that next to the idea of the Church as "the Mystical Body of Christ," vision "the People of God" should also be emphasized. This latter idea would take hold at the Council, and in the period following it, and would represent an important shift of perspective, perhaps too much so when viewed in a sociological context. The Melchite Bishop George Hakim, however, among other Council Fathers, considered the *schema* to be too "juridical."

Many Council Fathers nevertheless showed themselves to be favorable to the *schema*, even while other projects were increasingly coming before the Council. I can cite in this regard the idea of Cardinal Suenens to divide up the Council's work between internal questions, *ecclesia ad intra*, and external questions, *ecclesia ad extra*. Or again, there was the viewpoint of Cardinal Montini to the effect that the Council "lacked, or at any rate has not manifested, any overall organic ideal and logical plan on which to proceed." There were several expressions of concern, in fact, that the Council lacked an overall organic plan on the basis of which it could move forward. And this was the case, even though Pope John XXIII had approved the earlier draft of *De Ecclesia*, suggesting only minor changes in some details. Cardinal Lercaro of Bologna, though, added his adhesion to the Suenens-Montini request that the work of the Council be better organized; and a valuable contribution of his was to stress the mystery of Christ in the poor.

As a result of all these consolidation efforts, a total of some 20 subjects (later reduced to 17) were identified out of the 72 initial subjects—which sometimes up to that point were considered chapters of the same *schema*. Also, the primarily pastoral intent of the Council's work was reaffirmed. By this time, the jargon terms of "majority" and "minority" had come into use, referring to the existing innovative and conservative tendencies respectively. The risk here was for an artificial simplification of a reality that was much more complex and involved various convergences and divergences constantly in flux. What then came about, in fact, were the *clichés* of "two theologies" and "two ecclesiologies." These simplifications tended to weigh quite unfavorably on the work of the Council and on that of the theologians; it contributed to a conciliar hermeneutic that was simply not correct.

But to go on with the brief "history" of *Lumen Gentium* that chiefly concerns us here, in the meeting of January 23, 1963, of the Council's Central Coordinating Commission, Cardinal Suenens suggested a division of *De Ecclesia* into four chapters. This proposal was thoroughly debated, especially as far as the question of episcopal collegiality was concerned, thus confirming the centrality of this ecclesiological question at the Council. It was decided to introduce a chapter on the religious life into the document, and, later (on October 29), one on the Blessed Virgin Mary. This last proposal risked losing the "majority" (only 1114 *placet* as against 1074 *non placet* –that is a rejection).

The revision of the document—and we must be careful about what terms we employ here—was then given over to the Doctrinal Commission, which itself was divided into subcommissions. The basic text to be revised consisted of the most characteristic material selected from the original *schema* and from some other sources. This revision was basically the work of the theologian Monsignor Gérard Philips from Louvain. It is to be noted that he himself said that some 60 percent of the reworked *schema* was taken from the earlier draft.

At the Second Session of the Council there was a new pope as well as a new *edition altera recognita* of the Regulation of the Council. I take note here with reference to you laity, that it was at this point that the participation of lay experts in the work of the Council became officially approved; lay *auditores* would henceforth be able to attend all the conciliar meetings.

Through all of this, ecclesiology acquired a privileged position at the Council, and the revised *schema*, after two meetings, finally achieved the necessary "consensus" (2231 *placet* votes, out of 2301 voting members, in favor of going on with the plan of debating each chapter. The debate on the chapter on the hierarchy began on October 4, 1963; in this debate the divergences among the Council Fathers became more clearly manifest. An indication of this was the votes on the inquiry concerning the fundamental direction of the Council. It was on October 29 that a series of questions on this subject were presented for a vote (revised from an initial list of questions that had been originally suggested by Father Giuseppe Dossetti). There were eventually five questions presented, in all, including a vote asking for directions on the subject of the revival of the permanent diaconate. The destruction of the prepared ballots ordered by the pope on this occasion brought about the removal of the co-opted yet not forseen secretary to the group of Moderators of the trusted assistant to Cardinal Lercaro, Father Dossetti; contrary to the Regulation, he had created an alternative channel by-passing the authority of the Secretary General of the Council, Archbishop Pericle Felici. The pope himself remarked apropos of this: "This is not the place for Father Dossetti."

Following the reclassification and rearrangement of the various *schemata* that took place between Second and Third Sessions in accordance with the so-called Döpfner plan, the very important conciliar Central Coordinating Commission then made some new recommendations on such subjects as sacramentality and episcopal collegiality; these recommendations were in strict accord with the Constitution *Pastor Aeternus* of Vatican Council I.

There also came about at this time the transformation of the verb *est* into the verb *subsistit in*, referring to "the sole Church of Christ" that "subsists in the Catholic Church" (*Lumen Gentium* 8). This was a development destined to have great importance in post-conciliar ecumenism; much ink has been expended about it by commentators on the Council; one need think in this connection only of the intervention by Cardinal Ratzinger at the recent conference in Rome on the theme of the great Synod, or in the document *Dominus Iesus*, about which the cardinal gave his important interview in the *Frankfurter Allgemeine*. It is also worth mentioning here the rather negative initiative taken at the beginning of September, 1964, in which a number of influential Council Fathers, including many cardinals headed by Cardinal Arcadio Larraona, showed themselves to be quite critical of the doctrine of episcopal collegiality in a strict sense. But Pope Paul VI, respectful of the conciliar Regulation, let such developments concerning the *schema* play themselves out. When the vote on it came, there was a triple choice of *placet, non placet,* or *placet iuxta modum.* The pope continued, meanwhile, with his efforts to achieve a harmonious *consensus* during the Third Session, as he explained in his inaugural pontifical allocution of September 14 (see AS III/1, pp. 140-151).

If the voting on the first two chapters of the *schema* on the Church (that is, on the Church as "mystery" and as "People of God") were "easy," the vote on the third chapter on the subject of the hierarchy brought about a veritable drawing up of the opposing ranks of the majority and the minority at the Council which were by then well defined. We shall not pursue this debate in detail, although it was an interesting one. We shall instead turn to the *Nota Explicativa Praevia* that was brought forward during a very difficult week at the Council. The journalists styled it "Black Week," in fact [referring to the final week of the Third Session in 1964]. Today, with a bit of perspective, we can see that this week was decisive for the Council: it was required in order to make possible and finally reach a *consensus* and harmonization between *aggiornamento* and tradition at the Council. It would be worthwhile re-reading the text of this *Nota*, but we do not have the time here. Let it suffice for me to mention the concept of *hierarchical communion*, a concept connoting both reality and mystery, a concept exemplified in the history of both the First and Second Millennium of the Church—a concept which is very necessary for the Church to clarify today. My second point about the *Nota*, which for me is decisive, is the declaration of Monsignor Gérard Philips himself that there is no contradiction whatsoever between the text of the conciliar document and that of the *Nota*. It is worthwhile adding that even Father Edward Schillebeeckx, O.P., considered the *Nota* to be a necessary clarification, explaining the terms of the document itself so as to remove the confusion exhibited by many interested in promoting an idea of collegiality that would not be in harmony with the Catholic tradition; according to Schillebeeckx, some of these same people were deliberately promoting a variant idea of collegiality.

Lumen Gentium ended up with eight chapters, as follows: The Mystery of the Church; The People of God; The Church Is Hierarchical; The Laity; The Call to Holiness; Religious; The Pilgrim Church; and Our Lady. Of these chapters, the call to holiness, for example was specified as universal; that of the Pilgrim Church described in particular her eschatological nature as sojourning on the earth while united with the Church in heaven; and that of Our Lady treated the Virgin Mary, the Mother of God, in relation to the mystery of Christ and the Church. The definitive vote on this Constitution proved to be, I would say, virtually unanimous, and this was a perfectly extraordinary outcome when the opposition to the *schema* that emerged in the course of the debate is considered. It was to the very great credit of Pope Paul VI that this outcome was achieved. Pope Paul was decidedly not, as he himself had remarked on one occasion, merely the simple "notary" for the Council Fathers.

In the final part of my lecture, I would like to delineate briefly the main points of *Lumen Gentium* which have particular reference to you laity—whom have come out to hear me this evening. The fundamental theological elements concerning the laity are contained in Chapter IV of the Constitution, although we must keep in mind that Chapter II on the People of God and Chapter V on the universal vocation to holiness also bear upon the laity in an important sense. But let us begin with the Council's definition: "The term 'laity' is here understood to mean all the faithful except those in Holy Orders and those who belong to a religious state approved by the Church. That is, the faithful who by baptism are incorporated into Christ, are placed in the People of God, and in their own way share in the priestly, prophetic, and kingly office of Christ, and to the best of their ability carry on the mission of the whole Christian people in the Church and in the world" (LG 31).

Notwithstanding this initial rather negative and exclusionary definition of the laity, the intention of the Council Fathers was eminently positive, as is seen in their general approach and in what follows this definition, namely, that every baptized Christian participates in the *munera*, or offices of Christ, and in that respect, are not differentiated from those in the hierarchy, or religious life, nor do they participate at a more limited level of Christian existence, although they are distinguished by being engaged in "secular activities" (*Ibid.*). But this does not arise out of some characteristic that is added in the case of the laity and extends beyond their baptism, but rather arises from that baptism. That which distinguishes them from the non-laity and confers on them a positive situation is in fact common to all of the faithful, but it is not exercised in the case of the non-laity because the latter are removed from secular pursuits because of their particular charisms and ministries.

"But by reason of their special vocation, it belongs to the laity to seek the kingdom of God by engaging in temporal affairs and directing them according to God's will" (*Ibid.*). They are "closely associated... with temporal things...so that these may be affected and grow according to Christ and may be to the glory of the Creator and Redeemer" (*Ibid.*). "Even by their secular activity they [the laity] must aid one another to greater holiness of life so that the world may be filled with the spirit of Christ and may the more effectively attain its destiny in justice, love, and in peace" (LG 36). The text emphasizes the apostolic work of you laity (LG 33), as it does your witness to faith, hope and charity, particularly in social and family life (LG 31 and 35), and, especially, your "precious" activities in fostering evangelization. You are called to be the soul of the world, witnesses the resurrection and the life of the Lord Jesus and a sign of the living God (LG 38). Do you recall the Letter of Diognetus? What the soul is to the body, that is what Christians are to the world; they are the leaven in the dough. In particular, the Council exhorts you to realize that your competence in worldly disciplines and your secular activities, elevated in an intrinsic way by the grace of Christ, may result in effective work so that goods created through human and technical efforts and civil culture may be more justly distributed for the utility of men and society.

The conciliar text does not ignore the relationship between the laity and the hierarchy (LG 37); among other things, the pastors are invited to recognize and promote the dignity and responsibility of the laity in the Church (LG 32 and 37) and to make use willingly of the prudent counsels of the laity (LG 37), "always with truth, courage, and prudence and with reverence and charity towards those who, by reason of their office, represent the person of Christ" (*Ibid.*). The pastors should leave to the laity "freedom and scope for acting," encouraging them "to undertake works on their own initiative" (*Ibid.*).

On the other hand, "like all Christians the laity should promptly accept in Christian obedience what is decided by the pastors, who as teachers and rulers of the Church represent Christ" (LG 37).

30

Saving Truth (*Dei Verbum* 11): An Explanatory Note

In *Dei Verbum* 11 is God testified to as himself the cause of our salvation, or, rather, did God, "for the sake of our salvation" confide his truth "to the Sacred Scriptures"?

L'Osservatore Romano for November 22-23, 1965, published the Italian version of the text of Vatican II's Dogmatic Constitution on Divine Revelation, *Dei Verbum*. Number 11 of Chapter III of this document, dealing with the subject of divine inspiration and its interpretation, reads in the original Latin as follows: "*Inde Scripturae libri veritatem, quam Deus nostrae salutis causa litteris sacris consignari voluit, firmiter, fideliter, et sine errore doceri profitendi sunt*" ["The books of Scripture firmly, faithfully, and without error teach that truth which God for the sake of our salvation wished to see confided to the sacred Scriptures"]. The Italian translation, however, was done in a way that could not but interest us greatly, as follows: "Therefore, since…the truth that God, the cause of our salvation, wished to see confided to the sacred Scriptures."

There was a *peritus* (expert) from the Council's Doctrinal Commission—we know this from a note recorded by Archbishop Pericle Felici, Secretary General of the Council, which was dated November 24, 1965—who asked the Secretariat to clarify that the phrase "*nostrae salutis causa*" has to be translated "for the sake of our salvation." because the phrase could not be considered an attribute of the subject of the sentence, *Deus* (God), but rather had to be a complement of *veritatem*, truth—the truth that God had confided to the sacred "Letters" (Scriptures) for the sake of our salvation (see *Acta Synodalia*, Vol. VI, Part IV, pp. 648ff., edited by V. Carbone).

In truth, the Latin text, as it was printed in the fascicle provided to the Council Fathers themselves for their public meeting of November 18, 1965, allowed for both translations, which made possible two different meanings. Thus did the question arise concerning which translation should be adopted as the Council's official meaning.

If we seek to obtain the answer to this question by examining the fascicle containing the various *modi* or amendments offered—recall all the approvals voted under the heading of *placet iuxta modum*—we encounter the similar question of the *veritas salutaris*, the "saving truth," or "salvific truth," which God confided to the sacred Scriptures. In this latter case, 184 Council Fathers asked that the adjective *salutaris* (salvific, saving) be removed, while 73 of them proposed another reading, namely: "*veritatem qua, Deus, nostrae salutis causa libris sacris consignare*" ["The truth which God, the cause of our salvation, wished to confide to the sacred books"].

The Doctrinal Commission clarified the matter, stating that the word "*salutaris*" (salvific) "did not in any way suggest that sacred Scripture was not integrally inspired." This was what preoccupied many minds at the time, including especially those of the Council Fathers who were proposing the amendments just mentioned above. Cardinal Bea himself understood this (see AS, Vol. V., Part III, p. 465-466 ff). But in order "to avoid any possible abuse of interpretation," the Doctrinal Commission recommended the adoption of the amendment proposed by the 73 Council Fathers in such a way that the final text then read "*cum ergo...veritatem quam Deus nostrae salutis causa litteris sacris consignari voluit*," [as this has already been quoted and translated above].

Archbishop Felici observed concerning all this that "perhaps the mind of the Commission (taking into account what Father Tromp, its secretary, said) was to state that the truth was confided to the sacred Scriptures for the sake of our salvation, but that meaning, objectively speaking, was not in fact clearly stated, either in the final text or in the fascicle with the amendments, because attention was not being paid to the fact that the phrase *nostrae salutis causa* was susceptible of a double meaning" (*Ibid.* p. 649).

Archbishop Felici went on to say in his note that His Eminence the Cardinal Secretary of State [Amleto Cicognani] "in a letter dated October 18 to the Doctrinal Commission notified the Commission that he had been charged by the Holy Father to raise the question whether the elimination of the phrase *veritas salutaris* should not be considered in order not to allow the possibility of false interpretations being made concerning the inerrancy of the sacred books." Archbishop Felici then concluded: "This being the case, the opinion is that no clarification should be made; this was also the opinion of Father Sebastian Tromp, the secretary of the Doctrinal Commission" (*Ibid.*).

We know that this note of Archbishop Felici's was forwarded by its author to Pope Paul VI himself (the same day it was written). The pope, though, decided that the opinion of the Doctrinal Commission itself should be sought, and hence a query to this effect was sent to Cardinal Ottaviani on October 29 (see AS, Vol. V, Part III, pp. 635f.). The latter replied in the following terms: "In the expression, *'Deus nostrae salutis causa,'* the word *'causa'* is not nominative, but is ablative and is therefore not an attribute of *'Deus,'* and thus must be translated 'for the sake of our salvation.'" He added: "However, it does not seem opportune to publish any kind of rectification...leaving the remedy to show up in the definitive edition containing the Italian text, which will be published by the Vatican Polyglot Press" (AS, Vol. V., Part III, p. 641).

In a later annotation by Archbishop Felici made *ex audientia* (that is, as a result of an audience granted by Pope Paul VI on December 6, 1965), we learn that the pope decided on a correction of the text of the edition to be published by the Vatican Polyglot Press; in this later annotation it was added that "it will be seen in the future whether a note of clarification is called for" (AS, Vol. V, Part IV, note on p. 649). In this same Part IV of the *Acta Synodalia* (p. 756), we discover the final outcome of the whole question—which was not a trivial matter. This outcome is recorded in a letter from Father Tromp dated January 14, 1966, addressed to Archbishop Felici, in which it is officially communicated to the latter that there should be three important corrections to be made in the definitive text of the Dogmatic Constitution on Divine Revelation. The third of these corrections concerned our question here, precisely, and the decision was to regard *causa* in Latin as an ablative (hence, "for the sake of"), "so that no unprofitable disputes may arise."

Those who might wish to delve more deeply into the earlier instance of the debate, that is, over the question of "salvific truth" or "saving truth"—which had brought to the fore the question of what grammatical case was involved in the phraseology of *Dei Verbum*—the question which attracted my attention and motivated this Explanatory Note, may be referred to the *Notulae* of Monsignor G. Philips of the conciliar Doctrinal Commission (see the pertinent *adnexa* in the *Acta Synodalia:* Vol. VI. Part III, pp. 465ff.; and for the pertinent *modi*, or amendments, p. 467). The *adnexa* in question were forwarded to Paul VI by Cardinal Ottaviani. There will be found there also a debate on "the historicity of the Gospels."

Perhaps it is worth recalling here, in order to indicate the conciliar continuity which characterized the *aggiornamento* desired by the Blessed John XXIII, that even the Council of Trent referred to the Gospel as "the fount of every saving truth and of discipline as well" (Denz. 738-1501).

We conclude this Explanatory Note by referring back to the key word "salvation." Its various meanings pointed to the proper way for the Council to proceed as well—always an interesting consideration. There certainly does appear to be a link between truth and salvation, which I believe forms the fundamental nucleus of Christian thought, whether of salvation or of liberation. Then there is the Gospel saying, "You will know the truth and the truth will make you free" (Jn 8:32), so often echoed in the teaching of Pope John Paul II.

However, I hope these brief observations may provide a motivation to go back and revisit the Second Vatican Council. The Council was the "door" to the great Jubilee. The examples given here testify to the great wisdom and delicacy which these kinds of issues were treated by the Council. The concrete case we have considered in particular does honor both to the Council and to its protagonists. How it unfolded also testifies to the great care and solicitude which the great "manager" that Paul VI proved himself to be in more than one way, and certainly with respect to the way he navigated the waters in the coordination and direction that he gave to the Council. We find in all this a confirmation of the conciliar rule that goes back all the way to the primitive Council of Jerusalem, and is crystallized in the words "that it has seemed good to the Holy Spirit and to us" (Acts 15: 28).

In this regard, allow me to cite in conclusion another passage from *Dei Verbum* which shows how "connected and associated" are sacred Scripture, sacred Tradition, and the Magisterium of the Church. The passage in question is the conclusion of *Dei Verbum* Chapter II; it reads: "It is clear...that in the supremely wise arrangement of God, sacred Tradition, sacred Scripture, and the Magisterium of the Church are so connected and associated that one of them cannot stand without the others. Working together, each in its own way under the action of the one Holy Spirit, they all contribute effectively to the salvation of souls." (DV 10).

31

The Ministry of the Pope
in Ecumenical Perspective
(Vatican I and Vatican II
and the Encyclical *Ut Unum Sint*)

The title of this chapter is the one of the *Acts* of a colloquy held on this subject in Milan on April 16-18, 1998. Edited by Antonio Acerbi, these *Acts* were published in 1999 by *Vita e Pensiero* ["Life and Thought"] in Milan. They represent a new and solid contribution to the reflections that have been inspired by John Paul II's 1995 encyclical *Ut Unum Sint* ["That They May be One."]. They deal with the exercise of the primacy, but rather than treating this question *ad extra*, that is, primarily in connection with the Church's possible future relations with non-Catholic Churches and ecclesial Communities, they tend to focus on the exercise of the primacy within the Catholic Church herself. There are even a number of comments that call into question the biblical-traditional foundations of the primacy, its functioning, and, indeed, its very existence—contrary to what the encyclical itself plainly says about it. Much of what is said about the primacy by the scholars participating in this colloquy, in our way of thinking, could well apply to the Church's relations *ad extra*, but not to those *ad intra*. Moreover, in the desire to achieve ecumenical progress, renewed by the very serious appeal of Pope John Paul II, we must not lose sight of what is specifically Catholic, even with respect to the primacy. This primacy was significantly developed during the second millennium, especially where dogma was concerned, even though the reality of the pope as the Latin Patriarch was nevertheless not lost from sight, either; but meanwhile, as a result of the missionary impulse, the Latin rite came to be practiced throughout the entire world.

The theme of the patriarchates, and the many comments made about them in this Milanese colloquy, are many and are quite properly worthy of note. The special problems in these *Acts* to which I make reference, however, are clearly evident in the introduction and even more so in the conclusion of Acerbi's work (pp. 303-338). What stands at the base of his whole way of proceeding, in fact, is his conviction that one must enter into what he calls a "transition phase...beginning in the first place with Catholics," in order to arrive at a final stage, at the creation, that is, of a "world Christian consensus." He envisages perhaps "a pan-Christian council and an increasingly wide acceptance of an agreement to be forged at first among a number of Churches" (p. 3). To validate such an approach and point of view, this editor identifies in Vatican I what he calls "a single traditional line which is recognizable from the most ancient times in the history of the Church in Rome...but which is not the only line" (p. 5). This is the case because, in the first millennium, "the structure of ecclesial communion was synodal and polycentric; and this was the case in such a way that the authority of the Roman See found itself immersed in a system that was organic and organized from the bottom up" (*Ibid.*).

For us Catholics, however, the position of the Roman See was always inherent in the system, and the second millennium simply witnessed a development of what had been the case in the first millennium. With regard to the primacy, which remains our treasure, it was given by Christ to the Church, as we say, and represents an indispensable contributing factor to the internal cohesion of Catholicism. It now offers itself as a service of unity to all Christians— possibly through a new way of exercising the primacy as far as non-Catholics are concerned. For us, the opinion of Acerbi constitutes the fundamental plan for building the house—allow me this figure of speech!—"from the top down."

In this Colloquy, G. Wenz furnishes "An Evangelical Perspective," according to which "in view of an authentic unity of the Christian

Churches, it should be considered sufficient for the Gospel, rightly understood, to be preached and for the sacraments to be administered according to the Word of God" (p. 9). Again: "The canon [of Sacred Scripture]" needs to be "the criterion for any form of apostolic succession" (p. 11). As for what directly relates to the Petrine service and the papal ministry, Wenz distinguishes between them (p. 23), noting, however, "that already very early there was manifested a particular respect for the community of Rome; this became evident when, according to the model of the monarchical episcopate, there was attributed to the bishop of Rome a special relationship with the apostle and martyr, Peter, and with his apostolic service in favor of the unity of the apostles which is brought out in the Bible" (p. 24). Today, therefore, "it should not be disputed that the bishop of Rome occupies a special position...The alternatives, a 'Petrine service' that can be affirmed, a 'papal ministry' that must be denied, cannot be absolutely discounted, nor is this inevitable. Hence a ministry belonging to the pope can be recognized in principle, even in an evangelical context, as an ecclesiological form arising out of the Petrine function that was inherent in the apostle's own position" (*Ibid.*).

We believe, however, that this kind of statement represents the maximum that our evangelical brothers today are able to concede. We are confirmed in this judgment by the judgment that Wenz himself renders on the two Vatican Councils, on the *Nota Explicativa Praevia*, on infallibility, and on the pope's universal primacy of jurisdiction (pp. 25-30). It is to be noted, however, how a distinction is made "between the administrative rights and functions of the pope in his capacity as patriarch of the Latin Church, and his service of unity for the universal Church" (p. 29).

B. Pseftongas, however, presents the Eastern Orthodox position, which is very well known, and nothing new about it is revealed here. We do find two points of particular interest in the thought of this author, however, and hence they are worth special attention. The first of these points tends to cancel out the myth of the first millennium, when there supposedly existed an almost idyllic form of unity between the Christian East and West. In fact, during that era "unity was threatened in various ways, most of them well known to us today…However, the impulse towards unity resisted the obstacles encountered and focused on the one faith, the common dogmas, and the institution of synods of bishops who met with each other. This institution…characterized the pentarchy of five patriarchates" (p. 47).

The author's second important point, more personal, relates to this evaluation of "the small importance," in the current ecclesiastical situation, placed upon "research into the history of the period that aims at resolving the problems that are outstanding today" (p. 49; then see n. 19 on p. 71). The author goes on to speak of what he calls his profound respect for "the choices that history has made or that divine Providence has foreseen with regard to each Church today" (p. 49). Naturally, we cannot agree with Pseftongas about this.

"Synods, Patriarchates, and the Roman Primacy from the First to the Third Millennia" is the title of the intervention of the well-known Professor V. Peri. "Concerning the primacy, it is necessary to speak about it with other Christians and not merely in the way it has been in the past. The substance of the ancient doctrine is one thing…its reformulation today is something else. New formulations are required in this case, and also new forms for its canonical and spiritual exercise." In accordance with this premise, the author reminds us that "one cannot speak about the primacy without also speaking about the synodal system, the conciliar system, the hierarchy, and authority in general."

However, "the common tradition of the first millennium…can furnish significant conceptual and organizational schemes that are indispensable to the launching of a new ecclesial pluralism" (p. 55), where "a sense of unity would co-exist with the diversity of the various ecclesial expressions of the Churches" (p. 56). In this perspective, "the history of the Church is the indispensable instrument for any legitimate search for a theology of Christian unity" (pp. 58 and 71, n. 19, and 72ff.).

Moving from a "lexicon and historical phenomenology of the primatial function in the Church," and distinguishing *auctoritas* from *potestas*, Peri underlines "the persistence from the very beginning of a hierarchical structure geared to the integral transmission of the Gospel, and to the exercise of a concrete oversight concerning the collective fidelity to the *depositum fidei* in both doctrine and practice, and thus to the effective guidance, governance, and judgments of the community of the faithful" (p. 70).

He then goes on to examine "the apostolic succession in the historical forms arising out of the synodal constitution of the Church"; he pays particular attention to the Pentarchy and to what he calls the patriarchate of the West ("the title of Patriarch is preserved today in the Lateran palaces"). He concludes by saying that "the bishop of Rome understood himself to be one—although the first—of the five patriarchs of the *'oecumene,'* as this was understood in the Justinian Code of Laws. The Petrine charism of the unity of all the Churches, and of their visible communion, was both affirmed and vindicated, but it was exercised in diverse ways and in different ecclesial localities" (p. 81).

Peri then analyzes "the conditions according to which a council might be received...as ecumenical; they appeared to be canonically fixed, given certain conditions of fact and rights, as well as the dogmatic conditions of doctrine." He deals with "the presence and the 'personal' collaboration of the pope of Rome with the councils and also as he was represented by others or through letters, or through an expression of agreement with the acts of the councils, along with that of the other patriarchs of the Christian *oecumene*...On the other hand, harmony was required in the case of the definitions and prescriptions concerning the dogmas and doctrines decided upon in the series of preceding councils as they were diffused and universally applied in the Churches." (p. 89).

"Political Ideas and *Plenitudo Potestatis* from the Gregorian Era to the Eighteenth Century" is the focus of the contribution of Klaus Schatz. He examines the jurisdiction of the Church, comparing it with the political constitutions of secular kingdoms. But he concludes that "the 'absolutist' conception (that is, all power in the Church concentrated in the pope) was not developed out of or along with political developments"

(p. 101). He further states that "conciliarism did not presuppose only the political ideas of the time" (p. 104). He goes on to claim, rather too easily, that "the classic period for the transference of secular models of governance to those of the Church was the fifteenth century" (p. 106). This is questionable. And why try to restrict the ideas of Ultramontanism and Gallicanism to "the absolute or constitutional monarchies prevailing between the sixteenth and eighteenth centuries" (*Ibid.*)? Why continue down the same road of trying to see everything in today's terms, now that "what interests us more today is to understand where...the democratic element comes in" (p. 107)? When will it finally be understood that the Church is not a monarchy, either absolute or constitutional, nor is she a democracy? The Church is something different from any of these models: she is the Church.

T. Pruegel writes about "The Decree *Haec Sancta* of the Council of Constance and Its Reception by the Council of Basel." He states that the history of its interpretation and of its reception cannot be said to be conclusive" (p. 111). However, he does say that the Decree "was born of necessity" (p.113) and is "ambivalent" (p. 114) on the question of whether it was drafted in support of or in opposition to the papacy. The author goes on to say: "It seems that its unique aim was to give to the assembly gathered at the Council of Constance full jurisdictional powers only to bring an end to the Great Schism" (p. 115), even though it added a "however," when speaking of the reform of the Church *in capite et membris*. It was thus a compromise, a "victory of pragmatism." An appeal in favor of this conclusion is made to the work of W. Brandmüller, "considered today to be the foremost expert on the subject of the Council of Constance" (p. 116).

In any case, for Pruegel, the Decree in question represents "a fracture in the ecclesiology of the Latin Church" (*Ibid.*). To conclude he declares: "Up to our own days the opinion has been amply diffused that *Haec Sancta* was not proclaimed as a dogma, nor simply as an emergency measure, but rather it was a provision of canon law aimed at restoring the unity of the Church and effecting her reform in the most simple and secure way possible." Here again he quotes Brandmüller, and, less happily, Brian Tierney.

Following his examination of the Council of Basel, the author asserts that "it must be clearly recognized that the conciliar idea of the late medieval period failed because it insisted on its idea to an extensive degree. The Council of Basel became so fixated on the idea of a council as superior to a pope that it neglected to draw out adequately and place in relief its own theological foundations" (p. 127). What were the consequences of this? "The victorious papalists fought the exaggerations of the conciliarists, but in their fear of seeing the Church destabilized they allowed to fall into neglect certain valid ideas concerning the Church as 'conciliar.' They paid the price for this perhaps too high" (p. 128).

Marc Lienhard follows Pruegel with a contribution entitled "Protestant Reformers of the Sixteenth Century and the Papacy." He succeeds in making us see that their position was more nuanced than has generally been credited and also that it evolved in response to the developing situation and to the various diatribes being carried on. The author concludes that "even though they rejected the form which the papacy had assumed in the course of the centuries during which it had been developing, the Reformers did not exclude the idea of a reformed papacy. They envisaged a pastoral-type papacy which could function in harmony with the college of bishops; this papacy enjoyed a primacy of honor and would serve as a kind of spokesman for the college of bishops—but all of this was only on condition, of course, that it must carry out its ministry in fidelity to sacred Scripture" (p. 144).

H. J. Pottmeyer writes next on the subject of "The Influence of Political Thought on the Understanding of Vatican I and Its *Wirkungsgeschichte* in the Exercise of the Primacy." He continues along the same line as Schatz. For our part, it is sufficient to reaffirm the truth that it was not out of the concept of sovereignty that the primacy arose (see pp. 151-159). As for the minimalist and maximalist interpretations of Vatican I, "they cannot serve as the ultimate criteria, valid for all times, according to this author (p. 147). Moreover, the origin of the *plenitudo potestatis* is treated ideologically by him, and not according to its historical *substratum*—and this by an author who has covered this ground many times. What does it mean to say that "the theorists of Ultramontanism and the Church of Rome effectively assumed that the pope was an absolute sovereign" (p. 159)? Can it really be said that for the Dogmatic Preparatory Commission for Vatican I, "the Church constituted an absolute monarchy for the papacy"? (*Ibid.*). Actually, the answer to this question was provided by the German Bishops themselves in response to the similar question posed by Otto von Bismarck (p. 163). Pottmeyer himself reports on this. The viewpoint of the bishops was confirmed (and ours as well) by the declaration that Pope Pius IX made in response to the German bishops. Why then try to go on with the conclusion that this response did not "prevent maximalist interpretations in the years that followed" (p. 163)?

The treatment then given to "the Definition of the Infallibility of the Papal Magisterium" goes even further off the track. Laying out three interpretations of Vatican I—maximalist, intermediate, and a third way—the author opts for the third way, which he says "corresponds to that of the minority present at Vatican I" (p. 165). And for this author, this position was "confirmed by Vatican II." He writes: "In reality, the unilateral nature of the definition of Vatican I was in no way modified. However, the dogma of the infallibility of the papal magisterium came to be integrated into an ecclesiology of *communio*" (p. 166). The author is playing a game of hide-and-seek here, because he does not mention that the *communio* in question is a *hierarchical communion*. However, the author's personal and partial explanations of "sovereignty," "absolutism," and "Ultramontanism" do not square with Vatican II (nor with the *Nota Explicativa Praevia* in particular) nor with post-conciliar views. All this is brought out more clearly in the author's final *Wirkungsgeschichte* (pp. 166ff.).

In a long and rather well thought out essay, A. Zambarbieri writes about "A Problematic Service," namely, the service of unity offered by the papacy in the world of today. The summary on page 172 is quite well done; it lays out especially well the question of "temporalization," which was "imposed by the prevailing ideas of the times for which a merely spiritual authority was inconceivable" (p. 175). After a certain amount of attention given to Vatican I, the author treats the subject of the papacy in contemporary Catholicism, and generally with a good enough result, although with respect to the question of Modernism, he asks if a more in-depth treatment might be desirable (see p.88).

Quite original and again rather well done is his treatment of the papacy and the new types of world "communication," and, especially, of the new worldwide "political" dimension of the contemporary papal ministry. There are schools of thought today which incline towards considering even the merely "human" value of the universal pontifical ministry to be important; the Holy See's actions fit into today's world outlook quite well (see pp. 206ff.), although the author does not soft-pedal the continuing ecumenical difficulties. One thinks, for example, of the opinions of L. Vischer on the subject of the diplomacy of the Holy See today; but then those of P. A. D'Avack and Samuel Huntington certainly have to be viewed in a contrary vein (pp. 209ff.).

The next contribution by H. Legrand, however, appears to us to be quite extreme and excessive; he is intentionally quite critical [of the Holy See] and we believe unjustly so (p. 221). In effect, he wants to expand or enlarge the concept of episcopal collegiality to all the Churches, thus "Protestantizing" them (see pp. 216-217 and 220). This entails the loss of both universality and specificity, without making any distinctions between collegiality as understood in a broad or in a narrower sense (p. 223). Also, in whatever *communio ecclesiarum* that might eventually be brought about, the Catholic Church must preserve her own identity; this is demanded by Vatican II itself; but Legrand cites the "theological limits" of the Council instead, naturally from his own point of view (pp. 212ff, and 221ff.). More than that, he leaves out the two elements whose positions are defined in traditional language as *de iure divino*, namely, the pope and the bishops in their respective dioceses. Instead, he focuses on intermediate elements (see pp. 218-221 and 224-227). In his way of thinking, he opposes the movement that was already evident in the first millennium by which the pope was appealed to precisely as the defender of the bishops (in relation to their metropolitans, for example). One encounters in Legrand's account also the usual criticisms of titular bishops and of the current procedures by which bishops are named (p. 216ff.)—not to speak of his criticisms of the Code of Canon Law (p. 217), which, according to him, fails to "articulate the concepts of the *collegium episcoporum* and the *communio ecclesiarum*."

We have further grave reservations—and we are apparently not alone in having them (see pp. 281 and 294)—with regard to what is said about "overcoming the problem of a double meaning, inadequately distinguished, between the 'supreme' and the 'full' power of the pope over the Churches." The author thinks "it is necessary to re-read Vatican I."

The next study, by A. Maffeis on "The Ministry of Unity for the Universal Church in Ecumenical Dialogue," is a very good one. This exposition, very well focused, deals with the four common points of view that are prevalent today in treating the primacy in ecumenical dialogue; these four points are: the biblical ("the Petrine function"); the historical ("historical development and *ius divinum*"); the ecclesiological ("a ministry of unity for the universal Church"); and the practical ("a restructuring of the way in which the primacy is exercised"). Here again, as far as we are concerned, it should have been impossible to leave out the distinction already mentioned above, namely, between the exercise of the primacy *ad intra*, internally, or *ad extra*, externally. Making this distinction would have clarified what the author says about "the possibility of reaching an understanding concerning the primacy": he sees this possibility as based on overcoming what is called "the universalistic ecclesiology which has been dominant in the West since the days of the Gregorian Reform and which has deprived the local Church of possessing any theological significance," according to him (p. 259, and, again, p. 274). An ecclesiological harmony between the local and the universal Church must remain an important characteristic of a united Church. Some of the observations by L. Scheffczyk and W. Kasper which Maffeis quotes are very important in this regard.

With respect to what relates to "a restructuring of the way in which the primacy is exercised," the author opines that "it is certainly unacceptable to attempt an unhistorical 'return' to the origins of the

Church—a return which would ignore or cancel out the development which both the theory and practice of the primacy have undergone in the Occident" (p. 269). See also pages 296 and 300ff. for the treatment by G. Canobbio on the "essential aspects" of the papal ministry. We must bear in mind also what Joseph Ratzinger proposed in 1979, namely, that, "the East should cease to combat as 'heresy' developments in the West in the second millennium, and should accept the Catholic Church as orthodox and legitimate in the form she has assumed" (p. 269, n. 96). Moreover—if we are not going off the tracks in saying it, the distinction mentioned above concerning the *ad intra* and *ad extra* exercise of the primacy should be adopted; this would leave intact the question of the necessary examination in common of the way the primacy was exercised in the first millennium. On this subject, see once more the thought of G. Canobbio on page 300ff., which arises out of a reinterpretation of Vatican I. From page 270 on, Maffeis provides such a reinterpretation; he clarifies "the relationship between primacy and the patriarchates" (*Ibid.*), and he speaks of a possible papal "autolimitation"—which he sees as "a new way of exercising the papal ministry of unity" (pp. 271-275).

In the end, the author correctly observes "that the simple characterization of the primacy as 'pastoral,' or its definition in terms of 'charismatic leadership,' or even the underlining of its obvious character as a ministry of 'service', none of these amounts to an adequate response to the problem, since they all neglect the institutional structure of any real *communion*—or else they define it in such a weak way that it could not in any case ever be binding." Insofar as these elements might be considered new forms of the exercise of the papal ministry, however, they point to a "corrective" intention by comparison with the traditional Catholic model of the exercise of the primacy; but the element "constructive" nevertheless remains rather vague (p. 275).

G. Canobbio, in the contribution that comes next, treats "The Essential Aspects of a Dogmatic Teaching on the Papal Ministry." The notes he brings out prove to be almost more important than his actual text. His reflections are divided into three parts. He begins with methodological observations in order to bring out the doctrinal elements established by both Vatican I and Vatican II (particularly good in this regard are the nuances he discovers in comparing the teachings of the two Councils; see pp. 293-296). Then, he essays a re-reading in the light of the critical proposals that have been made as a result of the [post-Vatican II] ecumenical dialogue, or as a result of more recent research, in order to arrive at the "essential elements."

This author's way of proceeding is valid and constructive. We cannot go into detail concerning everything that he says, as we would like to do; it must suffice to indicate to the reader that the conclusions he reaches are particularly valuable, and that they are also very well balanced (see p. 300ff.).

A. Acerbi brings this Milan Colloquy to a close by launching an appeal for "a new form of the Petrine ministry." His text is in no way a panoramic representation of the interventions made at the Colloquy, but is rather a personal reflection on the current unlimited freedom and uncontrollable character of papal authority, as he sees it—in order to subject it to critical scrutiny. He returns to the ideas of an "absolute regime" or an "absolute papal monarchy," with confusion, ambivalence, and no little evidence of compulsion thereby. His criterion for reform, however, seems to be what he calls a "structural" episcopal collegiality; he considers himself in dialogue with both G. Colombo and G. Langevin, although this does not "resolve the question" for him.

We cannot tarry or linger to try to conduct a dialogue with this author, which would be very critical; we can only note that a decentralization legitimately carried out in the exercise of the primacy would be one thing, but simply dismantling it would be something else again. The same thing is true of the Latin patriarchate, which, on the model of the Eastern patriarchates, should remain intact. Perhaps the same thing would apply to the creation of any Anglican "patriarchate," or, eventually, one pertaining to other communions. In this regard, it is enough, while recognizing the personal preferences of this author in the various ways in which he issues his various judgments, to go back to the way indicated by the Council of Sardica. This would mean, in our view, that the relationship of the papacy to those Churches agreeing to re-establish Communion with Rome would not necessarily be the same as currently exists (*ad intra*) among the Churches already in communion with Rome. We end this review by simply indicating that Acerbi's proposal regarding the relations of a pope with a council seem to us even more problematical than some of his other views (see p. 334ff.).

32

Re-reading the Council Documents
(On the Role of the Pope)

Pottmeyer Hermann J., *Le rôle de la papauté au troisième millénaire. Une relecture de Vatican I et de Vatican II* [The Role of the Papacy in the Third Millennium: A Re-reading of Vatican I and Vatican II], Éditions du Cerf, Paris 2001, 188 pages.

This study came out as one of a number of studies produced recently in Catholic circles in response to Pope John Paul II's 1995 encyclical *Ut Unum Sint* on the Commitment of the Catholic Church to Ecumenism. It reconsiders the exercise of the papal primacy in the light of the pope's invitation to other Christian leaders regarding how the primacy might be better exercised from their point of view. The author of this study is H. J. Pottmeyer, who decided to "re-read" Vatican Councils I and II in response to the pope's invitation.

This slim volume, which originally appeared in English, illustrates the obstacles present today on the subject of any "ecumenical Petrine ministry," that is, one "susceptible of being recognized by all Christians as a gift of God to his Church." Naturally for Pottmeyer himself, "the first step should be taken by the Catholic Church herself" (p. 7). Here we encounter again, though, the same wearisome refrain about trying "to construct the house from the top down," because we should not anticipate a situation of union where one does not already exist; and the Catholic Church, meanwhile, has also the right to preserve her own "physiognomy," just as the other Churches and communions have that right as well, for that matter, in the case of any reunion that might possibly come about—certainly excluding, however, anything truly opposed to the *unitas in necessariis.*

Since the first obstacle to reunion, for many people, are "the dogmas of Vatican I, particularly those that were reaffirmed without modification by Vatican II," a re-reading of both Councils is called for. This author commits himself to undertaking such a re-reading. He begins with a chapter entitled "Challenges Calling for a New Dialogue on the Papacy." He then presents, in a way which seems quite one-sided and unilateral to us, Vatican I as a Council which did not take into account "the tradition of the communion that had existed during the first millennium" (p. 15). Vatican I was subject, he argues, to conditioning by the basic idea of "sovereignty," which was in vogue at that time. At the same time, however, "the social form of the Catholic Church has been profoundly modified in the twentieth century, having become more global" (p. 16).

This approach presents the same sociological hobgoblin that this author continually brings in whenever the "decisions" of Vatican II do not coincide with his own preferences. The idea of sovereignty is applied regularly by him as a principle, and supposedly it still rules today (see pp. 20, 46ff., 53, and, especially, 54, 57ff., 83ff., 120ff.,131, 133ff.,146, 148, 150, 153, and 171). But this approach amounts to an abdication of the real scholarly task before him in favor of "sociology" (see, also, pp. 77 and 15, on the subject of "the Catholic Ghetto"). We cannot but be highly critical of this approach. The same thing is true of some of the other subjects treated where an exaggerated vision of a Church "communion of particular Churches" results in a loss of a sense of the Church's universality.

Along the way, however, the author seeks to remove some misunderstandings which stand in the way of ecumenical dialogue. The first misunderstanding he takes up is that no reform of the papacy is possible which does not entail a relativization or abandonment of the normative character of the dogmas of Vatican I. However, the author claims that these dogmas are already "relative" from a certain point of view; and, in any case, they need not be considered "the only possible formulations" (p. 18). In fact, he says, "only those interpretations that have been specifically condemned can no longer be defended" (*Ibid.*). The second misunderstanding is that of believing that any reduction of Roman centralization would necessarily entail a weakening of the authority of the Petrine ministry. Rather, a distinction is possible here and has to be made between mere centralization and the exercise of the primacy in the true sense, focusing with wisdom on the concrete situation.

"From 'Witness' to 'Monarch'": a 'development' or a 'change' in the nature of the papal primacy"? The author examines this subject in the light of both the continuity and progress that would have accompanied any such development. However, Pottmeyer comes out in favor of a "break with venerable traditions" (see, for example, p. 31). For him, therefore, "it is not possible to discern a logical or organic continuity" (p. 24) in the primacy without bringing forward convincing proofs. This is supposedly the case the "deficiencies" in the forms in which the Petrine ministry has traditionally been expressed.

Certainly, we too can accept that there has been "a plurality of forms by which the Petrine ministry has been realized" (p. 24). In any case, it is not correct to radicalize the often-used expression that has been coined referring to the "papal monarchy" (p. 25). Nor can the author excuse himself by speaking of a "simplification." For him it is possible in any case to speak of "two paradigms concerning the consciousness that the Church has had of herself. The first has reference to the first millennium, the second to the second millennium. To each of these paradigms there is a corresponding conception and a specific realization of what the Petrine ministry has meant" (*Ibid.*). In the first, the role of the Church and papacy consisted of being "the guarantors and witnesses of the apostolic tradition" (*Ibid.*). (But the question then immediately arises: was this not true also in the case in the second millennium as well?) In this line of thoughts, "when the bishops emerged as the leaders and representatives of their local Churches, the particular situation which the Church of Rome enjoyed was transmitted to the authority of the bishop of Rome" (p. 26). Anyone who understands what is meant here knows what is implied in this kind of formulation, and what the "risks" are with this kind of approach.

However that may be, it is not possible to affirm with this author that it was only in the fifth century "that the bishop of Rome became the first among the bishops" (p. 26); nor does it make sense to refer to the *plenitudo potestatis* as applying in that era (see pp. 29, 31, 41, and 47), since this formula, in the beginning, referred only to the papal representatives in the Illyrian region (*vocatus in partem sollicitudinis*).

The formula had a long history and would have a longer one. The author, however, shows that he does not really understand this very well. He ignores completely the complicating factors arising out of the pseudo-Isidorian claims, which certainly influenced the exercise of the primacy and which deserve to be evaluated accordingly.

In this same vein of speaking about "the principle of supremacy," and thus of the unchangeableness of the tradition, Pottmeyer considers that "the collegiality of the bishops was the constitutive factor...as far as the apostolicity of the Church was concerned," and hence he concludes that "the unanimous testimony of the bishops had an authority greater than that of the pope by himself" (pp. 27, 34 and 89).

The author continues along the same lines: "It was a new paradigm for the Church to move to a monarchical primacy," entailing the same misunderstanding between the personal and the monarchical, and to this the idea of an "absolute" later became added, according to him (pp. 33, 48, 53ff., 61, 65) along with some other extraneous considerations (pp. 29-32). Among our many reservations concerning this particular account of things, we can at least speak positively about the thoughts included here concerning the role of the bishop of Rome as the patriarch of the West (p. 29), and also about some subsequent considerations that we shall note further on (see pp. 128 and 172ff.). In passing, however, we must repeat here what we have noted in other circumstances on this same subject, namely, that the dual role of the papacy becomes a positive factor when seeking new relationships with Churches and ecclesial communities that are currently not in full communion with us. Meanwhile, however, the traditional patriarchal rights and duties of the bishop of Rome remain operative in the region overseen by him as the Latin patriarch—even though the Latin Church has subsequently spread throughout the whole world as a result of the Western missionary impulse.

A subsequent step was what the author calls "the development that took place in the understanding of the primacy." By this he means that the Church gradually became more aware of the way in which she herself continually gave form to her own tradition in an active manner, by means of laws enacted and decisions adopted out of the necessities that arose" (p. 34). It was supposedly from this process that "the doctrine of the infallibility of the pope arose between the twelfth and sixteenth centuries" (p. 35). Given this conception, it should be added, in order to prevent misunderstandings, that the idea of a Roman See "without blemish" was not an idea of the second millennium.

There follows a chapter entitled "The Triple Traumas of Rome on the Eve of Vatican I." The first of these "traumas" concerned the consequences for the Church of Conciliarism, the Reformation, and Gallicanism. The second trauma was of a political nature and had to do with State Churches (*Staatskirchentum*) and the French Revolution. The third trauma was on an intellectual plane, and chiefly concerned rationalism, liberalism, and secularism. We cannot follow the author in what turns out to be his rather rambling treatment of all this; but it all certainly amounts to a "psychological" preparation of the reader in order to enable him to "understand" the process of the "conditioning" of the dogmas of Vatican I as well as their "unilateral" character (see, for example, esp. p. 73)—and also to understand the problem of Roman centralism. There is also an exaggerated tendency to see "parallels here between political developments and ecclesial developments" (pp. 44 and 46ff.) in what pertained to "the constitution of the Church" (p. 45).

With "Vatican I and the Pope's Primacy of Jurisdiction," the author arrives at the heart of his examination, following a long preamble on the subject of the Camaldolese Father Mauro Cappellari – later Pope Gregory XVI – and his thought. A great many things get mixed into this account, some of them of a rather disparate nature; there is included, for example, a presentation on the idea of "complex sovereignty" (pp.

60-65) of H. L. C. Maret, whose work was condemned at Vatican I.

However, the author admits that, in spite of the extreme Ultramontanism that was current—including that of Pope Pius IX himself (!)—the dogmatic conciliar text "does not define the primacy of jurisdiction as the sovereignty of an absolute monarch in the sense understood by Cappellari and Joseph de Maistre" (p 65). There is, then, what the author styles a "relative moderation" in the conciliar texts themselves; at the same time, though, the author speaks of "a maximalist interpretation of Vatican I that has held sway up to our own day, and which interprets the definition of the primacy of jurisdiction in a wholly unilateral way" (see, however, pp. 74 and 76), "in an Ultramontane sense" (p. 65). Pottmeyer recognizes, however, that "the desire of the bishops to see mentioned the fact that their college possessed a supreme jurisdiction was not accepted by the Council, nor was it rejected...There was, however, no question concerning their collegial co-responsibility for the universal Church." (pp. 67, 69, and 71). "The collegial cooperation of the episcopate in running the universal Church was not mentioned in the text" (p. 73ff.). Pottmeyer concludes, accordingly, that "the Council resisted the Ultramontane ideological pressures, and thus did not betray the original ecclesial and theological tradition concerning the episcopal and collegial constitution of the Church. The Council did not want to present the pope as a sovereign or an absolute monarch" (p. 79). Thus, according to this author, "Roman centralism cannot appeal theologically to Vatican I." The Council did not deny "the equally supreme authority of the college of bishops." More than that, "it made no affirmation to the effect that the jurisdiction of the bishops proceeded directly from that of the pope" (*Ibid.*).

From this and from some other considerations, the author deduces that "Vatican I was open, and was not an obstacle to the ecclesiology of communion which Vatican II attempted to formulate, and by which it hoped to reconnect to the tradition of the undivided Church of the first millennium" (p. 79). If we are not denying that the communion in question here is a "hierarchical communion," then we can agree with the author. Nevertheless, the true concept of collegiality still remains to be clarified, that is, whether or not we are taking it in a broad or in a narrow sense.

The Chapter entitled "Vatican I and the Infallibility of the Papal Magisterium" starts off with what the author styles the Pyrrhic victory of the maximalist interpretation of the dogma of papal infallibility. This, it is noted, "is not accepted by a majority of Catholics in many countries" (p. 81), certainly not in its "maximalist interpretation." The case of Hans Küng and what he called "rampant infallibility" is cited here (p. 82ff.).

For the author, however, the dogma does not constitute an insurmountable obstacle to ecumenism. He demonstrates this by explaining the three conceptions that were in conflict during the discussions at the Council itself. It does seem to us, however, speaking quite honestly, that Pottmeyer attempts to adopt an equilibrist's position, distinguishing in the conciliar majority what he styles a pragmatic school of thought ("pursued", "strategic"), and a theological one, which he identifies rather with the minority (p. 92). All this was supposedly clearly brought out in the intervention of Cardinal Guidi (pp. 92-95). We must insist, however, that the desire, "strategic' if you will, to condemn Gallicanism and strengthen the authority of the Roman pontiff, was also a theological issue and not simply a strategic one (see pp. 96ff., 106, 108, and 120). Even the idea of this author of seeing all this as "tactical" entails a certain risk (see p. 97, for example, where this is applied to the minority with regard to an infallibility that "was personal, separate, and absolute": cf. pp. 98ff., however). This application was an error which led to a hardening of the idea of *ex sese*, [and] with what was then added, namely, *non autem ex consensu Ecclesiae*—which the author thinks led to "a theological error" (p. 101). Pottmeyer claims, however, that his interpretation can be supported in the thought of Vatican I Bishop Vincent Gasser himself had.

Between the two Vatican Councils, however, there were three interpretations, occurring simultaneously with each other, of the dogma of papal infallibility—maximalist, middle-of-the-road, and the interpretation corresponding to the position of the minority at

Vatican I, the latter linked to an ecclesiology of communion among local Churches that was characteristic of the first millennium. "The first place for a magisterial decision, when one becomes necessary for the Church, is at a council...an *ex cathedra* definition has a subsidiary character to this" (p. 111). So the author concludes: "The majority at Vatican II took up again the preoccupation of the minority at Vatican I...and in this context, the dogma of papal infallibility, is perfectly compatible with an ecclesiology of communion" (p.114). We can agree with this if it is, once again, understood that the "communion" in question is "hierarchical."

That this may not be clearly the thought of this author, however, we gather from the next chapter title, namely, "Vatican II: the Unfinished Reform." Its subtitle is: "Exiting the Ghetto and Rising Up against Centralization." For Pottmeyer, as also is the case for Vatican I itself, Vatican II did not succeed in "completing its work"—that is, the work that this author, naturally, thinks was necessary. The way is still open, he believes, for a system of "communion between and among local Churches collegially managed" (p. 115). "We are waiting for a Church structure in the form of communion" (*Ibid.*, and esp. p. 133).

In effect, Vatican II got around "the 'spectre' of a participation of the college of bishops in the governance of the Church," that is, of a *congubernium* (p. 116); the Council simply did not succeed in "eliminating the fascination that the maximalist interpretation continues to have in the way in which it conceives authority" (p. 117). It is precisely for this reason that Pottmeyer objects to the idea of adding the adjective "hierarchical" to "communion" and, especially, to the *Nota Explicativa Praevia* itself. He gets the thought of Paul VI on this wrong, by the way (pp. 119, 146ff., and 175), and he opposes the position of Monsignor Gérard Philips as well. The latter, of course, considered the *Nota* to be completely in accord with the text of Chapter III of *Lumen Gentium*. However that may be, Pottmeyer is favorable to the idea of a permanent council or synod of bishops; this was supposedly the viewpoint of the majority of the Council Fathers, according to him. Such a permanent council of bishops would have the task of assisting the pope in the governance of the universal Church, and this was something he thinks "the Roman Curia had to impede at all costs" (p. 121).

Rather than distinguishing the meaning of collegiality in a broad or in a narrow sense, the author speaks instead of collegiality "from above" or "from below" (p. 122); he also underlines the "compromise" inherent in the distinction between *munera*, functions, and *potestates*, powers. He then advances his own idea of "a papal primacy of communion": the pope's task would be "to represent and maintain the universal communion of the Churches" (pp. 124, 127ff., 130, 137, 143, 153, 162, 165, 167ff., and 175).

Considering the importance that the author attributes to the type of primacy he envisages here, we need to describe it in greater detail, as he himself does in subsequent pages: "A Petrine ministry exercised as a primacy of communion...would give normative form to the reciprocal exchange of the agents of tradition and of the interpretation...that 'in the name of Christ' calls for fidelity to the Gospel and to reconciliation...and would also help to assure the necessary reforms for this"; it would offer "assurances that both continuity and vitality would be linked to tradition" (p. 167). This, in our view, would not amount to all that much, though, even with the greatest possible opening to "communion," especially when we think of what the author calls—though we do not agree with him here— "the juxtaposition in the texts of Vatican II documents of different ecclesiologies with diverse accents and priorities, which, in some cases, seem contradictory" (pp. 134 and 147). But in what pertains to "the infallibility of the papal magisterium," the hermeneutical line followed by Pottmeyer favors the idea that the position of the minority at Vatican I, with some changes, reappeared in the position of the majority at Vatican II (pp. 134-141). These are serious contentions, especially one passage where the author speaks of undue pastoral and doctrinal centralization, with the suggestion that "rampant infallibility" might truly be the problem.

The part of this work which we find to be really extreme in its "progressivism," however, and which contains some rather severe judgments, is the last chapter which bears the title: "Communion-Primacy: A Task for the Third Millennium." The chapter begins with the statement that "the two Vatican Councils were both open to the idea of a reform of the Petrine ministry" (p. 143). But the author shows here that he does not understand the fundamental importance of "consensus" in the Catholic Church. He is especially critical towards what he calls "an ecclesiology which, from a historical point of view, bears the marks of the Counter-Reformation"; this ecclesiology, "from a systematic point of view, presents itself one-sidedly as a juridical and social system which defines the Church and which from a theological point of view can be called 'Christomonist'" (p. 145). Approached in this way, there is "in a quintuple preeminence, as the universal Church in relation to the particular Churche; of the source of ministry with respect to the community; as the monarchical structure of this ministry (rather than a collegial structure); as the ministry in relation with to charisms in the members; and, finally, the source of unity rather than diversity" (p. 145). It seems to us that we are being overwhelmed with an excess of data and interpretation here, always in favor of "an ecumenical ecclesiology of communion" (p. 147ff.).

The author, however, believes that he has discovered signs of hope for the ecclesiology that he thinks is contained in the reflections issued by the Congregation for the Doctrine of the Faith, in the 1988 document entitled "The Primacy of the Successor of Peter in the Mystery of the Church" (pp. 148-152). He admits, however—rather euphemistically, we would say—that "some questions remain" (p. 152). I believe, that the reader will find that these questions are serious ones (see p.153 and also p. 159).

Confusing centralization with the primacy of jurisdiction, the author finally arrives at the principles that he advocates in order to start us down the road towards his "primacy of communion." He declares that "the universal Church and her institutions are nothing without the particular Churches in which this universal Church is embodied...All of the dispositions and functions which do not weaken or endanger the unity and the communion of the universal Church...

can be assumed by the particular Churches and the various groupings of these Churches. That which must remain outside the competence of the particular Churches and their groupings should not be defined exclusively by Rome...With regard to what pertains to the governance of the universal Church, this must be committed to the correlations and the inner structure that obtain between primacy and collegiality. As for the personal exercise of the primacy, this is constitutive of the task given to the successor of Peter, and it must be integrated into the tasks given to the college of the successors of the other apostles as well...The Church needs to be subject to a case of exceptional danger before the pope undertakes to act himself, without the participation of the episcopacy, and it must be a case which concerns the whole Church...[Moreover], an administration such as one where the Roman Curia inserts itself between the pope and the bishops is not compatible with the personal character of the internal relations within the episcopal college, nor with the responsibilities that are proper to the bishops...As for solemn dogmatic definitions, the rule should be that they are decided upon within the college of bishops and not outside of it. The episcopacy and the theologians of the universal Church should not ever be excluded from the decisions adopted by the ordinary papal magisterium when these are addressed to the whole Church and bear a normative character" (p. 169ff.).

The author goes on to recommend a number of structural changes, for example: "The establishment of a permanent council composed of cardinals and bishops from around the world which the pope would regularly consult...The choice of another method of operating for the present Synod of Bishops which would permit real exchanges of views among the participants, giving to the Synod a wider ability to take initiatives and make decisions...Encouraging a strengthened synodal practice and giving greater recognition to the proper responsibilities of the conferences of bishops...Naming bishops through a greater participation at all levels of the Church—local, regional, and universal...Returning to the classic triadic structure of the Church, namely, particular, regional, and universal..." (p.171ff.). All of these ideas are developed by the author, who also gives greater attention to the institution of the patriarchate (p. 173), as we have already noted above. He supplies a variety of reasons in support of this idea. But it is still important not to forget (-may I say-) the need to respect the two "poles" of the Church's structure that are of divine institution.

The volume concludes with a list of abbreviations, a good bibliography, and indexes, both general and of names.

33

Episcopal Ministry in the Postconciliar Era

Legrand H. and Theobald C., Eds., *Le Ministère des évêques au Concile Vatican II et depuis* [The Ministry of Bishops at Vatican II and Since], Éditions du Cerf, Paris 2001, 325 pages.

This book is the record of a colloquy dedicated to Bishop Guy Herbulot and his episcopacy of twenty-five years. It features an interdisciplinary approach that includes historical, canonical, and ecclesiological emphases. It also aims to look beyond the ecclesial situation in France.

Bishop Herbulot himself opened the colloquy. His words focused upon Vatican II as the road to follow both for today and for tomorrow. The first part of the book is devoted to the question of the renewal of the episcopacy desired by Vatican II. It begins with a study by Giuseppe Alberigo with the title, "The Bishops' Experience of Episcopal Responsibility," that is, their experiences when they were assembled at the Council itself, for which the author says he utilized "more than forty diaries written by bishops" of all ages, provenances, and orientations. He begins with "the statute of bishops in force at the end of the 1950s." He then goes on to the ante-preparatory consultations and the "wishes" of the bishops that were submitted in connection with these consultations. He follows this with an examination of the conciliar assembly itself and with the "institutional" occasions that were offered for taking episcopal responsibility. Among his other affirmations, two that particularly struck us made reference to October 13 and November 20, 1962, when, according to the author, "at least half of the bishops gave proofs of their autonomy and their liberty" (p. 33). We immediately asked ourselves if the other half was composed of bishops who were *not* free or autonomous! Did they not, in fact, also simply make use of *their* liberty or autonomy in another way than that favored by Alberigo? This comment of his was a sign, we thought, of an attitude of this particular author which has already been many times critiqued by us and which reappears here again in his use of the phrase "Black Week" (p. 38). The week in question turned out to be providential for the Council, in fact, in spite of the first over-emotional reactions to it.

Following his treatment of the topics mentioned, Alberigo goes on to deal with "The Challenge of Reception." This treatment is based on the postconciliar "careers" of some of the main protagonists of the great Synod. He then goes on to treat of the "destiny" of the particular Council Father who would eventually be called Pope John Paul II. This progression of his leaves us somewhat perplexed. And with regard to new movements, for example, he speaks of "ambiguous clouds" (p. 41). He tells too of the non-acceptance of the initiative proposed at the Council for the canonization of John XXIII, which according to him, was "blocked by authority" (p. 42). The motive for this blocking was supposedly so as not to provide a model for the postconciliar Church.

In the discussion at the colloquy that followed this presentation by this noted professor, except for the recurring question of the manner of naming bishops, which was not the focus here, we note only the fact that, for him, "there was no realization at the Council concerning the problem of the local communities which make up the Church, nor was adequate attention given to it. As a result, the entire Chapter III of the Dogmatic Constitution on the Church [on the subject of the hierarchy] is skewed in the wrong direction as far as the episcopacy and the universal Church are concerned" (p. 47).

Following this, G. Routhier takes up the theme, "Sacramentality of the Episcopacy and Hierarchical Communion: The Relationship of the Sacrament to Canon Law." This author begins his treatment with an examination of the first *schema* prepared by the Council's Theological Commission, the "approach" of which he describes as "entirely juridical" (p. 51). Then he deals very critically with the work of Monsignor Gérard Philips, who was chosen by Cardinal Suenens but put in place by Cardinal Cicognani. Philips adopted a course of not rejecting the "precedents" embodied in the original *schemata*, but instead worked to improve them—a process that was more suitable for a council and for arriving at a true consensus. It was a correct formula, in fact, although it is not correct to speak of it as a "second conciliar preparation." And how is it possible, in any case, to affirm that "the fundamental law of the Church is not dependent on any hierarchical relationship, but rather on communion with Christ and with all of us in the sacraments that should be considered as the fundamental processes of the Church" (p. 55)? This way of proceeding does not allow the necessary "fusion" between communion and hierarchy that is inherent in the very concept-reality of "hierarchical communion."

This author also refers, erroneously, to what he calls "the October Revolution." This reference was to the Council's meeting on October 30, 1963, when five crucial orientation votes were taken (p. 56; see also p. 68 and p. 59, where the author speaks of a "Copernican Revolution," although shortly afterwards, he states that it was "lacking in its reach"). Routhier further shows himself to be opposed to the universalistic perspective offered by Vatican Council I (p. 58). Moreover, he does not understand the reflected distinction, common from the thirteenth century on, between the power of order and that of jurisdiction; he actually speaks of "splitting" in this connection. He also seems to favor the pairing "primacy-bishop" rather than the more fruitful pairing represented by the concept of "bishop-Church" (*Ibid.*). This same deficiency applies to his treatment of the *Nota Explicativa Praevia*; this treatment calls for a further well-deserved critique, and, again, one must make reference here to the views of Philips, rather than to those of Grootaers, who is the one quoted by Routhier (p. 60). However, on page 62, writing about collegiality, and even citing *Apostolos Suos* (see also p. 74), this author's view is just not in line with what the Council actually decided, but accords rather with what the author, with the benefit of hindsight, thinks it should have decided. We are no longer dealing with the actual Council here, but rather with an imagined "other" Council, evidently, or else with the mere desire for what the Council's decisions should have "matured" into—that is, into the results desired by this author.

In speaking of a "Central Council for the World Episcopate" (pp. 63, 67, and 104), Routhier continues on with further judgments in the same vein (p. 64f.). He shows his incomprehension of the required distinction between collegiality as understood in a broader or in a narrower sense. He then speaks of the idea's "first reception in theology and in canon law," but always he exhibits the same confusion already mentioned above; and, moreover, he continues to show his incomprehension of the very idea of "hierarchical communion." He also criticizes the Extraordinary Synod Session of 1985 along with its *instrumentum laboris*, where the *mandatum docendi* of episcopal conferences was discussed. Routhier refers here to an imperfect form of collegiality, but it is not that. Rather, it is a question of collegiality in a broad sense, that is, true collegiality in that same sense.

"Is the Diocese a Local or a Particular Church?" This is the topic covered by L. Villemin, whose subtitle asks what was meant by these terms. In our view, it would be sufficient to quote *Christus Dominus*, which speaks in this connection of "a portion of the People of God... [which] constitutes one particular Church" (CD 11). In any case, the author does not succeed in getting around the difficulty (p. 86; Conclusion), although others do, including Routhier himself, farther along in the discussion (though, again, Routhier does not distinguish between the bishop's *munera* and his *potestates* (see p. 92ff.).

Next, Father Gustav Martelet treats in rather enthusiastic terms the topic of "The Cooperation between Theologians and Bishops at Vatican II." He showers praise right and left. It seems strange to us, however, to find him confessing that "I was in part theologically responsible for a group of bishops..." This seems to say it all, for us, and so we simply leave things there.

The Second Part of this volume bears the title: "The Ministry of Bishops after the Council: The Reception of the Council by the Church." The initial presentation here by J. Passicos seems to us both objective and honest. The particular topic he treats is "The Reception of the Conciliar Documents concerning the Episcopacy as Reflected in the Normative Texts Issued by the Holy See up to the Issuance of the Code of Canon Law in 1983 (Inclusive)." The interventions by Theobald, Routhier, and Legrand in the discussion which followed this presentation, however, evidence partiality and one-sidedness in a very pronounced degree. Passicos replies to them quite wisely, particularly in what concerns "the Latin patrimony, which surely must not disappear." It is otherwise described, in fact, as the "immense patriarchate of Rome" (p. 120).

The contribution which then follows is that of B. Sesboüé, and his topic takes up "The Official Reception of the Vatican II Documents on the Episcopacy in the Documents of the Holy See following the New Code-1983-1999." This presentation is very well done, and is even profound; but it is strongly, indeed, excessively, critical (see p. 122, for example); and, as far as we are concerned, not only relatively unimportant matters, or those pertaining only to discipline are involved here (see p. 132). We are greatly displeased with the entire outcome, as a matter of fact. In the eye of the storm is the Letter to the Bishops issued by the Congregation for the Doctrine of the Faith on May 8, 1992, entitled "Some Aspects of the Church Understood As Communion." This Document dealt with the question of the priority between the particular Churches and the universal Church, and supposedly it goes against the opinions of P. Tillard and "all the great theologians of our times" (p. 128) For the author, "the Church of Rome is a particular Church like all the others" (p. 127). The author thus forgets that all the other Churches are required to be in communion with *this* "particular Church," if they are to have any claim to being "Catholic." In this regard, it does not suffice to say that "Communion with the bishop of Rome constitutes the mediation that establishes full communion with the universal Church" (*Ibid.*). Rome does not just have an "essential role to play" here; Rome has a necessary, and for us, indispensable role.

The principal text aimed at by this author, however, is John Paul II's Apostolic Letter issued *Motu Proprio* on May 18, 1998, under the title *Ad Tuendam Fidem*. Among other things, this Letter reserved to the pope "the discernment of the ordinary and universal magisterium of the Church" (p. 133). We do not intend to enter into a discussion of this theme, but, on the other hand, we cannot agree that the way Sesboüé argues his case can be considered correct. He writes, for example, in the following way: "In order to be able to declare that a point belongs infallibly and in a definitive way to the deposit of faith or to the teaching of the Church, the pope no longer has to have recourse to a solemn *ex cathedra* definition. It is now sufficient that he should reaffirm and confirm what is being and has been taught in a definitive and infallible manner by the ordinary and universal magisterium of the pope and the bishops." The author does limit this to points "in the domain of the faith properly speaking." In order to support this assertion, he mistakenly appeals to Vacant's thoughts (of 1887).

In any case, for this author, we are said to be dealing here with a "magisterial novelty which, should it continue to stand, is infinitely greater than the definition of papal infallibility enacted at Vatican Council I, since nothing any longer limits the infallible acts of the pope" (p. 138). Finally, as regards the *Motu Proprio Apostolos Suos* cited above, Sesboüé does not understand and does not accept the distinction that continually needs to be made on the points presented by him between collegiality (a word that never appears in the conciliar texts) in a broader and a narrower sense. This is a question, by the way, which is not juridical but theological, yet from which the law must draw juridical consequences. But there is an incongruence implicit in the reasoning of Sesboüé and others who think like him because they are defending the particular Church against the universal Church, and they do not draw out the consequences regarding episcopal conferences.

In his conclusion, however, the author seeks to make a *captatio benevolentiae* which would respect the Roman intentions in all this and even the theological and pastoral foundations of the documents in question. But the effect is very strange, coming as it does after all that he has previously said (see pp. 144-146). The pendulum swings the other way in the discussion which follows, that is, towards the universal Church; and it does so through the intervention of Giuseppe Alberigo. He speaks of a lack of confidence on the part of Rome in the responsibility that the episcopacy can assume for the universal Church. Yet the bishop's link to his own particular Church should not be exaggerated at the expense of the link that he also has to the universal Church. H. Legrand thinks along the same lines as Alberigo, and he also shows very little historical sense with regard to the past (see p. 146) and takes up the cudgels for so-called "regional Churches" which, as far as we are concerned, are not "Churches" in the proper sense at all. It is in this skewed and distorted context that the question of new patriarchates is raised. Sesboüé responds to the comments and criticisms made, but not well. C. Theobald speaks along the same lines; for him, in *Lumen Gentium*, "the jurisdictional obscures the sacramental." For that matter, for Sesboüé, the "jurisdictional" provides a heavy counterweight to the great conciliar pronouncements on the subject of sacramentality (p. 152).

At the end of this part of the book, A. Vidal treats the topic of "The Reception of the Conciliar Documents concerning Their Ministry by the Bishops of France." Then there follows a gallery of French "figures in the episcopal ministry, both yesterday and today." Although this is quite interesting and is quite well done as well, we shall not go into it here, but instead we invite the patient reader to do so on his own. The portraits painted here include those of R. Rémond, F. Baldelli, M. Maziers, and G. Piroird.

H. Legrand then treats separately and at rather great length a topic that he entitles "Bishops, Local Churches, and the Whole Church: Institutional Developments following Vatican II, including Current Areas for Research" (pp. 201-260). He represents a brand of theology that always presses forward more prominently, while presenting itself as the most sophisticated and latest thing—but, in fact, it encroaches upon the territory of the magisterium as well.

In the course of his analysis, Legrand speaks of a supposed "ruinous" split, which has not been overcome yet, between the episcopal college and communion among the Churches; he discerns another split between the ideas of order and jurisdiction. However, these supposed gaps have been both clear and reflected in practice since around the thirteenth century. Legrand, again, does not recognize the two senses, wide and narrow, of the idea of collegiality; he also fails to understand the *Nota Explicativa Praevia* and the "reassuring" judgments about it made by Monsignor G. Philips.

He offers a strong critique of the new Code of Canon Law (C. I. C.) and of the use of the term "particular Church" to indicate the local diocese (which shows the way in which he understands the diocese as a "part" of the Church). His judgment on the 1990 Code of Canons for the Eastern Churches is quite severe, as are his judgments on *Apostolos Suos* (reflecting the *Instrumentum Laboris* of which we spoke above) and on *Ad Tuendam Fidem* as well.

The final question posed here—with the answer to it only too evident—is the following: "Is there a new centralization?" Even Legrand, like Sesboüé, is prepared to concede "good faith" to Rome, but I do not believe that this is sufficient. His conclusion is formulated as follows: "The Ecclesiology currently in vigor resembles the ecclesiology of forty years ago." We do not believe this is true at all.

At this point, the author indicates some directions for more long-range research, pointing out the deficiencies of the ecclesiology in vogue today and mentioning the antidotes for these deficiencies. It is necessary, the author thinks, to work in three major areas. They are: the traditional relationship between the college of bishops and the manifestations of the existing communion among the Churches they head; communion between and among regional Churches; and the kind of communion that extends beyond a purely hierarchical communion between the bishops in order to reach a 'corporate' type communion for the purpose of decision-making. This last undertaking is necessary, according to the author, "for a correct reception of the documents of Vatican II."

We cannot follow this author into these particular areas, and in part because to do so would overturn some of the very criticisms which he himself has previously formulated. But also Legrand himself asserts things which do not seem to accord with each other (see esp. pp. 232, 233ff., 237ff., 244ff., 247-251, and, in particular, 255). To conclude, the author summons Pope John XXIII to his side and lays out criteria for an ecclesiology that in his view would be capable of renewing the episcopacy. He derives the criteria for this ecclesiology from tradition, pastoral practice, the communion (primacy and conciliarity), ecumenism, missionary practice, and institutional factors. Who could possibly be opposed to such criteria? The question is, naturally, how they would be applied concretely and in practice.

After the veritable overflowing river provided here by Legrand, there are a number of other smaller streams. One of them is by J. P. Ricard; then, come two lectures from the diocese of Evry; and another contribution is by C. Theobald, along the same lines as mentioned above on the subject of Vatican II (covering the Council's principal driving forces). Then there is the contribution of Bishop Herbulot himself concerning his "experience as the bishop of a new diocese." The volume then winds up with an interview with him which appeared in the newspaper *La Croix* on the subject of the various factors that brought about both the original colloquy and the volume being presented here. The final conclusion to all of this is contributed by the vicar general Msgr. O. Morand.

34

Vatican II and Ecclesial Movements: A Charismatic Vision

Hegge Christoph, *Il Vaticano II e i movimenti ecclesiali. Una ricezione carismatica* [Vatican II and Ecclesial Movements: A Charismatic Reception], Città Nuova Editrice, Rome 2001, 240 pages.

This book comes with a good preface of Professor Gianfranco Ghirlanda, who situates the unexpected and novel development of charismatic movements in the life of the Church. For him this involved "questions, discomforts, tensions...and even presumptions and exaggerations on the one hand; and, on the other hand, not a few prejudices and reservations." All this occurred in the course of "the crisis through which the Church is living and in the midst of the galloping secularization that is also coming about" (p. 9). But it also took place in the context of Vatican Council II (see pp. 10ff.) and the pontifical magisterium (p. 12). Hegge believes that an ecclesial movement "is an existential locus for the application of the essential content of Vatican II" (p. 14), as well as for "the realization of the conciliar ecclesiology" (p. 17f.).

As the author himself writes: "In the first chapter, the concepts of both reception and charisma are analyzed in accordance with the content and the ecclesiology of the Council, and also with the aim of examining the relationship between the action of the Holy Spirit and the dynamics of the ecclesial reception of the Council—and also with reference to the possible significance of these charisms in relation to the ecclesial reception of the Council itself. Following an account of the post-conciliar discussions on the reception of the Council, there is presented a doctrinal analysis of the conciliar teaching on the subject of charisms. What needs to be underlined here is that the common and customary reception of the magisterium is in fact of the essence of these charisms, as it is of the charismatics themselves. On the other hand, it is the duty of the magisterium not to extinguish the Spirit—not to oppose the charisms that come, but rather to examine them and, indeed, to promote them" (p. 18).

In the second chapter, there is a presentation of the process of the ecclesial formation of the charisms themselves, as well as of the dynamics of their reception within the Church, according to the characteristic models provided by today's ecclesial movements. The author asserts that "they expand the 'space' of ecclesial life in which is realized their reception as part of the dialogue involved in following Christ and heeding both his service and his passion for his fellow men. It is in this context that the question of the juridical constitution of the various ecclesial movements in canon law arises, and this cannot ignore either their charismatic nature or the teachings of the Church which they are obliged to receive" (p. 18).

In his third chapter, Hegge is quite critical, in particular, about what relates to "the still incomplete reception of Vatican Council II in the provisions of the Code of Canon Law." He offers several proposals for amendments to the Code, based on the example of the Focolare Movement.

Speaking quite frankly, we find this book to be too critical, too partial and one-sided, and too imbued with a tendency to overrate charisms and, moreover, to equate the reception of Vatican II with these same highly touted charisms. The use of the term "charism" itself is not even quite exact. Nor does it have to apply to all ecclesial movements. What the Council desired in such movements was a renewal in fidelity and in continuity with the tradition of the Church—the whole Church. What is understated here is that Vatican II's communion is "hierarchical"; hence there is a certain imbalance in the presentation. To be brief, let us simply mention some reservations we have with regard to the following pages: pp. 22, 26f., 32, 34, n. 37, 37f., 40, 47, n. 79, 48, n. 81, 49, 52f., 54, 62f., 64, 65, n. 113, 66, 68-71,

73ff., 91, 94, 97ff., 100ff., 103f., 113, 125, 127, 155f., 163, 171, 178f., 181, 187, 201-206, 209ff., 213f., and 230.

The volume concludes with an Appendix bearing the significant title of: "A New Pentecost: the Communion of Ecclesial Movements in the One Church for the 'New Evangelization'"—this appears to be something of a manifesto for the future. The volume also contains a good bibliography, and also an Index of Names.

35

Vatican II and Ecclesial Movements: A Communal Vision[1]

A noted writer on theology and politics spoke as follows in connection with the last Meeting (of Communion and Liberation) held in Rimini: "Following Vatican II, Catholic theologians demanded and obtained the same liberty in all fields of theology that Protestant theologians already enjoyed, beginning with the field of biblical exegesis in which the Protestants already maintained a hegemony. There remained nothing left in Catholicism beyond the faith of the simple faithful, exhibited in such things as the call to 'adhere to Jesus' of Father Luigi Giussani, the brotherly love of Chiara Lubich, the severe Neocatechumenal movement of Kiko Argüello, and the birth of a neo-Protestant-type Pentecostal movement in what came to be called the Catholic Charismatic Renewal. All of these movements share a similar mode of existence in which theology counts for nothing. John Paul II himself entrusted the simple faithful to the Blessed Mother and to the saints and martyrs; he accorded to the faith of the simple faithful a primacy over the thinking of theologians engaged in a quest for modernity."[2]

Even taking into account the journalistic simplification evident here, as well as this writer's tendency to go to extremes, there is

---

[1]Intervention delivered on November 23, 2002, at the Meeting (in a series) organized by the Christian Russia Foundation on the topic: "Witnesses to Christ: In Memory of the Martyrs of the Twentieth Century and Christian Proclamation Today, in Confrontation with the Challenge of Secularism."

[2]See Gianni Baget Bozzo, "*The Primacy of Simple Faith over Theology*," in *Il Giornale*, August 20, 2002 (p. 10).

nevertheless some truth in the judgment he makes here—although there is also a grave error in imagining that there was no "theology" involved in the development of these ecclesial movements. In fact, they arose out of a theology thoroughly grounded in Vatican Council II as "received" in its entirety, that is, without the typical ideological distortions which have too often accompanied the presentation of the Council's teaching. This kind of correct "reception" entails an *aggiornamento* that has preserved fidelity to the great Tradition of the Church. The ideological distortions I refer to are principally those found in the ponderous five volumes of the *History of Vatican Council II* edited by Professor Giuseppe Alberigo.[3]

Vatican Council II was important for its doctrinal, spiritual, and pastoral value. It is a veritable icon of Catholicism, constitutionally and also in the way that it maintains communion with the past—with the origins of the Church, with the preservation of her identity in the course of her development, and with her fidelity as it has been maintained in the course of her renewal. This was, then, a very great Council. Its official Acts collected in 62 large volumes bear witness to this; these Acts provide a secure basis for the proper reception and a correct interpretation (hermeneutic) of the Council. However, many began writing the history of the Council before these volumes, fundamental for the proper comprehension of the Council, were yet available. They are indispensable for the understanding of the Council because they contain the records of all the official directive organs of the Council. Nevertheless, various historians embarked on their histories of the Council anyway, availing themselves of personal diaries and individual and private writings, and on contemporary journalistic accounts that contained many exaggerations. I am thinking here, for example, of the writings of Father Giovanni Caprile, S. J.

---

[3]*Storia del Concilo Vaticano II* [History of Vatican Council II], directed by G. Alberigo, 5 Volumes, Peeters, Il Mulino, Bologna 1995-2001. See also the critique of this history in my *Chiesa e Papato nella storia e nel diritto. 25 anni di studi critici* [Church and Papacy in History and in Law: 25 Years of Critical Studies], Vatican City, 2002 (see esp. pp. 235-279). And also, see, for example, my article in *L'Osservatore Romano*, February, 2000, p. 10. This article was expanded in *Apollinaris* LXXIV (2001), n. 1-4, pp. 811-825.

There is a very important question here of how well these individual and private writings are screened and evaluated, and of what critical criteria are employed when they are being used. A mere reading through of some of these sources reveals many discrepancies. There is a wide variety of attributions made and judgments rendered concerning the "merits" of certain positions [especially if they were "winning" ones]. There is also "information" or "knowledge" recorded that turns out to be quite partial, especially with regard to the complexities of the great conciliar event itself (the web of regulations; the various "pressures" and movements that predominated at the Council; the "battles" against "conservatism" or against the Roman Curia; the defense of Tradition; the significance of the magisterium; the schools of thought concerning the proper interpretation of the pastoral and ecumenical intentions of Pope John XXIII and so on.).

This is not said in order to deny the importance of what these diaries and journals bring to the historical research. They supply flavor and ingredients among other things; but they must be subordinated to the official Acts of the Council, or the history being written will slide into a fragmentary condition—or else it will simply be a "chronicle' or something of an "encyclopedia." The result will be off center, or will consist merely of a dissection, or a vivisection, or simply a peeling away of some of the layers involved in the real history of the Council. That this kind of thing can come about quite easily is shown by the most recent diary that has been published, namely, the *Journal* of Father Yves Congar, O. P. This book is severely critical, both in the phraseology it employs and in the names or epithets it applies to the adversaries, or supposed ones, of the author—they are all very revealing.

In fact, the editor of this *Journal*, Eric Mahieu, makes a point of including a reference on what Congar reports to the official *Acta Synodalia* as well; this makes it possible to identify many errors in Father Congar's own narrative. Unfortunately, however, these references pertain only to the interventions and discourses of the Council Fathers themselves, as they are reported by Father Congar. No similar references are included pertaining to the many rumors and bits of gossip that are mentioned, nor to the indiscretions and judgments of the author himself (even those subsequently corrected by him with the passage of time). Yet these latter assertions too should have been compared with the official records of the Council's directive organs, now available in published form, that pertain to what the author is writing about at any given point.

Another problem inherent in the utilization of diaries, in many cases, is the tendency to diminish the importance of the final documents issued by the Council, as compared with its supposed "spirit." For us the true spirit of the Council must naturally inhere in the corpus of documents finally issued; these documents represent the true synthesis of Tradition and of the renewal being effected by *aggiornamento*; they embody the concrete results of what was originally aimed at and enacted by the Council. Invoking the spirit of the Council rather than the authentic letter of these documents represents an ideological approach that looks only at the innovative aspects of the Council and emphasizes discontinuity with respect to the Tradition.

Focusing in this way on the spirit also comes about, I would say, today's general historiographical approach (following and also going against Braudel and the "Annales" model). This new approach favors the "event" in any historical interpretation. And the "event," in this context, is understood as discontinuity and as traumatic change. Now with regard to the Church, if such an "event" is not so much an important occurrence, but it is a break, a novelty—amounting, virtually, to the birth of a "new" Church, a kind of Copernican revolution, and to another and different kind of Catholicism, where the Church in fact has shed characteristics once thought to be essential to her—then the Church is no longer being understood and accepted as *Catholic*.

In any event, to return to the ponderous five-volume Alberigo *History* of the Council mentioned above, we encounter there a treatment that lacks a proper center, a monopolistic view that represents an extreme interpretation and that does not recognize that any true consensus was ever in fact achieved at the Council; rather, there was a "minority group" at the Council that remained wholly unassimilated to the so-called "majority group."

Then there is the question of the "reception" of the Council—fundamental to any success the Council might have. This is well known. Nor are we thinking of just any kind of "charismatic reception."[4] Such a "charismatic reception" is not the same as reception *tout court*. It cannot be a reception by which everybody can just interpret things as they please. Certainly, ecclesial movements possess and express and represent signs of various charisms, but they are not alone in this regard. We think, for example, of the charisms enjoyed by the simple faithful, even individually. Nor can we forget the postconciliar renewal of the religious life generally, which similarly went back to the charisms of the original Founders; these charisms are today also found in the new ecclesial movements. There are many things here worthy of examination in greater detail and greater depth, and Pope John Paul II has already moved in the proper direction in the way of reflection and guidance for us.[5]

But then there is the question of the relations of ecclesial movements with the particular Churches and with the Pastors of the particular Churches and not just with the Pastor of the universal Church. This is the case precisely because Vatican Council II brought to the fore the question of the "locality of the Churches."

Even though the new ecclesial movements constituted "unexpected novelties and were even sometimes breakthroughs," they were "officially recognized by ecclesiastical authority and were seen as forms of self-realization by the Church." Thus did Pope John Paul II characterize them in his important discourse of May 28,

---

[4]See Hegge, Christoph, *Il Vaticano II e i movimenti ecclesiali. Una ricenzione carismatica* [Vatican II and Ecclesial Movements: A Charismatic Reception], Città Nuova, Rome 2001, 240 pages. This book is interesting and I myself have profited by it, although I have many reservations about it as well, as expressed in my review in Apollinaris (see Chapter 34 in this book). Its valuable bibliography nevertheless merits careful attention, and I refer readers to that rather than burdening the text here.

[5]Cfr. John Paul II, To the Study Seminary for Bishops: *L'Osservatore Romano*, June 20, 1999.

1998, addressed to the Fourth World Congress of Movements and New Communities.[6] And thus too established authoritatively the link between the movements and the mystery of the Church—which in fact had stood at the center of the thinking and of the documents of the Council itself (*ad extra* and *ad intra*).

In this regard, the Council thus distanced itself somewhat— without, however, denying or rejecting it—from a rather societal and hierarchical vision, totalizing the ecclesial reality for considering its global mystery, that is, as a communion animated by the Holy Spirit through the Word, the Sacraments, and the communication of her charisms. This remained true even while these things continued to be parts of an organized and visible society, hierarchical in nature and, moreover, one that was organized juridically as well (cfr. *Lumen Gentium* 8).

The Church's *communio* is hierarchical even while it continues to remain a *communio*, its point of departure being found in the fundamental equality of all the faithful called to holiness; this equality is operative in both the dignity and the action of all, even though it is diversified in accordance with the vocations and charisms proper to each person; each is called to cooperation in the edification of the Body of Christ and the fulfillment of the mission that Christ committed to the Church to be carried out in this world (see *Lumen Gentium* 32). The Church at Vatican II found herself called not only to an internal unity within herself, but to the realization of a variety of ministries and charisms in relation to other Churches and ecclesial communities, and even to other religions. The Church found herself, in a word, in a relationship with all men of good will (cfr. *Gaudium et Spes* 40-45).

All of this can be verified in the new ecclesial movements. They represent, in effect, a new missionary impetus and in some of them a distinct ecumenical one. Characterizing these movements as "ecclesial" arises out of the fact that their aim and scope is to present and represent the Church in her relations as an organic communion and hence as a communion expressed through various vocations

---

[6] *L'Osservatore Romano*, June 1-2, 1998, n. 6.

within herself. In the end, it is the communitarian component that comes to the fore, as in fact occurred at the Council. Thus, number 29 of the apostolic exhortation *Christifidelis Laici*,[7] takes up number 18a of the Decree *Apostolicam Actuositatem* of Vatican II; and, referring in a general way to the associational apostolate, asserts that it is a "sign" that must manifest itself in the relationships that exist within the "communion." It is thus a communitarian component, and it applies both within and without the various forms of aggregation in the larger context of the entire Christian community.

A well-known canonist has written in this regard: "If the specific nature of the new ecclesial movements is to present the communion between the various vocations in the Church, this specific nature of theirs must especially manifest itself in their harmonious actions with other ecclesial components. This arises out of what is a necessity for the Church today, namely, that all of her components should act in harmony with one another, not only in proclaiming the Word of God but also in witnessing to her unity and love. Discerning the authenticity of the spirituality of an ecclesial movement today comes about through the proper reception of both the ecclesiology and the spirituality of Vatican II—all of this in relation to the activation of the Christian life in accordance with the experience of both reciprocity and complementarity of the diverse vocations within the Church...It is in this way that an ecclesial movement constitutes an existential locus for the reception of the essential content of Vatican II."[8]

At this point we can delve more deeply into the conciliar reception characteristic of the various ecclesial movements. The basis for this reception is always Vatican II's theology of communion, which more and more emerges as a principal "focus" of the Council, particularly following the results of the conciliar interpretations brought about by the Extraordinary Session of the Synod of Bishops held in 1985.

Let us, however, leave aside the simple notions of "reception" and

---

[7] *AAS* LXXXI (1989), pp. 393-521.
[8] Gianfranco Ghirlanda, S. J., in the Preface to the volume listed in note 4 above.

"charisma" as such in the context of conciliar ecclesiology.[9] Let us concentrate instead on the common characteristics derived from the Council that are found in these ecclesial movements, that is, on the elements that define them as what they are. In this context, we need to look on the one hand at types, whether associations, movements, groups, or communities; and, on the other hand, we need to look at them internally in themselves, that is, whether they are movements of the laity, of the spiritual life, or of the Church herself.

Regardless of the various circumstances of their foundings, we still need to single out their theological essence, as has already been explained to some extent up to this point; but it is also necessary to understand their character as movements, how they function and what they do, their connections with the Church, and their "charismatic" origins, as it were.[10] In order to know and understand all these things, we need to look at five elements specifically that pertain to ecclesial movements. They are as follows:

1) The Charism of the Founder which is at the origin and center of each movement; this becomes the representative source of the character of the members; it is the fountain, if we may so express ourselves of renewed conversions to the Gospel of Jesus Christ; it is a rediscovery of one's baptism in the midst of the new globalized and intercultural world of today, a world that is secularized in most places as well. One's personal vocation remains, but one is nevertheless assumed into the common spirituality of the movement along with all its members collectively. Conversion and baptism, we should remind ourselves, are the two fundamental poles of the spirituality that stems from Vatican Council II and from the *aggiornamento* launched by Pope John XXIII—"so that the world might believe"!

---

[9]See—although there are still a number of distinctions to be made as far as we are concerned—Chapter I in the book by C. Hegge referenced in note 4 above (pp. 21-72).

[10]Here we approach the treatment of L. Gerosa, *Charisma und Recht. Kirchenrechtliche Überlegungen zum Urcharisma der neuen Vereinigungsformen in der Kirche* [Charism and Law: Canonical Reflections on the Original Charisms of the New Movements in the Church], Einsiedeln-Trier, 1989, p. 93ff. However, we may not neglect the five criteria for ecclesial movements identified by John Paul II in *Christifideles Laici* (30).

2) From all this it follows that the members of a movement form a *quid* (a "something") potentially composed, if we may say so, of representatives of every category and status among the faithful, thus reflecting *in nuce* the communal essence of the Church herself. Once again, this is something—as we have already noted above—that was emphasized by the Council. The aim and scope of the members of these movements is to live out their special mission as Christian faithful in the image and reality of the Church. In this participation within and among the various components of the People of God, where priests and religious as well as laity can be involved, "ecclesial movements" must be distinguished from simple "lay" movements in the world as being "more amply linked with the Church."[11] On the spiritual plane, the communal unity of the various categories and states of the faithful goes beyond a spirituality that is predominantly individual, the spirituality of an individual person. Communal spirituality integrates the demands of the Gospel and of the communitarian character of the Church (which has its source and model in the Holy Trinity: see *Lumen Gentium* 1-4). At the social level, the communal unity of the various categories and states of the faithful creates the forms of common life which appear in many ecclesial movements. Moreover, a generous communion in the sharing of spiritual goods often results in a generous sharing of material goods as well. There is a relevance here that we would define as socio-cultural; for us it represents the expression, though not the unique expression, certainly, of the "Church of the poor" which created such echoes within the Council itself, as it still does in the context of today's globalized world (though it is not the same "Church of the poor" as was spoken of by the late Cardinal Lercaro).

3) A consequence of the working out of the original charisma of an ecclesial movement which unites the faithful in a common spirituality is that it becomes a factor or component in the structure of a unitary institution. Thus we would describe it. It implies a certain elasticity

---

[11]Cfr. J. Beyer, *"Novità dello Spirito"* [New Manifestations of the Spirit], in *Vita Consacrata*, [Consecrated Life], XIV (1978), p. 577.

or flexibility for those who belong, however. This is one thing that distinguishes "spiritual families" from "religious orders" (which also share a common spirituality) and from purely spiritual movements and apostolates. In the words of the late Father J. Beyer, it can be said of ecclesial movements that they "share a common spirit of a single association in order to live out the mystery of the Church today"[12] The central thought of Vatican Council II recurs here!

4) The spiritual communion brought about by the original charism of an ecclesial movement brings about in its turn, as we shall see, a particular understanding or comprehension of pastoral practice, of the apostolate, and of evangelization. This is one of the most important and sensitive aspects involved in the existence and development of any movement, because it is here that it enters into the life of a diocese as well as into that of the universal Church. We would even say that this entering in is analogous to the accommodations envisioned for religious by Vatican II (though in a broader sense). The bishop is always responsible for pastoral care on the local level, but he must respect the charisms proper to Institutes of Consecrated Life and to Societies of Apostolical Life. In effect, both evangelization and the various apostolates are carried out under the influence of their charisms, their communitarian witness, and the communal unity of a given movement. The latter enjoys "a true and proper spiritual pedagogy, both in its substance and in its methods, and also a particular form able to express the communitarian aspects of the Church, to make the Church present in places and situations in need of the testimony of the Gospels and of evangelization."[13]

5) We now arrive at the fifth element, that is, at the universality, or indeed the Catholicity, of these ecclesial movements. This is not to be confused with a tendency to internationalization or with a mere

---

[12] J. Beyer, *"Il diritto della Chiesa"* [The Law of the Church], in *Vita Consacrata* [Consecrated Life], XVIII (1982), p. 252.

[13] J. Castellano Cervera, *I movimento ecclesiali. Una presenza carismatica dell Chiesa di oggi* [Ecclesial Movements: A Charismatic Presence in the Church of Today], in *Rivista di vita spirituale* [Review of Religious Life], IV-V (1987), p. 507.

quantitative diffusion or expansion. Rather, universality aims, as P. J. Cordes attests, to establish "the universal relevance of the message of Christ."[14] This is realized in ecclesial movements as a structuring socio-cultural force that is operative in every sphere of life, a "force for the transformation of the Church through the spirit of the Gospels"[15] Universality thus entails dialogue between brothers and sisters, and among men and women, and in every situation of social and cultural life (whether inculturalization or inter-culturalization). It entails dialogue among Christians, that is, ecumenical dialogue, and this even extends to dialogue with non-believers. We must remember what Paul VI said about the importance of dialogue in his encyclical *Ecclesiam Suam*.

In summary, as Christoph Hegge, in particular, has noted, universality, or Catholicity, when applied to ecclesial movements, means to live in that tension towards the world and toward the men of today that the Church herself is called to live as the "sign and instrument, that is, of communion with God and of unity among all men" (*Lumen Gentium* 1; cfr. LG 9; 48; *Gaudium et Spes* 42; 45). It is precisely "this universality [that] is manifested as a particularly ecclesial note of the charisms of their ecclesial movements."[16] We would say simply of the "ecclesial movements," and this should be clearly understandable.

However, the very same author, C. Hegge, shortly after having covered the material on these movements that we have summarized in the five points, or elements, immediately above—in particular, how all of this is connected to Vatican II—then goes on to write that the possession of these various elements in no way impedes the ecclesial movements in question from being very diverse. They form "a very unhomogeneous pattern," he asserts. We would not be quite as radical as that, and, indeed, the author himself softens his position somewhat

---

[14]P. J. Cordes, *Den Geist nicht auslöschen. Charismen und Neuevangelisierung* [Do Not Extinguish the Spirit: Charisms and the New Evangelization], Freiburg-Basel-Wien, 1990, p. 101.

[15]*Ibid.*, p. 101.

[16]See C. Hegge, *op. cit.*, p. 94.

further on. We would, however, like to quote one of his final summary texts as follows: "The determining factor in these movements comes from the charisms which inspired them...and which give to them a socializing and structuring form that goes beyond the spiritual. They embody an existential and vital form of 'reception' of the essential content of Vatican II. Among the conciliar elements that can be mentioned in this connection are: the ecclesiology of *communion*, the doctrine pertaining to charisms, the common priesthood of all the faithful, the co-responsibility of the laity (in their sphere), the apostolate as a collective responsibility of the whole Church, the universal call to holiness of all the baptized, and the three great dialogues of the Church."[17] By this last phrase, namely, "the three great dialogues," the author is referring to the Council's Decree on Ecumenism, *Unitatis Redintegratio*, its Declaration on the Relation of the Church to Non-Christian Religions, *Nostra Aetate*, and its Pastoral Constitution on the Church in the Modern World, *Gaudium et Spes*. These documents cover the various "worlds" with which the ecclesial movements of today principally have to deal.[18]

If we had sufficient time, I would have liked to take up again the theme mentioned earlier of the sharing of material goods among the members of each movement, because this would indicate a radical kind of fidelity, which we can call "evangelical-apostolical"—and conciliar!— and which is strongly expressive, that is, of the reality of the *communion* of the movements themselves and of their reality in the context of today's "globalization." There is a certain realization here of a specific kind of social justice which provides an example for the life of the whole Church. In effect, in the documents of Vatican II, and with regard to the question of temporal goods, it remains necessary to go deeper into the question of actual practice, including that inspired by the primitive Christian community of which the Council provided an echo.[19]

I would like to conclude, though, with at least a brief mention of "the communion of the ecclesial movements in the one Church

---

[17]*Ibid*, p. 95ff.
[18]See, e. g., *Ibid.*, p. 186.
[19]*Ibid.*, pp. 188-192.

involved in the new evangelization." This clearly expands the horizon of the mission of these movements and of the new communities within the Church (as John Paul said on May 30, 1998, they are "united in the same communion for the same mission"[20]). Thus, there was necessarily a renewal of dialogue among them. At the same time, there became evident a new unity existing between and among them, one which had reference to the Holy Spirit and was based on the original charisms of the movements in question—and which had been operative before there was any diversification regarding specific missions.[21] Beyond what was characteristic of each, we note that there came about in various countries a kind of coordination that, while respectful of the characteristics of each movement, saw common kinds of missionary, apostolical, and social action taking place among them; they were evidently allowing themselves to be guided by the Spirit in reciprocal love.[22] It is a very consoling thing to see a new commitment in this way to evangelization, one which has come about among living members of a Church that is now renewed both in fidelity and in a common reception of the Second Vatican Council in its entirety.

At the end of this discourse of mine, you will permit me to add an appeal related to my current position as Secretary of the Pontifical Council for the Pastoral Care of Migrants and Itinerant People. This appeal is intended to inspire a greater commitment on the part of your various ecclesial movements in favor of migrants and itinerant people. The movement of people is certainly a characteristic of the world of today—which is also a markedly secularized world. The Council's documents fully recognized this (see *Gaudium et Spes* 65, 66, 87 and 27; and *Apostolicam Actuositatem* 10; and all this was also reflected from a pastoral standpoint in *Christus Dominus* 18).

---

[20]Pontifical Council for the Laity, *Movements in the Church: Acts of the World Congress of Ecclesial Movements,* Rome, May 27-29, 1998, Vatican City 1999, p. 221. With respect to the new evangelization and the common challenge to the Church, see the article—which is critical—of Gianni Colzani, *Nuova Evangelizzazione sfida Commune* [New Evangelization, Common Challenge], in *R.. Clero Ital.,* LXXXI (2000), pp. 646-665, but, especially, pp. 653-665.

[21]See C. Hegge, *op. cit.,* pp. 219-231.

[22]*Ibid.,* p. 231.

Courage, then! Take on and carry out these commitments that are so much in harmony with the signs of the times, with what the Council decided, and with what your movements are dedicated to carrying out!

VI

OFFICIAL AND PRIVATE CONCILIAR SOURCES

36

The Council As Seen by Cardinal Giuseppe Siri

Benny Lai, *Il Papa non eletto. Giuseppe Siri, Cardinale di Santa Romana Chiesa* [The Pope Not Elected: Giuseppe Siri, Cardinal of the Holy Roman Church], Laterza, Bari 1993. 416 pages.

We present this volume of "confessions" by the former archbishop of Genoa in particular for the pages included here from his "diary" of the Council. This book is by a journalist, which rather surprises us, even though he is a "loyal" one. The cardinal's "diary" was never completed, however. Evidently, he was thinking of putting together material for a biography to be done *post mortem*; this can be deduced from the way the presentation is made (see p. viii), though it is not given the title of such a presentation. A good part of the source material provided, however, consists of dialogues or colloquys with the cardinal or material in letters or other documents concerning him. This way of proceeding is not very pleasing to us.

But the book is nevertheless interesting. It is also true, and, in the end, rather brutally frank. It reveals a Siri who is very "human," with sensitivities which made him vulnerable. These contrast greatly with the rather cold manner of thought and ratiocination which he generally exhibited in public; he always wished to be identified with the *patrimonium fidei* (treasure of faith) of the Church.

The book begins by describing "the years of his infancy" and then those in the seminary and the university, culminating in his taking a degree. There follows a description of "his first experiences, his first successes, his first griefs and sadnesses." Then there were his "old acquaintances," which conditioned many future attitudes and judgments about him, some of them unfavorable, such as those of Cardinal Lercaro (see p. 17, n. 9; but also p. 85, n. 35) and of Bishops Emilio Guano and Franco Costa (see the pathetic attempt at a "memorial" on pp. 344-347, which is very significant). These unfavorable attitudes and judgments, along with some relatively "pitying" opinions, would later have serious consequences with regard to Siri's relations with Cardinal Montini; the relations with him, in fact, were very soon spoiled.

There follow the war and his appointment as auxiliary bishop. There was also his meeting, pregnant with consequences, with Pope Pius XII. Rather well delineated here is the rather strange wartime role of Siri "in trying to maintain good relations with the partisans as well as with the Germans and the Fascists" (p. 58). P. E. Taviani (an Italian politician) would later write that "the words of Siri were exact only in one face of the prism" (p. 69, n. 55).

And then he became archbishop of Genoa. This came about after the death of Cardinal Boetto as well as after various "intrigues" that were mounted against him. We report here two of the judgments he made about Fascism and Communism, respectively, among many: "The greatest fault that I attribute to Fascism in the period 1922-1939," he wrote, "is this: they lulled the episcopate and the priests into a condition of inaction" (p. 85, n. 41). As for Communism, he wrote that "the Communist danger was greatly feared" (p. 85, n. 42). It was in this context that he spoke of Luigi Gedda and his "anti-Communist function" (p. 87, esp. n. 44) and also about the "excommunication of the Communists" (p. 89). He expressed his conviction to Pope Pius XII that "the Communist militancy of many workers was devoid of ideological content." There is mention here too of the commitment of this archbishop of Genoa to the creation of an Italian Bishops' conference. He relied here on his "friend," Cardinal Ruffini of Palermo. Pius XII, however, remained distinctly "cool" to the idea of a bishops' conference, although he accepted it in part.

With Siri's elevation to the cardinalate, there began for him a long period in which he took on responsibilities for matters concerning Italy as a whole that went far beyond those pertaining to the archdiocese of Genoa alone. What was his opinion of Alcide De Gaspari? "He approved his moderate line" (p. 94). What about Socialism? He manifested various judgments with respect to Montini, who was supposedly "banished" from Rome on account of a letter of resignation from [Catholic Youth Action leader] Mario Rossi which Montini had simply "placed in a drawer" without action (see pp. 98ff.; and see also p. 100, n. 18 for a very characteristic judgment of Siri about the man who would become Pope Paul VI). Cardinal Siri agreed, though, to become the president of the episcopal commission for Catholic Action and thus he was the "channel" to and from the Holy See as far as Italian affairs were concerned. This book deals with all these things "from the point of view" of the archbishop of Genoa, and the interest inherent in this particular approach cannot be doubted.

At this point in the book, the question of "relations with the U.S.S.R." are covered, and in the course of this treatment we learn of the role of the religious man, Father Damasus da Celle Ligure (Secular name: Bernardo Testa), for which documentation is also provided (pp. 301-343). This documentation was given to the author by His Eminence "so that at least one day the truth will be known" (p. 113, n. 3). We take note also of the fact that the papal "secretariat of state believed it was opportune to reserve to itself everything related to this most delicate question" (p. 318). This was attested to by the aforementioned Father Damasus da Celle Ligure on February 25, 1957. Nevertheless, Soviet diplomats still continued to knock on the door of the archdiocese of Genoa.

May we be permitted simply to leave aside the material recorded here related to the conclave of October 28, 1958 (pp. 139-144), along with that linked to the one of 1978 (pp. 262-281), and also the unhappy declaration, as we judge it to be, that "I have asked for God's forgiveness" (pp. 296ff.) The same thing applies to Siri's statements that: "I have great remorse...I said no, and if you elect me I will again say no. I did wrong, and today I understand this. Just today? No, for several years now. I did wrong, because I should have avoided doing certain things. I wanted to own up to this, but I feared admitting certain errors" (p. 296).

Let us return, instead, to the questions related to Italian society. The chapter which is specifically dedicated to this (pp. 145-178) "reveals" a great deal about the "tasks" carried out by the cardinal of Genoa and also about political affairs in Italy generally, and not only in Italy. All this time, the rapport of mutual sympathy and esteem, not to speak of actual collaboration, between Cardinal Siri and Cardinal Domenico Tardini, grew apace ("I came to realize the extent of his stature. I don't know if he surpassed the famous Cardinal Pietro Gasparri, whom I knew when he was old, and no longer secretary of state; but of all those I knew [Tardini] was the greatest"—p. 148, n. 1). We are made witnesses here also to the affairs of the Christian Democrats in Italy, and to their difficult relations with the Socialists, beginning with Giovanni Gronchi. We also learn about the financial difficulties of Cardinal Roncalli in Venice...and about the advice given by Siri to the latter after he was elected pope about what to do in economic and financial matters (p. 155). Siri was good at juggling figures, as a matter of fact. There are evidences here also pointing to a "Johannine disengagement" from Italian politics (not that the pope was "indifferent," in this matter however). There are further evidences of contrasts of vision concerning the "center-left" between Montini, Ottaviani, Urbani, and Lercaro, the end results of which effectively left the responsibility for the direction of Italian Catholic Action in the hands of Cardinal Siri. Then there are the indications concerning the attitude of Pope John XXIII towards politics that do not tally with the "political" role that is generally attributed to him (p. 172). These indications arise from the evidence that he opposed the entrance of the Socialists into the governing majority. There are a number of memorable visions of this pope that are brought out here: "Have they deceived you up to this point, Holy Father?" Nevertheless, he was able to discern or detect evil when it appeared (p. 173). It seems too that there was a kind of conspiracy or plot against Cardinal Siri; things were being decided at his expense.

And at this point we arrive at the chapter bearing the title "The

Council of John XXIII" (pp. 179-198). To this is added the part of the Siri "diary" that relates to that same conciliar period (pp. 356-383). There are also a number of unpublished documents included here (pp. 348-355; see p. 372, n. 69, from which we learn that Monsignor A. Mauro functioned as secretary). These documents relate to the activity of the Council's Secretariat for Extraordinary Affairs, of which Cardinal Siri was a member. From all this there resulted the preoccupation of the Genoa cardinal with the "pastoral turn" of the Council which John XXIII so much desired, and there was also Cardinal Siri's perplexity with what is described as "the innovative theology that emerged in France and Germany after the Second World War along with all the ferment in the area of biblical studies" (p. 179). Then it was evident the role of Cardinal Ruffini, whether because of the earlier suggestion he had made to John XXIII to convene a council (*Ibid.*), or simply on account of his dynamism generally. Numerous opinions, votes, interventions, and explanations concerning the various roles of the archbishop of Genoa are reported on, some referred to "errors" he thought needed to be condemned by the Council. His views on the ambiguity of the term *"aggiornamento"* are also reported. At first he believed that the "Roman calm would prevail," but then he added later to some of the original thoughts in his diary a wise and prudent marginal note to the effect that "certain thoughts here and in the pages that follow are perhaps not completely certain or not completely objective." This certainly redounds to the great credit of the man; he was able to question himself as well as to articulate his views. Yet however that may be, it is worth reporting his thoughts on the pope's Opening Address to the Council: "I am fearful about two points that might be misused; perhaps it is this that prevented me from sleeping for a good while" (p. 184). He harbored doubts about the Council's initial Message to Humanity as well, perhaps because of the unhappy expression of Cardinal Confaloniere that this Message represented simply "a couple of pages thrown out to the world" (*Ibid.*). It is important to bear in mind also his disagreement with Montini concerning the election by the Italians of "foreign" members of the conciliar commissions—a situation which provoked discomfort and even stupefaction in him. He also deplored a lack of adequate "foundation, management, and direction" (p. 376). Siri basically wished to follow the Curia, while Montini wanted to search for the good of Italy (p. 192), "and appealed to him—rightly considered—in this regard, to work from what is already there and prepared" in the documents before them. Montini, meanwhile, sought the opinions of the presidents of the major bishops' conferences.

But John XXIII wanted to maintain a proper balance, perhaps because he was convinced that the Italians ought to seek actively to carry out balancing actions and to try to get things to dove-tail, as Cardinal Alfrink expressed it. Cardinal Siri agreed with him about this: "That is how we have always acted," he said (p. 194). The account of the meeting of the major Council figures at Santa Maria dell'Anima, to which Siri was also invited because of the suggestion of John XXIII, is quite interesting (p. 193). The Genoa cardinal had his own position on the question of the sources of revelation, *de fontibus revelationis* (see pp. 380ff. and 383 concerning what the Council had "revealed" in this regard). He wanted to go in three directions at once within the Italian episcopate: set up and maintain relations with European and American confreres as well, while at the same time establishing both a "study group" and an "oversight group" in order to be aware of what others were doing, and also to keep up with what was going on in Rome. Nothing was ever really done, however, about the first or third of these ideas.

The chapter entitled "The Council of Paul VI" (pp. 207-223) includes the material from the Siri "diary" on the Third Session. Once Montini "became pope, he was the one who henceforth guided the Council in practice" (p. 206, n. 17; see this also for the changes he introduced relating to the management of the assembly). Cardinal Siri immediately observed as follows concerning all this: "In contrast to what had taken place previously, the Italian episcopate began to deal with the new phase of the Council with more adequate positions on the issues being promoted by the president of the Italian bishops' conference" (p. 207).

The revised plan included seventeen *schemata* that "reflected the ideas of Paul VI when he was a cardinal" (*Ibid.*). His central concern was always the documents relating to the Church. But Cardinal Siri had reservations about some of these documents (see pp. 208ff.).

Following the "Dossetti crisis," things continued to look up for the cardinal, however, and his well being was actually restored somewhat. Though he remained "in reserve" for awhile, he was eventually paired with Cardinal Luigi Traglia and became the Pro-President of the Italian bishops' conference. He rejoiced at the end however for the *Nota Explicativa Praevia* (p. 219; but see also p. 234, n. 30). He expressed his sentiments on it as follows: "Everything has turned out for the better. The Holy Spirit has intervened at the Council. This morning the vote was nearly unanimous…Thus the watershed of the Council has been the pope who set the course and only he was in a position to do so. God has remained with his Church. Things are coming to be seen with clarity, and the importance of today's vote will result in its being seen as historical" (p. 402).

We would like to quote yet another judgment of his at this point, as follows: "The history of this Council has in large part been a history of the views of the various *periti*, since there turned out to be such a paucity of theological knowledge, both in the episcopate and in the sacred college" (p. 390). Paul VI, would remark in this regard that the Italian Council Fathers generally lacked an "historical sense" about theology.

"With his health restored, Siri went back full time to concerning himself with the Italian bishops' conference" (p. 222). He collaborated in the drafting of its new statutes and continued to work along these same lines until he received an "official communication that the pope had accepted his resignation from the presidency of the Italian bishops' conference—which he had never offered" (p. 222). We believe the case here was similar to that of Cardinal Lercaro's in Bologna (see pp. 239ff. in confirmation of this). In each case, however, the reality was somewhat different. To understand Siri's case, it is necessary to read page 204. The attempt to work with a pope he had so regularly complained about was finished.

"The End of the Council and Its Dangers" (pp. 224-244) covers the Fourth Session of the Council, which was the final one. It was characterized by "the activities of the conciliar commissions...engaged in the correction and finalizing of the eleven *schemata* which still had to be approved and also with the various votes that took place." As far as Italy was concerned, it was the time during which Bishop Costa was occupied with political contacts on behalf of the Italian bishops' conference; the latter's efforts were favorable to Aldo Moro and his governmental "experiment." The pages devoted to this subject make some interesting points, but also are quite painful. Nevertheless, the author continues to present the points of view, often critical, of Cardinal Siri at the Council (particularly on the subjects of tradition, religious liberty, and church-state relations in the contemporary world). He can be faulted for a number of "simplifications" here (see p. 233, n. 27), including his treatment of the subject of the journal *Renovatio*, which was supposed to rival the journal *Concilium*, as well as his treatment of the Synod of Bishops and the reform of the Roman Curia.

On the whole, however, Cardinal Siri maintained his distance from "extremist traditionalism" (p. 239). At the same time, however, he did oppose the "wave of dissent" which began to sweep over the Church (pp. 246ff.); he carefully identified the causes of it, paying special attention to the situation of Pope Paul VI to whom he had "become out of favor" (p. 249). Siri himself noted how he was out of favor at this point with the sacred college (p. 250). But the pope had meanwhile become a target of polemics on account of the encyclical *Humanae Vitae*, and "he then began to change his mind about the archbishop of Genoa" (p. 253). At the same time, the "star" of Bishop Franco Costa also began to sink as far as Italian affairs were concerned, and it shortly disappeared entirely and became extinct" (pp. 255ff.).

Then comes the chapter entitled "The End" (pp. 282-295). It did not come about, however, without the cardinal's attempt to mediate between Pope John Paul II and Archbishop Marcel Lefebvre. Siri had initially been quite enthusiastic about John Paul II, although he made a few "critical remarks" as well (see p. 290 in particular). He also had to deal with the Ballestrero era when the latter, Cardinal Anastasio

Ballestrero, O.C.D., was the head of the Italian bishops' conference. There was also the meeting at Loreto, not to speak of the publication of Cardinal Siri's book *Getsemani*. Finally, the pope accepted the Genoa cardinal archbishop's resignation (p. 293). This last was a bitter pill; the cardinal's action was based on pure obedience, as becomes apparent, if only when reading between the lines, in the following words which he addressed to the faithful of Genoa: "I am not abandoning you. I am only doing my duty. I am obeying...You may imagine that I am quitting but this is not the case. Don't even ask whether I have a heart of stone. I do not. Nobody can really imagine what a father feels, undergoes, when he is obliged to take leave of his own family" (p. 293). This pretty much expresses everything.

In addition to the appendices that we have already mentioned, the book concludes with an index both of names (pp. 407-414) and of works.

37

Council Notes of
Father Marie-Dominique Chenu

Chenu Marie-Dominique, O.P., *Notes quotidiennes au Concile (1962-1963)*
[Daily Notes at the Council (1962-1963)], Critical edition with an introduction
by Alberto Melloni, Éditions du Cerf, Paris 1995, 153 pages.

In looking at yet another work of this type concerning the on-
going historical research on the Second Vatican Council, we agree that
we have probably arrived at some kind of "diary phase" with regard
to the study of the Council. This is not a happy outcome because it
means a dizzying multiplication of information about the Council that
must be checked and verified against the official sources. A simple
reading of these private sources sometimes reveals discrepancies
and variations in the attribution of positions and the distribution of
"merits." As is well known, it is only all too "human" to attribute
virtues from the very outset to positions that eventually came to
dominate. Also, the knowledge of any one observer is always very
particular and partial, especially with respect to the complexity of the
events unfolding at the Council as well as its proceedings. There are
complicated interrelationships between all the regulation, "pressures,"
and movements, and also with respect to all the "battles" that had to
be organized against the "progressives," or the "conservatives," or
the Roman Curia. There is also the question of the *avant-garde* of
theologians and their special "magisterium" in contrast to the Church's
real magisterium; there is equally the question of interpreting the
pastoral and ecumenical directions being taken by various conciliar
figures, especially Pope John XXIII. We could go on enumerating

such points but we will stop here. Much more important is the task of discerning with a critical spirit the contributions of various voices to the history of Vatican II that has been developed up to this point, whether these contributions have been made by attentive observers at the Council or by active protagonists who were there.

Father M. D. Chenu, O.P., was one of the latter, and this book consists mainly of a few brief notes of his, scarcely a hundred pages in all. Most of them have reference to the First Session; there are only about ten pages referring to the Second Session, along with another ten references in the Notes (pp. 94-104). A document of Father Giuseppe Dossetti's is also reproduced, both in the original and in translation. All this is preceded by no less than 54 pages by Alberto Melloni on the subject of "diaries," as he calls them, which he considers to be basic "sources" (p. 7). We are supposed to single them out for their "great historical-critical importance," as he characterizes it (*Ibid.*). We respond immediately to say that this depends on a number of factors, and, most especially, on how these kinds of sources are used or applied in accordance with historical-critical criteria. That his affirmation of their great importance is "especially" applicable to a "modern" Council—which is one he defines as "not centered on a profession of faith or engaged principally in promulgating papal decrees" (*Ibid.*)—is a thesis that remains to be demonstrated, just as the chief distinction that needs to be made concerning Church synods and councils is not whether or not they are "modern," but whether or not they are ecumenical!

Moreover, the attention given to these conciliar "diaries" is hardly something new (see pp. 9 and 10). Melloni's discourse is interrupted at this point by his assertion that the diaries pertaining to Vatican II have been disregarded or "forgotten." Yet he prefers them as sources to the "objective" and "official" conciliar sources. He believes these latter ones have been wrongly overvalued, and he states that "the critical reliability of these official sources must be entirely re-evaluated" (p. 10). This is a very grave assertion. What we have here is a "fatal leap" from the official sources that are thus disvalued to private sources that mostly arose out of a lack of confidence in what the author calls "small Roman circles closed in upon themselves"; and, by contrast, in a plethora of blind confidence in what the author describes as "the echoes of the actual work that took place in a multi-lingual and variegated assembly such as the Council was" (p. 10). All this seems to us to be both "ideological" and based upon the author's "preconceived ideas." In any case, the publication of the Council's official acts in no way depended simply upon what Melloni several times calls the "Felici source," but rather it arose out of the wise and repeated dispositions made by Pope Paul VI to insure that everything related to the Council from all the various commissions, congregations, and other organizations was in fact collected and preserved. The purpose of this was precisely to avoid what had happened at Vatican I, for example, when much of this kind of material got dispersed. Pope Montini thereby showed himself to be a true "historian" by inclination, interest, and foresight; and, in this regard, the author's note 3 on page 10 indicates simple incomprehension of what the pope was about. Nevertheless, there are still those who stand aloof and try to preserve for themselves or for the positions they take a favored interpretation of the events of the Council; Father Dossetti himself did this with the "minutes" of the meetings of the Council Moderators which he prepared.

In order to defend his own point of view, the author speaks of a "shadow" cast over the use of diaries *stricto sensu* because of the partisan positions of their authors in the events they are describing. Passing on to a further analysis of the supposed neglect or disregard of these private sources, Melloni claims that as a result many protagonists fail to write their own accounts; the history of what happened is thus confined to what appears in books based on newspaper articles and those appearing in journals. He actually presents a "typology" of diaries (pp. 13-23), including a category of those of a more general nature that also happen to include references to the Council as well (e.g., the "agendas" of Pope Roncalli, both before and during the Council). Another category are those pertaining to the preparation of the Council (such as the "notes" of Father Sebastian Tromp); and yet another consists of those referring to the unfolding of the conciliar events as such. But it seems a bit much to say, as the author does say, that it is not false to formulate a hypothesis according to which each actor in the preparation of the Council kept a diary until it can be proved that some did not. He further speaks of a sub-type of "diary" made up from the writings of the Council leaders, theologians, or even the laity. This division of supposed different "types" of diaries seems quite excessive to us. What is the point of it? *Ad quid*?

Then there is Melloni's subtitle, "Character and Function of Diaries: The 'Test' of October 11, 1962." Here appear the final reflections of the author concerning the passage from an abstract evaluation of the character of various sources to a more concrete comparison of various approaches made and different perceptions recorded of the events that took place on the above-mentioned date [the opening day of the Council]. This is an example to which we would like to add an "objectifying" factor, even if it seems petty to do so. And so we ask what the various accounts in the diaries cited by the author really bring to the understanding of the conciliar *quid*, objectively speaking. Given the theme proposed by Melloni, what do the accounts by Bertetto, Jungmann, Bartoletti, and others really add? They say interesting things, which naturally reveal their own points of view, and even also perhaps their personalities. But how does all this really relate to objective facts of what took place on that first day of the Council? We ask this question so that the importance of what was said by any particular individual will not be exaggerated. (Would we consider them "triumphalist" if they wrote of a "glorious and historical day"?) In any case, the testimony of an individual can be presented in a misleading way which does not correspond to the text quoted (see, e.g., Labourdette, p. 35, and also a "magnificent" Congar whose first reaction is positive, but whose considered "reflections" are much more muted in the afternoon (pp. 37ff. and again p. 49).

Melloni finally gets around to dealing with the actual diary of Father Chenu (pp. 48-54). He finds it "typical" and "middle-of-the-road." It is neither voluminous, analytical, nor caught up with details. It comes from a private *peritus*. This very fact says something about its character; the press is one of the original factors present in this diary, along with reports of conversations with numerous people. Two things emerge from this text, and that is the role of Father Chenu in the formulation of the text of the Council's initial Message to Humanity, and his participation in the "Volk group" [of theologians gathered around the Bishop of Mainz, Hermann Volk]. Except in these cases, Chenu seemed to keep himself a bit distant from other "known" theologians with the exception of Yves Congar.

Melloni succeeds in presenting Chenu as a Council figure, both on the basis of this diary and on that of his two major interests, Africa and the East (see pp. 130ff., for example). He concludes with a long summary of the final significance of Chenu's participation: "All of this would require not a few *'conciliabuli"* where the Holy Spirit might be present, at least among the secondary causes, if not among the tertiary ones. After which, it would take a certain time in prayer to get back to the First Cause" (p. 54). This is well said.

The diary opens with a kind of presentation of the theologians most prominently in view at the Council, and then gives the background of the preparation of the Message to Humanity in which Father Chenu played a part, as we have already noted. We do, however, also have to take into account the somewhat different testimony about this of Archbishop Garrone as well as that of Father Congar (see esp. pp. 78-79, n. 1, not to speak of p. 82, n. 3; then see p. 129). There is also an account of the debates on the modification or rejection of the four dogmatic *schemata*, mentioning both the "German" and the "French" tactics on the subject of how to proceed (pp. 76 and 90; then see p. 124). Cardinal Ruffini referred to these activities as "revisions." There is an account here too of the famous election of the members of the ten conciliar commissions. Chenu also has words of praise for both Pope John XXIII and Archbishop Felici (p. 77, n. 1) and for the nominations made by the pope; but "the results were somewhat deceptive," he writes (p. 83, n. 3 and p. 84).

Then there is an account of the unfolding of the various meetings and encounters, with particular emphasis on those with Father Dossetti. The diary includes a text of Dossetti's which was given to

Chenu and which occupies around ten pages (pp. 94-104); the theme of this particular text is the pivot-question to the effect that "a council could never prepare itself." Here we encounter the same "despairing" Dossetti of the first part of the book, *Vaticano II. Frammenti di una riflessione* [Vatican II: Fragments of a Reflection] (Il Mulino, 1996). He was involved in the orientation votes in a spirit that excluded any compromises and looked to a subsequent council, if necessary, for vindication. Meanwhile he was involved in the battle over conciliar procedures and he actually had the courage—if that is what it was—to claim that it was by proceeding in this fashion that he always "won." Here Dossetti is encountered asking Chenu to send him "any pertinent information, notes, or documents."

It is worth recording that the Council's rejection and sending back of the documents already favorably commended by the pope is described in these notes with a translation into French which is sometimes misleading. This is one more indication of how this kind of private "testimony" that has not been published, but has remained in the hands of a few people, can impact negatively on our true knowledge of what actually took place.

However, the "strategy" adopted by Cardinal Ottaviani is well sketched out here (pp. 121-122). We think that the Latin originals of texts translated into French here might also have been included, as is the case with texts translated from other languages.

Quite notable here are the judgments of Father Chenu—which we do not share—on the subject of the supposed "two theologies" in the revised draft of the *Schema De Ecclesia* (p. 124; see, however, p. 135, n. 2, which contains a very different evaluation); on the subject of the "Latinism" of the Maronites (p. 124); on that of the influence of the positions of Cardinals Ruffini and Ottaviani in connection with the "stomach cancer" of Pope John XXIII (p. 133); on one of the key interventions of Cardinal Montini (p. 134); on another key intervention of Bishop Luigi Bettazzi, which drew much praise (p. 142); on the subject of the Church in Poland (p. 138ff.); on that of the unsuccessful attempt to create a new Secretariat for the problems of the modern world (pp. 125, 127, n. 1, with its criticisms of the Curia and of its filter on various proposals, mostly made by bishops, p. 133); and on the proposal to introduce the laity into the workings of the Council itself (pp. 136ff., including the negative reaction of Pope John XXIII). Finally, there is an account of the expression Paul VI is supposed to have uttered to the effect that the opposition was "beaten," as this manuscript reports it, or, in another version, that "we have won." This latter translation was supposedly intended to tone the pontiff's reaction down somewhat (p. 144), but it is not found in the version of the incident given by Cardinal Lercaro (*Ibid.*, n. 1). Certainly, it would seem to be more in conformity with the spirit of Pope Montini than the simple exclamation that the other side had been "beaten," as Dossetti would have it. Significantly, there is nothing in this account of Chenu's that bears on the subject of the questions that were posed to the Council Fathers, nor is there anything concerning the prepared ballots by Father Dossetti that were destroyed.

The volume concludes with an alphabetical index of the names mentioned and other subject matter (pp. 147-153).

38

Vatican II in the Diary of
Archbishop Neophytos Edelby

Edelby Neophytos, *Il Vaticano II nel diario di un vescovo arabo* [Vatican II in the Diary of an Arab Bishop]. Edited by Riccardo Cannelli, with an Introduction by Andrea Riccardi, Edizioni San Paolo, Cinisello Balsamo, 1996, 360 pages.

Historical research on the subject of the Second Vatican Council has now entered into a "diary phase" which does not make things easier because it means a rather considerable multiplication of the information that has to be verified and compared with the official sources. In effect, merely to read through some of this material turns up discrepancies and a variety of attributions and distributions of "merits." It is only human to claim that one always was correct with regard to positions and directions that ultimately proved to be those adopted by the Council. This is all the more true because the information and knowledge available to individuals is necessarily partial, particularly with respect to the complexity of all the conciliar issues and procedures. There is necessarily an intricate relationship between all the various regulations, "pressures," and movements, as well as the organizing of "battles" against the Curia and such that so characterized the Council. Then there were the *avant-garde* of theologians with their "magisterium" parallel to the official magisterium. There was also the question of how to interpret the pastoral and ecumenical directions being taken by the Council leaders, particularly the directions desired by Pope John XXIII himself. We could say more. It is better, however, to cultivate a critical spirit in evaluating the contributions to the history of the Council made by some of its participants who were particularly attentive to what was going on. One of these contributions is the diary of Archbishop Edelby, which has recently appeared. He was the titular Melchite archbishop of Edessa and an important Council Father in his own right.

To describe him as a member of the Eastern Catholic hierarchy already involves the situation within the Eastern Catholic Churches in communion with Rome. This impression is greatly reinforced by the reading of this text. At bottom, his is the voice of the Orthodox East, which thus was heard within the conciliar assembly itself as well as outside it, and which is also echoed in the pages of this book. Allow us to state this because it was also recognized by the late, venerated Orthodox Patriarch Athenagoras himself (see pp. 18, 23, 124, n. 123, 125, n. 124, 127ff., 159, n. 22, 183, 185, and 196). This book also brings out the "solitary nature" of the thoughts and positions of the Melchites at the Council as compared with the other Eastern Catholic Churches (see pp. 57, 73, 87, 89, n. 85, 126-127, 132, 157, 166, 220, n. 55, 246, 256, 258, and 260).

The book really constitutes an essay on the Eastern Christian mentality and sensitivity in a very strong way. It is an opening on the Christian East, as it were. It also explains the particular sensitivity and even touchingness of the Eastern Christians, which is easy to understand from a number of points of view (see pp. 34, 37, 42, 45, 66, 67, 126, 159, n. 22, 233, 309, and 314), though there is a certain internal contradiction involved here as well. Emblematic of the way Eastern Christians see themselves was the support given by them to the project for the idea of a "Church of the poor," which, however, was not ultimately to be realized as such, *qua talis* (see pp. 59, n. 49, 92, and 93, n. 89). Yet no mention is made of Cardinal Lercaro's promotion of this idea (p. 118). The felt need for a certain respectability and also a concern for appearances is palpable in the pages of Archbishop Edelby's diary, however, and it is also recognizable in what he himself calls "the great lesson that the American bishops have taught us, namely, simplicity" (p. 180; but see esp. pp. 319-321, on the "magical" moment of his visit to France).

In this small book, which is quite well written, we seem almost to be present at the veritable "panorama" of the various meetings and visits (paid and received) and of the many invitations to lunch and dinner and the like—all of which often constituted the background of the Council for many participants, at least from a human point of view. Moreover, the Melchite episcopacy proved in many respects to be the "connective tissue" for many of the relationships among the bishops—whom perhaps with not the greatest exactitude we could style "progressive" bishops (especially by comparison with some of the well known theologians involved). In this diary, however, to the great credit of its author, there is evident a very great pastoral preoccupation (almost calling their faithful by name), especially but not entirely with regard to the situation of the Melchite people now spread throughout the world (see p. 331). This preoccupation encountered its opposite, however, in the Council's commitment to deal with the relations between Christians and Jews. In the end, the archbishop notes, "It will be the Zionists who will be most unhappy" (see pp. 25, 202, 237, 240-242, 243, n. 12, 246, 287, 303, 308-309, n. 11, and 314-315). Yet it was the differences between the Eastern and Western Fathers on the need to deal with the Jews that resulted in raising and dealing with the question of Islam as well in *Nostra Aetate*.

Of particular importance in this contribution to conciliar history, however, is what we would call "the patriarchal mentality" (see pp. 23, 24, and 25). Reference is made to its "pedagogical function" (pp. 37, n. 10, 49, n. 28, 159, n. 22, 164, 167, 169, 170-173, 221, 248, 257, n. 24, 260). Then there is the question of what the author calls "the suppression of the Latin Patriarch of Jerusalem" (p. 263) which, according to him, "introduced into the West," a historical institution (the patriarchate) of great importance, the existence of which can be attributed to "divine Providence." This would be an ecumenical plus, he thinks (see pp. 38 and 172). He considers "erroneous," however, the idea that the pope might have "delegated" apostolic power to the patriarchs and to the bishops. Certainly it was not the Roman Curia that did so. He sees future relations with the Eastern Orthodox as heavily dependent upon how the Eastern Catholic Churches are treated (p. 42,

n. 20). But he believes in general that the relationships of the Eastern Catholic Patriarchs in communion with Rome represent a very special relationship (see pp. 24 and 51, n. 31).

Following the introduction of Andrea Riccardi, which succeeds in presenting the human and Christian figure of Archbishop Edelby as he presented himself in his Melchite and Arab identity, the preface of Riccardo Cannelli on the subject of this relatively young advisor and counselor of the aged Patriarch Maximos IV Saigh concludes with an important "note from the editor" (p. 26). He describes the quality of the text quite positively (p. 22); it is correctly styled a "synodal narrative," "a sort of diary of the Melchite community." This is an aspect of this work that we too much appreciate; it speaks favorably of "the conciliar spirit of the Melchites" (p. 23).

The "diary" itself begins by accurately reporting on the First Session (of the Council) and it culminates with the meeting where the strategy of the Melchites at the Council was decided (pp. 71-72, and, later, p. 95; as a "counterpoint" to this, there was the position of Archbishop Elias Zoghby, p. 72, n. 65). As the narrative proceeds, we note some negative judgments on Latin bishops that had emanated from behind the Iron Curtain (p. 47), as well as on what is called "the first defeat inflicted upon the Secretariat, which perhaps wished to run the Council the way a conductor conducts an orchestra" (p. 53). But which "Secretariat" is he even talking about? This mention of a "defeat" refers to the case of Bishop Sensi, who had offered a justified criticism of the adoption in the West of some Melchite ideas, and hence of Eastern ideas (p. 69, n. 61), on the subject of Latin. The subject of the liturgy itself represents a different case; we should recall, for example, that Old Slavonic is employed in the liturgy in the East; yet there is no mention of that here; the vernacular was even employed on occasion at the Council (pp. 75-76). Archbishop Edelby delivers himself of further negative judgments when he observes that "the members of the Curia attacked the Council Fathers more often than the latter attacked them" (p. 98). But were not the Curia bishops equally "Council Fathers"? Similarly, he asserts flatly that "there was no need for the Council to issue any dogmatic declarations" (p. 100).

And there are also some contradictions in what he himself asserts (pp. 113-114). Moreover, Archbishop Edelby sometimes says in vague and inexact language what he should have written in a much more straightforward and pointed fashion, and perhaps also with a little more humility. But can a historian legitimately raise this kind of question?

We also find some further imprecise writing of his on the subject of interpretation of some "applause" that was registered at a certain point (p. 131). He does better with his excellent description of the ecumenical method of the Melchite Patriarch Maximos IV Saigh (p. 134), and how it applies to the primacy of Peter.

The diary's treatment of the Second Session opens by evidencing some asperity on the part of Archbishop Edelby, who was working within the Commission for the Oriental Churches (see pp. 141, 145, 146, and 149). He eventually concludes that "the antagonistic groupings have reached an understanding and have ceased attacking each other" (p. 155). However, shortly after writing this, he adds that "Cardinal Ruffini and the Italian bishops in their entirety are dead set against any idea of episcopal collegiality...Thus the reactionary opposition has re-emerged. Still the progressive majority is alert to this" (p. 158). Why does he employ the adjective "reactionary"? Moreover, it is worth making mention of his interpretation of Vatican I's *ex sese et non ex consensu Ecclesiae* ["for themselves, and not from the consent of the Church"]. He becomes pretty ponderous, though, when he gets into rendering judgments not without a certain polemical spirit (see pp. 174-179, 185, 189, 190, and 191). And this is not to include anything about his mention of the "false steps" supposedly taken by the Council Moderators. The defense of Cardinal Döpfner is reported *post factum* (p. 207), but the author does not seem to realize how incongruous his judgments on the Spanish and Italian bishops and on the Roman Curia are when viewed in the context of the actual Council voting (pp. 192, 200, 204-205). He employs a double standard when dealing in one way with the Dossetti-Rugambwa collaboration and in another way with that of Ruffini-Siri-Batanian. The fact is that all sides "maneuvered" to advance their positions. Much more measured and impartial was the judgment of Cardinal Tisserant, who remarked that "if it were necessary to interrupt Cardinal Ruffini, it would have been equally necessary to interrupt the diatribe of Patriarch Maximos IV Saigh delivered the day before (pp. 206 and 217).

The Council's Third Session offers an opportunity to take note of the Melchite vision on the crucial point of the Council, namely, the subject of episcopal collegiality (p. 237). Actually, it seems to us that there was a change in attitude towards "the group of conservatives" who requested a clarification of the meaning of collegiality (p. 281). In any case, Edelby's interpretation of the *Nota Explicativa Praevia* leaves much to be desired (p. 285), as does his citation of Giuseppe Alberigo in note 49. The same thing is true of the archbishop's comments on the *schema De Sacra Revelatione.* Is it really true to state that Monsignor Antonio Romeo was "the ringleader in the Curia of the opposition to the Council"? Then there is the position on the Eastern Catholic Churches, which turns out to be surprising for a Melchite (pp. 271-272, nn. 37-38). In passing, his comments on the review *Concilium* in Italy seem excessive to us (p. 266). So do his comments on the scholastic idea of "mortal sin" (p. 267) and on birth control (pp. 269-270). Concerning this latter topic, he cites a letter which Maximos IV sent to the pope, and he remarks that "everybody was expecting a change." The language and expressions he reports concerning Bishop Carli merit blame (p. 273), even though they are not Archbishop Edelby's own words. Quite correct, however, is his judgment that "at the Council there can be neither victors nor vanquished" (p. 286).

The Fourth Session as covered here provides an occasion to revisit the subject of religious liberty, although Archbishop Edelby reveals a misunderstanding concerning the idea of a "right to existence" of non-Catholic religions (p. 294). There is also a clarification concerning the intervention of Archbishop Elias Zoghby on "the possibility of divorce in some cases in the Orthodox tradition" (pp. 302, 304, n. 8; and for the words of the patriarch, see p. 306, n. 9). Similarly, Eastern opinion on the subject of sacerdotal celibacy is mentioned (pp. 308, n. 11 and 310), the pope having reserved this subject to himself (p. 312, nn. 14-15). Other subjects dealt with include freedom in the election of bishops (p. 323) and indulgences (pp. 328ff.). A typical observation of Edelby's is his comment here claiming that "frightened by the intervention of the Patriarch, the Secretary General of the Council did not dare reply" (pp. 328ff.). Reported on here also is the *claque* expressly created in favor of Cardinal Döpfner. One begins immediately to understand why the President of the Council was obliged to insist that there be no applause in the *aula*. With all this, Edelby still actually approved the actions of the pope aimed at "maintaining the unanimity of the episcopacy in charity." He even adds: "Was there any better way to act?" (p. 333). He reports also on the announcement of the "lifting of the excommunication once directed against the Patriarch of Constantinople." In Istanbul, a comparable lifting of the excommunication of the pope was simultaneously announced. Archbishop Edelby's diary ends on this note.

Included, however, is a listing of the works of Archbishop Edelby, along with those of the principal exponents of the Melchite positions at the Council. There are also indexes both of names and of subjects. With regard to *errata*, we note: *al latinisti* (p. 57, n. 46), which should be *ai latinisti* ["to the Latinists"]; *Hevolino* (p. 130), which should be *Jervolino*; *valige* (p. 140), which should be *valigie* ["suitcases"]; *Roberts, former archbishop of Bombay* (p. 174), which should be: *Roberts, former apostolic vicar of Bombay*; *del grande e piccolo seminario* ["of the large and small seminary"] (p. 282) should be: *del seminario maggiore e minore* ["of the major and minor seminary"]; *alla Croce di legno* ["on the Cross of Wood"] (p. 286) should be *dalla croce di legno* ["with the cross of wood"].

39

Augustin Bea, Council Father

Schmidt Stjepan, *Agostino Bea, Cardinale dell'ecumenismo e del dialogo* [Augustin Bea: Cardinal of Ecumenism and the Dialogue], Edizioni San Paolo, Alba 1996, 197 pages.

Our interest in this volume, which is a condensation of a much larger tome entitled *Agostino Bea. Il Cardinale dell'unità* [Augustin Bea: the Cardinal of Unity] (Città Nuova Editrice, Rome 1987), lies principally in the part of Cardinal Bea's life related to his work at the Council. We note at the outset that the author, Stjepan Schmidt, is very well qualified for the task of writing this biography, since he was the secretary of the late cardinal.

Following a Preface by His Eminence Cardinal Edward Idris Cassidy, the author in his Introduction provides some biographical data on this illustrious man of the Church, Cardinal Bea. He includes a few judgments on him as well, i.e., that he was a "great personality," and he mentions some of his sources. In the first chapter, he discusses the "roots" of the cardinal's life, his upbringing in a "serene but demanding environment," his parental home (the "domestic Church"), his schooling in three different "gymnasiums," his theological studies, and, finally, his decision to join the Jesuits.

There followed "twelve years of ascetical and intellectual formation: 1902-1914." "Through difficulties he sought the light." There followed then the novitiate where he had to endure difficult associates. Then came the priesthood, specialized studies, and his

541

"third year of testing." After that, in the chapter which follows, there came "the vast and serious responsibilities of 1914-1930," when he was a Jesuit superior. This was during the war and afterwards he was a professor of Sacred Scripture. It is worth mentioning his method as a teacher: "I promised not to avoid or evade before my students any important modern controversy, but at the same time to offer them a solution based on a conscientious examination of all the elements of the problem, meanwhile respecting as faithfully as possible the tradition and the magisterium of the Church" (p. 36). Bea subsequently became the prefect of studies and a provincial superior, and, finally, in Rome, he was made responsible for the formation of future teachers of philosophy and theology. In the years from 1930 through 1949, he was a professor at the Pontifical Biblical Institute, of which he eventually became the rector. All this is covered in the book's fourth chapter.

He remained a teacher, and, in connection with this teaching commitment, Schmidt explains his "study of the ancient Near East, and its languages and civilizations." He was involved with both "the scholarly work of the Institute" and its personnel. We are particularly pleased to learn the conviction of the future Cardinal Bea to the effect that "a review should always contribute to the progress of scholarship" in its field (p. 52). At the Institute, he was also concerned with the new translation of Salterio in latin and also with extraordinarily good interpretations of Scripture. Writing in this context, the author pays a deserved tribute to Pope Pius XII, who, according to him, had the great task of "collecting and elaborating on the principal instances of Catholic scholarship on sacred Scripture as well as on liturgy and ecclesiology, and then publishing in 1943 his great encyclical *Divino Afflante Spiritu*; and, almost contemporaneously, his encyclical *Mystici Corporis* on the Church; and, four years later, another encyclical, *Mediator Dei,* on the liturgy" (p. 54). The author describes the contribution made by Bea to all this. The figure he cut is well described, also from a human point of view, when the author says that he was "always accessible" (pp. 57ff.).

Chapter V of the book is well written and very interesting, and bears the biblical title: "Leave Country and Your Kindred" (Gen 12:1).

It covers the years 1949-1959, when Bea essentially abandoned his own wishes and self to become a true servant of the truth and of the Church, and, indeed, of humanity. He became the confessor of Pope Pius XII at the same time that he was an advisor of the pontiff's. He was also an influential member of the eight-member commission appointed by Pius XII to prepare for a reform of the liturgy. "Ten years before Vatican II, it had laid the foundations for the Council's Constitution on the Sacred Liturgy" (p. 65). He was also a consulter for the Holy Office, "and more than once he praised both the seriousness of the method followed by this congregation as well as its actual work" (p. 66). His views in the matter were greatly respected (see p. 67). He occupied himself in particular with questions concerning Germany and the ecumenical movement (see pp. 69ff.).

Following the unexpected death of Pope Pius XII in 1958 he left not knowing where he would be going (1959-1960). In fact, he was made a cardinal by John XXIII on December 14, 1959. This was already after the announcement of the convoking of the Council, which had been made the previous January. On June 5, 1959, he was appointed president of a new Secretariat for Promoting Christian Unity. This was not a conciliar "commission" but a "secretariat" (p. 82). Almost immediately following this appointment, he wrote: "I am convinced that the Council, although not a Council of union, will nevertheless contribute to Christian unity." He suffered an illness for a time and then took the month of August off. After that he set to work. This history of the Secretariat project, in brief, was that it was to be an organism at the service of the Council: but from the time of the famous "incident of Rhodes," in which the cardinal had played a part, the Secretariat assumed an important role in the ongoing developments. There soon became evident "the first signs of the extraordinary understanding and confidence that existed between the pope and Cardinal Bea" (p. 82). And it was at this point too that another extraordinary figure entered upon the scene, namely Professor (Msgr.) Johannes Willebrands, who was provisionally named secretary general of the Secretariat for Promoting Christian Unity. The author notes that "the problems of the Church's relationship with the Hebrew people would henceforth be in the forefront." In this connection, it is worth recording a saying of John XXIII which the pope had made to Jules Isaac: "I am the head, but I must also consult the others, and also require the appropriate offices to study the problems that have been raised. We are not living in an absolute monarchy here" (p. 84). The author also does an excellent job in portraying the "spirit" of Bea, which was eminently "apostolical" spirit; his service was always "for souls." The German cardinal thought he had to "do everything possible so that they will desire unity...but especially I must show them my love." He was concerned with "interiority" and with "supernatural strength": "Everyone must see that in what I do there is no desire for power, no earthly interest, no simple activism, no routine, but only the true spirit of Christ" (p. 85).

Chapter VII of the book is dedicated to "the preparations for the Council in the ecumenical perspective (1960-1962)." Doubts concerning what the role of Bea was supposed to be were gradually cleared up, not always without difficulty. Eventually it was possible for him to develop all sorts of relationships and draw up drafts of documents (see p. 88, also with regard to his "method"). Problems arose because there was no established "canonical" way to do what he was doing; so he acted without communicating with the Secretariat of the Council concerning the assignments given to him directly by the Holy Father (p. 88). Certainly some of the subjects he was involved in were "upon the competence of this or that preparatory commission" beyond the Doctrinal Commission (*Ibid.*). Among the things explained here is the visit to Rome of [Archbishop of Canterbury] Dr. Fisher, as well as the roles of the representatives of other communions which led to the decision to send "Catholic observers" to New Delhi [for the meeting of the World Council of Churches]. There is an excellent exchange reported here between Cardinals Ottaviani and Bea (pp. 90ff.).

The latter became "the ambassador of unity," and he carried on "a personal activity aimed at sensitizing public opinion within the Church to the problem of ecumenism" (p. 92). A mere listing of all the meetings and media appearances in support of this activity is most impressive. At the same time, he undertook exploratory contacts that proved especially arduous in order to determine "whether and how other Christians might wish to be invited to the Council" (p. 95). His initial results were not entirely satisfactory.

The author then describes the *schemata* prepared by the Secretariat. They were prepared in a difficult environment owing to the necessity of maintaining good relations with the Council's Doctrinal Commission as well as with its other Commissions, including the Central Coordinating Commission. Cardinal Bea's contribution to the work of this last body is described.

"Ecumenism itself, meanwhile, was taking giant steps" (pp. 117ff.). The book's Chapter VIII, in fact, has the subtitle: "More Giant Steps." One important factor here was "that while all the conciliar preparatory commissions were being abolished, the pope had explicitly established the Secretariat with the provision that it was to maintain its original structure composed of the same members and consulters as had obtained in the preparatory phase" (pp. 103). As for the "observer delegates," the author explains both "their presence and their work" (p. 104: see also pp. 115ff.). Meanwhile, the Council itself was moving to approve its own principles of ecumenism (in 1962). There is something else to report here: "Bea and his collaborators were convinced that all the various themes to be treated by the Council would have their ecumenical dimension" (p. 107). This can be granted, even if we must add that all these themes would not necessarily have a "direct" ecumenical finality, and that "Catholic truth" would always be respected. The author discusses also the proposal of Cardinal Cicognani to "amalgamate all the ecumenical elements in all three *schemata* which had been prepared dealing with the subject."

Following all the preparatory work, the question arose of "the significance for ecumenism of the death of John XXIII and the election of Paul VI"—who forthwith went to Jerusalem to meet with the Eastern Orthodox Patriarch Athenagoras. Meanwhile the activities of "the indefatigable ambassador of unity continued." Indeed, "the Church herself was mobilized in favor of unity." The author explains the conciliar processes and also the fact of the pontifical interventions which Cardinal Bea considered to be a "right" of the pope (p. 114). The author's analysis is extended to explaining "the secret of the success of Cardinal Bea" (pp. 123ff.). We do not, however, consider it correct to refer to Pope John XXIII alone as "the pope of the Council." Was not Pope Paul VI also the "pope of the Council" (see p. 124)?

In Chapter IX of the book, the subject of the relationship of the Church to the Jews is taken up, along with the Church's relationships with non-Christian religions generally. We should recall that, in June 1962, the Central Preparatory Commission had rejected the draft *schema* on the Jews, and had removed the subject, temporarily, from the agenda of the Council. This was a tough defeat for the cardinal! Nevertheless, his strategy remained intact, namely, that anti-Semitism had to be condemned, and even the policy of John XXIII had to be clarified and revised accordingly (see p. 126). It was necessary "to go forward with new courage" (*Ibid.*), taking up again the renewed conciliar discussion and expending a "great deal of effort on a very brief text" (p. 129). Surprises were not lacking. December 1964, through September 1965, proved to be a very stormy period. The word "Deicide" was eliminated as the source of too many misunderstandings; but the "thing" itself, which was indicated by the use of this word in earlier drafts, was equivalently and exactly described in the language eventually employed in the final draft. The calm after the storm eventually came in the autumn of 1965.

The book's Chapter X deals with the question of religious liberty. The World Council of Churches had urged that this topic be treated. From the very first discussions on the subject, facing the difficulties that arose, Bea continued to be the "ambassador." This was true up until the final "victory" (p. 142). In our opinion, though, the author should have placed this word, "victory" between quotation marks. We note in passing that a fine reconstruction of the Council's Third Session is contained in this chapter (see p. 142). The role of the Council's Doctrinal Commission is described, as is that of the special mixed commission that was named. The document went through five drafts but finally obtained approval (p. 143) with less than 3 percent of the votes being negative. The author includes a judgment on the contribution made by Cardinal Bea to this successful end result (pp.

143ff.). He was the "guarantor," for everybody, from Pietro Pavan to Johannes Willebrands, of "the slow maturing of a subject that for the most part has not been assimilated by the Church yet" (p. 144).

We then arrive at the cardinal's "last three years"—1965-1968—which saw "incredible developments in ecumenism as well as a rich harvest of publications." These activities and publications dealt with the Anglican Communion, the Reformed Churches, and the pre-Chalcedonian Ancient Churches of the East (we do not believe it is correct to identify them as "Orthodox"). There were numerous examples of Bea's "method" manifested. There was his presentation on the occasion of the visit of Patriarch Athenagoras to Rome, as well as his presentations to the World Council of Churches and to various biblical societies. The author is justified in speaking of a virtual "ecumenical mobilization" of the Catholic Church in this connection. Permit us to quote at this point a decisive conviction of the man who was also an "indefatigable" interpreter of the Council: "Ecumenism should not be considered to be an activity carried out separately and apart from the life of the Church; it represents rather a new dimension that should be kept in mind in connection with every question, every prospect, every program, and every solution" (p. 165).

The final chapter in the book is entitled "Cardinal Bea Is Still with Us" (p. 171). The idea here is that the changes he wrought are still with us. As he approached the evening of his life of this earth, he experienced the warnings concerning his passage "beyond," and he received the sacrament of the Anointing of the Sick; he also experienced uncommon joy. In his last days, preparations were made for the final "voyage" of his mortal body back to his native land. The book concludes with a subtitle, "The Testimony of the Cardinal," which serves as a useful appendix summing up the activity of this "Council Father." His dates are given and also a brief bibliography pertaining to his life, along with the indexes.

40

Memories of the Council from Cardinal Joseph Ratzinger

Ratzinger, Joseph, *La Mia Vita. Ricordi* (1927-1977) [My Life: Memories (1927-1977)], Edizioni San Paolo, Mappano (To) 1997, 121 pages, with photographs.*

During a train trip, not a long one, I had a chance to look over these "notes," as the author calls them (p. 118). They are written in a pleasing and very "fine-spun" fashion. It is possible to read through this small book in one sitting. This provides an uncommon benefit.

We review this book here primarily for the part of it which concerns Vatican Council II, but it obviously possesses general interest as well. It covers the period of the cardinal's childhood between the Inn and Salzach rivers up to the years of his service as archbishop of Munich and Freising. We offer this review even though the cardinal makes clear that "the ecclesial and theological drama of those years is not the primary subject of these memories" (p. 86). However, as far as the Council is concerned, the author does ask the reader to allow two exceptions to this rule, which furnish the primary pretext for our intervention here. What the author says is worthwhile in itself as well as pointing towards the possibility that he might someday provide us with more ample and complete "memories" of his experience at the Council.

---

*Published in English as Ratzinger, Cardinal Joseph, *Milestones: Memoirs (1927-1977),* Ignatius Press: San Francisco, 1977, 156 pages.

The first of his two exceptions concerns the question of "how the Council should begin its work, what the precise task was that it needed to undertake" (*Ibid.*). Cardinal Ratzinger pursues this theme with great precision and objectivity, as follows: "Pope John XXIII had set forth in very general terms his intentions regarding the Council. He had left to the Council Fathers an almost unlimited space in which to work out its activity more concretely: the faith needed to speak to these times in a new way while fully maintaining the identity of its faith-content; and, following a period during which the Church had issued definitions based on defensive positions, it was time for the Church to leave off making condemnations and rely instead on 'the medicine of mercy.' There was tacit agreement that the principal theme of the Council was to be the Church herself so that the Council would take up again and complete what Vatican I had started...Cardinals Montini and Suenens elaborated ambitious plans on a vast theological plane...in accordance with which the theme of the Church would be extensively developed both *ad intra* (internally) and *ad extra* (externally)" (pp. 86ff.).

"The second part of this basic theme of focusing on the Church would permit the great questions of the present day to be brought out in the context of the relationship between the Church and the world" (p. 87).

And here the author introduces a theme which is particularly dear to him—and which is a source of great preoccupation for him as well—namely, the subject of the liturgy, about which he will return later with more force and radicality for "the Missal of Paul VI" (see pp. 110-113). The cardinal's point of view on this subject is as follows: "For the majority of the Council Fathers the reforms proposed by the liturgical movement were not a priority, indeed, for many of them the liturgy was not even a subject that they thought needed to be treated. For example, Cardinal Montini, who as Paul VI would become the true pope of the Council, had said very clearly in the thematic synthesis that he had put together at the beginning of the Council's work that he did not see the liturgy as one of the essential tasks for the Council. The liturgy and its reform...had become a pressing question only in France and Germany. More precisely, whatever reforms that were needed were seen as related to the purest possible restoration of the ancient Roman liturgy; in addition to this need, there was also the need to insure an active participation by the people in the liturgical event. These two countries, France and Germany, were in the forefront of modern theological developments (to which must be added Belgium and Holland as well); and in the preparatory phase of the Council, they succeeded in getting a *schema* on the liturgy added to the agenda. It fit naturally with the Council's general theme on the Church" (p. 87).

We may stop here at this point for a brief moment to take stock. It seems important to us in the midst of the veritable flood of ideological interpretations of the Council which we have today that someone should actually recall that the preparations for the Council were really not all so definite, and that this accorded with the Johannine idea of following the "spirit" of mercy and being primarily concerned with such things as "ecumenism" and "*aggiornamento*." It is equally important to recall that Pope Paul VI was indeed "the true pope of the Council," who carried it to term by completing the work of Vatican I.

As for the liturgy, however, allow us to note that although it was not immediately considered to be a high priority item, still the theme was present in many of the proposals that had come in, not only from Europe but especially from bishops in the mission territories. Thus, it is not entirely the case that for "many...the liturgy was not even a subject which they thought needed to be treated." Anyway, as far as Italy was concerned, Paul VI himself defended the liturgical reform when speaking to, for example, Cardinal Siri. However, we are certainly in agreement on the fact that the *schema* on the liturgy was "the first to be examined by the Council...[This] in no way indicated an increased interest on the part of a majority of the Council Fathers in the liturgy...but arose from the fact that the subject did not arouse great controversy or stir up polemics, but rather was considered to be an object that could allow the Fathers themselves to try out and test the best ways to proceed with their overall conciliar agenda."

We can, however, accept as valid these further considerations: "It would not have entered the minds of any of the Council Fathers to consider any of this a 'revolution,' or 'the end of the Middle Ages,' as some theologians have in the meantime come to consider it. The whole thing was in fact seen as a continuation of the liturgical reforms begun by Pius X and carried forward with prudence (although also with determination) by Pius XII...It naturally did involve going beyond some of the tendencies of the baroque liturgy as well as some of the devotional practices of the nineteenth century, while promoting a sober emphasis on the centrality of the mystery of the presence of Christ in his Church" (pp. 87ff.). "In this perspective," the cardinal adds, "it is not surprising that the *Missa normativa* which was developed to take the place of the earlier *Ordo Missae*, and in fact did take the place of it, was rejected by the majority of the bishops assembled at a special Synod of Bishops session in 1967" (p. 88). It is worth adding, however, that the new Mass came into force only after modifications had been made in it responding to the judgments of these bishops.

The author speaks of a "dramatic clash" that took place in the debate on the subject of "the sources of revelation" (his second exception to his otherwise remaining silent on the controversial aspects of the day). The question concerned the historical-critical method in biblical exegesis, which the cardinal remarks had "established a firm foothold also in Catholic theology." But he notes that "this method by its very nature does not tolerate any limitation placed upon it by an authoritative magisterium...As a result, the very concept of 'tradition' becomes problematical." Hence the cardinal concludes that with the conciliar text developed on the subject, "the whole problem of modern biblical interpretation was up for debate, and, especially, over the question of how history and spirit could relate to one another within the structure of the faith" (p. 89).

For Cardinal Ratzinger, one of the determining factors of this debate was a presumed historical discovery made by the theologian J. R. Geiselmann in the 1950s in the text of one of the documents of the Council of Trent. In this document, the idea that revelation was contained "partially in Scripture, and partially in Tradition" was replaced in Trent's final version by a simple "and." Geiselmann deduced from this that Trent's authoritative teaching was that there was no division between Scripture and Tradition in the context of the faith. From this he drew the further conclusion that there was a "material completeness" in the Bible in matters of faith. But such a formula—which was a wholly new idea—"became detached from its point of departure in the Tridentine decree," and the conclusion was then quickly drawn that the Church "could not teach anything that was not expressly contained in sacred Scripture" (*Ibid.*). "And given that the interpretation of Scripture and historical-critical exegesis had by now become identified as one and the same thing, this meant that the Church could not teach anything that could not be verified by the historical-critical method" (p. 90). The consequences? "The faith was obliged to retreat into indeterminacy and into accepting the continuing changes inherent in historical hypotheses or what was taken to be such." This was a stark conclusion, but it was a strictly logical one. "The Council naturally had to oppose such a conclusion, but the idea of the 'material completeness' of Scripture nevertheless remained present in opinion concerning the Church to a much greater degree than was the case in the document which the Council actually adopted."

And this latter phenomenon, namely, the opinion people have about the Church, is only all too real. We have right here a finger on the wound of so-called "ecclesial democracy," which is unfortunately accepted by too many people today. The cardinal notes that "the drama of the post-conciliar era has been largely determined by this kind of password ['material completeness'] and by the kinds of consequences that logically follow from it." He himself confesses that "initially, I too was fascinated, but it quickly leaped to the eye that the huge subject of the relationship between Scripture and Tradition could not be resolved in such a simplistic way. Subsequently, I carefully studied the Acts of the Council of Trent, and I was able to verify that the editorial variant that Geiselmann considered to be of such central importance was really nothing more than a rather insignificant and secondary aspect in the debate between the Council Fathers at Trent, which was more fundamentally concerned with how revelation could be expressed in human language at all, and hence by the written word" (p. 91). But let us leave aside at this point this excellent theological discourse of the cardinal on the subject of Revelation and move to his conclusion concerning it, which is always, "to gather and unite men, and hence this always involves the Church." From this, important further conclusions may be drawn, namely: "If this extension of revelation beyond Scripture is valid, then the ultimate analysis of the latter cannot be like the analysis of a mineral sample—by means, that is, of the historical-critical method alone. Rather, it forms part of a vital organism which is the faith of all past centuries. Precisely this kind of extension of Revelation beyond Scripture, which cannot be expressed merely by fixed formulas, is what we mean by Tradition" (pp. 91ff.). The author recognizes, though, that in the general climate of 1962, his general opposition to the existing *schema* was considered to be and was evaluated as, just another voice promoting the Geiselmann thesis.

A useful result came from what he calls the "brief *schema*" which he then prepared at the request of Cardinal Frings, in which he sought to express his real perspective on this subject. The cardinals present at the famous meeting in which he presented this paper "found it interesting but at that time they neither would nor could make a specific judgment concerning it" (p. 92). "It was thus established that, along with Karl Rahner, I would help draft another *schema* in greater depth" (*Ibid.*). Ratzinger here confesses that, in working with him, "I realized that Rahner and I, though agreeing on many things and desiring the same outcomes, from a theological point of view lived on two different planets" (*Ibid.*). We certainly agree with the author's characterization of Rahner's theology as different from his own—which we find to be very objective—but at this point we must move on to his conclusion that the Council's Constitution on Divine Revelation, *Dei Verbum*, "has not yet been truly received." Ratzinger generalizes this conclusion concerning the Council's documents as a whole, and he makes his case in terms that for us are critical with respect to the Church's situation today following the Council: "At first practically the only thing that emerged from the Council was the presumed novelty of what the Council Fathers were thinking on a variety of subjects. The task of communicating what the Council actually did say and forming thereby the consciousness of the Church about it is a task that remains to be carried out" (p. 93).

In the chapter of the book which follows, entitled "Münster and Tübingen," there is yet another mention of the conciliar climate that we would like to take note of. Ratzinger observes that "the Council went on...and every time I returned from Rome I found in the Church and among theologians a state of mind that was more and more agitated. More and more the impression grew that nothing in the Church remained stable any longer, that everything could be changed. More and more the Council came to resemble a great ecclesial parliament that could change everything and could even revolutionize everything in accordance with whatever it decided. The growth in resentment of Rome and the Roman Curia was increasingly evident; they appeared to be the enemies of everything that was new and progressive. Discussions concerning the Council were presented according to the partisan divisions typical of modern parliamentarianism...But there was in process something even more radical still: if the bishops meeting in Rome could change the Church in this way, then why was this legitimate just for the bishops?... By now it was understood that all the new things the bishops were adopting they had learned from the theologians...This fact created a new consciousness in the latter. They began to see themselves as the true custodians of knowledge, and hence they could no longer properly be placed *under* the bishops" (p. 98).

Rarely has it been given to read a typical analysis of the Council as clear as this one, and it applies to the post-conciliar era as well. And what the author then adds seems equally current and actual: "Behind these tendencies, and behind the new predominance of specialists, we begin to see emerging something very different, namely, the idea of a popular ecclesial sovereignty according to which it will be the people themselves who will establish what they want to understand by the term 'Church.' The latter, in any case, is now being defined as 'the people of God.' A Church 'from below' is thus proclaimed, a 'Church of the people,' which, especially in the perspective of the theology of liberation, becomes the aim and end of the reform" (p. 99). The circle is closed: this is still our situation today.

Faced with these changes being produced in the ecclesial climate in which he then found himself, the young theologian, Joseph Ratzinger, experienced what he called "a profound inquietude." This impelled him to follow the line which would lead him on to the positions he would continue to occupy in his seventies.

41

Vatican II in the Diary of Bishop André Charue

Carnets conciliares de l'évêque de Namur A.-M. Charue [Conciliar Notebooks of the Bishop of Namur, A.-M. Charue], eds. L. Declerck and C. Soetens, Publications of the Faculty of Theology, New Louvain 2000, 316 pages (In the series, *Cahiers de la Revue Théologique de Louvain*, Number 32).

In presenting yet another volume of this type, we note again that in the field of research on Vatican Council II, we have reached the phase of consulting "diaries." This is not an entirely happy outcome because it represents a spiralling multiplication of data and knowledge which must then be compared with what is in the official sources. Merely to read through these diaries, in effect, reveals discrepancies and a great variety of attributions and distributions of "merits." It is humanly understandable too that there would be claims to have championed from the beginning the positions that were eventually "victorious" at the Council. Also, the information and knowledge available to individuals is necessarily partial, particularly with respect to the complexity of the questions being considered by the Council—all the various processes and interrelations amid the existing regulations, "pressures," movements, and efforts to organize "battles" against progressivism, conservatism, the Roman Curia, etc. Then there were the *avant-garde* of theologians with their special "magisterium" supposedly predominating over the Church's magisterium. There was also the problem of interpreting the ecumenical and pastoral directions desired, especially by Pope John XXIII. We could go on but will stop here. It is more important to develop and exercise a critical spirit capable of properly discerning and judging the contributions of those who have created the actual history of Vatican II that we have up to this point, including those who were attentive observers at the Council, or were even protagonists there (see esp. p. 216, n. 64, and p. 272, n. 38).

In the case of these "Notebooks," however, we must be especially attentive and receptive—even though they contain many instances of "it seems" and "it was said"—when we consider the central role their author played in the development of various conciliar *schemata*, particularly those on the subject of the Church (*Lumen Gentium* and *Gaudium et Spes*).

In this perspective, we may recall two other related publications, namely: 1) The *Inventaire des Papiers Conciliares du Cardinal L.-J. Suenens* [Inventory of the Conciliar Papers of Cardinal L.-J. Suenens], eds. L. Declerck and E. Louchez, Publications of the Faculty of Theology, New Louvain 1998 (In the series, *Cahiers de la Revue Théologique de Louvain,* Number 31); and 2) De Smedt, Émile-Jozeph, *Papers. Vatican II. Inventory*, Leuven 1999. We are also currently awaiting the publication of the papers of Monsignor Gérard Philips, at which point we will have a pretty complete rundown of the papers of the "Belgian team" at the Council (as at one point it was styled). We should be no less eager to have in hand other memoirs of the Council by important conciliar personages; we think, for example, of Archbishop Péricle Felici himself. Such contributions could represent a new turning point in the history of the "diaries" of the Council.

The reading of this one, however, is not easy, particularly with regard to passages that relate to the texts of conciliar documents. Also, Charue turns out to be both "passionate" and "subjective." He does not always display equanimity, and he seems to harbor obvious prejudices against those who disagree with him. There appears in this diary no little insensitivity and even some animosity towards those whom we can call "conservatives," and particularly against Archbishop Felici himself. Perhaps these feelings were reciprocated. Still, Charue appears to be much too partisan in his prejudices and his judgments. At the same time, we find considerable references to his spiritual elevation and his faith in God. These are perhaps not as frequent as is the case in Pope John XXIII's *Journal of a Soul*, for example. Yet the attitude of *Deo Gratias* predominates.

In particular, this diary reveals the special interest of the former bishop of Namur in the topics of collegiality, divine revelation, and *Schema XIII* (especially on the subject of culture). He was also interested in Marian mediation and in the exemptions granted to religious; indeed, he was interested in the religious life in general, as treated in an entire chapter in *Lumen Gentium*. On all these themes the diary contributes to our understanding, even while making the proper distinctions.

These Notebooks succeed in presenting the personality of Bishop Charue, and they throw light on that of Monsignor Philips as well, whom Paul VI praised in Bishop Charue's presence (see p. 211). On nearly every page the bishop's work proves to be both fundamental and decisive. There are, understandably, many reverberations related to the famous Theological Commission (which the bishop calls the Doctrinal Commission or the Commission on Faith). Bishop Charue was made its vice-president on December 2, 1963. In these Notebooks there is evident the fact that the author had a hard time maintaining them; he generally employs a "telegraphic style" (see pp. 214, 221ff., 265, 278, n. 53, and 283, n. 60). Some of his notes (a minimal number) were added *post factum* (see p. 278, n. 53). We would delete the "probably" added by the editors with regard to certain additions and corrections. The author recorded nothing at all during the Second Session of the Council, nor during the month of November 1964.

The Introduction by C. Troisfontaines precedes the text itself. He divides things up among the following subjects: "The situation in Rome during the Council" (*Sitz im Leben*); and "The Content of the Diary." We cannot agree, however with some of the conclusions of Troisfontaines, particularly with reference to so-called "Black Week," as it has been regularly but incorrectly labeled. Similarly, we cannot agree with his views on the *Nota Explicativa Praevia*, particularly since the text of Bishop Charue is almost entirely silent on this issue. Further subdivisions in the Introduction by Troisfontaines include "The Role of Bishop Charue," and "Some Characteristics of His Behavior." The bishop is described as "both serious and jovial at one and the same time; he was timid but could also be audacious; he exhibited firmness but he was able to listen...He exhibited deep piety as well, and was profoundly loyal to the Church." And so on (esp. p. 23).

The text of the Notebooks is presented following the Introduction. We must be grateful to Bishop A. M. Leonard for having encouraged and authorized this publication, and to L. Declerck and C. Soetens for having so carefully transcribed and annotated the bishop's text. Research on Vatican II continues apace.

42

Conciliar Papers of
Monsignor Gérard Philips

Inventaire des papiers conciliares de Monseigneur Gérard Philips, Secrétaire Adjoint de la Commission Doctrinale [Inventory of the Conciliar Papers of Monsignor Gérard Philips, Adjunct Secretary of the Doctrinal Commission], eds. L. Declerck and W. Verschooten, with an Introduction by J. Grootaers, Bibliotheek van de Faculteit Godgeleerdheid, Uitgeverij Peeters, Leuven 2001, LIII, 260 pages.

The publication of this volume is an event, even though up now it has been passed over in silence in Italy. But only those who understand the extraordinary role this particular "personage" played at the Council can really appreciate the truth of what we are saying here. Gérard Philips was the "conciliator" (*homo conciliaris*—see pp. XXXVIII and XLI). He was the "patron" *par excellence* (pp. XXXVI, XXV, and XXIX). He coined the significant expression, "neither victors nor vanquished." All this was true, especially with regard to *Lumen Gentium, Dei Verbum, Gaudium et Spes*, and *Sacrosanctum Concilium*. His interests helped define Vatican Council II and his influence was limited only by his illness (see p. XXXVI, n. 41).

Thus, the publication of these papers is a good and useful work of its kind in its own right. This is not true, however, of the Introduction to the book. We now have available at our disposition, without having to travel to Belgium, the complete papers of Philips—and I say "at our disposition" because the careful work of the editors has supplied us with a notation on each of these papers, and, more than that—the most useful thing of all—the editors have provided a summary note of the contents of each paper. May they be abundantly thanked for such good work and positive zeal!

More than that, the work provides useful references to other works related to the documents in this exceptional archive. There are references to the diary of Philips himself, and to the diaries of Congar, Charue, and Prignon, and also to the "background" papers of Cardinal Suenens and Cardinal Léger as well as those of De Smedt, Dupont, and Prignon. There are yet more references here to the excellent *Relationes* of Father Sebastian Tromp and to the book of Umberto Betti; there is even mention of that of Burigana, if only to rectify an incorrect dating. It covers everything!

The arrangement of the documents is chronological. There are 2,729 of them! Their reading is facilitated by the inclusion of many important notes (see pp. 54, 81, 115, 151, 171ff., 174, 176, 178, 204, 228, and 235). These notes are very helpful to the reader at sea in such a vast ocean of documentation.

Of particular interest, we hasten to say, is for us the material related to the *Nota Explicativa Praevia* that was appended to Chapter III of *Lumen Gentium*. This remains the case even though, in general, this material duplicates that prepared by Philips himself, which was included in the volume collected and edited by Jan Grootaers (and reviewed in Chapter 28 of this book). However, Grootaers gives it an interpretation opposite to what emerges here in agreement with the conciliar note itself (see p. 81, Document n. 1922). Monsignor Albert Prignon, by the way, is of this same opinion. The editor, Declerck, for his part, seems inclined to consider Colombo/Bertrams, the scribes of the *Nota*, an opinion which we too are inclined to adopt (see pp. 179 and 181, and Documents nn. 1899 and 1920, respectively).

Moving now to the Introduction provided by Grootaers (pp. XXIII-XXXVIII), we are obliged to report his anti-curial sentiments once again (pp. XXIIIff., XXVIII, XXXII, and XXXVII). This remains the case even though it was Cardinal Cicognani himself who suggested that there should be a new basic text for the *schema De Ecclesia*, while retaining from the previous text what could be retained (and this was not merely an account of *captatio benevolentiae*, as Grootaers writes—pp. XXXIIff.). He speaks, in effect, of an "alternative project" of Philips (pp. XXVff., which is in contradiction to what Grootaers himself says on pp. XXXIIff.). But he does not make clear that this was a "mixed" and recombined text.

Moreover, this author alters our perspective on the famous "Belgian team at the Council." He speaks instead of what he calls the "Belgian college at the Council" (see p. XXXI). But this expression does not seem to be exact. The "circle" was wider than this (see p. XXXI), while the commonality of shared opinions (by all?) is raised to the level of "the sense of the assembly" as a whole, that is, of the bishops. There is, however, recognition that "a Council is an assembly of bishops making pastoral decisions and commitments. In no way is it a congress where the positions of various 'schools' confront each other" (*Ibid.*). There is an excellent note (n. 30) included here concerning an agreement concluded between Congar and Rahner not to mention the author[s] of the various parts of the *schema* but rather to present it as a unified whole.

And once again Grootaers employs the erroneous terminology of a "second conciliar preparation" (p. XXXII) as well as the journalistic expression, "Black Week" (p. 44, n. 44). This has no reason to be used at all, considering that the seven days in question turned out to be positive. It is praiseworthy, however, that the existence of a "radical left" among the majority is recognized and identified by the author (p. XXXVI). This fact has long been noted by us and is amply confirmed in the *History of Vatican Council II* of Giuseppe Alberigo. This tendency created tensions within the central nucleus that was the Theological Commission, and also in relation to the work of Philips (p. XXXVI; the name of Congar arises here). Finally, the promotion by Grootaers of the work of Prignon, following upon Congar himself, does not seem conclusive. Prignon was a very different type than Philips.

Following the Introduction comes the "Note on the Conciliar Archive of G. Philips" (pp. XXXIX-LIII). This is by the editors, L. Declerck and W. Verschooten. They describe the state of the papers and the importance of the *schema De Ecclesia*: "The text is a tributary to the streams of two different tendencies and two different terminologies." Thus wrote Bishop Joseph Heuschen of Liège. In the course of the various Council sessions and the intersessions between them are covered the *schemata De Revelatione* (pp. XLIIff.) and *De Ecclesia in mundo huius temporis* (pp. XLVIff.).

The editors explain their method of proceeding in the classification of Philips' papers which, as we mentioned above, is chronological but is also thematic for certain things. In order to establish the proper chronology, they have utilized various books on the history of the Council. From a scholarly point of view, however, we regret that they have placed the official *Acta Synodalia* edited by Monsignor Vincenzo Carbone, in the second rank in this regard. With respect to some of the other works they cite, our point of view as a critic is well known. There is also a bibliography covering the conciliar work of Philips and there are some technical clarifications as well, among which we should take note of the editors' decision not to insist on uniformity in spelling and in the use of certain terms and formulas. Very important and useful in this particular text is what is included within parentheses or brackets or in graphs in the course of the work. And very useful indeed, as one can well understand, is also the index of names that is included. As for *errata*, we noted only a few words in documents numbered 388, 407, 995, 1017, 1469, 2563, 2585, and 2665, and also in the title *De Populo Dei* on page 93.

Good reading!

43

Notes of Monsignor Albert Prignon
on the Fourth Session

Prignon Monseigneur Albert, *Journal Conciliare de la 4ième Session* [Conciliar Journal of the Fourth Session], ed. L. Declerck and A. Haquin, Publications of the Faculty of Theology, New Louvain 2003, 280 pages.

The labors of Monsignor L. Declerck, this time assisted by A. Haquin, in helping us uncover the "hidden" facts of Vatican Council II continue apace. The focus is on the private writings of some of the Council's "protagonists," as they are called. This time it is the "diary" of Monsignor Albert Prignon, which was dictated, and which is confined to the Fourth Session only. He appears to have provided solid support and perhaps even more than that to the efforts of the Belgian Cardinal Suenens, who was certainly one of the major figures at the Council (see pp. 190, 240, and esp. p. 258 for examples of how the votes of the bishops were influenced).

It is pleasing to be able to report, in the case of this publication, how the editors have consulted and compared this text with the official Council records contained in the *Acta Synodalia*; these latter official sources remain the reference works *par excellence* for the history of the Council. All other sources need to be reconciled with them.

Of particular interest in this work are the echoes coming from Cardinal Suenens or Bishop Charue concerning the meetings that the Council Moderators had with Pope Paul VI, though these encounters must be judged while taking into account the perspective of these prelates (see, e.g., pp. 154-158, 177, 250, 159ff., 165 and 174). In any case, these encounters seem unduly dramatized. Of special interest also is the material related to the subject of birth control, which figures prominently from page 223 through page 260; to that of what is called "the most tragic day of the Council" (p. 223); to that of the text of *Schema* XIII which eventually became *Gaudium et Spes*; to that of the role of the observers and the "tactic" of the conciliar majority (see pp. 67, 209, 211, 240 and 268); and, finally, to the subject of the "pressures" of both sides that were being exerted on Pope Paul VI—not to speak of "the fortunes of the Curia after the Council."

As for the so-called "most tragic day of the Council" just mentioned, however, it is incorrectly characterized by Prignon employing the usual term of "Black Week." The editors print this term in italics, but it is not clear whether it actually was employed in that way by the author in the course of his dictation.

And as for the mention of a certain "personage" who later became pope, the two positions of Karol Wojtyla which elicited the author's critical comments here (although these positions were shared by his fellow Polish bishops) stand out and are definitely worthy of notice (see pp. 195ff. and 219).

Then there is the question of the network of the relationships of Monsignor Prignon. From this diary he appears to have been in frequent touch with Etchegaray, Medina, Bonet, Moeller, Delhaye, Martimort, and Molari. Of these, Martimort appears to have functioned as something of a "brake" on the activities of the *Consilium ad exequendam Constitutionem de sacra Liturgia* (see p. 177, for example). For "passages going from one extreme to another" by those whom at one time he had had to "drag" along, see those related from a certain standpoint to Molari here.

It is worth reporting that rather often in this diary the well-known proverb is quoted: "The best is the enemy of the good." I believe the same general line was generally followed by G. Philips as well with regard to the drafting of the conciliar texts in a way which would result in the desired conciliar *consensus*.

To conclude, we are obliged to formulate a question that applies many times in the case of the private texts that are similar to this one. The question is this: beyond the mere increase of the historical knowledge of what happened at the Council, what hermeneutical or interpretive value does a diary such as this contribute to the understanding of the conciliar texts? Does it help us to understand them or perhaps "receive" them better or in greater depth? I leave to the attentive reader of this diary the reply to this question, as I do in the case of the other diaries of this type. In any case, there is a certain degree of sheer fatigue involved in going through all these diaries, with their varying points of view that hardly ever accord with each other, and also with their various relationships with the official conciliar sources. In a certain respect we are obviously dealing here with "petty history" as opposed to "grand history," as Yves Congar himself wrote apropos of his own diary of the Council (preseated in Chapter 45 of the present volume).

This book concludes with an Index of names (pp. 271-278) as well as with a Subject Index. There is a Preface by Bishop Jousten of Liège and an Introduction by C. Troisfontaines which is limited in its value as analysis (see pp. 12, 15ff., and 20), and there is also a note pertaining to this edition. A comparison arises from a judgment made by Declerck and Haquin in relation with to the view of Troisfontaines. They say: "Monsignor Prignon was wiser and more prudent than Cardinal Suenens, less optimistic and more critical than Bishop Émile De Smedt, less 'catastrophic' than Monsignor Philippe Delhaye, and more passionate than Father Yves Congar" (p. 24). Nevertheless, there was a certain "radicalism" in him as well, particularly as regards certain subjects. Now we are in a position to know him better, however. With this book he emerges from the shadows where he had been before.

44

The Council According to
Father Umberto Betti

Betti Umberto, *Diario del Concilio*, 11 Ottobre 1962-Natale 1978) [Diary of the Council from October 11, 1962, until Christmas 1978], EDB, Bologna, 2003, 282 pages.

I mention at the outset what the cover of this book announces, namely, that what we have here are principally the Betti-Florit papers, the latter name referring to the cardinal archbishop of Florence, Ermenegildo Florit, who, among other roles, was a member of Vatican II's Doctrinal Commission, as well as of the Council's subcommission charged with drafting the key Chapter III of *Lumen Gentium*, and also the subcommission responsible for producing the final version of *Dei Verbum*. All this is the case, in fact, even as regards the title appearing here, although what we do have, primarily, is the Florit-Betti correspondence (dating from Christmas 1962 until Christmas 1978). Nevertheless, much in the volume has reference to Vatican Council II, and it is this, in particular, in which we are most interested.

Let us grant, on the other hand, that the book is primarily a kind of *apologia pro vita sua* of Father Betti, in which many aspects of his personal life appear. Certainly the question arises of how all this fits into the history of the great Council and, in particular, how it applies to the reception of the Council (see, for example, all the material relating to the new journal *Concilium*, as well as to the Isolotto case). Indeed, the relationship itself between Betti and Florit, which began on the morning of October 11, 1962 (see p. 15), when the archbishop asked Father Betti to be his personal theologian at the Council. This invitation came about "without any preamble" or previous awareness on the part of either of them. The result amounts to a very detailed treatment of, I would say, virtually everything, that Cardinal Florit did at the Council that also was recorded in his notes or letters. Yet somehow it all becomes not the record of the Cardinal's concerns so much as those of Father Betti himself.

If it is legitimate to say this, it seems to me that this particular expert does not reveal very much from a scholarly point of view about the prelate who called him into his service. In fact, this case illustrates some of the difficulties inherent in the relationship between theologians and the magisterium—even when, as is the case for me, Church teaching is entirely accepted. But then there arises the case of a Council father in whom there is to be found deviations in thinking. And if this should occur, then well...

It is worth noting that beyond the Florit-Betti "correspondence" just mentioned (pp. 183-244), which was "edited on the basis of the original letters by Vilma Occhipinti" (p. 7), in this book, among the other contributions included, there are four articles signed by Father Betti that previously appeared in *L'Osservatore Romano*. Three of these articles are concerned with the primacy of Peter and hence they were ideally suited for the conciliar debates. But it is naturally not on these particular articles that our critical attention becomes focused here. The last appendix in the book, in any case, is a bibliography of the author's many works (pp. 275-279). This bibliography follows a general Index of subjects. There is no Index of names, however, which constitutes a distinct lack for the serious researcher.

The notes in the diary that have reference to the Council (see also the first Index related to *Dei Verbum* on pp. 247-252) add up to only two for the year 1962; very few for the year 1963 (pp. 26-27); but a rather abundant harvest for 1964 (pp. 28-61); and, finally, a reduced number for the year 1965 (pp. 62-84).

May we be permitted a few observations and a criticism concerning these conciliar notes? We believe they might be useful.

We begin with the statement that "the Council when seen as a school is more valuable than any other school we know about. To imagine that we have nothing to learn from it would stultify our mind and send it into early retirement on grounds of senility" (p. 28).

In this "school," Father Betti undertakes to teach us a number of lessons concerning collegiality and tradition, all of it in the context of the development of *Lumen Gentium* and *Dei Verbum* respectively. From these conciliar notes one gathers that these documents were collectively produced. This comes out more clearly here than in the *Journal* of Congar (see the comment on page 90). In this connection, the author's role becomes more clearly delineated with respect to his part in the drafting of several texts, whereas the role of Philips in this drafting is less visible. Naturally, the role of Father Betti (and that of Carlo Colombo) receive greater emphasis here; that is only human; but it takes us back to the fundamental question of the historical value of these diaries which we have previously raised. Squaring these accounts with the official Acts of the Council remains necessary; yet these latter Acts are cited only once in connection with the Florit papers here (p. 249).

There is more than a bit of disappointment in the way that Father Betti deals with the *Nota Explicativa Praevia*, for he limits himself simply to announcing it (p. 59). There is a certain crudity in his treatment of the *Coetus Internationalis Patrum* and of Bishop Luigi Carli (p. 68). Then there is his mention of being "in the shadow of the Holy Office" when speaking of a letter from Cardinal Cicognani which seemed to amount to disapproval of all the conciliar 'commissions' (*Ibid.*).

Nevertheless, we are pleased to be able to conclude our comments by noting the author's magnanimous judgment on his old mentor, Father Damiano Van den Eyden, who taught him "so much" (p. 141). But he did suffer from a defect that was "more instinctive than reflexive: a self-sufficient paternalism that was almost universal and was further colored by a rather impertinent anti-Italianism...But no defect"—Father Betti concludes—"was enough to destroy a single good quality of his, and he possessed numerous such qualities" (p.

142). This represents a word of consolation for all of us, and not merely in what concerns the Council and its human "protagonists": for the Holy Spirit who had guided the Church down through the centuries was also present at the Council.

45

Father Yves Congar and Vatican II
(according to His Diary)

Congar Yves, *Mon Journal du Concile* [My Journal of the Council], Volumes I and II, Edited and Annotated with an Introduction by Eric Mahieu; Preface by Bernard Dupuy, O. P., Éditions du Cerf, Paris 2002, 595 and 632 pages.

After a very long delay lasting up to the year 2000, designated by the author as the time after which this *Journal* could appear in print, this long-awaited account of the Council by Father Yves Congar, O.P., has finally been published. Bits and pieces of it had already been leaked for ideological purposes. The result now, though, is two thick volumes, with a Preface by Bernard Dupuy, which we shall leave aside, since there is too much Dupuy in it; and, also, there is a rather better Introduction by Eric Mahieu, the editor, anyway (see p. XXX for a realistic picture of the "sentiments" of Congar and pages LVI-LXIII for his most pointed attitudes on the "economy" of the Council). Mahieu has provided generally excellent notes, in the course of which he has made significant and necessary corrections, based on the official conciliar Acts (*Acta Synodalia*).[1] Unfortunately, he has not made similar use of the official "Acts" of the Council's directive Organs found in some further indispensable volumes; these latter sources also throw important light

---

[1] Page numbers in Volume II will be indicated by a Roman numeral II following the reference to the page. Significant and important corrections are to be found on pages 183, 200, 232, 240, 264, 278, 313, 316, 320, 332, 370, 412ff., 470, 485, 487, 502ff., 511, 514, 570, 579, 62II, 79II, 122II, 135II, 149II, 174II, 179II, 192II, 205II, 210ff.II, 221II, 223II, 236II, 239II, 256II, 265II, 287II, 293II, 317II, 403II, 453II, 466II, 490II, 500II. On page 20II the confusion between Giacomo and Gustavo Testa is not corrected.

on our understanding of Vatican Council II, and they thus go beyond all the murmurs and whispers that have abounded. Mahieu does heed and follows up on, at least up to a certain point, our regular refrain to the effect that private "diaries" must be checked against the official conciliar "Acts." Among the rich and interesting appendices included in this work, there is lacking a subject Index as well as one referring to the various conciliar *schemata*. Yet we fully realize the difficulties that would have been inherent in compiling these Indexes.

The Author

But let us turn to the "diary" itself and to its author, who in this diary appears in all his greatness as well as in his pettiness—and also in his weakness and fragility, if one may so speak. Quite beyond any admiring or critical views that we might have of him, and also beyond the question of whether or not these views might be rooted in either sympathy or antipathy (in turn based either on his character or his theology), we shall seek here above all to present him as he appears in this particular piece of his writing. This will not be an easy task because his personality turns out to be an extremely complex one. In fact, on the one hand, he appears to be caustic, ironic, garrulous, sarcastic, excessive, and even ferocious and pitiless towards his adversaries or those he judges to be such; he regularly labels them as "miserable," "cretins," or "imbeciles," and he thereby evinces a kind of thinly veiled pride or ambition of his own which ill accords with his many declarations of humility.[2] Yet, at the same time, he comes across as what we would call a very spiritual man. He is literally enamored of poverty and of liberty, and he presents a simply enormous zeal for Christian unity and for what he believes to be the truth.[3]

However that may be, it is important to take note of the attitudes

---

[2]He regularly labels Cardinal Giuseppe Pizzardo an "imbecile," for example, as he does Archbishop Dino Staffa and the biblical scholar Monsignor Antonio Romeo [all of them in the Congregation for Seminaries and Universities at the time]; see pp. 51, 53, 30II, 80II, 176ff.II, 243II, 341II, 377II, 383II, and 518II. Archbishop Staffa is described as "obsessed" with the notion of a papal monarchy (see pp. 516 and 143II) and as a tireless advocate of Thomism (pp. 415II and 422II).

[3]For the Spirituality of Congar, we refer the reader to pp. 573, 577, 130II,

of theological experts such as Congar, whose task it was to present to the various Council Fathers who were members of the conciliar commissions texts which were then subject to discussion by these same Council Fathers in the commissions and later in the conciliar assembly as a whole. They were also regularly revised and voted on and *modi* or amendments were regularly proposed for them—not to speak of the consideration and evaluation of them by the pope.[4] It was inevitable that theological experts such as these should have harbored no little frustration with this whole process along with many disapprovals, disappointments, and regrets. This was the case with Congar.[5] He vividly expressed his feelings of "powerlessness" and his disappointments with the outcomes of various conciliar actions at the same time as he could assert that "this Council will prove to be primarily one of theologians."[6] However, he could also remark with respect to the necessary mediations concerning the texts proposed to the Council Fathers that "I find that too many theologians at the present time in France seem to forget that we are the Church."[7]

Precisely because of the "powerlessness" the author speaks of, it seems to us that he sins by exaggeration when he does speak also of his contribution to various conciliar texts.[8] Mahieu, in his

---

288II, 320II, 340II, 385II, 397II, 409f.II, 440ff.II, 471II, 473II, 487II, 489II, 493II, 502ff.II, and 526II. Moreover, he is very conscious of the kindness of others (see pp. 30II and 391II). His own sufferings from his various health problems are revealed on many pages of this "diary"; see, e.g., pp. 516, 529, 589, 523II, and 573II.

[4] See pp. 340II, 348II, 406II, and 410II.

[5] See pp. XXXIVff., XLI, XLIIff., and LV (because his drafts were not used); LXff., 181ff., 189, 193, 201ff., 213, 233ff., 280, 325, 328ff., 335, 370, 382, 399, 475, 489, 499, 508, 521, 19II, 51ff.II, 54II, 57II, 119II, 176II (on the subject of *modi*); 184II, 199II, 212II, 221II, 223II, 227II, 230II, 235II, 181II (on the experts not being allowed to speak); 240II ("I am not able to defend a text that is important for me"); 250II, 252II, 255II, 327II, 332II, 337II, 344II, 345II, 348f.II, 355II, 370II, 373II, 405II, 427ff.II, 430II, 439II, 444f.II, 451II, 453II, 457II, 460II, 467II, 481ff.II. All this must be seen in the context of the author's intense work for the Council; see pp. 459ff.II, 462II, 482II, 484II, 498II, 500II, and 504II.

[6] See pp. 421II and 81II.

[7] See pp. 442, 444II, 469II, 473II, and 481II.

[8] See p. 511II: "It appears that what was read out today came very largely from me." See also p. 405II.

Introduction, writes about the same thing when he notes how difficult it is to evaluate the nevertheless undeniable influence that theologians did have on a conciliar text. Speaking frankly, what came to mind for me about all this was a remark of Mahatma Gandhi in his "Words to a Friend," when the Indian leader said that "we do not know how to resist the temptation to exaggerate."[9] It is indicative that, on page 445II, Congar quotes a bishop saying: "You theologians be quiet! It's for the bishops to decide!" Although this is crudely put, it nevertheless reflects the reality.

For the fact is that while the bishops in Council do accept what the theologians have to contribute, it is not ultimately the theologians who "make up" the Council, as occasionally appears to be the suggestion that is made in this particular book under review. In this regard, there is even a Freudian slip or two here and there (see pp. 457II and 501II). It is certain, however, that Father Congar's greatest contributions are to be found in the texts of *Ad Gentes* and *Presbyterorum Ordinis*.[10]

However that may be, Father Congar is nevertheless conscious of recording what he knows about the "minor history" of the Council with a view towards contributing to its "major history." His "minor history," however, is quite interesting, particularly as regards his judgments on various conciliar figures. Let us look at some of these judgments, beginning with those he makes on some of the Roman pontiffs of the recent past mentioned in the diary, for us not often impartially.

His Judgments on Roman Pontiffs

Leaving aside the mentions made of earlier popes, which are nevertheless interesting, I only cite here at the outset Father Congar's judgment on Pope Pius IX—"petty and catastrophic," who "understood nothing of the movement of history"[11]—and his judgment on Pope Pius XII—"a diplomat" who conducted a "suffocating regime."[12]

---

[9]Mahatma Gandhi, *Chi segue il cammino della verità non inciampa. Parole a un amico* [Who Follows the Way of Truth Will Not Stumble: Words to a Friend], Editions San Paolo, Cinisello Balsamo, 2002, p. 33. See, e.g., the illusions of Congar concerning the *schema De Presbyteris*, pp. 443ff.II and 446ff.II.

[10]See pp. 473II, 475II, 499II, and 505II.

[11]See pp. 109, 115, 137, 228II, and 453II.

[12]See pp. 5, 419, and 453II.

We need to look more closely, however, at his ideas on the "conciliar popes," beginning with John XXIII, about whom his judgment moves back and forth. His general tone, in which disappointment prevails, becomes immediately evident when he writes of this pontiff's "extremely sympathetic words and actions," although "his actual decisions ended up largely giving the lie to the hopes he himself had aroused" (pp. 5-7). Moreover, there was an "original sin" involved in the organization of the Council itself.[13] This went back to the fact that "the conciliar commissions corresponded with the Roman congregations."[14] This gave rise to various Congarian criticisms,[15] the most serious of which concerned the fact that "the Council was never properly conceived and directed."[16] It is hard not to discern here a certain extremism in judgments such as these, even though, in other places in the diary, the author shows an appreciation for the person and the work of Pope Roncalli.[17]

Similarly, moving back and forth like a pendulum are Father Congar's judgments on Pope Paul VI, who received him in a private audience (see p. 113II). We do not so much stress his initial favorable judgments—"a well-informed man of superior intelligence; gives an impression of profound sanctity; has taken up the program of John XXIII" (p. 385)—as we need to follow him more closely and laboriously in judging the concrete decisions the pope made with regard to the Council,[18] as well as in relation to the discussion of the negative influence of Dossetti and even Alberigo.[19] Monsignor Gérard Philips himself saw Paul VI as "authoritarian" (p. 278II), while Father Louis Bouyer considered him open to ecumenism.[20] Congar himself,

---

[13]See pp. 89, 99, 109, and 158.

[14]P. 585; see, however, pp. 369 and 374.

[15]See pp. 151, 207, 232 (concerning Father Roberto Tucci), 282, 344, and 373.

[16]See pp. 302II and 202II, 204, 256, 272, and 453II.

[17]See pp. 321ff., 383ff., 397, 467ff., 276 ("they didn't understand me") and 357 ("I want to shake off the imperial dust which, since Constantine, has settled on the throne of Peter").

[18]See pp. 584, 588, 243II, esp. 32II, 291II ("give satisfaction to everybody"), 84II, 117ff.II, 133II, 289II, 303II, and 467II.

[19]See pp. 361ff., 364, 583, and 168II: "The always greater distinction from John XXIII."

[20]See pp. 100II, 467, and 486.

however, praised him in this same regard on other occasions.[21] On the other hand, this pope "appeared on the ecclesiological plane not to have the kind of vision his approach called for; he was too wedded to a purely Roman vision" (p. 118II). This conclusion was confirmed by the fact that "he did not possess the ecclesiology that was indicated and called for by his grand ecumenical gestures."[22]

Father Congar continues in such a vacillating, "pendulum" mode, and even increasingly so, in his judgments and evaluations concerning the man who would eventually become Pope John Paul II. The future Cardinal Karol Wojtyla, while he was still merely the capitular vicar of the diocese of Cracow submitted to Father Congar texts "drafted by him that were confused and full of imprecisions and inexactitudes, if not of actual errors and misinformation." However, Congar writes that he himself was "happy to enter into contact with the Polish episcopacy" (p. 464), but on which, he rendered a rather negative judgment on account of its "nationalistic foundations."[23] Yet he does mention that "Archbishop Karol Wojtyla is in favor of the text *De Populo Dei* in Chapter II [of *Lumen Gentium*], preceding the chapter *De s. Hierarchia*. This required a revision of Chapter I, and consists of what had in part been passed to me, though it had been corrected" (p. 488). Here we are recording the kind of note that Father Congar was accustomed to make, at least some of the time, on the interventions in the *aula* by various Council Fathers when they took the floor.

Everything changed, however, at least in part, with the emergence of a Polish project inherent to the conciliar *Schema* XIII, "revised by them in accordance with the observations made by the Council Fathers." "They read and revised it themselves in accordance with their own situation in a Communist society." Archbishop Wojtyla read

---

[21]See pp. 77ff.II, 333II, 486II ("never would John XXIII himself have gone so far"), 519II, 512II, 515II, 421ff.II, 333II, 336II, 345ff.II, 481II, and 484II.

[22]P. 269II; see also pp. 274II, 279II ("rather, he espoused a contrary theology"), 514II, 291II ("neither the theology nor the intellectual structure matched his gestures"), 388II ("and his messages"), and 99II ("what was necessary was to have a theology of communion of the Churches").

[23]P. 575; see, however, pp. 480ff.II: "A separate people with whom it is difficult to come to an understanding. They have their own ideas and do not seek to come to an understanding with anybody."

out the initial draft and explained the subsequent revisions. Congar wrote apropos of this: "It has been revised and redrafted by them *from the point of view of the Church herself*; *her* principles and *her* justifications are included. It is going to be necessary to take all of this into account. However, this text in particular cannot serve as the basis for our general discussions in preference to the text that has been elaborated by the authority of the mixed commission" (p. 309II).

The author went on to writes about of the Poles that theirs was "a text very well constructed. It shows *doctrinally* the principles and gives the justifications *of the Church*. But this text does not speak to men today...There is more of Pius XII in it than there is of John XXIII" (pp. 311ff.II). On the same subject, Archbishop Wojtyla "made several observations of extreme gravity on the subject of Chapter II [of what would become *Gaudium et Spes*]. He noted that we must consider the new situation of the world described in the *schema*'s Chapter I; yet the same modern world offers its own answers to these questions. But it is necessary [for the Church] to provide responses to those answers" (p. 312II). Father Congar goes on here to write: "Archbishop Wojtyla made a great impression. His personality is imposing. One derives from it a certain attraction, a prophetic strength which is nevertheless quite calm; but which is undeniable...Father Jean Daniélou appeared ready to pursue this question; he should have drafted something in conjunction with Archbishop Wojtyla. In the event, however, almost all the theological experts doubted that Daniélou was the one capable. Quick and adaptable as he is, is he the right man?...Archbishop Wojtyla said that, in his opinion, the soteriological and salvific dimension has not been sufficiently brought out" (*Ibid.*; see also pp. 313ff.II).

Following all this, Archbishop Wojtyla read various chapters from the Cracow document (thus does Father Congar now characterize the document, which he had previously called "Polish"). Congar writes: "Thus comes the reaction: with great and admirable frankness, Haubtmann says: 'It is an option,' but the orientation of the Cracow text, and my own view of things is such that, this Cracow text and my own view are so different as to be judged incompatible" (p. 314II). What came out of all this is well known.[24]

---

[24]See, however, p. 326II: "Archbishop Wojtyla defends his text"; and also, p. 338.

Judgments concerning Council Fathers

We cannot go deeply in this study into the relations of Father Congar with the various Council Fathers. We shall limit ourselves to take notice of some of the more prominent and indicative cases without aiming at completeness. We shall try to identify, however, relations and the ones which were more or less negative, if they did not go up to the point of outright contempt. We shall have to omit some nuances and shadings in this regard, but we will attempt to take note also of the "mixed feelings" harbored by Congar towards various Fathers in at least some cases.

Let us begin with his marked *appreciation* for Cardinal Suenens. Even though the latter was isolated from the other Belgian bishops (see p. 154 and also 142II), he was decisive in his orientation aimed at seeing the Council's work divided up between *ad intra* and *ad extra* issues (see p. 293). The same thing was true of Cardinal Montini.[25] For Congar, Cardinal Suenens was a very positive figure; he was well organized and he interacted freely with his "interlocutors" (p. 399). He proposed to the whole Council the idea of canonizing Pope John XXIII by acclamation (see p. 175II). Father Congar was against this effort and opposed the "custom" of canonizing the popes (see p. 478II).

The author's appreciation of the Belgian cardinal did not prevent him, however, from disapproving of the fact that "Suenens is more or less directing the whole Council along with the small group of Belgians who are managing practically everything" (see p. 574). I find this characterization much exaggerated. Along with his appreciation for Cardinal Suenens, there is also his marked appreciation for Joseph Cardijn after the latter was named a cardinal.[26]

Let us take note of Congar's views on Cardinal Liénart (see p. 171II and 193II); Patriarch Maximos IV;[27] Bishop Elchinger;[28]

---

[24] See, however, p. 326II: "Archbishop Wojtyla defends his text"; and also, p. 338.

[25] See pp. 296ff., 300, and 397ff.; the author is excessive in the judgments recorded on pp. 324 and 397, however.

[26] See pp. 383II, 390II, and 404II: "Cardijn speaks like a tribune but that does not compensate for not having a prepared text in hand."

[27] See p. 82II. Further judgments are found on pp. 335II and 425II, where the patriarch is charged with "an anti-Semitic reaction."

[28] See pp. 102, 121II, 136II, and 386f.II ("excessive though").

Archbishop Villot (see p. 193II); Archbishop Hermaniuk (see p. 411ff.); Bishop McGrath;[29] Bishop Guano (see p. 264; deemed "very open"); Archbishop Hurley;[30] Bishop Willebrands (see pp. 427II and 479II); and Bishop Reuss (see pp. 380IIff.).

Within the Roman Curia, Father Congar regarded Archbishop Dell'Acqua favorably.[31] He also had a basic high regard for Archbishop Garrone—which gradually increased with time.[32]

It is worth adding that thanks to Roger Etchegaray, Father Congar was well informed about and close to the group of bishops that "privately" met (see p. 480II) in the *Domus Mariae* (sometimes called "the group of 22").[33]

As for *critical or negative judgments* on Council Fathers by Congar, we may note that some of these were quite severe. Again, we make no claim to completeness, but in alphabetical order, for the convenience of the reader, we may list: Agagianian;[34] Batanian (see pp. 523ff.); Bea;[35] Browne;[36] Carli ("anti-collegial");[37] Cicognani;[38] De Smedt;[39] Döpfner (246II), "along with his reductionism"; Aniceto Fernandez, Master General of the Friars Preachers (Dominicans);[40] Franić;[41] Gori (see p. 135II); Heenan;[42] Jaeger (see p. 343II; "incompetent"); Larraona;[43] Lokuang;[44] Marcel Lefebvre (see pp. 77 and 433II); Marella (see p.

---

[29]See pp. 452, 129II, and 252II.
[30]See pp. 276, 291, and 326ff.II.
[31]See pp. 62II, 194II, and 208II; he saw him as a possible replacement for Archbishop Felici!
[32]See pp. 193, 195, 239, 328, 330, 191II, 328II ("he's a power"), 359II, 460II, 468II, 519II, and 532II.
[33]See pp. 133ff.II, 147ff.II, 160II, 266II, 418II, and 484II.
[34]See pp. 585, 241II, 245II, and 283II.
[35]See pp. 254, 257 ("It is his Council"!), 311 ("rather conservative"!), 315, 97II, 446II, 449II, 458II (however, Bea was considered "an absolutely providential man"!), and 342II.
[36]See p. 321, but with a favorable mention on pp. 380 and 42II.
[37]See pp. 423, 443, 531, 560, 73II, 144II, 147II, and 433II.
[38]See pp. 539, 23II, 191II, 464II (from Father Tucci).
[39]See pp. 285, 338II, 344II, 376II, 397II, and 415ff.II.
[40]See pp.100II, 129II, 448II, 488II, and for St. Sabina, pp. 367II and 373ff.II.
[41]See pp. 337, 356, 137II, 147II, and 253II.
[42]See pp. 247, 278, 552 ("sensational"), and 218II.
[43]See pp. 97, 151, 171, 198, and 189II.
[44]See pp. 301II, 355II (a positive note), and 357II ("confused").

585); Marty;[45] Ottaviani;[46] Parente;[47] Peruzzo (see p. 160); Roberti (see p. 506II); Ruffini;[48] Samoré (see p. 179); Proença Sigaud (see p. 447); Siri;[49] Tardini;[50] Tisserant;[51] Vagnozzi;[52] Veuillot (see p. 512II); Vilnet (see pp. 481ff.II); and Weber (see pp. 98 and 170).

In a category set apart as a regular target for criticism by Father Congar, most of it harsh and unjust, is the Secretary General of the Second Vatican Council, Archbishop Pericle Felici.[53]

We need to take note here also of the author's many arrows directed towards the Holy Office,[54] the Roman Curia,[55] the apostolic nuncios,[56] "papists,"[57] "integralists,"[58] the conciliar minority,[59] the Eastern bishops in general (see p. 247), and the *Coetus Internationalis Patrum*.[60] Among the national episcopates,[61] the author criticizes in particular the French episcopate and the German episcopate.[62]

---

[45]See pp. 204II, 453II, 481ff.II, and 505II.

[46]See pp. 37, 165, 205, 209, 257, 268, 272, 279, 313, 344, 468 ("a child"), 522 ("treacherous"), 525, 528, 581, 77ff.II, 171II, and, for a favorable mention, p. 495II.

[47]See pp. 6-7, 227, 268, 314, 69II, 91II, and with a slight change of judgment, pp. 347ff., 37II, and 250II.

[48]See pp. 415, 433 ("a shotgun blast"), 478, 578, 126II, 154II ("an old fighter"), 430II, and 504II.

[49]See pp. 438, 17II ("an old fighter"), 430II, and 504II.

[50]See pp. 373 (for the influence of Dossetti), and 23II.

[51]See pp. 440, 453ff., 432II, and 512II.

[52]See pp. 258, 375II, and 506II.

[53]See pp. 260, 583, 15II, 62II, 147II, 168II, 172ff., 190ff.II, 208ff.II (serious), 287II, 320II, 324II, 380ff.II, 466II, 476II, and 499II.

[54]See pp. 73, 343, 346, 369, 525 ("Frings") and 128II.

[55]See pp. 8ff., 114, 169ff., 180, 191 (against the power of the officials of the Roman Curia), 234, 343, 466, 472, 490, 527, 532, 534ff., 585 (serious criticisms of Marella, Ottaviani, and Pizzardo), 11II, 98II, 177II, 185ff.II, 191II, 243II, and 518II.

[56]See pp. 179, 181II, and 185ff.II.

[57]See pp. 353, 356, and 128II.

[58]See pp. 238II, 404II, and 433II.

[59]See pp. 466, 573, 153II ("as recalcitrant as children"), 361II, 391II, and 464II.

[60]See pp. 189II, 317II, and 433II.

[61]See pp. 191II, 324II, 439II, 442II ("the more mystical of the Germans"), 451II, and 481II.

[62]See pp. 83II and 482II.

In concluding this part of our inquiry, we list those Council Fathers about whom, in our opinion, Father Congar had *"mixed feelings."* Once again, we list them in alphabetical order, and, among others, they include: Ancel;[63] Bertoli (see p. 272); Charue (see p. 101II); Colombo;[64] Florit (see pp. 407 and 67ff.); Léger;[65] Lercaro;[66] and Rugambwa (see p. 523).

Judgments on Theologians Present at the Council

In this section, we will list theologians, whether official or not (see p. 422II), in three categories: those whose relations with Father Congar, as indicated in his remarks about them in this diary, are negative, or who are actually rejected by him, even to the point of contempt; those who, on the other hand, are evaluated by him positively; and, finally, those in the category already utilized above, namely, those about whom he harbored "mixed feelings." We shall not go into fine distinctions or details here.

Let us begin with those who enjoyed Congar's favorable *appreciation*. We list them in alphabetical order so as to facilitate for the patient reader the task of checking on any of these references. They are: Aubert (see p. 230); Benoit;[67] Chenu in particular;[68] Cottier (see pp. 394 and 120II); de Lubac;[69] Ferrari Toniolo (see p. 387); Hamer (see p. 169II); Jedin (see pp. 163 and 584); Lambruschini (see pp. 527 and 163II); Le Guillou (see p. 169II); Lebret (see pp. 125II and 131II); Medina;[70] Meersseman (see p. 513II); Moeller;[71] Onclin;[72] Philips;[73]

---

[63]See pp. 237, 102II, and 191II.

[64]See pp. 83, 42II ("a mistaken prophecy"), 153II, 178II, 279II, 411II, 427II, 436II, and 495II.

[65]See pp. 161, 197, 276, 341ff., 344, 357, 426 (against Suenens), and 66II.

[66]See pp. 138, 303ff., and 362II.

[67]See pp. 123II, 125II, and 127II.

[68]See pp. 590ff., 64II, 128f.II (how he was co-opted), 131II, and 263f.II ("sensational").

[69]See pp. 21ff., 573, 145II, and 253II.

[70]See pp. 41II, 54II, 68II, 253II and 489II.

[71]See pp. 335, 54II, 68II, 360II, 493II, and 519f.II.

[72]See pp. 73II, 478II, 481II, 497II, and 505II.

[73]See pp. 68, 92ff., 151ff., 156, 188 (Philips text), 318ff., 330, 333, 335,

Prignon;[74] Ratzinger;[75] Schillebeeckx;[76] Smulders (see p. 218II and 407II); Spiazzi (see p. 371II, and Tucci.[77]

Regarding *critical and negative judgments on theologians*, some of which could be quite severe, Congar placed the following in this category: Balić;[78] Carbone (see p. 109II); Ciappi (see pp. 359 and 288II); Daniélou;[79] Delhaye (see p. 74); Del Portillo (see p. 249ff. II); D'Ercole;[80] Dhanis (see p. 353); Fenton (see pp. 16ff. and 94); Garofalo;[81] Herranz (see p. 250II); Küng;[82] Lattanzi (see pp. 93ff.); Laurentin;[83] Lio (see p. 315II); Martelet (see page 449II); Molinari (see p. 181II); Piolanti (see p. 163II); Ramirez (see p. 65II); Romeo (see pp. 50ff.); Schauf;[84] Schütte (see p. 350II): Seumois;[85] Stickler (see p. 274II); Tillmann (see p. 451II); and Tromp.[86]

339ff., 343, 398, 513, 537, 549 ("providential," "takes on everything"), 567 ("is soft, however"), 576, 583, 55ff.II, 57II ("does not seek the 'victory' of any theological school as such"), 72II, 117II, 130II, 148II (replaces Häring), 220II ("clarifier and pacifier"), 227II, 242II ("Philips is followed almost without question"), 275II ("does not want to go back to zero"), 283II ("mostly utilizes the original text of De Ecclesia"), 359II ("he does what he wants to do"), 360II ("decisive"), 412II, 454II, 465II, 489II, 510II ("the one who worked the hardest"), and, in addition, pp. 186ff.II. Philips accepted recommendations and *modi* from Congar, p. 230II.

[74]See pp. 335, 54II ("Suenens' agent"), and 73II.

[75]See pp. 201, 355f.II, and 498II.

[76]See pp. 345II, 448II, 480II, and 498II.

[77]See pp. 232, 243, 54II, 317II ("the pope has been right nine times out of ten times"), 326II (criticizes his Latin), 450II, 464II (against Cicognani), and 483 ("on the subject of Communism at the Council he showed himself not well informed").

[78]See pp. 333, 561, 572, 14II (against his "Marianist" Christianity), and 90II (insulting).

[79]See pp. 151, 181, 317, 328ff. (however Daniélou urged Congar to come to Rome and even found him a place), 332, 335, 354, 368f., 459, 493, 81II, 122II, 314II, 429II, 434II, 440II, 459II.

[80]See pp. 353f., 38II, 107II, and 145II.

[81]See pp. 198, 337, and 81II.

[82]See pp. 101, 465f. ("a very demanding revolutionary type"), 336II, and 497f.II ("very radical").

[83]See pp. 105, 180, 188, 435, 85II, 143II, 463II, 471II, and 497II.

[84]See pp. 81f., 338, 550, 103II, and 407II.

[85]See pp. 283II, 349ff.II, 355f.II, 445II, and 537II.

[86]See pp. 48, 61f., 69 ("a decisive role at the beginning"), 82f., 182 ("tyrant"), 338 ("redivivus"), 356 ("sceptre in the hands of others"), 442, 492, 514 ("out of his role"), 549f., 39II, 315II.

At the end of this list of theologians whom he basically disapproved, it is also necessary to mention Father Congar's theological *"bête noire,"* as becomes clear in this diary, namely, the Pontifical Lateran University.[87]

It remains only to list those theologians who aroused "mixed feelings" in Father Congar. They were: Bertrams;[88] Betti;[89] Cerfaux;[90] Dossetti;[91] Dupuis (see pp. 146II and 169II); Féret;[92] Gagnebet;[93] Gauthier (see pp. 564 and 500II); Häring;[94] Haubtmann;[95] Journet;[96] Jungmann (see p. 533II); Lécuyer (see pp. 249ff.II); Maccarone;[97] Martimort (see p. 465); Murray;[98] Pavan;[99] and Rahner.[100]

At the end of this presentation concerning the conciliar theologians, as they are treated in the diary of Yves Congar, it is necessary to record his praise, even though it is somewhat mitigated, for the work of the Belgians at the Council; in this connection, he actually goes so far as to speak of the Second Vatican Council, at least as far as theology is concerned, as "the First Council of Louvain"![101] In his view, the Belgians were "everywhere,"[102] employing both strategy and tactics

---

[87]See pp. 26ff., 49 ("obscurantist"), 74 ("did not submit proposals but rather long dissertations"), 86 ("miserable"), 121, 387 ("offensive integralist"), 390, and 515 ("Your work be positive"—Paul VI).

[88]See pp. 254II, 266II, and 268ff.II.

[89]See pp. 67ff., 218II, and 514II.

[90]See pp. 227, 33II, and 169II.

[91]See pp. 361ff., 364, 583, 194II, and 253II.

[92]See pp. 130II. Yet Congar wanted to co-opt him and he introduced him to Archbishop Felici at a favorable moment; see 242II, 382II ("not conciliar"), and 390II ("dogmatized against dogmatism").

[93]See pp. 69, 364 (negative judgment on Dossetti), 81II, and 345II.

[94]See pp. 79 ("takes things tragically"), 44II, 100II ("harms the cause somewhat"), 110II, 498ff.II.

[95]See pp. 294II (replaced Häring, "Philips will help him"), 325II, 328II, 332II, 465II, and 467II.

[96]See pp. 48, 69, 334II, 426II ("prisoner of Maritain"), 432II ("poor and simple"—this is intended as a compliment), and 474II.

[97]See pp. 104II, 145II, 230II ("frank???"), and 507II.

[98]See pp. 333II, 337II, and 340II.

[99]See pp. 367 ("against (his) natural law"), 383 ("too abstract"), 10II, 25II, 162II, 202II, 343II, 363II, 370II, and 428II.

[100]See pp. 54, 197, 201ff., 182 ("indiscreet"), 479 ("monopolizes the dialogue"), 496, 440II, and 532II.

[101]See pp. 10II, 45II, 53f.II, 67II, and 72II.

[102]See pp. 53f.II, 262II, and 311II.

well developed for the Council,[103] which they successfully imposed both on the majority of the Council Fathers and on Congar himself.

Also interesting in this diary is the question of the relations between the theologians and the bishops. From the very beginning, Father Congar expresses a rather negative viewpoint concerning "the great number of incapable bishops…with a deficient vision of the outstanding questions and particularly of their ideological and theological aspects…For the most part, they have lost the capacity to study and decide things for themselves. They are wholly accustomed to receiving ready-made decisions from Rome" (p. 9 and also p. 224II). Unfortunately even Pietro Parente thought that the bishops were "novices in all these questions" (p. 348). Nevertheless the *periti* needed to speak their minds when they were asked to do so (see pp. 95II and 358II). Even Congar was against the inflation in the number of *periti* present (see p. 424), but he was not entirely consistent here.

Certainly theological research has its role and task in the Church (see p. 340II), but it is not the case that this role and this task are equivalent to those possessed by our Protestant brethren, for example (see p. 467). Nor it is possible to say, as Congar does, that the theologians "made the Council."[104] Rather, and properly so, Congar later makes the point that theologians must not forget that they are part of the Church (see p. 469II); and he even confesses that, if he were a bishop, there would be a number of questions, for example, those concerned with the *schema De libertate*, for which he would have "a pastoral responsibility to view very carefully"; he would have to take into account "both the threats of the sects and the possibility that the absolute convictions of Catholics could become unraveled" (p. 469II; see also p. 58II). Certainly the relations of the Council Fathers and their *periti* could not but be delicate.[105] Their diverse criteria and methods of examining *modi*, for example, had to be taken into account.[106]

At a certain point, however, it became possible to invite to

---

[103]See pp. 123, 324, 66II, 88II ("like a battle"), 211II, and also 224, 259, 463, 275II, 393f.II, 406II, and 438II ("If you can win Italy, you have won a great deal").

[104]P. 81II; see, however, pp. 421f.II, 465II, and 480II.

[105]See pp. 181II, 187II, 406f.II, 410II, and 518II.

[106]See pp. 176II, 187II, 340II, and 348II.

participate in the work of the Council experts who were not official (see p. 396II). The conciliar freedom of the theologians! However that may be, Father Congar had words of appreciation for the conciliar Doctrinal Commission, which he found to be "broad and accessible" (especially by comparison with the other conciliar commissions). He frequently had words of praise for it,[107] even though it sometimes met without any *periti* present (see pp. 267II and 440II).

Certain Important Conciliar Topics in the Congarian Vision

As for the conciliar themes and topics, that is, the contents of the dialogues and the discussions that led to the final documents, I am pleased to be able to comment here on some of the more interesting of them as they are treated in this diary.

Among the first of these topics mentioned is that of *collegiality*.[108] In discussing it, we need to understand that when Congar refers to the "anti-collegiality" Fathers, this term must be understood to mean those who were opposed to a certain type of collegiality; Congar himself distinguished between "broad" and "narrow" collegial acts.[109] In dealing with this subject in general, we find it useful to check for references in the diary to the *Nota Explicativa Praevia* attached to Chapter III of *Lumen Gentium*.[110]

In this connection too, it needs to be stressed that Father Congar did not find the *Nota Explicativa Praevia* to be in contrary to collegiality or to the Church's doctrine. What this means, and what we have confirmed and verified in this text, is that Father Congar did not belong to the extremist fringe within the conciliar majority which we have identified with Dossetti,[111] and, later, with Alberigo.

---

[107]See pp. 263, 57II, 109II, 359II, 412II, and 505II ("nostalgia").

[108]See pp. 118, 263, 298ff., 301, 347, 353, 469, 37II, 128II, 134II, 145II, 227II, and 371II.

[109]See pp. 456ff., 248II, and 266II.

[110]See pp. 126II, 148II, 152ff.II, 178ff.II, 242II, 248ff.II, 251II, 253ff. II ("it does not go against collegiality"), 266ff.II, 269f.II ("it does not go against the doctrine"), 272II, 274II, 325II, 344ff.II, 440II ("like Zinelli at Vatican I"), and 518II.

[111]See pp. 145II, 260II, 262II, 269ff.II ("the Nota does not change anything...Although it is not part of the text as voted, it does convey the sense of it").

As regards the topic of the *papacy*, however, the situation is more complicated, especially in view of the many "hard sayings" of the author on this particular subject. He launched not a few arrows against the "system" which he characterized variously, as "Constantinian," "Renaissance," "lordly," "Roman," or perhaps sometimes as simply "Italian." The "system" in question, of course, was nothing else but the primacy of the bishop of Rome in the Church, understood in a religious and Catholic sense.[112]

It is clear that the "modern papacy," for Congar is "Tridentine and post-Tridentine" (see p. 370II), if it is not actually "medieval," and "linked to Augustinianism" (see pp. 453ff.II). He cites two interventions of Onclin (see p. 73II) and D'Ercole (see p. 107II), respectively, on the papal *plenitudo potestatis* and on the Pseudo-Isidorian Decretals which had such a great influence on the development of the exercise of the primacy. The Roman Church supposedly thought of nothing but "her own authority during the entire course of her history" (see p. 537II). Similarly, a critical note is lodged also against Vatican Council I,[113] on account of what is styled the papal "usurpation" with respect to the Church and the bishops (see p. 526); or worse, on account of what the popes supposedly "robbed" in the course of the centuries (see p. 586 and also p. 535). Various arrows are also launched against what Congar calls "plain Ultramontanism," for which he convicts various people unjustly.[114] He accuses others of "papalotry" (idolatry).[115]

And on the subject of the *papal primacy*, in order to deepen our knowledge of the viewpoint of Father Congar on this subject, one can read with profit several of his notes on the matter of the relationship of the pope with the Church (see esp. p. 180) and on that of the pope's relationship with the patriarchs as well.[116] The same thing is

---

[112]See pp. 71, 74, 78, 107, 115, 312, 345, 358, 401ff., 502, 506, 523ff., 535, 576, 14II, 31II, 224II (where he takes up the cause of Lamennais), 243II, 322II, 334f.II, and 523II.

[113]See pp. 106II ("a surpassing," without any contradiction), 156ff.II ("a rebalancing"), and 262II.

[114]See pp. 312 (Italy), 535, 559, 22II, 24II, and 26II.

[115]See pp. 301, 345, 587, and 42II.

[116]See, for example, pp. 68, 408, 565, 569, 584, and 588.

true with regard to the formula to be employed to express the papal confirmation of the Council's documents; on this subject, Congar expresses satisfaction with the formula finally chosen by Paul VI; in. this he diverges from the position of Dossetti, who was in opposition to this formula.[117] Linked to the hierarchical question was the one of the inclusion in the draft *schema De Ecclesia* of the chapter *De Populo Dei*, which by a decision of the Council's Central Coordinating Commission, was placed ahead of the chapter on the hierarchy in what became *Lumen Gentium*. This was done for reasons that were described as "logical." Father Congar was not alone in believing that there were other motives at work in this placement. However that may be, it is evident in Congar's diary that the chapter on "the People of God" was properly "structured," for it also includes the hierarchy.[118] For this reason, no one should oppose the placement of these two chapters, nor try to establish any theological precedence on the basis of this placement.

Closely related to this same idea, it seems, are the number of passages in the diary related to *the Church of the poor*. This topic was not honored with treatment in a *schema* by itself, as Cardinal Lercaro had requested; but it was certainly one of the major interests of Father Congar; because of this he was asked by Bishop Alfred Ancel to be the latter's conciliar *peritus*, for Bishop Ancel too was much taken with the question.[119]

Following this, we are happy to report that the topic of *the unity of Christians* is a constant in the zealous spirit of Father Congar, who, for that matter, was always a convinced ecumenist and a leader in promoting ecumenism. The passages in which he refers to the subject are thus quite numerous.[120] So are the references he makes to persons involved in ecumenism (although they also mostly fall into

---

[117]See pp. 461, 465, 565, 569, 584, and 588.
[118]See pp. xxxvii, 47, 284, 289, 449ff., 470, 475, 480, 488 (Wojtyla), 13II, and 349II.
[119]See pp. 231II and also 280, 472 484, 543, 7II, 188II, 228II, 237II, 252II, and 500II.
[120]See, for example, pp. 116, 418, 490, 106II, 156II, 279f.II, 282II, 287II, 290ff.II, 295II, 331II, 490II, 492II, 501ff.II, and 506ff.II.

the category of those about whom he had "mixed feelings"). They include: Cullmann;[121] Schlink (see p. 459II); Schutz (see p. 498II); Visser't Hooft (see p. 165II), and Barth.[122]

What is to be underlined, however, is the playing down, in effect, of the papal interventions in view of the importance of the approval of the final document on ecumenism in the end (see pp. 280II and 331II). This was the true issue, even if Congar too spoke at a certain point of a "catastrophic morning" for the ecumenical climate.[123]

We do not travel far from the theme of ecumenism before we arrive at the related theme of *religious liberty*. These were two themes that conditioned the dialogue, as did ecumenical collaboration. Both themes were followed closely by the author; this comes out clearly in this diary. It was also quite natural.[124]

We need to bring out, in this regard, that Paul VI very clearly insisted that the "logical" continuity of the Church's teaching [on religious liberty] needed to be shown (see p. 415II). This was not a question that greatly concerned Father Congar (see pp. 451ff.II and 545), but it was well brought out in the formula concerning "immunity from coercion."[125] It was important to eliminate the idea that religious liberty was equivalent to "ecclesiastical liberty."[126] At this point the *proemium* of Father Congar was eliminated (see pp. 376ff.II and 397II), although his text affirmed that the idea of religious liberty did not threaten the truth that there was a single unique true religion and Church (see pp. 424ff.II). Also, his text recognized the existence at the Council of a beneficent conciliar presence in the form of a minority able to clarify and improve the text.[127] All of this amounts to saying

---

[121]See pp. 272, 390 ("contrary to Bultmann"), 8ff.II, 118II, and 263II.

[122]See p. 533II (not like the Protestants, either in his identity or openness).

[123]P. 282II; see also pp. 287II ("lost virginity"), and 290II.

[124]See pp. 545, 159ff.II, 163II, 202II, 222II, 330II, 333II, 337ff.II, 340II, 344II, 363II, 370II, 376II, 397II, 401II, 411II, 416II, 424ff.II, 428II, 451II, and 469II.

[125]See pp. 330II and 340II.

[126]See pp. 372II and 376II, and also pp. 310II and 391II—Congar was in the minority here.

[127]See pp. 250II, 329ff.II, 333II, and 495II

that we need not adopt the journalistic appellation of a "black week" [when the pope intervened and caused the postponement of votes on ecumenism and religious liberty]; for this postponement was decisive for the improvement of the conciliar text on religious liberty—and not only the text on that subject.[128]

It seems opportune to insert at this point the conciliar treatment of ecumenism, as it refers to the *Word of God*, particularly for what concerns the relationship between Scripture and Tradition and the *historia salutis* (history of salvation), and the historicity of the Gospels. The points of view of the Council Fathers and of the members of the Commission were not necessarily "*opposed*,"[129] even though the question of "Tradition" brought out several other questions.[130]

But, in fact, papal interventions were made (on the historicity of the Gospels, for example—see pp. 101ff.II). With regard to Tradition, however, I am pleased to cite an expression of Archbishop Edelby reported by Congar, namely, that all this was "like an epiclesis in the history of salvation" (see p. 180II). Meanwhile, the question of the "truth which saves" continued to figure in the text.[131]

It is not possible to deny, however, that the Council's discussion on the subject of *Mariology* was necessarily conditioned by the Council's approach to ecumenism. It was certainly true in Father Congar's case.[132] However, it must be recorded that his reaction was quite negative towards the pontifical proclamation of Mary as "the Mother of the Church."[133]

As for ecumenism, we find passages in the diary referring to the long and rather tortuous progression of the *schema De Iudeis*[134]

---

[128]See pp. 403II, 281II, and 295II.

[129]See pp. 230, 237, and 240ff.

[130]See pp. 331, 348, 437, 48II, 65II, 101II, 216II, 416II, 420II, 423II, and 436II.

[131]See pp. 417II, 421II, and 446II (and my explanatory note, "The Truth which Saves," in *Bailamme*, January-December, 2001, pp. 34-42 (in this book, Chapter 30).

[132]See pp. 65ff., 71, 89, 496, 507, 543, 52II, 86f.II, 90fII, 92ff.II, 118II, 143f.II, 151II, and 200II.

[133]See pp. 557 ("a cancer for Mariology"), 138II, 278II, and 290II.

[134]See pp. 70ff.II, 82II, 119II, 182ff.II, 300II, 320II, 339II, 342II, 364ff., and 427II.

and also of the texts concerning other non-Christian religions. These posed difficulties for Congar, particularly where the Muslims were concerned.[135]

Nevertheless, the "ecumenical" vision did not prevent the Council from treating the question of the *missions* at length. There were various developments here, including interventions by Congar himself. He provided a decisive contribution, especially in one of the chapters of the approved document.[136]

The Church is in a state of *mission also in the atheist world*, not merely in the traditional mission fields. One topic that gets frequent mention here is the question of whether or not the Council should have condemned Communism explicitly by name, as a considerable number of Council Fathers wished; but it becomes clear that this author was really not very well informed about this topic when his words about it are checked with the *Acta Synodalia*.[137] Repeated here, again while adequate knowledge was lacking, is the case of the famous questions posed to the Council Fathers on *De Ecclesia*.[138]

Particular attention would be called for here on the subject of the author's many references to *Schema XVII* (later Schema XIII)—which became *Gaudium et Spes*.[139] We have to limit ourselves, however, to suggesting to the patient reader to check in particular the theme of *war and peace* (see, for example, p. 505II) and that of *family morality* (see, for instance, p. 372).

Our author is well informed in the line of *Pacem in Terris* (see pp. 249II and 505II), but he was not completely in agreement with the magisterial norms on the subject of conjugal relations.[140] However that may be, *Schema XIII* helped Congar understand how difficult it was to treat the connection between the Church and the temporal world (see p. 479II).

---

[135]See pp. 71II, 260II, 394II, and 427II.

[136]See pp. 249II, 257II, 287II, 292II, 294II, 298II, and 472ff.II.

[137]See pp. 346, 371, 450II, 454II, and 483II.

[138]See pp. 476, 482, 491, 493, 497, 503, 505ff., 583, 585, and 15ff.II.

[139]See, for example, pp. 365ff., 34ff.II, 99II, 126II, 130II, 148II, 196II, 307ff.II, 310II, 314ff.II, 318ffII, 325II, 327ff.II, 386ff.II, 395ff.II, 406II, 465II, 467II, 475II, and 497II.

[140]See p. 215II, and also pp. 347II, 490II, and 495II.

With regard to the Church's relations *ad extra*, that is, with the temporal world, the Council's "Closing Messages" were particularly significant. At first, Congar had a rather ambivalent attitude towards such messages, as the one at the beginning of the Council that had been promoted by his friend and confrere Father Chenu, although the commitment of Archbishop Garrone to all this was clear from the start.[141] The same thing was true of the "Closing Messages," even though the author did not find himself "completely at ease" with them (see pp. 515ff.II). For him *Gaudium et Spes* itself was the Council's true—and great—"message to the modern world" (see p. 516II).

Moderate Aspects in the Congarian Positions

Before looking at how Father Congar saw the future from the standpoint of forty years ago, we would like to conclude this part by looking at several aspects in the diary which incline one to think that Congar was not just another progressive theologian wholly at home in the ranks of the "conciliar majority," but rather was quite variable in certain ways.

I begin this discussion by recalling how important he considered the reaching of a true consensus among the Council Fathers,[142] and also how he declined to see any separation between the *pastoral* aspects and the *doctrinal* ones. This latter distinction was particularly important as regards how the Council of Trent was viewed—for Congar it was "certainly pastoral, though above all doctrinal" (p. 225 and see also, however, p. 372).

We note as well that he thought the Catholic Church rightly included a Cardinal Ottaviani as well as an Archbishop Parente (see p. 466). He also recognized the beneficent role played by the conciliar minority (see pp. 329II and 263II), and he was not always exaggeratedly suspicious of his adversaries (see pp. 236 and 238).

A *fundamental moderation*, in fact, is to be seen in his judgments on the *papal interventions* in the work of the Council—and not only the one regarding the question of sacerdotal celibacy (see pp. 426II and

---

[141]See pp. 99ff., 102, 104ff., 112, 121, 125, and 131.
[142]See pp. 235, 241, 272, 387, 152II, and 355II.

430II). He understood the need for obtaining a consensus for the final documents on *ecumenism*,[143] *collegiality*,[144] and the *Word of God* (see pp. 102II and 437II)—not to speak of that concerning the question of the suspension of the discussion on *religious liberty* (see pp. 281II and 377II), which brought about the journalistic formula "Black Week" (p. 403II). In general, his judgments on the formulas employed by the press was negative.[145] His fundamental balance further showed itself in his reaction to the idea of a *Church of the poor*.[146] The same balance is evident, as we have seen, in the case of the "structured" vision of "the People of God" and in defense of "the ordinary pontifical magisterium" (see p. 475II, n. 1).

The same balanced position characterized Congar's repeated invitation to all to respect the continuity of conciliar texts that were. not yet complete,[147] and to respect the mind of the Council and of the Council Fathers, particularly in view of the difficult materials concerning the relationships between the conciliar commissions and the conciliar assembly itself.[148]

In any case, Father Congar believed that the *Holy Spirit* did make use of human beings (see p. 261). He made mention of both the "*spirit*" and "*mind*"[149] of the Council itself, suggesting that these could be determined by theologians (see p. 465II). For us, however, the "spirit" of the Council is definitely to be found in the *corpus* of the Council's own final documents, approved by the pope and the bishops.

Certainly it was all a question of "something remarkably new or renewed" (pp. 488II and 72II), even though Congar often considered the texts themselves "banal" or "mediocre" (see p. 72II). However, he thought they contained "germs" capable of bearing fruit (*Ibid.*). In fact, he thought such fruits could already be descried, for example, in

---

[143]See pp. 280II, 290ff., and 331II.

[144]See pp. 250II, 260II, 266II, 269ff.II, and 270II.

[145]See pp. 295II, 337, and 189II.

[146]See p. 484 and also p. 525II.

[147]See pp. 151, 201ff., 319, 343ff., 387, 283II, 309II, 326ff.II, 359II, 395ff. II, 451ff.II, and 482II.

[148]See pp. 163 (Hubert Jedin), 274, 387, 452, 492, 105II, 187II, and 452II.

[149]See pp. 339II, 372II, 374II, 465II, and 478II.

the *liturgies* in St. Peter's.[150] However, he failed to see any such fruits in the liturgy of a parish he visited (see p. 494II).

I would like, finally, to include two quotations from the author here. One of them made reference to the movement of the Council, which supposedly consisted of "applying purely juridical-type judgments to a supernatural ontology" (p. 354II). This observation sums up Congar completely for us. Then there was his claim to the effect that: "I am a man who strives to bring about peace" (p. 355II). This claim is not far from the truth, in fact; though it is amazing that he should be able to advance such a claim in spite of everything, including especially the frequent invective contained in this diary—which hardly does him honor—yet he evidently sincerely believed that things must be accomplished by going through necessary stages. This position was precisely contrary to that of Hans Küng (see p. 466 and 355II).

Perhaps it is opportune to recall at this point, looking at the *Journal* as a whole, the state of the author's health, which he frequently complained about, throughout the whole of the Council, in fact. He often considered himself, as a result of his infirmity, to have been "silent," "inactive," "without initiatives," "too prudent," "timorous," and "timid." This was not true, for the most part, especially during the early phases of the Council.[151] Yet the author's *psychological state* during the Council can be considered to have been a heavy burden for him; the diary contains passages indicating pronounced changes of mood.[152] Such changes, for example, impelled him to decline to swear the obligatory oath, though he signed the related document anyway (see p. 33); all this has to be seen in the context of the spiritual aspects also revealed in the diary (see above). Moreover, his many notes on the various interventions of the Fathers, to the extent that he recorded them, exhibit his intense reactions and his usual critical passion: "fiction," he writes, "unreality," "abstractions," "outmoded." Or else:

---

[150]See pp. 132II, 389II, and 393II.

[151]See pp. 102ff., 396, 437, 466, 479, 151ff.II, 89II ("my absolute silence"?), 133II, and 431II. Proof of his considerable activity can be found especially on pp. 122ff.II, 131II, 133II, 136II, 140II, 143II, 147II, 176ff.II, and 178II.

[152]See pp. 516ff., 589, 113ffII, 116II, 156II, 188II, 223II, and 405ff.II.

"What world is he living in?" (See, for example, p. 490). To be noted also is a progressive hardening of his own positions.[153] Then, thanks to him, there was the co-optation of various theologians at the Council: M.-D. Chenu himself (see pp. 129II and 131II), Pierre Benoit (see pp. 123II and 129II), and the attempt made in the case of Henri-Marie Féret (see p. 242II). He found self-criticism to be "difficult" (see p. 72II).

A final touch in our attempt to portray the "person" of this author can be found in the often beautiful writing and phraseology he produced in this diary. His descriptions, often sketched in miniature, as well as his capturing of both *places* and *situations*, often reflect his state of mind and soul. This is an author who knew how to write.[154]

Towards the Future

We do not want to employ the term "prophet," but we must nevertheless concede that Father Congar was right on the mark when he wrote about how *difficult* it would be to write the history of the Council (see p. 281). He himself was a historian and he knew what he was talking about.[155]

He was also right when he spoke about the need for theological, juridical, and historical studies on the subject of collegiality (see p. 164II). For him, in future years, "the history of ecclesiology should count as urgent priority number one" (p. 291II). And he saw the subject as one requiring an "ecclesiology of communion" (p. 115II).

He was again on the right track as far as we are concerned when he called for a the Roman Curia to be "more international" (see p. 518II). This is something that, in effect, has been realized.

And Father Congar was surely right on the mark once again when he called for moving beyond the mistaken division into separate camps or domains representing questions of principle and those of practice, of competences and of cares or concerns. This division, he declared, was "the most decisive fault or vice of the entire institution" (pp. 247 and 68).

---

[153]See pp. 62II, 67II, and 33II.
[154]See pp. 69ff., 80, 92, 106, 178, 312, 329, 334, 378, 487ff., 565, 590, 27II, 118II, 289II, 384II, 463II, 484ff.II, 487ff.II, 494II, and 496II.
[155]See p. 259II: "I have not 'done' ecclesiology."

Again, he touches upon the question of *ecclesiology*, when considering the relationship between the hierarchy and the theologians,[156] that has not been resolved yet. But how is it to be resolved? Certainly, "men [the Council Fathers] would not have done what they did without the help of their experts."[157] For Congar, one of the major problems of the whole post-conciliar era was going to be "maintaining the organic cooperation between bishops and theologians which only the event of the Council itself had brought about" (p. 518II). Our judgment about this, speaking as a historian, is that the theologians and exegetes—not to speak of the historians themselves—have in large part elected to go their own way, seemingly unconcerned about what the real meaning of *aggiornamento* required of them.

In this connection, we would like to recall a profound conviction, expressed in words by Romano Guardini, first in 1952, and later again in 1965—words which I now hereby adopt as my own. The words in question were addressed to a certain personage, one Giovanni Batista Montini, who later became "His Holiness." They are the following: "Coming to know the Church has been the determining motive and reason of my entire life. Even back when I was a student of political science, it became clear to me that the choice of the Christian was not merely based on one's conception of God nor even just on the figure of Christ, but, rather, it fundamentally entailed the question of the Church. From that time on I knew that an authentic and efficacious understanding was possible only in union with the Church...What can be convincing to modern man is not a 'modernized' version of Christianity refashioned in accordance with historical, or psychological, or any other kind of knowledge, but purely and simply the affirmation without limits or interruptions of what has been revealed to us in Christ. Naturally it is also the task of whoever makes this affirmation to be able to express it in relation to the problems and needs of our time. I myself have tried to do this in various times and places...But my experience has always been the same. What contemporary man wants and needs to hear is the pure and whole Christian proclamation

---

[156]See p. 518II and 340II: An examination of conscience by a theologian.
[157]See p. 518II, but compare this with contradictory passages on pp. 177 and 81II.

of the Good News. Perhaps he will then react negatively, but at least he will know what the whole thing is all about. In every case and in every test, this is the consideration that has always proved to be the' correct one."[158]

Father Congar, always in the context of his strong commitment in favor of the Council, mentioned the possibility of a subsequent great Synod, during which the treasury of Vatican Council II would be exploited (see p. 108). This was one of the reasons he opposed any such thing as a "Council" consisting only of "written contributions" sent in (see p. 145).

One final mention in the field of ecumenism must be permitted. It points to the fundamental importance for the Catholic reality of *dialogue*. I refer chiefly to the Eastern Catholic Churches here which, according to Congar, "will not enjoy their full status in the Church until the unity of the Orthodox is achieved" (see p. 270).

At this point I would like to formulate in my turn a judgment on the many expressed by Congar, as we have presented them, not without a few discordant notes. But I would like to refer the patient reader to the continuing critical "counterpoint" we have produced in opposition to the widely distributed *History of Vatican Council II* produced by Professor Giuseppe Alberigo and his associates—which often used and cited this *Journal* of Father Yves M.-J. Congar, O.P., as one of its sources and authorities. I accordingly refer the reader to my volume entitled *Church and Papacy in History and Law: 25 Years of Critical Studies*;[159] and also to the *L'Osservatore Romano*;[160] to the *Annuarium Historiae Conciliorum*;[161] to *Apollinaris*;[162] and, finally, to *Ius Ecclesiae*.[163]

---

[158]See the *Notiziario* of the Paul VI Institute, n. 44, pp. 86 and 91.

[159]*Chiesa e Papato nella Storia e nel Diritto*, published by the Libreria Editrice Vaticana in 2002. See also the reviews contained in this book beginning with Chapter 10.

[160]See *L'Oss. Rom.* for 11/13/97, 6/10/98, and 2/1/02.

[161]See *AHC* XXX (1998). And also *Apollinaris* LXXI (1998).

[162]See *Apollinaris* LXIX (1996); LXX (1997); LXXIII (2000); LXXIV (2001); and LXXV (2002).

[163]See *Ius Ecclesiae* XV (2003).

In any case, however, the perusal of this *Journal* has confirmed for us the complexity of the personality of Yves Congar—if added confirmation of that fact were needed. The Council which he chronicled was also complex, notwithstanding the ideological simplifications that have too often been applied to it.

46

Private Conciliar Sources

Faggioli Massimo, Turbanti Giovanni, eds., *Il Concilio inedito. Fonti del Vaticano II* [The Unpublished Council: Sources of Vatican II], Società Editrice Il Mulino, Bologna 2001, 164 pages.

It is always a pleasure to be able to take note of a commitment to serious research regarding Vatican Council II, particularly its "roots," that is to say, its sources. These materials are indispensable for understanding the great conciliar event more fully and correctly— but it is also always necessary to distinguish the "hierarchy" of these sources, in particular whether they are private or official. There is no doubt, of course, that private sources help give the savor and the aroma of the actual event, and even add important personal touches, depending upon who wrote them or saved them up. They often describe moods, reactions, tastes, "plots," and, also, they generally repeat many, many rumors. With hindsight they have no wisdom contained therein. Very often very little reflection has gone into them, either. The proof of their unevenness comes when a given "scribe" or writer, sometimes even an eminent one, after the actual publication of his words, is often obliged to make excuses or ask pardon for his own hasty, amateurish, or even mistaken judgments, not to speak of his possible rashness, in order to set things right. Unfortunately, though, many writers never get around to doing this, or do not want to do it. Others allow a sufficient number of years to pass after the event before allowing their "revelations" to surface. As often as not, this shows respect for the reputations of persons still living, who might otherwise be embarrassed by what is recounted.

As their point of departure, the authors look at the unfortunate case of the records of Vatican Council I, which motivated the wish, from the outset of Vatican II, to collect and preserve all the conciliar documents with the greatest care, and to prevent their dispersion at the end of the Council.

A note that is perhaps not without some malicious intent expresses this concern as well as anything: "Regulation and control of the documentation has always been an important element in the reception of conciliar documentation; this has been the case even when there was a willingness to pass over and forget certain documents, or to place obstacles in the way of full publication of them" (p. 8). This tendency becomes more marked when such things as the "polemics" of Paolo Sarpi [historian of the Council of Trent] are recalled.

In what follows in this volume, the authors present "the Archives" of Vatican II in Rome. They refer to Alberigo concerning the question of whether or not the great Synod was an "event" (Note 5, p. 9). We have many times encountered this question in the course of following modern historiography. For us, however, it can in no way be a question of an "event" that represents a "break" with the past, of an ecclesial revolution which somehow amounts to the birth of a new Church or a new Catholicism. Yet Vatican Council II has sometimes been presented in precisely this way.

In this regard, the Archives covered here owe much to the "praiseworthy work of Monsignor Carbone," who is credited with the systematization of the Council's Archives. "Thanks to him, scholars have had access to the conciliar documents, although [as of the end of 1999] with some limitations owing to the lack of a detailed inventory. Consulting the documents thus requires collaboration in order to find the documents desired" (p. 10).

But it is on the basis of these documents that this edition of the *Acta* of the Council has been published. It follows chronological order. A critical reading requires one to refer to the notes (n. 10, p. 10). It is also to be noted, however, that the Acts of the individual conciliar commissions have not been included in this publication, but only the *schemata* that these commissions produced.

For the authors, however, "this focusing of the work on the final results risks neglecting or passing over other possible developments that might have taken place...The various *schemata* are put together and lined up in such a way that variant readings between one draft and another are undervalued. In this way, an image of the Council is created that sees it as an institution strongly conditioned by the direction provided by its central organs, while all those aspects and initiatives taken by the Council Fathers themselves are correspondingly downgraded. The interactions between bishops, theologians, observers, and other protagonists—some of which took place outside the *aula* of the Council—are similarly undervalued" (pp. 12ff.).

Although we do not agree with this characterization, we have quoted this entire passage in full in order to bring out one of the ways in which contemporary conciliar hermeneutics is really quite mistaken in its view of the Council and is also unsympathetic, in fact, to the real nature of the Church.

On this very important subject of hermeneutics, the authors go on as follows: "The systematization of the Archives and the official publication of the conciliar Acts seems to be aiming at establishing a favored 'authentic' position, concerning the possible interpretations of the Council itself. In effect, Paul VI always evidenced a great preoccupation, and even revealed a rather lively inquietude, regarding what he considered to be 'partial' or one-sided interpretations of the documents which might bear upon ecclesiastical discipline; he feared that in the process of reception, radical tendencies might prevail, bringing about disarray in Church structures" (p. 13). But was this not a legitimate concern for a pope?

The authors concede this at least in part, since "the way in which the available documents have been organized and presented results in a rather precise picture of the Council that might differ considerably in the light of other sources and itself seem to be a 'partial' view." In what sense, may we be permitted to ask? Certainly, what emerges from consideration of the official documents still allows for other possible interpretations in the light of other real evidence from "diverse sources." But such "diverse sources" surely cannot simply go against what clearly emerges *ex actis et probatis* (from the facts).

Under a subtitle, the authors present what they call "local sources." But these turn out to be rather equivocal because it turns out that these sources are private sources. And also to be avoided here is the introduction of the famous ecclesial dichotomy—at least it is such in the eyes of some—of the "universal" Church versus the "local" one.

Brought out here is the difficulty of making a commitment to publish a history of the Second Vatican Council, as Professor Giuseppe Alberigo and his associates undertook to do at the end of the 1980s, "not so much because of the relatively brief time since the end of the Council, but rather because of the inaccessibility of essential sources. We realize the limits imposed, in spite of everything, by the fact that the *Acta* were merely in the process of being published; several volumes were still lacking"—among which were some of the most important, in our view. "This fact left without proper documentation some of the crucial points in the work of the Council, in particular matters which concerned the conciliar commissions" (p. 14).

"There thus came about a systematic examination of the sources that were available, including at the local level and including private sources…[the latter] representing a different type of documentation, in the eyes of some, a complementary version of the events set forth in the records preserved in Rome…Many factors important in the decision-making process were not known to the Council's Secretary General and hence were not recorded in the Archives maintained in Rome. Rather, they only came out into the light of day through the abundance of the accounts produced by various Council Fathers and theologians" (p. 15). We ask how anybody knew that what was contained in these private sources was necessarily "unknown" to the Secretary General, if the official records of the latter had not yet been published?

"The Council appeared [to the Council Fathers and theologians] as an occasion of discussion and reflection much more than as an institutional organ designed to issue doctrinal definitions…The character of the Council that emerged from these variant sources proved to be very different from the one derived from the records in the Vatican Archives…Nobody, certainly not the Council's central directing organs, and not the Secretariat, either, could be considered the expression of the Council as a whole" (p. 16).

Here, again, we are obliged to note that in the background of all this there lurks the famous question of the Council as an "event" (see, again, p. 16, where the Council is expressly spoken of as an "event"). The question also arises, of whether the essence of the Council is not to be located in the "consensus" represented by the documents issued by it, which are, precisely, "conciliar," and not merely "personal." The mistake of the authors here seems evident, as does the critical point that we too would make, namely, that to move the center of gravity of the Council from the assembly of the Council Fathers, who, after all, voted on and passed the conciliar documents, to the conciliar commissions which merely existed to serve the Council and the Fathers who composed it, in truth and charity, was indeed a mistake.

We shall not linger over the question of the establishment of "a typology of sources." For the most part, this seems to us to be a vain enterprise, with too much importance given to private diaries (pp. 19 and 23, n. 38). Nor shall we pause over what the authors call a "functional plan" in which are included indications useful in connection with the conciliar commissions. There is also "a geographical plan" as well as "a list of local sources." There are limitations in the latter, which the authors admit with some frankness, as they do with regard to the information they utilize drawing upon studies conducted some time back.

"This list aims to provide information available at this time. It can be verified only marginally and in connection with research conducted in view of this publication...This list thus does not claim to be exhaustive, nor, certainly, to be definitive" (p. 31).

Then, for the most part, this reading of "the summary of the sources utilized for the history of Vatican Council II" confirms a negative conclusion regarding the many attempts at more direct contact and research. Others, however, arrive at a rather different conclusion about all this, and end up with rather strange and even vague conclusions. For example, "the material in question is surely preserved in the diocesan archives of..." Moreover, both the ecclesiastical terms and titles employed here leave something to be desired.

We conclude with the citation of an important notice that pertains to the *History of Vatican Council II* prepared by Giuseppe Alberigo and his associates. It is this: "In effect, the studies conducted up to this point have utilized a relatively reduced amount of the massive documentation that exists" (p. 33). In their Note 65 the authors add: "The sources gathered along the way by the team that has collaborated on the production of this *History of Vatican Council II* have generally been made available to all. But that does not alter the fact that each collaborator on the project of this *History* has utilized what was wanted from these common sources according to his own individual discretion, meanwhile drawing upon other sources of various types as well." It is good to know this since it confirms our judgment concerning the choice *ad usum delphini* [for a certain purpose] of the sources that have in fact been used. This is one of the great weaknesses—which from the outset we have also characterized as "ideological"—of the *History* in question. Its correspondence with the official sources is both difficult and labored.

A final quotation in the nature of an *excusatio non petita* [excuse not requested] is the following: "On the subject of current research on Vatican II, some have spoken about limiting what is described as a certain partiality or bias. But this tendency should have been attributed to the fact that not all of the archival sources have been accessible, and a true verification of historiographical interpretations can only be properly made on the basis of the accessibility of the instruments for the required research."

We are inclined to think in this regard that it is possible to affirm, considering the way in which the five volumes of the Alberigo *History* in question have turned out, that the ideological position of the authors has impeded, and continues to impede, their having recourse to a much larger field of research. Accessibility to solid sources can only grow, and has already grown. We might wish to be contradicted by the facts about this in the future, but the situation on all this remains what it is. To have gone forward with the project of the publication of this *History*, at a time when the publication of the official *Acta* of the Council was not yet complete, demonstrates how dependent the authors were on the idea of the Council that they had in their minds, rather than relying on the humble quest for the actual historical truth—not to speak of objectivity.

47

Official Conciliar Sources:
Synodal Acts from the Secretariat General

Part A: Carbone Monsignor Vincenzo, ed., *Acta Synodalia Sacrosancti Concilii Oecumenici Vaticani II. Volumen VI, Acta Secretariae Generalis, Pars III, Periodus Tertia*, MCMLXIV, *Typis Vaticanis 1998* [Synodal Acts of the Sacred Ecumenical Council of Vatican II, Volume 6, Acts of the Secretariat General, Part 3, Third Session, 1964, Vatican Press, 1998], 757 pages. [Monsignor Carbone was charged with responsibility for the Vatican Council II Archives.]

There has now appeared the sixty-first volume in the series of the official sources of the great Council. This is a work that may justly be styled "titanic." It attests at one and the same time to both the greatness and the providence of the historical vision of Pope Paul VI, who ardently wished to see the publication of this material carried out. It attests also to the industrious fidelity of the one to whom the pope assigned the task of realizing this project (see pp. 46ff., 134, and 149ff.). We understand that we have now arrived at the penultimate volume of this invaluable collection of documents, which will make possible the writing of the true history of the great conciliar event, based on these official sources in particular (which are in Latin). The Council has already had an enormous influence as our century now moves to its close. Pope John Paul II considers it to have been the "gate" to what is now looming before us as the great Jubilee for which we are making preparations.

The "purpose and the mind" for this book by the general editor of these volumes is clear (see pp. 7ff.). It has been prepared in continuity with the already published Acts of the Council's Central Coordinating Commission, as well as of those of the meetings of the Council Moderators. This book consists of a selection of documents from the Council's Secretariat General. Appearing here, in fact, are the documents which explain and interpret the *res gestas* (the facts) of the important Third Session of the Council. Added are two very interesting *Appendices* which have reference to the very fundamental Chapter III of the *Schema De Ecclesia* on the one hand (pp. 639-648); and, on the other hand, to the pope's m*otu proprio* entitled *Sacram Liturgiam*, which was decisive for the development of the liturgical reform desired by the Council. As always in this series, the order is chronological, and the text is enriched by useful notes. What is decisive, however, especially on certain major themes—and what the editor has helpfully provided—are the formulas, notes, and decisions handwritten by Pope Paul VI himself. These show, or rather confirm, the guidance that the pope provided to the Council at decisive moments in the course of the great "conciliar journey."

It is clear that we cannot spell out in any way that is exhaustive and useful, all of the new roads that are now open to historical research as a result of the publication of this series. We limit ourselves, therefore, to mentioning just a few of those that are contained in this volume.

The most important and decisive documents among those in this volume, in fact, are those connected with the *schema De Ecclesia*, that is, concerning the text which became Chapter III [of *Lumen Gentium*], and, in particular, concerning the subject of collegiality (n. 22). And in this regard, the text of greatest interest is that entitled the "Personal Note Reserved to the Holy Father on the *Schema Constitutionis De Ecclesia*" ("*Quidam Patres Cardinales*": see pp. 316, 322-338, and, in particular, also pp. 339ff., 136-148, 166, 231, 244, 274ff.). In this document, at least an important segment of the conciliar "minority" is seen to go on record in rather dramatic terms explaining the motives for their "very serious reservations" concerning the *schema*. The pope's point-by-point reply to them is quite extraordinary in its depth. The authoritative position which the pope takes is also strongly supported by a very significant and illuminating *pro-memoria* by Archbishop

Felici prepared at what was obviously a difficult and delicate moment (see pp. 357ff., and also p. 128ff., which, however, presents a rather different tone). A reading of this latter document prepared by the Council's Secretary General suffices as a response to the hostile and ill-disposed judgments often made about him branding him as an "extremist" of the conciliar minority (even if in this regard some distinctions are brought out here). We need only cite his conclusion to show this: "It is necessary to repose confidence in the consciences of the Fathers," he writes, "and in the strength of the truth, and in the help of the Holy Spirit" (p. 358; see also pp. 184ff.).

Yet always on the subject of this same key point, decisive for the ultimate destiny of Vatican II, in fact, the present volume contains important notes referring to the famous *Nota Explicativa Praevia* which help to explain it. It was requested that it be published along with the approved text of *Lumen Gentium* (as emerges *ex Actis Concilii* on pp. 560ff. and also on p. 529). Paul VI wrote in his own hand: "We agree, without ascribing a polemical character to a *Nota* which is merely explanatory. Nevertheless, it does possess an official character among the Acts of the Council, and, as such, it is authoritative" (p. 561). See also on this same subject pages 575, 583ff., 615ff., 629, and, especially pages 643-648: "The Vicar of Christ, wishing to promulgate the new text and make it his own, has nevertheless expressed the wish that the text be preceded by an explanatory Note from the Doctrinal Commission on the significance and value of the emendations made in the text. By means of such an explanation, it will be opportune to bear in mind the method followed by Vatican Council I" (p. 643). This quotation comes from a letter from His Eminence Amleto Cardinal Cicognani, Secretary of State, addressed to His Eminence, Alfredo Cardinal Ottaviani, President of the Council's Doctrinal Commission on Faith and Morals. Of great importance for the clarity and strength found in one of the attachments to this letter is what is described as "the text of an opinion requested on this subject from the Reverend Father Wilhelm Bertrams, S.J." This opinion is an excellent commentary showing that it is to Bertrams that we owe the introduction of the key concept of a "hierarchical communion" (p. 647). Elsewhere this same concept is indicated as capable of providing a fruitful synthesis between the First and Second Millennium [of Christianity] as far as the organic constitution of the Church is concerned.

Much clear light reflected from the conciliar documents contained in this collection is also thrown upon the complicated and intricate debate on the subject of *religious liberty*. Here, again, "pressures" on the pope were not lacking, and the pontifical decisions contributing to the final and happy result embodied in the conciliar document itself are brought out here (see pp. 113-122, 417ff., 440-443, 501ff., 522, 525, 530, 557, 564, 605, and 610). The pope's interventions are both vigorous and convincing, and they are usually quite explicitly stated (p. 502). On September 29, 1964, for example, Paul VI wrote: "As regards the *schema* entitled *De libertate religiosa*, it is necessary to redo it, associating with this effort competent persons in the process of revision, especially those with competencies in theology and sociology" (p. 418). This papal will is confirmed in a document dated November 15, 1964, in which, among other things, it is ordered that "consideration of this document is to be postponed to the Fourth Session for its definitive approval"; this is accompanied by a note from Johannes Willebrands in which he declares himself "entirely in agreement" (p. 530). Now we finally know from this book that the number of Council Fathers who appealed to the Holy Father opposing any postponement of the *schema* on religious liberty was 441; according to Monsignor Carbone, they were more than 450, and indeed 457 (pp. 605 and 610).

Also on the subject of ecumenism, this volume presents additional authentic new light. We limit ourselves to mentioning the "emendations ordered by the Supreme Authority in the *schema* entitled *De Oecumenismo*"—characterized here as "helpful suggestions authoritatively expressed" (p. 563), and included among other reactions (see pp. 563ff., 558, and 562). And, further, there are numerous documents on the subject of the Jews; they are so numerous, in fact, that we shall not attempt to enumerate or describe them; the same thing applies to the many documents on mixed marriages to be found here.

It could be interesting to follow in this volume the history of the title *Mater Ecclesiae* (Mother of the Church), which Pope Paul VI eventually bestowed on the Blessed Virgin Mary on his own authority—even after so many in the Council had declared themselves "displeased" with this idea. There was even a judgment from the Holy Office of that day to the effect that conferring such a title was inopportune (see, for example, pp. 358, 378, 402, 466 [on the proposal by the Polish Episcopate], 469, 533, 575, and 581).

In conclusion, we would like to say a word in favor of the value of reading the notes which from time to time Archbishop Felici addressed to the Holy Father to apprise him of the current conciliar situation. The historian can utilize these notes to very good effect in seeking the path to follow among the many paths involved in the history of the Council (see, for example, pp. 507-512 and pp. 634-636).

The volume concludes with an Index which divides up the material covered by months during the year 1964, and also describes the contents of the two *Appendices*.

Part B: Carbone Monsignor Vincenzo, ed., *Acta Synodalia Sacrosancti Concilii Oecumenici Vaticani II. Volumen VI, Acta Secretariae Generalis, Pars IV, Periodus quarta* MCMLXV, *Typis Vaticanis* 1999 [Synodal Acts of the Sacred Ecumenical Council of Vatican II, Volume 6, Acts of the Secretariat General, Part 4, Fourth Session, 1965, Vatican Press 1999], 877 pages. [Monsignor Carbone was charged with responsibility for the Vatican Council II Archives.]

The sixty-second volume in the series of the official sources of the great Synod that was Vatican Council II has recently become available for use by scholars. It is part of the series that has been correctly styled a "titanic" enterprise. It truly is a testimonial to the greatness and providence of vision of Pope Paul VI. It similarly illustrates the diligence and industriousness of the man, Vincenzo Carbone, to whom Paul VI confided the realization of this gigantic task (see pp. 695, 704ff., 724, 729ff., 743, 750, 771, 777, 798, 812, 814ff., and 818-837). It was a work entailing great difficulties, as becomes clear from the readings of the pages just referenced; it involved the bringing together under "one roof" of all the various archives of the different conciliar commissions. All this was only possible with the patronage provided by the Holy Father's wish that it be done; it furnished the proof of how "dear" to some are the "files" they happen to have. There were further difficulties in the arrangements, treatment, and control of the texts themselves, as can be seen from the documentation included in this volume (see pp. 601, 614, 648, 735, 746, 756, 774, 780ff., 787, 797, 801ff., 806ff., and 817; on this last page is explained the question of an "analytical index" of the "typical editions" of the conciliar decrees). In addition, speaking of a combination of both topical subjects and the difficulties involving them, there are included here documents covering the work of the Secretariat General relative to the institution of the post-conciliar organs set up to implement the Council (see pp. 634ff., 694ff., 710ff., 719, 722-725, and 742ff.).

However, this present volume, unfortunately, marks the end of the work once confided to Monsignor Carbone, who has now turned the whole enterprise over to the Secret Archives of the Vatican, coinciding with his own arrival at the age of eighty (though he is still hale and hearty). All his work remains available to scholars, however. And we still hope that the Indexes of Volumes V-VI of the *Acta Synodalia* will soon appear, and that there will be yet another volume dedicated to the immediate post-conciliar era; the latter is rather important in order to have before us all the definitive texts pertaining to the Council.

The Purpose and the Mind

The "purpose and mind" of the editor is made quite plain once again (pp. 7ff.) It is in clear continuity with the basic "Acts" of the Central Coordinating Commission already published, as well as with those of some of the meetings of the Council Moderators. This volume contains a selection of the documents of the Secretariat General pertaining to the final and Fourth Session of the Council (September 14-December 8, 1965). Among those documents appearing here of particular interest are the notes and records of Archbishop Felici himself (see, for example, pp. 138, 258ff., 430ff., 501, 511ff. (with observations of Paul VI), 578ff., 634ff., 628-635, 639, and 687ff.). Worthy of much praise are the documents published from page 688 on—in connection with the approach of the closing of the Council—and, more than that, in connection with the interventions of Pope Paul VI, including some that were made in his own handwriting. They were generally aimed at overcoming difficulties that had arisen concerning Council procedures as well as accurately amending the *schemata* under discussion. The pope generally wished to see these in draft before they were printed up for distribution (see pp. 13, 312, 318ff., 570, 572, 587, and also, for the *modi*, p. 554).

More than that, during this final Fourth Session, the pope arranged that the presidents of the episcopal conferences (*consilium episcoporum o coetus praesidum conferentiarum episcoporum*) should meet together in order to express their opinions on various questions not treated in the conciliar *schemata* themselves (pp. 419, 421ff., with handwritten notes by Paul VI, pp. 435, 462, 469ff., 473, 488, 577, and 586; also pp. 511ff.).

The organization of the meetings of such episcopal bodies was entrusted to the Secretary General, and the documents relative to this are published here. We thus have true and correct indications of the thoughts of Pope Paul VI on such subjects as mixed marriages (see pp. 38-46, 60, 66, 77, 86-90, 104ff., 112ff., 131, 137-147, 149, 151, 157ff., 258ff., 162-176, 179-181, 187-190, 192ff., 195-202, 211ff., 217-220, 224ff., 228-239, 245ff., 251, 253-256, 258-260, 285ff., 3037, 313ff., 332, 342, 470, 535, 661ff.); on the subject of birth control (see p. 470, 535, 539, 651 and 655); on fast and abstinence and penitential discipline (pp. 490ff., 522-529, 543ff., and 568); and on indulgences (see pp. 556, 608ff., 621ff., 638, 663-667, 676-679, 786ff.). All these references are of great interest.

In the final part of the tome are included some documents that have relation to the Fourth Session, but are actually dated after the closure of the Council (pp. 731-837). There is also a very brief *Appendix* (pp. 839-843). As always, the order followed by the editor is chronological (see the *Index*, pp. 845-877, which is organized month by month). The entire text is enriched with useful notes.

Paths to Historical Objectivity

Most certainly, we cannot here enumerate and explain all the various paths open to historical objectivity that are opened up for us with the publication of this series. We shall therefore limit ourselves to mentioning only a few of them in this volume beginning with a letter (pp. 17ff.) pertaining to what became an established custom in conciliar historiography of opposing unduly John XXIII to Paul VI. See, for example, the book entitled *The Difficult Choice: The Church and the Council between John XXIII and Paul VI*, the Italian edition of "The Pilgrim" which was published by Feltrinelli. It is thus very worthwhile to read the letter of Archbishop Felici to Paul VI, dated November 19, 1965, which mentions the initiative that was announced in order to try to begin the process of beatification of John XXIII, along with that of Pius XII (see pp. 627ff.).

Also important are the intentions to alleviating the constant pressures being exerted by various groupings and "alliances" discouraging them. I refer in particular to the *Coetus Internationalis Patrum* (pp. 410ff., concerning the very strong letter of the Secretary of State to Bishop Luigi Carli; pp. 373ff., concerning the origins of the *Coetus*; and, finally, p. 540, about some consequent diverse attitudes of consequences for those involved). I also refer to the "conference" the *Domus Mariae* (see p. 607, writings on the subject of Paul VI, and the reactions of a number of Council Fathers; also pp. 610ff., and, finally, pp. 624ff.).

In connection with all this, it is useful to record the positions, at opposite ends of the spectrum, of the Italian cardinals Giuseppe Siri and Ernesto Ruffini (see pp. 480ff., and 668). The same thing is true of the accusations lodged against the Roman Curia, indirectly revealed in yet another letter of the Secretary of State, Cardinal Amleto Cicognani (pp. 20ff., pp. 58ff., and pp. 217, 241ff., and 246ff.). Also of interest in this connection is what arises naturally out of the preoccupation of various members of the conciliar minority with where they believed the ordinary magisterium was going (pp. 640, 669 and p. 28) and with what some asserted was a "discontinuity" in its teaching (p. 617, and, especially, p. 481).

Standing out here too are declarations by prominent progressive theologians such as Hans Küng (pp. 109ff. and 136) and Edward Schillebeeckx (pp. 115ff.).

Clarifications on the Development of Texts

Under this heading we shall indicate some of the clarifications that emerge from these pages. Among the most interesting for us are some arising in connection with what became the Constitution on Divine Revelation, *Dei Verbum*. Illustrative passages are not lacking, beginning with the *Annotationes* of Archbishop Felici addressed to the pope or the Secretary of State (pp. 51, 132ff., and 152ff.), along with various references to the relationship between sacred Scripture and sacred Tradition (pp. 482, 549, and 51), and also to irregular procedures being followed by the Doctrinal Commission (see pp. 548ff.), as well as to other mixed materials. We also find in this tome questions linked with the *salutis causa* and to the differing interpretations of its meaning (pp. 648ff. and 756ff.)—all this in the context of "that truth which God, for the sake of our salvation, wished to see confided to the sacred Scriptures" (DV#11). (See Chapter 30 in this book on this same topic.)

As for what concerned the famous *Nota Explicativa Praevia*, there is in this volume a note of Archbishop Felici prepared for the pope on the subject of an article by Archbishop Pietro Parente, in which the Secretary General warns of the "danger that erroneous opinions might be formed about the interpretation of the *Nota*—opinions not in conformity with the truth of the matter, which is clear in the Acts of the Council" (p. 34). This subject is taken up again by Cardinal Siri (pp. 92ff. and 102ff.) and yet again by another note of the Secretary General transmitting the cardinal's letter. The importance of all this arose out of an article by Edward Schillebeeckx, translated only in part and sent to Paul VI (pp. 115ff.), according to which "the *Nota Praevia* leaves the conciliar text intact as written, but simply frees it from any 'hidden implications.' That is all that was said. Thus, the conciliar minority can also accept the text of the Constitution as written. For the conciliar minority is not opposed to the *schema* as such, but is rather opposed to possible hidden implications which they think can be drawn from it, even though there is no basis for this in the text itself" (p. 116). In the end, the situation truly was exactly what Father Yves Congar said it was when he told the bishops around him: "Vote for it! Vote for it! Later on, we theologians will decide what the *Nota Explicativa Praevia* means"! Schillebeeckx concluded that it meant "the elimination of a certain equivocal character that in the beginning was deliberate, if I may be permitted at this time to express myself in a way that is both clear and forceful" (p. 117).

All this was taken up again by Cardinal Cicognani, who, having consulted the pope, believed that it was "necessary to issue a clarification in order to eliminate any ambiguity." He therefore gave the necessary authorization (p. 122), and the record of the execution of his order is included in this volume (pp. 130ff.). Thus, the Secretary General arranged that the *Nota Explicativa Praevia* should be included and published alongside of the various translations of the Constitution (p. 257).

Another interpretation of the various conciliar discussions is that related to the subject of *religious liberty*. Pertinent, necessary, and even illuminating views on this important subject are also found in this volume. There are the "notes" of Archbishop Felici himself (pp. 51, 135, and 501; see p. 500, however, for the views of the Cardinal Secretary of State). There is also here the correspondence between Cardinals Cicognani and Bea with Msgrs. Johannes Willebrands and Pasquale Macchi [private secretary of the pope] (pp. 213, 275, 460ff., 465, 480, 561ff., 570, and 580). But especially, there are the handwritten notes of Paul VI himself (pp. 276ff. and 499), which make more intelligible his convictions about intervening in the Council, even in the case when an "orientation" vote was being called for on the subject of where the Council was going. This vote "reaffirmed the teaching of our true religion and still made possible a vote on other amendments to the text itself" (p. 499).

Moreover, it would be carried out within "the terms which had been decided upon in the meeting of the directive organs of the Council," and not merely on the terms of the Secretariat for Promoting Christian unity (p. 501). "The Holy Father desires that sound theologians and experts in the subject matter should be involved in the work of revision" (*Ibid.*). Archbishop Felici, who earlier had had the occasion to take note of the disorganization of the preparatory work on the *schema* as it then stood, strongly insisted that the subsequent work should be carried out harmoniously, in good faith, and with real cooperation between the Secretariat and the Doctrinal Commission" (*Ibid.*).

Pope Paul VI, in the *Annotationes Manu Scriptae* for November 15, 1965, gave this directive: "Archbishop Pericle Felici is requested to pass on these few tranquilizing retouches, but then the *schema* must be printed immediately (this evening) in order to be distributed on Wednesday the 17th and voted on on Friday the 19th. I have already telephoned Archbishop Dell'Acqua about this" (p. 617). And at the same time the pope wrote: "From Bishop Colombo...This text is to be inserted into the final text of the *schema* on *De libertate religiosa* in order to reply to the objections concerning a discontinuity of the magisterium" (*Ibid.*). I believe all this is highly significant for anyone truly wishing to understand what really happened.

Another very delicate point for the Council—as everyone knows—was the question of the Church's relationship with *Judaism*. In this regard, the volume provides important points for reflection based on the Council's original documents. Thus, the context of the reaction of the Arab countries is provided from the outset (pp. 11, 37, 70ff., 73ff., 83ff., 117ff., 194, and 405ff.), and these references provide insight into the persistence of "the perplexities and reservations concerning several expressions used in the text, particularly those on the subject of the Jews" (p. 52). Various proposals emerged out of all this, up to and including one offered by the Melchite Patriarch, Maximos IV Saigh, who proposed that "the entire question should be referred to His Holiness" (pp. 118 and 129). The pope followed this whole question quite closely (see, for example, pp. 225ff. and 278).

One subject in particular, finally, which provided controversial material for "political" debate, especially in Italy, is the subject of *Communism*. This question is also covered in the tome. We shall limit ourselves to citing a few page references on this subject (see pp. 618ff., 622, 628f., 630-635). Much attention is given to the appeal of Bishop Carli, which Msgr. Felici described to the pope, who then replied: "Should we accept the appeal or should it be returned to him? Did the Mixed Commission do anything wrong here? Following the intervention *iuxta modum*, the appeal of the petitioners should be brought to the attention of the Fathers, with appropriate comments." Or again, the pope asked: "Is this prudent? One: If we reject it, it will appear that the Council has refused to condemn Communism (already condemned by the Church); if we accept it, how will that affect Catholics in Communist countries? Two: Does this fit with the aims of the Council? not to get into politics? not to issue condemnations and anathemas? Not, in fact, to talk about Communism?" (pp. 619ff.). Anyone wishing to show the acuteness of thought and the pastoral vision of Paul VI, as well as the largeness of his views, could perhaps not do better than to cite these observations of his.

48

Vatican II: Preparation of the Church for the Third Millennium

Carbone Vincenzo, *Il Concilio Vaticano II. Preparazione della Chiesa al Terzo Millennio* [Vatican Council II: Preparation of the Church for the Third Millennium], Vatican City 1998, 202 pages. (Notebooks from *L'Osservatore Romano*, N. 42)

Even a broken piece from a mosaic can allow the beauty of the whole to be seen. Yet the splendor of the whole in its diversity can sometimes represent yet a greater vision before our very eyes.

This thought presents itself to the eyes of the mind when reading this important and charming collection of articles from *L'Osservatore Romano* by the well-known professor, Monsignor Vincenzo Carbone, diligent custodian of the Vatican II Archives and the faithful and indefatigable editor of the Acts of Vatican Council II. The publication of these articles is owed to the historical sensitivity and the concern to get the great Council "right" of the *L'Osservatore Romano* Director, Professor Mario Agnes.

A Preface to the work has been contributed by the Reverend Father Gianfranco Grieco, who quite correctly praises the author for his scholarly writing; he finds the key to the work in the "joining of the old and the new, the true and the curious, the present and both the recent and the remote past, as well as actualities and prospects" (p. 5).

With happy intuition, these contributions of Monsignor Carbone have been written within a logical and temporal framework that extends beyond the times and occasions when the articles themselves appeared. What we have here are true and solid, though partial, views on such subjects as "The History of Vatican II," "The Humble Resolution of a Great Announcement," and "From Vatican Council II to the Synod of Bishops." We simply note in passing such further titles as "Preparation for Vatican Council II" (including the "spiritual" aims of John XXIII), "The Council's First Day," "Actions of John XXIII at the First Session," "The Length of the Council: in Expectation and in Reality," "The First Fruits of the Council" (the Constitution *Sacrosanctum Concilium*), "*Lumen Gentium*: Fidelity to Sacred Principles and Immutable Doctrine," "Mary, Mother of the Church," and "The Decree *Ad Gentes Divinitus*: the Vocation of the Church."

Characteristic of Monsignor Carbone's brand of "history"—it is not necessarily obvious at first sight—is his fidelity to his sources, which is extraordinary both in its precision and in its scholarly method. He bases his work on the official conciliar documents, both in their vastness and in their splendid clarity; and, while working in such a wide field, this author leaves aside the kind of biased, partial, or ideological viewpoints that are unfortunately so common today. His outlook is calm and serene (see, for example, pp. 79ff., 95, 127, 150, and pp. 69ff., 71, and 129). This is notably true concerning the "note personally reserved" to the pope from a group of cardinals and superiors general. Sometimes the tone is actually "pious." This is a very valuable work, in other words, particularly since it has been drawn mainly from the clear waters of the Council's official records, "prophetically" preserved at the wish of Pope Paul VI, who foresaw the dangers of wayward and erring interpretations of the Council.

On a number of sensitive and delicate points, in fact, we have here both clarifying and authoritative interpretations. I refer, for example, to the pope's Opening Address to the Council (p. 38), to the famous "second day" of the Council (p. 42), and to all the vast and important conciliar preparation (pp. 24 and 124). On this last topic, the author notes: "The Council modified (while improving) the earlier preparatory work; this was both necessary and was foreseen; and it constituted the basis for the Council's subsequent work." Other interpretations of Carbone's include: the role of Tardini (his "immediate, full, and convinced assent" to the pope's plan, which constituted both a "support and a comfort for the pope in his enterprise"—p. 14); the Roman Curia ("a complex and many-sided reality, which cannot be reduced to the actions of one or another person; thus it is impossible to refer simplistically to the Roman Curia"—p. 42); and, finally, to Archbishop Felici himself ("he earned the confidence of the pope"— pp. 45 and 59).

I make reference also to the famous vote suspended by Pope Paul VI on October 16, 1963. Carbone observes apropos of this: "The vote involved problems of content in the text and it also raised procedural questions; these needed to be clarified in order to preclude them from taking on an importance which at the time they did not have; the postponement made it possible for the Doctrinal Commission to amend the *schema* and it also preserved the liberty of the Council Fathers to review and pass on it"—p. 68; see, however, p. 95. The *Nota Explicativa Praevia* in *Lumen Gentium* is also covered here (pp. 96ff.).

Very pertinent and valid are the scholarly contributions of Monsignor Carbone clarifying the key points of the Council related to the questions: of its primarily "pastoral" character (pp. 57, 11, 15, 113, and 121ff.); of renewal and *aggiornamento* (pp. 58 and 112ff.); of the development of doctrine in continuity with established doctrine and not as a "break" with it (pp. 58, 114, 122, 132, 134, 146, and 165); of its serving as a Council for reunion, though not, unfortunately, as a Council *of* reunion (pp. 58 and 123); related also to the character of the great Synod as one "of the Church of Christ and all mankind" (p. 135); and to other specific characteristics of Vatican II. This Council, like other ecumenical ones, marked "the opening of a new era" (pp. 132 and 165), in which "the Church moved ahead into the future in carrying out her mission" (pp. 133ff.). In these cases, it is necessary to follow developments a step at a time—which is impossible for us here—as the author carefully lays them out. He quite dispassionately analyzes tendencies that are usually characterized as "progressive" or "conservative." "These classifications," he writes, "are guilty of being too simplistic" (pp. 83ff., and also pp. 134, 146, 150, and 165). He moreover deals with the clashes at the Council and the comparisons between the personalities of the various popes: "always difficult," he remarks about the latter (p. 146, and also 124, 128, 76, and 127).

In this book of Monsignor Carbone, there are included articles which spell out a proper relationship between the Second Vatican Council and conciliar and papal history generally. What we have here is a contribution to the kind of research which sees the great Synod as "light for the Church and for the modern world as well"; as "a time for God in the life of the Church"; and "as a fundamental event in the life of the contemporary Church." All of these formulations are related as well to the Tridentine past, and to "the developments in continuity" that arose out of it.

This volume is moreover of interest, we think, for the history of the popes. Even though the articles collected here primarily pertain to the Council, they still explain much about the pontificates of John XXIII and Paul VI respectively. I refer, for example, to the chapter which concerns the encyclical *Pacem in Terris* and to what is styled here "the pontificate of the Council" (that of John XXIII); and also to the chapter in which Monsignor Carbone describes the election of Paul VI to be "head of the Church at a solemn hour of her history... whose first thought and primary commitment was to the Council with the aim of promoting the evangelization of the contemporary world."

Montini is also presented as the pope of the "transformation" and he is lauded for his encyclical *Populorum Progressio* as well. This is described as one which "draws from the Gospel a global vision for the economy and for the common good for all humanity"; the encyclical is, in fact, "an extension of Vatican II"; it is "a universal guide for the elevation of all peoples."

There is another article, also primarily about the Council, which nevertheless relates to Pope John Paul II. It covers the first fifteen years of his pontificate, and it is entitled: "Fidelity to the Council and to the Mission of a Pastor"; its subtitles are "His Election," "Bringing to Fruition the Seeds of the Council," and "The Mystery of Love in the Service of the Faith."

Finally, among all the many things that are worthy of praise, we touch upon one point which, in our opinion, should be developed further.

We refer to that "inspiration from on high" (p. 10) to which Pope John XXIII ascribed his "idea," as we shall call it for the moment, of convoking the great Vatican Synod. In order to maintain the idea as a divine inspiration, Monsignor Carbone holds that we cannot "connect this idea with the previous attempt of Pope Pius XII" (not to speak of that of Pope Pius XI). To maintain this position, he writes that "perhaps John XXIII did not even have any idea about this" (see p. 13 and also pp. 57 and 120ff.). However, we do not see how this could have been possible when we recall that, in the case of Pius XII, in the author's own words, "a central commission was set up along with several subcommissions. The principal subjects to be considered were also spelled out" (p. 13). It would greatly surprise us if none of this ever came to the attention of Pope Roncalli, who was noted for his "curiosity"; he was also himself a historian. And if memory serves in this case, it was none other than Cardinal Ruffini himself—not to venture farther afield—who tells us that he proposed the idea of the convocation of a Council to Pope John XXIII.

Is there not a contradiction here, considering that Pope Roncalli declared himself "the first to be surprised by this proposal of mine... since no one had spoken to me about it" (*Ibid.*; and p. 21, n. 3)? Actually, we think there was really no contradiction, considering the complexity of human psychology, as well as what is conscious and unconscious in the mind and the memory. We should also not forget the analogy, *mutatis mutandis*, with the *acceptio rerum* that applies to the "inspiration" of sacred Scripture.

We should be grateful to Monsignor Carbone for these profound and incisive articles. They throw much light on the subject for anyone who is studying Vatican Council II. That, in fact, should be all of us, considering it constitutes the "door" that leads us into the Third Millennium of Christianity—take careful note of the subtitle of this book in this regard!

VII

FOR A CORRECT INTERPRETATION OF THE COUNCIL

49

Towards a Correct Interpretation
of Vatican Council II

Scheffczyk Leo, *La Chiesa. Aspetti della crisi post-conciliare e corretta interpretazione del Vaticano II* [The Church: Aspects concerning the Post-conciliar Crisis and a Correct Interpretation of Vatican II], Introduction by Joseph Ratzinger, Jaca Book, Como 1998. 183 pages.

In his Introduction to this work by the well-known Professor Scheffczyk, Cardinal Joseph Ratzinger, very realistically, observes that "often partial and one-sided interpretations of the principal documents of Vatican Council II have resulted in certain fruits in the post-conciliar era which have produced a profound crisis in ecclesiological consciousness in various sectors of Catholic life. This crisis is ultimately rooted in a widely diffused loss of a 'Catholic' sense that applies to the reality of the Church" (p. 9). The cardinal makes this observation after noting the predominance of ecclesiastical themes in the post-conciliar period.

The cardinal thus puts his finger squarely on the wound. At the same time he points to the methods followed by Professor Scheffczyk in attempting to heal the wound. This is a collection of the latter's "interventions," already published in part between 1985 and 1990 in somewhat simplified form, in which he undertakes to show the full continuity of the teachings of Vatican II with the Church's earlier ecclesiological teachings. He provides evidence for this at the same time as he shows evidence of both development and progress in understanding the mystery of the Church herself.

The other fundamental aspect of this analysis by Professor

Scheffczyk is his description of the divergences between what Vatican II proposed, and what in the post-conciliar era has too often been taken to be what Vatican II proposed. We believe for our part that these divergences have arisen out of unilateral, selective, and ultimately misleading interpretations of the true thought of the Council. Scheffczyk, however, allows us to discern again the revealed truth about the Church. He provides a comprehensive overview of the essential aspects of the mystery of the Church. The points he makes constitute of reference, and they are also particularly well founded.

In his own Preface, the author delineates the problematical contemporary ecclesial situation, which he describes as "an uncritical and even rash fraternization of Christianity with the spirit of the times…in which occur many irrational and post-modern developments such as a vague religiosity and even some gnostical tendencies." His own theological work, by contrast, is based upon fidelity to the true identity of the Church, a creation of the Word. Her origins are found in the supertemporality of divine Revelation, notwithstanding her relationship with these present times. What is at stake here is the continuity of the Catholic Church herself, even though she is in contemporary contact with "progress."

The author's basic undertaking here is to go back to the documents of the Council and re-examine them in the light of today's ecclesial questions. These occur within a network of related themes and also within the context of a complete ecclesial vision. The only aspect that we find treated here in perhaps too minor tone is that of the primacy of the bishop of Rome, the "Petrine principle" (pp. 103ff.).

In his first chapter, Scheffczyk takes as his point of departure "the crisis in the Church—a crisis of both consciousness and comprehension." It is a crisis which pertains to what is today called "the open Church" (see also p. 67), and Scheffczyk proposes to deal with it by means of "the teachings of Vatican II," both with regard to "progress" and to the "continuity" of Church teachings—and also with regard to the Council's synthesis of the old and the new. His intention is to respond to the slogan, "Christ, yes! Church, no!" In the end, the kind of understanding that is inherent in such a slogan issues in an image of Jesus which is a purely human construction, and in which "every interpreter and even every group accept only what corresponds to their own preconceptions" (p. 21), or perhaps merely to those of "the majority." This is "the error inherent in the call to 'democratize' the Church," as a matter of fact (see, however, pp. 67ff.).

The chapter that follows is a very good one. It treats of the Church as the sacrament of Jesus Christ. Its Christological roots are found in this precise idea, which is applied to the Church as the body of Christ. This image, the body of Christ, is considered to be "the most mature of the New Testament ideas on the nature of the Church," according to the thinking of Rudolph Schnackenburg. In reality, it is "the strongest definition expressing the sacramental substance of the nature of the Church" (p. 36), but it is also very far from being any kind of "ecclesiological monophysitism" (p. 38).

This "Monophysite" preoccupation recurs in the book's Chapter III, which bears the title, "Christ and the Church: Identity in Diversity." Brought out here is the question of whether or not the Church was willed and founded by the actual "historical Jesus"—"a question which only began to be asked with the rise of Modernism" (p. 44). Our author replies again by relying on the help of Schnackenburg, for whom "it is not possible to understand how the community could have been completely closed up within Judaism, and yet have then developed as it did without taking into account the work of Jesus of Nazareth...For the primitive community, the focus on the 'historical Jesus' was both vital and inevitable" (p. 47). On this point, however, Scheffczyk links the foundation of the Church with "a prior understanding of the faith" (p. 48). This is a solution which he returns to later (see p. 91). His way of putting it does entail some risks, however, and it is not exactly the way Schnackenburg himself deals with the question.

Following this comes the chapter entitled: "The Church and the Holy Spirit." It treats the role of the Spirit in the salvation effected by Jesus Christ. It is well and precisely done and does not raise the question of any false alternative between Christology and Pneumatology: "The Church exists within a unity because of the link with Christ and the Spirit" (p. 61); she exists in "the people of God, which did not receive its formal structural constitution from the Holy Spirit; the Holy Spirit did *not* become man, and hence could not be the cause of the divine-human disposition of the Church" (*Ibid.*). In effect, what the Church receives from the Spirit is her supernatural character, her divine vitality, her strength, and her spiritual holiness" (*Ibid.*). In this same vein, it is asserted that "Christ constitutes the first principle of the existence of the Church, of both her visibility and her sacramentality, her historical tangibility and her continuity. The Holy Spirit, however, is the essential principle of the Church in the strength of her interiority, in her immediate relationship with God, and in her intimacy with Him...Thus it is necessary to ascribe all the phenomena of the Spirit in the Church to Christ and to his 'body,' because the Holy Spirit does not proceed only from Christ, nor is 'sent' only by him, but is also from the Father. Yet all this pertains to the concrete historical Christ as well" (p. 62). This chapter's subtitles, "The Operations of the Spirit," and "the Spirit of Multiplicity and Unity," thus point to a very precious teaching.

With his next chapter entitled "The Church as *Communio*," the author moves more deeply into the subject of the great Synod itself. There are many well-written pages on conciliar doctrine here, and there is yet more besides. The author assigns proper value to the important question of *hierarchical communion*, though without any "pretension to exclusivity," which some have claimed for this formulation. With great clarity, Scheffczyk examines the erroneous post-conciliar interpretations of Hoffman, Duquoc, Schillebeeckx, and Bühlmann on the subjects both of *Communio* and of the *Nota Explicativa Praevia* (p. 74). The proper response to the post-conciliar decline of the reality-mystery concept of the Church, as we have written elsewhere, is here presented in "the developed form of *communio*—indeed, of the *communio sanctorum*" (see pp. 78-79 in particular). There is a very acute analysis of "the actuality of the Church" which follows (pp. 81-84). We repeat only one very indicative quotation, which opens a window on the whole question of a "vertical schism" (see, however, p. 177): "The reforming forces never managed to escape from the ranks of diligent technicians laying out new models of the Church, and they did not necessarily belong to the ranks of those living and witnessing to the supernatural faith present in the communion of saints" (p. 83).

In his Chapter VI entitled *"Communio*: Ministry and Priestly People," the author analyzes in particular the original apostolic ministry, which was not founded on charism—as H. Schlier well attests—although St. Paul, for example, as this very same exegete also attests, certainly practiced it in a charismatic fashion. But its principal characteristic was *auctoritas*. This did not mean, however, domination, but rather service, *diakonia*. From dealing with the "apostolate," the author goes on to discuss the ministries of the Church and the charisms inherent in them; these are viewed along the same lines as those found in Schnackenburg's original judgment, namely, that "the structure of the community was not primarily of a charismatic type" (p. 92). The treatment of the ministerial (to be preferred to the particular) and universal (of the faithful) priesthood begins on a good note, and issues in a very positive one, namely, the well-established "link with the male sex of the sacrament of Holy Orders" (pp. 97-102).

But the author then treats the question of women in the following chapter, which has the title "Mary and the Church: the Marian Dimension of the Church." He explains the distinction between the "Marian" and "Petrine" principles in the People of God quite well; he thinks the original image of the Church takes the form of an *oecumene*, and he writes of Mary as "the *typus* of the Church...constituting a perspective that is not far from the theological thought of the Gospels" (p. 109).

More urgently from the point of view of the present crisis in the Church, are the two chapters which then follow. They include: 1) "Church and World: the Task of the Church in the World": this is directly linked to Vatican Council II, which is the "first" Church Council which ever specifically taught on this subject; 2) "Church and Liberation." This latter chapter contains an excellent synthesis of the Council's thought on the subject and on the problems related to it (there is an aside on the subject of culture). These pages are quite illuminating, although they do not contain a great deal that is new, even in the parts dedicated to the so-called "theology of liberation"—we would put this term in the plural! According to the author, the theology of liberation "raises fundamental problems, the answers to which have an inherently decisive character, whether for the fundamental order of the Church, or for the form of her life in the world" (p. 126).

We are pleased to be able to note here a formulation of the author's with which we are in full agreement: he speaks of what he calls "the viscosity of ideologies," and what he means by this is their tendency to be "substitutes for a faith that has become secularized." Unfortunately, he writes, "they rarely completely lose their power to attract in this form" (p. 130).

The two chapters which follow are dedicated to ecumenism. They include 1) "The Church and the Churches." This chapter in turn is divided into the following sections: "The Claim of the Catholic Church to Be the One, True Church"; "The Relationship between the Church and the 'Churches' (and ecclesial Communities) following Vatican Council II"; and "The Relationship between Unity and Multiplicity." Unfortunately, the level of discourse falls off in this last section, and there are some inexactitudes as well (see pp. 146-147). Then there is 2) the chapter entitled: "The Church and Other Religions." This includes a series of profound analyses. We also find here a strong and justified critique of Hans Küng in particular, developed in the light of the Council's own teaching.

Can we cite for the reader some indication of the author's approach in these two chapters of ecumenism? Perhaps the following quotation will serve: "Contrary to the received opinion accepted by many that Vatican II produced radical changes in our understanding of the nature of the Church, we can confirm from the outset that the Council remained firmly within traditional bounds in its teaching on the Church. However, this does not mean that, within these same bounds, the Council did not produce new ideas and approaches" (p. 141). This is expressive of the same basic "binomial" between the new and the traditional that we regularly encounter. "This Church (then) subsists in the Catholic Church" (LG#8). "This unique Church of Christ finds its realization, its existence, and its stability in the Catholic Church... whose essential unity has not been annulled by the many separations from it that have occurred" (p. 142). This is confirmed, for that matter, by the Council's own linguistic usage, which indicates the differences which exist between the various Christian confessions, even while the state of "being Church" subsists (p. 146).

As for the non-Christian religions, the author confirms the vision of "the fullness, completeness, and universality that is present only in Christianity" (p. 157). In effect, "a religion that believes that God became man, and then draws out the consequences of that belief, is by its very nature different from other religions" (p. 158). For the Church, "the action of dispensing divine grace beyond the visible boundaries of the Church does not come about except through the Church (in Christ) and hence [this dispensing of grace] is not truly outside the Church. The Church remains the universal sacrament of salvation, through which grace comes and towards which grace is directed" (p. 162).

Dulcis in fundo (sweet at the end) is the way we read the final chapter in Professor Scheffczyk's book. It is entitled: "The Church of the Future and the Fulfillment of the Church." It consists of a profound and closely argued critique of human futurologies, and is thus not merely a discussion of the "future" of God. The author finds a big difference between "future" and "fulfillment" (pp. 164-167), and his critique is directed towards those who believe that "the Church was not created in a state of fulfillment, but rather is oriented towards fulfillment and is on the way to fulfillment in history" (p. 163; see also p. 167 for "the two hopes"). In this connection, the author mentions the names of Rahner, Zulehner, Duquoc, Küng, and Bühlmann. The author notes at the same time that "Vatican Council II placed a new emphasis on the historical constitution of the Church in which there exists a clear recognition of the Church's weakness, fragility, and provisory nature, this was not done in order to diminish the Church, but to orient her towards what her fulfillment is truly supposed to be and towards which she must move" (*Ibid.*; see also *Gaudium et Spes* #40 and #43 and *Unitatis Redintegratio* #3).

By contrast, there are the "futurologists," with their "models" and their "data." These futurologists claim to want "to remedy what the existing Church supposedly lacks, but in reality they themselves exhibit the symptoms of the very illness which they claim they can cure in the case of the Church" (p. 175). Many of their "futuristic dreams…have as their aim the creation of another and different faith as well" (here the case of Eugen Drewermann is cited along with all his impressive statistics regarding the state of the Church in Germany). If it is dogmatic theology itself which is engaged in relativizing the questions of truth and morality, then the author considers that we are in a situation identical to that of an organism no longer able to throw off the poisons which afflict it. And it is necessary to recognize in the end that "sociological-type prognoses concerning the Church's future fail to take into account the reality of the faith" (p. 181). In such cases, as Altermatt attests, "Catholicism appears to be coming a type of religion comparable to Western European Protestantism" (p. 178). In affirming such positions as the absolute primacy of conscience as supposedly transcending the Church's fundamental teachings on faith and morals, the promotion of an undifferentiated priesthood of the faithful, and the imposition of the principle of *Sola Scriptura* (subject to what must be considered hypercritical interpretations)…Protestantism at the height of its influence was closer to the modern world than to historic Christianity, and those who advocate such positions today within the Catholic Church are simply promoting an uncritical policy of adaptation and accommodation to the modern world."

Hence, "only those who realize the fact that the Catholic faith does not coincide with the modern spirit, but rather itself has the power to modify and assimilate it, can resist the modern tendency to water down the faith." And here the author quotes a prophecy from the great John Henry Newman.

Let us conclude by turning our gaze to the whole question of "fulfillment" (pp. 180-183): "The believer contemplates the state of the Church in every era only through the lens of 'Christian time,' which is determined by two dates, namely: the coming of Christ in the 'fullness of time,' and the eschatological advent that will mark the return of the transfigured Lord as the judge of the world. It is between these two pillars that we live in an 'intermediate time.' It is a dialectical time between the 'already' and the 'not yet' in the life of the Church, and we are carried along through it in hope. It is also a time for the *mea culpa* of the People of God, of a critical-type contemplation conducted by means of the gift of discernment. But this kind of honest critique is by no means to be compared with the present-day common *pathological* critique that is directed towards the very substance of the Church and aims at the creation of another and different and 'future' Church" (p. 182).

"The Church's opening to her true 'fulfillment' not only allows us to contemplate a realistic vision of the Church's actual wounds caused by the sins and weaknesses of men; it also allows us to view the trials and damages, as well as an apostolic type of suffering" (*Ibid.*), which can even take the form of martyrdom. Such a martyrdom is "not compatible with the idea of a Church which tells people only what they want to hear (and which they basically get from the media today anyway); nor is it compatible with the spirit of the times" (p. 183). Nevertheless, the close link between natural creation and supernatural redemption still requires both Christians and the pilgrim Church to turn towards the world" (*Ibid.*).

There is a final and important brushstroke to be added to this picture: "The pilgrim Church does indeed have a task that we can style 'political,' but this task possesses its own character and is not exactly comparable to secular politics. The Church's 'political' task cannot be carried out solely with respect to the temporal future to come, but in the end it must be inspired by the ultimate end of the Church's 'fulfillment.' This means that even her earthly task has a different content. Alongside the promotion of temporal things, supertemporal things must also be kept in view; the Church in her very nature is obliged to deal with and make a record of them as well" (p. 183).

50

Tradition and Renewal Together:
The Second Vatican Council

I do not believe that I have to convince any of my gentle readers of the doctrinal, spiritual, and pastoral value of the Second Vatican Council. The Council is surely an "Icon" of the Catholic Church herself; it partakes of the essence of Catholicism, is communion with the past, and also with the origins of this Church, which has preserved her identity in the course of her long development—just as she has also preserved fidelity to her own tradition in the course of constantly renewing herself. She is an abundantly leafy tree sprung from the seed which was planted with tears two millennia ago with the redemptive death of the Savior followed by his burial, but which also then burst forth in her own perpetual springtime with the resurrection of that same Christ. Since then the vine of the Lord has extended its branches throughout the whole world.[1]

---

[1]A testimonial to this flowering of the Catholic Church can be found in *Le Chiese Cristiane del Duemila* [Christian Churches in the Year 2000], published by the J. A. Moehler Institute, Brescia, in 1998: "The Catholic Church still remains, apart from and beyond all the changes which have occurred in her diverse history, in uninterrupted continuity with the apostolic Church" (p. 13). In this regard, I am much taken with the admiring remarks of Olivier Clément, writing about "The Chapel of Painted Stones" in the Vatican (see B. Forte in *Il Sole—24 Ore*, for November 14, 1999, p. 36). Clément remarked: "I marvel before the extraordinary dynamism rooted in this Tradition." The ecumenical vision experienced in the Vatican Chapel, viewed through an association of images, is the same as what Klaus Schatz noted about the bishop of Rome in relation to Tradition. He wrote: "Thanks to the structure of the Primacy, the Catholic Church has had the opportunity to link together both stability and tradition, on the one hand, and dynamism and innovation on the other" (see page 26 of *Papato ed Ecumenismo. Il*

The conciliar event of the twentieth century truly was a great one, and some of you who are reading me now will most certainly recall it. 3068 Council Fathers participated, coming from nearly every country in the world. In the four Sessions of the Council held between October 11, 1962, and December 8, 1965, there were no less than 168 general congregations (or meetings) and 10 public ones. Sixteen conciliar documents were promulgated: 4 constitutions, 9 decrees, and 3 declarations.

I add, in order to convey the vastness of the whole enterprise, that if we think only of the official "Acts" of the Council, I can see lined up on my bookshelves no less than 61 large volumes bound in a vivid red. Never fear, however, because we are nearly at the end of this titanic effort: there is only one more volume scheduled to come out at the end of the current year. We also hope, however, that indexes to the last eleven volumes will appear. Monsignor Vincenzo Carbone has been the indefatigable editor of this whole series.

But there have also begun to appear the journals or diaries of a number of well-known "personages" who participated in the work of the Council, or who at any rate followed its progress closely. These kinds of sources must be scrupulously examined and always with a critical eye. This will require an effort that will be both long and difficult. These kinds of sources can certainly add both flavor and many personal elements to the history of the Council; but they must be judged in the light of the official Acts (facts) of the Council itself. It is clear that there is a danger here of sliding into a fragmentary kind of history of the Council, that would find it hard to escape from being a mere narrative or "chronicle." Anyone who is following the conciliar hermeneutic that has been developing in today's climate cannot fail to have the impression that too often it shows itself to be divided up and even diverted into a multitude of different streams and rivulets. There has even been a kind of dissection, if not vivisection—or even a veritable peeling off of the skin—of the basic ecclesial events that took place.

---

ministero petrino al servizio dell'unità [Papacy and Ecumenism: The Petrine Ministry at the Service of Unity], edited by P. Huenermann and published in Bologna in 1999.)

I. Underlying Problems

In effect, there has been an effort on the part of many to downgrade the importance of the actual Council documents, even though they represent a synthesis of the Church's tradition as it is linked with the contemporary *aggiornamento* being undertaken by the Church through the Council. Instead, there has been an effort, which for a good while I have been defining as "ideological," to emphasize only the new and innovative aspects of the Council, and, in effect, to present the Council as discontinuous with the Church's true Tradition.

This tendency is very clearly brought out in a recent volume strongly characterized by the general historiographical theory prominent today, which emphasizes the important historical occurrences as "events."[2] This theory looks for change and discontinuity in history, indeed, for traumatic transformations. But this approach is in contrast to that of the famous historiographical tendency of the "Annales," which instead covers long periods of time, and underline the historical continuities to be found in them. For Fernand Braudel, for example, history is "a social science which aims at bringing to light perennial structures, models, and systems which at first sight might even be invisible." The new historiography does not admit—or perhaps does not want to realize—that what is involved in being an "event" is just a simple happening "worthy of note." So also, where the Church is concerned, an "event" is seen as a break, an absolute novelty; it is supposed to mean a kind of "Copernican revolution," a new Church, in effect, a passage from one type of Catholicism to another [and different] in which it loses its essential attributes. But this way of proceeding cannot and should not be considered acceptable, as far as the Catholic Church is concerned—and as far as history is concerned, or at least history that truly takes into account the Church's specific nature as well as the continuity of her Tradition. This continuity is present in the documents issued by the Council, and hence it must also be reflected in the interpretation of them.

---

[2]Fattori Maria Teresa, Melloni Alberto, eds., *L'Evento e le decisioni. Studi sulle dinamiche del Concilio Vaticano II* [The Event and the Decisions: Studies in the Dynamics of Vatican Council II], Il Mulino, Imola, 1997, 534 pages. Reviewed in Chapter 23 of this volume.

In this regard, reading the contributions to conciliar research in the volume just cited, one is surprised by the very radical critiques in it offered of the work of three illustrious figures: Hubert Jedin, Joseph Ratzinger, and Walter Kasper (the last with his four excellent hermeneutical rules, to which we fully subscribe. Rules such as Kasper's are in this book considered to be too abstract, however, and hence they are set aside, also because of the emphasis put in the peculiarity of Vatican II). This book, however, is also critical of the work of Émile Poulat. The aim does seem to be to promote the idea of the Council as an "event," understood as we have explained it, and always with the "ideological" character that we have indicated is present as well.

Taking a wholly unprejudiced view, it is not hard to realize that what has been brought to the fore here, and enshrined in this study as normal, are positions that within the so-called "majority" at the Council itself would have been considered extreme positions, if not radically extreme ones. On the contrary, the Council constituted a constant and active search for a "consensus" because of the need to harmonize *aggiornamento* with established Tradition. These extremist authors are simply bent on imposing their own point of view; they are oblivious to the constant and careful work of Paul VI as he tried to "sew" things together. After the Council, authors with this point of view have pretty much monopolized the way it has been interpreted since—namely, as an "event." Divergent views have simply been rejected, and those holding them attacked as "anti-conciliar."

The true underlying basis for interpreting the Council as an "event," as is consistently done in this volume, has been noted by E. Fouilloux, as follows: "The category of an 'event,' its revival, as E. Morin has attested, has been taken from recent French historiography"—that is, history written over the last fifty years approximately. "The possibility of an analysis of the strict link between the historical existence of the event and the way it is mediated is not lacking," Fouilloux writes. "As P. Nora has said, 'Because there is an event, it must come about that it becomes known.' And Vatican Council II fits perfectly with this mediating definition of an event."

Always in this same volume, P. Huenermann invokes the method of Georg Gadamer and concludes, summing up, that "the event of the Council can be understood by thinking of the practice which is expressed conceptually as 'topical dialectics' (this phrase is taken from the *Philosophical Investigations* of Ludwig Wittgenstein). It is this which makes possible a consensus; it constitutes, in renewed and radicalized form, the basic movement of the Council; it consists of a unitary movement which brought together the innumerable individual conciliar activities, and then placed them in a flux, which then produced, as its result and fruit, the new vision of the Church and of divine revelation which is found at various sedimentary layers in the texts of the Council" (*Ibid.*, p. 92).

II. The Intentions of Pope John and the Meaning of Tradition (with both a capital 'T' and a small 't')

But let us return to the original idea of Newman, which saw the Church as a living organism in continual growth and development, both internally and externally, while always remaining herself. Certainly, such a conception of development entails many possible problems concerning doctrine, cult, morality, discipline, and the apostolate.

In general, as is well known, though, it is the Church's magisterium that provides the answers to these problems—the ordinary magisterium of the pastors, assisted by theologians in union with the People of God and united with them. At times, however, either the complexity of the material involved, or the seriousness of the historical circumstances, call for extraordinary interventions by the magisterium.

Among these extraordinary interventions, we must consider the Church's Councils, which treat and develop in fidelity to the Church's Tradition, doctrinal developments, liturgical and disciplinary reforms, and, in general, apostolic efforts coinciding with the needs of the times. In this category are "the signs of the times" mentioned by Vatican Council II (GS #4). These "signs," however, do not constitute a new Revelation; and, in this perspective, the Church's Councils must be seen as milestones on her road through history.

At this point, I pause in order to explain the meaning of "Tradition" with a capital "T," as contrasted with many "traditions," spelled with a small "t" and also appearing in the plural. All this must also be viewed today in ecumenical perspective, and this must itself be explained for the sake of our readers. For this purpose, I refer to a recent hermeneutical reflection which has been published, and which bears the title "A Treasure in Earthen Vessels."[3] In this work, an effort is made to formulate "a common understanding of Tradition as 'one.'" This formulation comprises the first part of this document. Then, an effort is made to explain the many "traditions" as well as how the ancient councils of the Church fit into the picture. However, merely to stay rooted in the vision of Tradition found in this "instrument," or "working paper," without moving forward into the fullness of Christianity as we Catholics understand it, is to miss the whole point. In fact those who seriously and sincerely seek and find Christ understand that it is precisely Christ himself who speaks through Tradition with a capital "T." This Tradition reflects the "one" Gospel; it is the living "Word of God."[4]

---

[3] "A Treasure in Earthen Vessels: An Instrument for Ecumenical Reflection on Hermeneutics," Faith and Order, Byalystok, 1998, p. 42. [This title given in English in the original]. This should be compared on the Catholic side with the now "traditional" treatment of the same subject by Father Yves Congar, O.P., La Tradition et les traditions [Tradition and traditions]. This latter study has appeared in two volumes in Italian, i.e., in 1961, 409 pages "Historical Essay," and 1965, 527 pages "Theological Essay." Of particular interest is the first chapter of the second volume entitled, "Analysis and Synthesis of the Idea of Tradition" (pp. 15-19); and also the pages dedicated to "Apostolic Traditions" (pp. 108-112); and, finally, the overall scheme of the work (pp. 140ff.). For the ecumenical dimension of the problem, see Chapter VII of the second volume entitled "Contemporary Protestant Thought on the Problem of Tradition" (pp. 407-468). For the situation following the issuance of Pope John Paul II's encyclical Ut Unum Sint, see Paolo Ricca, "La Papauté en discussion. Attentes et perspectives pour le IIIe millénaire" ["The Papacy under Discussion: Expectations and Perspectives for the Third Millenium"], in Irenikon 70 (1997), pp. 31-40. Covered here is the distinction between traditions and the "great Tradition" spoken about by the pope in Number 39 of the encyclical just cited. This Tradition with a capital "T" is identified with the "Tradition of the ancient Church to which all the Churches ought to refer back to." With regard to Judaism, see N. Rotenstreich, "On the Notion of Tradition in Judaism," Journal of Religion 28 (1948), pp. 28-36.

[4] See op. cit., "A Treasure in Earthen Vessels," nn. 15 and 8, not to speak of pp. 18, 19, 27, and 32.

Taking up again our narrative following this brief interruption, in order to indicate the distinction between Tradition and the traditions, and, especially, the ecumenical dimensions of this important topic, we must now emphasize that the idea of convoking a council as it arose in the mind of John XXIII went back to the pope's consciousness of the crisis resulting from the widespread decadence of spiritual and moral values in contemporary society.

The truth of the matter is that convoking a council was also something that was considered and evaluated by the pope's immediate predecessors. Pope Pius XI, at the beginning of his pontificate, in his encyclical *Ubi Arcano*, expressed his desire to promote by such conciliar means the cooperation of the whole episcopate in his program to re-establish all things in Christ and achieve peace among peoples. However, the times were not propitious for this to be carried out.

During the pontificate of Pope Pius XII, in 1948, the idea of holding a council re-emerged. Pope Pacelli was very conscious of the difficulties that would be involved, however, even though he had ordered the Congregation of the Holy Office begin preparations for such an assembly. A central commission was instituted to carry out these preparations, along with several subcommissions. Some of the principal subjects to be covered were also laid out. However, in 1951, Pius XII definitively suspended these preparations for an ecumenical council.

Pope John XXIII, though, brushed aside these hesitations and delays; and to the cardinals who were assembled in the Benedictine monastery adjoining the Roman Basilica of St. Paul's-outside-the-Walls, he announced on January 25, 1959, the "good news" of the Council he planned to convoke. He specified that the Synod in question was being called principally for the purpose of promoting an increase in faith, a renewal of customs and practices, and the *aggiornamento*, or bringing up to date, of ecclesiastical discipline. The gathering was intended to be a demonstration of truth, unity, and charity for the Church; it was also to be an invitation to our separated brethren to come to unity with us in Christ.[5] The pope had in mind a Council that would be both pastoral, and would bring about an

[5] *Acta et Documenta* (AD), Series I, Vol. I, p. 46.

aggiornamento, or "updating," of the Church's practices. This Italian word, *aggiornamento,* in fact, became the key word for defining the purpose of the Council in many languages; but it was certainly never intended to signify anything that was purely practical and dynamic and somehow divorced from Catholic doctrine. A purely "pastoral" plan not related to doctrine and to the Tradition of the Church was, in fact, inconceivable for him.

John XXIII treated these questions quite clearly in his first encyclical, *Ad Petri Cathedram.* He spoke about the lack of knowledge of, and, indeed, the outright ignorance of the truth, if not an actual contempt for it on the part of many; and he saw this as lying at the root of the modern evils poisoning individuals, peoples, and nations, and, certainly, as adversely affecting the minds of many. But the pope thought that everybody should instead be encouraged to accept the Gospel. Not to do so—to reject the Gospel—he thought was to imperil the foundations of truth, honesty, and civility.

The same pontiff, in his Opening Address to the Council, delivered on October 11, 1962,[6] affirmed that the principal concern of the Council was "that the sacred deposit of Christian doctrine should be guarded and taught more efficaciously"—that is, that "Tradition" should thus be guarded and taught. It was not just a question of this sacred deposit merely being guarded and taught, however; nor was it merely a question of just repeating what the Fathers of the Church and Catholic theologians had already transmitted to us; rather, it was a question of promulgating to all men, in continuity with the ecclesiastical magisterium, the Church's entire doctrine, without watering it down or misrepresenting it in any way—while taking into account, of course, the deviations, the requirements, and the particular opportunities of our own day. "The substance of the ancient doctrine of the deposit of faith is one thing," the pope said. "The way in which it is presented is another."[7]

---

[6] *Acta Synodalia Sacrosancti Concilii Oecumenici Vaticani II* (AS), edited by V. Carbone, Volume I, Part I, pp. 170ff.

[7] On the question of the original text of this famous Opening Address to the Council, see Carbone Vincenzo, *Il Concilio Vaticano II. Preparazione della Chiesa al Terzo Millennio* [Vatican Council II: Preparations by the

He thus distinguished between Catholic doctrine in its integrity, completeness, and immutability, and in its presentation or formulation. In line with his general pastoral approach, Pope John XXIII set forth his own preferences concerning the way in which errors ought to be corrected. He preferred what he called "the medicine of mercy" to what he characterized as the Church's former "severity," and he thought that a positive teaching ought to be given in order to show forth to the men of today the sacred truth in the teaching of the Church illuminated by the light of Christ so that the men of today might be "even more deeply convinced of the paramount dignity of the human person and of his perfections, as well as of the duties which that implies." The wish for an *aggiornamento* was thus clear, and it was indeed supposed to come from the Council; but this in no way implied any break with the past, nor did it imply any contradiction with regard to historical positions; rather, it called for growth and for the perfecting of the goods and truths already present in the Church. The renewal of the Church was to be a "permanent one."

III. The Intentions of Pope Paul VI

Faithful interpreter of his immediate predecessor,[8] Pope Montini,

---

Church for the Third Millennium], Vatican City 1998 (pp. 35-39). (Reviewed in Chapter 48 of the present book.). Carbone concludes his treatment by stating that "the substantial identity of the Italian text with the Latin text is established and is certain, because the differences do not touch upon the sense and meaning of the speech. Besides, John XXIII himself cited the Italian version of the speech when it was published in *L'Osservatore Romano*, thus "authoritatively accrediting" it (*Ibid.*, p. 39). The importance of the speech is underlined by the references made to it by both Paul VI and John Paul II (*Ibid.*, p. 33).

[8]Archbishop Loris Capovilla [private secretary of Pope John XXIII], in a recent interview which appeared in *Corsera* on August 3, 1999 (page 27, column VIII), has confirmed that the synthesis of the Johannine pontificate can be summed up in the phrase, "fidelity and renewal." Pope John, he noted, "was not aiming at innovations...but he did like to say, 'Don't hide any part of the flag.' But he knew that 'fidelity' alone could have reduced the Church to the status of a museum, while 'renewal' alone could have resulted in anarchy. He tried to inspire the Council to steer a course between these two poles." Paul VI tried to do the same, for that matter; his approach was that of the line also adopted by the Belgians at the Council, namely, to retain what was possible in the preparatory documents of the Council as the basis for further work (see *The Event and the Decisions*, cited in

in his allocution to the Council Fathers of November 18, 1965, affirmed that "John XXIII, in employing the term *aggiornamento*, did not give it the same meaning that some have attempted to give it since, even using it to justify the relativization of the Church's dogmas, laws, structures, and traditions in accordance with the spirit of the times. John XXIII, however, retained a firm and vital sense of the doctrinal and structural stability of the Church; it formed the basis of his entire thought and his work."[9]

In fact, Paul VI, although his own formation and character were very different from those of John, nevertheless maintained his orientation by the latter's polar star consisting of "development within continuity"; with him the Council would go on pursuing the same pastoral hopes and aims.[10] "It would not be the truth," Paul VI held, "for anybody to imagine that Vatican II represented any kind of a break, interruption, or 'liberation' from the teaching of the Church; or that the Council promoted or authorized any kind of accommodation or conformism with the mentality of our times in its negative and ephemeral aspects."[11]

In support of what is contended here, we need only refer back to what Paul VI said on the day of his coronation (thus was the initiation of the pastoral mission of the popes designated at that time). He said: "We are taking up...the work of our predecessors: we are defending the holy Church from the errors of either doctrine or practice that today threaten her integrity both from within and without and spoil

Note 2 above, pp. 186-187, 152, 162 and 340). Indicative in this regard is the following statement of Monsignor Gérard Philips concerning the pope's conciliation efforts (p. 154; the statement was strongly criticized by Father Giuseppe Dossetti, by the way): "It was not a question of seeing one's own personal ideas and positions prevail; rather, it was a question of arriving at a consensus that the whole Church could accept as an authentic expression of her common faith...but without making any compromises on fundamental principles." Perhaps there will be no objection if I conclude here by citing [the Protestant] Oscar Cullmann on this subject as well: "He represented a much more pragmatic attitude determined to maintain a respect for theological tradition and for the 'genius' of Catholicism" (*op. cit.*, p. 257). I believe these views on ecumenical aspects continue to be very useful.

[9]AS, Volume IV, Part VI, pp. 693ff.

[10]*Ibid.*, Volume II, Part VI, p. 568; and Volume IV, Part VII, pp. 660ff.

[11]See *Insegnamenti Insegnamenti di Paolo VI* [Teachings of Paul VI], Volume IV, 1966, p. 699.

her beauty; we shall seek to augment the pastoral virtues of the Church."[12] And he remained faithful to this commitment. On June 29, 1978, virtually at the end of his pontificate, he provided something of a summing up of his work. He said: "This has been my tireless and watchful motive: I have kept the faith! I can say today with a humble but firm conscience that I have not betrayed the *holy truth*."[13]

And what Paul VI thus attributes to himself in the way of fidelity, can also be affirmed of Vatican Council II, which followed with a pastoral spirit the line of promoting the Catholic faith while renewing the customs and ecclesiastical disciplines which had been undertaken by the Councils which preceded it. In confirmation of this line, I cite what Paul VI said on March 8, 1964, to a group of pilgrims from Trent in the Basilica of St. Peter: "The spirit of the Council of Trent inspires and reanimates the current assembly, Vatican Council II. This Council is linked to Trent, and from that former Council it derives the motive to face and deal with problems, both old and new, which remain unsolved, including many of the latter which have emerged with the passage of time."[14]

Certainly, by the will of Pope John XXIII, Vatican II was a great pastoral synod which pursued an *aggiornamento*. But this *aggiornamento* was not a rupture with the past; nor was it contrary to various historical developments, as has been claimed; rather, it represented the growth and perfecting of elements always present in the Church. Its renewal was therefore continuous with the creative and sanctifying action of the Spirit, and it was also in harmony with the doctrinal and disciplinary tradition of the Church. Yet the Council dealt with vast horizons in its documents on the Church, Revelation, Liturgy, the Eastern Churches, the Bishops, the Priests, Religious Missions, etc. But it is not legitimate to interpret all this in

[12]*Ibid.*, Volume I, 1963, p. 26.

[13]*Ibid.* Volume XVI, 1978, p. 521.

[14]*Ibid.*, Volume II, 1964, pp. 156ff. G. Ruggieri does not agree with this. In his contribution to *The Event and the Decisions*, to which reference is made in Note 2 above—it is entitled "Times for Debates, Time of the Council"— he first presents John XXIII and Paul VI as opposed to each other; and then he critiques Hubert Jedin for having defended the "continuity" of Vatican II with the Council of Trent: "It was not a revision, but a completion," Jedin wrote (see pp. 459-462).

too simplistic a fashion or to present the great Synod as primarily an arena for "battles" between "conservatives" and "progressives."

In this connection, it would seem to me to be worthwhile to employ language less partisan or one-sided. It would be more respectful of everybody involved to understand "conservatives" as desirous of preserving what exists and "innovators" as also dealing with an existing situation for which they could also be seen as simply wishing to validate an older tradition. But it is important to get beyond confused and imprecise terminology which distinguishes so poorly between traditionalists, traditionals, "integrists," integrals and progressives, with "extremists" also among them, as there were among the conservatives.

IV. Some Test Cases of Tradition and Renewal Together: Collegiality and Papal Primacy

Without being able to go into many of the key issues in much detail here, I think it is opportune to do so in the case of a couple of them, notably how the *nova et vetera,* the new *and* the old, were put together at the Council, both in what was decided and also in the way in which Pope Paul VI guided the conciliar progress. Hans Urs von Balthasar has written about how the conjunction "and" is so "Catholic."

Monsignor Carbone sums up, in a number of very objectively presented pages, how the episcopacy fits together with the primacy: "In the very first days of the Second Session...Pope Paul VI, remaining above all the 'parties,' intervened with promptness to suspend the vote on four propositions which had been scheduled by the Moderators for October 17, 1963. As things stood, this vote raised questions about the content of the text; there were procedural questions which needed to be clarified as well. To have gone forward with the vote at that stage would have ascribed to the text being voted on a value which it did not have. Thus, the pope's action gave the Doctrinal Commission the chance to amend this text, and it also preserved the liberty of the Council Fathers to examine and vote on a text which had been properly vetted."

With both tenacity and patience, Paul VI worked so that the problems that arose in the course of the debates could be clarified and developed in greater depth, so that the greatest possible majority could be achieved. He followed the work of the individual conciliar commissions with both prudence and discretion; and although he did not attempt to substitute his judgment for theirs, he did work steadily to improve the *schemata* being considered. He was firm in his interventions, but at the same time he was both sensitive and respectful. He managed to harmonize contrasting positions in favor of greater unity within the assembly, and he regularly achieved a consensus on the documents that was morally "unanimous." This was fully recognized by some of the Council Fathers themselves who had been at odds with each other, and this result was all the more important because the pope's interventions had not been welcomed by many of these same Council Fathers at first. The pope's work in this regard was long and difficult, and it sometimes caused no little grief and suffering to the gentle and patient pontiff. Cardinal Franziskus König [of Vienna] actually called him "the martyr of the Council."

A moment of particular suffering of this kind for him was occasioned by the communication he received on the eve of the Third Session, on September 13, 1964. It was entitled, "Note Addressed Personally to the Holy Father." It was signed by eighteen cardinals, an archbishop, and four superiors general of religious orders. On the subject of the *schema* on the Church, in particular its Chapter III on the hierarchy, these prelates informed the Holy Father that the text in question was "novel, not certain, not even solidly probable"; it was also judged to be "vague," and its argumentation "weak, one-sided, and even fallacious."

Grave reservations were expressed concerning the way in which the teaching on the primacy of the pope was being presented, as well as how the teaching on the powers and collegiality of the bishops was set forth. The same doubts were presented on the subject of the way in which the college of bishops succeeded to the College of the Apostles. It was contended that the Church was being transformed from a monarchy into a kind of oligarchy of the bishops, where the primacy of the pope was not sufficiently brought out. It was suggested that Chapter III of the *schema* on the Church should be separated from the rest of the text, or even that a new draft entirely should be prepared, with the discussion of the whole subject postponed to another time.

Paul VI, who had attentively followed the debate on collegiality as well as the drafting of the *schema*, was "surprised and disturbed" by this Note and, especially, by the number and dignity of the prelates who had signed it. He was particularly concerned by what the reactions would be if he were ever to accept such suggestions. In a truly noble letter dated October 18, 1963, consisting of eight pages in his own handwriting, the pope replied to each and every one of the points in the Note without exhibiting either bitterness or resentment towards those who had drawn up and sent such a Note to him.

He replied with both courtesy and serenity to the criticisms that had been made on the contents of the *schema* as well as on the maneuvers and pressures that, it was asserted, had accompanied the drafting of the text. He mentioned his own interventions aimed at guaranteeing the integrity and orthodoxy of the doctrine set forth in the *schema*, and then he added: "We are sensitive to the claim addressed in such an extraordinary way concerning our own responsibility to be vigilant in accordance with the express prayers of the Lord. We are equally sensitive to the sacrifice that we ourselves have humbly made to offer up our own life in order that this testimony will prove faithful to the purity of the teachings of the Lord and will redound to the greater good of his holy Church." He promised that his commitment to follow closely the preparation of this *schema* would continue, and that suitable amendments would be made if required for the orthodoxy of the doctrines contained in the *schema*, or for the clarity of the exposition of those doctrines. The proof of his seriousness in this regard was confirmed in the drafting of the *Nota Explicativa Praevia* which he directed to be added to Chapter III of this *schema* on the Church.[15]

---

[15]Cfr. V. Carbone, *Il Concilio Vaticano II* [Vatican Council II], pp. 69ff. and 95 (reviewed in Chapter 48 of this book). See also Tagle, L. A., "Paul VI and the Council in 1964," in *The Event and the Decisions* referenced in Note 2 above. In these accounts, a particularly difficult conciliar period is covered, namely, the last days of the Third Session. At the center of everything, the figure of Paul VI stands out. He is seen as "judging carefully" and also as "scrupulous," and he originated certain actions and decisions that created anxieties in some. L. A. Tagle asks: "Why did Paul VI act in this way?" He replies to his own question by describing the pope's actions taken near the end

The *Nota* freed the text from potential implications and suggestions that could have given rise to distorted interpretations of the document. But it was not in contradiction to the conciliar text itself, according to the judgment that Monsignor Gérard Philips later rendered on it. He, of course, was the noted theologian and skilled "re-weaver" of the text of *Lumen Gentium*. With this *Nota Explicativa Praevia*, perplexities and hesitations were at an end for most of the Council Fathers, and when the vote was taken at the plenary public meeting on November 21, 1964, the result was that there were 2141 *placet* votes and only 5 *non placet*.

With the end of the Council in view, Pope Paul VI undertook to set in motion the reform of the liturgy, the revision of the Code of Canon Law, the reform of the Roman Curia, the setting up of other new entities and organisms, and the initiation of the meetings of the new Synod of Bishops. It was a crucial and decisive period, but also

---

of the Third Session as in accordance with "his understanding of the theology contained in *Lumen Gentium*, but with special reference to the difficulties of safeguarding the papal prerogatives included there...Without discounting the very real influences of his own temperament, of the formation he had received, and of his personal predispositions towards the events of 1964, I believe it can be said" —Tagle opines—"that his acts simply reflected the dynamic tensions and the hesitations inherent in the teaching of the Council itself on the subject of the episcopal college and on the head of the latter" (*Ibid.*, pp. 357ff.). The author attempts to prove this (see, esp. pp. 360ff.); but to do so adequately he would need to bring out more clearly the question of the "sacramental conferring of the power of jurisdiction along with the power of orders itself" (p. 361). The author concludes: "Nobody suffered any 'defeat' on this; all ended up convinced" (p. 368). I believe that this sums up the commitment that Paul VI assumed, although there were those who were dissatisfied then and those who continue to be dissatisfied now. Among the admirers of Paul VI, it is worth remembering, as we know so well from *Vatican II in Moscow*, edited by A. Melloni and published in Leuven in 1997 (reviewed in Chapter 18 of this book), there was the archpriest Vitalj Borovoij. As is indeed well known, he was the Russian Orthodox observer most prominently in view at the Council. Having presented his view of the great significance of the Council, he also manifested great sympathy and, indeed, "compassion" for Paul VI personally: "We could see, understand, and sympathize with the great solicitude of the pope for the maintenance of unity and for conciliation within the Council. He navigated skillfully between the diverse tendencies, preserving thereby, along with a true liberty of discussion, the possibility of arriving at decisions on which all could agree" (p. 87). Or again: "The experience of the Second Vatican Council was a school and a laboratory for both 'conciliarity' and for conciliation in the Catholic Church" (*Ibid.*).

a very delicate and sensitive one. In the course of what followed upon all of these new directions and initiatives, there were many reactions, including attempts to go back to the way things had been before or to leap forward too precipitously.

Certainly the near unanimous conciliar consensus which had been achieved was soon put to new and hard tests, since practically everybody had a propensity to follow what he believed to be the best path. This is certainly still true today. The propensity in question usually entails deciding for oneself or for the community what accords with one's own vision, or worse, one's own "ideology"—meanwhile not accepting the whole *corpus* of the sixteen Council documents. Yet it was these documents which the Council, for better or for worse, agreed to adopt. They are rightly invoked, therefore, as the expression of the Council's true intentions and decisions.[16]

[16] See, in *The Event and the Decisions*, referred to in Note 2 above, the article entitled "Historiographical Reflections on Vatican II as an Event," by J. A. Komonchak. This contribution elucidates the problem of conciliar "exegesis." We add, however, that among the various broad "types of interpretation" that might apply to the Council, according to this author (p. 420), there is lacking one by which it might be considered to be a "great happening." It may have been an "event" all right, but it was a "Catholic event," by which I mean one capable of combining, as I have often said, the *nova et vetera*, the new and the old. Can I say that I find myself dealing with such an assembly in this case? Let me cite an example in order to make myself better understood. In the Constitution *Dei Verbum*, the author notes that the final text "was certainly intended to express something different than a 'simple' reconfirmation of the continuity of Catholicism" (p. 424). It seems evident, though, that the adjective "simple" here was misleadingly introduced, since the other necessary word that also belongs here, namely *aggiornamento*, was left out. However, the author goes on to state in an attempt to recover his ground "that the two camps...perhaps had more in common than seems to be the case at first sight" (p. 434; and see also the further contribution to the question on pp. 443 and 450). But the two aspects go together (the same thing is true for what is said on p. 426). Along the same general line of thinking, it seems to me, is the contribution of G. Routhier in the cited volume; his essay is entitled, "Orientation for the study of Vatican II's Reception." This is a theme on which much has been said over the past twenty years, a fact which may have led to "the neglect of the processes of reception which were already operative within the Council" (p. 466). The author speaks of the reception of Scripture, the Creeds, previous councils, the teaching of the ordinary Magisterium, customs, the life of the Church herself, and of culture (where the author attempts to deal with "democratic culture"—p. 484). He also speaks of "the negative reception exercised by

V. Dialogue and Consensus at the Council Resulting in a Proper Combination of Tradition and Renewal

I referred above to the conciliar "consensus" which Pope Paul VI pursued tirelessly as a proper expression of the *Catholica*, that is, of the *unitas in necessariis* (unity in necessary things). For us, this consensus represented the acceptance of the necessary combination of Tradition with the renewal launched by the great Synod.

Certainly, this kind of consensus represents a category different from the *consensus unanimis* considered a *conditio sine qua non* of conciliar dogmatic decisions at Vatican Council I.[17] Still, both the occasion and the opportunity for manifesting the spirit of truth remain the essential way of proceeding for a Council. Its absence or

the Council itself. This latter subject includes that which the Council did not wish to receive by applying it wrongly" (pp. 484ff.). Then there was the question of the internal reception, consisting of what was contained in the documents of previous councils. Certainly, reception is profoundly linked to the theme of this article. In spite of my great reservations for many of the affirmations of the various authors, I must nevertheless also cite the volume entitled *Recezione e comunione tra le chiese* [Reception and Communion among the Churches], Acts of the International Colloquium at Salamanca, April 8-14, 1996, edited by H. Legrand, J. Manzanares, Á García y García, published in Bologna in 1998 (I refer in particular to pp. 51ff., 105ff., 108, 344, and, especially p. 438). On this last page, it is stated that "the normative role belongs to tradition and not to reception." (Along the same lines, see p. 440). It is worthwhile adding one last citation. It is one of Scheffczyk Leo, *La Chiesa. Aspetti della crisi post-conciliare e corretta interpretazione del Vaticano II* [The Church: Aspects concerning the Post-Conciliar Crisis and a Correct Interpretation of Vatican II], published in Como in 1998 (reviewed in Chapter 49 of this book). This author states that "every interpreter and even every group accept only what corresponds to their own preconceptions" (p. 21), or perhaps merely to those of the "majority." This volume, however, is intended to present "the doctrine of Vatican II accurately, including both "continuity and progress." It demonstrates the complete continuity of the full teaching of the great Synod with the Church's preceding ecclesiology, evidencing at the same time the development and progress in understanding the mystery of the Church. The other fundamental aspect is the author's analysis of the divergences, between the proposals for renewal before the Council, and what often took place after the Council as a consequence (I would add) of unilateral, one-sided, and, ultimately, deviant interpretations of the Council's actual teachings.

[17]Cfr. K. Schatz, *Storia dei Concili. La Chiesa nei suoi punti focali* [A History of the Councils: The Church in Her Focal Points], EDB, Bologna, 1999, p. 233.

failure would be something that would have to be paid for dearly, as the history of Church Councils attests. In fact, "the example of many important Councils, from Chalcedon to Vatican II itself, and including the Council of Trent, records the exertion of tireless efforts in order to achieve a consensus, and this in turn demonstrates the importance of such a consensus as a sign, especially in showing that truth is not so much 'decided' by voting as it is 'attested to' by the existence of such a consensus."[18]

And what constitutes the path to follow in order to achieve this if it is not *dialogue*? This is especially the case when we recall the richness as well as the contradictions of modern culture, its aspirations and hopes, its sadnesses and joys, as well as all the disappointments and difficulties of modern man.[19] Pope Paul VI, following an interior

---

[18]*Ibid.*, p. 233.

[19]Leo Scheffczyk, *op. cit.*, Note 16 above (and also see Chapter 49 of this book), in his preface delineates the problematical contemporary ecclesiastical situation, which he describes as "an uncritical and even rash fraternization of Christianity with the spirit of the times...in which occur many irrational and post-modern developments such as a vague religiosity and even some Gnostical tendencies." His own theological work, by contrast, is based upon fidelity to the true identity of the Church, a creation of the Word. Her origins are found in the supertemporality of divine Revelation, notwithstanding her relationship with these present times. What is at stake here is the continuity of the Catholic Church, even though at the present time she is involved with "progress." In his conclusion, Scheffczyk fixes his "gaze on the whole question of fulfillment" (pp. 180-183). He writes that "the believer contemplates the state of the Church in every era only through the lens of 'Christian time,' which is determined by two dates: the coming of Christ in the 'fullness of time,' and the eschatological advent that will mark the return of the transfigured Lord as the judge of the world. It is between these two pillars that we live in an 'intermediate time.' It is a dialectical time between the 'already' and the 'not yet' in the life of the Church, and we are carried along through it in hope. It is also a time for the *mea culpa* of the People of God, of a critical-type contemplation conducted by means of the gift of discernment. But this kind of honest critique is by no means to be compared with the present-day *pathological* critique directed towards the very substance of the Church and aiming at the creation of another and different and 'future' Church" (p. 182). "The Church's opening to her true 'fulfillment' not only allows us to contemplate a realistic vision of the Church's actual wounds caused by the sins and weaknesses of men; it also allows us to view the trials and damages, as well as an apostolic type of suffering" (*Ibid.*), which can take the form of martyrdom. Such a martyrdom is "not compatible with the idea of a Church which tells people only what

impulse of charity, sought to involve himself regularly in this dialogue, since, as he said, "the world is not saved from outside."

Paul VI was an assiduous announcer and promoter of dialogue with all men of good will, including separated Christians, non-Christians, and even non-believers. "The Church," he said, "should enter into dialogue with the world in which she finds herself; the Church has something to say; the Church has a message to deliver; the Church is committed to dialogue."[20] Subsequently, the same pope expressly affirmed: "It is particularly upon us, the pastors of the Church, that rests the responsibility for seeking boldly though wisely, the most adaptable and the most effective methods in order to communicate the evangelical message to the men of our time, while remaining wholly faithful to the content of the faith."[21] It is a question of the dialogue of salvation itself, which takes its transcendent origin from the will of God. It is characterized by clarity, gentleness, faith, and prudence. "It is in dialogue, conducted in this way, that the union of truth with charity is realized, as is the union of truth with love."[22]

Pope Paul VI insisted strongly that the dialogue must be immune from today's relativism, which would undermine faith and morals.

they want to hear (and they basically get that from the media today anyway); it is not compatible with the spirit of the times" (p. 183). Nevertheless, "the close link between natural creation and supernatural redemption still requires both Christians and the pilgrim Church to turn towards the world" (*Ibid.*). There is a final and important brushstroke to be added to this picture: "The pilgrim Church does have a task that we can style 'political,' but this task possesses its own character and is not exactly comparable to secular politics. The Church's 'political' task cannot be carried out solely with respect to the temporal future to come, but must be inspired by the ultimate end of her 'fulfillment.' This means that even her earthly task has a different content; alongside the promotion of temporal things, supertemporal things must also be kept in view; the Church in her very nature is obliged to deal with and make a record of them as well" (p. 183). Useful in this regard is my own critical review which appeared in *L'Osservatore Romano* of June 10, 1998 (p. 10)—and is reprinted in Chapter 24 of this book—of the volume entitled *Vatikanum II und Modernisierung. Historische, Theologische, und soziologische Perspektive* [Vatican II and Modernization: Historical, Theological, and Sociological Perspectives], edited by F. X. Kaufmann and Arnold Zingerle, Paderborn, 1996, p. 423.

[20]Pope Paul VI, Encyclical *Ecclesiam Suam*: AAS 56 (1964), p. 639.

[21]Apostolic Exhortation *Evangelii Nuntiandi*, 40, AAS 68 (1976), p. 31.

[22]Encyclical *Ecclesiam Suam*, *loc. cit.*, Note 20, p. 645.

"Our solicitude to communicate our message to our brothers must not result in an attenuation or diminishing of the truth". "Our dialogue must not stem from any weakness with respect to our commitment to our faith". "We cannot compromise on either the theory or the practice of our Christian profession."[23]

May our patient reader thus recognize all the many ties between Vatican Council II, its operating procedures, its quest for a fruitful dialogue within the Catholic Church, its fervent and equally constant search for a proper consensus, and its desire continually renewed and acted upon to insure a dialogue between renewal and tradition, a melding of the old and the new. Vatican II sanctioned theological developments and translated them into pastoral action in response to the exigencies of our times, and in continuity with the teaching of the Church.

Thus, the Church—immutable in her intrinsic vitality stemming from Christ the head of the mystical body and the Holy Spirit and always in fidelity to the Father—nevertheless continues to perfect herself through the Council, even while she remains essentially the same. Yet she is also enriched by new doctrines and ordinances even while she retains the sacred deposit of the faith confided to her by Christ himself. Bishop Bossuet, for example, wrote: "We must hold as certain that we do not admit any new revelation, and that the faith as propounded by the Council of Trent is guaranteed to have come down to us intact; in this fact lies the source of the expression that dominated that Tridentine Council, namely, that the dogmas it proclaimed must be considered to be *sicut Ecclesia Catholica semper intellexit*, that is, what the Catholic Church has always understood. It is in accordance with this rule that it must be held for certain that ecumenical councils, when they make a pronouncement concerning a truth, do not thereby propound new dogmas but only declare what has always been believed, while they explicate it in terms that are more clear and more precise."[24]

---

[23]*Ibid.*, p. 647.

[24]Bishop Jacques-Bénigne Bossuet, Letter n. 32 to Leibniz, in *Oeurres*, Paris, 1846, p. 716.

I would not like to conclude here without issuing an invitation—if this is permitted to me—to the effect that, just as at the time of the Council, there should continue to be carried on in the Church today a dialogue which seeks consensus on the basis of the eternal truth and beauty of the Church, always ancient and always new, in fidelity to Tradition and to the renewal that is inherent in *aggiornamento*.

51

Vatican Council II:
Hermeneutical Tendencies
from 1990 to 2000

I certainly do not have to convince anybody of the doctrinal, spiritual, and pastoral value of the Second Vatican Council. It is surely enough to be able to say that the Council is an "icon" of the Catholic Church herself, of what Catholicism simply *is*, constitutionally, that is, a "communion." It is a communion with its own origins and its own past: the Church retains her identity even as she develops in time; she remains faithful even as she renews herself.

The principal image which comes to mind to illustrate this concept is that of a leafy tree sprung from a humble seed planted two thousand years ago and buried in the earth—because of the death of Christ—but only to burst forth in a perennial springtime with the resurrection of that same Christ. This vine of the Lord has in fact spread its roots throughout the entire world. We can only recall this with joy and gratitude in this year of the Jubilee.

The conciliar event was undeniably a great event. For my part, speaking as a historian, and in order to underline the vastness of the event in question, I need only mention the official *Acts* of the Council collected in no less than 62 large volumes (the major enterprise of the publication of all these *Acts* has only been recently brought to a happy conclusion owing to the diligence, application, and many years of excellent work on the part of Monsignor Vincenzo Carbone). All this constitutes a solid basis on which everybody can now construct and deal with the reception and the correct interpretation of the great Council. However, the fact is that many have instead proceeded to construct their own conciliar hermeneutic almost without regard to these official *Acts*—in fact, not yet entirely complete with regard to the Council's directive organs. Many have based their interpretations on "private" writings (personal diaries mostly), contemporary newspapers and journals, and various other accounts or "chronicles" (at times with exaggerated and distorted viewpoints). It was not the case, however, for the work of Father Giovanni Caprile, S. J.

Moreover, in recent years, there has begun to appear the publication of diaries on the Council kept by well-known figures who participated in the Council in various ways or at least followed its work. It should go without saying that such sources ought to be subjected to a particularly careful screening. Even a superficial reading of such sources often reveals discrepancies and a variety of other questionable attributions and "merits." As is well known, it is only human to believe that one is at the center of what is "really happening," that one is "in the know" with regard to the directions and positions being taken, especially those which then turn out after debate to have been "victorious" or to have "won out." This is true even though one's positions may in fact be very one-sided and partial, especially with regard to the real complexity of the issues being considered. Then there is the interaction of the whole range of regulations, "pressures" and movements, and also the prevalence of the idea that "battles" are being fought for or against "conservatism," for or against the Church's "Tradition," for or against brilliant ideas, for or against certain theologians, especially those thought to be "*avant-garde*, or, finally, for or against the Magisterium itself. Above all, there is the widespread belief that this or that initiative was truly in accordance with the mind and intentions of Pope John XXIII. We could go on citing such examples...The careful screening which must surely be applied to all such sources is thus necessarily going to be a long and difficult task. These kinds of personal experiences and sources certainly add personal flavor and other ingredients to any history of the Council, but they must only be used in strict conformity with the official *Acts* of the Council. These are the principal *facts* concerning the Council.

The same kind of careful screening is also needed because of the preponderance of the "personal" in diaries, at least in many of them. There is also the risk of sliding into a kind of narrative which is fragmentary, and which does not easily escape from being either a mere narrative or "chronicle" or perhaps even a kind of encyclopedia article. Anyone who has attentively followed the conciliar history that has predominated up to now cannot but have the impression that, often, there is a kind of diversion into numerous by-paths that are off the main road. There is sometimes even a detailed dissection or taking apart of the great event of the twentieth century that was Vatican Council II.

With regard to these diaries, I shall limit myself to calling attention only to those of Father Marie-Dominique Chenu, O.P.[1] and Archbishop Neophytos Edelby.[2] In addition, I will make mention of four other volumes of a literary *genre* somewhat similar to a diary. The first three of these latter books are somewhat different from each other but are all quite interesting. I refer to books by Stjepan Schmidt,[3] Benny Lai,[4] and Joseph Ratzinger.[5] This last title, even though the author declares that "the ecclesial and theological drama of these years is not the primary subject of these memories," contains a request from the author to the reader to allow two exceptions, one on the purpose of the Council and another on "the sources of revelation." These are

---

[1]Chenu Marie-Dominique, O.P., *Notes quotidiennes au Concile* (1962-1963) [Daily Notes of the Council (1962-1963)], edited by Albert Melloni, Cerf, Paris 1995. See my review in *Apollinaris* LXX (1997), pp. 421-425, and in Chapter 37 of this book.

[2]Edelby Neophytos, *Il Vaticano II nel diario di un vescovo arabo* [Vatican II in the Diary of an Arab Bishop], edited by Riccardo Cannelli, San Paolo, Cinisello Balsamo 1996. See *Apollinaris* LXX (1997), pp. 888-891, and Chapter 38 of this book.

[3]Schmidt Stjepan, *Agostino Bea, Cardinale dell'ecumenismo e del dialogo* [Augustin Bea: Cardinal of Ecumenism and the Dialogue], San Paolo, Alba 1996. See my review in *Apollinaris*, LXX, 1997, pp. 409-413, and also in Chapter 39 in this book.

[4]Lai Benny, *Il Papa non eletto. Giuseppe Siri, Cardinale di Santa Romana Chiesa* [The Pope Not Elected: Giuseppe Siri, Cardinal of the Holy Roman Church], Laterza, Bari 1993. See *Apollinaris,* LXX (1997), pp. 413-417, and also Chapter 36 in this book.

[5]Ratzinger Joseph, *La mia vita. Ricordi* (1927-1977) [My Life: Memories (1927-1977)], Edizioni San Paolo, Mappano 1997. See my review in *Apollinaris* LXX (1997), pp. 417-421, and in Chapter 40 of this book.

happy exceptions! But I add to the listing of these three books, the "memoirs" of Cardinal Suenens as well.[6]

Problems Underlying the Publication of Diaries

Concerning the research and use of various "diaries" about the Council collected with the help of various "friends," when there was almost a "neutral" time as far as the hermeneutical question—there still remains the aim of many to downgrade the importance of the conciliar documents themselves which, for us, remain the true synthesis of Tradition and *aggiornamento*. Research focused in this way, which we have long characterized as "ideological," aims solely at the new or the novel or innovative aspects which emerged at the Council; it thus focuses upon discontinuity with regard to the Catholic Tradition generally.

There is, in fact, a book which views the Council in this perspective. It is entitled *The Event and the Decisions: Studies on the Dynamics of Vatican Council II*, edited by Maria Teresa Fattori and Alberto Melloni, it was published by Il Mulino in Imola in 1997.[7]

By focusing so much of conciliar hermeneutics on discontinuity, today's general historiographical tendency thereby privileges the idea of an "event" in historical interpretation, and this tendency, precisely, thus favors discontinuity—that is, "change," if not actual traumatic mutations. This tendency thus goes counter to the famous idea of "Annales" in historiography, for this latter theory looks at long periods of history and underlines the evidence of continuity found in them. For Fernand Braudel, history is "an applied social science which brings out structures, systems, and perennial models which at first sight were invisible." It is often not seen in the case of the history of the Church—or else one does not want to realize that by

---

[6]Suenens Leo J., *Souvenirs et Espérances* [Memories and Hopes], Fayard, 1991. See the review by Father G. Caprile in *Civiltà Cattolica,* n. 3433, July 3, 1993, pp. 91ff.

[7]See on this my article entitled, "Concerning a 'Thesis' on Vatican Council II." This article appeared in the *Annuarium Historiae Conciliorum* (AHC) XXX (1998), pp. 132-142; see also *Apollinaris* LXXI (1998), pp. 324-337 and Chapter 23 in this book.

"event" is meant not so much just a notable happening, but rather a complete break with the past, an absolute novelty, the coming to birth of what is seen as a new ecclesial entity, in fact, a kind of "Copernican revolution," the passage from one type of Catholicism to another and new type—which, however, does not shed its original unmistakable characteristics. All this represents a tendency in historiography which cannot and must not be accepted, at least not as far as the Catholic Church is concerned—and as far as any history which takes into account her specific nature. I refer to the continuity of her own mysterious reality, which must always be borne in mind, even in the interpretation of her documents.

In this connection, reading over the contributions to *The Event and the Decisions*, one is surprised by the radical critiques offered, in the name of the "event," against the hermeneutics of Jedin, Ratzinger, and Kasper (this last with his four hermeneutical rules, which are considered abstractly in the referenced volume, or are otherwise neglected, stressing the peculiarities of Vatican II in comparison with various earlier councils). The same kind of mask against critique is present in the work of Émile Poulat. This choice of method has the aim of promoting the view of the Council as an event, understood in accordance with the ideological assumptions that we have mentioned above.

It is not difficult to realize that, without prejudice, this position at the time of the Council was not frequent but rather an extreme one among those who made up the conciliar majority. I would even characterize it as an "extremist" position; it went contrary to the more flexible one that was prepared to seek a possible compromise in the search for consensus and for the proper combination between Tradition and renewal. The "extremists," however, were always determined to impose their own point of view, turning a deaf ear to the need for discussion or for the work of "mending" or "re-weaving" that was constantly carried out by Pope Paul VI. Following the Council, the adherents of this extremist point of view succeeded in henceforth virtually monopolizing the interpretation of the Council, even attacking contrary positions as "anti-conciliar." Very revealing in this connection is the book by Giuseppe Dossetti entitled *Il Concilio Vaticano II, Frammenti di una riflessione* [Vatican Council II: Fragments of a Reflection] published by Il Mulino, in Bologna, in 1996. Father Dossetti was the famous "secretary" of the Council Moderators. Paul VI himself was moved to remark about him that this role was "not a proper position for him."

However, the true background of the idea of an "event" in history is brought out in the study entitled "The Category of 'Event' in Recent French Historiography" by E. Fouilloux. This study is included in *The Event and the Decisions*, the volume referred to above (and in which the author mentions "its return" attested by E. Morin). By "recent" in this title is meant roughly from the 1950s. Nor does the author fail to mention the strict link between the actual historical existence of an event and the way it has been mediated. The view of P. Nora is cited to the effect that "in order that there be an event, it is necessary that it should become known." Supposedly, "Vatican II responds very well to this 'media' definition of what constitutes an event."

Then there is P. Hünermann, writing in the same volume. He recommends the method of G. Gadamer and concludes that "the event of the Council can be understood as the formation of the practice that can be expressed conceptually as 'subject dialectics' (described in the language of the *Philosophical Investigations* of Ludwig Wittgenstein). This 'subject dialectics,' which makes possible a consensus, constitutes in a radical and renewed form the true foundation of the Council; it consists of a unitary movement which has tightly linked together innumerable individual activities, inserting them into a flux, which then produced as its fruit and result the new vision of the Church and of divine revelation which are now to be found embedded in the various texts of the Council."[8]

---

[8]See Fattori Maria Teresa and Melloni Alberto, eds., *L'evento e le decisioni. Studi sulle dinamiche del Concilio Vaticano II* [The Event and the Decisions: Studies on the Dynamics of Vatican Council II], Il Mulino, Imola 1997, p. 92.

The Intentions of John XXIII and Paul VI

But let us return to the original idea of Newman, which saw the Church as a living organism in continual growth, both internally and externally, even while always remaining herself. Certainly, such a conception of development entails many possible problems concerning doctrine, cult, morality, discipline, and the apostolate.

In general, the solution to such problems is provided by the Church's ordinary Magisterium residing in her pastors and, especially, in the papal ministry. This Magisterium is assisted by theologians working in unity with the whole people of God, always in communion with the pastors. At times, however, either the complexity of the material or the gravity of the historical circumstances calls for extraordinary interventions, general or ecumenical councils, for example. These doctrinal developments, promote liturgical and other adaptations and reforms, foster a disciplinary *aggiornamento*, and, in general, make other apostolical choices—all in consideration of the time in which the Church happens to be living (the famous "signs of the times," which, however, do not constitute some kind of a new Revelation!).

Viewed in this perspective, Popes John XXIII and Paul VI shared the same outlook and sought the same aims: specifically, *aggiornamento* in fidelity to the Church's Tradition. I myself have furnished a demonstration of this in an article entitled "Tradition and Renewal Together: The Second Vatican Council."[9] I will cite only one passage. Paul VI wrote: "It would not be the truth for anybody to imagine that Vatican Council II represented any kind of a break, interruption, or 'liberation' from the teaching of the Church, or that it authorized or promoted any kind of accommodation or conformism with the mentality of our times, in its negative or ephemeral aspects."[10]

---

[9]*"Tradizione e rinnovamento si sono abbracciati: il Concilio Vaticano II,"* in *Rivista della Diocesi di Vicenza,* XC (1999), pp. 1232-1245; reprinted in Chapter 50 of this book.
[10]See *Insegnamenti di Paolo VI* [Teachings of Paul VI], Volume IV, 1966, p. 699.

Situation in the Last Ten Years

Since we are on this subject, what can we say about the conciliar hermeneutics of the last ten years? Not very much that is favorable: I must reply in this vein at the outset. There appears, in effect, to be a one-sided school of interpretation which, however, is not in the line of seeing renewal in the light of Church Tradition—but which, we contend, is characteristic of the Church and her Councils generally. The fact is that "the School of Bologna," guided by Professor Giuseppe Alberigo, has mostly succeeded in monopolizing the whole subject and in imposing a distorted view on how things are to be seen. This is especially the case owing to the publication of the projected five-volume *History of Vatican Council II* edited by him and published by Peeters/Il Mulino, of which four of the volumes in the Italian version have already appeared. In order to indicate the wide scope of the influence of this work, and the financial capacity of the publisher—as well as his high protections—it should be noted that translations of the work are in progress in French, English, German, Spanish, and Portuguese. In fact, some of the volumes that comprise this work have already appeared in some of these languages.

The seriousness of the meaning of this for sound conciliar hermeneutics, from our point of view, can be gathered by reading my reviews of the four volumes that have already appeared in Italy.[11] Needless to say, I cannot here repeat all that I have said in these critical reviews. I will accordingly just limit myself to some illustrative examples. One is the paragraph I wrote in reviewing the fourth volume (which, however, is indicative of all that had appeared in the series up to that point). I quote: "As has been the case for the previous volumes in the series, this large volume, well made and presented, constitutes a notable encyclopedic effort on the subject of the great Vatican Synod…" And I would underline the word "encyclopedic" here.

What continued to characterize this *History*, though, was an element which from the start we have defined as "ideological." It becomes only too evident in the animosity shown against some of the

---

[11]See *Apollinaris* LXIX (1996), pp. 305-317 and Chapter 10 of this book; *Apollinaris* LXX (1997), pp. 331-351, and also *L'Osservatore Romano* for August 28, 1996, and for January 31-February 1, 2000, p. 10. See also Chapters 11-13 in this book.

prominent persons in the Council's "minority"; this animosity is neither justified, nor is it scholarly; but on this particular score this *History* is consistently one-sided. For it, again, the "true" Second Vatican Council is the one thought to have been envisaged by Pope John XXIII, who is seen as an entirely "progressive" pope and as an "innovator," and this "Johannine" Council supposedly lasted until September 1964, when the "other" Council of Paul VI supposedly took over. The fact of the matter, of course, is that the great Synod was always one and indivisible and was never anything but quite simply "Vatican II."

Along these same subjective and wholly unfounded interpretive lines, there appears an idea which underlies the kind of synodal hermeneutic presented here, and which clearly characterizes this study as a whole and marks it as a history that sees the Council generally as an "event." The idea in question is the one of the "novelty" or "newness" of everything that had to be decided at the Council; this supposedly represented a break with the past and thereby by-passed the ideas of continuity and Tradition that in fact need to be taken into account in cases of true *aggiornamento*. Again, as has been the case previously, it is strictly necessary to point out the harsh judgments rendered on the performance of the Secretary General of the Council, Archbishop Pericle Felici (the same thing is true of the judgments rendered on some other conciliar figures). Little account is made or attention paid to the papal *mens* in all this, particularly with respect to the period unfortunately still commonly referred to as "Black Week" (in November, 1964).[12] This "journalistic" expression, which is quite erroneous, continues to be widely employed, even though it is sometimes placed between quotation marks. In fact, it was during this precise period of time that the pope made a number of decisions and judgments now recognized to have been both correct and necessary for the whole synodal "economy." These can be followed in the *Adnotationes* contained in the Council records ("Handwritten Notes by the Supreme Pontiff, Pope Paul VI"). He noted, for example, on September 24, 1964, on the subject of the *schema De Libertate Religiosa*, that "it did not seem to be well-prepared." On September 29, he wrote that "(1) It is necessary to redo it; and (2) to draw in to

---

[12]See *L'Osservatore Romano* for January 31-February 1, 2000, p. 10.

associate with the Commission other persons competent in theology and sociology."[13] This is just one example!

But the volumes published under the direction of Professor Alberigo have been put together utilizing materials from various meetings and conferences held in different places which themselves had their own specific publications. These results have to be considered because they are characterized by the tendencies described above.

I limit myself to citing the titles of several of them, making reference also to my [critical] relative reviews. Thus:

1) *Towards Vatican Council II (1960-1962): Passages and Problems related to the Preparation for the Council.*[14]

2) *On the Eve of Vatican Council II:* Vota *and Reactions in Europe and Eastern Catholicism.*[15]

3) *Christianity and the Churches of Latin America on the Eve of Vatican II.*[16]

4) *Expectations from and Celebration of Vatican Council II.*[17]

5) *Vatican II in Moscow.*[18]

---

[13]*Acta Synodalia* (AS), VI/3, p. 418.

[14]Alberigo G., and Melloni A., eds., with Various Authors, *Verso il Concilio Vaticano II* (1960-1962). *Passagi e problemi della preparazione concliare* [Towards Vatican Council II (1960-1962): Extracts and Problems related to Preparation for the Council], Marietti, Genoa, 1993, 503 pages. See my reviews in *Apollinaris* LXVIII (1995), pp. 848-854, and in Chapter 6 of this book.

[15]Lamberigts M., and Soetens C., eds., with Various Authors, *À la Veille du Concile Vatican II:* Vota *et reactions en Europe et dans le catholicisme oriental* [On the Eve of Vatican Council II: *Vota* and Reactions in Europe and Eastern Catholicism], Bibliotheek van de Faculteit der Godgeleerdheid, Leuven 1992, 277 pages. See my review in *Apollinaris* LXIX (1996), pp. 444-453, and in Chapter 7 of this book.

[16]Beozzo José Oscar, ed., with Various Authors, *Cristianismo e eglesias de América Latina en visperas del Vaticano II* [Christianity and the Churches of Latin America on the Eve of Vatican II], Cehila-Editorial D. E. I., San José, Costa Rica 1992, 216 pages. See my review in *Apollinaris* LXX (1997), pp. 881-883, and in Chapter 8 of this book.

[17]Alberigo Giuseppe, ed., with Various Authors. *Il Vaticano II fra attese e celebrazione* [Expectations from and celebration of Vatican Council II], Il Mulino, Imola 1995, 250 pages. See my review in *Apollinaris* LXX (1997), 883-888, and in Chapter 9 of this book.

[18]Melloni A., ed., *Vatican II in Moscow* (1959-1965), Leuven, 1997, 352 pages. See my review in *L'Osservatore Romano*, August 22, 1998, p. 6, and in Chapter 18 of this book.

Comprehensive Investigations of the Council

Contemporaneously, beginning around 1995, it became apparent that a different type of research or investigation on the Council was beginning to be carried out, namely, studies of the Council as a whole. Some of this new research appeared to be quite provisional, however, and even to have been carried out in haste.

The risks in this approach have not been lacking, particularly since some of the authors involved have remained wedded to their one-sided views; hence truly scholarly results have been difficult to achieve. Such results generally require some distance from the subject matter, along with some time for the understanding of past events to become settled; they also require a long and patient work of assimilation and sorting out of the various existing accounts and "chronicles" of what happened, as well as of the various journalistic reports contemporary with the events themselves; these latter have exerted a great and unfortunate influence on the histories of the Council. Properly speaking, all these sources have to be combined and compared with the official *Acta Synodalia*, and these have only been complete as of this year. Of course, it is not difficult merely to cite these *Acta*; what is difficult is to draw the appropriate critical and comparative conclusions and consequences from them.

Let us take a look from this perspective at the second section of Part I of the work, *The Church of Vatican II (1958-1978)*, edited by Guasco, Guerriero, and Traniello.[19] Part II of this book is actually better than Part I; it treats the post-conciliar situation, and is edited by the same team and published in the same year as Part I. Both of these volumes comprise Volume *XXV* (1 and 2) of the Fliche-Martin *History of the Church*. This huge work has been completely translated into Italian and brought up to date by the San Paolo Editions publishers.

The treatment of Vatican Council II in this particular work was assigned to R. Aubert; he is the author of a preface and four chapters

---

[19]Guasco Maurilio, Guerriero Elio, and Traniello Francesco, eds., *La Chiesa del Vaticano II (958-1978)* [The Church of Vatican II (1958-1978)], Part I, Editions San Paolo, Cinisello Balsamo 1994, 594 pages (Volume XXVI of the Fliche-Martin *History of the Church*). See my review in *Apollinaris* LXVIII (1995), pp. 425-433, and in Chapter 16 of this book.

in the book (pp. 119-388); and he is, of course, a well-known Belgian historian. His treatment allows us to follow the work of "the group of Louvain," which has also collaborated with the enterprise of Giuseppe Alberigo. It even seems to me that there has been a kind of alliance formed between these two groups of Bologna and Louvain.

In my review of this work,[20] I noted part of the same defects as those found in the work of the School of Bologna, although Aubert is somewhat more balanced. He nevertheless still exhibits part of the same prejudices towards various men and institutions involved in the Council. Certainly, in his Chapter VI, entitled "The Unfolding of the Council," this author provides a valid and concise compendium of the history of the Council up to that point of the research (he was writing in 1994). He also covers the conciliar discussions well enough, though not without raising some questions that are in need of more critical judgments.

However, Aubert's final conclusion placing Paul VI "entirely in the line traced by John XXIII" tells us a great deal about his viewpoint, which in this case is contrary to that of Alberigo, as it is contrary to some of the others in the Belgian group.

Aubert's Chapter VII is on the subject of the conciliar texts themselves. In our view, much greater account needed to be taken of these documents which, after all, are the texts of an ecumenical Council of the Catholic Church. This is all the more important in the context of the widely hoped-for "reception" of the documents. They should be kept in a class apart from and beyond all partiality or one-sided views. However, by continually underlining the supposed deficiencies of these documents, does not an author such as Aubert, we ask, compromise or undermine the acceptance of the products of the Church's "doctrinal magisterium in a pastoral context" which precisely was the characteristic of Vatican II? This is a question which applies generally, and it remains one of the critical questions of our time, even when, as is the case today, it is accepted that "the force and authority of documents is judged on the basis of their literary *genre* and on that of obligatory criteria, and on the nature of the subjects covered in them."

---

[20]*Ibid.*

Always on the subject of correct conciliar hermeneutics, which is what concerns us here, we ask if it is really appropriate to assert, as Aubert does, that "numerous ambiguities remain in the text, where traditional statements are melded with innovative ones; they are simply juxtaposed with each other rather than being truly integrated." Or again: "Such a lack of coherence often produces divergent interpretations, with the result that some passages came to be unilaterally insisted upon more than other passages. In this situation, a historical study serenely carried out can decide to try to ascertain the deeper intentions of the great majority of the assembly beyond the efforts that were exerted to obtain a broader consensus."

However, we do not believe that it is possible to arrive at conciliar thinking as such (the "deeper intentions"), while prescinding from the constant conciliar preoccupation of achieving a true consensus; this latter preoccupation was an integral part of the Council and it was not sought after merely for its own sake, but rather because this was the way to insure fidelity to the Church's Tradition, even while effecting the desired *aggiornamento*. In any case, only the definitive texts approved by the Council and promulgated by the pope "count" as true conciliar thinking. Many may "receive" them as they will, in accordance with their own personal viewpoints or experiences, their theological preferences, or even the "school" to which they belong. However—we must constantly repeat—the Council represented an experience of communion within the whole Church, where, in the end, both the old and the new were bound to meet and meld and fecundate each other. It is here that is encountered what is always present and yet is quite new: a characteristic of the Catholic Church—of her deposit of faith from which is drawn both *nova et vetera* (new and old things together). Here we are obliged to view things with a theological eye rather than with the eye of a historian or that of a conciliar alone, if we are not to fall ourselves into a partisan or ideological position. But we shall also pause here, even while we continue to consider important what we observed a long time ago with regard to *Lumen Gentium*, namely, its actuation, one of the true conciliar dispositions as they actually were decided by the Council.

Alberigo speaks of this same subject in the volume entitled *A History of the Councils*.[21] In our review of this work, we found that, by comparison with some earlier books, the research somewhat improved: "It is less 'journalistic,' more concise and measured, and in the end more objective. Nevertheless, we should note the presence of some *clichés*—which are not always easy to overcome, even for well-trained authors." Nothing needs to be added to this judgment.

Professor Alberigo himself ventured upon an effort of synthesis during the same decade of the 1990s. This was the work of his *History of the Ecumenical Councils*, published in Brescia in 1990.[22] It was written by several hands, who covered the Church's general Councils up to those held at the Vatican; these latter were reserved to treatment by Professor Alberigo himself. Nearly fifty pages are devoted to Vatican II alone. We reviewed this book too, as noted, and there is nothing to add to what we have already said in our review and elsewhere about both the methods and contents of Professor Alberigo's historical research: this volume too exhibits the well-known "filters" through which the Bologna professor habitually sifts his material, his typical one-sided sensibility, and the same prejudices and preconceptions that he regularly adopts in all his writings.

Last year [1999] there was published in Italy another *History of the Councils*, this one written by Klaus Schatz.[23] While awaiting the publication of my review of this book in *Apollinaris*, I shall limit myself here merely to mentioning some of my reservations and perplexities regarding this particular work which point to the author's ambiguities, prejudices, and confusions. I refer, for example to his use of the concept of "Ultramontanism" and also to his idea about "We

---

[21] R. Aubert, G. Fedalto, D. Quaglioni, *Storia dei Concili* [A History of the Councils], Edizioni San Paolo, Cinisello Balsamo 1995. See my review in *Apollinaris* LXIX (1996), pp. 453-460, and in Chapter 2 of this book.

[22] Alberigo Giuseppe, with Various Authors, *Storia dei Concilii ecumenici* [A History of the Ecumenical Councils], Brescia 1990. See my review in *Apollinaris* LXV (1992), pp. 665-689, and in Chapter 1 of this book.

[23] Schatz Klaus, *Storia dei Concili. La Chiesa nei suoi punti focali* [A History of the Councils: The Church in Her Focal Points], EDB, Bologna 1999. My review is found in Chapter 3 of this book.

are the Church," as well as to his assertions concerning "the minority at Vatican II." Also, his judgments on the *Nota Explicativa Praevia* are far from balanced, and, in any case, he makes no reference to the recent volumes of the conciliar *Acta et Documenta* (AD) or the conciliar *Acta Synodalia* (AS) prepared by Monsignor Carbone. These "Acts," particularly with reference to the *Nota*, provide the key to any objective interpretation.

I cannot fail to mention at this point the volume on *Vatican II and Modernization*.[24] I am not a sociologist and hence I make no attempt to provide a critique in depth of this work, but there are still many things that can be said, particularly with regard to its one-sided (and for us, arbitrary) interpretation of the nature of the Council itself. This is especially the case with regard to the contribution by Professor Klinger here, as it is for that of Doctor Pottmeyer.

In this regard, and speaking about sociology, we reject the idea that this discipline is any kind of a "queen" of the sciences, taking precedence over theology, and we are therefore obliged to keep our distance from the sociological "turn" of theology. This appears to be the proper position to take. Moreover, "Montanism," and even "neo-Montanism," are historico-theological concepts, not sociological concepts. Historians and theologians certainly have something to say about them (here it is claimed that they lead to a "ghetto"). The same thing is true of the idea of a "hierocracy" mentioned here. With all of that, however, we do not wish to undervalue an interdisciplinary study—as this one is presented as being. Nevertheless, it is important to recognize the risks inherent in producing such a study.

Finally, in order not to neglect the whole spectrum of opinions, we must also make mention of a modest bi-monthly publication that has been coming out in Rome for the last twenty-five years. It bears the title, *Si si, No no*, and it is frankly traditionalist in orientation. To get an idea about it, it is enough to look at the issue of March 15,

---

[24]Kaufmann Franz-Xaver, and Zingerle Arnold, eds., *Vatikanum II und Modernisierung. Historische, Theologische, und Soziologische Perspektive* [Vatican II and Modernization: Historical, Theological, and Sociological Perspectives], F. Schöningh, Paderborn 1996. See *L'Osservatore Romano*, June 10, 1998, and Chapter 24 of this book for my review.

2000, the most recent one. It features an article entitled, "Council or Secret Meeting?" It treats of the question of the possible invalidity of Vatican II. It considers the Constitution on the Sacred Liturgy to be "the prologue to revolution."

For a Correct Interpretation

Faced with such a vast hermeneutical spectrum, even though it is mostly one-dimensional as far as the orientation of most of the authors is concerned, we could perhaps even feel ourselves to be somewhat isolated in our own interpretations of the Council—although we could surely derive some consolation from the consideration of the case of the Council of Trent. We need think only of Paolo Sarpi (even though his extremist interpretation finally did get superseded). We are, however, convinced that the judgments of future histories based *ex actis et probatis* will prove to be more correct with time. Meanwhile, patience is required, as well as commitment; also, much work, and recourse to the proper means.

A new phase of interpretation has begun to emerge in the last decade, in fact. For instance, I may mention the book of the well-known Professor Leo Scheffczyk entitled *The Church: Aspects concerning the Post-conciliar Crisis and a Correct Interpretation of Vatican II*.[25] In this book, we see a recovery of a true "Catholic" sense based on the reality of the Church. This follows upon the lengthy period of the post-conciliar crisis. I refer interested persons to my review of this book so as not to prolong unduly the present treatment. I do believe, however, that the author correctly puts his finger on the deficiencies of contemporary conciliar hermeneutics when he observes that "every interpreter and every group accept only what corresponds to their own preconceptions"—or perhaps merely to the preconceptions of "the conciliar majority."

An exception to this tendency is the editor of the "Acts" of the

---

[25]Scheffczyk Leo, *La Chiesa. Aspetti della crisi post-conciliare e corretta interpretazione del Vaticano II* [The Church: Aspects Concerning the Post-conciliar Crisis and a Correct Interpretation of Vatican II], Jaca Book, Como 1998. For my review, see *L'Osservatore Romano*, January 22, 1999, p. 6, and Chapter 49 in this book.

Council that are preserved in the Vatican archives. I refer to Monsignor Vincenzo Carbone, who was placed in the position he occupied through the providential foresight of Pope Paul VI. I do not make reference here to all his various contributions to clarity in the field of conciliar hermeneutics, but merely to one small volume of his, modest in appearance but exceptionally important; it is entitled *Vatican Council II: Preparation of the Church for the Third Millennium.*[26] This book consists of articles of the author previously published in *L'Osservatore Romano* on the subject of the great Synod. The book represents a shaft of light all by itself, illustrating how research can be wholly objective, free of preconceptions, and carried out beyond any ideological vision. The author's pen, in effect, proves to be quite balanced throughout.

Also representing a very positive interpretive line among works of history of the Church's Councils generally is the book on *The Vatican Councils* by Annibale Zambarbieri.[27] As far as we are concerned, this is the best general history of the Council published so far in Italian. The author covers both Vatican I (pp. 31-118) and Vatican II (pp. 119-351). This volume is also exceptional for the "historical sense" which pervades it. The author however does exhibit some occasional "indulgences" for positions characteristic of the School of Bologna; the book's principal deficiency, in fact, comes precisely on the subject of the *Nota Explicativa Praevia.* Nevertheless, I can report with great satisfaction that the book combines good research with a careful underpinning of facts and a good presentation of all the various pertinent documents. All of this also demonstrates a mastery of an excellent bibliography on the subject. The presentation is straightforward and its judgments are balanced. The author avoids a too "journalistic" style and he follows the guidance of Father Giovanni Caprile, S.J., in chronicling the events

---

[26]Carbone Vincenzo, *Il Concilio Vaticano II. Preparazione della Chiesa al Terzo Millenio* [Vatican Council II: Preparation of the Church for the Third Millennium], Vatican City 1998. See my review in *L'Osservatore Romano*, January 20, 1999, and in Chapter 48 of this book.

[27]Zambarbieri Annibale, *I Concili del Vaticano* [The Vatican Councils], Edizioni San Paolo, Cinisello Balsamo, 1995. For my review see *Apollinaris* LXVIII (1995), pp. 433-438, and Chapter 4 of this book.

he covers, as he also adheres in his concrete references to the conciliar "Acts" prepared by Monsignor Carbone.

It would seem unjust not to refer also in a positive way here to two volumes published by the Paul VI Institute in Brescia. One is on the subject of "Paul VI and the Relationships between the Church and the World at the Council" (1991); and the other deals with "Paul VI and Ecclesiological Problems at the Council" (1989). These two volumes extend a bit beyond the decade of the 1990s which we have been covering here; but along with another study from the Paul VI Institute on the subject of Pope Montini's interventions at the Council, they constitute a valuable "trilogy" arising out of the international colloquies held at the Institute. They are of great importance in our view.

Beyond this we cannot go with regard to Paul VI, because we would then have to get into the subject of the vast bibliography that exists on him. This represents a huge field in itself, even though it also includes his conciliar actions as well as the post-conciliar interpretation of them.

Also, it is not possible to get into the hermeneutical questions regarding papal primacy and the relation of the primacy to collegiality that have been extensively researched over these past ten years. These are two subjects intimately related to the Council, of course—which, moreover, have given rise to many and varied different interpretations and emphases [but we must leave them aside].

I will make two exceptions, however, mentioning especially the "Acts" of the important Theological Symposium which took place in the Vatican, in December, 1996. The subject was: "The Primacy of the Successor of Peter." The publication on this came out in 1998. We authored a presentation in *L'Osservatore Romano* for November 27, 1998.

My second exception is the very complete study by J.-M. R. Tillard on *The Local Church*.[28] I mention this work because it illustrates how far one can go in the direction of "localism," even when taking as one's starting point Vatican II itself. It represents a very considerable swing

---

[28]Tillard Jean-Marie R., *L'Église locale. Ecclésiologie de communion et catholicité* [The local Church: Ecclesiology of Communion and Catholicity], Cerf, Paris 1995. See my "Nota" in *Apollinaris* LXX (1997), pp. 625-632.

of the theological pendulum, one deliberately chosen perhaps in order to right the balance from the earlier idea of "universality," which was sometimes excessive and even "discarnate" and almost abstract. Still, excesses are excesses, no matter in which direction they tend.

Also, I do not want to wind up this paper without informing the reader of two other recent positive events which raise hopes for a general change of tone and emphasis in the field of conciliar hermeneutics. I bring this up not merely because I wish to conclude on a note of *dulcis in fundo* (sweet at the end) at all costs, but because I believe that these two events represent a true positive change.

Thus, a new Center for Research on Vatican Council II has been established at the Pontifical Lateran University. While it is still a new and very fragile entity, it has issued its first promising Bulletin for its first year, beginning in January, 2000. At the same time, it has organized for that same month an international study conference on the subject of "The Lateran University and the Preparation for Vatican Council II."[29]

But even more satisfying, as far as we are concerned, was the international conference on the subject of the "Implementation of Vatican Council II" which took place in February, 2000, as part of the program for that Jubilee Year. At this Conference, we found being addressed at long last many of the hermeneutical issues which have long concerned us. While awaiting the publication of the "Acts" of this particular conference, one can read an account of it in *L'Osservatore Romano* for January 29, 2000.

I quote one passage of Pope John Paul II herewith from this press account: "The Church has always understood the rules for a sound hermeneutic of the contents of Catholic dogma. These rules arise internally out of the very fabric of the Catholic faith; they do not come from sources outside the faith. To read the Council's documents and then to imagine that this Council somehow represents a break with the past is to be seriously mistaken. In reality, the documents fall wholly within the line of the faith of all time."

---

[29]See *L'Osservatore Romano*, January 29, 2000.

52

Vatican Council II:
Considerations concerning
Hermeneutical Tendencies in Recent Years

I shall begin here by noting the importance of the vital link between history and law. I have worked in support of this link for the past thirty years. One of the fruits of this labor has been my book: *Chiesa e Papato nella storia e nel diritto* [Church and Papacy in History and Law: 25 Years of Critical Studies] (Editrice Vaticana, 2002).

I add here an expression of my profound conviction of how important it has been and is to base the Church's canonical renewal on the actual texts of the documents of Vatican II of course derived from a correct hermeneutic. With this observation we enter immediately into the subject of our discussion, and I want to underline at the outset both the importance and the doctrinal, spiritual, and pastoral value of the Second Vatican Council: it is the "icon" of Catholicism, constitutionally speaking, and it also represents communion with the Church's whole past, including her remote origins. She has preserved her identity in the course of her development, and has been faithful in this even while she renews herself.

The Council was undeniably a great one. Its official *Acts* alone fill 62 large volumes, which provide a secure basis both for the Council's "reception" and for developing a correct hermeneutic of its documents. Many nevertheless have attempted to paint the whole picture of the Council even before its official *Acts,* as far as the directive organs are concerned, were published; they generally based their accounts on records from the private diaries and contemporary publications and chronicles; however, that of Father Giovanni Caprile, S.J., was good.

But the question arises concerning methods and criteria employed in the writing of such diaries. A simple reading of them reveals discrepancies and a great variety of approaches in the attribution of merits and credit (particularly where positions thought to have "won out" against opposition are concerned). Then there is the evidence of various partial and one-sided positions that sometimes fail to appreciate the complexity of the conciliar questions treated; this complexity inevitably arose from out of the veritable web of conciliar regulations, from the "pressures" that were exerted, and from the movements at the Council representing various positions. Many "battles" were supposedly fought, whether against the Roman Curia or against the "conservatives," whether in defense of either Tradition or the theological *avant-garde*, for or against the Magisterium, or else on what Pope John XXIII intended when he convoked the Council.

Certainly, diaries are not to be rejected as conciliar sources. One prime example of a diary as a valuable source is the *Journal* of Father Yves Congar, so capably edited by Éric Mahieu [see Chapter 45 of this book]. Diaries provide flavor and personal ingredients to a text, but they need to be checked with the official conciliar sources if they are not to cause slippage into a fragmentary type of history, whether that of a simple "chronicle" type, or of an "encyclopedia article." These types of history can result in a simple dissection of the Council or even a veritable peeling off of various "layers" of "facts." Besides the *Journal* of Congar, we have also reviewed [in this book] the diaries or papers of Archbishop Neophytos Edelby [Chapter 38], Father M.-D. Chenu [Chapter 37], Bishop André Charue, [Chapter 41] along with the inventories of Bishop De Smedt and Cardinal Suenens, Monsignor Albert Prignon [Chapter 43], Monsignor Gérard Philips [Chapter 42], Father Umberto Betti [Chapter 44], Archbishop Pericle Felici in a certain sense [Chapter 47], and Cardinal Joseph Ratzinger [Chapter 40]. We have also reviewed Schmidt's biography of Cardinal Bea [Chapter 39] and Lai's biography of Cardinal Siri [Chapter 36].

One underlying problem with the use of such diaries and papers as these as sources for the history of the Council, however, is the widespread tendency that became evident in the post-conciliar era of using these sources in order to undermine the importance of the Council's own official documents. The "spirit of the Council" reigned! But the proper "spirit" here should have been that of the *corpus* (body) of these conciliar texts; they represent a synthesis of Tradition and renewal adding up to a true *aggiornamento.* The following "the spirit of the Council" instead, however, resulted in an agenda-driven type of research that was "ideological" from the start. This type of research focused solely on the innovative aspects of the Council; it emphasized discontinuity with regard to Catholic Tradition. The most salient example of this tendency can be found in the volume *The "Event" and the "Decisions,"* edited by Maria Teresa Fattori and Alberto Melloni [see Chapter 23 of this book].

Focusing on discontinuity is actually one of the chief general tendencies in historiography today. It goes against Braudel and the school of the "Annales," and it favors a historical interpretation which looks primarily at "events." It looks at them not so much as important happenings, or facts, but rather as absolute novelties, "new things." In Church history terms, this means a "new Church," a "Copernican Revolution" in the history of the Church; it amounts to nothing else but a new Catholicism, in which some characteristics once thought essential to or inseparable from authentic Catholicism are suddenly found to have been dropped. But this approach to Church history cannot and must not find acceptance. In the volume just mentioned, the hermeneutics of men who were in no way against or closed to the authentic message of Vatican II are severely criticized—men such as Jedin, Kasper, Ratzinger, and even Poulat. The result of this biased way of proceeding has been that what was an extreme, if not an extremist, position within the ranks of the conciliar majority at the time of the Council has become, after the Council, practically a "monopoly" viewpoint among historians of the Council. Certainly there were extremist views among the conciliar minority as well, as we have seen with the schism of Archbishop Lefebvre, but this "monopoly" viewpoint among the historians of the Council today rejects every other point of view or interpretation of the Council besides its own. More than that, it vituperates as "anti-conciliar" anyone who departs from the "monopoly" line. (In this regard, see the book by Father Dossetti, *Il Vaticano II. Frammenti di una riflessione* [Vatican II: Fragments of a Reflection]).

In the light of all this, it is necessary to go back and examine the intention of both John XXIII and Paul VI with regard to the Council—I purposely employ the word "intention" in the singular here, although many use it in the plural to imply that the intentions of the two pontiffs for the Council somehow differed. Following an initial bout of perplexity, however, Pope Paul VI went on to adhere with all his heart to the original purpose of the Council, that is, true *aggiornamento*, as John XXIII proposed it. One need think in this regard only of Cardinal Montini's letter to Cardinal Cicognani of how to secure unity for the Council's deliberations (using the concepts *ad intra* and *ad extra*). For both John XXIII and Paul VI, the desired *aggiornamento* was pastoral in nature—and it always aimed to remain faithful to the deposit of faith. To illustrate what I mean here I refer to my *"Tradizione e rinnovamento si sono abbracciati: il Concilio Vaticano II* [Tradition and Renewal Together: Vatican Council II]" (published in the *Rivista della Diocesi di Vicenza*, no. 9, 1999, pp. 1232-1245; and in *Bailamme*, no 26/4, June-December, 2000, pp. 51-64) [and in Chapter 50 of this book]. Let me summarize the content of this article by listing the subtitles I employed in it: "Underlying Problems"; "The Intentions of Pope John and the Meaning of 'Tradition' (with Both a Capital and a Small 't')"; "The Intentions of Pope Paul VI"; "Some Test Cases: Collegiality and Papal Primacy" and "Dialogue and Consensus at the Council Resulting in a Proper Combination of Tradition and Renewal."

I cite one passage only. Paul VI wrote: "It would not be the truth for anybody to imagine that Vatican II represented any kind of a break, interruption, or 'liberation' from the teaching of the Church; or that the Council promoted or authorized any kind of accommodation or conformism with the mentality of our times in its negative or ephemeral aspects" (*Insegnamenti di Paolo VI* [Teachings of Paul VI], Volume IV, 1966, p. 699).

It is within this basic framework that we can place the hermeneutical background ranging from the 1990s up to the present day. And as far as we are concerned, it does not constitute the most desirable of backgrounds because there is both disequilibrium and a lack of balance in it. The dominant interpretation of the Council plays out on almost one note, and it is not a note which sees Tradition and renewal as being combined in any kind of proper balance, such as we have indicated to be necessary from the very beginning.

The "School of Bologna"

The writers and scholars who have been brought together into what we have called "the school of Bologna," headed by Professor Giuseppe Alberigo—which also includes scholars from Louvain, among other places—all follow the same fundamental line of thought. Moreover, they have succeeded by means of the wealth of resources of which they dispose, by their own industriousness, and by their wide network of friends and contacts, in monopolizing and imposing the hermeneutical position they represent on the whole field of conciliar studies. This is the case, primarily, because of the importance of the five-volume *History of Vatican Council II* which they have produced through the work of various collaborative hands, and which has been published not only in Italian, but also in French, English, Spanish, German, and Portuguese. There seems to be a plan afoot as well to bring the work out in Russian.

I have underlined the gravity of the situation which results from this "monopoly" in my reviews of all the volumes comprising this massive five-volume work (see, for example, my book *Chiesa e Papato nella storia e nel diritto* [Church and Papacy in History and Law], pp. 235-279: *L'Osservatore Romano*, January 2, 2000, p. 10, as well as an article expanded and printed in *Apollinaris* LXXIV (2001), pp. 811-825, and see also Chapters 10-14 in this book). There is yet to be published my critique of the fifth volume, especially of the chapter entitled "Conclusions and the First Indications of the Council's Reception." This particular research was taken by Professor Alberigo himself.

What one finds here, as is the case throughout all his voluminous work, is that Professor Giuseppe Alberigo consistently sticks to his well-known positions, which by now we have exhaustively critiqued. For example, he places John XXIII and Paul VI in opposition to each other on the question of "modernity." What is it? He does the same thing with the notion of "humanity" which these pontiffs held. Then there are his typical displacement of the conciliar "center of gravity," moving it from the conciliar assembly itself (and relative *Acta Synodalia*) to the conciliar commissions (and consequently to personal diaries!); his tendency to consider certain drafts to be new *schemata* but which were not such; his judgment that the Council was a "headless" operation; and his erroneous understanding of religious liberty.

We can go on to mention Alberigo's further tendency to downgrade the *Synodus Episcoporum* and his mistaken view of "a disparity between the various Acts that were approved...Their degree of elaboration and their correspondence with the basic line set forth for Vatican II are quite visibly unequal." But then who has established what the Council's "basic line" was, we ask? Alberigo further devalues the Code of Canon Law, while at the same time favoring "master" laws. And I have many times had to critique his advocacy of the idea that there was a "black week" at the Council in 1964; the week in question was actually a week in which many things got clarified. Then there is his view of the *Nota Explicativa Praevia*, which was supposedly "a hermeneutical norm." Again, Alberigo is mistaken in believing that there was a long waiting period between the decisions made by the Council and their implementation in and by the Church (this delay supposedly justified "spontaneous uprisings" against the authority of the Church). Another mistake is his view that the reform of the Roman Curia was not based upon a "decentralization," and hence, according to him, it was "incoherent and not in accord with Vatican II." Then there is also his mistaken view concerning a supposed "silence of Vatican II"; he thinks that in some respects the Council was "mute." But is this true? Again, he was wrong about "the trauma throughout the Christian world which came about because of the encyclical *Humanae Vitae*"—which presumably invalidated the Church's teaching on the ends of marriage, responsible procreation, and priestly celibacy. He was and is equally mistaken concerning the need for new criteria for the interpretation of Vatican II, and he is quite obstinate in his continued advocacy of the need for a conciliar canonization of Pope John XXIII. The same thing is true of his consistent devaluing of the conciliar texts. On top of all this, there is his focus on the Council as an "event" and his critique of the "typical edition" of the Council's documents as well as his criticism of Monsignor Carbone's editor of the *Acta Synodalia* (the latter effected through third persons).

But the big question, whether or not the Council represented "an epochal of transition," was replied to in the affirmative in the chapter which follows, placed there by Professor Alberigo himself. In this chapter, the typical thought of this author is perhaps a little less drastic than usual, as it is more limited in expression in some cases, than has typically been the case previously for this author. Take, for example, his basically correct affirmation that "there did not exist a Council of the majority and a Council of the minority, much less a Council of victors and one of vanquished. Vatican II was the result of all the factors which came together in it." We take note of this particular statement with singular pleasure, after having encountered so many references in the preceding volumes, to a supposed "anti-conciliar minority." But if Alberigo is correct in what he is now asserting here, then the previous four volumes should be reworked!

However that may be, again in this final chapter, Alberigo continues to expound his typical points of view. We have amply critiqued these views as being saturated with quite evident ideology. But let us leave aside other questions and focus on the author's view that Vatican II was "above all an event," and that only after that came "the *corpus* of its decisions." This priority is precisely wrong and indeed is the reverse of what is the case. If what is intended by an "event" here corresponds to how such an "event" is now being viewed in secular historiography—that is, as we have already noted, as a break with the past—then we cannot accept such an interpretation (in this connection, see our article on "The 'Event' and the 'Decisions'" in *AHC* 1998, pp. 131-142 and in *Apollinaris* LXXI [1998], pp. 325-337) [and in Chapter 23 of this book].

The "event" in question is correctly presented as a link with *aggiornamento*, but then it is filtered through the screen provided by Father Chenu emphasizing what is called "pastorality," or a purely "pastoral" approach. This latter emphasis is in turn treated as contrary to the "research methods" of the late lamented Michele Maccarrone.

What is called "pastorality," along with *aggiornamento*, for this author, supposedly entails the premise that it is proper and valid "to go beyond the hegemony of theology." By theology is understood "the isolated doctrinal dimension of the faith" and what is also called its "abstract conceptualization" together with "Juridicalism" But the author makes serious errors here, stating, for example, that "the Church and the faith do not appear to be co-extensive with doctrine, which in any case does not constitute [the Church's] most important dimension...Adhesion to doctrine, or, particularly to *one single* formulation of doctrine, cannot possibly be the ultimate criterion in order to determine who belongs to the *Unam Sanctam*..."

However, and on the further subject of ecumenism, Alberigo holds that the non-Catholic observers at the Council were substantially "members" of the Council, even though it was in their own way, that is, "informally." He even thinks there was a real *communicatio in sacris*, even though it was an "imperfect" one. He writes: "It is in this way that there emerged at the Council, even if only in germ, a sacramental-pastoral conception of Christianity and of the Church that can take the place of the old doctrinal and disciplinary conception." Take the place of?

There follows, in a chapter entitled "Physiognomy of the Church and the Dialogue with the World,"—and although with some ambiguities to begin with—which a marked differentiation made by this author between Pope John and Pope Paul. He notes this in particular with respect to Vatican I. "Thus, Pope Paul went so far as to insist that there was a 'hierarchical communion.' From this arose a full-fledged difference from the ecclesiology of the conciliar majority. The conciliar majority decided not to continue with the idea of the Church as the 'mystical body,' a tendency which had culminated in the *Nota Explicativa Praevia* in the third chapter of *Lumen Gentium*." The author certainly makes an amazing somersault here in order to differentiate between the two popes!

Another burning question is covered under the subtitle "Vatican II and the Tradition." Here the author claims that there was "substantial continuity" between the initial and the final drafts of texts. At the same time, he says that there was "discontinuity with respect to the Christianity of the Middle Ages and of the Post-Tridentine period. It wasn't that substantial novelties emerged, but rather that there was an effort…to propose once again the ancient faith in terms that were comprehensible to contemporary man." However, immediately after stating this, he gets into the distinction between the Church and the Kingdom of God; and this theme is treated in such a way that, for him, the Church cannot be considered the germ and beginning of the Kingdom. Rather, the author's conception is supposedly based on "the premise that it is necessary to go beyond ecclesiocentrism and thereby achieve a relativization of ecclesiology itself—that is, a re-centering of Christian thought and reflection."

The author thus introduces a vision of a "parallelism of forces: episcopate-papacy-curia-public opinion." One detects an indulgence on his part for certain "psychological" factors (fear, fatigue, apathy, marginalization). Alberigo makes the Continental episcopal conferences (which did not exist) a party to his suit; and, without any basis for doing so, he considers these conferences to be analogous to parliamentary lobbies or to the "nations" of the late medieval Councils. He mentions the warning of Paul VI against organizing groups or factions within the Council, but he appears to mean by this that only the conservative *Coetus* is really out of bounds on this score. He also speaks of what he calls the "rivalry test," which he thinks impeded the work of nearly all the conciliar commissions.

The treatment he reserves for the Roman Curia turns out to be along his usual lines. According to him, the Roman Curia "exercised a hegemony over both the ante-preparatory and the preparatory phases of the Council." It "occupied this position throughout the entire life of the Council…[It was] a position which entailed a particular vision of the Church, of which it was envious…" At this point the names of Cardinal Ottaviani and Archbishop Felici surface, with those of the Secretaries of State. According to Alberigo, they "had an enormous influence on the Council, either directly or by influencing the pope in their favor." Nor does Alberigo admit or even seem to realize that the Secretary of State was among the closest actual collaborators of the pope, his "pair of hands." According to him, "the greatest incidence of the curial conditioning of the Council came in connection with the weight which the first preparatory *schemata* continued to have in the drafting of the final texts." This "curial conditioning" supposedly went on throughout the entire Council, and thus, according to this author, the Council documents continued to be products of the "Curia" to much too great an extent.

In his thought and reflection, Alberigo claims to accord first place in the influence primarily exerted on the Council "not to the pope or to the Church or by its doctrinal universe," but rather to the Holy Spirit ([as was said of] at the very first primitive Council of Jerusalem they were put together "and…and.."). This was also true of this particular Council, which was "guided" in its methods, he thinks, by its encounter with modern secular science and knowledge, as well as with Protestant thought, all of which had to be reflected upon theologically. This, for Alberigo, adds up to what he calls "an acceptance of history." He speaks of an "organic relationship between history and salvation," and this, he thinks, supersedes "the dichotomy between sacred history and profane history." Thus, in his view, history itself comes to be recognized in its theological dimension. Important aspects of his thought focus upon the rigorous use of the historico-critical method; but then he also thinks that Vatican II was weighed down to some extent by "a certain number of inspirations that were pre-conciliar in origin." He nevertheless, at the same time, concedes that the Council "exceeded expectations" for the most part.

Our critique of Alberigo's thought has consistently focused upon his exaggerated idea of the "novelty" of the Council and of its work. Although it is true that it countenanced a certain legitimate diversity by comparison with what the earlier councils had done, the idea that its "pastorality," or pastoral character, along with the *aggiornamento* could be considered during such a long time and even "alien" to "Catholicism," is something that cannot stand. The same thing applies to the author's idea of the Council's supposed "non-juridical" nature, that is, with decisions which were merely "orientative and not prescriptive."

And always on the subject of the Church as an institution, the author, again erroneously, believes that there was "an overturning of the Church's priorities...an abandonment of the custom of always referring back to the Church as an institution, to its authority and effectiveness as the measure and center of the faith." This, of course, is a very seriously unbalanced judgment, especially when we consider that it was Alberigo himself who earlier wrote as follows: "The hegemony of the institution on the Christian life...reached its peak with the dogmatic claims of the magisterial infallibility of the bishop of Rome." He went on to add: "It was the faith itself, internal communion, and the Church's availability to render service that made the Church what it became; these are the values in accordance with which the evangelical inadequacy of the institutional structures and operations can be seen." But why oppose these values to the institution?

From all of this, Alberigo draws the conclusion that "the reception of Vatican II—and perhaps the true understanding of it—remain both uncertain and in an embryonic state." We would never be able to take as radical a stance as this. And in any case, Alberigo himself can surely not take the Extraordinary Synod of 1985 as in any way supportive of his own radical views. It was diametrically opposed to a hermeneutic such as his, as a matter of fact. And how, for questions linked with secular institutions, can he accuse the church of going down the same road, while he himself at the same time goes on proposing a "democratization" of the Church?

Could the Council have done more? This is the question that the author ultimately arrives at. "The question is troubling, and its answer tentative," he replies to himself. But in thus replying to, he reveals two illusions to which he is subject: First, he thinks that "Vatican II was not truly ecumenical in a strict sense." Why not? Because the Council ended up with a Church that had become very different from the one it had started out with, according to him. At this point, he attempts to call to witness for his way of thinking such figures as Jedin, Rahner, Chenu, Pesch, Vilanova, and Dossetti. He does so in order to introduce us to what he calls "the third epoch of the Church" (Pesch) and, at the same time, to define the event that was Vatican II as one of "epochal change" or as an "epochal transition." "On the one hand, it represents the arrival at the end of the Tridentine and 'controversialist' era; and, on the other hand, it represents the anticipation and the point of departure for a new historical era."

So what must we say in response to all this? First of all, we repeat what we have often said, namely, that it is not acceptable to separate the "event" that was Vatican II from the Council's "decisions." After that, we must insist yet one more time that, although the Council was indeed a great event, it was in no way a break with Tradition or a revolution or the creation of a new Church; nor was it the rejection of the great Tridentine Synod or of Vatican Council I or of any of the other ecumenical Councils of the Church that preceded it. It certainly represented a turn in the road, if we may continue using the imagery of roads, but it was in no way a "U-turn." At the same time, it did represent an *aggiornamento*, or a bringing of things up to date; but this term comprehends the co-presence of both the new and the old, the *nova et vetera*, and also of fidelity along with openness. This is amply demonstrated, for that matter, in the documents approved by the Council, and I mean in *all* the documents.

The "event" that was Vatican II, then, was indeed another one of the Church's ecumenical Councils (on this subject, see M. Deneken's "*L'engagement oecuménique de Jean XXIII* [The Ecumenical

Commitment of John XXIII] in the *Revue des Sciences Religieuses, 2001*, pp. 82-86) and therefore should be analyzed as such without any kind of prejudgment. It should be accepted as based on the Catholic faith. Even though it had its own particular characteristics, it could not really contradict anything that earlier Councils had decided. It was, in any case, based on unity, on consensus. Moreover, although the Church has always been the true friend of humanity, this does not necessarily entail friendship for modernity as such. But in what sense then? Alberigo is inclined to think that "the elements of continuity with the tradition are considerable, but the elements of newness are at least as relevant and perhaps more so." It is not a question of quantity here but of quality; and we are concerned with faithful development or evolution, not with some kind of a subversive revolution. All we have to do is patiently wait for a true, correct, and authentic "reception" of the Council, and this means a reception not merely of what it produced that was new, but also in what it produced in continuity with the great Catholic ecclesial tradition.

For a better treatment of the continuity exhibited by Vatican II, we refer to the volume edited by Massimo Faggioli and Giovanni Turbanti, *Il Concilio inedito. Fonti del Vaticano II* [The Unpublished Council: Sources of Vatican II]. A further treatment of this subject written by me is also soon to be published but we may here quote two passages from this particular volume which are indicative. The first concerns "the systematization of the Archives and the official publication of the conciliar Acts [which] seem to be aiming at establishing a favored, 'authentic' position concerning the possible interpretations of the Council itself. In effect, Paul VI always evidenced a great preoccupation, and even revealed a rather lively inquietude, concerning what he regarded as 'partial' or one-sided interpretations of the documents which might bear upon ecclesiastical discipline. The pope feared that in the process of reception, radical tendencies might prevail, bringing about disarray in Church structures." But was this not a legitimate preoccupation for a pope? The authors concede this at least in part, since "the way in which the available documents have been organized and presented results in a rather precise picture of the

Council that might differ considerably in the light of other sources, and which might itself be seen to be a 'partial' view." In what sense, may we be permitted to ask? Certainly, what emerges from consideration of the official documents still allows for other possible interpretations in the light of other real evidence from "diverse sources." But surely cannot simply go against what clearly emerges *ex actis et probatis*.

The second citation from the Faggioli-Turbanti book is concerned with an important mention of *The History of Vatican Council II,* series edited by Alberigo; it notes that "the studies conducted up to this point have utilized a relatively reduced amount of the massive documentation that exists." These authors note further that "the sources gathered along the way by the team that has collaborated on the production of this *History of Vatican Council II* have generally been made available to all. But that does not alter the fact that each collaborator working on the project of this *History* has utilized what he wanted from these common sources according to his own individual discretion, meanwhile drawing upon other sources of various types as well." It is good to know this, since it confirms our own judgment concerning the choice *ad usum delphini* of the sources that have in fact been used. This is one of the great weaknesses—which from the outset we have also characterized as "ideological"—of the *History* in question, in which the combination with the official sources is both difficult and labored.

The volumes edited under the direction of Professor Alberigo have also been produced following various conferences or colloquies held in [various] different places, after which specific publications of varying importance often followed; but these also exhibited some of the same characteristics already delineated above. Those who wish to follow up on these references can do so, basing themselves on what I have stated in my reviews. But I would also like to mention a work such as Á *la Veille du Concile Vatican II* [On the Eve of Vatican Council II], edited by M. Lamberigts and Cl. Soetens, and published in Leuven in 1992 [see my review in Chapter 7 of this book]. It is in this latter book that Alberigo furnishes his personal "hermeneutical criteria" for the history of Vatican II (he lays them out elsewhere as well, of course). I have strongly critiqued these criteria. One meeting of some importance on this subject was held at Klingenthal (Strasbourg) in 1999; it produced the volume edited by J. Doré and A. Melloni entitled *Studi di storia e teologia sulla conclusione del Vaticano II* [Studies of the History and Theology on the Conclusion of Vatican II]. Monsignor Doré contributes the final study in this particular volume, and he thus gets involved in a very difficult effort of synthesis, trying to put together things that others have kept separate. I have also reviewed this book in *Apollinaris* LXXIV (2001), pp. 789-799 [See Chapter 15 in this book].

General Research on the Council

It was around 1995 that the bold enterprise of writing comprehensive histories of the Council was seriously taken up. "Narrative" histories aiming at a synthesis of the event "as a whole" were produced, some of them seeming to be somewhat provisory in nature and even seeming to have been composed in haste. Were there risks involved in this? Yes. The authors involved generally remained tied down to their original conciliar visions, sometimes quite "partial" ones. Research of a truly scholarly nature proved difficult in that there was no proper distance from the events being covered, which requires certain sedimentary layers of the facts. A long and patient work of checking and assimilation of the various "chronicles" against the "Acts" especially for the "journalistic" accounts which have already had such an unfortunate influence, is surely necessary for a work of this kind. All of these sources need to be checked with the official "Acts" of the Council, which were only completed in 1999.

Limiting ourselves to Italy alone, we find in this same *genre* Volume XXV, 1 and 2, of the Fliche-Martin *History of the Church* edited by Guasco, Guerriero, and Traniello. It is entitled *La Chiesa del Vaticano II (1958-1978)* [The Church of Vatican II-1958-1978] [See my review in Chapter 16 of this book]. In this particular volume, the treatment of Vatican Council II was confided to Roger Aubert, the well-known Belgian historian. In my review, I emphasized the same faults of this author that are found in the work of the School of Bologna. However, Aubert is somewhat more balanced in his judgments.

The author's eventual conclusion, in fact, which places Paul VI "fully in the line traced by John XXIII," and which speaks volumes concerning his final convictions, goes contrary to those Alberigo, from whom he diverges quite markedly, along with the entire Belgian group of historians. Aubert's Chapter VII in this book includes his evaluation of the "theological merit" of the Council documents. These, in our view, ought to be accorded greater weight than he allows, if only to contribute to the proper "reception" of the Council, extending beyond any partial or one-sided view. Everybody hopes for such a proper reception. However, by continually criticizing the supposed shortcomings or deficiencies in the conciliar documents, this author may not be allowing sufficient room for the acceptance of "the doctrinal magisterium in a pastoral context" that actually characterized Vatican II. This is a general problem, even if of course "the force and authority of these documents is too often judged on the basis of their literary *genre*, on the basis of obligatory engagements, or on the nature of the subjects covered." Always on the subject of conciliar hermeneutics, though, which is what we are most concerned with here, we ask if Aubert is really correct in asserting that "numerous ambiguities remain in the texts, where traditional statements are melded with innovative ones; they are juxtaposed with each other rather than being truly integrated." Or yet again: "Such a lack of coherence often produces divergent interpretations, with the result that some passages come to be unilaterally insisted upon more than other passages. In this situation, a historical study serenely carried out can decide to try to ascertain the deeper intentions of the great majority of the assembly— beyond the efforts that were exerted to obtain a broader consensus."

However, we do not believe that it is possible to arrive at the "real" conciliar thought *qua talis* (in itself), while prescinding from the preoccupations that made a search for consensus necessary. Reaching such a consensus is a characteristic of any Council; it is not sought for its own sake but in order to remain faithful to Tradition and bring about *aggiornamento* at the same time. Only the definitive texts approved by the Council and promulgated by the Supreme Pastor *are* the conciliar texts, in fact. Otherwise, everyone would simply "receive" the Council in his own fashion and in accordance with his own preferences, whether theological or personal—or according to the "school" to which he belongs.

Aubert deals with the same subject elsewhere: in another work by three hands, namely, the 1995 *Storia dei Concili* [History of the Councils] by himself along with G. Fedalto and D. Quaglioni [see Chapter 2 of this book]; and also in the volume published in 2000 edited by Jean-Marie Mayeur, and entitled *Crise et Renouveau de 1958 à nos Jours* [Crisis and Renewal from 1958 to our Days], to which he and Claude Soetens both contribute [see my review in Chapter 25 of this book]. This latter work is Volume XIII of the *Histoire du Christianisme* [History of Christianity], an Italian translation of which will soon be published, along with all the volumes in the series. In comparing these two efforts, we find that the second and later book, in which Aubert collaborated with Soetens, does not seem to have provided great benefit to the former.

More recently, in a study which goes a bit beyond that of Aubert, and perhaps also moves in a more positive direction, there is the work of Joseph Thomas, S.J., to whom was confided the treatment of Vatican II in the book *I Concili Ecumenici* [The Ecumenical Councils], published in 2001, in Brescia by Queriniana (it was edited by Antonio Zani). It is a translation into Italian from the French. I will be reviewing it in *Apollinaris*, but I can say now that it is not sufficiently fair and balanced [see Chapter 26 of this book].

Then, there is Giuseppe Alberigo himself, who ventured upon a comprehensive synthesis type of history in the book he edited that included other collaborators and was entitled *Storia dei Concili ecumenici* [A History of the Ecumenical Councils]. It was published in 1990 in Brescia [see my review in Chapter 1 of this book]. About fifty pages in this volume are dedicated to Vatican II. I have spoken sufficiently elsewhere about this author, and even about this book, and I have nothing further to add here.

I cannot fail to mention, however—leaving Italy for the moment—the book *Vatikanum II und Modernisierung. Historische, theologische, und soziologische Perspektive* [Vatican II and Modernization:

Historical, Theological, and Sociological Perspectives]. Edited by Franz Xaver Kaufmann and Arnold Zingerle, it was published in Paderborn in 1996. It features a combination of mostly theological and sociological perspectives. I am not a sociologist, and hence I cannot properly judge some of this material; nevertheless, there are things that must be said, even if we limit ourselves to noting the one-dimensional and, in our view, arbitrary judgment rendered here on what the Council was supposed to be all about. This is certainly true of the contribution of Professor Klinger and also that of Professor Pottmeyer, though perhaps to a lesser extent in the case of the latter. In no way can we accept the idea that sociology could somehow be considered the "mistress" of theology; nor can we accept the idea of the sociological "turn" in contemporary theology. This seems to us to be the most solid and correct position to take. Moreover, the terms "Montanism" and "Neo-Montanism" are primarily historico-theological concepts. Yet in this book, it is contended that they lead to a "ghetto." But historians and theologians should have been allowed to have their say about these terms. The same thing is true of the term "hierocracy" that is employed here. We do not wish to undervalue an interdisciplinary project by raising such points; nevertheless, the risks that underlie such a project need to be recognized.

For a Correct Interpretation

Faced with such a vast hermeneutical effort, even though it is largely one-dimensional and proceeds along similar interpretive lines, we cannot but feel somewhat isolated in espousing the views which we nevertheless feel are the correct ones. We are somewhat consoled, however, when we consider what happened after the Council of Trent. We think of the "exegesis" of Paolo Sarpi, which, however, was finally superseded. We are thus convinced that history and the documentation that exists on the Council will in time eventually result in a sounder hermeneutic and sounder judgments on it based *ex actis et probatis* (from the facts). Meanwhile, much patience is required. And much work, firm commitments, and proper means are necessary as well. A new era has in fact already dawned over the past decade, we believe, and we mention here, for starters, the volume of the well-known Professor Leo Scheffczyk [later made a cardinal] entitled *La Chiesa. Aspetti della crisi post-conciliare e corretta interpretazione del Vaticano II* [The Church: Aspects concerning the Post-conciliar Crisis and a Correct Interpretation of Vatican II] [See Chapter 49 of this book]. This work of Scheffczyk represents a recovery of the "Catholic" sense of the true "reality" of the Church following what the author himself describes as the great "post-conciliar crisis." He has put his finger squarely on the wound of post-conciliar hermeneutics with the following words, namely, that "every interpreter, and even every group, accept only what corresponds to their own preoccupations"— or perhaps only to the preoccupations of what is taken to have been those of the conciliar "majority."

In addition to this book of Leo Scheffczyk, there is the work of the custodian of the collections in the Archives of Vatican Council II, who is also the editor of those vast collections, namely, Monsignor Vincenzo Carbone, whom Pope Paul VI had providentially appointed to this task. I shall not go into all his various enlightening studies in the field of conciliar hermeneutics, but will mention only his small volume, published in 1998, modest in appearance but exceptionally important, namely, *Il Concilo Vaticano II. Preparazione della Chiesa al Terzo Millenio* [Vatican Council II: Preparation of the Church for the Third Millennium] [see Chapter 48 in this book]. This small publication brings together his major articles on the great Synod that were previously published in *L'Osservatore Romano*.

Also in a positive vein, and always in the field of "comprehensive" conciliar investigations, there is the 1995 work of Annibale Zambarbieri, *I Concili del Vaticano* [The Vatican Councils]. With this book, we are dealing with the best contemporary work of synthesis concerning the history of the councils that has been published to date in the Italian language. The same thing is true of the good "historical sense" that pervades it. There is found in it at times, however, a certain "indulgence," or toleration, for some of the ideological positions taken by the writers of the School of Bologna. The greatest lack or deficiency, in any case, lies in the book's treatment of the *Nota*

Explicativa Praevia. However, we gladly repeat what we have said before about this book, namely, that we are dealing here with a good synthesis along with rapid summaries and a good presentation of the various documents—all of it is based on an in-depth bibliographical knowledge. The discourse is clear, the judgments are balanced, and a "journalistic" style is avoided. Zambarbieri relies on the sure guidance provided by Father Giovanni Caprile, S.J., in the matter of the chronicling of events. The author also makes precise and concrete references to the *Acta* of the Council edited by Monsignor Carbone [see my review in Chapter 4 of this book].

While we are in a positive judgment, it would be unfair not to refer here to the two volumes published by the Paul VI Institute in Brescia: "Paul VI and the Relationships between the Church and the World at the Council" and "Paul VI and Ecclesiological Problems at the Council." These two volumes conclude what proved to be a valuable "trilogy" of studies arising out of the international colloquies held at the aforementioned Institute. They deal with Paul VI's various interventions at the Council, and this is a subject of great importance, in our view.

Beyond this we cannot go with regard to Paul VI, because we would then have to get into the subject of the vast bibliography that exists on him. This one presents a huge field in itself, even though it also includes his conciliar actions and the post-conciliar interpretation of them. Also, it is not possible to get into the hermeneutical questions regarding papal primacy and the relation of the primacy to collegiality that have been researched over these past ten years. These are two subjects intimately related to the Council, and they have given rise to many and varied different interpretations and emphases [but we cannot go into them here.

I will, however, make three exceptions, mentioning especially the "Acts" of the important Theological Symposium which took place in the Vatican, in December, 1996. The subject was: "The Primacy of the Successor of Peter." Then, secondly, there is the very complete 1995 study published by J.-M. R. Tillard, *L'Église locale. Ecclésiologie de communion et catholicité* [The Local Church: Ecclesiology of

Communion and Catholicity]. I cite this work because it illustrates how far one can go in the direction of "localism," even when taking as one's starting point Vatican II itself. It represents a very considerable swing of the theological pendulum, a swing which was quite deliberately chosen, perhaps, in order to right the balance in relation to the earlier common idea of "universality." This was sometimes quite excessive and even "disincarnate"; it was perhaps almost wholly abstract. Still, excesses are excesses.

My third exception is the 2001 book by Hermann J. Pottmeyer, *Le rôle de la papauté au troisième millénaire. Une relecture de Vatican I et de Vatican II* [The Role of the Papacy in the Third Millennium: A Re-reading of Vatican I and Vatican II] [see my review in Chapter 32 of this book]. This work in French of Pottmeyer actually appeared first in English but has now, I believe, also been translated into Italian. What is of special interest for us here is its interpretation of Vatican II, which shows how a papal "primacy of communion" arose out of the Council. What this meant was that the pope has to "represent and maintain the unity of universal communion of the Churches." But there is also another part of the book, the last one, which we consider to be "progressive," indeed extremely so, and which also contains some rather harsh judgments. But while agreeing with his overall presentation, I found the author's proposals for structural changes in the Church to be truly too much.

I do not want to terminate this presentation without speaking about two other rather positive recent developments which give rise to hope that a general change of tone and emphasis in conciliar hermeneutics may be in the offing. I actually conclude on this note not because I want to respect the principle of *dulcis in fundo* (sweet at the end) at all costs, but because I believe this new tone represents the truth.

There has been established at the Pontifical Lateran University, a new Center for Research on Vatican Council II. In the year 2000, this Center organized an interesting international Conference on the subject of "The Lateran University and the Preparation for Vatican Council II." More recently [in 2003] it has repeated this scholarly effort with yet another Congress, this one on the theme of "John

XXIII and Paul VI: The Two Popes of the Council." The very title of this event points to the positive commitment not to place these two great pontiffs in opposition to each other. This fact itself is significant, quite apart from the actual program and the interventions that were featured at the Conference.

But even more positive and "pleasing" was the international Conference on the subject of the "Implementation of Vatican Council II" which took place in February, 2000, as part of the program for the Jubilee Year. We finally found here a proper attention given to some of our own hermeneutical concerns. It is only necessary to read the papal discourse on this subject, that appeared in *L'Osservatore Romano* for February 28-29, 2000, in order to understand what I am talking about. I will quote only one passage from this press account: "The Church has always understood the rules for a sound hermeneutic of the contents of Catholic dogma. These rules arise internally out of the very fabric of the Catholic faith; they do not come from sources outside the faith. To read the Council's documents and then to imagine that this Council somehow represents a break with the past is to be seriously mistaken. In reality, the conciliar documents fall into the line of the faith of all time."

LIST OF WORKS REVIEWED
AND/OR
SUBJECTS DISCUSSED
(See each referenced chapter for complete
bibliographical information on the works listed)

Acerbi Antonio, *Paolo VI. Il papa che baciò la terra* [Paul VI: the Pope Who Kissed the Ground] — Chapter 22.

Acerbi Antonio, ed., *Acts* of a Colloquy on "The Ministry of the Pope in Ecumenical Perspective"— Chapter 31.

Alberigo Giuseppe, ed., with Various Authors, *Storia dei Concili ecumenici* [A History of the Ecumenical Councils] — Chapter 1.

Alberigo Giuseppe, ed., with Various Authors, *Chiese italiane a concilio* [Italian Churches at the Council] — Chapter 5.

Alberigo Giuseppe, and Melloni Alberto, eds., with Various Authors, *Verso il Concilio Vaticano II (1960-1962): Passagi e problemi della preparazione conciliare* [Towards Vatican Council II (1960-1962): Passages and Problems Related to the Preparation for the Council] — Chapter 6.

Alberigo Giuseppe, ed., with Various Authors, *Il Vaticano II fra attese e celebrazione* [Expectations from and Celebration of Vatican Council II] — Chapter 9.

Alberigo Giuseppe, ed., with Various Authors, *Il cattolicesimo verso una nuova stagione. L'annuncio e la preparazione, gennaio 1959-settembre 1962* [Towards a New Season for Catholicism: The Announcement and the Preparations, January, 1959-September, 1962]. Volume I of the *Storia del Concilio Vaticano II* [History of Vatican Council II] — Chapter 10.

Alberigo Giuseppe, ed., with Various Authors, *La formazione della coscienza conciliare* [The Formation of the Conciliar Conscience]. Volume II of the *Storia del Concilio Vaticano II* [History of Vatican Council II] — Chapter 11.

Alberigo Giuseppe, ed., with Various Authors, *Il Concilio adulto. Il secondo periodo e la seconda intersessione, settembre 1963-settembre 1964* [The Adult Council: The Second Session and the Second Intersession]. Volume III of the *Storia del Concilio Vaticano II* [History of Vatican Council II] — Chapter 12.

Alberigo Giuseppe, ed., with Various Authors, *La Chiesa come comunione. Il terzo periodo e la terza intersessione, settembre 1964-settembre 1965* [The Church as Communion: The Third Session and the Third Intersession, September, 1964-September, 1965]. Volume IV of the *Storia del Concilio Vaticano II* [History of Vatican Council II] — Chapter 13.

Alberigo Giuseppe, ed., with Various Authors, *Concilio di transizione. Il quarto periodo e la conclusione del concilio, 1965* [A Transition Council: The Fourth Session and the Conclusion of the Council, 1965]. Volume V of the *Storia del Concilio Vaticano II* [History of Vatican Council II] — Chapter 14.

Alberigo Giuseppe, *Papa Giovanni (1881-1963)* [Pope John (1881-1963)] — Chapter 19.

Aubert R., Fedalto G., and Quaglioni D., *Storia dei Concili* [A History of the Councils] — Chapter 2.

Beozzo José Oscar, Ed., with Various Authors, *Cristianismo e iglesias de América Latina en visperas del Vaticano II* [Christianity and Churches of Latin America on the Eve of Vatican II] — Chapter 8.

Betti Umberto, *Diario del Concilio, 11 Ottobre 1962-Natale 1978* [Diary of the Council from October 11, 1962 till Christmas 1978] — Chapter 44.

Buonasorte Nicla, *Tra Roma e Lefebvre. Il tradizionalismo cattolico italiano e il concilio Vaticano II* [Between Rome and Lefebvre: Italian Catholic Traditionalism and Vatican Council II] — Chapter 27.

Carbone Vincenzo, Ed. *Acta Synodalia Sacrosancti Concilii Oecumenici Vaticani II, Volumen VI* [Synodal Acts of the Sacred Ecumenical Council of Vatican II, Volume 6] — Chapter 47.

Carbone Vincenzo, *Il Concilio Vaticano II. Preparazione della Chiesa al Terzo Millennio* [Vatican Council II: Preparation of the Church for the Third Millennium] — Chapter 48.

Chenu Marie-Dominique, O.P., *Notes quotidiennes au Concile (1962-1963)* [Daily Notes at the Council 1962-1963] — Chapter 37.

Congar Yves, O.P., *Mon Journal du Concile* [My Journal of the Council] — Chapter 45.

Declerck L., and Soetens C., eds., *Carnets conciliares de l'évêque de Namur, A.-M. Charue* [Conciliar Notebooks of the Bishop of Namur, A.-M. Charue] — Chapter 41.

Declerck L., and Verschooten W., eds., *Inventaire des papiers conciliares de Monsigneur Gérard Philips* [Inventory of the Conciliar Papers of Monsignor Gérard Philips] — Chapter 42.

Doré J., and Melloni A., eds., *Studi di storia e teologia sulla conclusione del Vaticano II* [Studies of the History and Theology on the Conclusion of the Second Vatican Council] — Chapter 15.

Edelby Neophytos, *Il Vaticano II nel diario di un vescovo arabo* [Vatican II in the Diary of an Arab Bishop] — Chapter 38.

Faggioli Massimo and Turbanti Giovanni, eds., *Il Concilio inedito. Fonti del Vaticano II* [The Unpublished Council: Sources of the Vatican II] — Chapter 46.

Fattori Maria Theresa, and Melloni Alberto, eds., *L'Evento e le decisioni. Studi sulle dinamiche del Concilio Vaticano II* [The Event and the Decisions: Studies on the Dynamics of the Vatican Council II] — Chapter 23.

Garzaniga Gianni, ed., *Giovanni XXIII e il Vaticano II* [John XXIII and Vatican II] — Chapter 21.

Giovanni XXIII e il Concilio [John XXIII and the Council] from the Series *Duemila anni di Cristianesimo* [Two Thousand Years of Christianity] — Chapter 17.

Roncalli Marco, ed., *Giovanni XXIII. Nostra pace è la volonta di Dio* [John XXIII: Our Peace Is the Will of God] — Chapter 20.

Grootaers Jan, ed., *Primauté et Collégialité. Le dossier de Gérard Philips sur la* Nota Explicativa Praevia [Primacy and Collegiality: The Dossier of Gérard Philips on the *Nota Explicativa Praevia*] — Chapter 28.

Guasco Maurilio, Guerriero Elio, and Traniello Francesco, eds., *La Chiesa del Vaticano II (1958-1978)* [The Church of Vatican II (1958-1978)] — Chapter 16.

Hegge Christoph, *Il Vaticano II e i movimenti ecclesiali* [Vatican II and Ecclesial Movements] — Chapter 34.

Kaufmann Franz-Xaver and Zingerle Arnold, eds., *Vatikanum II und Modernisierung. Historische, theologische und soziologische Perspektive* [Vatican II and Modernization: Historical, Theological, and Sociological Perspectives] — Chapter 24.

Legrand H. and Theobald C., eds., *Le Ministère des évêques au Concile Vatican II et depuis* [The Ministry of Bishops at Vatican II and since] — Chapter 33.

Lamberigts M., and Soetens Cl., eds, with Various Authors, *Á la Veille du Concile Vatican II: Vota et reactions en Europe et dans le catholicisme oriental* [On the Eve of Vatican Council II: *Vota* and Reactions in Europe and Eastern Catholicism] — Chapter 7.

Lai Benny, *Il Papa non eletto. Giuseppe Siri, cardinale di Santa Romana Chiesa* [The Pope Not Elected: Giuseppe Siri, Cardinal of the Holy Roman Church] — Chapter 36.

Marchetto Agostino, "*Lumen Gentium*: A Brief History of the Document" — Chapter 29.

Marchetto Agostino, "*Dei Verbum*: An Explanatory Note" — Chapter 30.

Marchetto Agostino, "Vatican II and Ecclesial Movements: A Communal Vision" — Chapter 35.

Marchetto Agostino, "Tradition and Renewal Together: The Second Vatican Council" — Chapter 50.

Marchetto Agostino, "Vatican Council II: Hermeneutical Tendencies from 1990 to 2000" — Chapter 51.

Marchetto Agostino, "Vatican Council II: Hermeneutical Tendencies in Recent Years" — Chapter 52.

Mayeur Jean-Marie, ed., *Crise et Renouveau de 1958 à nos jours* [Crisis and Renewal from 1958 to Our Days] — Chapter 25.

Melloni Alberto, ed., *Vatican II in Moscow (1959-1965)* — Chapter 18.

Pottmeyer Hermann J., *Le rôle de la papauté au troisième millénaire* [The Role of the Papacy in the Third Millennium] — Chapter 32.

Prignon Monsignor Albert, *Journal conciliare de la 4 ème Session* [Conciliar Journal of the Fourth Session] — Chapter 43.

Ratzinger Joseph, *La mia vita. Ricordi (1927-1977)* [My Life: Memories (1927-1977)] — Chapter 40.

Schatz Klaus, S*toria dei Concili. La Chiesa nei suoi punti focali* [A History of the Councils: The Church Viewed in Her Focal Points] — Chapter 3.

Scheffczyk Leo, *La Chiesa. Aspetti della crisi post-conciliare e corretta interpretazione del Vaticano II* [The Church: Aspects Concerning the Post-conciliar Crisis and a Correct Interpretation of Vatican II] — Chapter 49.

Schmidt Stjepan, *Agostino Bea, Cardinale dell'ecumenismo e del dialogo* [Augustin Bea: Cardinal of Ecumenism and Dialogue] — Chapter 39.

Various Authors (esp. Joseph Thomas, S.J.) *I Concili Ecumenici* [The Ecumenical Councils] — Chapter 26.

Zambarbieri Annibale, *I Concili del Vaticano* [The Vatican Councils] — Chapter 4.

INDEX

Monachino V., 10
Monticone A., 363
Montini G.B., 75, 79, 80, 84, 104,
116, 159, 161, 169, 170, 176, 192,
198, 218, 229, 233, 237, 238, 296,
297, 303, 315, 324, 369, 370, 371,
373, 378, 380, 393, 415, 446, 514,
515, 516, 518, 525, 528, 529, 548,
579, 597, 622, 644, 674, 680
Montréal, 131
Morand O., 495
Morin E., 385, 639, 662
Moro A., 378, 520
Morone (Card.), 55
Morozzo della Rocca R., 106, 109,
433
Moscow, 333, 334, 335, 336, 337,
338, 339, 341, 343, 344, 390, 650,
667
Moses, 208
Mozzoni U., 121
Munich, 149, 547
Münster, 553
Murray J.C., 222, 223, 243, 405,
585

Namur, 555, 557
Naples, 75, 83, 84
Nestorius, 8, 9, 51
New Delhi, 115, 150, 542
Newman (Card.), 632, 639, 663
Nicaragua, 319
Nicholas I, 13
Nicomedia, 7
Niero A., 75, 80
Nikodim (Rotov), 169, 337, 339,
344
Nissiotis N., 285, 389, 444
Noël P.C., 285
Nora P., 385, 639, 662

North America, 60, 319
Norway, 359

Occhipinti V., 568
Oesterreicher J.M., 222
Olivier B., 391
Onclin W., 583, 588
Origen, 11
Ottaviani (Card.), 92, 93, 98, 129,
156, 157, 159, 160, 161, 162, 169,
173, 199, 201, 204, 267, 303, 341,
373, 392, 455, 456, 516, 528, 542,
581, 594, 609, 686
Outler A., 248

Paiano M., 90
Paleologus (Emperor), 25
Papen (von), 351
Paraguay, 121,
Parente P., 308, 309, 581, 586, 594,
615
Paris, 295, 339, 356, 423, 473, 485,
523, 571, 656, 659, 675
Passicos J., 489
Paul (Saint), 63, 307, 375, 629, 642
Paul III, 27
Paul VI, 31, 43, 44, 45, 47, 67,
140, 177, 188, 191, 193, 197, 198,
204, 206, 208, 209, 211, 214,
218, 219, 220, 221, 222, 224, 227,
228, 229, 230, 231, 234, 235,
238, 241, 242, 244, 246, 247,
248, 252, 253, 254, 255, 257,
260, 261, 265, 266, 273, 279,
282, 285, 294, 296, 297, 298,
299, 301, 303, 306, 307, 312, 313,
315, 316, 320, 321, 324, 325, 328,
329, 330, 338, 340, 342, 343, 355,
365, 369, 370, 371, 372, 373, 374,
375, 376, 377, 378, 379, 380, 383,